"I've never purchased a better programming book... This book proved to be the most informative, easiest to follow, and had the best examples of any other computer-related book I have ever purchased. The text is very easy to follow!"

—Nick Landman

"...the Sams book by Welling & Thomson is the only one which I have found to be indispensable. The writing is clear and straightforward but never wastes my time. The book is extremely well laid out. The chapters are the right length and chapter titles quickly take you where you want to go."

—Wright Sullivan, President, A&E Engineering, Inc., Greer South Carolina

"I just wanted to tell you that I think the book *PHP and MySQL Web Development* rocks! It's logically structured, just the right difficulty level for me (intermediate), interesting and easy to read, and, of course, full of valuable information!"

—CodE-E, Austria

"There are several good introductory books on PHP, but Welling & Thomson is an excellent handbook for those who wish to build up complex and reliable systems. It's obvious that the authors have a strong background in the development of professional applications and they teach not only the language itself, but also how to use it with good software engineering practices."

—Javier Garcia, senior telecom engineer, Telefonica R&D Labs, Madrid

"I picked up this book two days ago and I am half way finished. I just can't put it down. The layout and flow is perfect. Everything is presented in such a way so that the information is very palatable. I am able to immediately grasp all the concepts. The examples have also been wonderful. I just had to take some time out to express to you how pleased I have been with this book."

—Jason B. Lancaster

"This book has proven a trusty companion, with an excellent crash course in PHP and superb coverage of MySQL as used for Web applications. It also features several complete applications that are great examples of how to construct modular, scalable applications with PHP. Whether you are a PHP newbie or a veteran in search of a better desk-side reference, this one is sure to please!"

—WebDynamic

"The true PHP/MySQL bible, *PHP and MySQL Web Development* by Luke Welling and Laura Thomson, made me realize that programming and databases are now available to the commoners. Again, I know 1/10000th of what there is to know, and already I'm enthralled."

—Tim Luoma, TnTLuoma.com

"Welling and Thomson's book is a good reference for those who want to get to grips with practical projects straight off the bat. It includes webmail, shopping cart, session control, and web-forum/weblog applications as a matter of course, and begins with a sturdy look at PHP first, moving to MySQL once the basics are covered."

—twilight30 on Slashdot

"This book is absolutely excellent, to say the least.... Luke Welling and Laura Thomson give the best in-depth explanations I've come across on such things as regular expressions, classes and objects, sessions etc. I really feel this book filled in a lot of gaps for me with things I didn't quite understand.... This book jumps right into the functions and features most commonly used with PHP, and from there it continues in describing real-world projects, MySQL integration, and security issues from a project manager's point of view. I found every bit of this book to be well organized and easy to understand."

—notepad on codewalkers.com

"A top-notch reference for programmers using PHP and MySQL. Highly recommended."

—*The Internet Writing Journal*

"This book rocks! I am an experienced programmer, so I didn't need a lot of help with PHP syntax; after all, it's very close to C/C++. I don't know a thing about databases, though, so when I wanted to develop a book review engine (among other projects) I wanted a solid reference to using MySQL with PHP. I have O'Reilly's *mSQL and MySQL* book, and it's probably a better pure-SQL reference, but this book has earned a place on my reference shelf...Highly recommended."

—Paul Robichaux

"One of the best programming guides I've ever read."

—jackofsometrades from Lahti, Finland

"This is a well-written book for learning how to build Internet applications with two of the most popular open-source Web development technologies....The projects are the real jewel of the book. Not only are the projects described and constructed in a logical, component-based manner, but the selection of projects represents an excellent cross-section of common components that are built into many web sites."

—Craig Cecil

"The book takes an easy, step-by-step approach to introduce even the clueless programmer to the language of PHP. On top of that, I often find myself referring back to it in my Web design efforts. I'm still learning new things about PHP, but this book gave me a solid foundation from which to start and continues to help me to this day."

—Stephen Ward

"This book is one of few that really touched me and made me 'love' it. I can't put it in my bookshelf; I must put it in a touchable place on my working bench as I always like to refer from it. Its structure is good, wordings are simple and straight forward, and examples are clear and step by step. Before I read it, I knew nothing of PHP and MySQL. After reading it, I have the confidence and skill to develop any complicated Web application."

—Power Wong

"This book is God.... I highly recommend this book to anyone who wants to jump in the deep end with database driven Web application programming. I wish more computer books were organized this way."

—Sean C Schertell

PHP and MySQL Web Development

Third Edition

Luke Welling
Laura Thomson

DEVELOPER'S
LIBRARY

Sams Publishing, 800 East 96th Street, Indianapolis, Indiana 46240

PHP and MySQL Web Development
Third Edition

Copyright © 2005 by Sams Publishing

International Standard Book Number: 0-672-32672-8

Library of Congress Catalog Card Number: 2003099244

Printed in the United States of America

First Printing: October 2004

07   06   05   4   3   2

Trademarks

Warning and Disclaimer

Bulk Sales

Sams Publishing offers excellent discounts on this book when ordered in quantity for bulk purchases or special sales. For more information, please contact

U.S. Corporate and Government Sales
1-800-382-3419
corpsales@pearsontechgroup.com

For sales outside the U.S., please contact

International Sales
1-317-428-3341
international@pearsoned.com

Acquisitions Editor
Shelley Johnston

Development Editor
Scott Meyers

Managing Editor
Charlotte Clapp

Copy Editor
Chuck Hutchinson

Indexer
Mandie Frank

Proofreader
Paula Lowell

Technical Editors
Sara Golemon
Chris Newman

Media Specialist
Dan Scherf

Design
Gary Adair

Page Layout
Cheryl Lynch
Michelle Mitchell

❖

To our Mums and Dads

❖

Contents at a Glance

Table of Contents

About the Authors

Laura Thomson is a lecturer in the School of Computer Science and Information Technology at RMIT University in Melbourne, Australia. She is also a partner in the award-winning web development firm Tangled Web Design. Laura has previously worked for Telstra and the Boston Consulting Group. She holds a Bachelor of Applied Science (Computer Science) degree and a Bachelor of Engineering (Computer Systems Engineering) degree with honors, and is currently completing her Ph.D. in Adaptive Web Sites. In her spare time, she enjoys sleeping. Laura can be reached via email at laura@tangledweb.com.au.

Luke Welling is a senior web developer at MySQL AB, the company behind the MySQL database. He has previously taught engineering and computer science at RMIT University in Melbourne, Australia and worked as a computer programmer for many years. He holds a Bachelor of Applied Science (Computer Science) degree. In his spare time, he attempts to perfect his insomnia. Luke can be reached via email at luke@tangledweb.com.au.

Both authors have attained the MySQL Core Certification offered by MySQL AB and the Zend Certified PHP Engineer offered by Zend Technologies Ltd.

About the Contributors

Israel Denis Jr. is a freelance consultant working on e-commerce projects throughout the world. He specializes in integrating ERP packages such as SAP and Lawson with custom web solutions. When he is not busy designing software or writing books, Israel enjoys traveling to Italy, a place he considers home. Israel obtained a master's degree in Electrical Engineering from Georgia Tech in Atlanta, Georgia, in 1998. He is the author of numerous articles about Linux, Apache, PHP, and MySQL. He has worked for companies such as GE and Procter & Gamble with mainly Unix-based computer systems. Israel can be reached via email at idenis@ureach.com.

Chris Newman is a consultant programmer specializing in the development of dynamic Internet applications. He has extensive commercial experience using PHP and MySQL to produce a wide range of applications for an international client base. A graduate of Keele University, Chris lives in Stoke-on-Trent, England, where he runs Lightwood Consultancy Ltd., the company he founded in 1999 to further his interest in Internet development. Chris became fascinated with the potential of the Internet while at the university and is thrilled to be working with cutting-edge technology. More information on Lightwood Consultancy Ltd. can be found at http://www.lightwood.net, and Chris can be contacted at chris@lightwood.net.

Acknowledgments

We would like to thank the team at Sams for all their hard work. In particular, we would like to thank Shelley Johnston without whose dedication and patience this book would not have been possible. We would also like to thank Israel Denis Jr. and Chris Newman for their valuable contributions.

We appreciate immensely the work done by the PHP and MySQL development teams. Their work has made our lives easier for a number of years now and continues to do so on a daily basis.

We thank Adrian Close at eSec for saying "You can build that in PHP" back in 1998. He said we would like PHP, and it seems he was right.

Finally, we would like to thank our family and friends for putting up with us while we have been repeatedly antisocial while working on books. Specifically, thank you for your support to our family members: Julie, Robert, Martin, Lesley, Adam, Paul, Archer, and Barton.

We Want to Hear from You!

As the reader of this book, *you* are our most important critic and commentator. We value your opinion and want to know what we're doing right, what we could do better, what areas you'd like to see us publish in, and any other words of wisdom you're willing to pass our way.

You can email or write me directly to let me know what you did or didn't like about this book—as well as what we can do to make our books stronger.

Please note that I cannot help you with technical problems related to the topic of this book, and that due to the high volume of mail I receive, I might not be able to reply to every message.

When you write, please be sure to include this book's title and authors as well as your name and phone or email address. I will carefully review your comments and share them with the authors and editors who worked on the book.

Email: opensource@samspublishing.com
Mail: Mark Taber
              Associate Publisher
              Sams Publishing
              800 East 96th Street
              Indianapolis, IN 46240 USA

Reader Services

For more information about this book or others from Sams Publishing, visit our Web site at www.samspublishing.com. Type the ISBN (excluding hyphens) or the title of the book in the Search box to find the book you're looking for.

Introduction

Welcome to *PHP and MySQL Web Development*. Within its pages, you will find distilled knowledge from our experiences using PHP and MySQL, two of the hottest web development tools around.

In this introduction, we cover

- Why you should read this book
- What you will be able to achieve using this book
- What PHP and MySQL are and why they're great
- What the new features of PHP 5.0 and MySQL 5.0 are
- How this book is organized

Let's get started.

Why You Should Read This Book

This book will teach you how to create interactive websites from the simplest order form through to complex, secure e-commerce sites. What's more, you'll learn how to do it using open source technologies.

This book is aimed at readers who already know at least the basics of HTML and have done some programming in a modern programming language before but have not necessarily programmed for the Internet or used a relational database. If you are a beginning programmer, you should still find this book useful, but digesting it might take a little longer. We've tried not to leave out any basic concepts, but we do cover them at speed. The typical readers of this book want to master PHP and MySQL for the purpose of building a large or commercial website. You might already be working in another web development language; if so, this book should get you up to speed quickly.

We wrote the first edition of this book because we were tired of finding PHP books that were basically function references. These books are useful, but they don't help when your boss or client has said, "Go build me a shopping cart." In this book, we have done our best to make every example useful. You can use many of the code samples directly in your website, and you can use many others with only minor modifications.

What You Will Be Able to Achieve Using This Book

Reading this book will enable you to build real-world, dynamic websites. If you've built websites using plain HTML, you realize the limitations of this approach. Static content from a pure HTML website is just that—static. It stays the same unless you physically update it. Your users can't interact with the site in any meaningful fashion.

Using a language such as PHP and a database such as MySQL allows you to make your sites dynamic: to have them be customizable and contain real-time information.

We have deliberately focused this book on real-world applications, even in the introductory chapters. We begin by looking at a simple online ordering system and work our way through the various parts of PHP and MySQL.

We then discuss aspects of electronic commerce and security as they relate to building a real-world website and show you how to implement these aspects in PHP and MySQL.

In the final part of this book, we describe how to approach real-world projects and take you through the design, planning, and building of the following projects:

- User authentication and personalization
- Shopping carts
- Content-management systems
- Web-based email
- Mailing list managers
- Web forums
- PDF document generation
- Web services with XML and SOAP

You should be able to use any of these projects as is, or you can modify them to suit your needs. We chose them because we believe they represent some the most common web-based applications built by programmers. If your needs are different, this book should help you along the way to achieving your goals.

What Is PHP?

PHP is a server-side scripting language designed specifically for the Web. Within an HTML page, you can embed PHP code that will be executed each time the page is visited. Your PHP code is interpreted at the web server and generates HTML or other output that the visitor will see.

PHP was conceived in 1994 and was originally the work of one man, Rasmus Lerdorf. It was adopted by other talented people and has gone through four major rewrites to bring us the broad, mature product we see today. As of August 2004, it was installed on more than 17 million domains worldwide, and this number is growing rapidly. You can see the current number at

http://www.php.net/usage.php

PHP is an Open Source product, which means you have access to the source code and can use, alter, and redistribute it all without charge.

PHP originally stood for *Personal Home Page* but was changed in line with the GNU recursive naming convention (GNU = Gnu's Not Unix) and now stands for *PHP Hypertext Preprocessor*.

The current major version of PHP is 5. This version has seen a complete rewrite of the underlying Zend engine and some major improvements to the language.

The home page for PHP is available at
http://www.php.net

The home page for Zend Technologies is
http://www.zend.com

What Is MySQL?

MySQL (pronounced *My-Ess-Que-Ell*) is a very fast, robust, *relational database management system (RDBMS)*. A database enables you to efficiently store, search, sort, and retrieve data. The MySQL server controls access to your data to ensure that multiple users can work with it concurrently, to provide fast access to it, and to ensure that only authorized users can obtain access. Hence, MySQL is a multiuser, multithreaded server. It uses *Structured Query Language (SQL)*, the standard database query language worldwide. MySQL has been publicly available since 1996 but has a development history going back to 1979. It is the world's most popular open source database and has won the Linux Journal Readers' Choice Award on a number of occasions.

MySQL is available under a dual licensing scheme. You can use it under an open source license (the GPL) free as long as you are willing to meet the terms of that license. If you want to distribute a non-GPL application including MySQL, you can buy a commercial license instead.

Why Use PHP and MySQL?

When setting out to build an e-commerce site, you could use many different products. You need to choose the following:

- Hardware for the web server
- An operating system
- Web server software
- A database management system
- A programming or scripting language

Some of these choices are dependent on the others. For example, not all operating systems run on all hardware, not all scripting languages can connect to all databases, and so on.

In this book, we do not pay much attention to hardware, operating systems, or web server software. We don't need to. One of the best features of both PHP and MySQL is that they work with any major operating system and many of the minor ones.

To demonstrate this, we have written the examples in this book and tested them on two popular setups:

- Linux using the Apache web server
- Microsoft Windows XP using Microsoft Internet Information Server (IIS)

Whatever hardware, operating system, and web server you choose, we believe you should seriously consider using PHP and MySQL.

Some of PHP's Strengths

Some of PHP's main competitors are Perl, Microsoft ASP.NET, JavaServer Pages (JSP), and ColdFusion.

In comparison to these products, PHP has many strengths, including the following:

- High performance
- Interfaces to many different database systems
- Built-in libraries for many common web tasks
- Low cost
- Ease of learning and use
- Strong object-oriented support
- Portability
- Availability of source code
- Availability of support

A more detailed discussion of these strengths follows.

Performance

PHP is very efficient. Using a single inexpensive server, you can serve millions of hits per day. If you use large numbers of commodity servers, your capacity is effectively unlimited. Benchmarks published by Zend Technologies (http://www.zend.com) show PHP outperforming its competition.

Database Integration

PHP has native connections available to many database systems. In addition to MySQL, you can directly connect to PostgreSQL, mSQL, Oracle, dbm, FilePro, Hyperwave, Informix, InterBase, and Sybase databases, among others. PHP 5 also has a built-in SQL interface to a flat file, called SQLite.

Using the *Open Database Connectivity Standard (ODBC)*, you can connect to any database that provides an ODBC driver. This includes Microsoft products and many others.

Built-in Libraries

Because PHP was designed for use on the Web, it has many built-in functions for performing many useful web-related tasks. You can generate GIF images on the fly, connect to web services and other network services, parse XML, send email, work with cookies, and generate PDF documents, all with just a few lines of code.

Cost

PHP is free. You can download the latest version at any time from http://www.php.net for no charge.

Ease of Learning PHP

The syntax of PHP is based on other programming languages, primarily C and Perl. If you already know C or Perl, or a C-like language such as C++ or Java, you will be productive using PHP almost immediately.

Object-Oriented Support

PHP version 5 has well-designed object-oriented features. If you learned to program in Java or C++, you will find the features (and generally the syntax) that you expect, such as inheritance, private and protected attributes and methods, abstract classes and methods, interfaces, constructors, and destructors. You will even find some less common features such as built-in iteration behavior. Some of this functionality was available in PHP versions 3 and 4, but the object-oriented support in version 5 is much more complete.

Portability

PHP is available for many different operating systems. You can write PHP code on free Unix-like operating systems such as Linux and FreeBSD, commercial Unix versions such as Solaris and IRIX, or on different versions of Microsoft Windows.

Well-written code will usually work without modification on a different system running PHP.

Source Code

You have access to PHP's source code. With PHP, unlike commercial, closed-source products, if you want to modify something or add to the language, you are free to do so.

You do not need to wait for the manufacturer to release patches. You also don't need to worry about the manufacturer going out of business or deciding to stop supporting a product.

Availability of Support

Zend Technologies (www.zend.com), the company behind the engine that powers PHP, funds its PHP development by offering support and related software on a commercial basis.

What Is New in PHP 5.0?

You may have recently moved to PHP 5.0 from one of the PHP 4.x versions. As you would expect in a new major version, it has some significant changes. The Zend engine beneath PHP has been rewritten for this version. Major new features are as follows:

- Better object-oriented support built around a completely new object model (see Chapter 6, "Object-Oriented PHP")
- Exceptions for scalable, maintainable error handling (see Chapter 7, "Exception Handling")
- SimpleXML for easy handling of XML data (see Chapter 33, "Connecting to Web Services with XML and SOAP")

Other changes include moving some extensions out of the default PHP install and into the PECL library, improving streams support, and adding SQLite.

Some of MySQL's Strengths

MySQL's main competitors are PostgreSQL, Microsoft SQL Server, and Oracle. MySQL has many strengths, including the following:

- High performance
- Low cost
- Ease of configuration and learning
- Portability
- Availability of source code
- Availability of support

A more detailed discussion of these strengths follows.

Performance

MySQL is undeniably fast. You can see the developers' benchmark page at http://web.mysql.com/benchmark.html. Many of these benchmarks show MySQL to be orders of magnitude faster than the competition. In 2002, *eWeek* published a benchmark comparing five databases powering a web application. The best result was a tie between MySQL and the much more expensive Oracle.

Low Cost

MySQL is available at no cost under an open source license or at low cost under a commercial license. You need a license if you want to redistribute MySQL as part of an application and do not want to license your application under an Open Source license. If you do not intend to distribute your application or are working on Free Software, you do not need to buy a license.

Ease of Use

Most modern databases use SQL. If you have used another RDBMS, you should have no trouble adapting to this one. MySQL is also easier to set up than many similar products.

Portability

MySQL can be used on many different Unix systems as well as under Microsoft Windows.

Source Code

As with PHP, you can obtain and modify the source code for MySQL. This point is not important to most users most of the time, but it provides you with excellent peace of mind, ensuring future continuity and giving you options in an emergency.

Availability of Support

Not all open source products have a parent company offering support, training, consulting, and certification, but you can get all of these benefits from MySQL AB (www.mysql.com).

What Is New in MySQL 5.0?

Major changes introduced for MySQL 5.0 include

- Stored procedures (see Chapter 13, "Advanced MySQL Programming")
- Cursor support

Other changes include more ANSI standard compliance and speed improvements. If you are still using an early 4.x version or a 3.x version of the MySQL server, you should know that the following features were added to various versions from 4.0:

- Subquery support
- GIS types for storing geographical data
- Improved support for internationalization
- The transaction-safe storage engine InnoDB included as standard
- The MySQL query cache, which greatly improves the speed of repetitive queries as often run by web applications

How Is This Book Organized?

This book is divided into five main parts:

Part I, "Using PHP," provides an overview of the main parts of the PHP language with examples. Each example is a real-world example used in building an e-commerce site rather than "toy" code. We kick off this section with Chapter 1, "PHP Crash Course." If you've already used PHP, you can whiz through this chapter. If you are new to PHP or new to programming, you might want to spend a little more time on it. Even if you are quite familiar with PHP, you will want to read Chapter 6, "Object-Oriented PHP," because the object-oriented functionality has changed significantly in PHP5.

Part II, "Using MySQL," discusses the concepts and design involved in using relational database systems such as MySQL, using SQL, connecting your MySQL database to the world with PHP, and employing advanced MySQL techniques, such as security and optimization.

Part III, "E-commerce and Security," covers some of the general issues involved in developing an e-commerce site using any language. The most important of these issues is security. We then discuss how you can use PHP and MySQL to authenticate your users and securely gather, transmit, and store data.

Part IV, "Advanced PHP Techniques," offers detailed coverage of some of the major built-in functions in PHP. We have selected groups of functions that are likely to be useful when building an e-commerce site. You will learn about interaction with the server, interaction with the network, image generation, date and time manipulation, and session variables.

Part V, "Building Practical PHP and MySQL Projects," is our favorite section. It deals with practical real-world issues such as managing large projects and debugging, and provides sample projects that demonstrate the power and versatility of PHP and MySQL.

Finally

We hope you enjoy this book and enjoy learning about PHP and MySQL as much as we did when we first began using these products. They are really a pleasure to use. Soon, you'll be able to join the thousands of web developers who use these robust, powerful tools to easily build dynamic, real-time websites.

I

Using PHP

1

PHP Crash Course

THIS CHAPTER GIVES YOU A QUICK OVERVIEW of PHP syntax and language constructs. If you are already a PHP programmer, it might fill some gaps in your knowledge. If you have a background using C, Active Server Pages (ASP), or another programming language, it will help you get up to speed quickly.

In this book, you'll learn how to use PHP by working through lots of real-world examples taken from our experiences in building e-commerce sites. Often, programming textbooks teach basic syntax with very simple examples. We have chosen not to do that. We recognize that often what you want to do is get something up and running, to understand how the language is used, instead of plowing through yet another syntax and function reference that's no better than the online manual.

Try the examples. Type them in or load them from the CD-ROM, change them, break them, and learn how to fix them again.

This chapter begins with the example of an online product order form to show how variables, operators, and expressions are used in PHP. It also covers variable types and operator precedence. You learn how to access form variables and manipulate them by working out the total and tax on a customer order.

You then develop the online order form example by using a PHP script to validate the input data. You examine the concept of Boolean values and look at examples using if, else, the ?: operator, and the switch statement. Finally, you explore looping by writing some PHP to generate repetitive HTML tables.

Key topics you learn in this chapter include

- Embedding PHP in HTML
- Adding dynamic content
- Accessing form variables

- Understanding identifiers
- Creating user-declared variables
- Examining variable types
- Assigning values to variables
- Declaring and using constants
- Understanding variable scope
- Understanding operators and precedence
- Evaluating expressions
- Using variable functions
- Making decisions with `if`, `else`, and `switch`
- Taking advantage of iteration using `while`, `do`, and `for` loops

Using PHP

To work through the examples in this chapter and the rest of the book, you need access to a web server with PHP installed. To gain the most from the examples and case studies, you should run them and try changing them. To do this, you need a testbed where you can experiment.

If PHP is not installed on your machine, you need to begin by installing it or having your system administrator install it for you. You can find instructions for doing so in Appendix A, "Installing PHP5 and MySQL5." Everything you need to install PHP under Unix or Windows can be found on the accompanying CD-ROM.

Creating a Sample Application: Bob's Auto Parts

One of the most common applications of any server-side scripting language is processing HTML forms. You'll start learning PHP by implementing an order form for Bob's Auto Parts, a fictional spare parts company. You can find all the code for the examples used in this chapter in the directory called `chapter01` on the CD-ROM.

Creating the Order Form

Bob's HTML programmer has set up an order form for the parts that Bob sells. This relatively simple order form, shown in Figure 1.1, is similar to many you have probably seen while surfing. Bob would like to be able to know what his customers ordered, work out the total prices of their orders, and determine how much sales tax is payable on the orders.

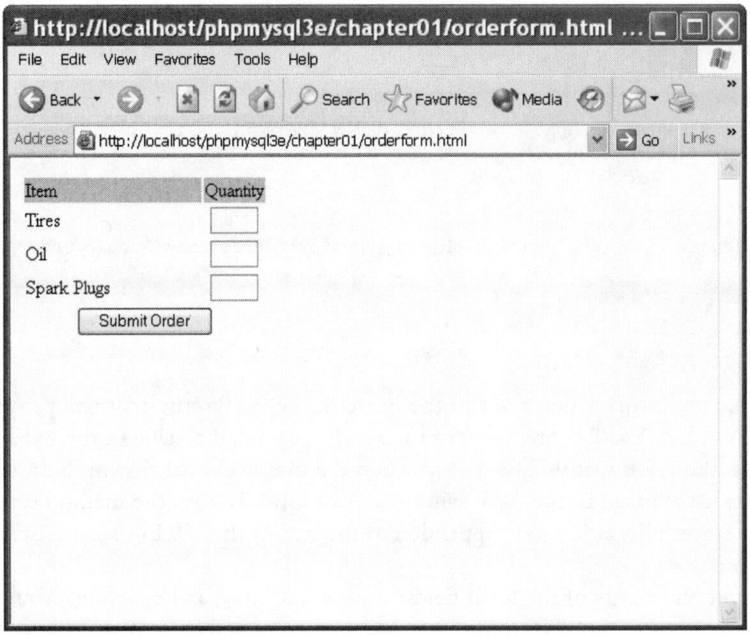

Figure 1.1   Bob's initial order form records only products and quantities.

Part of the HTML for this form is shown in Listing 1.1.

Listing 1.1   `orderform.html`— **HTML for Bob's Basic Order Form**

```
<form action="processorder.php" method="post">
<table border="0">
<tr bgcolor="#cccccc">
  <td width="150">Item</td>
  <td width="15">Quantity</td>
</tr>
<tr>
  <td>Tires</td>
  <td align="center"><input type="text" name="tireqty" size="3"
      maxlength="3" /></td>
</tr>
<tr>
  <td>Oil</td>
  <td align="center"><input type="text" name="oilqty" size="3"
      maxlength="3" /></td>
</tr>
```

Listing 1.1 **Continued**

```
<tr>
  <td>Spark Plugs</td>
  <td align="center"><input type="text" name="sparkqty" size="3"
    maxlength="3" /></td>
</tr>
<tr>
  <td colspan="2" align="center"><input type="submit" value="Submit Order" /></td>
</tr>
</table>
</form>
```

Notice that the form's action is set to the name of the PHP script that will process the customer's order. (You'll write this script next.) In general, the value of the `action` attribute is the URL that will be loaded when the user clicks the Submit button. The data the user has typed in the form will be sent to this URL via the method specified in the `method` attribute, either `get` (appended to the end of the URL) or `post` (sent as a separate message).

Also note the names of the form fields: `tireqty`, `oilqty`, and `sparkqty`. You'll use these names again in the PHP script. Because the names will be reused, it's important to give your form fields meaningful names that you can easily remember when you begin writing the PHP script. Some HTML editors generate field names like `field23` by default. They are difficult to remember. Your life as a PHP programmer will be easier if the names you use reflect the data typed into the field.

You might want to consider adopting a coding standard for field names so that all field names throughout your site use the same format. This way, you can more easily remember whether, for example, you abbreviated a word in a field name or put in underscores as spaces.

Processing the Form

To process the form, you need to create the script mentioned in the `action` attribute of the `form` tag called `processorder.php`. Open your text editor and create this file. Then type in the following code:

```
<html>
<head>
  <title>Bob's Auto Parts - Order Results</title>
</head>
<body>
<h1>Bob's Auto Parts</h1>
<h2>Order Results</h2>
</body>
</html>
```

Notice how everything you've typed so far is just plain HTML. It's now time to add some simple PHP code to the script.

Embedding PHP in HTML

Under the `<h2>` heading in your file, add the following lines:

```
<?php
  echo '<p>Order processed.</p>';
?>
```

Save the file and load it in your browser by filling out Bob's form and clicking the Submit Order button. You should see something similar to the output shown in Figure 1.2.

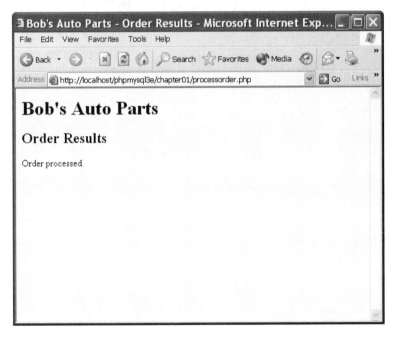

Figure 1.2   Text passed to PHP's `echo` construct is echoed to the browser.

Notice how the PHP code you wrote was embedded inside a normal-looking HTML file. Try viewing the source from your browser. You should see this code:

```
<html>
<head>
```

```
   <title>Bob's Auto Parts - Order Results</title>
</head>
<body>
<h1>Bob's Auto Parts</h1>
<h2>Order Results</h2>
<p>Order processed.</p>
</body>
</html>
```

None of the raw PHP is visible because the PHP interpreter has run through the script and replaced it with the output from the script. This means that from PHP you can produce clean HTML viewable with any browser; in other words, the user's browser does not need to understand PHP.

This example illustrates the concept of server-side scripting in a nutshell. The PHP has been interpreted and executed on the web server, as distinct from JavaScript and other client-side technologies interpreted and executed within a web browser on a user's machine.

The code that you now have in this file consists of four types of text:

- HTML
- PHP tags
- PHP statements
- Whitespace

You can also add

- Comments

Most of the lines in the example are just plain HTML.

Use of PHP Tags

The PHP code in the preceding example began with <?php and ended with ?>. This is similar to all HTML tags because they all begin with a less than (<) symbol and end with a greater than (>) symbol. These symbols (<?php and ?>) are called *PHP tags*. They tell the web server where the PHP code starts and finishes. Any text between the tags is interpreted as PHP. Any text outside these tags is treated as normal HTML. The PHP tags allow you to *escape* from HTML.

You can choose different tag styles. Let's look at these tags in more detail.

PHP Tag Styles

There are actually four different styles of PHP tags. Each of the following fragments of code is equivalent:

- **XML style**

```
<?php echo '<p>Order processed.</p>'; ?>
```

This is the tag style that we use in this book; it is the preferred PHP tag style. The server administrator cannot turn it off, so you can guarantee it will be available on all servers, which is especially important if you are writing applications that may be used on different installations. This tag style can be used with Extensible Markup Language (XML) documents. If you plan to serve XML on your site, you should definitely use this tag style.

- **Short style**

```
<? echo '<p>Order processed.</p>'; ?>
```

This tag style is the simplest and follows the style of a Standard Generalized Markup Language (SGML) processing instruction. To use this type of tag—which is the shortest to type—you either need to enable the `short_open_tag` setting in your config file or compile PHP with short tags enabled. You can find more information on how to use this tag style in Appendix A. The use of this style is not recommended because, although this tag style is currently enabled by default, system administrators occasionally disable it because it interferes with XML document declarations.

- **SCRIPT style**

```
<SCRIPT LANGUAGE='php'> echo '<p>Order processed.</p>'; </SCRIPT>
```

This tag style is the longest and will be familiar if you've used JavaScript or VBScript. You might use it if you're using an HTML editor that gives you problems with the other tag styles.

- **ASP style**

```
<% echo '<p>Order processed.</p>'; %>
```

This tag style is the same as used in Active Server Pages (ASP) or ASP.NET. You can use it if you have enabled the `asp_tags` configuration setting. You might want to use this style of tag if you are using an editor that is geared toward ASP or ASP.NET or if you already program in ASP or ASP.NET. Note that, by default, this tag style is disabled.

PHP Statements

You tell the PHP interpreter what to do by including PHP statements between your opening and closing tags. The preceding example used only one type of statement:

```
echo '<p>Order processed.</p>';
```

As you have probably guessed, using the `echo` construct has a very simple result: It prints (or echoes) the string passed to it to the browser. In Figure 1.2, you can see the result is that the text `Order processed.` appears in the browser window.

Notice that a semicolon appears at the end of the `echo` statement. It separates statements in PHP much like a period separates sentences in English. If you have programmed in C or Java before, you will be familiar with using the semicolon in this way.

Leaving off the semicolon is a common syntax error that is easily made. However, it's equally easy to find and to correct.

Whitespace

Spacing characters such as newlines (carriage returns), spaces, and tabs are known as *whitespace*. As you probably already know, browsers ignore whitespace in HTML. So does the PHP engine. Consider these two HTML fragments:

```
<h1>Welcome to Bob's Auto Parts!</h1><p>What would you like to order today?</p>
```

and

```
<h1>Welcome          to Bob's
Auto Parts!</h1>
<p>What would you like
to order today?</p>
```

These two snippets of HTML code produce identical output because they appear the same to the browser. However, you can and are encouraged to use whitespace in your HTML as an aid to humans—to enhance the readability of your HTML code. The same is true for PHP. You don't need to have any whitespace between PHP statements, but it makes the code much easier to read if you put each statement on a separate line. For example,

```
echo 'hello ';
echo 'world';
```

and

```
echo 'hello ';echo 'world';
```

are equivalent, but the first version is easier to read.

Comments

Comments are exactly that: Comments in code act as notes to people reading the code. Comments can be used to explain the purpose of the script, who wrote it, why they wrote it the way they did, when it was last modified, and so on. You generally find comments in all but the simplest PHP scripts.

The PHP interpreter ignores any text in comments. Essentially, the PHP parser skips over the comments, making them equivalent to whitespace.

PHP supports C, C++, and shell script–style comments.

The following is a C-style, multiline comment that might appear at the start of a PHP script:

```
/* Author: Bob Smith
   Last modified: April 10
   This script processes the customer orders.
*/
```

Multiline comments should begin with a /* and end with */. As in C, multiline comments cannot be nested.

You can also use single-line comments, either in the C++ style:

```
echo '<p>Order processed.</p>'; // Start printing order
```

or in the shell script style:

```
echo '<p>Order processed.</p>'; # Start printing order
```

With both of these styles, everything after the comment symbol (# or //) is a comment until you reach the end of the line or the ending PHP tag, whichever comes first.

In the following line of code, the text before the closing tag, `here is a comment`, is part of a comment. The text after the closing tag, `here is not`, will be treated as HTML because it is outside the closing tag:

```
// here is a comment ?> here is not
```

Adding Dynamic Content

So far, you haven't used PHP to do anything you couldn't have done with plain HTML.

The main reason for using a server-side scripting language is to be able to provide dynamic content to a site's users. This is an important application because content that changes according to users' needs or over time will keep visitors coming back to a site. PHP allows you to do this easily.

Let's start with a simple example. Replace the PHP in `processorder.php` with the following code:

```
<?php
  echo '<p>Order processed at ';
  echo date('H:i, jS F');
  echo '</p>';
?>
```

In this code, PHP's built-in `date()` function tells the customer the date and time when his order was processed. This information will be different each time the script is run. The output of running the script on one occasion is shown in Figure 1.3.

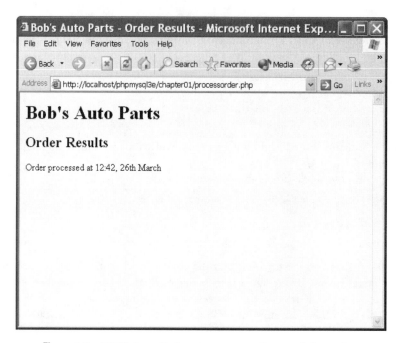

Figure 1.3   PHP's date() function returns a formatted date string.

Calling Functions

Look at the call to date(). This is the general form that function calls take. PHP has an extensive library of functions you can use when developing web applications. Most of these functions need to have some data passed to them and return some data.

Now look at the function call again:

```
date('H:i, jS F')
```

Notice that it passes a string (text data) to the function inside a pair of parentheses. The element within the parentheses is called the function's *argument* or *parameter*. Such arguments are the input the function uses to output some specific results.

Using the date() Function

The date() function expects the argument you pass it to be a format string, representing the style of output you would like. Each letter in the string represents one part of the date and time. H is the hour in a 24-hour format with leading zeros where required, i is the minutes with a leading zero where required, j is the day of the month without a leading zero, S represents the ordinal suffix (in this case th), and F is the full name of the month.

For a full list of formats supported by date(), see Chapter 20, "Managing the Date and Time."

Accessing Form Variables

The whole point of using the order form is to collect customers' orders. Getting the details of what the customers typed is easy in PHP, but the exact method depends on the version of PHP you are using and a setting in your php.ini file.

Form Variables

Within your PHP script, you can access each form field as a PHP variable whose name relates to the name of the form field. You can recognize variable names in PHP because they all start with a dollar sign ($). (Forgetting the dollar sign is a common programming error.)

Depending on your PHP version and setup, you can access the form data via variables in three ways. These methods do not have official names, so we have nicknamed them *short*, *medium*, and *long style*. In any case, each form field on a page submitted to a PHP script is available in the script.

You can access the contents of the field tireqty in the following ways:

```
$tireqty                      // short style
$_POST['tireqty']             // medium style
$HTTP_POST_VARS['tireqty']    // long style
```

In this example and throughout this book, we have used the medium style (that is, $_POST['tireqty']) for referencing form variables, but we have created short versions of the variables for ease of use. (This has been the recommended approach since PHP version 4.2.0.)

For your own code, you might decide to use a different approach. To make an informed choice, look at the different methods:

- Short style ($tireqty) is convenient but requires the register_globals configuration setting be turned on. Whether it is on or off by default depends on the version of PHP. In all versions since 4.2.0, it has been off by default. Previously, it was on by default, and most PHP programmers used the short tag style. This change caused quite a lot of confusion at the time it was made. This style also allows you to make errors that could make your code insecure, which is why it is no longer the recommended approach.

- Medium style ($_POST['tireqty']) is now the recommended approach. It is fairly convenient but came into existence only with PHP 4.1.0, so it does not work on older installations.

■ Long style ($HTTP_POST_VARS['tireqty']) is the most verbose. Note, however, that it is deprecated and is therefore likely to be removed in the long term. This style used to be the most portable but can now be disabled via the register_long_arrays configuration directive, which improves performance.

When you use the short style, the names of the variables in the script are the same as the names of the form fields in the HTML form. You don't need to declare the variables or take any action to create these variables in your script. They are passed into your script, essentially as arguments are passed to a function. If you are using this style, you can use a variable such as $tireqty. The field tireqty in the form creates the variable $tireqty in the processing script.

Such convenient access to variables is appealing, but before you simply turn on register_globals, it is worth considering why the PHP development team set it to off.

Having direct access to variables like this is very convenient, but it does allow you to make programming mistakes that could compromise your scripts' security. With form variables automatically turned into global variables like this, there is no obvious distinction between variables that you have created and untrusted variables that have come directly from users.

If you are not careful to give all your own variables a starting value, your scripts' users can pass variables and values as form variables that will be mixed with your own. If you choose to use the convenient short style of accessing variables, you need to give all your own variables a starting value.

Medium style involves retrieving form variables from one of the arrays $_POST, $_GET, or $_REQUEST. One of the $_GET or $_POST arrays holds the details of all the form variables. Which array is used depends on whether the method used to submit the form was GET or POST, respectively. In addition, all data submitted via GET or POST is also available through $_REQUEST.

If the form was submitted via the POST method, the data entered in the tireqty box will be stored in $_POST['tireqty']. If the form was submitted via GET, the data will be in $_GET['tireqty']. In either case, the data will also be available in $_REQUEST['tireqty'].

These arrays are some of the *superglobal* arrays. We will revisit the superglobals when we discuss variable scope.

If you are using an older version of PHP, you might not have access to $_POST or $_GET. Prior to version 4.1.0, this information was stored in arrays named $HTTP_POST_VARS and $HTTP_GET_VARS. We call this the long style. As mentioned previously, this style has been deprecated. There is no equivalent of $_REQUEST in this style.

If you are using long style, you can access a user's response through $HTTP_POST_VARS['tireqty'] or $HTTP_GET_VARS['tireqty'].

The examples in this book were tested with PHP version 5.0 and will sometimes be incompatible with older versions of PHP prior to version 4.1.0. We recommend that, where possible, you use the current version.

Let's look at another example. Because the long and medium style variable names are somewhat cumbersome and rely on a variable type known as *arrays*, which are not covered properly until Chapter 3, "Using Arrays," you can start by creating easier-to-use copies.

To copy the value of one variable into another, you use the assignment operator, which in PHP is an equal sign (=). The following statement creates a new variable named `$tireqty` and copies the contents of `$ POST ['tireqty']` into the new variable:

```
$tireqty = $_POST['tireqty'];
```

Place the following block of code at the start of the processing script. All other scripts in this book that handle data from a form contain a similar block at the start. Because this code will not produce any output, placing it above or below the `<html>` and other HTML tags that start your page makes no difference. We generally place such blocks at the start of the script to make them easy to find.

```php
<?php
  // create short variable names
  $tireqty = $_POST['tireqty'];
  $oilqty = $_POST['oilqty'];
  $sparkqty = $_POST['sparkqty'];
?>
```

This code creates three new variables—`$tireqty`, `$oilqty`, and `$sparkqty`—and sets them to contain the data sent via the POST method from the form.

To make the script start doing something visible, add the following lines to the bottom of your PHP script:

```php
echo '<p>Your order is as follows: </p>';
echo $tireqty.' tires<br />';
echo $oilqty.' bottles of oil<br />';
echo $sparkqty.' spark plugs<br />';
```

At this stage, you have not checked the variable contents to make sure sensible data has been entered in each form field. Try entering deliberately wrong data and observe what happens. After you have read the rest of the chapter, you might want to try adding some data validation to this script.

If you now load this file in your browser, the script output should resemble what is shown in Figure 1.4. The actual values shown, of course, depend on what you typed into the form.

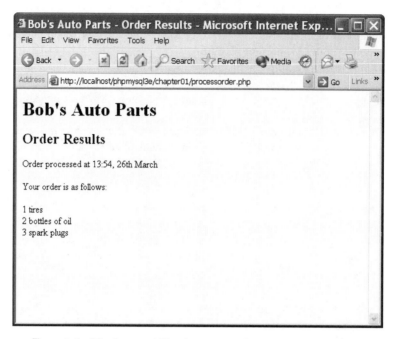

Figure 1.4   The form variables the user typed in are easily accessible in
processorder.php.

The following subsections describe a couple of interesting elements of this example.

String Concatenation

In the sample script, echo prints the value the user typed in each form field, followed by some explanatory text. If you look closely at the echo statements, you can see that the variable name and following text have a period (.) between them, such as this:

```
echo $tireqty.' tires<br />';
```

This period is the string concatenation operator, which adds strings (pieces of text) together. You will often use it when sending output to the browser with echo. This way, you can avoid writing multiple echo commands.

You can also place any nonarray variables inside a double-quoted string to be echoed. (Arrays are somewhat more complicated, so we look at combining arrays and strings in Chapter 4, "String Manipulation and Regular Expressions.") Consider this example:

```
echo "$tireqty tires<br />";
```

This is equivalent to the first statement shown in this section. Either format is valid, and which one you use is a matter of personal taste. This process, replacing a variable with its contents within a string, is known as interpolation.

Note that interpolation is a feature of double-quoted strings only. You cannot place variable names inside a single-quoted string in this way. Running the following line of code

```
echo '$tireqty tires<br />';
```

simply sends `"$tireqty tires<br />"` to the browser. Within double quotation marks, the variable name is replaced with its value. Within single quotation marks, the variable name or any other text is sent unaltered.

Variables and Literals

The variables and strings concatenated together in each of the `echo` statements in the sample script are different types of things. Variables are symbols for data. The strings are data themselves. When we use a piece of raw data in a program like this, we call it a *literal* to distinguish it from a variable. `$tireqty` is a variable, a symbol that represents the data the customer typed in. On the other hand, `' tires<br />'` is a literal. You can take it at face value. Well, almost. Remember the second example in the preceding section? PHP replaced the variable name `$tireqty` in the string with the value stored in the variable.

Remember the two kinds of strings mentioned already: ones with double quotation marks and ones with single quotation marks. PHP tries to evaluate strings in double quotation marks, resulting in the behavior shown earlier. Single-quoted strings are treated as true literals.

Recently, a third way of specifying strings was added. The heredoc syntax (<<<), familiar to Perl users, was added to PHP4. Heredoc syntax allows you to specify long strings tidily, by specifying an end marker that will be used to terminate the string. The following example creates a three-line string and echoes it:

```
echo <<<theEnd
  line 1
  line 2
  line 3
theEnd
```

The token `theEnd` is entirely arbitrary. It just needs to be guaranteed not to appear in the text. To close a heredoc string, place a closing token at the start of a line.

Heredoc strings are interpolated, like double-quoted strings.

Understanding Identifiers

Identifiers are the names of variables. (The names of functions and classes are also identifiers; we look at functions and classes in Chapters 5, "Reusing Code and Writing Functions," and 6, "Object-Oriented PHP.") You need to be aware of the simple rules defining valid identifiers:

- Identifiers can be of any length and can consist of letters, numbers, and underscores.

- Identifiers cannot begin with a digit.

- In PHP, identifiers are case sensitive. `$tireqty` is not the same as `$TireQty`. Trying to use them interchangeably is a common programming error. Function names are an exception to this rule: Their names can be used in any case.

- A variable can have the same name as a function. This usage is confusing, however, and should be avoided. Also, you cannot create a function with the same name as another function.

Creating User-Declared Variables

You can declare and use your own variables in addition to the variables you are passed from the HTML form.

One of the features of PHP is that it does not require you to declare variables before using them. A variable is created when you first assign a value to it. See the next section for details.

Assigning Values to Variables

You assign values to variables using the assignment operator (=) as you did when copying one variable's value to another. On Bob's site, you want to work out the total number of items ordered and the total amount payable. You can create two variables to store these numbers. To begin with, you need to initialize each of these variables to zero.

Add these lines to the bottom of your PHP script:

```
$totalqty = 0;
$totalamount = 0.00;
```

Each of these two lines creates a variable and assigns a literal value to it. You can also assign variable values to variables, as shown in this example:

```
$totalqty = 0;
$totalamount = $totalqty;
```

Examining Variable Types

A variable's type refers to the kind of data stored in it. PHP provides a growing set of data types. Different data can be stored in different data types.

PHP's Data Types

PHP supports the following basic data types:

- **Integer**—Used for whole numbers
- **Float** (also called **double**)—Used for real numbers
- **String**—Used for strings of characters
- **Boolean**—Used for true or false values
- **Array**—Used to store multiple data items (see Chapter 3, "Using Arrays")
- **Object**—Used for storing instances of classes (see Chapter 6)

Two special types are also available: NULL and resource. Variables that have not been given a value, have been unset, or have been given the specific value NULL are of type NULL. Certain built-in functions (such as database functions) return variables that have the type resource. They represent external resources (such as database connections). You will almost certainly not directly manipulate a resource variable, but frequently they are returned by functions and must be passed as parameters to other functions.

Type Strength

PHP is a very weakly typed language. In most programming languages, variables can hold only one type of data, and that type must be declared before the variable can be used, as in C. In PHP, the type of a variable is determined by the value assigned to it.

For example, when you created $totalqty and $totalamount, their initial types were determined as follows:

```
$totalqty = 0;
$totalamount = 0.00;
```

Because you assigned 0, an integer, to $totalqty, this is now an integer type variable. Similarly, $totalamount is now of type float.

Strangely enough, you could now add a line to your script as follows:

```
$totalamount = 'Hello';
```

The variable $totalamount would then be of type string. PHP changes the variable type according to what is stored in it at any given time.

This ability to change types transparently on the fly can be extremely useful. Remember PHP "automagically" knows what data type you put into your variable. It returns the data with the same data type when you retrieve it from the variable.

Type Casting

You can pretend that a variable or value is of a different type by using a type cast. This feature works identically to the way it works in C. You simply put the temporary type in parentheses in front of the variable you want to cast.

For example, you could have declared the two variables from the preceding section using a cast:

```
$totalqty = 0;
$totalamount = (float)$totalqty;
```

The second line means "Take the value stored in $totalqty, interpret it as a float, and store it in $totalamount." The $totalamount variable will be of type float. The cast variable does not change types, so $totalqty remains of type integer.

Variable Variables

PHP provides one other type of variable: the variable variable. Variable variables enable you to change the name of a variable dynamically.

As you can see, PHP allows a lot of freedom in this area. All languages enable you to change the value of a variable, but not many allow you to change the variable's type, and even fewer allow you to change the variable's name.

A variable variable works by using the value of one variable as the name of another. For example, you could set

```
$varname = 'tireqty';
```

You can then use $$varname in place of $tireqty. For example, you can set the value of $tireqty as follows:

```
$$varname = 5;
```

This is exactly equivalent to

```
$tireqty = 5;
```

This approach might seem somewhat obscure, but we'll revisit its use later. Instead of having to list and use each form variable separately, you can use a loop and variable to process them all automatically. You can find an example illustrating this in the section on for loops.

Declaring and Using Constants

As you saw previously, you can readily change the value stored in a variable. You can also declare constants. A constant stores a value just like a variable, but its value is set once and then cannot be changed elsewhere in the script.

In the sample application, you might store the prices for each item on sale as a constant. You can define these constants using the `define` function:

```
define('TIREPRICE', 100);
define('OILPRICE', 10);
define('SPARKPRICE', 4);
```

Now add these lines of code to your script. You now have three constants that can be used to calculate the total of the customer's order.

Notice that the names of the constants appear in uppercase. This convention borrowed from C makes it easy to distinguish between variables and constants at a glance. Following this convention is not required but will make your code easier to read and maintain.

One important difference between constants and variables is that when you refer to a constant, it does not have a dollar sign in front of it. If you want to use the value of a constant, use its name only. For example, to use one of the constants just created, you could type

```
echo TIREPRICE;
```

As well as the constants you define, PHP sets a large number of its own. An easy way to obtain an overview of them is to run the `phpinfo()` command:

```
phpinfo();
```

This function provides a list of PHP's predefined variables and constants, among other useful information. We will discuss some of them as we go along.

One other difference between variables and constants is that constants can store only boolean, integer, float, or string data. These types are collectively known as scalar values.

Understanding Variable Scope

The term *scope* refers to the places within a script where a particular variable is visible. The six basic scope rules in PHP are as follows:

- Built-in superglobal variables are visible everywhere within a script.
- Constants, once declared, are always visible globally; that is, they can be used inside and outside functions.
- Global variables declared in a script are visible throughout that script, but *not inside functions*.

- Variables used inside functions that are declared as global refer to the global variables of the same name.
- Variables created inside functions and declared as static are invisible from outside the function but keep their value between one execution of the function and the next. (We explain this idea fully in Chapter 5.)
- Variables created inside functions are local to the function and cease to exist when the function terminates.

In PHP 4.1 onward, the arrays $_GET and $_POST and some other special variables have their own scope rules. They are known as *superglobals* and can be seen everywhere, both inside and outside functions.

The complete list of superglobals is as follows:

- $GLOBALS—An array of all global variables (Like the global keyword, this allows you to access global variables inside a function—for example, as $GLOBALS['myvariable'].)
- $_SERVER—An array of server environment variables
- $_GET—An array of variables passed to the script via the GET method
- $_POST—An array of variables passed to the script via the POST method
- $_COOKIE—An array of cookie variables
- $_FILES—An array of variables related to file uploads
- $_ENV—An array of environment variables
- $_REQUEST—An array of all user input including the contents of input including $_GET, $_POST, and $_COOKIE
- $_SESSION—An array of session variables

We come back to each of these types throughout the book as they become relevant.

We cover scope in more detail when we discuss functions. For the time being, all the variables we use are global by default.

Using Operators

Operators are symbols that you can use to manipulate values and variables by performing an operation on them. You need to use some of these operators to work out the totals and tax on the customer's order.

We've already mentioned two operators: the assignment operator (=) and the string concatenation operator (.). In the following sections, we describe the complete list.

In general, operators can take one, two, or three arguments, with the majority taking two. For example, the assignment operator takes two: the storage location on the left side of the = symbol and an expression on the right side. These arguments are called *operands*—that is, the things that are being operated upon.

Arithmetic Operators

Arithmetic operators are straightforward; they are just the normal mathematical operators. PHP's arithmetic operators are shown in Table 1.1.

Table 1.1 **PHP's Arithmetic Operators**

Operator	Name	Example
+	Addition	$a + $b
–	Subtraction	$a - $b
*	Multiplication	$a * $b
/	Division	$a / $b
%	Modulus	$a % $b

With each of these operators, you can store the result of the operation, as in this example:

```
$result = $a + $b;
```

Addition and subtraction work as you would expect. The result of these operators is to add or subtract, respectively, the values stored in the $a and $b variables.

You can also use the subtraction symbol (-) as a unary operator—that is, an operator that takes one argument or operand—to indicate negative numbers, as in this example:

```
$a = -1;
```

Multiplication and division also work much as you would expect. Note the use of the asterisk as the multiplication operator rather than the regular multiplication symbol, and the forward slash as the division operator rather than the regular division symbol.

The modulus operator returns the remainder calculated by dividing the $a variable by the $b variable. Consider this code fragment:

```
$a = 27;
$b = 10;
$result = $a%$b;
```

The value stored in the $result variable is the remainder when you divide 27 by 10—that is, 7.

You should note that arithmetic operators are usually applied to integers or doubles. If you apply them to strings, PHP will try to convert the string to a number. If it contains an e or an E, it will be read as being in scientific notation and converted to a float; otherwise, it will be converted to an integer. PHP will look for digits at the start of the string and use them as the value; if there are none, the value of the string will be zero.

String Operators

You've already seen and used the only string operator. You can use the string concatenation operator to add two strings and to generate and store a result much as you would use the addition operator to add two numbers:

```
$a = "Bob's ";
$b = "Auto Parts";
$result = $a.$b;
```

The $result variable now contains the string "Bob's Auto Parts".

Assignment Operators

You've already seen the basic assignment operator (=). Always refer to this as the assignment operator and read it as "is set to." For example,

```
$totalqty = 0;
```

This line should be read as "$totalqty is set to zero." We explain why when we discuss the comparison operators later in this chapter, but if you call it equals, you will get confused.

Values Returned from Assignment

Using the assignment operator returns an overall value similar to other operators. If you write

```
$a + $b
```

the value of this expression is the result of adding the $a and $b variables together. Similarly, you can write

```
$a = 0;
```

The value of this whole expression is zero.

This technique enables you to form expressions such as

```
$b = 6 + ($a = 5);
```

This line sets the value of the $b variable to 11. This behavior is generally true of assignments: The value of the whole assignment statement is the value that is assigned to the left operand.

When working out the value of an expression, you can use parentheses to increase the precedence of a subexpression, as shown here. This technique works exactly the same way as in mathematics.

Combination Assignment Operators

In addition to the simple assignment, there is a set of combined assignment operators. Each of them is a shorthand way of performing another operation on a variable and assigning the result back to that variable. For example,

```
$a += 5;
```

This is equivalent to writing

```
$a = $a + 5;
```

Combined assignment operators exist for each of the arithmetic operators and for the string concatenation operator. A summary of all the combined assignment operators and their effects is shown in Table 1.2.

Table 1.2   **PHP's Combined Assignment Operators**

Operator	Use	Equivalent To
+=	$a += $b	$a = $a + $b
-=	$a -= $b	$a = $a - $b
*=	$a *= $b	$a = $a * $b
/=	$a /= $b	$a = $a / $b
%=	$a %= $b	$a = $a % $b
.=	$a .= $b	$a = $a . $b

Pre- and Post-Increment and Decrement

The pre- and post-increment (++) and decrement (--) operators are similar to the += and -= operators, but with a couple of twists.

All the increment operators have two effects: They increment and assign a value. Consider the following:

```
$a=4;
echo ++$a;
```

The second line uses the pre-increment operator, so called because the ++ appears before the $a. This has the effect of first incrementing $a by 1 and second, returning the incremented value. In this case, $a is incremented to 5, and then the value 5 is returned and printed. The value of this whole expression is 5. (Notice that the actual value stored in $a is changed: It is not just returning $a + 1.)

If the ++ is after the $a, however, you are using the post-increment operator. It has a different effect. Consider the following:

```
$a=4;
echo $a++;
```

In this case, the effects are reversed. That is, first, the value of $a is returned and printed, and second, it is incremented. The value of this whole expression is 4. This is the value that will be printed. However, the value of $a after this statement is executed is 5.

As you can probably guess, the behavior is similar for the -- operator. However, the value of $a is decremented instead of being incremented.

References

The reference operator (&, an ampersand) can be used in conjunction with assignment. Normally, when one variable is assigned to another, a copy is made of the first variable and stored elsewhere in memory. For example,

```
$a = 5;
$b = $a;
```

These code lines make a second copy of the value in $a and store it in $b. If you subsequently change the value of $a, $b will not change:

```
$a = 7; // $b will still be 5
```

You can avoid making a copy by using the reference operator. For example,

```
$a = 5;
$b = &$a;
$a = 7; // $a and $b are now both 7
```

References can be a bit tricky. Remember that a reference is like an alias rather than like a pointer. Both $a and $b point to the same piece of memory. You can change this by unsetting one of them as follows:

```
unset($a);
```

Unsetting does not change the value of $b (7) but does break the link between $a and the value 7 stored in memory.

Comparison Operators

The comparison operators compare two values. Expressions using these operators return either of the logical values true or false depending on the result of the comparison.

The Equals Operator

The equals comparison operator (==, two equal signs) enables you to test whether two values are equal. For example, you might use the expression

```
$a == $b
```

to test whether the values stored in $a and $b are the same. The result returned by this expression is true if they are equal or false if they are not.

You might easily confuse == with =, the assignment operator. Using the wrong operator will work without giving an error but generally will not give you the result you wanted. In general, nonzero values evaluate to true and zero values to false. Say that you have initialized two variables as follows:

```
$a = 5;
$b = 7;
```

If you then test $a = $b, the result will be true. Why? The value of $a = $b is the value assigned to the left side, which in this case is 7. Because 7 is a nonzero value, the expression evaluates to true. If you intended to test $a == $b, which evaluates to false, you have introduced a logic error in your code that can be extremely difficult to find. Always check your use of these two operators and check that you have used the one you intended to use.

Using the assignment operator rather than the equals comparison operator is an easy mistake to make, and you will probably make it many times in your programming career.

Other Comparison Operators

PHP also supports a number of other comparison operators. A summary of all the comparison operators is shown in Table 1.3. One to note is the identical operator (===), which returns true only if the two operands are both equal and of the same type. For example, 0=='0' will be true, but 0==='0' will not because one zero is an integer and the other zero is a string.

Table 1.3 **PHP's Comparison Operators**

Operator	Name	Use
==	Equals	$a == $b
===	Identical	$a === $b
!=	Not equal	$a != $b
!==	Not identical	$a !== $b
<>	Not equal (comparison operator)	$a <> $b
<	Less than	$a < $b
>	Greater than (comparison operator)	$a > $b
<=	Less than or equal to	$a <= $b
>=	Greater than or equal to	$a >= $b

Logical Operators

The logical operators combine the results of logical conditions. For example, you might be interested in a case in which the value of a variable, $a, is between 0 and 100. You would need to test both the conditions $a >= 0 and $a <= 100, using the AND operator, as follows:

```
$a >= 0 && $a <=100
```

PHP supports logical AND, OR, XOR (exclusive or), and NOT.

The set of logical operators and their use is summarized in Table 1.4.

Table 1.4 **PHP's Logical Operators**

Operator	Name	Use	Result
!	NOT	!$b	Returns true if $b is false and vice versa
&&	AND	$a && $b	Returns true if both $a and $b are true; otherwise false
||	OR	$a || $b	Returns true if either $a or $b or both are true; otherwise false
and	AND	$a and $b	Same as &&, but with lower precedence
or	OR	$a or $b	Same as ||, but with lower precedence

The and and or operators have lower precedence than the && and || operators. We cover precedence in more detail later in this chapter.

Bitwise Operators

The bitwise operators enable you to treat an integer as the series of bits used to represent it. You probably will not find a lot of use for the bitwise operators in PHP, but a summary is shown in Table 1.5.

Table 1.5 **PHP's Bitwise Operators**

Operator	Name	Use	Result
&	Bitwise AND	$a & $b	Bits set in $a and $b are set in the result.
|	Bitwise OR	$a | $b	Bits set in $a or $b are set in the result.
~	Bitwise NOT	~$a	Bits set in $a are not set in the result and vice versa.
^	Bitwise XOR	$a ^ $b	Bits set in $a or $b but not in both are set in the result.
<<	Left shift	$a << $b	Shifts $a left $b bits.
>>	Right shift	$a >> $b	Shifts $a right $b bits.

Other Operators

In addition to the operators we have covered so far, you can use several others.

The comma operator (,) separates function arguments and other lists of items. It is normally used incidentally.

Two special operators, `new` and `->`, are used to instantiate a class and access class members, respectively. They are covered in detail in Chapter 6.

There are a few others that we discuss briefly here.

The Ternary Operator

The ternary operator (`?:`) works the same way as it does in C. It takes the following form:

```
condition ? value if true : value if false
```

This operator is similar to the expression version of an `if-else` statement, which is covered later in this chapter.

A simple example is

```
($grade >= 50 ? 'Passed' : 'Failed')
```

This expression evaluates student grades to `'Passed'` or `'Failed'`.

The Error Suppression Operator

The error suppression operator (@) can be used in front of any expression—that is, anything that generates or has a value. For example,

```
$a = @(57/0);
```

Without the @ operator, this line generates a divide-by-zero warning. With the operator included, the error is suppressed.

If you are suppressing warnings in this way, you should write some error handling code to check when a warning has occurred. If you have PHP set up with the `track_errors` feature enabled, the error message will be stored in the global variable `$php_errormsg`.

The Execution Operator

The execution operator is really a pair of operators—a pair of backticks (`` `` ` ``) in fact. The backtick is not a single quotation mark; it is usually located on the same key as the ~ (tilde) symbol on your keyboard.

PHP attempts to execute whatever is contained between the backticks as a command at the server's command line. The value of the expression is the output of the command.

For example, under Unix-like operating systems, you can use

```
$out = `ls -la`;
echo '<pre>'.$out.'</pre>';
```

Or, equivalently on a Windows server, you can use

```
$out = `dir c:`;
echo '<pre>'.$out.'</pre>';
```

Either version obtains a directory listing and stores it in `$out`. It can then be echoed to the browser or dealt with in any other way.

There are other ways of executing commands on the server. We cover them in Chapter 18, "Interacting with the File System and the Server."

Array Operators

There are a number of array operators. The array element operators (`[]`) enable you to access array elements. You can also use the `=>` operator in some array contexts. These operators are covered in Chapter 3.

You also have access to a number of other array operators. We cover them in detail in Chapter 3 as well, but we included them here for completeness.

Table 1.6 **PHP's Array Operators**

Operator	Name	Use	Result
+	Union	$a + $b	Returns an array containing everything in $a and $b
==	Equality	$a == $b	Returns true if $a and $b have the same elements
===	Identity	$a === $b	Returns true if $a and $b have the same elements in the same order
!=	Inequality	$a != $b	Returns true if $a and $b are not equal
<>	Inequality	$a <> $b	Returns true if $a and $b are not equal
!==	Non-identity	$a !== $b	Returns true if $a and $b are not identical

You will notice that the array operators in Table 1.6 all have equivalent operators that work on scalar variables. As long as you remember that + performs addition on scalar types and union on arrays—even if you have no interest in the set arithmetic behind that behavior—the behaviors should make sense. You cannot usefully compare arrays to scalar types.

The Type Operator

There is one type operator: `instanceof`. This operator is used in object-oriented programming, but we mention it here for completeness. (Object-oriented programming is covered in Chapter 6.)

The `instanceof` operator allows you to check whether an object is an instance of a particular class, as in this example:

```
class sampleClass{};
$myObject = new sampleClass();
if ($myObject instanceof sampleClass)
  echo "myObject is an instance of sampleClass";
```

Using Operators: Working Out the Form Totals

Now that you know how to use PHP's operators, you are ready to work out the totals and tax on Bob's order form. To do this, add the following code to the bottom of your PHP script:

```
$totalqty = 0;
$totalqty = $tireqty + $oilqty + $sparkqty;
echo 'Items ordered: '.$totalqty.'<br />';

$totalamount = 0.00;

define('TIREPRICE', 100);
define('OILPRICE', 10);
define('SPARKPRICE', 4);

$totalamount = $tireqty * TIREPRICE
             + $oilqty * OILPRICE
             + $sparkqty * SPARKPRICE;

echo 'Subtotal: $'.number_format($totalamount,2).'<br />';

$taxrate = 0.10;  // local sales tax is 10%
$totalamount = $totalamount * (1 + $taxrate);
echo 'Total including tax: $'.number_format($totalamount,2).'<br />';
```

If you refresh the page in your browser window, you should see output similar to Figure 1.5.

As you can see, this piece of code uses several operators. It uses the addition (+) and multiplication (*) operators to work out the amounts and the string concatenation operator (.) to set up the output to the browser.

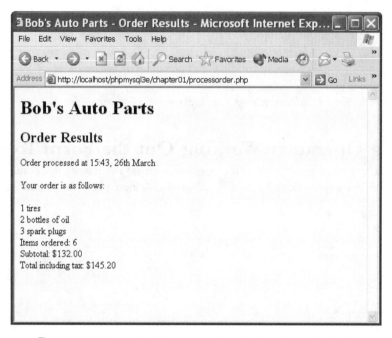

Figure 1.5   The totals of the customer's order have been calculated, formatted, and displayed.

It also uses the `number_format()` function to format the totals as strings with two decimal places. This is a function from PHP's Math library.

If you look closely at the calculations, you might ask why the calculations were performed in the order they were. For example, consider this statement:

```
$totalamount = $tireqty * TIREPRICE
            + $oilqty * OILPRICE
            + $sparkqty * SPARKPRICE;
```

The total amount seems to be correct, but why were the multiplications performed before the additions? The answer lies in the precedence of the operators—that is, the order in which they are evaluated.

Understanding Precedence and Associativity: Evaluating Expressions

In general, operators have a set precedence, or order, in which they are evaluated. Operators also have an associativity, which is the order in which operators of the same precedence are evaluated. This order is generally left to right (called *left* for short), right to left (called *right* for short), or *not relevant*.

Table 1.7 shows operator precedence and associativity in PHP. In this table, operators with the lowest precedence are at the top, and precedence increases as you go down the table.

Table 1.7 **Operator Precedence in PHP**

Associativity	Operators
left	,
left	or
left	xor
left	and
right	print
left	= += -= *= /= .= %= &= |= ^= ~= <<= >>=
left	? :
left	||
left	&&
left	|
left	^
left	&
n/a	== != === !==
n/a	< <= > >=
left	<< >>
left	+ - .
left	* / %
right	! ~ ++ -- (int) (double) (string) (array) (object) @
right	[]
n/a	new
n/a	()

Notice that we haven't yet covered the operator with the highest precedence: plain old parentheses. The effect of using parentheses is to raise the precedence of whatever is contained within them. This is how you can deliberately manipulate or work around the precedence rules when you need to.

Remember this part of the preceding example:

```
$totalamount = $totalamount * (1 + $taxrate);
```

If you had written

```
$totalamount = $totalamount * 1 + $taxrate;
```

the multiplication operation, having higher precedence than the addition operation, would be performed first, giving an incorrect result. By using the parentheses, you can force the subexpression 1 + $taxrate to be evaluated first.

You can use as many sets of parentheses as you like in an expression. The innermost set of parentheses is evaluated first.

Also note one other operator in this table we have not yet covered: the `print` language construct, which is equivalent to `echo`. Both constructs generate output.

We generally use `echo` in this book, but you can use `print` if you find it more readable. Neither `print` nor `echo` is really a function, but both can be called as a function with parameters in parentheses. Both can also be treated as an operator: You simply place the string to work with after the keyword `echo` or `print`.

Calling `print` as a function causes it to return a value (1). This capability might be useful if you want to generate output inside a more complex expression but does mean that `print` is marginally slower than `echo`.

Using Variable Functions

Before we leave the world of variables and operators, let's look at PHP's variable functions. PHP provides a library of functions that enable you to manipulate and test variables in different ways.

Testing and Setting Variable Types

Most of the variable functions are related to testing the type of function. The two most general are `gettype()` and `settype()`. They have the following function prototypes; that is, this is what arguments expect and what they return:

```
string gettype(mixed var);
int settype(mixed var, string type);
```

To use `gettype()`, you pass it a variable. It determines the type and returns a string containing the type name: `boolean`, `integer`, `double` (for floats), `string`, `array`, `object`, `resource`, or `NULL`. It returns `unknown type` if it is not one of the standard types.

To use `settype()`, you pass it a variable for which you want to change the type and a string containing the new type for that variable from the previous list.

> **Note**
>
> This book and the php.net documentation refer to the data type mixed. There is no such data type, but because PHP is so flexible with type handling, many functions can take many (or any) data types as an argument. Arguments for which many types are permitted are shown with the pseudo-type mixed.

You can use these functions as follows:

```
$a = 56;
echo gettype($a).'<br />';
settype($a, 'double');
echo gettype($a).'<br />';
```

When `gettype()` is called the first time, the type of `$a` is integer. After the call to `settype()`, the type is changed to `double`.

PHP also provides some specific type-testing functions. Each takes a variable as an argument and returns either `true` or `false`. The functions are

- `is_array()`
- `is_double()`, `is_float()`, `is_real()` (All the same function)
- `is_long()`, `is_int()`, `is_integer()` (All the same function)
- `is_string()`
- `is_object()`
- `is_resource()`
- `is_null()`
- `is_scalar()`—Checks whether the variable is a scalar, that is, an integer, boolean, string, or float.
- `is_numeric()`—Checks whether the variable is any kind of number or a numeric string.
- `is_callable()`—Checks whether the variable is the name of a valid function.

Testing Variable Status

PHP has several functions for testing the status of a variable. The first is `isset()`, which has the following prototype:

```
boolean isset(mixed var);
```

This function takes a variable name as an argument and returns `true` if it exists and `false` otherwise. You can also pass in a comma-separated list of variables, and `isset()` will return `true` if all the variables are set.

You can wipe a variable out of existence by using its companion function, `unset()`, which has the following prototype:

```
void unset(mixed var);
```

This function gets rid of the variable it is passed.

The `empty()` function checks to see whether a variable exists and has a nonempty, nonzero value; it returns `true` or `false` accordingly. It has the following prototype:

```
boolean empty(mixed var);
```

Let's look at an example using these three functions.

Try adding the following code to your script temporarily:

```
echo 'isset($tireqty): '.isset($tireqty).'<br />';
echo 'isset($nothere): '.isset($nothere).'<br />';
echo 'empty($tireqty): '.empty($tireqty).'<br />';
echo 'empty($nothere): '.empty($nothere).'<br />';
```

Refresh the page to see the results.

The variable $tireqty should return 1 (true) from isset() regardless of what value you entered in that form field and regardless of whether you entered a value at all. Whether it is empty() depends on what you entered in it.

The variable $nothere does not exist, so it generates a blank (false) result from isset() and a 1 (true) result from empty().

These functions can be handy when you need to make sure that the user filled out the appropriate fields in the form.

Reinterpreting Variables

You can achieve the equivalent of casting a variable by calling a function. The following three functions can be useful for this task:

```
int intval(mixed var[, int base]);
float floatval(mixed var);
string strval(mixed var);
```

Each accepts a variable as input and returns the variable's value converted to the appropriate type. The intval() function also allows you to specify the base for conversion when the variable to be converted is a string. (This way, you can convert, for example, hexadecimal strings to integers.)

Implementing Control Structures

Control structures are the structures within a language that allow you to control the flow of execution through a program or script. You can group them into conditionals (or branching) structures and repetition structures (or loops). We consider the specific implementations of each of them in PHP next.

Making Decisions with Conditionals

If you want to sensibly respond to your users' input, your code needs to be able to make decisions. The constructs that tell your program to make decisions are called *conditionals*.

if Statements

You can use an if statement to make a decision. You should give the if statement a condition to use. If the condition is true, the following block of code will be executed. Conditions in if statements must be surrounded by parentheses ().

For example, if a visitor orders no tires, no bottles of oil, and no spark plugs from Bob, it is probably because she accidentally clicked the Submit Order button before she had finished filling out the form. Rather than telling the visitor "Order processed," the page could give her a more useful message.

When the visitor orders no items, you might like to say, "You did not order anything on the previous page!" You can do this easily by using the following `if` statement:

```
if( $totalqty == 0 )
  echo 'You did not order anything on the previous page!<br />';
```

The condition you are using here is `$totalqty == 0`. Remember that the equals operator (`==`) behaves differently from the assignment operator (`=`).

The condition `$totalqty == 0` will be `true` if `$totalqty` is equal to zero. If `$totalqty` is not equal to zero, the condition will be `false`. When the condition is `true`, the `echo` statement will be executed.

Code Blocks

Often you may have more than one statement you want executed according to the actions of a conditional statement such as `if`. You can group a number of statements together as a *block*. To declare a block, you enclose it in curly braces:

```
if( $totalqty == 0 )
{
  echo '<font color=red>';
  echo 'You did not order anything on the previous page!<br />';
  echo '</font>';
}
```

The three lines enclosed in curly braces are now a block of code. When the condition is `true`, all three lines are executed. When the condition is `false`, all three lines are ignored.

Note

As already mentioned, PHP does not care how you lay out your code. However, you should indent your code for readability purposes. Indenting is used to enable you to see at a glance which lines will be executed only if conditions are met, which statements are grouped into blocks, and which statements are parts of loops or functions. In the previous examples, you can see that the statement depending on the `if` statement and the statements making up the block are indented.

`else` Statements

You may often need to decide not only whether you want an action performed, but also which of a set of possible actions you want performed.

An `else` statement allows you to define an alternative action to be taken when the condition in an `if` statement is `false`. Say you want to warn Bob's customers when they do not order anything. On the other hand, if they do make an order, instead of a warning, you want to show them what they ordered.

If you rearrange the code and add an `else` statement, you can display either a warning or a summary:

```
if( $totalqty == 0 )
{
  echo 'You did not order anything on the previous page!<br />';
}
else
{
  echo $tireqty.' tires<br />';
  echo $oilqty.' bottles of oil<br />';
  echo $sparkqty.' spark plugs<br />';
}
```

You can build more complicated logical processes by nesting `if` statements within each other. In the following code, the summary will be displayed only if the condition `$totalqty == 0` is true, and each line in the summary will be displayed only if its own condition is met:

```
if( $totalqty == 0)
{
  echo 'You did not order anything on the previous page!<br />';
}
else
{
  if ( $tireqty>0 )
    echo $tireqty.' tires<br />';
  if ( $oilqty>0 )
    echo $oilqty.' bottles of oil<br />';
  if ( $sparkqty>0 )
    echo $sparkqty.' spark plugs<br />';
}
```

elseif **Statements**

For many of the decisions you make, you have more than two options. You can create a sequence of many options using the `elseif` statement, which is a combination of an `else` and an `if` statement. When you provide a sequence of conditions, the program can check each until it finds one that is true.

Bob provides a discount for large orders of tires. The discount scheme works like this:

- Fewer than 10 tires purchased—No discount
- 10–49 tires purchased—5% discount
- 50–99 tires purchased—10% discount
- 100 or more tires purchased—15% discount

You can create code to calculate the discount using conditions and `if` and `elseif` statements. In this case, you need to use the AND operator (`&&`) to combine two conditions into one:

```
if( $tireqty < 10 )
  $discount = 0;
elseif( $tireqty >= 10 && $tireqty <= 49 )
  $discount = 5;
elseif( $tireqty >= 50 && $tireqty <= 99 )
  $discount = 10;
elseif( $tireqty >= 100 )
  $discount = 15;
```

Note that you are free to type `elseif` or `else if`—versions with or without a space are both correct.

If you are going to write a cascading set of `elseif` statements, you should be aware that only one of the blocks or statements will be executed. It did not matter in this example because all the conditions were mutually exclusive; only one can be true at a time. If you write conditions in a way that more than one could be true at the same time, only the block or statement following the first true condition will be executed.

`switch` **Statements**

The `switch` statement works in a similar way to the `if` statement, but it allows the condition to take more than two values. In an `if` statement, the condition can be either `true` or `false`. In a `switch` statement, the condition can take any number of different values, as long as it evaluates to a simple type (integer, string, or float). You need to provide a `case` statement to handle each value you want to react to and, optionally, a default case to handle any that you do not provide a specific `case` statement for.

Bob wants to know what forms of advertising are working for him, so you can add a question to the order form. Insert this HTML into the order form, and the form will resemble Figure 1.6:

```
<tr>
  <td>How did you find Bob's?</td>
  <td><select name="find">
      <option value = "a">I'm a regular customer</option>
      <option value = "b">TV advertising</option>
      <option value = "c">Phone directory</option>
      <option value = "d">Word of mouth</option>
    </select>
  </td>

</tr>
```

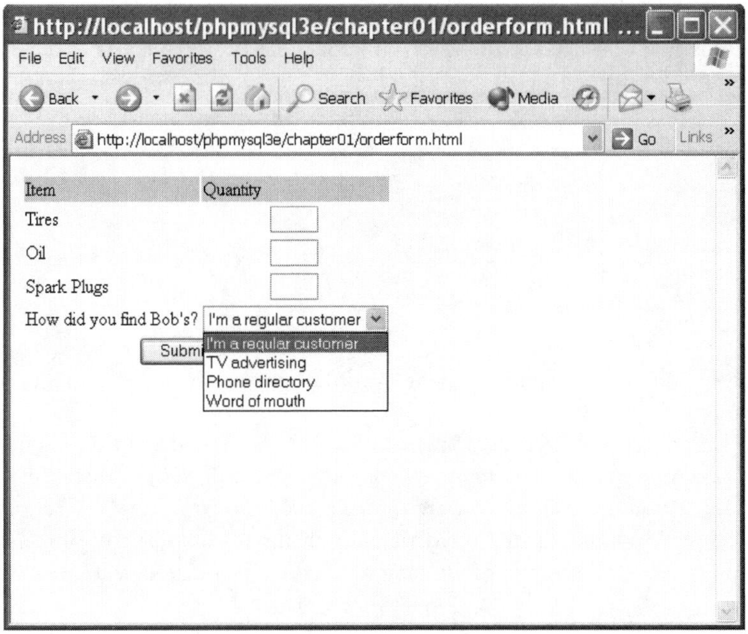

Figure 1.6 The order form now asks visitors how they found Bob's Auto Parts.

This HTML code adds a new form variable (called find) whose value will either be 'a', 'b', 'c', or 'd'. You could handle this new variable with a series of if and elseif statements like this:

```
if($find == 'a')
  echo '<p>Regular customer.</p>';
elseif($find == 'b')
  echo '<p>Customer referred by TV advert.</p>';
elseif($find == 'c')
  echo '<p>Customer referred by phone directory.</p>';
elseif($find == 'd')
  echo '<p>Customer referred by word of mouth.</p>';
else
  echo '<p>We do not know how this customer found us.</p>';
```

Alternatively, you could write a switch statement:

```
switch($find)
{
  case 'a' :
    echo '<p>Regular customer.</p>';
```

```
      break;
    case 'b' :
      echo '<p>Customer referred by TV advert.</p>';
      break;
    case 'c' :
      echo '<p>Customer referred by phone directory.</p>';
      break;
    case 'd' :
      echo '<p>Customer referred by word of mouth.</p>';
      break;
    default :
      echo '<p>We do not know how this customer found us.</p>';
      break;
}
```

(Note that both of these examples assume you have extracted $find from the $_POST array.)

The switch statement behaves somewhat differently from an if or elseif statement. An if statement affects only one statement unless you deliberately use curly braces to create a block of statements. A switch statement behaves in the opposite way. When a case statement in a switch is activated, PHP executes statements until it reaches a break statement. Without break statements, a switch would execute all the code following the case that was true. When a break statement is reached, the next line of code after the switch statement is executed.

Comparing the Different Conditionals

If you are not familiar with the statements described in the preceding sections, you might be asking, "Which one is the best?"

That is not really a question we can answer. There is nothing that you can do with one or more else, elseif, or switch statements that you cannot do with a set of if statements. You should try to use whichever conditional will be most readable in your situation. You will acquire a feel for which suits different situations as you gain experience.

Repeating Actions Through Iteration

One thing that computers have always been very good at is automating repetitive tasks. If you need something done the same way a number of times, you can use a loop to repeat some parts of your program.

Bob wants a table displaying the freight cost that will be added to a customer's order. With the courier Bob uses, the cost of freight depends on the distance the parcel is being shipped. This cost can be worked out with a simple formula.

You want the freight table to resemble the table in Figure 1.7.

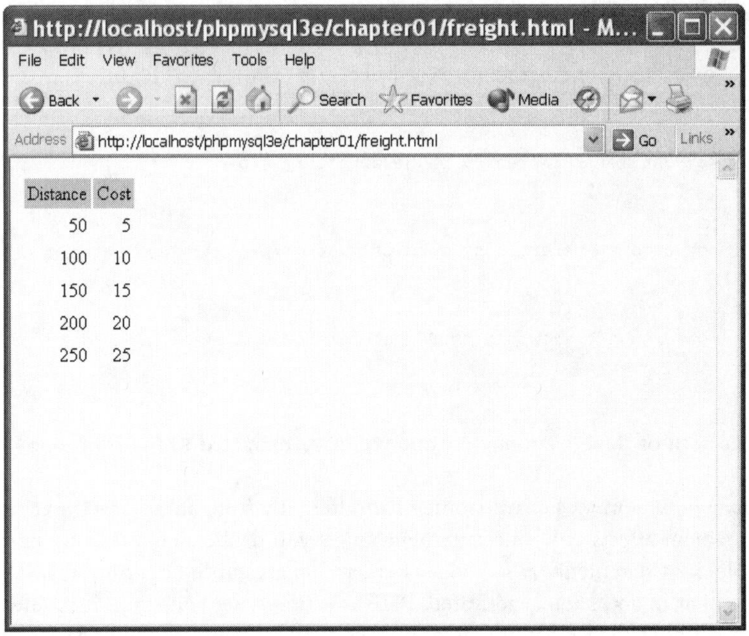

Figure 1.7 This table shows the cost of freight as distance increases.

Listing 1.2 shows the HTML that displays this table. You can see that it is long and repetitive.

Listing 1.2 `freight.html`— HTML for Bob's Freight Table

```html
<html>
<body>
<table border="0" cellpadding="3">
<tr>
  <td bgcolor="#CCCCCC" align="center">Distance</td>
  <td bgcolor="#CCCCCC" align="center">Cost</td>
</tr>
<tr>
  <td align="right">50</td>
  <td align="right">5</td>
</tr>
<tr>
  <td align="right">100</td>
  <td align="right">10</td>
</tr>
```

Listing 1.2   **Continued**

```
<tr>
  <td align="right">150</td>
  <td align="right">15</td>
</tr>
<tr>
  <td align="right">200</td>
  <td align="right">20</td>
</tr>
<tr>
  <td align="right">250</td>
  <td align="right">25</td>
</tr>
</table>
</body>
</html>
```

Rather than requiring an easily bored human—who must be paid for his time—to type the HTML, having a cheap and tireless computer do it would be helpful.
Loop statements tell PHP to execute a statement or block repeatedly.

while **Loops**

The simplest kind of loop in PHP is the while loop. Like an if statement, it relies on a condition. The difference between a while loop and an if statement is that an if statement executes the following block of code once if the condition is true. A while loop executes the block repeatedly for as long as the condition is true.

You generally use a while loop when you don't know how many iterations will be required to make the condition true. If you require a fixed number of iterations, consider using a for loop.

The basic structure of a while loop is

```
while( condition ) expression;
```

The following while loop will display the numbers from 1 to 5:

```
$num = 1;
while ($num <= 5 )
{
  echo $num."<br />";
  $num++;
}
```

At the beginning of each iteration, the condition is tested. If the condition is false, the block will not be executed and the loop will end. The next statement after the loop will then be executed.

You can use a while loop to do something more useful, such as display the repetitive freight table in Figure 1.7. Listing 1.3 uses a while loop to generate the freight table.

Listing 1.3 `freight.php`—**Generating Bob's Freight Table with PHP**

```
<html>
<body>
<table border="0" cellpadding="3">
<tr>
  <td bgcolor="#CCCCCC" align="center">Distance</td>
  <td bgcolor="#CCCCCC" align="center">Cost</td>
</tr>
<?php
$distance = 50;
while ($distance <= 250 )
{
  echo "<tr>\n  <td align = 'right'>$distance</td>\n";
  echo "  <td align = 'right'>". $distance / 10 ."</td>\n</tr>\n";
  $distance += 50;
}
?>
</table>
</body>
</html>
```

To make the HTML generated by the script readable, you need to include newlines and spaces. As already mentioned, browsers ignore this whitespace, but it is important for human readers. You often need to look at the HTML if your output is not what you were seeking.

In Listing 1.3, you can see \n inside some of the strings. When inside a double-quoted string, this character sequence represents a newline character.

for **and** foreach **Loops**

The way that you used the while loops in the preceding section is very common. You set a counter to begin with. Before each iteration, you test the counter in a condition. And at the end of each iteration, you modify the counter.

You can write this style of loop in a more compact form by using a for loop. The basic structure of a for loop is

```
for( expression1; condition; expression2)
  expression3;
```

- *expression1* is executed once at the start. Here, you usually set the initial value of a counter.

- The `condition` expression is tested before each iteration. If the expression returns `false`, iteration stops. Here, you usually test the counter against a limit.

- `expression2` is executed at the end of each iteration. Here, you usually adjust the value of the counter.

- `expression3` is executed once per iteration. This expression is usually a block of code and contains the bulk of the loop code.

You can rewrite the `while` loop example in Listing 1.3 as a `for` loop. In this case, the PHP code becomes

```php
<?php
for($distance = 50; $distance <= 250; $distance += 50)
{
  echo "<tr>\n  <td align = 'right'>$distance</td>\n";
  echo "  <td align = 'right'>". $distance / 10 ."</td>\n</tr>\n";
}
?>
```

Both the `while` and `for` versions are functionally identical. The `for` loop is somewhat more compact, saving two lines.

Both these loop types are equivalent; neither is better or worse than the other. In a given situation, you can use whichever you find more intuitive.

As a side note, you can combine variable variables with a `for` loop to iterate through a series of repetitive form fields. If, for example, you have form fields with names such as `name1`, `name2`, `name3`, and so on, you can process them like this:

```php
for ($i=1; $i <= $numnames; $i++)
{
  $temp= "name$i";
  echo $$temp.'<br />'; // or whatever processing you want to do
}
```

By dynamically creating the names of the variables, you can access each of the fields in turn.

As well as the `for` loop, there is a `foreach` loop, designed specifically for use with arrays. We discuss how to use it in Chapter 3.

`do..while` Loops

The final loop type we describe behaves slightly differently. The general structure of a `do..while` statement is

```php
do
  expression;
while( condition );
```

A `do..while` loop differs from a `while` loop because the condition is tested at the end. This means that in a `do..while` loop, the statement or block within the loop is always executed at least once.

Even if you consider this example in which the condition will be `false` at the start and can never become `true`, the loop will be executed once before checking the condition and ending:

```
$num = 100;
do
{
  echo $num.'<br />';
}
while ($num < 1 ) ;
```

Breaking Out of a Control Structure or Script

If you want to stop executing a piece of code, you can choose from three approaches, depending on the effect you are trying to achieve.

If you want to stop executing a loop, you can use the `break` statement as previously discussed in the section on `switch`. If you use the `break` statement in a loop, execution of the script will continue at the next line of the script after the loop.

If you want to jump to the next loop iteration, you can instead use the `continue` statement.

If you want to finish executing the entire PHP script, you can use `exit`. This approach is typically useful when you are performing error checking. For example, you could modify the earlier example as follows:

```
if( $totalqty == 0)
{
  echo 'You did not order anything on the previous page!<br />';
  exit;
}
```

The call to `exit` stops PHP from executing the remainder of the script.

Employing Alternative Control Structure Syntax

For all the control structures we have looked at, there is an alternative form of syntax. It consists of replacing the opening brace (`{`) with a colon (`:`) and the closing brace with a new keyword, which will be `endif`, `endswitch`, `endwhile`, `endfor`, or `endforeach`, depending on which control structure is being used. No alternative syntax is available for `do...while` loops.

For example, the code

```
if( $totalqty == 0)
{
  echo 'You did not order anything on the previous page!<br />';
  exit;
}
```

could be converted to this alternative syntax using the keywords `if` and `endif`:

```
if( $totalqty == 0):
  echo 'You did not order anything on the previous page!<br />';
  exit;
endif;
```

Using `declare`

One other control structure in PHP, the `declare` structure, is not used as frequently in day-to-day coding as the other constructs. The general form of this control structure is as follows:

```
declare (directive)
{
// block
}
```

This structure is used to set *execution directives* for the block of code—that is, rules about how the following code is to be run. Currently, only one execution directive, called `ticks`, has been implemented. You set it by inserting the directive `ticks=n`. It allows you to run a specific function every *n* lines of code inside the code block, which is principally useful for profiling and debugging.

The `declare` control structure is mentioned here only for completeness. We consider some examples showing how to use `tick` functions in Chapters 24, "Using PHP and MySQL for Large Projects," and 25, "Debugging."

Next: Saving the Customer's Order

Now you know how to receive and manipulate the customer's order. In the next chapter, you learn how to store the order so that it can be retrieved and fulfilled later.

2

Storing and Retrieving Data

Now that you know how to access and manipulate data entered in an HTML form, you can look at ways of storing that information for later use. In most cases, including the example from the previous chapter, you'll want to store this data and load it later. In this case, you need to write customer orders to storage so that they can be filled later.

In this chapter, you learn how to write the customer's order from the previous example to a file and read it back. You also learn why this isn't always a good solution. When you have large numbers of orders, you should use a database management system such as MySQL instead.

Key topics you learn in this chapter include

- Saving data for later
- Opening a file
- Creating and writing to a file
- Closing a file
- Reading from a file
- Locking files
- Deleting files
- Using other useful file functions
- Doing it a better way: using database management systems

Saving Data for Later

You can store data in two basic ways: in flat files or in a database.

A flat file can have many formats, but in general, when we refer to a *flat file*, we mean a simple text file. For this chapter's example, you will write customer orders to a text file, one order per line.

Writing orders this way is very simple, but also reasonably limiting, as you'll see later in this chapter. If you're dealing with information of any reasonable volume, you'll probably want to use a database instead. However, flat files have their uses, and in some situations you need to know how to use them.

The processes of writing to and reading from files in PHP are virtually identical to the ways you write and read in C. If you've done any C programming or Unix shell scripting, these procedures will all seem reasonably familiar to you.

Storing and Retrieving Bob's Orders

In this chapter, you use a slightly modified version of the order form you looked at in the preceding chapter. Begin with this form and the PHP code you wrote to process the order data.

> **Note**
> You can find the HTML and PHP scripts used in this chapter in the `chapter02/` folder of this book's CD-ROM.

We've modified the form to include a quick way to obtain the customer's shipping address. You can see this modified form in Figure 2.1.

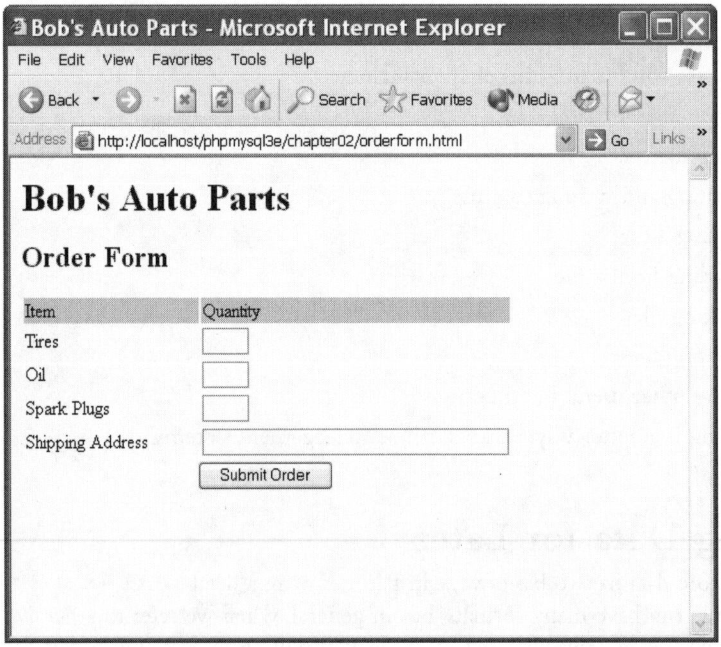

Figure 2.1 This version of the order form gets the customer's shipping address.

The form field for the shipping address is called `address`. This gives you a variable you can access as `$_REQUEST['address']` or `$_POST['address']` or `$_GET['address']`, depending on the form submission `METHOD`. (See Chapter 1, "PHP Crash Course," for details.)

In this chapter, you write each order that comes in to the same file. Then you construct a web interface for Bob's staff to view the orders that have been received.

Processing Files

Writing data to a file requires three steps:

1. Open the file. If the file doesn't already exist, you need to create it.
2. Write the data to the file.
3. Close the file.

Similarly, reading data from a file takes three steps:

1. Open the file. If you cannot open the file (for example, if it doesn't exist), you need to recognize this and exit gracefully.
2. Read data from the file.
3. Close the file.

When you want to read data from a file, you have choices about how much of the file to read at a time. We describe each choice in detail. For now, we start at the beginning by opening a file.

Opening a File

To open a file in PHP, you use the `fopen()` function. When you open the file, you need to specify how you intend to use it. This is known as the *file mode*.

Choosing File Modes

The operating system on the server needs to know what you want to do with a file that you are opening. It needs to know whether the file can be opened by another script while you have it open and whether you (or the script owner) have permission to use it in that way. Essentially, file modes give the operating system a mechanism to determine how to handle access requests from other people or scripts and a method to check that you have access and permission to a particular file.

You need to make three choices when opening a file:

1. You might want to open a file for reading only, for writing only, or for both reading and writing.
2. If writing to a file, you might want to overwrite any existing contents of a file or append new data to the end of the file. You also might like to terminate your program gracefully instead of overwriting a file if the file already exists.

3. If you are trying to write to a file on a system that differentiates between binary and text files, you might want to specify this fact.

The `fopen()` function supports combinations of these three options.

Using `fopen()` to Open a File

Assume that you want to write a customer order to Bob's order file. You can open this file for writing with the following:

```
$fp = fopen("$DOCUMENT_ROOT/../orders/orders.txt", 'w');
```

When `fopen()` is called, it expects two, three, or four parameters. Usually, you use two, as shown in this code line.

The first parameter should be the file you want to open. You can specify a path to this file, as in the preceding code; here, the `orders.txt` file is in the `orders` directory. We used the PHP built-in variable `$_SERVER['DOCUMENT_ROOT']` but, as with the cumbersome full names for form variables, we assigned a shorter name.

This variable points at the base of the document tree on your web server. This code line uses `..` to mean "the parent directory of the document root directory." This directory is outside the document tree, for security reasons. In this case, we do not want this file to be web accessible except through the interface that we provide. This path is called a *relative path* because it describes a position in the file system relative to the document root.

As with the short names given form variables, you need the following line at the start of your script

```
$DOCUMENT_ROOT = $_SERVER['DOCUMENT_ROOT'];
```

to copy the contents of the long-style variable to the short-style name.

Just as there are different ways to access form data, there are different ways to access the predefined server variables. Depending on your server setup (refer to Chapter 1 for details), you can get at the document root through

- `$_SERVER['DOCUMENT_ROOT']`
- `$DOCUMENT_ROOT`
- `$HTTP_SERVER_VARS['DOCUMENT_ROOT']`

As with form data, the first style is preferred.

You could also specify an *absolute path* to the file. This is the path from the root directory (`/` on a Unix system and typically `c:\` on a Windows system). On our Unix server, this path would be `/home/book/orders`. The problem with using this approach is that, particularly if you are hosting your site on somebody else's server, the absolute path might change. We once learned this the hard way after having to change absolute paths in a large number of scripts when the system administrators decided to change the directory structure without notice.

If no path is specified, the file will be created or looked for in the same directory as the script itself. The directory used will vary if you are running PHP through some kind of CGI wrapper and depends on your server configuration.

In a Unix environment, you use forward slashes (/) in directory paths. If you are using a Windows platform, you can use forward (/) or backslashes (\). If you use backslashes, they must be escaped (marked as a special character) for `fopen()` to understand them properly. To escape a character, you simply add an additional backslash in front of it, as shown in the following:

```
$fp = fopen("$DOCUMENT_ROOT\\..\\orders\\orders.txt", 'w');
```

Very few people use backslashes in paths within PHP because it means the code will work only in Windows environments. If you use forward slashes, you can often move your code between Windows and Unix machines without alteration.

The second `fopen()` parameter is the file mode, which should be a string. This string specifies what you want to do with the file. In this case, we are passing `'w'` to `fopen()`; this means "open the file for writing." A summary of file modes is shown in Table 2.1.

Table 2.1   **Summary of File Modes for** `fopen()`

Mode	Mode Name	Meaning
r	Read	Open the file for reading, beginning from the start of the file.
r+	Read	Open the file for reading and writing, beginning from the start of the file.
w	Write	Open the file for writing, beginning from the start of the file. If the file already exists, delete the existing contents. If it does not exist, try to create it.
w+	Write	Open the file for writing and reading, beginning from the start of the file. If the file already exists, delete the existing contents. If it does not exist, try to create it.
x	Cautious write	Open the file for writing, beginning from the start of the file. If the file already exists, it will not be opened, `fopen()` will return `false`, and PHP will generate a warning.
x+	Cautious write	Open the file for writing and reading, beginning from the start of the file. If the file already exists, it will not be opened, `fopen()` will return `false`, and PHP will generate a warning.
a	Append	Open the file for appending (writing) only, starting from the end of the existing contents, if any. If it does not exist, try to create it.
a+	Append	Open the file for appending (writing) and reading, starting from the end of the existing contents, if any. If it does not exist, try to create it.
b	Binary	Used in conjunction with one of the other modes. You might want to use this mode if your file system differentiates between binary and text files. Windows systems differentiate; Unix systems do not. The PHP developers recommend you always use this option for maximum portability. It is the default mode.
t	Text	Used in conjunction with one of the other modes. This mode is an option only in Windows systems. It is not recommended except before you have ported your code to work with the b option.

The file mode you use in the example depends on how the system will be used. We used 'w', which allows only one order to be stored in the file. Each time a new order is taken, it overwrites the previous order. This usage is probably not very sensible, so you would better off specifying append mode (and binary mode, as recommended):

```
$fp = fopen("$DOCUMENT_ROOT/../orders/orders.txt", 'ab');
```

The third parameter of fopen() is optional. You can use it if you want to search the include_path (set in your PHP configuration; see Appendix A, "Installing PHP5 and MySQL5") for a file. If you want to do this, set this parameter to 1. If you tell PHP to search the include_path, you do not need to provide a directory name or path:

```
$fp = fopen('orders.txt', 'ab', true);
```

The fourth parameter is also optional. The fopen() function allows filenames to be pre-fixed with a protocol (such as http://) and opened at a remote location. Some protocols allow for an extra parameter. We look at this use of the fopen() function in the next section of this chapter.

If fopen() opens the file successfully, a resource that is effectively a pointer to the file is returned and should be stored in a variable—in this case, $fp. You use this variable to access the file when you actually want to read from or write to it.

Opening Files Through FTP or HTTP

In addition to opening local files for reading and writing, you can open files via FTP, HTTP, and other protocols using fopen(). You can disable this capability by turning off the allow_url_fopen directive in the php.ini file. If you have trouble opening remote files with fopen(), check your php.ini file.

If the filename you use begins with ftp://, a passive mode FTP connection will be opened to the server you specify and a pointer to the start of the file will be returned.

If the filename you use begins with http://, an HTTP connection will be opened to the server you specify and a pointer to the response will be returned. When using HTTP mode with older versions of PHP, you must specify trailing slashes on directory names, as shown in the following:

http://www.example.com/

not
http://www.example.com

When you specify the latter form of address (without the slash), a web server normally uses an HTTP redirect to send you to the first address (with the slash). Try it in your browser.

Prior to PHP 4.0.5, the fopen() function did not support HTTP redirects, so you had to specify URLs that referred to directories with a trailing slash.

As of PHP 4.3.0, you can now open files over SSL as long as you have compiled or enabled support for OpenSSL and you begin the name of the file with https://.

Remember that the domain names in your URL are not case sensitive, but the path and filename might be.

Addressing Problems Opening Files

An error you might make is trying to open a file you don't have permission to read from or write to. (This error occurs commonly on Unix-like operating systems, but you may also see it occasionally under Windows.) When you do, PHP gives you a warning similar to the one shown in Figure 2.2.

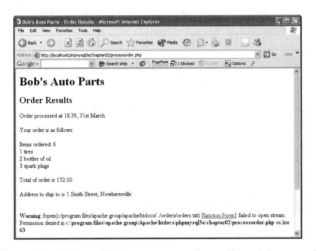

Figure 2.2   PHP specifically warns you when a file can't be opened.

If you receive this error, you need to make sure that the user under which the script runs has permission to access the file you are trying to use. Depending on how your server is set up, the script might be running as the web server user or as the owner of the directory where the script is located.

On most systems, the script runs as the web server user. If your script is on a Unix system in the ~/public_html/chapter2/ directory, for example, you could create a world-writeable directory in which to store the order by typing the following:

```
mkdir ~/orders
chmod 777 ~/orders
```

Bear in mind that directories and files that anybody can write to are dangerous. In particular, directories that are accessible directly from the Web should not be writeable. For this reason, our orders directory is two subdirectories back, above the public_html directory. We discuss security more in Chapter 15, "E-commerce Security Issues."

Incorrect permission setting is probably the most common thing that can go wrong when opening a file, but it's not the only thing. If you can't open the file, you really need to know this so that you don't try to read data from or write data to it.

If the call to fopen() fails, the function will return false. You can deal with the error in a more user-friendly way by suppressing PHP's error message and giving your own:

```
@ $fp = fopen("$DOCUMENT_ROOT/../orders/orders.txt", 'ab');
if (!$fp)
{
  echo '<p><strong> Your order could not be processed at this time.  '
       .'Please try again later.</strong></p></body></html>';
  exit;
}
```

The @ symbol in front of the call to fopen() tells PHP to suppress any errors resulting from the function call. Usually, it's a good idea to know when things go wrong, but in this case we're going to deal with that problem elsewhere.

You can also write this line as follows:

```
$fp = @fopen("$DOCUMENT_ROOT/../orders/orders.txt", 'a');
```

Using this method tends to make it less obvious that you are using the error suppression operator, so it may make your code harder to debug.

The method described here is a simplistic way of dealing with errors. We look at a more elegant method for error handling in Chapter 7, "Exception Handling." But one thing at a time.

The if statement tests the variable $fp to see whether a valid file pointer was returned from the fopen call; if not, it prints an error message and ends script execution. Because the page finishes here, notice that we have closed the HTML tags to give reasonably valid HTML.

The output when using this approach is shown in Figure 2.3.

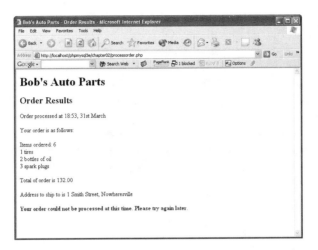

Figure 2.3   Using your own error messages instead of PHP's can be more user friendly.

Writing to a File

Writing to a file in PHP is relatively simple. You can use either of the functions `fwrite()` (file write) or `fputs()` (file put string); `fputs()` is an alias to `fwrite()`. You call `fwrite()` in the following way:

```
fwrite($fp, $outputstring);
```

This function call tells PHP to write the string stored in `$outputstring` to the file pointed to by `$fp`.

One new alternative to `fwrite()` is the `file_put_contents()` function. It has the following prototype:

```
int file_put_contents ( string filename,
                        string data
                        [, int flags
                        [, resource context]])
```

This function writes the string contained in `data` to the file named in `filename` without any need for an `fopen()` (or `fclose()`) function call. This function is new in PHP5, and is a matched pair for `file_get_contents()`, which we discuss shortly. You most commonly use the `flags` and `context` optional parameters when writing to remote files using, for example, HTTP or FTP. (We discuss these function in Chapter 19, "Using Network and Protocol Functions.")

Parameters for `fwrite()`

The function `fwrite()` actually takes three parameters, but the third one is optional. The prototype for `fwrite()` is

```
int fwrite ( resource handle, string string [, int length])
```

The third parameter, *length*, is the maximum number of bytes to write. If this parameter is supplied, `fwrite()` will write *string* to the file pointed to by *handle* until it reaches the end of *string* or has written *length* bytes, whichever comes first.

You can obtain the string length by using PHP's built-in `strlen()` function, as follows:

```
fwrite($fp, $outputstring, strlen($outputstring));
```

You may want to use this third parameter when writing in binary mode because it helps avoid some cross-platform compatibility issues.

File Formats

When you are creating a data file like the one in the example, the format in which you store the data is completely up to you. (However, if you are planning to use the data file in another application, you may have to follow that application's rules.)

Now construct a string that represents one record in the data file. You can do this as follows:

```
$outputstring = $date."\t".$tireqty." tires \t".$oilqty." oil\t"
               .$sparkqty." spark plugs\t\$".$totalamount
               ."\t". $address."\n";
```

In this simple example, you store each order record on a separate line in the file. Writing one record per line gives you a simple record separator in the newline character. Because newlines are invisible, you can represent them with the control sequence `"\n"`.

Throughout the book, we write the data fields in the same order every time and separate fields with a tab character. Again, because a tab character is invisible, it is represented by the control sequence `"\t"`. You may choose any sensible delimiter that is easy to read back.

The separator or delimiter character should be something that will certainly not occur in the input, or you should process the input to remove or escape out any instances of the delimiter. We look at processing the input in Chapter 4, "String Manipulation and Regular Expressions." For now, you can assume that nobody will place a tab into the order form. It is difficult, but not impossible, for a user to put a tab or newline into a single-line HTML input field.

Using a special field separator allows you to split the data back into separate variables more easily when you read the data back. We cover this topic in Chapter 3, "Using Arrays," and Chapter 4. Here, we treat each order as a single string.

After a few orders are processed, the contents of the file look something like the example shown in Listing 2.1.

Listing 2.1   `orders.txt`—**Example of What the Orders File Might Contain**

```
20:30, 31st March  4 tires   1 oil  6 spark plugs  $434.00  22 Short St, Smalltown
20:42, 31st March  1 tires   0 oil  0 spark plugs  $100.00  33 Main Rd, Newtown
20:43, 31st March  0 tires   1 oil  4 spark plugs  $26.00   127 Acacia St,
Springfield
```

Closing a File

After you've finished using a file, you need to close it. You should do this by using the `fclose()` function as follows:

```
fclose($fp);
```

This function returns `true` if the file was successfully closed or `false` if it wasn't. This process is much less likely to go wrong than opening a file in the first place, so in this case we've chosen not to test it.

   The complete listing for the final version of `processorder.php` is shown in Listing 2.2.

Listing 2.2   `processorder.php`—**Final Version of the Order Processing Script**

```php
<?php
  // create short variable names
  $tireqty = $_POST['tireqty'];
  $oilqty = $_POST['oilqty'];
  $sparkqty = $_POST['sparkqty'];
  $address = $_POST['address'];

  $DOCUMENT_ROOT = $_SERVER['DOCUMENT_ROOT'];
?>
<html>
<head>
  <title>Bob's Auto Parts - Order Results</title>
</head>
<body>
<h1>Bob's Auto Parts</h1>
<h2>Order Results</h2>
<?php
$date = date('H:i, jS F');

echo '<p>Order processed at ';
echo $date;
echo '</p>';
```

Listing 2.2 **Continued**

```php
echo '<p>Your order is as follows: </p>';

$totalqty = 0;
$totalqty = $tireqty + $oilqty + $sparkqty;
echo 'Items ordered: '.$totalqty.'<br />';

if( $totalqty == 0)
{
  echo 'You did not order anything on the previous page!<br />';
}
else
{
  if ( $tireqty>0 )
    echo $tireqty.' tires<br />';
  if ( $oilqty>0 )
    echo $oilqty.' bottles of oil<br />';
  if ( $sparkqty>0 )
    echo $sparkqty.' spark plugs<br />';
}

$totalamount = 0.00;

define('TIREPRICE', 100);
define('OILPRICE', 10);
define('SPARKPRICE', 4);

$totalamount = $tireqty * TIREPRICE
             + $oilqty * OILPRICE
             + $sparkqty * SPARKPRICE;

$totalamount=number_format($totalamount, 2, '.', ' ');

echo '<p>Total of order is '.$totalamount.'</p>';
echo '<p>Address to ship to is '.$address.'</p>';

$outputstring = $date."\t".$tireqty." tires \t".$oilqty." oil\t"
              .$sparkqty." spark plugs\t\$".$totalamount
              ."\t". $address."\n";

// open file for appending
@ $fp = fopen("$DOCUMENT_ROOT/../orders/orders.txt", 'ab');
```

Listing 2.2 **Continued**

```php
if (!$fp)
{
  echo '<p><strong> Your order could not be processed at this time. '
      .'Please try again later.</strong></p></body></html>';
  exit;
}

fwrite($fp, $outputstring, strlen($outputstring));
fclose($fp);

echo '<p>Order written.</p>';
?>
</body>
</html>
```

Reading from a File

Right now, Bob's customers can leave their orders via the Web, but if Bob's staff members want to look at the orders, they have to open the files themselves.

Let's create a web interface to let Bob's staff read the files easily. The code for this interface is shown in Listing 2.3.

Listing 2.3 `vieworders.php`—**Staff Interface to the Orders File**

```php
<?php
  //create short variable name
  $DOCUMENT_ROOT = $HTTP_SERVER_VARS['DOCUMENT_ROOT'];
?>
<html>
<head>
  <title>Bob's Auto Parts - Customer Orders</title>
</head>
<body>
<h1>Bob's Auto Parts</h1>
<h2>Customer Orders</h2>
<?php
@  $fp = fopen("$DOCUMENT_ROOT/../orders/orders.txt", 'r');

   if (!$fp)
   {
     echo '<p><strong>No orders pending.'
         .'Please try again later.</strong></p></body></html>';
     exit;
   }
```

Listing 2.3 **Continued**

```
  while (!feof($fp))
  {
     $order= fgets($fp, 999);
     echo $order.'<br>';
  }

  fclose($fp);
?>
</body>
</html>
```

This script follows the sequence we described earlier: open the file, read from the file, close the file. The output from this script using the data file from Listing 2.1 is shown in Figure 2.4.

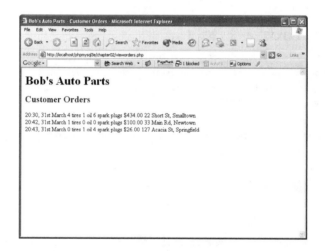

Figure 2.4   The `vieworders.php` script displays all the orders currently in the `orders.txt` file in the browser window.

Let's look at the functions in this script in detail.

Opening a File for Reading: `fopen()`

Again, you open the file by using `fopen()`. In this case, you open the file for reading only, so you use the file mode `'rb'`:

```
$fp = fopen("$DOCUMENT_ROOT/../orders/orders.txt", 'rb');
```

Knowing When to Stop: `feof()`

In this example, you use a `while` loop to read from the file until the end of the file is reached. The `while` loop tests for the end of the file using the `feof()` function:

```
while (!feof($fp))
```

The `feof()` function takes a file handle as its single parameter. It returns `true` if the file pointer is at the end of the file. Although the name might seem strange, you can remember it easily if you know that `feof` stands for File End Of File.

In this case (and generally when reading from a file), you read from the file until EOF is reached.

Reading a Line at a Time: `fgets()`, `fgetss()`, and `fgetcsv()`

In this example, you use the `fgets()` function to read from the file:

```
$order= fgets($fp, 999);
```

This function reads one line at a time from a file. In this case, it reads until it encounters a newline character (\n), encounters an EOF, or has read 998 bytes from the file. The maximum length read is the length specified minus 1 byte.

You can use many different functions to read from files. The `fgets()` function, for example, is useful when you're dealing with files that contain plain text that you want to deal with in chunks.

An interesting variation on `fgets()` is `fgetss()`, which has the following prototype:

```
string fgetss(resource fp, int length, string [allowable_tags]);
```

This function is similar to `fgets()` except that it strips out any PHP and HTML tags found in the string. If you want to leave in any particular tags, you can include them in the `allowable_tags` string. You would use `fgetss()` for safety when reading a file written by somebody else or one containing user input. Allowing unrestricted HTML code in the file could mess up your carefully planned formatting. Allowing unrestricted PHP could give a malicious user almost free rein on your server.

The function `fgetcsv()` is another variation on `fgets()`. It has the following prototype:

```
array fgetcsv ( resource fp, int length [, string delimiter
            [, string enclosure]])
```

This function breaks up lines of files when you have used a delimiting character, such as the tab character (as we suggested earlier) or a comma (as commonly used by spreadsheets and other applications). If you want to reconstruct the variables from the order separately rather than as a line of text, `fgetcsv()` allows you to do this simply. You call it in much the same way as you would call `fgets()`, but you pass it the delimiter you used to separate fields. For example,

```
$order = fgetcsv($fp, 100, "\t");
```

This code would retrieve a line from the file and break it up wherever a tab (\t) was encountered. The results are returned in an array ($order in this code example). We cover arrays in more detail in Chapter 3.

The *length* parameter should be greater than the length in characters of the longest line in the file you are trying to read.

The *enclosure* parameter specifies what each field in a line is surrounded by. If not specified, it defaults to " (a double quotation mark).

Reading the Whole File: readfile(), fpassthru(), and file()

Instead of reading from a file a line at a time, you can read the whole file in one go. There are four different ways you can do this.

The first uses readfile(). You can replace the entire script you wrote previously with one line:

```
readfile("$DOCUMENT_ROOT/../orders/orders.txt");
```

A call to the readfile() function opens the file, echoes the content to standard output (the browser), and then closes the file. The prototype for readfile() is

```
int readfile(string filename, [int use_include_path[, resource context]] );
```

The optional second parameter specifies whether PHP should look for the file in the include_path and operates the same way as in fopen(). The optional *context* parameter is used only when files are opened remotely via, for example, HTTP; we cover such usage in more detail in Chapter 19. The function returns the total number of bytes read from the file.

Second, you can use fpassthru(). To do so, you need to open the file using fopen() first. You can then pass the file pointer as an argument to fpassthru(), which dumps the contents of the file from the pointer's position onward to standard output. It closes the file when it is finished.

You can replace the previous script with fpassthru() as follows:

```
$fp = fopen("$DOCUMENT_ROOT/../orders/orders.txt", 'rb');
fpassthru($fp);
```

The function fpassthru() returns true if the read is successful and false otherwise.

The third option for reading the whole file is using the file() function. This function is identical to readfile() except that instead of echoing the file to standard output, it turns it into an array. We cover this function in more detail when we look at arrays in Chapter 3. Just for reference, you would call it using

```
$filearray = file($DOCUMENT_ROOT/../orders/orders.txt");
```

This line reads the entire file into the array called $filearray. Each line of the file is stored in a separate element of the array. Note that this function is not binary safe.

Finally, as of PHP 4.3.0, you can use the file_get_contents() function. This function is identical to readfile() except that it returns the content of the file as a string instead of outputting it to the browser. The advantage of this new function is that it is binary safe, unlike the file() function.

Reading a Character: fgetc()

Another option for file processing is to read a single character at a time from a file. You can do this by using the fgetc() function. It takes a file pointer as its only parameter and returns the next character in the file. You can replace the while loop in the original script with one that uses fgetc(), as follows:

```
while (!feof($fp))
{
  $char = fgetc($fp);
  if (!feof($fp))
    echo ($char=="\n" ? '<br />': $char);
}
```

This code reads a single character at a time from the file using fgetc() and stores it in $char, until the end of the file is reached. It then does a little processing to replace the text end-of-line characters (\n) with HTML line breaks (<br />).

This is just to clean up the formatting. If you try to output the file with newlines between records, the whole file will be printed on a single line. (Try it and see.) Web browsers do not render whitespace, such as newlines, so you need to replace them with HTML linebreaks (<br />) instead. You can use the ternary operator to do this neatly.

A minor side effect of using fgetc() instead of fgets() is that fgetc() returns the EOF character, whereas fgets() does not. You need to test feof() again after you've read the character because you don't want to echo the EOF to the browser.

Reading a file character by character is not generally sensible or efficient unless for some reason you want to process it character by character.

Reading an Arbitrary Length: fread()

The final way you can read from a file is to use the fread() function to read an arbitrary number of bytes from the file. This function has the following prototype:

```
string fread(resource fp, int length);
```

It reads up to length bytes, to the end of the file or network packet, whichever comes first.

Using Other Useful File Functions

Numerous other file functions are useful from time to time. Some are described next.

Checking Whether a File Is There: `file_exists()`

If you want to check whether a file exists without actually opening it, you can use `file_exists()`, as follows:

```
if (file_exists("$DOCUMENT_ROOT/../orders/orders.txt"))
    echo 'There are orders waiting to be processed.';
else
    echo 'There are currently no orders.';
```

Determining How Big a File Is: `filesize()`

You can check the size of a file by using the `filesize()` function:

```
echo filesize("$DOCUMENT_ROOT/../orders/orders.txt");
```

It returns the size of a file in bytes and can be used in conjunction with `fread()` to read a whole file (or some fraction of the file) at a time. You can even replace the entire original script with the following:

```
$fp = fopen("$DOCUMENT_ROOT/../orders/orders.txt", 'rb');
echo nl2br(fread( $fp, filesize("$DOCUMENT_ROOT/../orders/orders.txt" )));
fclose( $fp );
```

The `nl2br()` function converts the `\n` characters in the output to HTML line breaks (`<br />`).

Deleting a File: `unlink()`

If you want to delete the order file after the orders have been processed, you can do so by using `unlink()`. (There is no function called delete.) For example,

```
unlink("$DOCUMENT_ROOT/../orders/orders.txt");
```

This function returns `false` if the file could not be deleted. This situation typically occurs if the permissions on the file are insufficient or if the file does not exist.

Navigating Inside a File: `rewind()`, `fseek()`, and `ftell()`

You can manipulate and discover the position of the file pointer inside a file by using `rewind()`, `fseek()`, and `ftell()`.

The `rewind()` function resets the file pointer to the beginning of the file. The `ftell()` function reports how far into the file the pointer is in bytes. For example, you can add the following lines to the bottom of the original script (before the `fclose()` command):

```
echo 'Final position of the file pointer is '.(ftell($fp));
echo '<br />';
rewind($fp);
echo 'After rewind, the position is '.(ftell($fp));
echo '<br />';
```

The output in the browser should be similar to that shown in Figure 2.5.

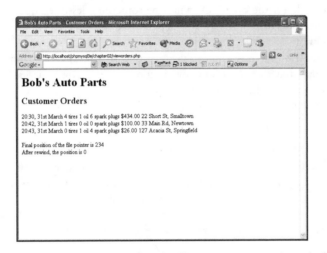

Figure 2.5 After reading the orders, the file pointer points to the end of the file, an offset of 234 bytes. The call to rewind sets it back to position 0, the start of the file.

You can use the function `fseek()` to set the file pointer to some point within the file. Its prototype is

```
int fseek ( resource fp, int offset [, int whence])
```

A call to `fseek()` sets the file pointer *fp* at a point starting from *whence* and moving *offset* bytes into the file. The optional *whence* parameter defaults to the value `SEEK_SET`, which is effectively the start of the file. The other possible values are `SEEK_CUR` (the current location of the file pointer) and `SEEK_END` (the end of the file).

The `rewind()` function is equivalent to calling the `fseek()` function with an offset of zero. For example, you can use `fseek()` to find the middle record in a file or to perform a binary search. Often, if you reach the level of complexity in a data file where you need to do these kinds of things, your life will be much easier if you use a database.

Locking Files

Imagine a situation in which two customers are trying to order a product at the same time. (This situation is not uncommon, especially when your website starts to get any kind of traffic volume.) What if one customer calls `fopen()` and begins writing, and then the other customer calls `fopen()` and also begins writing? What will be the final contents of the file? Will it be the first order followed by the second order, or vice versa? Will it be one order or the other? Or will it be something less useful, such as the two orders interleaved somehow? The answer depends on your operating system but is often impossible to know.

To avoid problems like this, you can use file locking. You use this feature in PHP by using the `flock()` function. This function should be called after a file has been opened but before any data is read from or written to the file.

The prototype for `flock()` is

```
bool flock (resource fp, int operation [, int &wouldblock])
```

You need to pass it a pointer to an open file and a constant representing the kind of lock you require. It returns true if the lock was successfully acquired and false if it was not. The optional third parameter will contain the value true if acquiring the lock would cause the current process to block (that is, have to wait).

The possible values for *operation* are shown in Table 2.2. The possible values changed at PHP 4.0.1, so both sets of values are shown in the table.

Table 2.2   `flock()` **Operation Values**

Value of Operation	Meaning
LOCK_SH (formerly 1)	Reading lock. The file can be shared with other readers.
LOCK_EX (formerly 2)	Writing lock. This operation is exclusive; the file cannot be shared.
LOCK_UN (formerly 3)	The existing lock is released.
LOCK_NB (formerly 4)	Blocking is prevented while you are trying to acquire a lock.

If you are going to use `flock()`, you need to add it to all the scripts that use the file; otherwise, it is worthless.

Note that `flock()` does not work with NFS or other networked file systems. It also does not work with older file systems that do not support locking, such as FAT. On some operating systems, it is implemented at the process level and does not work correctly if you are using a multithreaded server API.

To use it with the order example, you can alter `processorder.php` as follows:

```
$fp = fopen("$DOCUMENT_ROOT/../orders/orders.txt", 'ab');
flock($fp, LOCK_EX); // lock the file for writing
fwrite($fp, $outputstring);
flock($fp, LOCK_UN);  // release write lock
fclose($fp);
```

You should also add locks to `vieworders.php`:

```
$fp = fopen("$DOCUMENT_ROOT /../orders/orders.txt", 'r');
flock($fp, LOCK_SH);  // lock file for reading
// read from the file
flock($fp, LOCK_UN);  // release read lock
fclose($fp);
```

The code is now more robust but still not perfect. What if two scripts tried to acquire a lock at the same time? This would result in a race condition, in which the processes compete for locks but it is uncertain which will succeed. Such a condition could cause more problems. You can do better by using a database management system (DBMS).

Doing It a Better Way: Database Management Systems

So far, all the examples we have looked at use flat files. In the next part of this book, we look at how to use MySQL, a relational database management system (RDBMS), instead. You might ask, "Why would I bother?"

Problems with Using Flat Files

There are a number of problems in working with flat files:

- When a file grows large, working with it can be very slow.
- Searching for a particular record or group of records in a flat file is difficult. If the records are in order, you can use some kind of binary search in conjunction with a fixed-width record to search on a key field. If you want to find patterns of information (for example, you want to find all the customers who live in Smalltown), you would have to read in each record and check it individually.
- Dealing with concurrent access can become problematic. You have seen how to lock files, but locking can cause the race condition we discussed earlier. It can also cause a bottleneck. With enough traffic on a site, a large group of users may be waiting for the file to be unlocked before they can place their order. If the wait is too long, people will go elsewhere to buy.
- All the file processing you have seen so far deals with a file using sequential processing; that is, you start from the beginning of the file and read through to the end. Inserting records into or deleting records from the middle of the file (random access) can be difficult because you end up reading the whole file into memory, making the changes, and writing the whole file out again. With a large data file, having to go through all these steps becomes a significant overhead.
- Beyond the limits offered by file permissions, there is no easy way of enforcing different levels of access to data.

How RDBMSs Solve These Problems

Relational database management systems address all these issues:

- RDBMSs can provide much faster access to data than flat files. And MySQL, the database system we use in this book, has some of the fastest benchmarks of any RDBMS.
- RDBMSs can be easily queried to extract sets of data that fit certain criteria.
- RDBMSs have built-in mechanisms for dealing with concurrent access so that you, as a programmer, don't have to worry about it.
- RDBMSs provide random access to your data.
- RDBMSs have built-in privilege systems. MySQL has particular strengths in this area.

Probably the main reason for using an RDBMS is that all (or at least most) of the functionality that you want in a data storage system has already been implemented. Sure, you could write your own library of PHP functions, but why reinvent the wheel?

In Part II of this book, "Using MySQL," we discuss how relational databases work generally, and specifically how you can set up and use MySQL to create database-backed websites.

If you are building a simple system and don't feel you need a full-featured database but want to avoid the locking and other issues associated with using a flat file, you may want to consider using PHP's new SQLite extension. This extension provides essentially an SQL interface to a flat file. In this book, we focus on using MySQL, but if you would like more information about SQLite, you can find it at http://sqlite.org/ and http://www.php.net/sqlite.

Further Reading

For more information on interacting with the file system, you can go straight to Chapter 18, "Interacting with the File System and the Server." In that part of the book, we talk about how to change permissions, ownership, and names of files; how to work with directories; and how to interact with the file system environment.

You may also want to read through the file system section of the PHP online manual at http://www.php.net/filesystem.

Next

In the next chapter, you learn what arrays are and how they can be used for processing data in your PHP scripts.

3

Using Arrays

THIS CHAPTER SHOWS YOU HOW TO USE AN important programming construct: arrays. The variables used in the previous chapters were *scalar* variables, which store a single value. An *array* is a variable that stores a set or sequence of values. One array can have many elements, and each element can hold a single value, such as text or numbers, or another array. An array containing other arrays is known as a *multidimensional array*.

PHP supports both numerically indexed and associative arrays. You are probably familiar with numerically indexed arrays if you've used any programming language, but unless you use PHP or Perl, you might not have seen associative arrays before. Associative arrays allow you to use more useful values as the index. Rather than each element having a numeric index, it can have words or other meaningful information.

In this chapter, you continue developing the Bob's Auto Parts example using arrays to work more easily with repetitive information such as customer orders. Likewise, you write shorter, tidier code to do some of the things you did with files in the preceding chapter.

Key topics covered in this chapter include

- Numerically indexed arrays
- Non-numerically indexed arrays
- Array operators
- Multidimensional arrays
- Array sorting
- Array functions

What Is an Array?

You learned about scalar variables in Chapter 1, "PHP Crash Course." A scalar variable is a named location in which to store a value; similarly, an array is a named place to store a *set* of values, thereby allowing you to group scalars.

Bob's product list is the array for the example used in this chapter. In Figure 3.1, you can see a list of three products stored in an array format. These three products are stored in a single variable called $products. (We describe how to create a variable like this shortly.)

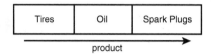

Figure 3.1   Bob's products can be stored in an array.

After you have the information as an array, you can do a number of useful things with it. Using the looping constructs from Chapter 1, you can save work by performing the same actions on each value in the array. The whole set of information can be moved around as a single unit. This way, with a single line of code, all the values in the array can be passed to a function. For example, you might want to sort the products alphabetically. To achieve this, you could pass the entire array to PHP's sort() function.

The values stored in an array are called the array *elements*. Each array element has an associated *index* (also called a *key*) that is used to access the element. Arrays in most programming languages have numerical indices that typically start from zero or one.

PHP allows you to use numbers or strings as the array indices. You can use arrays in the traditional numerically indexed way or set the keys to be whatever you like to make the indexing more meaningful and useful. (This approach may be familiar to you if you have used associative arrays or maps in other programming languages.) The programming approach may vary a little depending on whether you are using standard numerically indexed arrays or more interesting index values.

We begin by looking at numerically indexed arrays and then move on to using user-defined keys.

Numerically Indexed Arrays

Numerically indexed arrays are supported in most programming languages. In PHP, the indices start at zero by default, although you can alter this value.

Initializing Numerically Indexed Arrays

To create the array shown in Figure 3.1, use the following line of PHP code:

```
$products = array( 'Tires', 'Oil', 'Spark Plugs' );
```

This code creates an array called $products containing the three values given: 'Tires', 'Oil', and 'Spark Plugs'. Note that, like echo, array() is actually a language construct rather than a function.

Depending on the contents you need in your array, you might not need to manually initialize them as in the preceding example. If you have the data you need in another array, you can simply copy one array to another using the = operator.

If you want an ascending sequence of numbers stored in an array, you can use the range() function to automatically create the array for you. The following statement creates an array called numbers with elements ranging from 1 to 10:

```
$numbers = range(1,10);
```

The range() function has an optional third parameter that allows you to set the step size between values. For instance, if you want an array of the odd numbers between 1 and 10, you could create it as follows:

```
$odds = range(1, 10, 2);
```

The range() function can also be used with characters, as in this example:

```
$letters = range('a', 'z');
```

If you have information stored in a file on disk, you can load the array contents directly from the file. We look at this topic later in this chapter under the heading "Loading Arrays from Files."

If you have the data for your array stored in a database, you can load the array contents directly from the database. This process is covered in Chapter 11, "Accessing Your MySQL Database from the Web with PHP."

You can also use various functions to extract part of an array or to reorder an array. We look at some of these functions later in this chapter under the heading "Performing Other Array Manipulations."

Accessing Array Contents

To access the contents of a variable, you use its name. If the variable is an array, you access the contents using the variable name and a key or index. The key or index indicates which of the values in the array you access. The index is placed in square brackets after the name.

Type $products[0], $products[1], and $products[2] to use the contents of the $products array.

By default, element zero is the first element in the array. The same numbering scheme is used in C, C++, Java, and a number of other languages, but it might take some getting used to if you are not familiar with it.

As with other variables, you change array elements' contents by using the = operator. The following line replaces the first element in the array `'Tires'` with `'Fuses'`:

```
$products[0] = 'Fuses';
```

You can use the following line to add a new element—`'Fuses'`—to the end of the array, giving a total of four elements:

```
$products[3] = 'Fuses';
```

To display the contents, you could type this line:

```
echo "$products[0] $products[1] $products[2] $products[3]";
```

Note that although PHP's string parsing is pretty clever, you can confuse it. If you are having trouble with array or other variables not being interpreted correctly when embedded in a double-quoted string, you can either put them outside quotes or look up complex syntax in Chapter 4, "String Manipulation and Regular Expressions." The preceding `echo` statement works correctly, but in many of the more complex examples later in this chapter, you will notice that the variables are outside the quoted strings.

Like other PHP variables, arrays do not need to be initialized or created in advance. They are automatically created the first time you use them.

The following code creates the same `$products` array created previously with the `array()` statement:

```
$products[0] = 'Tires';
$products[1] = 'Oil';
$products[2] = 'Spark Plugs';
```

If `$products` does not already exist, the first line will create a new array with just one element. The subsequent lines add values to the array. The array is dynamically resized as you add elements to it. This resizing capability is not present in most other programming languages.

Using Loops to Access the Array

Because the array is indexed by a sequence of numbers, you can use a `for` loop to more easily display its contents:

```
for ( $i = 0; $i<3; $i++ )
  echo "$products[$i] ";
```

This loop provides similar output to the preceding code but requires less typing than manually writing code to work with each element in a large array. The ability to use a simple loop to access each element is a nice feature of arrays. You can also use the `foreach` loop, specially designed for use with arrays. In this example, you could use it as follows:

```
foreach ($products as $current)
  echo $current.' ';
```

This code stores each element in turn in the variable `$current` and prints it out.

Arrays with Different Indices

In the $products array, you allowed PHP to give each item the default index. This meant that the first item you added became item 0; the second, item 1; and so on. PHP also supports arrays in which you can associate any key or index you want with each value.

Initializing an Array

The following code creates an array with product names as keys and prices as values:

```
$prices = array( 'Tires'=>100, 'Oil'=>10, 'Spark Plugs'=>4 );
```

The symbol between the keys and values is simply an equal sign immediately followed by a greater than symbol.

Accessing the Array Elements

Again, you access the contents using the variable name and a key, so you can access the information stored in the prices array as $prices['Tires'], $prices['Oil'], and $prices['Spark Plugs'].

The following code creates the same $prices array. Instead of creating an array with three elements, this version creates an array with only one element and then adds two more:

```
$prices = array( 'Tires'=>100 );
$prices['Oil'] = 10;
$prices['Spark Plugs'] = 4;
```

Here is another slightly different but equivalent piece of code. In this version, you do not explicitly create an array at all. The array is created for you when you add the first element to it:

```
$prices['Tires'] = 100;
$prices['Oil'] = 10;
$prices['Spark Plugs'] = 4;
```

Using Loops

Because the indices in an array are not numbers, you cannot use a simple counter in a for loop to work with the array. However, you can use the foreach loop or the list() and each() constructs.

The foreach loop has a slightly different structure when using associative arrays. You can use it exactly as you did in the previous example, or you can incorporate the keys as well:

```
foreach ($prices as $key => $value)
  echo $key.'=>'.$value.'<br />';
```

The following code lists the contents of the $prices array using the each() construct:

```
while( $element = each( $prices ) )
{
  echo $element[ 'key' ];
  echo ' - ';
  echo $element[ 'value' ];
  echo '<br />';
}
```

The output of this script fragment is shown in Figure 3.2.

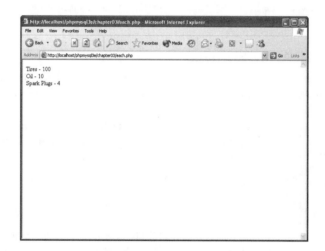

Figure 3.2   An each() statement can be used to loop through arrays.

In Chapter 1, you looked at while loops and the echo statement. The preceding code uses the each() function, which you have not used before. This function returns the current element in an array and makes the next element the current one. Because you are calling each() within a while loop, it returns every element in the array in turn and stops when the end of the array is reached.

In this code, the variable $element is an array. When you call each(), it gives you an array with four values and the four indices to the array locations. The locations key and 0 contain the key of the current element, and the locations value and 1 contain the value of the current element. Although the one you choose makes no difference, we chose to use the named locations rather than the numbered ones.

There is a more elegant and more common way of doing the same thing. The construct `list()` can be used to split an array into a number of values. You can separate two of the values that the `each()` function gives you like this:

```
list( $product, $price ) = each( $prices );
```

This line uses `each()` to take the current element from `$prices`, return it as an array, and make the next element current. It also uses `list()` to turn the 0 and 1 elements from the array returned by `each()` into two new variables called `$product` and `$price`.

You can loop through the entire `$prices` array, echoing the contents using this short script:

```
while ( list( $product, $price ) = each( $prices ) )
  echo "$product - $price<br />";
```

It has the same output as the previous script but is easier to read because `list()` allows you to assign names to the variables.

When you are using `each()`, note that the array keeps track of the current element. If you want to use the array twice in the same script, you need to set the current element back to the start of the array using the function `reset()`. To loop through the `prices` array again, you type the following:

```
reset($prices);
while ( list( $product, $price ) = each( $prices ) )
  echo "$product - $price<br />";
```

This code sets the current element back to the start of the array and allows you to go through again.

Array Operators

One set of special operators applies only to arrays. Most of them have an analogue in the scalar operators, as you can see by looking at Table 3.1.

Table 3.1 **PHP's Array Operators**

Operator	Name	Example	Result
+	Union	`$a + $b`	Union of $a and $b. The array $b is appended to $a, but any key clashes are not added.
==	Equality	`$a == $b`	True if $a and $b contain the same elements.
===	Identity	`$a === $b`	True if $a and $b contain the same elements in the same order.
!=	Inequality	`$a != $b`	True if $a and $b do not contain the same elements.
<>	Inequality	`$a <> $b`	Same as !=.
!==	Non-identity	`$a !== $b`	True if $a and $b do not contain the same elements in the same order.

These operators are mostly fairly self-evident, but union requires some further explanation. The union operator tries to add the elements of $b to the end of $a. If elements in $b have the same keys as some elements already in $a, they will not be added. That is, no elements of $a will be overwritten.

You will notice that the array operators in Table 3.1 all have equivalent operators that work on scalar variables. As long as you remember that + performs addition on scalar types and union on arrays—even if you have no interest in the set arithmetic behind that behavior—the behaviors should make sense. You cannot usefully compare arrays to scalar types.

Multidimensional Arrays

Arrays do not have to be a simple list of keys and values; each location in the array can hold another array. This way, you can create a two-dimensional array. You can think of a two-dimensional array as a matrix, or grid, with width and height or rows and columns.

If you want to store more than one piece of data about each of Bob's products, you could use a two-dimensional array. Figure 3.3 shows Bob's products represented as a two-dimensional array with each row representing an individual product and each column representing a stored product attribute.

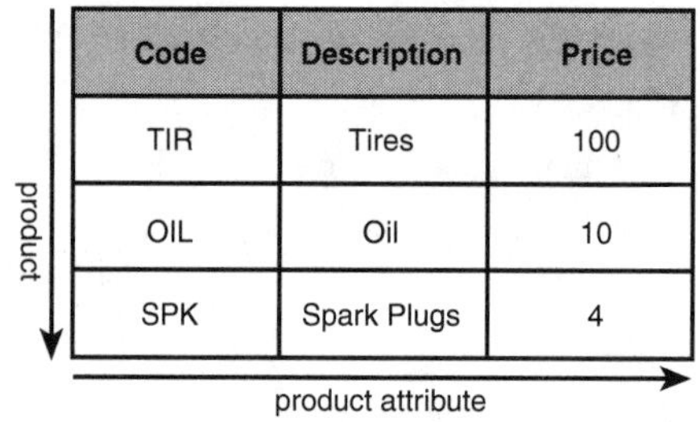

	Code	Description	Price
	TIR	Tires	100
	OIL	Oil	10
	SPK	Spark Plugs	4

product

product attribute

Figure 3.3   You can store more information about Bob's products in a two-dimensional array.

Using PHP, you would write the following code to set up the data in the array shown in Figure 3.3:

```
$products = array( array( 'TIR', 'Tires', 100 ),
                   array( 'OIL', 'Oil', 10 ),
                   array( 'SPK', 'Spark Plugs', 4 ) );
```

You can see from this definition that the $products array now contains three arrays.

To access the data in a one-dimensional array, recall that you need the name of the array and the index of the element. A two-dimensional array is similar, except that each element has two indices: a row and a column. (The top row is row 0, and the far-left column is column 0.)

To display the contents of this array, you could manually access each element in order like this:

```
echo '|'.$products[0][0].'|'.$products[0][1].'|'.$products[0][2].'|<br />';
echo '|'.$products[1][0].'|'.$products[1][1].'|'.$products[1][2].'|<br />';
echo '|'.$products[2][0].'|'.$products[2][1].'|'.$products[2][2].'|<br />';
```

Alternatively, you could place a `for` loop inside another `for` loop to achieve the same result:

```
for ( $row = 0; $row < 3; $row++ )
{
  for ( $column = 0; $column < 3; $column++ )
  {
    echo '|'.$products[$row][$column];
  }
  echo '|<br />';
}
```

Both versions of this code produce the same output in the browser:

```
|TIR|Tires|100|
|OIL|Oil|10|
|SPK|Spark Plugs|4|
```

The only difference between the two examples is that your code will be shorter if you use the second version with a large array.

You might prefer to create column names instead of numbers, as shown in Figure 3.3. To store the same set of products, with the columns named as they are in Figure 3.3, you would use the following code:

```
$products = array( array( 'Code' => 'TIR',
                          'Description' => 'Tires',
                          'Price' => 100
                        ),
                   array( 'Code' => 'OIL',
                          'Description' => 'Oil',
                          'Price' => 10
                        ),
```

```
        array( 'Code' => 'SPK',
               'Description' => 'Spark Plugs',
               'Price' =>4
             )
      );
```

This array is easier to work with if you want to retrieve a single value. Remembering that the description is stored in the Description column is easier than remembering it is stored in column 1. Using descriptive indices, you do not need to remember that an item is stored at [x][y]. You can easily find your data by referring to a location with meaningful row and column names.

You do, however, lose the ability to use a simple for loop to step through each column in turn. Here is one way to write code to display this array:

```
for ( $row = 0; $row < 3; $row++ )
{
  echo '|'.$products[$row]['Code'].'|'.$products[$row]['Description'].
       '|'.$products[$row]['Price'].'|<br />';
}
```

Using a for loop, you can step through the outer, numerically indexed $products array. Each row in the $products array is an array with descriptive indices. Using the each() and list() functions in a while loop, you can step through these inner arrays. Therefore, you need a while loop inside a for loop:

```
for ( $row = 0; $row < 3; $row++ )
{
  while ( list( $key, $value ) = each( $products[ $row ] ) )
  {
    echo "|$value";
  }
  echo '|<br />';
}
```

You do not need to stop at two dimensions. In the same way that array elements can hold new arrays, those new arrays, in turn, can hold more arrays.

A three-dimensional array has height, width, and depth. If you are comfortable thinking of a two-dimensional array as a table with rows and columns, imagine a pile or deck of those tables. Each element is referenced by its layer, row, and column.

If Bob divided his products into categories, you could use a three-dimensional array to store them. Figure 3.4 shows Bob's products in a three-dimensional array.

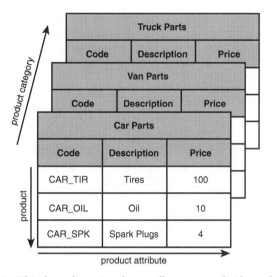

Figure 3.4   This three-dimensional array allows you to divide products into categories.

From the code that defines this array, you can see that a three-dimensional array is an array containing arrays of arrays:

```
$categories = array( array ( array( 'CAR_TIR', 'Tires', 100 ),
                             array( 'CAR_OIL', 'Oil', 10 ),
                             array( 'CAR_SPK', 'Spark Plugs', 4 )
                           ),
                     array ( array( 'VAN_TIR', 'Tires', 120 ),
                             array( 'VAN_OIL', 'Oil', 12 ),
                             array( 'VAN_SPK', 'Spark Plugs', 5 )
                           ),
                     array ( array( 'TRK_TIR', 'Tires', 150 ),
                             array( 'TRK_OIL', 'Oil', 15 ),
                             array( 'TRK_SPK', 'Spark Plugs', 6 )
                           )
                   );
```

Because this array has only numeric indices, you can use nested `for` loops to display its contents:

```
for ( $layer = 0; $layer < 3; $layer++ )
{
  echo "Layer $layer<br />";
  for ( $row = 0; $row < 3; $row++ )
  {
    for ( $column = 0; $column < 3; $column++ )
    {
      echo '|'.$categories[$layer][$row][$column];
    }
    echo '|<br />';
  }
}
```

Because of the way multidimensional arrays are created, you could create four-, five-, or even six-dimensional arrays. There is no language limit to the number of dimensions, but it is difficult for people to visualize constructs with more than three dimensions. Most real-world problems match logically with constructs of three or fewer dimensions.

Sorting Arrays

Sorting related data stored in an array is often useful. You can easily take a one-dimensional array and sort it into order.

Using `sort()`

The following code showing the `sort()` function results in the array being sorted into ascending alphabetical order:

```
$products = array( 'Tires', 'Oil', 'Spark Plugs' );
sort($products);
```

The array elements will now appear in the order Oil, Spark Plugs, Tires.

You can sort values by numerical order, too. If you have an array containing the prices of Bob's products, you can sort it into ascending numeric order as follows:

```
$prices = array( 100, 10, 4 );
sort($prices);
```

The prices will now appear in the order 4, 10, 100.

Note that the `sort()` function is case sensitive. All capital letters come before all low-ercase letters. So *A* is less than *Z*, but *Z* is less than *a*.

The function also has an optional second parameter. You may pass one of the constants SORT_REGULAR (the default), SORT_NUMERIC, or SORT_STRING. The ability to specify the sort type is useful when you are comparing strings that might contain numbers, for example, 2 and 12. Numerically, 2 is less than 12, but as strings `'12'` is less than `'2'`.

Using `asort()` and `ksort()` to Sort Arrays

If you are using an array with descriptive keys to store items and their prices, you need to use different kinds of sort functions to keep keys and values together as they are sorted.

The following code creates an array containing the three products and their associated prices and then sorts the array into ascending price order:

```
$prices = array( 'Tires'=>100, 'Oil'=>10, 'Spark Plugs'=>4 );
asort($prices);
```

The function `asort()` orders the array according to the value of each element. In the array, the values are the prices, and the keys are the textual descriptions. If, instead of sorting by price, you want to sort by description, you can use `ksort()`, which sorts by key rather than value. The following code results in the keys of the array being ordered alphabetically—`Oil`, `Spark Plugs`, `Tires`:

```
$prices = array( 'Tires'=>100, 'Oil'=>10, 'Spark Plugs'=>4 );
ksort($prices);
```

Sorting in Reverse

The three different sorting functions—`sort()`, `asort()`, and `ksort()`—sort an array into ascending order. Each function has a matching reverse sort function to sort an array into descending order. The reverse versions are called `rsort()`, `arsort()`, and `krsort()`.

You use the reverse sort functions in the same way you use the ascending sort functions. The `rsort()` function sorts a single-dimensional numerically indexed array into descending order. The `arsort()` function sorts a one-dimensional array into descending order using the value of each element. The `krsort()` function sorts a one-dimensional array into descending order using the key of each element.

Sorting Multidimensional Arrays

Sorting arrays with more than one dimension, or by something other than alphabetical or numerical order, is more complicated. PHP knows how to compare two numbers or two text strings, but in a multidimensional array, each element is an array. PHP does not know how to compare two arrays, so you need to create a method to compare them. Most of the time, the order of the words or numbers is fairly obvious, but for complicated objects, it becomes more problematic.

User-Defined Sorts

The following is the definition of a two-dimensional array used earlier. This array stores Bob's three products with a code, a description, and a price for each:

```
$products = array( array( 'TIR', 'Tires', 100 ),
                   array( 'OIL', 'Oil', 10 ),
                   array( 'SPK', 'Spark Plugs', 4 ) );
```

If you sort this array, in what order will the values appear? Because you know what the contents represent, there are at least two useful orders. You might want the products sorted into alphabetical order using the description or by numeric order by the price. Either result is possible, but you need to use the function usort() and tell PHP how to compare the items. To do this, you need to write your own comparison function.

The following code sorts this array into alphabetical order using the second column in the array—the description:

```
function compare($x, $y)
{
  if ( $x[1] == $y[1] )
    return 0;
  else if ( $x[1] < $y[1] )
    return -1;
  else
    return 1;
}

usort($products, 'compare');
```

So far in this book, you have called a number of the built-in PHP functions. To sort this array, you need to define a function of your own. We examine writing functions in detail in Chapter 5, "Reusing Code and Writing Functions," but here is a brief introduction.

You define a function by using the keyword function. You need to give the function a name. Names should be meaningful, so you can call it compare() for this example. Many functions take parameters or arguments. This compare() function takes two: one called $x and one called $y. The purpose of this function is to take two values and determine their order.

For this example, the $x and $y parameters are two of the arrays within the main array, each representing one product. To access the Description of the array $x, you type $x[1] because the Description is the second element in these arrays, and numbering starts at zero. You use $x[1] and $y[1] to compare each Description from the arrays passed into the function.

When a function ends, it can give a reply to the code that called it. This process is called *returning* a value. To return a value, you use the keyword return in the function. For example, the line return 1; sends the value 1 back to the code that called the function.

To be used by usort(), the compare() function must compare $x and $y. The function must return 0 if $x equals $y, a negative number if it is less, or a positive number if it is greater. The function will return 0, 1, or -1, depending on the values of $x and $y.

The final line of code calls the built-in function usort() with the array you want sorted ($products) and the name of the comparison function (compare()).

If you want the array sorted into another order, you can simply write a different comparison function. To sort by price, you need to look at the third column in the array and create this comparison function:

```
function compare($x, $y)
{
if ( $x[2] == $y[2] )
  return 0;
else if ( $x[2] < $y[2] )
  return -1;
else
  return 1;
}
```

When `usort($products, 'compare')` is called, the array is placed in ascending order by price.

The *u* in `usort()` stands for *user* because this function requires a user-defined comparison function. The `uasort()` and `uksort()` versions of `asort` and `ksort` also require user-defined comparison functions.

Similar to `asort()`, `uasort()` should be used when sorting a non-numerically indexed array by value. Use `asort` if your values are simple numbers or text. Define a comparison function and use `uasort()` if your values are more complicated objects such as arrays.

Similar to `ksort()`, `uksort()` should be used when sorting a non-numerically indexed array by key. Use `ksort` if your keys are simple numbers or text. Define a comparison function and use `uksort()` if your keys are more complicated objects such as arrays.

Reverse User Sorts

The functions `sort()`, `asort()`, and `ksort()` all have a matching reverse sorts with an *r* in the function name. The user-defined sorts do not have reverse variants, but you can sort a multidimensional array into reverse order. Because you provide the comparison function, you can write a comparison function that returns the opposite values. To sort into reverse order, the function needs to return 1 if $x is less than $y and -1 if $x is greater than $y. For example,

```
function reverse_compare($x, $y)
{
if ( $x[2] == $y[2] )
  return 0;
else if ( $x[2] < $y[2] )
  return 1;
else
  return -1;
}
```

Calling `usort($products, 'reverse_compare')` would now result in the array being placed in descending order by price.

Reordering Arrays

For some applications, you might want to manipulate the order of the array in other ways. The function `shuffle()` randomly reorders the elements of your array. The function `array_reverse()` gives you a copy of your array with all the elements in reverse order.

Using `shuffle()`

Bob wants to feature a small number of his products on the front page of his site. He has a large number of products but would like three randomly selected items shown on the front page. So that repeat visitors do not get bored, he would like the three chosen products to be different for each visit. He can easily accomplish his goal if all his products are in an array. Listing 3.1 displays three randomly chosen pictures by shuffling the array into a random order and then displaying the first three.

Listing 3.1 `bobs_front_page.php`—**Using PHP to Produce a Dynamic Front Page for Bob's Auto Parts**

```php
<?php
  $pictures = array('tire.jpg', 'oil.jpg', 'spark_plug.jpg',
                    'door.jpg', 'steering_wheel.jpg',
                    'thermostat.jpg', 'wiper_blade.jpg',
                    'gasket.jpg', 'brake_pad.jpg');

  shuffle($pictures);
?>
<html>
<head>
  <title>Bob's Auto Parts</title>
</head>
<body>
  <center>
    <h1>Bob's Auto Parts</h1>
    <table width = '100%'>
      <tr>
<?php
  for ( $i = 0; $i < 3; $i++ )
  {
    echo '<td align="center"><img src="';
    echo $pictures[$i];
    echo '" width="100" height="100"></td>';
```

Listing 3.1   **Continued**

```
 }
?>
     </tr>
   </table>
 </center>
</body>
</html>
```

Because the code selects random pictures, it produces a different page nearly every time you load it, as shown in Figure 3.5.

Figure 3.5   The shuffle() function enables you to feature three randomly chosen products.

In older versions of PHP, the shuffle() function required that you seed the random number generator first by calling srand(). This step is no longer required.

The shuffle() function has not had a very illustrious history. In older versions of PHP, it did not shuffle very well, giving a result that was not very random. In version 4.2.x on Windows, for instance, it did not shuffle at all, giving a result that was exactly what you started with. In version 5, it seems to work. If this function is important to you, test it on your server before employing it in your applications.

Because you do not really need the whole array reordered, you can achieve the same result using the function array_rand().

Using `array_reverse()`

The function `array_reverse()` takes an array and creates a new one with the same contents in reverse order. For example, there are a number of ways to create an array containing a countdown from 10 to 1.

Using `range()` usually creates an ascending sequence, which you could place in descending order using `array_reverse()` or `rsort()`. Alternatively, you could create the array one element at a time by writing a `for` loop:

```
$numbers = array();
for($i=10; $i>0; $i--)
  array_push( $numbers, $i );
```

A `for` loop can go in descending order like this: You set the starting value high and at the end of each loop use the `--` operator to decrease the counter by one.

Here, you create an empty array and then use `array_push()` for each element to add one new element to the end of an array. As a side note, the opposite of `array_push()` is `array_pop()`. This function removes and returns one element from the end of an array.

Alternatively, you can use the `array_reverse()` function to reverse the array created by `range()`:

```
$numbers = range(1,10);
$numbers = array_reverse($numbers);
```

Note that `array_reverse()` returns a modified copy of the array. If you do not want the original array, as in this example, you can simply store the new copy over the original.

If your data is just a range of integers, you can create it in reverse order by passing −1 as the optional step parameter to `range()`:

```
$numbers = range(10, 1, -1);
```

Loading Arrays from Files

In Chapter 2, "Storing and Retrieving Data," you learned how to store customer orders in a file. Each line in the file looked something like this:

```
15:42, 20th April 4 tires 1 oil 6 spark plugs $434.00 22 Short St, Smalltown
```

To process or fulfill this order, you could load it back into an array. Listing 3.2 displays the current order file.

Listing 3.2 `vieworders.php`— **Using PHP to Display Orders for Bob**

```
<?php
//create short variable name
$DOCUMENT_ROOT = $_SERVER['DOCUMENT_ROOT'];
```

Listing 3.2   **Continued**

```php
$orders= file("$DOCUMENT_ROOT/../orders/orders.txt");

$number_of_orders = count($orders);
if ($number_of_orders == 0)
{
  echo '<p><strong>No orders pending.
      Please try again later.</strong></p>';
}
for ($i=0; $i<$number_of_orders; $i++)
{
  echo $orders[$i].'<br />';
}
?>
```

This script produces almost exactly the same output as Listing 2.3 in the preceding chapter, which was shown in Figure 2.4. This time, the script uses the function file(), which loads the entire file into an array. Each line in the file becomes one element of an array. This code also uses the count() function to see how many elements are in an array.

Furthermore, you could load each section of the order lines into separate array elements to process the sections separately or to format them more attractively. Listing 3.3 does exactly that.

Listing 3.3   `vieworders2.php`— **Using PHP to Separate, Format, and Display Orders for Bob**

```php
<?php
  //create short variable name
  $DOCUMENT_ROOT = $_SERVER['DOCUMENT_ROOT'];
?>
<html>
<head>
  <title>Bob's Auto Parts - Customer Orders</title>
</head>
<body>
<h1>Bob's Auto Parts</h1>
<h2>Customer Orders</h2>
<?php
  //Read in the entire file.
  //Each order becomes an element in the array
  $orders= file("$DOCUMENT_ROOT/../orders/orders.txt");
```

Listing 3.3 **Continued**

```
  // count the number of orders in the array
  $number_of_orders = count($orders);
  if ($number_of_orders == 0)
  {
    echo '<p><strong>No orders pending.
          Please try again later.</strong></p>';
  }
  echo "<table border='1'>\n";
  echo '<tr><th bgcolor="#CCCCFF">Order Date</th>
            <th bgcolor="#CCCCFF">Tires</th>
            <th bgcolor="#CCCCFF">Oil</th>
            <th bgcolor="#CCCCFF">Spark Plugs</th>
            <th bgcolor="#CCCCFF">Total</th>
            <th bgcolor="#CCCCFF">Address</th>
          <tr>';
  for ($i=0; $i<$number_of_orders; $i++)
  {
    //split up each line
    $line = explode( "\t", $orders[$i] );
    // keep only the number of items ordered (discard other stored data)
    $line[1] = intval( $line[1] );
    $line[2] = intval( $line[2] );
    $line[3] = intval( $line[3] );
    // output each order
    echo "<tr><td>$line[0]</td>
              <td align='right'>$line[1]</td>
              <td align='right'>$line[2]</td>
              <td align='right'>$line[3]</td>
              <td align='right'>$line[4]</td>
              <td>$line[5]</td>
          </tr>";
  }
  echo '</table>';
?>
</body>
</html>
```

The code in Listing 3.3 loads the entire file into an array, but unlike the example in Listing 3.2, here you use the function explode() to split up each line so that you can apply some processing and formatting before printing. The output from this script is shown in Figure 3.6.

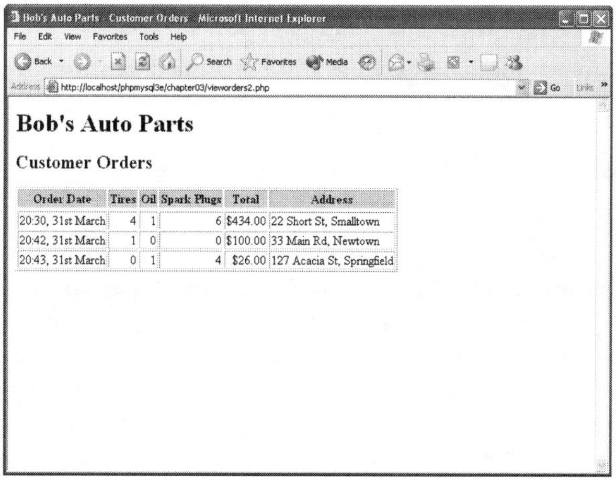

Figure 3.6 After splitting order records with `explode()`, you can put each part of an order in a different table cell for better-looking output.

The `explode` function has the following prototype:

```
array explode(string separator, string string [, int limit])
```

In the preceding chapter, you used the tab character as a delimiter when storing this data, so here you call

```
explode( "\t", $orders[$i] )
```

This code "explodes" the passed-in string into parts. Each tab character becomes a break between two elements. For example, the string

```
"15:42, 20th April\t4 tires\t1 oil\t6 spark plugs\t$434.00\t
22 Short St, Smalltown"
```

is exploded into the parts `"15:42, 20th April"`, `"4 tires"`, `"1 oil"`, `"6 spark plugs"`, `"$434.00"`, and `"22 Short St, Smalltown"`.

Note that the optional *limit* parameter can be used to limit the maximum number of parts returned.

This example doesn't do very much processing. Rather than output tires, oil, and spark plugs on every line, this example displays only the number of each and gives the table a heading row to show what the numbers represent.

You could extract numbers from these strings in a number of ways. Here, you use the function `intval()`. As mentioned in Chapter 1, `intval()` converts a string to an integer. The conversion is reasonably clever and ignores parts, such as the label in this example, which cannot be converted to an integer. We cover various ways of processing strings in the next chapter.

Performing Other Array Manipulations

So far, we have covered only about half the array processing functions. Many others will be useful from time to time; we describe some of them next.

Navigating Within an Array: `each()`, `current()`, `reset()`, `end()`, `next()`, `pos()`, and `prev()`

We mentioned previously that every array has an internal pointer that points to the current element in the array. You indirectly used this pointer earlier when using the `each()` function, but you can directly use and manipulate this pointer.

If you create a new array, the current pointer is initialized to point to the first element in the array. Calling `current( $array_name )` returns the first element.

Calling either `next()` or `each()` advances the pointer forward one element. Calling `each( $array_name )` returns the current element before advancing the pointer. The function `next()` behaves slightly differently: Calling `next( $array_name )` advances the pointer and then returns the new current element.

You have already seen that `reset()` returns the pointer to the first element in the array. Similarly, calling `end( $array_name )` sends the pointer to the end of the array. The first and last elements in the array are returned by `reset()` and `end()`, respectively.

To move through an array in reverse order, you could use `end()` and `prev()`. The `prev()` function is the opposite of `next()`. It moves the current pointer back one and then returns the new current element.

For example, the following code displays an array in reverse order:

```
$value = end ($array);
while ($value)
{
  echo "$value<br />";
  $value = prev($array);
}
```

For example, you can declare $array like this:

```
$array = array(1, 2, 3);
```

In this case, the output would appear in a browser as follows:

```
3
2
1
```

Using `each()`, `current()`, `reset()`, `end()`, `next()`, `pos()`, and `prev()`, you can write your own code to navigate through an array in any order.

Applying Any Function to Each Element in an Array: `array_walk()`

Sometimes you might want to work with or modify every element in an array in the same way. The function `array_walk()` allows you to do this. The prototype of `array_walk()` is as follows:

```
bool array_walk(array arr, string func, [mixed userdata])
```

Similar to the way you called `usort()` earlier, `array_walk()` expects you to declare a function of your own. As you can see, `array_walk()` takes three parameters. The first, *arr*, is the array to be processed. The second, *func*, is the name of a user-defined function that will be applied to each element in the array. The third parameter, *userdata*, is optional. If you use it, it will be passed through to your function as a parameter. You see how this works shortly.

A handy user-defined function might be one that displays each element with some specified formatting. The following code displays each element on a new line by calling the user-defined function `my_print()` with each element of `$array`:

```
function my_print($value)
{
  echo "$value<br />";
}
array_walk($array, 'my_print');
```

The function you write needs to have a particular signature. For each element in the array, `array_walk` takes the key and value stored in the array, and anything you passed as *userdata*, and calls your function like this:

```
yourfunction(value, key, userdata)
```

For most uses, your function will be using only the values in the array. For some, you might also need to pass a parameter to your function using the parameter *userdata*. Occasionally, you might be interested in the key of each element as well as the value. Your function can, as with `MyPrint()`, choose to ignore the key and *userdata* parameter.

For a slightly more complicated example, you can write a function that modifies the values in the array and requires a parameter. Although you may not interested in the key, you need to accept it to accept the third parameter:

```
function my_multiply(&$value, $key, $factor)
{
  $value *= $factor;
}
array_walk(&$array, 'my_multiply', 3);
```

This code defines a function, my_multiply(), that will multiply each element in the array by a supplied factor. You need to use the optional third parameter to array_walk() to take a parameter to pass to the function and use it as the factor to multiply by. Because you need this parameter, you must define the function, my_multiply(), to take three parameters: an array element's value ($value), an array element's key ($key), and the parameter ($factor). You can choose to ignore the key.

A subtle point to note is the way $value is passed. The ampersand (&) before the variable name in the definition of my_multiply() means that $value will be *passed by reference*. Passing by reference allows the function to alter the contents of the array.

We address passing by reference in more detail in Chapter 5. If you are not familiar with the term, for now just note that to pass by reference, you place an ampersand before the variable name.

Counting Elements in an Array: count(), sizeof(), and array_count_values()

You used the function count() in an earlier example to count the number of elements in an array of orders. The function sizeof() serves exactly the same purpose. Both of these functions return the number of elements in an array passed to them. You get a count of one for the number of elements in a normal scalar variable and zero if you pass either an empty array or a variable that has not been set.

The array_count_values() function is more complex. If you call array_count_values($array), this function counts how many times each *unique* value occurs in the array named $array. (This is the *set cardinality* of the array.) The function returns an associative array containing a frequency table. This array contains all the unique values from $array as keys. Each key has a numeric value that tells you how many times the corresponding key occurs in $array.

For example, the code

```
$array = array(4, 5, 1, 2, 3, 1, 2, 1);
$ac = array_count_values($array);
```

creates an array called $ac that contains

Key	Value
4	1
5	1
1	3
2	2
3	1

This result indicates that 4, 5, and 3 occurred once in $array, 1 occurred three times, and 2 occurred twice.

Converting Arrays to Scalar Variables: extract()

If you have a non-numerically indexed array with a number of key value pairs, you can turn them into a set of scalar variables using the function extract(). The prototype for extract() is as follows:

```
extract(array var_array [, int extract_type] [, string prefix] );
```

The purpose of extract() is to take an array and create scalar variables with the names of the keys in the array. The values of these variables are set to the values in the array.

Here is a simple example:

```
$array = array( 'key1' => 'value1', 'key2' => 'value2', 'key3' => 'value3');
extract($array);
echo "$key1 $key2 $key3";
```

This code produces the following output:

```
value1 value2 value3
```

The array has three elements with keys: key1, key2, and key3. Using extract(), you create three scalar variables: $key1, $key2, and $key3. You can see from the output that the values of $key1, $key2, and $key3 are 'value1', 'value2', and 'value3', respectively. These values come from the original array.

The extract() function has two optional parameters: extract_type and prefix. The variable extract_type tells extract() how to handle collisions. These are cases in which a variable already exists with the same name as a key. The default response is to overwrite the existing variable. The allowable values for extract_type are shown in Table 3.2.

Table 3.2 **Allowed** extract_type **Parameters for** extract()

Type	Meaning
EXTR_OVERWRITE	Overwrites the existing variable when a collision occurs.
EXTR_SKIP	Skips an element when a collision occurs.
EXTR_PREFIX_SAME	Creates a variable named $prefix_key when a collision occurs. You must supply prefix.
EXTR_PREFIX_ALL	Prefixes all variable names with prefix. You must supply prefix.
EXTR_PREFIX_INVALID	Prefixes variable names that would otherwise be invalid (for example, numeric variable names) with prefix. You must supply prefix.
EXTR_IF_EXISTS	Extracts only variables that already exist (that is, writes existing variables with values from the array). This parameter was added at version 4.2.0 and is useful for converting, for example, $_REQUEST to a set of valid variables.

Table 3.2 **Continued**

Type	Meaning
EXTR_PREFIX_IF_EXISTS	Creates a prefixed version only if the nonprefixed version already exists. This parameter was added at version 4.2.0.
EXTR_REFS	Extracts variables as references. This parameter was added at version 4.3.0.

The two most useful options are EXTR_OVERWRITE (the default) and EXTR_PREFIX_ALL. The other options might be useful occasionally when you know that a particular collision will occur and want that key skipped or prefixed. A simple example using EXTR_PREFIX_ALL follows. You can see that the variables created are called *prefix-underscore-keyname*:

```
$array = array( 'key1' => 'value1', 'key2' => 'value2', 'key3' => 'value3');
extract($array, EXTR_PREFIX_ALL, 'my_prefix');
echo "$my_prefix_key1 $my_prefix_key2 $my_prefix_key3";
```

This code again produces the following output:

```
value1 value2 value3
```

Note that for extract() to extract an element, that element's key must be a valid variable name, which means that keys starting with numbers or including spaces are skipped.

Further Reading

This chapter covers what we believe to be the most useful of PHP's array functions. We have chosen not to cover all the possible array functions. The online PHP manual available at http://www.php.net/array provides a brief description for each of them.

Next

In the next chapter, you learn about string processing functions. We cover functions that search, replace, split, and merge strings, as well as the powerful regular expression functions that can perform almost any action on a string.

4

String Manipulation and Regular Expressions

IN THIS CHAPTER, WE DISCUSS HOW YOU can use PHP's string functions to format and manipulate text. We also discuss using string functions or regular expression functions to search (and replace) words, phrases, or other patterns within a string.

These functions are useful in many contexts. You often may want to clean up or reformat user input that is going to be stored in a database. Search functions are great when building search engine applications (among other things).

Key topics covered in this chapter include

- Formatting strings
- Joining and splitting strings
- Comparing strings
- Matching and replacing substrings with string functions
- Using regular expressions

Creating a Sample Application: Smart Form Mail

In this chapter, you use string and regular expression functions in the context of a Smart Form Mail application. You then add these scripts to the Bob's Auto Parts site you've been building in preceding chapters.

This time, you build a straightforward and commonly used customer feedback form for Bob's customers to enter their complaints and compliments, as shown in Figure 4.1. However, this application has one improvement over many you will find on the Web. Instead of emailing the form to a generic email address like feedback@example.com, you'll attempt to put some intelligence into the process by searching the input for key words and phrases and then sending the email to the appropriate employee at Bob's company. For example, if the email contains the word *advertising*, you might send the feedback to the Marketing department. If the email is from Bob's biggest client, it can go straight to Bob.

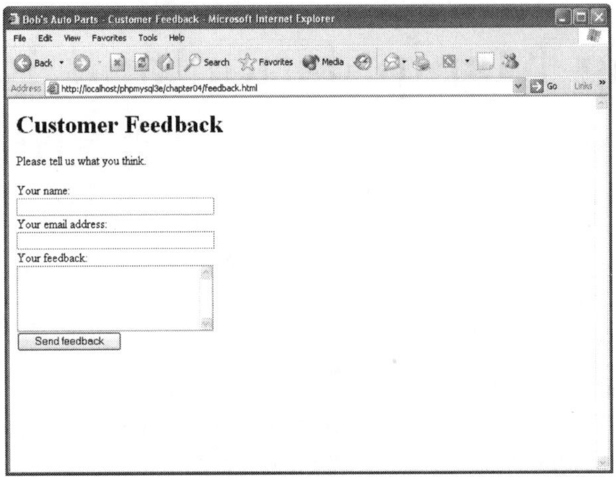

Figure 4.1   Bob's feedback form asks customers for their name, email address, and comments.

Start with the simple script shown in Listing 4.1 and add to it as you read along.

Listing 4.1 `processfeedback.php`—**Basic Script to Email Form Contents**

```php
<?php
  //create short variable names
  $name=$_POST['name'];
  $email=$_POST['email'];
  $feedback=$_POST['feedback'];

  $toaddress = 'feedback@example.com';
  $subject = 'Feedback from web site';
  $mailcontent = 'Customer name: '.$name."\n"
              .'Customer email: '.$email."\n"
              ."Customer comments: \n".$feedback."\n";
  $fromaddress = 'From: webserver@example.com';

  mail($toaddress, $subject, $mailcontent, $fromaddress);
?>
<html>
<head>
```

Listing 4.1   **Continued**

```
  <title>Bob's Auto Parts - Feedback Submitted</title>
</head>
<body>
<h1>Feedback submitted</h1>
<p>Your feedback has been sent.</p>
</body>
</html>
```

Generally, you should check that users have filled out all the required form fields using, for example, isset().We have omitted this function call from the script and other examples for the sake of brevity.

In this script, you can see that we have concatenated the form fields together and used PHP's mail() function to email them to feedback@example.com.This is a sample email address. If you want to test the code in this chapter, substitute your own email address here. Because we haven't yet used mail(), we need to discuss how it works.

Unsurprisingly, this function sends email.The prototype for mail() looks like this:

```
bool mail(string to, string subject, string message,
          string [additional_headers [, string additional_parameters]]);
```

The first three parameters are compulsory and represent the address to send email to, the subject line, and the message contents, respectively.The fourth parameter can be used to send any additional valid email headers.Valid email headers are described in the document RFC822, which is available online if you want more details. (RFCs, or Requests for Comment, are the source of many Internet standards; we discuss them in Chapter 19, "Using Network and Protocol Functions.") Here, the fourth parameter adds a "From:" address for the mail.You can also use it to add "Reply-To:" and "Cc:" fields, among others. If you want more than one additional header, just separate them by using newlines and carriage returns (\n\r) within the string, as follows:

```
$additional_headers="From: webserver@example.com\r\n "
                    .'Reply-To: bob@example.com';
```

The optional fifth parameter can be used to pass a parameter to whatever program you have configured to send mail.

To use the mail() function, set up your PHP installation to point at your mail-sending program. If the script doesn't work for you in its current form, double-check Appendix A, "Installing PHP5 and MySQL5."

Throughout this chapter, you enhance this basic script by making use of PHP's string handling and regular expression functions.

Formatting Strings

You often need to tidy up user strings (typically from an HTML form interface) before you can use them. The following sections describe some of the functions you can use.

Trimming Strings: `chop()`, `ltrim()`, and `trim()`

The first step in tidying up is to trim any excess whitespace from the string. Although this step is never compulsory, it can be useful if you are going to store the string in a file or database, or if you're going to compare it to other strings.

PHP provides three useful functions for this purpose. You can use the `trim()` function to tidy up your input data as follows:

```
$name=trim($name);
$email=trim($email);
$feedback=trim($feedback);
```

The `trim()` function strips whitespace from the start and end of a string and returns the resulting string. The characters it strips by default are newlines and carriage returns (`\n` and `\r`), horizontal and vertical tabs (`\t` and `\x0B`), end-of-string characters (`\0`), and spaces. You can also pass it a second parameter containing a list of characters to strip instead of this default list. Depending on your particular purpose, you might like to use the `ltrim()` or `rtrim()` functions instead. They are both similar to `trim()`, taking the string in question as a parameter and returning the formatted string. The difference between these three is that `trim()` removes whitespace from the start and end of a string, `ltrim()` removes whitespace from the start (or left) only, and `rtrim()` removes whitespace from the end (or right) only.

Formatting Strings for Presentation

PHP includes a set of functions that you can use to reformat a string in different ways.

Using HTML Formatting: The `nl2br()` Function

The `nl2br()` function takes a string as a parameter and replaces all the newlines in it with the XHTML `<br />` tag (or the HTML `<br>` tag in versions prior to 4.0.5). This capability is useful for echoing a long string to the browser. For example, you can use this function to format the customer's feedback to echo it back:

```
<p>Your feedback (shown below) has been sent.</p>
<p><?php echo nl2br($mailcontent); ?> </p>
```

Remember that HTML disregards plain whitespace, so if you don't filter this output through `nl2br()`, it will appear on a single line (except for newlines forced by the browser window). The result is illustrated in Figure 4.2.

Formatting a String for Printing

So far, you have used the `echo` language construct to print strings to the browser. PHP also supports a `print()` construct, which does the same thing as `echo`, but returns a value (`true` or `false`, denoting success).

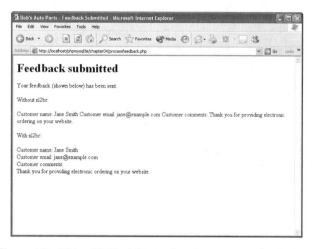

Figure 4.2   Using PHP's `nl2br()` function improves the display of long strings within HTML.

Both of these techniques print a string "as is." You can apply some more sophisticated formatting using the functions `printf()` and `sprintf()`. They work basically the same way, except that `printf()` prints a formatted string to the browser and `sprintf()` returns a formatted string.

If you have previously programmed in C, you will find that these functions are conceptually similar to the C versions. Be careful, though, because the syntax is not exactly the same. If you haven't, they take getting used to but are useful and powerful.

The prototypes for these functions are

```
string sprintf (string format [, mixed args...])
void printf (string format [, mixed args...])
```

The first parameter passed to both of these functions is a format string that describes the basic shape of the output with format codes instead of variables. The other parameters are variables that will be substituted in to the format string.

For example, using `echo`, you can use the variables you want to print inline, like this:

```
echo "Total amount of order is $total.";
```

To get the same effect with `printf()`, you would use

```
printf ("Total amount of order is %s.", $total);
```

The `%s` in the format string is called a *conversion specification*. This one means "replace with a string." In this case, it is replaced with `$total` interpreted as a string. If the value stored in `$total` was 12.4, both of these approaches would print it as `12.4`.

The advantage of `printf()` is that you can use a more useful conversion specification to specify that `$total` is actually a floating-point number and that it should have two decimal places after the decimal point, as follows:

```
printf ("Total amount of order is %.2f", $total);
```

Given this formatting, and 12.4 stored in `$total`, this statement will print as `12.40`.

You can have multiple conversion specifications in the format string. If you have *n* conversion specifications, you will usually have *n* arguments after the format string. Each conversion specification will be replaced by a reformatted argument in the order they are listed. For example,

```
printf ("Total amount of order is %.2f (with shipping %.2f) ",
        $total, $total_shipping);
```

Here, the first conversion specification uses the variable `$total`, and the second uses the variable `$total_shipping`.

Each conversion specification follows the same format, which is

```
%['padding_character][-][width][.precision]type
```

All conversion specifications start with a `%` symbol. If you actually want to print a `%` symbol, you need to use `%%`.

The *padding_character* is optional. It is used to pad your variable to the width you have specified. An example would be to add leading zeros to a number like a counter. The default padding character is a space. If you are specifying a space or zero, you do not need to prefix it with the apostrophe (`'`). For any other padding character, you need to prefix it with an apostrophe.

The - symbol is optional. It specifies that the data in the field will be left-justified rather than right-justified, which is the default.

The *width* specifier tells `printf()` how much room (in characters) to leave for the variable to be substituted in here.

The *precision* specifier should begin with a decimal point. It should contain the number of places after the decimal point you would like displayed.

The final part of the specification is a type code. A summary of these codes is shown in Table 4.1.

Table 4.1 **Conversion Specification Type Codes**

Type	Meaning
b	Interpret as an integer and print as a binary number.
c	Interpret as an integer and print as a character.
d	Interpret as an integer and print as a decimal number.
f	Interpret as a double and print as a floating-point number.
o	Interpret as an integer and print as an octal number.
s	Interpret as a string and print as a string.

Table 4.1   **Continued**

Type	Meaning
u	Interpret as an integer and print as an unsigned decimal.
x	Interpret as an integer and print as a hexadecimal number with lowercase letters for the digits a–f.
X	Interpret as an integer and print as a hexadecimal number with uppercase letters for the digits A–F.

Since PHP version 4.0.6, you can use argument numbering, which means that the arguments don't need to be in the same order as the conversion specifications. For example,

```
printf ("Total amount of order is %2\$.2f (with shipping %1\$.2f) ",
        $total_shipping, $total);
```

Just add the argument position in the list directly after the % sign, followed by an escaped $ symbol; in this example, 2\$ means "replace with the second argument in the list." This method can also be used to repeat arguments.

Two alternative versions of these functions are called vprintf() and vsprintf(). These variants accept two parameters: the format string and an array of the arguments rather than a variable number of parameters.

Changing the Case of a String

You can also reformat the case of a string. This capability is not particularly useful for the sample application, but we'll look at some brief examples.

If you start with the subject string, $subject, which you are using for email, you can change its case by using several functions. The effect of these functions is summarized in Table 4.2. The first column shows the function name, the second describes its effect, the third shows how it would be applied to the string $subject, and the last column shows what value would be returned from the function.

Table 4.2   **String Case Functions and Their Effects**

Function	Description	Use	Value
		$subject	Feedback from web site
strtoupper()	Turns string to uppercase	strtoupper($subject)	FEEDBACK FROM WEB SITE
strtolower()	Turns string to lowercase	strtolower($subject)	feedback from web site
ucfirst()	Capitalizes first character of string if it's alphabetic	ucfirst($subject)	Feedback from web site

Table 4.2 **Continued**

Function	Description	Use	Value
ucwords()	Capitalizes first character of each word in the string that begins with an alphabetic character	ucwords($subject)	Feedback From Web Site

Formatting Strings for Storage: addslashes() and stripslashes()

In addition to using string functions to reformat a string visually, you can use some of these functions to reformat strings for storage in a database. Although we don't cover actually writing to the database until Part II, "Using MySQL," we cover formatting strings for database storage now.

Certain characters are perfectly valid as part of a string but can cause problems, particularly when you are inserting data into a database because the database could interpret these characters as control characters. The problematic ones are quotation marks (single and double), backslashes (\), and the NULL character.

You need to find a way of marking or *escaping* these characters so that databases such as MySQL can understand that you meant a literal special character rather than a control sequence. To *escape* these characters, add a backslash in front of them. For example, " (double quotation mark) becomes \" (backslash double quotation mark), and \ (backslash) becomes \\ (backslash backslash). (This rule applies universally to special characters, so if you have \\ in your string, you need to replace it with \\\\.)

PHP provides two functions specifically designed for escaping characters. Before you write any strings into a database, you should reformat them with addslashes(), as follows:

```
$feedback = addslashes($feedback);
```

Like many of the other string functions, addslashes() takes a string as a parameter and returns the reformatted string.

Figure 4.3 shows the actual effects of using these functions on the string.

You may try these functions on your server and get a result that looks more like Figure 4.4.

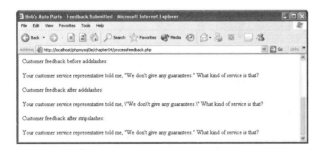

Figure 4.3   After the `addslashes()` function is called, all the quotation marks have been slashed out. `stripslashes()` removes the slashes.

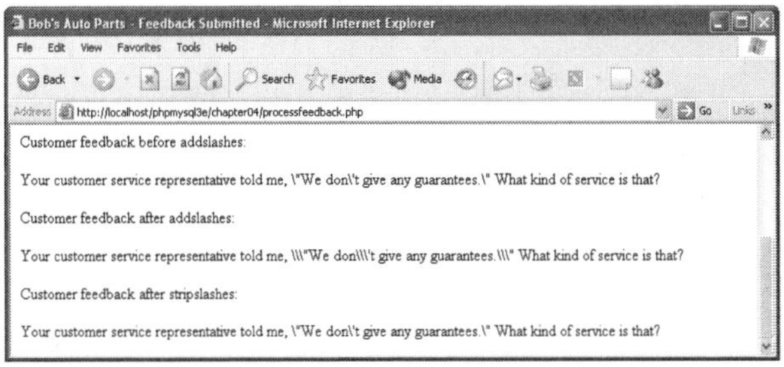

Figure 4.4   All problematic characters have been escaped twice; this means the magic quotes feature is switched on.

If you see this result, it means that your configuration of PHP is set up to add and strip slashes automatically. This capability is controlled by the `magic_quotes_gpc` configuration directive. This directive is now on by default in new versions of PHP. The letters *gpc* stand for *GET, POST,* and *cookie*. This means that variables coming from these sources are automatically quoted. You can check whether this directive is switched on in your system by using the `get_magic_quotes_gpc()` function, which returns `true` if strings from these sources are being automatically quoted for you. If this directive is on in your system, you need to call `stripslashes()` before displaying user data; otherwise, the slashes will be displayed.

Using magic quotes allows you to write more portable code. You can read more about this feature in Chapter 23, "Other Useful Features."

Joining and Splitting Strings with String Functions

Often, you may want to look at parts of a string individually. For example, you might want to look at words in a sentence (say, for spellchecking) or split a domain name or email address into its component parts. PHP provides several string functions (and one regular expression function) that allow you to do this.

In the example, Bob wants any customer feedback from `bigcustomer.com` to go directly to him, so you can split the email address the customer typed into parts to find out whether he or she works for Bob's big customer.

Using `explode()`, `implode()`, and `join()`

The first function you could use for this purpose, `explode()`, has the following proto-type:

```
array explode(string separator, string input [, int limit]);
```

This function takes a string *input* and splits it into pieces on a specified *separator* string. The pieces are returned in an array. You can limit the number of pieces with the optional *limit* parameter, added in PHP 4.0.1.

To get the domain name from the customer's email address in the script, you can use the following code:

```
$email_array = explode('@', $email);
```

This call to `explode()` splits the customer's email address into two parts: the username, which is stored in `$email_array[0]`, and the domain name, which is stored in `$email_array[1]`. Now you can test the domain name to determine the customer's origin and then send the feedback to the appropriate person:

```
if ($email_array[1]=='bigcustomer.com')
  $toaddress = 'bob@example.com';
else
  $toaddress = 'feedback@example.com';
```

If the domain is capitalized, however, this approach will not work. You could avoid this problem by converting the domain to all uppercase or all lowercase and then checking, as follows:

```
$email_array[1] = strtolower ($email_array[1]);
```

You can reverse the effects of `explode()` by using either `implode()` or `join()`, which are identical. For example,

```
$new_email = implode('@', $email_array);
```

This statement takes the array elements from `$email_array` and joins them with the string passed in the first parameter. The function call is similar to `explode()`, but the effect is the opposite.

Using `strtok()`

Unlike `explode()`, which breaks a string into all its pieces at one time, `strtok()` gets pieces (called *tokens*) from a string one at a time. `strtok()` is a useful alternative to using `explode()` for processing words from a string one at a time.

The prototype for `strtok()` is

```
string strtok(string input, string separator);
```

The separator can be either a character or a string of characters, but the input string is split on each of the characters in the separator string rather than on the whole separator string (as `explode` does).

Calling `strtok()` is not quite as simple as it seems in the prototype. To get the first token from a string, you call `strtok()` with the string you want tokenized and a separator. To get the subsequent tokens from the string, you just pass a single parameter—the separator. The function keeps its own internal pointer to its place in the string. If you want to reset the pointer, you can pass the string into it again.

`strtok()` is typically used as follows:

```
$token = strtok($feedback, ' ');
echo $token.'<br />';
while ($token!='')
{
  $token = strtok(' ');
  echo $token.'<br />';
};
```

As usual, it's a good idea to check that the customer actually typed some feedback in the form, using, for example, the `empty()` function. We have omitted these checks for brevity.

The preceding code prints each token from the customer's feedback on a separate line and loops until there are no more tokens. Note that prior to version 4.1.0, PHP's `strtok()` didn't work exactly the same as the one in C. If two instances of a separator appeared *in a row* in your target string (in this example, two spaces in a row), `strtok()` would return an empty string. You could not differentiate this from the empty string returned when you got to the end of the target string. Also, if one of the tokens was zero, the empty string was returned. This made PHP's `strtok()` somewhat less useful than the one in C. The new version works correctly, skipping empty strings.

Using `substr()`

The `substr()` function enables you to access a substring between given start and end points of a string. It's not appropriate for the example used here but can be useful when you need to get at parts of fixed format strings.

The `substr()` function has the following prototype:

```
string substr(string string, int start[, int length] );
```

This function returns a substring copied from within *string*.

The following examples use this test string:

```
$test = 'Your customer service is excellent';
```

If you call it with a positive number for *start* (only), you will get the string from the *start* position to the end of the string. For example,

```
substr($test, 1);
```

returns `our customer service is excellent`. Note that the string position starts from 0, as with arrays.

If you call `substr()` with a negative *start* (only), you will get the string from the end of the string minus *start* characters to the end of the string. For example,

```
substr($test, -9);
```

returns `excellent`.

The *length* parameter can be used to specify either a number of characters to return (if it is positive) or the end character of the return sequence (if it is negative). For example,

```
substr($test, 0, 4);
```

returns the first four characters of the string—namely, `Your`. The code

```
echo substr($test, 5, -13);
```

returns the characters between the fourth character and the thirteenth-to-last character—that is, `customer service`. The first character is location 0. So location 5 is the sixth character.

Comparing Strings

So far, we've just shown you how to use `==` to compare two strings for equality. You can do some slightly more sophisticated comparisons using PHP. We've divided these comparisons into two categories for you: partial matches and others. We deal with the others first and then get into partial matching, which we need to further develop the Smart Form example.

Performing String Ordering: `strcmp()`, `strcasecmp()`, and `strnatcmp()`

The `strcmp()`, `strcasecmp()`, and `strnatcmp()` functions can be used to order strings. This capability is useful when you are sorting data.

The prototype for `strcmp()` is

```
int strcmp(string str1, string str2);
```

The function expects to receive two strings, which it compares. If they are equal, it will return 0. If `str1` comes after (or is greater than) `str2` in lexicographic order, `strcmp()` will return a number greater than zero. If `str1` is less than `str2`, `strcmp()` will return a number less than zero. This function is case sensitive.

The function `strcasecmp()` is identical except that it is not case sensitive.

The function `strnatcmp()` and its non–case sensitive twin, `strnatcasecmp()`, were added in PHP 4. These functions compare strings according to a "natural ordering," which is more the way a human would do it. For example, `strcmp()` would order the string `"2"` as greater than the string `"12"` because it is lexicographically greater. `strnatcmp()` would order them the other way around. You can read more about natural ordering at

http://www.naturalordersort.org/

Testing String Length with `strlen()`

You can check the length of a string by using the `strlen()` function. If you pass it a string, this function will return its length. For example, `strlen('hello')` returns 5.

You can use this function for validating input data. Consider the email address on the sample form, stored in `$email`. One basic way of validating an email address stored in `$email` is to check its length. By our reasoning, the minimum length of an email address is six characters—for example, *a@a.to* if you have a country code with no second-level domains, a one-letter server name, and a one-letter email address. Therefore, an error could be produced if the address is not at least this length:

```
if (strlen($email) < 6)
{
  echo 'That email address is not valid';
  exit;  // finish execution of PHP script
}
```

Clearly, this approach is a very simplistic way of validating this information. We look at better ways in the next section.

Matching and Replacing Substrings with String Functions

Checking whether a particular substring is present in a larger string is a common operation. This partial matching is usually more useful than testing for complete equality in strings.

In the Smart Form example, you want to look for certain key phrases in the customer feedback and send the mail to the appropriate department. If you want to send emails discussing Bob's shops to the retail manager, for example, you want to know whether the word *shop* or derivatives thereof appear in the message.

Given the functions you have already looked at, you could use `explode()` or `strtok()` to retrieve the individual words in the message and then compare them using the == operator or `strcmp()`.

You could also do the same thing, however, with a single function call to one of the string-matching or regular expression-matching functions. They search for a pattern inside a string. Next, we look at each set of functions one by one.

Finding Strings in Strings: `strstr()`, `strchr()`, `strrchr()`, and `stristr()`

To find a string within another string, you can use any of the functions `strstr()`, `strchr()`, `strrchr()`, or `stristr()`.

The function `strstr()`, which is the most generic, can be used to find a string or character match within a longer string. In PHP, the `strchr()` function is exactly the same as `strstr()`, although its name implies that it is used to find a character in a string, similar to the C version of this function. In PHP, either of these functions can be used to find a string inside a string, including finding a string containing only a single character.

The prototype for `strstr()` is as follows:

```
string strstr(string haystack, string needle);
```

You pass the function a *haystack* to be searched and a *needle* to be found. If an exact match of the *needle* is found, the function returns the *haystack* from the *needle* onward; otherwise, it returns `false`. If the *needle* occurs more than once, the returned string will start from the first occurrence of *needle*.

For example, in the Smart Form application, you can decide where to send the email as follows:

```
$toaddress = 'feedback@example.com';  // the default value

// Change the $toaddress if the criteria are met
if (strstr($feedback, 'shop'))
  $toaddress = 'retail@example.com';
else if (strstr($feedback, 'delivery'))
  $toaddress = 'fulfillment@example.com';
else if (strstr($feedback, 'bill'))
  $toaddress = 'accounts@example.com';
```

This code checks for certain keywords in the feedback and sends the mail to the appropriate person. If, for example, the customer feedback reads "I still haven't received delivery of my last order," the string "delivery" will be detected and the feedback will be sent to `fulfillment@example.com`.

There are two variants on `strstr()`. The first variant is `stristr()`, which is nearly identical but is not case sensitive. This variation is useful for this application because the customer might type `'delivery'`, `'Delivery'`, or `'DELIVERY'`.

The second variant is `strrchr()`, which is again nearly identical, but returns the *haystack* from the last occurrence of the *needle* onward.

Finding the Position of a Substring: `strpos()` and `strrpos()`

The functions `strpos()` and `strrpos()` operate in a similar fashion to `strstr()`, except, instead of returning a substring, they return the numerical position of a *needle* within a *haystack*. Interestingly enough, the PHP manual now recommends using `strpos()` instead of `strstr()` to check for the presence of a string within a string because it runs faster.

The `strpos()` function has the following prototype:

```
int strpos(string haystack, string needle, int [offset] );
```

The integer returned represents the position of the *first* occurrence of the *needle* within the *haystack*. The first character is in position 0 as usual.

For example, the following code echoes the value 4 to the browser:

```
$test = 'Hello world';
echo strpos($test, 'o');
```

This code passes in only a single character as the *needle*, but it can be a string of any length.

The optional *offset* parameter specifies a point within the *haystack* to start searching. For example,

```
echo strpos($test, 'o', 5);
```

This code echoes the value 7 to the browser because PHP has started looking for the character o at position 5 and therefore does not see the one at position 4.

The `strrpos()` function is almost identical but returns the position of the last occurrence of the *needle* in the *haystack*.

In any of these cases, if the *needle* is not in the string, `strpos()` or `strrpos()` will return `false`. This result can be problematic because `false` in a weakly typed language such as PHP is equivalent to 0—that is, the first character in a string.

You can avoid this problem by using the === operator to test return values:

```
$result = strpos($test, 'H');
if ($result === false)
  echo 'Not found';
else
  echo "Found at position $result";
```

Note that this approach works only in PHP 4 and later; in earlier versions, you could test for `false` by testing the return value to see whether it was a string (that is, `false`).

Replacing Substrings: `str_replace()` **and** `substr_replace()`

Find-and-replace functionality can be extremely useful with strings. You can use find and replace for personalizing documents generated by PHP—for example, by replacing <<name>> with a person's name and <<address>> with her address. You can also use it for censoring particular terms, such as in a discussion forum application, or even in the Smart Form application. Again, you can use string functions or regular expression functions for this purpose.

The most commonly used string function for replacement is `str_replace()`. It has the following prototype:

```
mixed str_replace(mixed needle, mixed new_needle, mixed haystack[, int &count]));
```

This function replaces all the instances of `needle` in `haystack` with `new_needle` and returns the new version of the `haystack`. The optional fourth parameter, `count`, contains the number of replacements made. Note that `count` was added in PHP5.

> **Note**
>
> As of PHP 4.0.5, you can pass all parameters as arrays, and the `str_replace()` function works remarkably intelligently. You can pass an array of words to be replaced, an array of words to replace them with (respectively), and an array of strings to apply these rules to. The function then returns an array of revised strings.

For example, because people can use the Smart Form to complain, they might use some colorful words. As a programmer, you can easily prevent Bob's various departments from being abused in that way if you have an array `$offcolor` that contains a number of offensive words. Here is an example using `str_replace()` with an array:

```
$feedback = str_replace($offcolor, '%!@*', $feedback);
```

The function `substr_replace()` finds and replaces a particular substring of a string based on its position. It has the following prototype:

```
string substr_replace(string string, string replacement,
                      int start, int [length] );
```

This function replaces part of the string `string` with the string `replacement`. Which part is replaced depends on the values of the `start` and optional `length` parameters.

The `start` value represents an offset into the string where replacement should begin. If it is zero or positive, it is an offset from the beginning of the string; if it is negative, it is an offset from the end of the string. For example, this line of code replaces the last character in `$test` with `"x"`:

```
$test = substr_replace($test, 'X', -1);
```

The `length` value is optional and represents the point at which PHP will stop replacing. If you don't supply this value, the string will be replaced from `start` to the end of the string.

If `length` is zero, the replacement string will actually be *inserted* into the string without overwriting the existing string. A positive `length` represents the number of characters that you want replaced with the new string; a negative `length` represents the point at which you would like to stop replacing characters, counted from the end of the string.

Introducing Regular Expressions

PHP supports two styles of regular expression syntax: POSIX and Perl. The POSIX style of regular expression is compiled into PHP by default, but you can use the Perl style by compiling in the Perl-compatible regular expression (PCRE) library. We cover the simpler POSIX style here, but if you're already a Perl programmer or want to learn more about PCRE, read the online manual at http://php.net.

> **Note**
>
> POSIX regular expressions are easier to learn faster, but they are not binary safe.

So far, all the pattern matching you've done has used the string functions. You have been limited to exact matches or to exact substring matches. If you want to do more complex pattern matching, you should use regular expressions. Regular expressions are difficult to grasp at first but can be extremely useful.

The Basics

A regular expression is a way of describing a pattern in a piece of text. The exact (or literal) matches you've seen so far are a form of regular expression. For example, earlier you searched for regular expression terms such as `"shop"` and `"delivery"`.

Matching regular expressions in PHP is more like a `strstr()` match than an equal comparison because you are matching a string somewhere within another string. (It can be anywhere within that string unless you specify otherwise.) For example, the string `"shop"` matches the regular expression `"shop"`. It also matches the regular expressions `"h"`, `"ho"`, and so on.

You can use special characters to indicate a meta-meaning in addition to matching characters exactly. For example, with special characters you can indicate that a pattern must occur at the start or end of a string, that part of a pattern can be repeated, or that characters in a pattern must be of a particular type. You can also match on literal occurrences of special characters. We look at each of these variations next.

Character Sets and Classes

Using character sets immediately gives regular expressions more power than exact matching expressions. Character sets can be used to match any character of a particular *type*; they're really a kind of wildcard.

First, you can use the . character as a wildcard for any other single character except a newline (\n). For example, the regular expression

`.at`

matches the strings `'cat'`, `'sat'`, and `'mat'`, among others. This kind of wildcard matching is often used for filename matching in operating systems.

With regular expressions, however, you can be more specific about the type of character you would like to match and can actually specify a set that a character must belong to. In the preceding example, the regular expression matches 'cat' and 'mat' but also matches '#at'. If you want to limit this to a character between *a* and *z*, you can specify it as follows:

```
[a-z]at
```

Anything enclosed in the square brackets ([and]) is a *character class*—a set of characters to which a matched character must belong. Note that the expression in the square brackets matches only a single character.

You can list a set; for example,

```
[aeiou]
```

means any vowel.

You can also describe a range, as you just did using the special hyphen character, or a set of ranges, as follows:

```
[a-zA-Z]
```

This set of ranges stands for any alphabetic character in upper- or lowercase.

You can also use sets to specify that a character cannot be a member of a set. For example,

```
[^a-z]
```

matches any character that is *not* between *a* and *z*. The caret symbol (^) means *not* when it is placed inside the square brackets. It has another meaning when used outside square brackets, which we look at shortly.

In addition to listing out sets and ranges, you can use a number of predefined *character classes* in a regular expression. These classes are shown in Table 4.3.

Table 4.3 **Character Classes for Use in POSIX-Style Regular Expressions**

Class	Matches
[[:alnum:]]	Alphanumeric characters
[[:alpha:]]	Alphabetic characters
[[:lower:]]	Lowercase letters
[[:upper:]]	Uppercase letters
[[:digit:]]	Decimal digits
[[:xdigit:]]	Hexadecimal digits
[[:punct:]]	Punctuation
[[:blank:]]	Tabs and spaces
[[:space:]]	Whitespace characters
[[:cntrl:]]	Control characters
[[:print:]]	All printable characters
[[:graph:]]	All printable characters except for space

Repetition

Often, you may want to specify that there might be multiple occurrences of a particular string or class of character. You can represent this using two special characters in your regular expression. The * symbol means that the pattern can be repeated zero or more times, and the + symbol means that the pattern can be repeated one or more times. The symbol should appear directly after the part of the expression that it applies to. For example,

```
[[:alnum:]]+
```

means "at least one alphanumeric character."

Subexpressions

Being able to split an expression into subexpressions is often useful so that you can, for example, represent "at least one of these strings followed by exactly one of those." You can split expressions using parentheses, exactly the same way as you would in an arithmetic expression. For example,

```
(very )*large
```

matches 'large', 'very large', 'very very large', and so on.

Counted Subexpressions

You can specify how many times something can be repeated by using a numerical expression in curly braces ({}). You can show an exact number of repetitions ({3} means exactly three repetitions), a range of repetitions ({2, 4} means from two to four repetitions), or an open-ended range of repetitions ({2,} means at least two repetitions).

For example,

```
(very ){1, 3}
```

matches 'very ', 'very very ' and 'very very very '.

Anchoring to the Beginning or End of a String

The pattern [a-z] will match any string containing a lowercase alphabetic character. It does not matter whether the string is one character long or contains a single matching character in a longer string.

You also can specify whether a particular subexpression should appear at the start, the end, or both. This capability is useful when you want to make sure that only your search term and nothing else appears in the string.

The caret symbol (^) is used at the start of a regular expression to show that it must appear at the beginning of a searched string, and $ is used at the end of a regular expression to show that it must appear at the end.

For example, the following matches bob at the start of a string:

^bob

This pattern matches com at the end of a string:

com$

Finally, this pattern matches a string containing only a single character from *a* to *z*:

^[a-z]$

Branching

You can represent a choice in a regular expression with a vertical pipe. For example, if you want to match com, edu, or net, you can use the following expression:

com|edu|net

Matching Literal Special Characters

If you want to match one of the special characters mentioned in the preceding sections, such as ., {, or $, you must put a backslash (\) in front of it. If you want to represent a backslash, you must replace it with two backslashes (\\).

Be careful to put your regular expression patterns in single-quoted strings in PHP. Using regular expressions in double-quoted PHP strings adds unnecessary complications. PHP also uses the backslash to escape special characters—such as a backslash. If you want to match a backslash in your pattern, you need to use two to indicate that it is a literal backslash, not an escape code.

Similarly, if you want a literal backslash in a double-quoted PHP string, you need to use two for the same reason. The somewhat confusing, cumulative result of these rules is that a PHP string that represents a regular expression containing a literal backslash needs four backslashes. The PHP interpreter will parse the four backslashes as two. Then the regular expression interpreter will parse the two as one.

The dollar sign is also a special character in double-quoted PHP strings and regular expressions. To get a literal $ matched in a pattern, you would need "\\\$". Because this string is in double quotation marks, PHP will parse it as \$, which the regular expression interpreter can then match against a dollar sign.

Reviewing the Special Characters

A summary of all the special characters is shown in Tables 4.4 and 4.5. Table 4.4 shows the meaning of special characters outside square brackets, and Table 4.5 shows their meaning when used inside square brackets.

Table 4.4 **Summary of Special Characters Used in POSIX Regular Expressions Outside Square Brackets**

Character	Meaning
\	Escape character
^	Match at start of string
$	Match at end of string
.	Match any character except newline (\n)
|	Start of alternative branch (read as OR)
(	Start subpattern
)	End subpattern
*	Repeat zero or more times
+	Repeat one or more times
{	Start min/max quantifier
}	End min/max quantifier
?	Mark a subpattern as optional

Table 4.5 **Summary of Special Characters Used in POSIX Regular Expressions Inside Square Brackets**

Character	Meaning
\	Escape character
^	NOT, only if used in initial position
–	Used to specify character ranges

Putting It All Together for the Smart Form

There are at least two possible uses of regular expressions in the Smart Form application. The first use is to detect particular terms in the customer feedback. You can be slightly smarter about this using regular expressions. Using a string function, you would have to perform three different searches if you wanted to match on 'shop', 'customer service', or 'retail'. With a regular expression, you can match all three:

```
shop|customer service|retail
```

The second use is to validate customer email addresses in the application by encoding the standardized format of an email address in a regular expression. The format includes some alphanumeric or punctuation characters, followed by an @ symbol, followed by a string of alphanumeric and hyphen characters, followed by a dot, followed by more alphanumeric and hyphen characters and possibly more dots, up until the end of the string, which encodes as follows:

```
^[a-zA-Z0-9_\-.]+@[a-zA-Z0-9\-]+\.[a-zA-Z0-9\-.]+$
```

The subexpression `^[a-zA-Z0-9_\-.]+` means "start the string with at least one letter, number, underscore, hyphen, or dot, or some combination of those." Note that when a dot is used at the beginning or end of a character class, it loses its special wildcard meaning and becomes just a literal dot.

The `@` symbol matches a literal `@`.

The subexpression `[a-zA-Z0-9\-]+` matches the first part of the hostname including alphanumeric characters and hyphens. Note that you slash out the hyphen because it's a special character inside square brackets.

The `\.` combination matches a literal dot (.). We are using a dot outside character classes, so we need to escape it to match only a literal dot.

The subexpression `[a-zA-Z0-9\-\.]+$` matches the rest of a domain name, including letters, numbers, hyphens, and more dots if required, up until the end of the string.

A bit of analysis shows that you can produce invalid email addresses that will still match this regular expression. It is almost impossible to catch them all, but this will improve the situation a little. You can refine this expression in many ways. You can, for example, list valid top-level domains (TLDs). Be careful when making things more restrictive, though, because a validation function that rejects 1% of valid data is far more annoying than one that allows through 10% of invalid data.

Now that you have read about regular expressions, you're ready to look at the PHP functions that use them.

Finding Substrings with Regular Expressions

Finding substrings is the main application of the regular expressions you just developed. The two functions available in PHP for matching POSIX-style regular expressions are `ereg()` and `eregi()`. The `ereg()` function has the following prototype:

```
int ereg(string pattern, string search, array [matches]);
```

This function searches the *search* string, looking for matches to the regular expression in *pattern*. If matches are found for subexpressions of *pattern*, they will be stored in the array *matches*, one subexpression per array element.

The `eregi()` function is identical except that it is not case sensitive.

You can adapt the Smart Form example to use regular expressions as follows:

```
if (!eregi('^[a-zA-Z0-9_\-.]+@[a-zA-Z0-9\-]+\.[a-zA-Z0-9\-\.]+$', $email))
  {
    echo 'That is not a valid email address.  Please return to the'
        .' previous page and try again.';
    exit;
  }
$toaddress = 'feedback@example.com';  // the default value
if (eregi('shop|customer service|retail', $feedback))
    $toaddress = 'retail@example.com';
else if (eregi('deliver|fulfill', $feedback))
```

```
    $toaddress = 'fulfillment@example.com';
  else if (eregi('bill|account', $feedback))
    $toaddress = 'accounts@example.com';

  if (eregi('bigcustomer\.com', $email))
    $toaddress = 'bob@example.com';
```

Replacing Substrings with Regular Expressions

You can also use regular expressions to find and replace substrings in the same way as you used str_replace(). The two functions available for this task are ereg_replace() and eregi_replace(). The function ereg_replace() has the following prototype:

```
string ereg_replace(string pattern, string replacement, string search);
```

This function searches for the regular expression *pattern* in the *search* string and replaces it with the string *replacement*.

The function eregi_replace() is identical but, again, is not case sensitive.

Splitting Strings with Regular Expressions

Another useful regular expression function is split(), which has the following prototype:

```
array split(string pattern, string search[, int max]);
```

This function splits the string *search* into substrings on the regular expression *pattern* and returns the substrings in an array. The *max* integer limits the number of items that can go into the array.

This function can be useful for splitting up email addresses, domain names, or dates. For example,

```
$address = 'username@example.com';
$arr = split ('\.|@', $address);
while (list($key, $value) = each ($arr))
  echo '<br />'.$value;
```

This example splits the hostname into its five components and prints each on a separate line.

Comparing String Functions and Regular Expression Functions

In general, the regular expression functions run less efficiently than the string functions with similar functionality. If your task is simple enough to use a string expression, do so. This may not be true for tasks that can be performed with a single regular expression but multiple string functions.

Further Reading

PHP has many string functions. We covered the more useful ones in this chapter, but if you have a particular need (such as translating characters into Cyrillic), check the PHP manual online to see whether PHP has the function for you.

The amount of material available on regular expressions is enormous. You can start with the man page for regexp if you are using Unix, and you can also find some terrific articles at devshed.com and phpbuilder.com.

At Zend's website, you can look at a more complex and powerful email validation function than the one we developed here. It is called MailVal() and is available at http://www.zend.com/codex.php?id=88&single=1.

Regular expressions take a while to sink in; the more examples you look at and run, the more confident you will be using them.

Next

In the next chapter, we discuss several ways you can use PHP to save programming time and effort and prevent redundancy by reusing pre-existing code.

5

Reusing Code and Writing Functions

THIS CHAPTER EXPLAINS HOW REUSING CODE leads to more consistent, reliable, maintainable code, with less effort. We demonstrate techniques for modularizing and reusing code, beginning with the simple use of `require()` and `include()` to use the same code on more than one page. We explain why these includes are superior to server-side includes. The example given here covers using include files to get a consistent look and feel across your site. We also explain how you can write and call your own functions using page and form generation functions as examples.

Key topics covered in this chapter include

- Reusing code
- Using `require()` and `include()`
- Introducing functions
- Defining functions
- Using parameters
- Understanding scope
- Returning values
- Calling by reference versus calling by value
- Implementing recursion

Reusing Code

One of the goals of software engineers is to reuse code in lieu of writing new code. The reason for this is not that software engineers are a particularly lazy group. Reusing existing code reduces costs, increases reliability, and improves consistency. Ideally, a new project is created by combining existing reusable components, with a minimum of development from scratch.

Cost

Over the useful life of a piece of software, significantly more time will be spent maintaining, modifying, testing, and documenting it than was originally spent writing it. If you are writing commercial code, you should attempt to limit the number of lines in use within the organization. One of the most practical ways to achieve this goal is to reuse code already in use instead of writing a slightly different version of the same code for a new task. Less code means lower costs. If existing software meets the requirements of the new project, acquire it. The cost of buying existing software is almost always less than the cost of developing an equivalent product. Tread carefully, though, if existing software *almost* meets your requirements. Modifying existing code can be more difficult than writing new code.

Reliability

If a module of code is in use somewhere in your organization, it has presumably already been thoroughly tested. Even if this module contains only a few lines, there is a possibility that, if you rewrite it, you will either overlook something that the original author incorporated or something that was added to the original code after a defect was found during testing. Existing, mature code is usually more reliable than fresh, "green" code.

Consistency

The external interfaces to your system, including both user interfaces and interfaces to outside systems, should be consistent. Writing new code consistent with the way other parts of the system function takes a will and a deliberate effort. If you are reusing code that runs another part of the system, your functionality should automatically be consistent.

On top of these advantages, reusing code is less work for you, as long as the original code was modular and well written. While you work, try to recognize sections of your code that you might be able to call on again in the future.

Using `require()` and `include()`

PHP provides two very simple, yet very useful, statements to allow you to reuse any type of code. Using a `require()` or `include()` statement, you can load a file into your PHP script. The file can contain anything you would normally type in a script including PHP statements, text, HTML tags, PHP functions, or PHP classes.

These statements work similarly to the server-side includes offered by many web servers and `#include` statements in C or C++.

require()

The following code is stored in a file named `reusable.php`:

```php
<?php
  echo 'Here is a very simple PHP statement.<br />';
?>
```

The following code is stored in a file named main.php:

```php
<?php
  echo 'This is the main file.<br />';
  require( 'reusable.php' );
  echo 'The script will end now.<br />';
?>
```

If you load `reusable.php`, you probably won't be surprised when the message `Here is a very simple PHP statement.` appears in your browser. If you load `main.php`, something a little more interesting happens. The output of this script is shown in Figure 5.1.

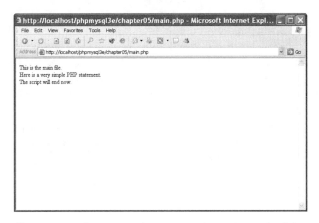

Figure 5.1   The output of `main.php` shows the result of the require() statement.

A file is needed to use a `require()` statement. In the preceding example, you used the file named `reusable.php`. When you run the script, the `require()` statement

```php
require( 'reusable.php' );
```

is replaced by the contents of the requested file, and the script is then executed. This means that when you load `main.php`, it runs as though the script were written as follows:

```php
<?php
  echo 'This is the main file.<br />';
  echo 'Here is a very simple PHP statement.<br />';
  echo 'The script will end now.<br />';
?>
```

When using `require()`, you need to note the different ways filename extensions and PHP tags are handled.

Filename Extensions and `require()`

PHP does not look at the filename extension on the required file. This means that you can name your file whatever you choose as long as you do not plan to call it directly. When you use `require()` to load the file, it effectively becomes part of a PHP file and is executed as such.

Normally, PHP statements would not be processed if they were in a file called, for example, `page.html`. PHP is usually called upon to parse only files with defined extensions such as `.php`. (This may be changed in your web server configuration file.) However, if you load `page.html` via a `require()` statement, any PHP inside it will be processed. Therefore, you can use any extension you prefer for include files, but sticking to a sensible convention such as `.inc` or `.php` would be a good idea.

One issue to be aware of is that if files ending in `.inc` or some other nonstandard extension are stored in the web document tree and users directly load them in the browser, they will be able to see the code in plain text, including any passwords. It is therefore important to either store included files outside the document tree or use the standard extensions.

PHP Tags and `require()`

In the example, the reusable file (`reusable.php`) was written as follows:

```php
<?php
  echo 'Here is a very simple PHP statement.<br />';
?>
```

The PHP code was placed within the file in PHP tags. You need to follow this convention if you want PHP code within a required file treated as PHP code. If you do not open a PHP tag, your code will just be treated as text or HTML and will not be executed.

Using `require()` for Website Templates

If your company's web pages have a consistent look and feel, you can use PHP to add the template and standard elements to pages using `require()`.

For example, the website of fictional company TLA Consulting has a number of pages, all with the look and feel shown in Figure 5.2. When a new page is needed, the developer can open an existing page, cut out the existing text from the middle of the file, enter new text, and save the file under a new name.

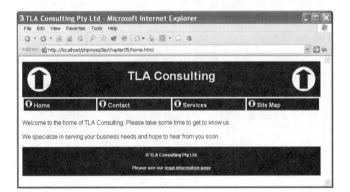

Figure 5.2   TLA Consulting has a standard look and feel for
all its web pages.

Consider this scenario: The website has been around for a while, and the company now has tens, hundreds, or maybe even thousands of pages all following a common style. A decision is made to change part of the standard look; the change might be something minor, such as adding an email address to the footer of each page or adding a single new entry to the navigation menu. Do you want to make that minor change on tens, hundreds, or even thousands of pages?

Directly reusing the sections of HTML common to all pages is a much better approach than cutting and pasting on tens, hundreds, or even thousands of pages. The source code for the home page (`home.html`) shown in Figure 5.2 is given in Listing 5.1.

Listing 5.1   `home.html`—The HTML That Produces TLA Consulting's Home Page

```
<html>
<head>
  <title>TLA Consulting Pty Ltd</title>
  <style type="text/css">
    h1 {color:white; font-size:24pt; text-align:center;
        font-family:arial,sans-serif}
```

Listing 5.1 **Continued**

```
    .menu {color:white; font-size:12pt; text-align:center;
          font-family:arial,sans-serif; font-weight:bold}
    td {background:black}
    p {color:black; font-size:12pt; text-align:justify;
      font-family:arial,sans-serif}
    p.foot {color:white; font-size:9pt; text-align:center;
           font-family:arial,sans-serif; font-weight:bold}
    a:link,a:visited,a:active {color:white}
  </style>
</head>
<body>

  <!-- page header -->
  <table width="100%" cellpadding="12" cellspacing="0" border="0">
  <tr bgcolor="black">
    <td align="left"><img src="logo.gif" alt="TLA logo" height="70"
width="70"></td>
    <td>
        <h1>TLA Consulting</h1>
    </td>
    <td align="right"><img src="logo.gif" alt="TLA logo" height="70"
width="70"></td>
  </tr>
  </table>

  <!-- menu -->
  <table width="100%" bgcolor="white" cellpadding="4" cellspacing="4">
  <tr >
    <td width="25%">
      <img src="s-logo.gif" alt="" height="20" width="20">
      <span class="menu">Home</span></td>
    <td width="25%">
      <img src="s-logo.gif" alt="" height="20" width="20">
      <span class="menu">Contact</span></td>
    <td width="25%">
      <img src="s-logo.gif" alt="" height="20" width="20">
      <span class="menu">Services</span></td>
    <td width="25%">
      <img src="s-logo.gif" alt="" height="20" width="20">
      <span class="menu">Site Map</span></td>
  </tr>
  </table>
```

Listing 5.1   **Continued**

```
  <!-- page content -->
  <p>Welcome to the home of TLA Consulting.
  Please take some time to get to know us.</p>
  <p>We specialize in serving your business needs
  and hope to hear from you soon.</p>

  <!-- page footer -->
  <table width="100%" bgcolor="black" cellpadding="12" border="0">
  <tr>
    <td>
      <p class="foot">&copy; TLA Consulting Pty Ltd.</p>
      <p class="foot">Please see our
        <a href="legal.php">legal information page</a></p>
    </td>
  </tr>
  </table>
</body>
</html>
```

You can see in Listing 5.1 that a number of distinct sections of code exist in this file. The HTML head contains cascading style sheet (CSS) definitions used by the page. The section labeled "page header" displays the company name and logo, "menu" creates the page's navigation bar, and "page content" is text unique to this page. Below that is the page footer. You can usefully split this file and name the parts header.inc, home.php, and footer.inc. Both header.inc and footer.inc contain code that will be reused on other pages.

The file home.php is a replacement for home.html and contains the unique page content and two require() statements shown in Listing 5.2.

Listing 5.2   home.php—**The PHP That Produces TLA's Home Page**

```
<?php
  require('header.inc');
?>
  <!-- page content -->
  <p>Welcome to the home of TLA Consulting.
  Please take some time to get to know us.</p>
  <p>We specialize in serving your business needs
  and hope to hear from you soon.</p>
<?php
  require('footer.inc');
?>
```

The `require()` statements in `home.php` load `header.inc` and `footer.inc`.

As mentioned previously, the name given to these files does not affect how they are processed when you call them via `require()`. A common, but entirely optional, convention is to call the partial files that will end up included in other files *something*`.inc` (here, `inc` stands for include). It is also common, and a good idea, to place your include files in a directory that can be seen by your scripts but does not permit your include files to be loaded individually via the web server—that is, outside the web document tree. This setup prevents these files from being loaded individually, which would either (a) probably produce some errors if the file extension is `.php` but contains only a partial page or script, or (b) allow people to read your source code if you have used another extension.

The file `header.inc` contains the CSS definitions that the page uses, the tables that display the company name, and navigation menus, as shown in Listing 5.3.

Listing 5.3 `header.inc`—**The Reusable Header for All TLA Web Pages**

```
<html>
<head>
  <title>TLA Consulting Pty Ltd</title>
  <style type="text/css">
    h1 {color:white; font-size:24pt; text-align:center;
        font-family:arial,sans-serif}
    .menu {color:white; font-size:12pt; text-align:center;
          font-family:arial,sans-serif; font-weight:bold}
    td {background:black}
    p {color:black; font-size:12pt; text-align:justify;
       font-family:arial,sans-serif}
    p.foot {color:white; font-size:9pt; text-align:center;
           font-family:arial,sans-serif; font-weight:bold}
    a:link,a:visited,a:active {color:white}
  </style>
</head>
<body>

  <!-- page header -->
  <table width="100%" cellpadding="12" cellspacing="0" border="0">
  <tr bgcolor="black">
    <td align="left"><img src="logo.gif" alt="TLA logo" height="70"
width="70"></td>
    <td>
        <h1>TLA Consulting</h1>
    </td>
    <td align="right"><img src="logo.gif" alt="TLA logo" height="70"
width="70"></td>
  </tr>
  </table>
```

Listing 5.3   **Continued**

```
<!-- menu -->
<table width="100%" bgcolor="white" cellpadding="4" cellspacing="4">
<tr >
  <td width="25%">
    <img src="s-logo.gif" alt="" height="20" width="20">
    <span class="menu">Home</span></td>
  <td width="25%">
    <img src="s-logo.gif" alt="" height="20" width="20">
    <span class="menu">Contact</span></td>
  <td width="25%">
    <img src="s-logo.gif" alt="" height="20" width="20">
    <span class="menu">Services</span></td>
  <td width="25%">
    <img src="s-logo.gif" alt="" height="20" width="20">
    <span class="menu">Site Map</span></td>
</tr>
</table>
```

The file `footer.inc` contains the table that displays the footer at the bottom of each page. This file is shown in Listing 5.4.

Listing 5.4   `footer.inc`— **The Reusable Footer for All TLA Web Pages**

```
<!-- page footer -->
  <table width="100%" bgcolor="black" cellpadding="12" border="0">
  <tr>
    <td>
      <p class="foot">&copy; TLA Consulting Pty Ltd.</p>
      <p class="foot">Please see our <a href="legal.php">
      legal information page</a></p>
    </td>
  </tr>
  </table>
</body>
</html>
```

This approach gives you a consistent-looking website very easily, and you can make a new page in the same style by typing something like this:

```
<?php require('header.inc'); ?>
Here is the content for this page
<?php require('footer.inc'); ?>
```

Most importantly, even after you have created many pages using this header and footer, you can easily change the header and footer files. Whether you are making a minor text change or completely redesigning the look of the site, you need to make the change only once. You do not need to separately alter every page in the site because each page is loading in the header and footer files.

The example shown here uses only plain HTML in the body, header, and footer. This need not be the case. Within these files, you could use PHP statements to dynamically generate parts of the page.

If you want to be sure that a file will be treated as plain text or HTML, and not have any PHP executed, you may want to use `readfile()` instead. This function echoes the content of a file without parsing it. This can be an important safety precaution if you are using user-provided text.

Using `include()`

The statements `require()` and `include()` are almost identical. The only difference between them is that when they fail, the `require()` construct gives a fatal error, whereas the `include()` construct gives only a warning.

Using `require_once()` and `include_once()`

There are two variations on `require()` and `include()`, called `require_once()` and `include_once()`, respectively. The purpose of these constructs is, as you might guess, to ensure that an included file can be included only once. For the examples we have looked at so far—headers and footers—this functionality is not particularly useful.

This functionality becomes useful when you begin using `require()` and `include()` to include libraries of functions. Using these constructs protects you from accidentally including the same function library twice, thus redefining functions and causing an error.

Using `auto_prepend_file` and `auto_append_file`

If you want to use `require()` or `include()` to add your header and footer to every page, you can do it another way. Two of the configuration options in the `php.ini` file are `auto_prepend_file` and `auto_append_file`. By setting these options to point to the header and footer files, you ensure that they will be loaded before and after every page. Files included using these directives behave as though they had been added using an `include()` statement; that is, if the file is missing, a warning will be issued.

For Windows, the settings resemble the following:

```
auto_prepend_file = "c:/Apache/include/header.inc"
auto_append_file = "c:/Apache/include/footer.inc"
```

For Unix, they resemble the following:

```
auto_prepend_file = "/home/username/include/header.inc"
auto_append_file = "/home/username/include/footer.inc"
```

If you use these directives, you do not need to type `include()` statements, but the headers and footers will no longer be optional on pages.

If you are using an Apache web server, you can change various configuration options like these for individual directories. To do this, you must have your server set up to allow its main configuration file(s) to be overridden. To set up auto prepending and appending for a directory, create a file called `.htaccess` in the directory. The file needs to contain the following two lines:

```
php_value auto_prepend_file "/home/username/include/header.inc"
php_value auto_append_file "/home/username/include/footer.inc"
```

Note that the syntax is slightly different from the same option in `php.ini`: As well as `php_value` at the start of the line, there is no equal sign. A number of other `php.ini` configuration settings can be altered in this way, too.

Setting options in the `.htaccess` file rather than in either `php.ini` or your web server's configuration file gives you a lot of flexibility. You can alter settings on a shared machine that affect only your directories. You do not need to restart the web server, and you do not need administrator access. A drawback to the `.htaccess` method is that the files are read and parsed each time a file in that directory is requested rather than just once at startup, so there is a performance penalty.

Using Functions in PHP

Functions exist in most programming languages; they separate code that performs a single, well-defined task. This makes the code easier to read and allows you to reuse the code each time you need to perform the same task.

A function is a self-contained module of code that prescribes a calling interface, performs some task, and optionally returns a result.

You have seen a number of functions already. In preceding chapters, we routinely called a number of the functions built into PHP. We also wrote a few simple functions but glossed over the details. In the following sections, we cover calling and writing functions in more detail.

Calling Functions

The following line is the simplest possible call to a function:

```
function_name();
```

This line calls a function named `function_name` that does not require parameters. This line of code ignores any value that might be returned by this function.

A number of functions are called in exactly this way. The function `phpinfo()` is often useful in testing because it displays the installed version of PHP, information about PHP, the web server setup, and the values of various PHP and server variables. This function does not take any parameters, and you generally ignore its return value, so a call to `phpinfo()` is simply as follows:

```
phpinfo();
```

Most functions, however, do require one or more parameters, which are the inputs to functions. You pass parameters by placing data or the name of a variable holding data inside parentheses after the function name. You could call a function that accepts a single parameter as follows:

```
function_name('parameter');
```

In this case, the parameter used is a string containing only the word `parameter`, but the following calls may also be fine depending on what parameters the function expects:

```
function_name(2);
function_name(7.993);
function_name($variable);
```

In the last line, `$variable` might be any type of PHP variable, including an array.

A parameter can be any type of data, but particular functions usually require particular data types.

You can see how many parameters a function takes, what each represents, and what data type each needs to be from the function's *prototype*. We often show the prototype when we describe a function.

This is the prototype for the function `fopen()`:

```
resource fopen ( string filename, string mode
                [, bool use_include_path [, resource zcontext]])
```

The prototype tells you a number of things, and it is important that you know how to correctly interpret these specifications. In this case, the word `resource` before the function name tells you that this function will return a resource (that is, an open file handle). The function parameters are inside the parentheses. In the case of `fopen()`, four parameters are shown in the prototype. The parameters `filename` and `mode` are strings, the parameter `use_include_path` is a Boolean, and the parameter `zcontext` is a resource. The square brackets around `use_include_path` and `zcontext` indicate that these parameters are optional. You can provide values for optional parameters, or you can choose to ignore them and the default value will be used. Note, however, that for a function with more than one optional parameter, you can only leave out parameters from the right. For example, when using `fopen()`, you can leave out `zcontext` or you can leave out both `use_include_path` and `zcontext`; however, you cannot leave out `use_include_path` but provide `zcontext`.

After reading the prototype for this function, you know that the following code fragment is a valid call to `fopen()`:

```
$name = 'myfile.txt';
$openmode = 'r';
$fp = fopen($name, $openmode);
```

This code calls the function named `fopen()`. The value returned by the function will be stored in the variable `$fp`. For this example, we chose to pass to the function a variable called `$name` containing a string representing the file we want to open and a variable called `$openmode` containing a string representing the mode in which we want to open the file. We chose not to provide the optional third and fourth parameters.

Calling an Undefined Function

If you attempt to call a function that does not exist, you will get an error message, as shown in Figure 5.3.

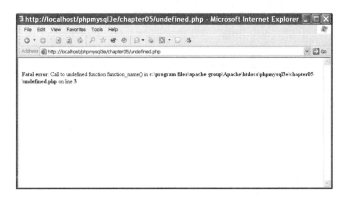

Figure 5.3   This error message is the result of calling a function that does not exist.

The error messages that PHP gives are usually very useful. The one in the figure tells you exactly in which file the error occurred, in which line of the script it occurred, and the name of the function you attempted to call. This information should make it fairly easy to find and correct the problem.

Check these two things if you see this error message:

- Is the function name spelled correctly?
- Does the function exist in the version of PHP you are using?

You might not always remember how a function name is spelled. For instance, some two-word function names have an underscore between the words, and some do not. The function `stripslashes()` runs the two words together, whereas the function `strip_tags()` separates the words with an underscore. Misspelling the name of a function in a function call results in an error, as shown in Figure 5.3.

Some functions used in this book do not exist in PHP4 because this book assumes that you are using PHP5. In each new version, new functions are defined, and if you are using an older version, the added functionality and performance justify an upgrade. To see when a particular function was added, you can check the online manual. Attempting to call a function that is not declared in the version you are running results in an error such as the one shown in Figure 5.3.

One other reason you may see this error message is that the function you are calling is part of a PHP extension that is not loaded. For example, if you try to use functions from the gd (image manipulation) library and you have not installed gd, you will see this message.

Understanding Case and Function Names

Note that calls to functions are *not* case sensitive, so calls to `function_name()`, `Function_Name()`, or `FUNCTION_NAME()` are all valid and all have the same result. You are free to capitalize in any way you find easy to read, but you should aim to be consistent. The convention used in this book, and most other PHP documentation, is to use all lowercase.

It is important to note that function names behave differently to variable names. Variable names *are* case sensitive, so `$Name` and `$name` are two separate variables, but `Name()` and `name()` are the same function.

Understanding Why You Should Define Your Own Functions

In the preceding chapters, you saw many examples using some of PHP's built-in functions. However, the real power of a programming language comes from being able to create your own functions.

The functions built into PHP enable you to interact with files, use a database, create graphics, and connect to other servers. However, in your career, you often may need to do something that the language's creators did not foresee.

Fortunately, you are not limited to using the built-in functions; you can write your own to perform any task that you like. Your code will probably be a mixture of existing functions combined with your own logic to perform a task for you. If you are writing a block of code for a task that you are likely to want to reuse in a number of places in a script or in a number of scripts, you would be wise to declare that block as a function.

Declaring a function allows you to use your own code in the same way as the built-in functions. You simply call your function and provide it with the necessary parameters. This means that you can call and reuse the same function many times throughout your script.

Examining Basic Function Structure

A function declaration creates or *declares* a new function. The declaration begins with the keyword `function`, provides the function name and parameters required, and contains the code that will be executed each time this function is called.

Here is the declaration of a trivial function:

```
function my_function()
{
  echo 'My function was called';
}
```

This function declaration begins with `function` so that human readers and the PHP parser know that what follows is a user-defined function. The function name is `my_function`. You can call the new function with the following statement:

```
my_function();
```

As you probably guessed, calling this function results in the text `My function was called.` appearing in the viewer's browser.

Built-in functions are available to all PHP scripts, but if you declare your own functions, they are available only to the script(s) in which they were declared. It is a good idea to have a file or set of files containing your commonly used functions. You can then have a `require()` statement in your scripts to make your functions available when required.

Within a function, curly braces enclose the code that performs the task you require. Between these braces, you can have anything that is legal elsewhere in a PHP script, including function calls, declarations of new variables, functions, `require()` or `include()` statements, class declarations, and plain HTML. If you want to exit PHP within a function and type plain HTML, you do so the same way as anywhere else in the script—with a closing PHP tag followed by the HTML. The following is a legal modification of the preceding example and produces the same output:

```php
<?php
  function my_function()
  {
?>
My function was called
<?php
  }
?>
```

Note that the PHP code is enclosed within matching opening and closing PHP tags. For most of the small code fragment examples in this book, we do not show these tags. We show them here because they are required within the example as well as above and below it.

Naming Your Function

The most important point to consider when naming your functions is that the name should be short but descriptive. If your function creates a page header, `pageheader()` or `page_header()` might be good names.

A few restrictions follow:

- Your function cannot have the same name as an existing function.
- Your function name can contain only letters, digits, and underscores.
- Your function name cannot begin with a digit.

Many languages do allow you to reuse function names. This feature is called *function over-loading*. However, PHP does not support function overloading, so your function cannot have the same name as any built-in function or an existing user-defined function. Note that although every PHP script knows about all the built-in functions, user-defined functions exist only in scripts where they are declared. This means that you could reuse a function name in a different file, but this would lead to confusion and should be avoided.

The following function names are legal:

```
name()
name2()
name_three()
_namefour()
```

These names are illegal:

```
5name()
name-six()
fopen()
```

(The last would be legal if it didn't already exist.)

Note that although $name is not a valid name for a function, a function call like

```
$name();
```

may well execute, depending on the value of $name. The reason is that PHP takes the value stored in $name, looks for a function with that name, and tries to call it for you. This type of function is referred to as a *variable function* and may occasionally be useful to you.

Using Parameters

To do their work, most functions require one or more parameters. A parameter allows you to pass data into a function. Here is a sample function that requires a parameter; it takes a one-dimensional array and displays it as a table:

```
function create_table($data)
{
  echo '<table border = 1>';
  reset($data); // Remember this is used to point to the beginning
  $value = current($data);
  while ($value)
  {
    echo "<tr><td>$value</td></tr>\n";
    $value = next($data);
  }
  echo '</table>';
}
```

If you call the `create_table()` function

```
$my_array = array('Line one.','Line two.','Line three.');
create_table($my_array);
```

you see output as shown in Figure 5.4.

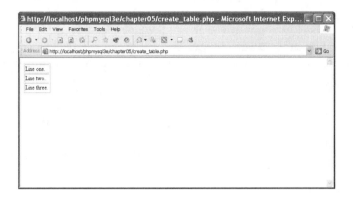

Figure 5.4   This HTML table is the result of calling `create_table()`.

Passing a parameter allows you to get data created outside the function—in this case, the array `$data`—into the function.

As with built-in functions, user-defined functions can have multiple parameters and optional parameters. You can improve the `create_table()` function in many ways, but one way might be to allow the caller to specify the border or other attributes of the table. Here is an improved version of the function; it is similar but allows you to optionally set the table's border width, cellspacing, and cellpadding.

```
function create_table2( $data, $border = 1, $cellpadding = 4, $cellspacing = 4 )
{
  echo "<table border = $border cellpadding = $cellpadding"
      ." cellspacing = $cellspacing>";
  reset($data);
  $value = current($data);
  while ($value)
  {
    echo "<tr><td>$value</td></tr>\n";
    $value = next($data);
  }
  echo '</table>';
}
```

The first parameter for `create_table2()` is still required. The next three are optional because default values are defined for them. You can create similar output to that shown in Figure 5.4 with this call to `create_table2()`:

```
create_table2($my_array);
```

If you want the same data displayed in a more spread-out style, you could call the new function as follows:

```
create_table2($my_array, 3, 8, 8);
```

Optional values do not all need to be provided; you can provide some and ignore some. Parameters are assigned from left to right.

Keep in mind that you cannot leave out one optional parameter but include a later listed one. In this example, if you want to pass a value for cellspacing, you will have to pass one for cellpadding as well. This is a common cause of programming errors. It is also the reason that optional parameters are specified last in any list of parameters.

The function call

```
create_table2($my_array, 3);
```

is perfectly legal and results in $border being set to 3 and $cellpadding and $cellspacing being set to their defaults.

You also can declare functions that accept a variable number of parameters. You can find out how many parameters have been passed and what their values are with the aid of three helper functions: func_num_args(), func_get_arg(), and func_get_args().

For example, consider this function:

```
function var_args()
{
  echo "Number of parameters:";
  echo func_num_args();

  echo '<br />';
  $args = func_get_args();
  foreach ($args as $arg)
    echo $arg.'<br />';
}
```

This function reports the number of parameters passed to it and prints out each of them. The func_num_args() function returns the number of arguments passed in. The func_get_args() function returns an array of the arguments. Alternatively, you can access the arguments one at a time using the func_get_arg() function, passing it the argument number you want to access. (Arguments are numbered starting from zero.)

Understanding Scope

You might have noticed that when we needed to use variables inside a required or included file, we simply declared them in the script before the require() or include() statement. When using a function, we explicitly passed those variables into the function partly because no mechanism exists for explicitly passing variables to a required or included file and partly because variable scope behaves differently for functions.

A variable's scope controls where that variable is visible and usable. Different programming languages have different rules that set the scope of variables. PHP has fairly simple rules:

- Variables declared inside a function are in scope from the statement in which they are declared to the closing brace at the end of the function. This is called *function scope*. These variables are called *local variables*.

- Variables declared outside functions are in scope from the statement in which they are declared to the end of the file, but *not inside functions*. This is called *global scope*. These variables are called *global variables*.

- The special superglobal variables are visible both inside and outside functions. (See Chapter 1, "PHP Crash Course," for more information on these variables.)

- Using `require()` and `include()` statements does not affect scope. If the statement is used within a function, function scope applies. If it is not inside a function, global scope applies.

- The keyword `global` can be used to manually specify that a variable defined or used within a function will have global scope.

- Variables can be manually deleted by calling `unset($variable_name)`. A variable is no longer in scope if it has been unset.

The following examples might help to clarify scope further.

The following code produces no output. Here, you declare a variable called `$var` inside the function `fn()`. Because this variable is declared inside a function, it has function scope and exists only from where it is declared until the end of the function. When you again refer to `$var` outside the function, a new variable called `$var` is created. This new variable has global scope and will be visible until the end of the file. Unfortunately, if the only statement you use with this new `$var` variable is `echo`, it will never have a value.

```
function fn()
{
  $var = 'contents';
}
fn();
echo $var;
```

The following example is the inverse. Here, you declare a variable outside the function and then try to use it within a function:

```
function fn()
{
  echo 'inside the function, $var = '.$var.'<br />';
  $var = 'contents 2';
  echo 'inside the function, $var = '.$var.'<br />';
}
```

```
$var = 'contents 1';
fn();
echo 'outside the function, $var = '.$var.'<br />';
```

The output from this code is as follows:

```
inside the function, $var =
inside the function, $var = contents 2
outside the function, $var = contents 1
```

Functions are not executed until they are called, so the first statement executed is $var = 'contents 1';. This statement creates a variable called $var, with global scope and the contents "contents 1". The next statement executed is a call to the function fn(). The lines inside the statement are executed in order. The first line in the function refers to a variable named $var. When this line is executed, it cannot see the previous $var that was created, so it creates a new one with function scope and echoes it. This creates the first line of output.

The next line within the function sets the contents of $var to "contents 2". Because you are inside the function, this line changes the value of the local $var, not the global one. The second line of output verifies that this change worked.

The function is now finished, so the final line of the script is executed. This echo statement demonstrates that the global variable's value has not changed.

If you want a variable created within a function to be global, you can use the keyword global as follows:

```
function fn()
{
  global $var;
  $var = 'contents';
  echo 'inside the function, $var = '.$var.'<br />';
}

fn();
echo 'outside the function, $var = '.$var.'<br />';
```

In this example, the variable $var is explicitly defined as global, meaning that after the function is called, the variable will exist outside the function as well. The output from this script follows:

```
inside the function, $var = contents
outside the function, $var = contents
```

Note that the variable is in scope from the point in which the line global $var; is executed. You could declare the function above or below where you call it. (Note that function scope is quite different from variable scope!) The location of the function declaration is inconsequential; what is important is where you call the function and therefore execute the code within it.

You can also use the `global` keyword at the top of a script when a variable is first used to declare that it should be in scope throughout the script. This is possibly a more common use of the `global` keyword.

You can see from the preceding examples that it is perfectly legal to reuse a variable name for a variable inside and outside a function without interference between the two. It is generally a bad idea, however, because without carefully reading the code and thinking about scope, people might assume that the variables are one and the same.

Passing by Reference Versus Passing by Value

If you want to write a function called `increment()` that allows you to increment a value, you might be tempted to try writing it as follows:

```
function increment($value, $amount = 1)
{
  $value = $value +$amount;
}
```

This code is of no use. The output from the following test code will be `10`:

```
$value = 10;
increment ($value);
echo $value;
```

The contents of `$value` have not changed because of the scope rules. This code creates a variable called `$value`, which contains 10. It then calls the function `increment()`. The variable `$value` in the function is created when the function is called. One is added to it, so the value of `$value` is 11 inside the function, until the function ends; then you return to the code that called it. In this code, the variable `$value` is a different variable, with global scope, and therefore unchanged.

One way of overcoming this problem is to declare `$value` in the function as global, but this means that to use this function, the variable that you wanted to increment would need to be named `$value`. A better approach would be to use *pass by reference*.

The normal way that function parameters are called is through an approach dubbed *pass by value*. When you pass a parameter, a new variable is created containing the value passed in. It is a copy of the original. You are free to modify this value in any way, but the value of the original variable outside the function remains unchanged.

The better approach is to use *pass by reference*. Here, when a parameter is passed to a function, instead of creating a new variable, the function receives a reference to the original variable. This reference has a variable name, beginning with a dollar sign ($), and can be used in exactly the same way as another variable. The difference is that instead of having a value of its own, it merely refers to the original. Any modifications made to the reference also affect the original.

You specify that a parameter is to use pass by reference by placing an ampersand (&) before the parameter name in the function's definition. No change is required in the function call.

You can modify the preceding `increment()` example to have one parameter passed by reference, and it will work correctly:

```
function increment(&$value, $amount = 1)
{
  $value = $value +$amount;
}
```

You now have a working function and are free to name the variable you want to increment anything you like. As already mentioned, it is confusing to humans to use the same name inside and outside a function, so you can give the variable in the main script a new name. The following test code now echoes 10 before the call to `increment()` and 11 afterward:

```
$a = 10;
echo $a.'<br />';
increment ($a);
echo $a.'<br />';
```

Returning from Functions

The keyword `return` stops the execution of a function. When a function ends because either all statements have been executed or the keyword `return` is used, execution returns to the statement after the function call.

If you call the following function, only the first `echo` statement will be executed:

```
function test_return()
{
  echo 'This statement will be executed';
  return;
  echo 'This statement will never be executed';
}
```

Obviously, this is not a very useful way to use `return`. Normally, you want to return from the middle of a function only in response to a condition being met.

An error condition is a common reason to use a `return` statement to stop execution of a function before the end. If, for instance, you write a function to find out which of two numbers is greater, you might want to exit if any of the numbers are missing:

```
function larger( $x, $y )
{
  if (!isset($x)||!isset($y))
  {
    echo 'This function requires two numbers';
    return;
  }
  if ($x>=$y)
```

```
        echo $x;
    else
        echo $y;
}
```

The built-in function `isset()` tells you whether a variable has been created and given a value. This code gives an error message and returns if either of the parameters has not been set with a value. You test it by using `!isset()`, meaning "NOT `isset()`," so the `if` statement can be read as "if x is not set or if y is not set." The function returns if either of these conditions is true.

If the `return` statement is executed, the subsequent lines of code in the function will be ignored. Program execution returns to the point at which the function was called. If both parameters are set, the function will echo the larger of the two.

The output from the code

```
$a = 1;
$b = 2.5;
$c = 1.9;
larger($a, $b);
larger($c, $a);
larger($d, $a);
```

is as follows:

```
2.5
1.9
This function requires two numbers
```

Returning Values from Functions

Exiting from a function is not the only reason to use `return`. Many functions use `return` statements to communicate with the code that called them. Instead of echoing the result of the comparison in the `larger()` function, the function might have been more useful if it returned the answer. This way, the code that called the function can choose if and how to display or use it. The equivalent built-in function `max()` behaves in this way.

You can write the `larger()` function as follows:

```
function larger ($x, $y)
{
  if (!isset($x)||!isset($y))
    return false;
  else if ($x>=$y)
    return $x;
  else
    return $y;
}
```

Here, the function returns the larger of the two values passed in. It returns an obviously different value in the case of an error. If one of the numbers is missing, it returns `false`. (The only caveat with this approach is that programmers calling the function must test the return type with `===` to make sure that `false` is not confused with 0.)

For comparison, the built-in function `max()` returns nothing if both variables are not set and, if only one was set, returns that one.

The code

```
$a = 1; $b = 2.5; $c = 1.9;
echo larger($a, $b).'<br />';
echo larger($c, $a).'<br />';
echo larger($d, $a).'<br />';
```

produces this output because `$d` does not exist and `false` is not visible:

```
2.5
1.9
```

Functions that perform some task but do not need to return a value often return `true` or `false` to indicate whether they succeeded or failed. The boolean values `true` and `false` can be represented with integer values 1 and 0, respectively, although they are of different types.

Code Blocks

You declare that a group of statements is a block by placing them within curly braces. This does not affect most of the operation of your code but has specific implications, including the way control structures such as loops and conditionals execute.

The following two examples work very differently:

Example without code block:

```
for($i = 0; $i < 3; $i++ )
  echo 'Line 1<br />';
echo 'Line 2<br />';
```

Example with code block:

```
for($i = 0; $i < 3; $i++ )
{
  echo 'Line 1<br />';
  echo 'Line 2<br />';
}
```

In both examples, the `for` loop is iterated through three times. In the first example, only the single line directly below this is executed by the `for` loop. The output from this example is as follows:

```
Line 1
Line 1
```

```
Line 1
Line 2
```

The second example uses a code block to group two lines together. This means that both lines are executed three times by the `for` loop. The output from this example is as follows:

```
Line 1
Line 2
Line 1
Line 2
Line 1
Line 2
```

Because the code in these examples is properly indented, you can probably see the difference between them at a glance. The indenting of the code is intended to give readers a visual interpretation of what lines are affected by the `for` loop. However, note that spaces do not affect how PHP processes the code.

In some languages, code blocks affect variable scope. This is not the case in PHP.

Implementing Recursion

Recursive functions are supported in PHP. A *recursive function* is one that calls itself. These functions are particularly useful for navigating dynamic data structures such as linked lists and trees.

Few web-based applications, however, require a data structure of this complexity, so you have minimal use for recursion. It is possible to use recursion instead of iteration in many cases because both of these processes allow you to do something repetitively. However, recursive functions are slower and use more memory than iteration, so you should use iteration wherever possible.

In the interest of completeness, let's look at the brief example shown in Listing 5.5.

Listing 5.5 `recursion.php`—**Reversing a String Using Recursion and Iteration**

```
function reverse_r($str)
{
   if (strlen($str)>0)
     reverse_r(substr($str, 1));
   echo substr($str, 0, 1);
   return;
}

function reverse_i($str)
{
```

Listing 5.5   **Continued**

```
    for ($i=1; $i<=strlen($str); $i++)
    {
      echo substr($str, -$i, 1);
    }
    return;
}
```

Listing 5.5 implements two functions. Both of them print a string in reverse. The function reverse_r() is recursive, and the function reverse_i() is iterative.

The reverse_r() function takes a string as a parameter. When you call it, it proceeds to call itself, each time passing the second to last characters of the string. For example, if you call

```
reverse_r('Hello');
```

it will call itself a number of times, with the following parameters:

```
reverse_r('ello');
reverse_r('llo');
reverse_r('lo');
reverse_r('o');
reverse_r('');
```

Each call the function makes to itself makes a new copy of the function code in the server's memory, but with a different parameter. It is like pretending that you are actually calling a different function each time. This stops the instances of the function from getting confused.

With each call, the length of the string passed in is tested. When you reach the end of the string (strlen()==0), the condition fails. The most recent instance of the function (reverse_r('')) then goes on and performs the next line of code, which is to echo the first character of the string it was passed; in this case, there is no character because the string is empty.

Next, this instance of the function returns control to the instance that called it, namely reverse_r('o'). This function then prints the first character in its string—"o"—and returns control to the instance that called it.

The process continues—printing a character and then returning to the instance of the function above it in the calling order—until control is returned to the main program.

There is something very elegant and mathematical about recursive solutions. In most cases, however, you are better off using an iterative solution. The code for such a solution is also shown in Listing 5.5. Note that it is no longer (although this is not always the case with iterative functions) and does exactly the same thing. The main difference is that the recursive function makes copies of itself in memory and incurs the overhead of multiple function calls.

You might choose to use a recursive solution when the code is much shorter and more elegant than the iterative version, but it does not happen often in this application domain.

Although recursion appears more elegant, programmers often forget to supply a termination condition for the recursion. This means that the function will recur until the server runs out of memory, or until the maximum execution time is exceeded, whichever comes first.

Further Reading

The use of `include()`, `require()`, `function`, and `return` are also explained in the online manual. To find out more details about concepts such as recursion, pass by value or reference, and scope that affect many languages, you can look at a general computer science textbook, such as Dietel and Dietel's *C++ How to Program*.

Next

Now that you are using include files, require files, and functions to make your code more maintainable and reusable, the next chapter addresses object-oriented software and the support offered in PHP. Using objects allows you to achieve goals similar to the concepts presented in this chapter, but with even greater advantages for complex projects.

6

Object-Oriented PHP

THIS CHAPTER EXPLAINS CONCEPTS OF OBJECT-ORIENTED (OO) development and shows how they can be implemented in PHP. PHP5 introduces a new, more powerful object-oriented implementation, which makes classes and objects more useful.

Now PHP's OO implementation has all the features you would expect in a fully object-oriented language. We point out each of the new features as we go through this chapter for those of you who have previously used PHP4 or earlier.

Key topics covered in this chapter include

- Object-oriented concepts
- Classes, attributes, and operations
- Class attributes
- Per-class constants
- Class method invocation
- Inheritance
- Access modifiers
- Static methods
- Type hinting
- Object cloning
- Abstract classes
- Class design
- Implementation of your design
- Advanced OO functionality
- OO functionality new to PHP5

Understanding Object-Oriented Concepts

Modern programming languages usually support or even require an object-oriented approach to software development. Object-oriented development attempts to use the classifications, relationships, and properties of the objects in the system to aid in program development and code reuse.

Classes and Objects

In the context of OO software, an object can be almost any item or concept—a physical object such as a desk or a customer; or a conceptual object that exists only in software, such as a text input area or a file. Generally, you will be most interested in objects, including both real-world objects and conceptual objects, that need to be represented in software.

Object-oriented software is designed and built as a set of self-contained objects with both attributes and operations that interact to meet your needs. *Attributes* are properties or variables that relate to the object. *Operations* are methods, actions, or functions that the object can perform to modify itself or perform for some external effect. (You will hear the term *attribute* used interchangeably with the terms *member variable* and *property*, and the term *operation* used interchangeably with *method*.)

Object-oriented software's central advantage is its capability to support and encourage *encapsulation*—also known as *data hiding*. Essentially, access to the data within an object is available only via the object's operations, known as the *interface* of the object.

An object's functionality is bound to the data it uses. You can easily alter the details controlling how the object is implemented to improve performance, add new features, or fix bugs *without having to change the interface*. Changing the interface could have ripple effects throughout the project, but encapsulation allows you to make changes and fix bugs without your actions cascading to other parts of the project.

In other areas of software development, object orientation is the norm, and procedural or function-oriented software is considered old fashioned. Most web scripts are still designed and written using an *ad hoc* approach following a function-oriented methodology.

A number of reasons for using this approach exist. Many web projects are relatively small and straightforward. You can get away with picking up a saw and building a wooden spice rack without planning your approach, and you can successfully complete the majority of web software projects in the same way because of their small size. However, if you picked up a saw and attempted to build a house without formal planning, you wouldn't get quality results, if you got results at all. The same is true for large software projects.

Many web projects evolve from a set of hyperlinked pages to a complex application. Complex applications, whether presented via dialog boxes and windows or via dynamically generated HTML pages, need a properly thought-out development methodology.

Object orientation can help you to manage the complexity in your projects, increase code reusability, and thereby reduce maintenance costs.

In OO software, an object is a unique and identifiable collection of stored data and operations that operate on that data. For instance, you might have two objects that represent buttons. Even if both have a label "OK", a width of 60 pixels, a height of 20 pixels, and any other attributes that are identical, you still need to be able to deal with one button or the other. In software, separate variables act as *handles* (unique identifiers) for the objects.

Objects can be grouped into classes. Classes represent a set of objects that might vary from individual to individual, but must have a certain amount in common. A class contains objects that all have the same operations behaving in the same way and the same attributes representing the same things, although the values of those attributes vary from object to object.

You can think of the noun *bicycle* as a class of objects describing many distinct bicycles with many common features or *attributes*—such as two wheels, a color, and a size—and operations, such as move.

My own bicycle can be thought of as an object that fits into the class bicycle. It has all the common features of all bicycles, including a move operation that behaves the same as most other bicycles' move—even if it is used more rarely. My bicycle's attributes have unique values because my bicycle is green, and not all bicycles are that color.

Polymorphism

An object-oriented programming language must support *polymorphism*, which means that different classes can have different behaviors for the same operation. If, for instance, you have a class car and a class bicycle, both can have different move operations. For real-world objects, this would rarely be a problem. Bicycles are not likely to become confused and start using a car's move operation instead. However, a programming language does not possess the common sense of the real world, so the language must support polymorphism to know which move operation to use on a particular object.

Polymorphism is more a characteristic of behaviors than it is of objects. In PHP, only member functions of a class can be polymorphic. A real-world comparison is that of verbs in natural languages, which are equivalent to member functions. Consider the ways a bicycle can be used in real life. You can clean it, move it, disassemble it, repair it, or paint it, among other things.

These verbs describe generic actions because you don't know what kind of object is being acted on. (This type of abstraction of objects and actions is one of the distinguishing characteristics of human intelligence.)

For example, moving a bicycle requires completely different actions from those required for moving a car, even though the concepts are similar. The verb *move* can be associated with a particular set of actions only after the object acted on is made known.

Inheritance

Inheritance allows you to create a hierarchical relationship between classes using *subclasses*. A subclass inherits attributes and operations from its *superclass*. For example, car and bicycle have some things in common. You could use a class vehicle to contain the things such as a color attribute and a move operation that all vehicles have, and then let the car and bicycle classes inherit from vehicle.

You will hear *subclass*, *derived class*, and *child* used interchangeably. Similarly, you will hear *superclass* and *parent* used interchangeably.

With inheritance, you can build on and add to existing classes. From a simple base class, you can derive more complex and specialized classes as the need arises. This capability makes your code more reusable, which is one of the important advantages of an object-oriented approach.

Using inheritance might save you work if operations can be written once in a superclass rather than many times in separate subclasses. It might also allow you to more accurately model real-world relationships. If a sentence about two classes makes sense with "is a" between the classes, inheritance is probably appropriate. The sentence "a car is a vehicle" makes sense, but the sentence "a vehicle is a car" does not make sense because not all vehicles are cars. Therefore, car can inherit from vehicle.

Creating Classes, Attributes, and Operations in PHP

So far, we have discussed classes in a fairly abstract way. When creating a class in PHP, you must use the keyword `class`.

Structure of a Class

A minimal class definition looks like this:

```
class classname
{
}
```

To be useful, the classes need attributes and operations. You create attributes by declaring variables within a class definition using the keyword var. The following code creates a class called `classname` with two attributes, $attribute1 and $attribute2:

```
class classname
{
  var $attribute1;
  var $attribute2;
}
```

You create operations by declaring functions within the class definition. The following code creates a class named `classname` with two operations that do nothing. The operation `operation1()` takes no parameters, and `operation2()` takes two parameters:

```
class classname
{
  function operation1()
  {
  }
  function operation2($param1, $param2)
  {
  }
}
```

Constructors

Most classes have a special type of operation called a *constructor*. A constructor is called when an object is created, and it also normally performs useful initialization tasks such as setting attributes to sensible starting values or creating other objects needed by this object.

A constructor is declared in the same way as other operations, but has the special name `__construct()`. This is a change in PHP5. In previous versions, constructor functions had the same name as the class. For backward compatibility, if no function called `__construct()` is found in a class, PHP will search for a function with the same name as the class.

Although you can manually call the constructor, its main purpose is to be called automatically when an object is created. The following code declares a class with a constructor:

```
class classname
{
  function __construct($param)
  {
    echo "Constructor called with parameter $param <br />";
  }
}
```

PHP5 now supports function overloading, which means that you can provide more than one function with the same name and different numbers or types of parameters. (This feature is supported in many OO languages.) We discuss this later in this chapter.

Destructors

The opposite of a constructor is a *destructor*. Destructors are new in PHP5. They allow you to have some functionality that will be executed just before a class is destroyed, which will occur automatically when all references to a class have been unset or fallen out of scope.

Similar to the way constructors are named, the destructor for a class must be named ___destruct(). Destructors cannot take parameters.

Instantiating Classes

After you have declared a class, you need to create an object—a particular individual that is a member of the class—to work with. This is also known as *creating an instance of* or *instantiating* a class. You create an object by using the new keyword. When you do so, you need to specify what class your object will be an instance of and provide any parameters required by the constructor.

The following code declares a class called classname with a constructor and then creates three objects of type classname:

```
class classname
{
  function __construct($param)
  {
    echo "Constructor called with parameter $param <br />";
  }
}

$a = new classname('First');
$b = new classname('Second');
$c = new classname();
```

Because the constructor is called each time you create an object, this code produces the following output:

```
Constructor called with parameter First
Constructor called with parameter Second
Constructor called with parameter
```

Using Class Attributes

Within a class, you have access to a special pointer called $this. If an attribute of your current class is called $attribute, you refer to it as $this->attribute when either setting or accessing the variable from an operation within the class.

The following code demonstrates setting and accessing an attribute within a class:

```
class classname
{
  var $attribute;
  function operation($param)
  {
```

```
    $this->attribute = $param
    echo $this->attribute;
  }
}
```

Whether you can access an attribute from outside the class is determined by access modifiers, discussed later in this chapter. This example does not restrict access to the attributes, so you can access them from outside the class as follows:

```
class classname
{
  var $attribute;
}
$a = new classname();
$a->attribute = 'value';
echo $a->attribute;
```

It is not generally a good idea to directly access attributes from outside a class. One of the advantages of an object-oriented approach is that it encourages encapsulation. You can enforce this with the use of __get and __set functions. If, instead of accessing the attributes of a class directly, you write *accessor functions*, you can make all your accesses through a single section of code. When you initially write your accessor functions, they might look as follows:

```
class classname
{
  var $attribute;
  function __get($name)
  {
    return $this->$name;
  }
  function __set ($name, $value)
  {
    $this->$name = $value;
  }
}
```

This code provides minimal functions to access the attribute named $attribute. The function named __get() simply returns the value of $attribute, and the function named __set() assigns a new value to $attribute.

Note that __get() takes one parameter—the name of an attribute—and returns the value of that attribute. Similarly, the __set() function takes two parameters: the name of an attribute and the value you want to set it to.

You do not directly call these functions. The double underscore in front of the name shows that these functions have a special meaning in PHP, just like the __construct() and __destruct() functions.

How then do they work? If you instantiate the class

```
$a = new classname();
```

you can then use the __get() and __set() functions to check and set the value of any attributes.

If you type

```
$a->$attribute = 5;
```

this statement implicitly calls the __set() function with the value of $name set to "attribute", and the value of $value set to 5. You need to write the __set() function to do any error checking you want.

The __get() function works in a similar way. If, in your code, you reference

```
$a->attribute
```

this expression implicitly calls the __get() function with the parameter $name set to "attribute". It is up to you to write the __get() function to return the value.

At first glance, this code might seem to add little or no value. In its present form, this is probably true, but the reason for providing accessor functions is simple: You then have only one section of code that accesses that particular attribute.

With only a single access point, you can implement validity checks to make sure that only sensible data is being stored. If it occurs to you later that the value of $attribute should only be between 0 and 100, you can add a few lines of code *once* and check before allowing changes. You could change the __set() function to look as follows:

```
function __set ($name, $value)
{
  if( $name='attribute' && $value >= 0 && $value <= 100 )
    $this->attribute = $value;
}
```

With only a single access point, you are free to change the underlying implementation. If, for some reason, you choose to change the way $attribute is stored, accessor functions allow you to do this and change the code in only one place.

You might decide that, instead of storing $attribute as a variable, you will retrieve it from a database only when needed, calculate an up-to-date value every time it is requested, infer a value from the values of other attributes, or encode the data as a smaller data type. Whatever change you decide to make, you can simply modify the accessor functions. Other sections of code will not be affected as long as you make the accessor functions still accept or return the data that other parts of the program expect.

Controlling Access with private and public

PHP5 introduces access modifiers. They control the visibility of attributes and methods, and are placed in front of attribute and method declarations. PHP5 supports the following three different access modifiers:

- The default option is `public`, meaning that if you do not specify an access modifier for an attribute or method, it will be `public`. Items that are public can be accessed from inside or outside the class.

- The `private` access modifier means that the marked item can be accessed only from inside the class. You might use it on all attributes if you are not using `__get()` and `__set()`. You may also choose to make some methods private, for example, if they are utility functions for use inside the class only. Items that are private will not be inherited (more on this issue later in this chapter).

- The `protected` access modifier means that the marked item can be accessed only from inside the class. It also exists in any subclasses; again, we return to this issue when we discuss inheritance later in this chapter. For now, you can think of `protected` as being halfway in between `private` and `public`.

To add access modifiers to the sample class, you can alter the code as follows:

```
class classname
{
  public $attribute;
  public function __get($name)
  {
    return $this->$name;
  }
  public function __set ($name, $value)
  {
    $this->$name = $value;
  }
}
```

Here, each class member is prefaced with an access modifier to show whether it is private or public. You could leave out the `public` keyword because it is the default, but the code is easier to understand with it in if you are using the other modifiers.

Notice that we removed the `var` keyword in front of the attribute; it is replaced with the access modifier `public`. In this case, we made everything public.

Calling Class Operations

You can call class operations in much the same way that you call class attributes. Say you have the class

```
class classname
{
  function operation1()
  {
  }
```

```
function operation2($param1, $param2)
{
}
}
```

and create an object of type `classname` called $a as follows:

```
$a = new classname();
```

You then call operations the same way that you call other functions: by using their name and placing any parameters that they need in brackets. Because these operations belong to an object rather than normal functions, you need to specify to which object they belong. The object name is used in the same way as an object's attributes, as follows:

```
$a->operation1();
$a->operation2(12, 'test');
```

If the operations return something, you can capture that return data as follows:

```
$x = $a->operation1();
$y = $a->operation2(12, 'test');
```

Implementing Inheritance in PHP

If the class is to be a subclass of another, you can use the `extends` keyword to specify this use. The following code creates a class named B that inherits from some previously defined class named A:

```
class B extends A
{
  var $attribute2;
  function operation2()
  {
  }
}
```

If the class A was declared as

```
class A
{
  var $attribute1;
  function operation1()
  {
  }
}
```

all the following accesses to operations and attributes of an object of type B would be valid:

```
$b = new B();
$b->operation1();
$b->attribute1 = 10;
$b->operation2();
$b->attribute2 = 10;
```

Note that because class B extends class A, you can refer to operation1() and $attribute1, although they were declared in class A. As a subclass of A, B has all the same functionality and data. In addition, B has declared an attribute and an operation of its own.

It is important to note that inheritance works in only one direction. The subclass or child inherits features from its parent or superclass, but the parent does not take on features of the child. This means that the last two lines in this code are wrong:

```
$a = new A();
$a->operation1();
$a->attribute1 = 10;
$a->operation2();
$a->attribute2 = 10;
```

The class A does not have an operation2() or an attribute2.

Controlling Visibility Through Inheritance with `private` and `protected`

You can use the access modifiers private and protected to control what is inherited. If an attribute or method is specified as private, it will not be inherited. If an attribute or method is specified as protected, it will not be visible outside the class (like a private element) but *will* be inherited.

Consider the following example:

```php
<?php
class A
{
  private function operation1()
  {
    echo "operation1 called";
  }
  protected function operation2()
  {
    echo "operation2 called";
  }
  public function operation3()
  {
    echo "operation3 called";
  }
}
```

```
class B extends A
{
  function __construct()
  {
    $this->operation1();
    $this->operation2();
    $this->operation3();
  }
}

$b = new B;

?>
```

This code creates one operation of each type in class A: `public`, `protected`, and `private`. B inherits from A. In the constructor of B, you then try to call the operations from the parent.

The line

```
$this->operation1();
```

produces a fatal error as follows:

Fatal error: Call to private method A::operation1() from context 'B'

This example shows that private operations cannot be called from a child class.

If you comment out this line, the other two function calls will work. The `protected` function is inherited but can be used only from inside the child class, as done here. If you try adding the line

```
$b->operation2();
```

to the bottom of the file, you will get the following error:

Fatal error: Call to protected method A::operation2() from context ''

However, you can call `operation3()` from outside the class, as follows:

```
$b->operation3();
```

You can make this call because it is declared as `public`.

Overriding

In this chapter, we have shown a subclass declaring new attributes and operations. It is also valid and sometimes useful to redeclare the same attributes and operations. You might do this to give an attribute in the subclass a different default value to the same attribute in its superclass or to give an operation in the subclass different functionality to the same operation in its superclass. This action is called *overriding*.

For instance, say you have a class A:

```
class A
{
  var $attribute = 'default value';
  function operation()
  {
    echo 'Something<br />';
    echo "The value of \$attribute is $this->attribute<br />";
  }
}
```

If you want to alter the default value of $attribute and provide new functionality for operation(), you can create the following class B, which overrides $attribute and operation():

```
class B extends A
{
  var $attribute = 'different value';
  function operation()
  {
    echo 'Something else<br />';
    echo "The value of \$attribute is $this->attribute<br />";
  }
}
```

Declaring B does not affect the original definition of A. Now consider the following two lines of code:

```
$a = new A();
$a -> operation();
```

These lines create an object of type A and call its operation() function. This produces

```
Something
The value of $attribute is default value
```

proving that creating B has not altered A. If you create an object of type B, you will get different output.

This code

```
$b = new B();
$b -> operation();
```

produces

```
Something else
The value of $attribute is different value
```

In the same way that providing new attributes or operations in a subclass does not affect the superclass, overriding attributes or operations in a subclass does not affect the superclass.

A subclass will inherit all the attributes and operations of its superclass, unless you provide replacements. If you provide a replacement definition, it takes precedence and overrides the original definition.

The `parent` keyword allows you to call the original version of the operation in the parent class. For example, to call `A::operation` from within class `B`, you would use

```
parent::operation();
```

The output produced is, however, different. Although you call the operation from the parent class, PHP uses the attribute values from the current class. Hence, you get the following output:

```
Something
The value of $attribute is different value
```

Inheritance can be many layers deep. You can declare a class imaginatively called `C` that extends `B` and therefore inherits features from `B` and from `B`'s parent, `A`. The class `C` can again choose which attributes and operations from its parents to override and replace.

Preventing Inheritance and Overriding with `final`

PHP5 introduces the keyword `final`. When you use this keyword in front of a function declaration, that function cannot be overridden in any subclasses. For example, you can add it to class `A` in the previous example, as follows:

```
class A
{
  var $attribute = 'default value';
  final function operation()
  {
    echo 'Something<br />';
    echo "The value of \$attribute is $this->attribute<br />";
  }
}
```

Using this approach prevents you from overriding `operation()` in class `B`. If you attempt to do so, you will get the following error:

Fatal error: Cannot override final method A::operation()

You can also use the `final` keyword to prevent a class from being subclassed at all. To prevent class `A` from being subclassed, you can add it as follows:

```
final class A
{...}
```

If you then try to inherit from A, you will get an error similar to

Fatal error: Class B may not inherit from final class (A)

Understanding Multiple Inheritance

A few OO languages (most notably C++ and Smalltalk) support multiple inheritance, but like most, PHP does not. This means that each class can inherit from only one parent. No restrictions exist for how many children can share a single parent. What this means might not seem immediately clear. Figure 6.1 shows three different ways that three classes named A, B, and C can inherit.

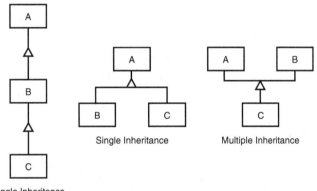

Figure 6.1   PHP does not support multiple inheritance.

The left combination shows class C inheriting from class B, which in turn inherits from class A. Each class has at most one parent, so this is a perfectly valid single inheritance in PHP.

The center combination shows classes B and C inheriting from class A. Each class has at most one parent, so again this is a valid single inheritance.

The right combination shows class C inheriting from both class A and class B. In this case, class C has two parents, so this is multiple inheritance and is invalid in PHP.

Implementing Interfaces

PHP5 introduces *interfaces*. They are seen as workarounds for multiple inheritance and are similar to the interface implementation supported by other object-oriented languages, including Java.

The idea of an interface is that it specifies a set of functions that must be implemented in classes that implement that interface. For instance, you might decide that you have a set of classes that need to be able to display themselves. Instead of having a parent class with a `display()` function that they all inherit from and override, you can implement an interface as follows:

```
interface Displayable
{
```

```
    function display();
}

class webPage implements Displayable
{
  function display()
  {
  // ...
  }
}
```

This example illustrates a roundabout kind of multiple inheritance because the webPage class can inherit from one class and implement one or more interfaces.

If you do not implement the methods specified in the interface (in this case, display()), you will get a fatal error.

Designing Classes

Now that you know some of the concepts behind objects and classes and the syntax to implement them in PHP, it is time to look at how to design useful classes.

Many classes in your code will represent classes or categories of real-world objects. Classes you might use in Web development might include pages, user interface components, shopping carts, error handling, product categories, or customers.

Objects in your code can also represent specific instances of the previously mentioned classes—for example, the home page, a particular button, or the shopping cart in use by Fred Smith at a particular time. Fred Smith himself can be represented by an object of type customer. Each item that Fred purchases can be represented as an object, belonging to a category or class.

In the preceding chapter, you used simple include files to give the fictional company TLA Consulting a consistent look and feel across the different pages of its website. Using classes and the timesaving power of inheritance, you can create a more advanced version of the same site.

Now you want to be able to quickly create pages for TLA that look and behave in the same way. You should be able to modify those pages to suit the different parts of the site.

For purposes of this example, you are going to create a Page class. The main goal of this class is to limit the amount of HTML needed to create a new page. It should allow you to alter the parts that change from page to page, while automatically generating the elements that stay the same. The class should provide a flexible framework for creating new pages and should not compromise your freedom.

Because you are generating the page from a script rather than with static HTML, you can add any number of clever things including functionality to

- Enable you to alter page elements in only one place. If you change the copyright notice or add an extra button, you should need to make the change in only a single place.

- Have default content for most parts of the page but be able to modify each element where required, setting custom values for elements such as the title and metatags.

- Recognize which page is being viewed and alter navigation elements to suit; there is no point in having a button that takes you to the home page located on the home page.

- Allow you to replace standard elements for particular pages. If, for instance, you want different navigation buttons in sections of the site, you should be able to replace the standard ones.

Writing the Code for Your Class

Having decided what you want the output from your code to look like and a few features you would like for it, how do you implement it? Later in the book, we discuss design and project management for large projects. For now, we concentrate on the parts specific to writing object-oriented PHP.

The class needs a logical name. Because it represents a page, you can call it `Page`. To declare a class called `Page`, type

```
class Page
{
}
```

The class needs some attributes. For this example, set elements that you might want changed from page to page as attributes of the class. The main contents of the page, which are a combination of HTML tags and text, are called `$content`. You can declare the content with the following line of code within the class definition:

```
public $content;
```

You can also set attributes to store the page's title. You will probably want to change this title to clearly show what particular page the visitor is looking at. Rather than have blank titles, you can provide a default title with the following declaration:

```
public $title = 'TLA Consulting Pty Ltd';
```

Most commercial web pages include metatags to help search engines index them. To be useful, metatags should probably change from page to page. Again, you can provide a default value:

```
public $keywords = 'TLA Consulting, Three Letter Abbreviation,
                    some of my best friends are search engines';
```

The navigation buttons shown on the original page in Figure 5.2 (see the preceding chapter) should probably be kept the same from page to page to avoid confusing people, but to change them easily, you can make them an attribute, too. Because the number of buttons might be variable, you can use an array and store both the text for the button and the URL it should point to:

```
public $buttons = array( 'Home'     => 'home.php',
                         'Contact'  => 'contact.php',
                         'Services' => 'services.php',
                         'Site Map' => 'map.php'
                       );
```

To provide some functionality, the class also needs operations. You can start by providing accessor functions to set and get the values of the attributes you defined:

```
public function __set($name, $value)
{
  $this->$name = $value;
}
```

The __set() function does not contain error checking (for brevity), but this capability can be easily added later, as required. Because it is unlikely that you will be requesting any of these values from outside the class, you can elect not to provide a __get() function, as done here.

The main purpose of this class is to display a page of HTML, so you need a function. We called ours Display(), and it is as follows:

```
public function Display()
{
  echo "<html>\n<head>\n";
  $this -> DisplayTitle();
  $this -> DisplayKeywords();
  $this -> DisplayStyles();
  echo "</head>\n<body>\n";
  $this -> DisplayHeader();
  $this -> DisplayMenu($this->buttons);
  echo $this->content;
  $this -> DisplayFooter();
  echo "</body>\n</html>\n";
}
```

The function includes a few simple echo statements to display HTML but mainly consists of calls to other functions in the class. As you have probably guessed from their names, these other functions display parts of the page.

Breaking up functions like this is not compulsory. All these separate functions might simply have been combined into one big function. We separated them out for a number of reasons.

Each function should have a defined task to perform. The simpler this task is, the easier writing and testing the function will be. Don't go too far; if you break up your program into too many small units, it might be hard to read.

Using inheritance, you can override operations. You can replace one large `Display()` function, but it is unlikely that you will want to change the way the entire page is displayed. It will be much better to break up the display functionality into a few self-contained tasks and be able to override only the parts that you want to change.

This `Display()` function calls `DisplayTitle()`, `DisplayKeywords()`, `DisplayStyles()`, `DisplayHeader()`, `DisplayMenu()`, and `DisplayFooter()`. This means that you need to define these operations. You can write operations or functions in this logical order, calling the operation or function before the actual code for the function. In many other languages, you need to write the function or operation before it can be called. Most of the operations are fairly simple and need to display some HTML and perhaps the contents of the attributes.

Listing 6.1 shows the complete class, saved as `page.inc` to include or require into other files.

Listing 6.1 `page.inc`— The Page Class Provides an Easy and Flexible Way to Create TLA Pages

```php
<?php
class Page
{
  // class Page's attributes
  public $content;
  public $title = 'TLA Consulting Pty Ltd';
  public $keywords = 'TLA Consulting, Three Letter Abbreviation,
                 some of my best friends are search engines';
  public $buttons = array( 'Home'     => 'home.php',
                      'Contact'  => 'contact.php',
                      'Services' => 'services.php',
                      'Site Map' => 'map.php'
                   );

  // class Page's operations
  public function __set($name, $value)
  {
    $this->$name = $value;
  }

  public function Display()
  {
    echo "<html>\n<head>\n";
    $this -> DisplayTitle();
    $this -> DisplayKeywords();
    $this -> DisplayStyles();
```

Listing 6.1 **Continued**

```php
    echo "</head>\n<body>\n";
    $this -> DisplayHeader();
    $this -> DisplayMenu($this->buttons);
    echo $this->content;
    $this -> DisplayFooter();
    echo "</body>\n</html>\n";
  }

  public function DisplayTitle()
  {
    echo '<title> '.$this->title.' </title>';
  }

  public function DisplayKeywords()
  {
    echo "<meta name=\"keywords\" content=\
        "".htmlentities($this->keywords)."\" />";
  }

  public function DisplayStyles()
  {
?>
  <style>
<!--
    h1 {color:white; font-size:24pt; text-align:center;
        font-family:arial,sans-serif}
    .menu {color:white; font-size:12pt; text-align:center;
           font-family:arial,sans-serif; font-weight:bold}
    td {background:black}
    p {color:black; font-size:12pt; text-align:justify;
       font-family:arial,sans-serif}
    p.foot {color:white; font-size:9pt; text-align:center;
            font-family:arial,sans-serif; font-weight:bold}
    a:link,a:visited,a:active {color:white}
-->
  </style>
<?php
  }

  public function DisplayHeader()
  {
?>
  <table width="100%" cellpadding ="12" cellspacing ="0" border ="0">
  <tr bgcolor ="black">
    <td align ="left"><img src = "logo.gif" /></td>
```

Listing 6.1 **Continued**

```php
   <td>
       <h1>TLA Consulting Pty Ltd</h1>
   </td>
   <td align ="right"><img src = "logo.gif" /></td>
 </tr>
 </table>
<?php
 }

 public function DisplayMenu($buttons)
 {
   echo "<table width='100%' bgcolor='white' cellpadding='4'
              cellspacing='4'>\n";
   echo "   <tr>\n";

   //calculate button size
   $width = 100/count($buttons);

   foreach ($buttons as $name=>$url)
   {
     $this -> DisplayButton($width, $name, $url,
                         !$this->IsURLCurrentPage($url));
   }
   echo "   </tr>\n";
   echo "</table>\n";
 }

 public function IsURLCurrentPage($url)
 {
   if(strpos($_SERVER['PHP_SELF'], $url )==false)
   {
     return false;
   }
   else
   {
     return true;
   }
 }

 public function DisplayButton($width, $name, $url, $active = true)
 {
   if ($active)
   {
     echo "<td width ='".htmlentities($width)."%'>
```

Listing 6.1 **Continued**

```
              <a href ='".htmlentities($url)."'>
              <img src ='s-logo.gif' alt ='".htmlentities($name)."' border
              ='0' /></a>
              <a href ='".htmlentities($url)."'><span class='menu'>$name</span>
              </a></td>";
      }
      else
      {
        echo "<td width ='".htmlentities($width)."%'>
              <img src ='side-logo.gif'>
              <span class='menu'>$name</span></td>";
      }
    }

    public function DisplayFooter()
    {
?>
      <table width = "100%" bgcolor ="black" cellpadding ="12" border ="0">
      <tr>
        <td>
          <p class="foot">&copy; TLA Consulting Pty Ltd.</p>
          <p class="foot">Please see our
                      <a href ="legal.php">legal information page</a></p>
        </td>
      </tr>
      </table>
<?php
    }
}
?>
```

When reading this class, note that DisplayStyles(), DisplayHeader(), and
DisplayFooter() need to display a large block of static HTML, with no PHP process-
ing. Therefore, you simply use an end PHP tag (?>), type your HTML, and then re-enter
PHP with an open PHP tag (<?php) while inside the functions.

Two other operations are defined in this class. The operation DisplayButton() outputs a single menu button. If the button is to point to the page you are on, you display
an inactive button instead, which looks slightly different and does not link anywhere.
This way, you can keep the page layout consistent and provide visitors with a visual
location.

The operation IsURLCurrentPage() determines whether the URL for a button points to the current page. You can use several techniques to discover this information. Here, you use the string function `strpos()` to see whether the URL given is contained in one of the server set variables. The statement `strpos( $_SERVER['PHP_SELF']`, `$url )` returns a number if the string in `$url` is inside the superglobal variable `$_SERVER['PHP_SELF']` or `false` if it is not.

To use this `Page` class, you need to include `page.inc` in a script and call `Display()`.

The code in Listing 6.2 creates TLA Consulting's home page and gives output similar to that previously generated in Figure 5.2. The code in Listing 6.2 does the following:

1. Uses `require` to include the contents of `page.inc`, which contains the definition of the class `Page`.

2. Creates an instance of the class `Page`. The instance is called `$homepage`.

3. Sets the content, consisting of some text and HTML tags to appear in the page. (This implicitly invokes the `__set()` method.)

4. Calls the operation `Display()` within the object `$homepage` to cause the page to be displayed in the visitor's browser.

Listing 6.2   home.php—This Home Page Uses the `Page` Class to Do Most of the Work Involved in Generating the Page

```php
<?php
  require ('page.inc');

  $homepage = new Page();

  $homepage->content =' <p>Welcome to the home of TLA Consulting.
                        Please take some time to get to know us.</p>
                        <p>We specialize in serving your business needs
                        and hope to hear from you soon.</p>';
  $homepage->Display();
?>
```

You can see in Listing 6.2 that you need to do very little work to generate new pages using this `Page` class. Using the class in this way means that all your pages need to be very similar.

If you want some sections of the site to use a variant of the standard page, you can simply copy `page.inc` to a new file called `page2.inc` and make some changes. This means that every time you update or fix parts of `page.inc`, you need to remember to make the same changes to `page2.inc`.

A better course of action is to use inheritance to create a new class that inherits most of its functionality from `Page` but overrides the parts that need to be different. For the TLA site, require that the services page include a second navigation bar. The script shown in Listing 6.3 does this by creating a new class called `ServicesPage` that inherits from `Page`. You provide a new array called `$row2buttons` that contains the buttons and links you want in the second row. Because you want this class to behave in mostly the same ways, you override only the part you want changed: the `Display()` operation.

Listing 6.3 `services.php`— **The Services Page Inherits from the** `Page` **Class but Overrides** `Display()` **to Alter the Output**

```php
<?php
  require ('page.inc');

  class ServicesPage extends Page
  {
    private $row2buttons = array( 'Re-engineering' => 'reengineering.php',
                                  'Standards Compliance' => 'standards.php',
                                  'Buzzword Compliance' => 'buzzword.php',
                                  'Mission Statements' => 'mission.php'
                                );
    public function Display()
    {
      echo "<html>\n<head>\n";
      $this -> DisplayTitle();
      $this -> DisplayKeywords();
      $this -> DisplayStyles();
      echo "</head>\n<body>\n";
      $this -> DisplayHeader();
      $this -> DisplayMenu($this->buttons);
      $this -> DisplayMenu($this->row2buttons);
      echo $this->content;
      $this -> DisplayFooter();
      echo "</body>\n</html>\n";
    }
  }

  $services = new ServicesPage();
  $services -> content ='<p>At TLA Consulting, we offer a number of services.
          Perhaps the productivity of your employees would
          improve if we re-engineered your business.
          Maybe all your business needs is a fresh mission
          statement, or a new batch of buzzwords.</p>';
  $services -> Display();
?>
```

The overriding `Display()` is similar but contains one extra line:

```
$this -> DisplayMenu($this->row2buttons);
```

This line calls `DisplayMenu()` a second time and creates a second menu bar.

Outside the class definition, you create an instance of the `ServicesPage` class, set the values for which you want nondefault values, and call `Display()`.

As you can see, Figure 6.2 shows a new variant of the standard page. You needed to write new code only for the parts that were different.

Figure 6.2   The services page is created using inheritance to reuse most of the standard page.

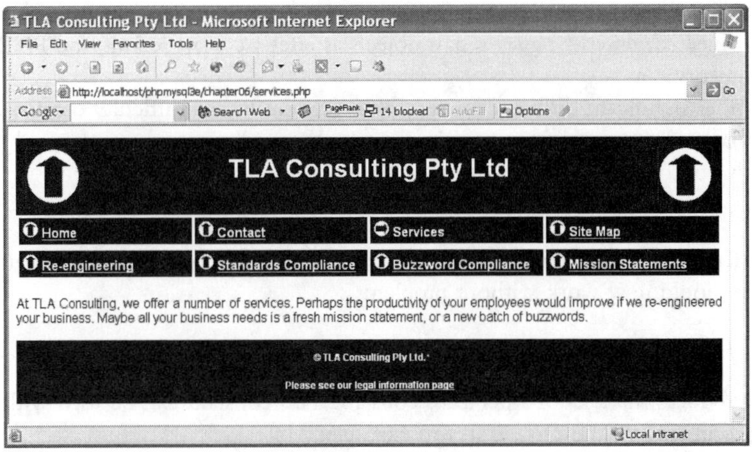

Creating pages via PHP classes has obvious advantages. With a class to do most of the work for you, you need to do less work to create a new page. You can update all your pages at once by simply updating the class. Using inheritance, you can derive different versions of the class from the original without compromising the advantages.

As with most things in life, these advantages do not come without cost. Creating pages from a script requires more computer processor effort than simply loading a static HTML page from disk and sending it to a browser. On a busy site, this will be important, and you should make an effort to either use static HTML pages or cache the output of your scripts where possible to reduce the load on the server.

Understanding Advanced and New Object-Oriented Functionality in PHP

In the following sections, we discuss PHP's advanced OO features, most of which are new in PHP5.

Note: PHP4 Versus PHP5

If you have used previous versions of PHP, you should be aware of a couple of important differences.

In PHP4, objects were passed by value, and they are now passed around by reference. Writing your code this way should not break any old code, and in fact many programmers wrote inefficient code without realizing it. For example, even writing

```
$c = new myClass;
```

created a new class and then copied the instance into $c (effectively creating two copies but immediately losing the handle to one of them). This behavior can cause problems if you assume that objects are being passed by reference, particularly when you are passing objects to functions.

Most object-oriented languages pass objects as references by default, and PHP is now in this category.

The other significant difference is that PHP previously had difficulty dereferencing objects that were returned from functions, typically to call methods on those objects. Previously, you could not write, for example,

```
select_object()->display();
```

where `select_object()` returned an object that had a method called `display()`. This statement should now work without problems.

Using Per-Class Constants

PHP5 introduces the idea of a per-class constant. This constant can be used without your needing to instantiate the class, as in this example:

```
<?php
class Math {
    const pi = 3.14159;
}
echo 'Math::pi = '.Math::pi."\n";
?>
```

You can access the per-class constant by using the `::` operator to specify the class the constant belongs to, as done in this example.

Implementing Static Methods

PHP5 also introduces the `static` keyword. It is applied to methods to allow them to be called without instantiating the class. This is the method equivalent of the per-class constant idea. For example, consider the `Math` class created in the preceding section. You could add a `squared()` function to it and invoke it without instantiating the class as follows:

```
class Math
{
```

```
static function squared($input)
{
  return $input*$input;
}
}
echo Math::squared(8);
```

Note that you cannot use the `this` keyword inside a static method because there may be no object instance to refer to.

Checking Class Type and Type Hinting

Also new in PHP5 are the `instanceof` keyword and the concept of *type hinting*.

The `instanceof` keyword allows you to check the type of an object. You can check whether an object is an instance of a particular class, whether it inherits from a class, or whether it implements an interface. The `instanceof` keyword is effectively a conditional operator. For instance, with the previous examples in which you implemented class B as a subclass of class A, then

`($b instanceof B)`	would be true.
`($b instanceof A)`	would be true.
`($b instanceof Displayable)`	would be false.

All these examples assume that A, B, and `Displayable` are in the current scope; otherwise, an error will be triggered.

Also new in PHP5 is the idea of class type hinting. Normally, when you pass a parameter to a function in PHP, you do not pass the type of that parameter. With class type hinting, you can specify the type of class that ought to be passed in, and if that is not the type actually passed in, an error will be triggered. The type checking is equivalent to `instanceof`. For example, consider the following function:

```
function check_hint(B $someclass)
{
  //...
}
```

This example suggests that `$someclass` needs to be an instance of class B. If you then pass in an instance of class A as

```
check_hint($a);
```

you will get the following fatal error:

Fatal error: Argument 1 must be an instance of B

Note that if you had hinted A and passed in an instance of B, no error would have occurred because B inherits from A.

Cloning Objects

PHP5 introduces the `clone` keyword, which allows you to copy an existing object. For example,

```
$c = clone $b;
```

would create a copy of object $b of the same class, with the same attribute values.

You can also change this behavior. If you need nondefault behavior from `clone`, you need to create a method in the base class called __clone(). This method is similar to a constructor or destructor in that you do not call it directly. It is invoked when the `clone` keyword is used as shown here. Within the __clone() method, you can then define exactly the copying behavior that you want.

The nice thing about __clone() is that it will be called after an exact copy has been made using the default behavior, so at that stage you are able to change only the things you want to change.

The most common functionality to add to __clone() is code to ensure that attributes of the class that are handled as references are copied correctly. If you set out to clone a class that contains a reference to an object, you are probably expecting a second copy of that object rather than a second reference to the same one, so it would make sense to add this to __clone().

You may also choose to change nothing but perform some other action, such as updating an underlying database record relating to the class.

Using Abstract Classes

Another new feature in PHP5 is abstract classes. These classes cannot be instantiated.

PHP5 also offers abstract methods, which provide the signature for a method but no implementation, as in this example:

```
abstract operationX($param1, $param2);
```

Any class that contains abstract methods must itself be abstract, as shown in this example:

```
abstract class A
{
  abstract function operationX($param1, $param2);
}
```

The main use of abstract methods and classes is in a complex class hierarchy where you want to make sure each subclass contains and overrides some particular method; this can also be done with an interface.

Overloading Methods with __call()

We previously looked at a number of class methods with special meanings whose names begin with a double underscore (__), such as __get(), __set(), __construct(), and __destruct(). Another example is the method __call(), which is used in PHP to implement method overloading.

Method overloading is common in many object-oriented languages but is not as useful in PHP because you tend to use flexible types and the (easy-to-implement) optional function parameters instead.

To use it, you implement a __call() method, as in this example:

```
public function __call($method, $p)
{
  if ($method == 'display')
    if (is_object($p[0]))
        $this->displayObject($p[0]);
    else if (is_array($p[0]))
        $this->displayArray($p[0]);
    else
        $this->displayScalar($p[0]) ;
}
```

The __call() method should take two parameters. The first contains the name of the method being invoked, and the second contains an array of the parameters passed to that method. You can then decide for yourself which underlying method to call. In this case, if an object is passed to method display(), you call the underlying displayObject() method; if an array is passed, you call displayArray(); and if something else is passed, you call displayScalar().

To invoke this code, you would first instantiate the class containing this __call() method (name it overload) and then invoke the display() method, as in this example:

```
$ov = new overload;
$ov->display(array(1, 2, 3));
$ov->display('cat');
```

The first call to display() invokes displayArray(), and the second invokes displayScalar().

Note that you do not need any underlying implementation of the display() method for this code to work.

Using __autoload()

Another of the special functions is __autoload(). It is not a class method but a standalone function; that is, you declare it outside any class declaration. If you implement it, it will be automatically called when you attempt to instantiate a class that has not been declared.

The main use of __autoload() is to try to include or require any files needed to instantiate the required class. Consider this example:

```
function __autoload($name)
{
   include_once $name.'.php';
}
```

This implementation tries to include a file with the same name as the class.

Implementing Iterators and Iteration

One clever feature of the new object-oriented engine is that you can now use a
`foreach()` loop to iterate through the attributes of an object as you would an array.
Here's an example:

```
class myClass
{
  public $a=5;
  public $b=7;
  public $c=9;
}
$x = new myClass;
foreach ($x as $attribute)
  echo $attribute.'<br />';
```

(At the time of writing, the PHP manual suggests that you need to implement the
empty interface `Traversable` for the `foreach` interface to work, but doing so causes a
fatal error. Not implementing it seems to work just fine, though.)

If you need more sophisticated behavior than this, you can implement an *iterator*. To
do this, you make the class that you want to iterate over implement the
`IteratorAggregate` interface and give it a method called `getIterator` that returns an
instance of the iterator class. That class must implement the `Iterator` interface, which
has a series of methods that must be implemented. An example of a class and iterator is
shown in Listing 6.4.

Listing 6.4 `iterator.php`— **A Sample Base Class and Iterator Class**

```php
<?php
class ObjectIterator implements Iterator {

    private $obj;
    private $count;
    private $currentIndex;

    function __construct($obj)
    {
      $this->obj = $obj;
      $this->count = count($this->obj->data);
    }
    function rewind()
    {
      $this->currentIndex = 0;
    }
    function valid()
    {
      return $this->currentIndex < $this->count;
```

Listing 6.4 **Continued**

```
    }
    function key()
    {
      return $this->currentIndex;
    }
    function current()
    {
      return $this->obj->data[$this->currentIndex];
    }
    function next()
    {
      $this->currentIndex++;
    }
}

class Object implements IteratorAggregate
{
  public $data = array();

  function __construct($in)
  {
    $this->data = $in;
  }

  function getIterator()
  {
    return new ObjectIterator($this);
  }
}

$myObject = new Object(array(2, 4, 6, 8, 10));

$myIterator = $myObject->getIterator();
for($myIterator->rewind(); $myIterator->valid(); $myIterator->next())
{
  $key = $myIterator->key();
  $value = $myIterator->current();
  echo "$key => $value <br />";
}
?>
```

The ObjectIterator class has a set of functions as required by the Iterator interface:

- The constructor is not required but is obviously a good place to set up values for the number of items you plan to iterate over and a link to the current data item.

- The rewind() function should set the internal data pointer back to the beginning of the data.
- The valid() function should tell you whether more data still exists at the current location of the data pointer.
- The key() function should return the value of the data pointer.
- The value() function should return the value stored at the current data pointer.
- The next() function should move the data pointer along in the data.

The reason for using an iterator class like this is that the interface to the data will not change even if the underlying implementation changes. In this example, the IteratorAggregate class is a simple array. If you decide to change it to a hash table or linked list, you could still use a standard Iterator to traverse it, although the Iterator code would change.

Converting Your Classes to Strings

Another of the new "magical" functions is __toString(). If you implement a function called __toString() in your class, it will be called when you try to print the class, as in this example:

```
$p = new Printable;
echo $p;
```

Whatever the __toString() function returns will be printed by echo. You might, for instance, implement it as follows:

```
class Printable
{
  var $testone;
  var $testtwo;
  public function __toString()
  {
    return(var_export($this, TRUE));
  }
}
```

(The var_export() function prints out all the attribute values in the class.)

Using the Reflection API

An exciting new feature in PHP5 is the *reflection API*. Reflection is the ability to interrogate existing classes and objects to find out about their structure and contents. This capability can be useful when you are interfacing to unknown or undocumented classes, such as when interfacing with encoded PHP scripts.

The API is extremely complex, but we will look at a simple example to give you some idea of what it can be used for. Consider the `Page` class defined in this chapter, for example. You can get all the information about this class from the Reflection API, as shown in Listing 6.5.

Listing 6.5 `reflection.php`—**Displays Information About the Page Class**

```php
<?php
require_once('page.inc');
$class = new ReflectionClass('Page');
echo '<pre>';
echo $class;
echo '</pre>';
?>
```

Here, you use the `__toString()` method of the `Reflection` class to print out this data. Note that the `<pre>` tags are on separate lines so as not to confuse the `__toString()` method.

The first screen of output from this code is shown in Figure 6.3.

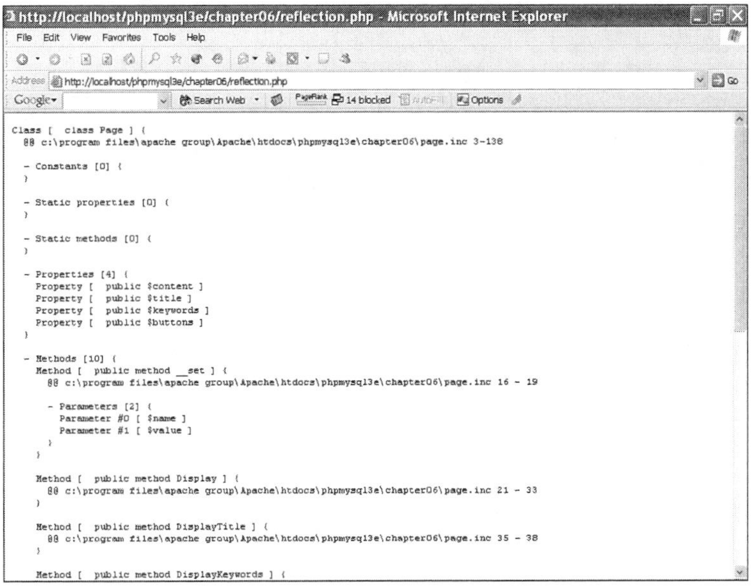

Figure 6.3   The output from the reflection API is surprisingly detailed.

Next

The next chapter explains PHP's new exception handling capabilities. Exceptions provide an elegant mechanism for dealing with runtime errors.

7

Exception Handling

I N THIS CHAPTER, WE EXPLAIN THE CONCEPT OF exception handling and the way it is implemented in PHP. Exceptions are a new and important feature in PHP5. They provide a unified mechanism for handling errors in an extensible, maintainable, and object-oriented way.

Key topics covered in this chapter include

- Exception handling concepts
- Exception control structures: `try...throw...catch`
- The `Exception` class
- User-defined exceptions
- Exceptions in Bob's Auto Parts
- Exceptions and PHP's other error handling mechanisms

Exception Handling Concepts

The basic idea of exception handling is that code is executed inside what is called a *try block*. That's a section of code that looks like this:

```
try
{
  // code goes here
}
```

If something goes wrong inside the `try` block, you can do what is called *throwing an exception*. Some languages, such as Java, throw exceptions automatically for you in certain cases. In PHP, exceptions must be thrown manually. You throw an exception as follows:

```
throw new Exception('message', code);
```

The keyword `throw` triggers the exception handling mechanism. It is a language construct rather than a function, but you need to pass it a value. It expects to receive an object. In the simplest case, you can instantiate the built-in `Exception` class, as done in this example.

The constructor for this class takes two parameters: a message and a code. They are intended to represent an error message and an error code number. Both of these parameters are optional.

Finally, underneath your `try` block, you need at least one *catch block*. A catch block looks like this:

```
catch (typehint exception)
{
  // handle exception
}
```

You can have more than one `catch` block associated with a single `try` block. Using more than one would make sense if each `catch` block is waiting to catch a different type of exception. For example, if you want to catch exceptions of the `Exception` class, your catch block might look like this:

```
catch (Exception $e)
{
  // handle exception
}
```

The object passed into (and caught by) the `catch` block is the one passed to (and thrown by) the `throw` statement that raised the exception. The exception can be of any type, but it is good form to use either instances of the `Exception` class or instances of your own user-defined exceptions that inherit from the `Exception` class. (You see how to define your own exceptions later in the chapter.)

When an exception is raised, PHP looks for a matching `catch` block. If you have more than one `catch` block, the objects passed in to each should be of different types so that PHP can work out which `catch` block to fall through to.

One other point to note is that you can raise further exceptions within a `catch` block.

To make this discussion a bit clearer, let's look at an example. A simple exception handling example is shown in Listing 7.1.

Listing 7.1 `basic_exception.php`— **Throwing and Catching an Exception**

```php
<?php

try
{
  throw new Exception('A terrible error has occurred', 42);
}
catch (Exception $e)
{
  echo 'Exception '. $e->getCode(). ': '. $e->getMessage()
       .' in '. $e->getFile(). ' on line '. $e->getLine(). '<br />';
}
?>
```

In Listing 7.1, you can see that we used a number of methods of the `Exception` class, which we discuss shortly. The result of running this code is shown in Figure 7.1.

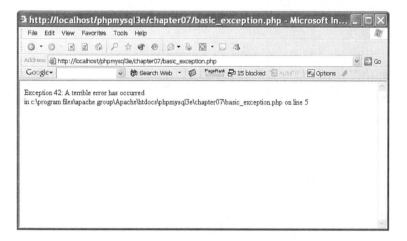

Figure 7.1   This `catch` block reports the exception error message and notes where it occurred.

In the sample code, you can see that we raise an exception of class `Exception`. This built-in class has methods you can use in the `catch` block to report a useful error message.

The `Exception` **Class**

PHP5 comes with a built-in class called `Exception`. The constructor takes two parameters, as we discussed previously: an error message and an error code.

In addition to the constructor, this class comes with the following built-in methods:

- `getCode()`—Returns the code as passed to the constructor
- `getMessage()`—Returns the message as passed to the constructor
- `getFile()`—Returns the full path to the code file where the exception was raised
- `getLine()`—Returns the line number in the code file where the exception was raised
- `getTrace()`—Returns an array containing a backtrace where the exception was raised
- `getTraceAsString()`—Returns the same information as `getTrace`, formatted as a string
- `__toString()`—Allows you to simply echo an `Exception` object, giving all the information from the above methods

You can see that we used the first four of these methods in Listing 7.1. You could obtain the same information (plus the backtrace) by executing

```
echo $e;
```

A *backtrace* shows which functions were executing at the time the exception was raised.

User-Defined Exceptions

Instead of instantiating and passing an instance of the base `Exception` class, you can pass any other object you like. In most cases, you will extend the `Exception` class to create your own exception classes.

You can pass any other object with your `throw` clause. You may occasionally want to do this if you are having problems with one particular object and want to pass it through for debugging purposes.

Most of the time, however, you will extend the base `Exception` class. The PHP manual provides code that shows the skeleton of the `Exception` class. This code, taken from http://www.php.net/zend-engine-2.php, is reproduced in Listing 7.2. Note that this is not the actual code but represents what you can expect to inherit.

Listing 7.2 `Exception` **class—This Is What You Can Expect to Inherit**

```php
<?php
class Exception {
    function __construct(string $message=NULL, int $code=0) {
        if (func_num_args()) {
            $this->message = $message;
        }
        $this->code = $code;
        $this->file = __FILE__; // of throw clause
        $this->line = __LINE__; // of throw clause
        $this->trace = debug_backtrace();
        $this->string = StringFormat($this);
    }

    protected $message = 'Unknown exception';  // exception message
    protected $code = 0; // user defined exception code
    protected $file;    // source filename of exception
    protected $line;    // source line of exception

    private $trace;     // backtrace of exception
    private $string;    // internal only!!

    final function getMessage(){
        return $this->message;
    }
    final function getCode() {
```

Listing 7.2   **Continued**

```
        return $this->code;
    }
    final function getFile() {
        return $this->file;
    }
    final function getTrace() {
        return $this->trace;
    }
    final function getTraceAsString() {
        return self::TraceFormat($this);
    }
    function _toString() {
        return $this->string;
    }
    static private function StringFormat(Exception $exception) {
        // ... a function not available in PHP scripts
        // that returns all relevant information as a string
    }
    static private function TraceFormat(Exception $exception) {
        // ... a function not available in PHP scripts
        // that returns the backtrace as a string
    }
}
? >
```

The main reason we are looking at this class definition is to note that most of the public methods are final: That means you cannot override them. You can create your own sub-class Exceptions, but you cannot change the behavior of the basic methods. Note that you can override the __toString() function, so you can change the way the exception is displayed. You can also add your own methods.

An example of a user-defined Exception class is shown in Listing 7.3.

Listing 7.3 user_defined_exception.php—**An Example of a User-Defined** Exception **Class**

```
<?php

class myException extends Exception
{
  function __toString()
  {
      return '<table border><tr><td><strong>Exception '. $this->getCode()
             . '</strong>: '. $this->getMessage().'<br />'.' in '
             . $this->getFile(). ' on line '. $this->getLine()
             . '</td></tr></table><br />';
```

Listing 7.3   **Continued**

```
  }
}

try
{
  throw new myException('A terrible error has occurred', 42);
}
catch (myException $m)
{
    echo $m;
}


?>
```

In this code, you declare a new exception class, called myException, that extends the
basic Exception class. The difference between this class and the Exception class is that
you override the __toString() method to provide a "pretty" way of printing the
exception. The output from executing this code is shown in Figure 7.2.

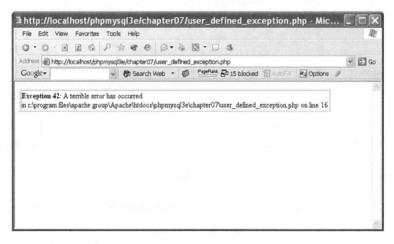

Figure 7.2   The myException class provides exceptions with
"pretty printing."

This example is fairly simple. In the next section, we look at ways to create different
exceptions to deal with different categories of error.

Exceptions in Bob's Auto Parts

Chapter 2, "Storing and Retrieving Data," described how you could store Bob's order data in a flat file. You know that file I/O (in fact, any kind of I/O) is one area in programs where errors often occur. This makes it a good place to apply exception handling.

Looking back at the original code, you can see that three things are likely to go wrong with writing to the file: the file cannot be opened, a lock cannot be obtained, or the file cannot be written to. We created an exception class for each of these possibilities. The code for these exceptions is shown in Listing 7.4.

Listing 7.4   `file_exceptions.php`—**File I/O-Related Exceptions**

```php
<?php

class fileOpenException extends Exception
{
  function __toString()
  {
      return 'fileOpenException '. $this->getCode()
             . ': '. $this->getMessage().'<br />'.' in '
             . $this->getFile(). ' on line '. $this->getLine()
             . '<br />';
  }
}


class fileWriteException extends Exception
{
  function __toString()
  {
      return 'fileWriteException '. $this->getCode()
             . ': '. $this->getMessage().'<br />'.' in '
             . $this->getFile(). ' on line '. $this->getLine()
             . '<br />';
  }
}


class fileLockException extends Exception
{
  function __toString()
  {
      return 'fileLockException '. $this->getCode()
             . ': '. $this->getMessage().'<br />'.' in '
             . $this->getFile(). ' on line '. $this->getLine()
             . '<br />';
  }
}

?>
```

These Exception subclasses do not do anything particularly interesting. In fact, for the purpose of this application, you could leave them as empty subclasses or use the provided Exception class. We have, however, provided a __toString() method for each of the subclasses that explains what type of exception has occurred.

We rewrote the processorder.php file from Chapter 2 to incorporate the use of exceptions. The new version is shown in Listing 7.5.

Listing 7.5 processorder.php—**Bob's Order-Processing Script with Exception Handling Included**

```php
<?php

  require_once('file_exceptions.php');

  // create short variable names
  $tireqty = $_POST['tireqty'];
  $oilqty = $_POST['oilqty'];
  $sparkqty = $_POST['sparkqty'];
  $address = $_POST['address'];

  $DOCUMENT_ROOT = $_SERVER['DOCUMENT_ROOT'];
?>
<html>
<head>
  <title>Bob's Auto Parts - Order Results</title>
</head>
<body>
<h1>Bob's Auto Parts</h1>
<h2>Order Results</h2>
<?php
$date = date('H:i, jS F') ;

echo '<p>Order processed at ';
echo $date;
echo '</p>';

echo '<p>Your order is as follows: </p>';

$totalqty = 0;
$totalqty = $tireqty + $oilqty + $sparkqty;
echo 'Items ordered: '.$totalqty.'<br />';

if( $totalqty == 0)
{
  echo 'You did not order anything on the previous page!<br />';
}
```

Listing 7.5 **Continued**

```php
else
{
  if ( $tireqty>0 )
    echo $tireqty.' tires<br />';
  if ( $oilqty>0 )
    echo $oilqty.' bottles of oil<br />';
  if ( $sparkqty>0 )
    echo $sparkqty.' spark plugs<br />';
}

$totalamount = 0.00;

define('TIREPRICE', 100);
define('OILPRICE', 10);
define('SPARKPRICE', 4);

$totalamount = $tireqty * TIREPRICE
             + $oilqty * OILPRICE
             + $sparkqty * SPARKPRICE;

$totalamount=number_format($totalamount, 2, '.', ' ');

echo '<p>Total of order is '.$totalamount.'</p>';
echo '<p>Address to ship to is '.$address.'</p>';

$outputstring = $date."\t".$tireqty." tires \t".$oilqty." oil\t"
                .$sparkqty." spark plugs\t\$".$totalamount
                ."\t". $address."\n";

// open file for appending
try
{
  if (!($fp = @fopen("$DOCUMENT_ROOT/../orders/orders.txt", 'ab')))
      throw new fileOpenException();

  if (!flock($fp, LOCK_EX))
    throw new fileLockException();

  if (!fwrite($fp, $outputstring, strlen($outputstring)))
    throw new fileWriteException();
  flock($fp, LOCK_UN);
  fclose($fp);
  echo '<p>Order written.</p>';
}
```

Listing 7.5   **Continued**

```
catch (fileOpenException $foe)
{
   echo '<p><strong>Orders file could not be opened.  '
         .'Please contact our webmaster for help.</strong></p>';
}
catch (Exception $e)
{
   echo '<p><strong>Your order could not be processed at this time.  '
         .'Please try again later.</strong></p>';
}


?>
</body>
</html>
```

You can see that the file I/O section of the script is wrapped in a `try` block. It is generally considered good coding practice to have small `try` blocks and catch the relevant exceptions at the end of each. This makes your exception handling code easier to write and maintain because you can see what you are dealing with.

If you cannot open the file, you throw a `fileOpenException`; if you cannot lock the file, you throw a `fileLockException`; and if you cannot write to the file, you throw a `fileWriteException`.

Look at the `catch` blocks. To illustrate a point, we have included only two: one to handle `fileOpenExceptions` and one to handle `Exceptions`. Because the other exceptions inherit from `Exception`, they will be caught by the second `catch` block. `Catch` blocks are matched on the same basis as the `instanceof` operator. This is a good reason for extending your own exception classes from a single class.

One important warning: If you raise an exception for which you have not written a matching catch block, PHP will report a fatal error.

Exceptions and PHP's Other Error Handling Mechanisms

In addition to the exception handling mechanism discussed in this chapter, PHP has complex error handling support, which we consider in Chapter 25, "Debugging." Note that the process of raising and handling exceptions does not interfere or prevent this error handling mechanism from operating.

In Listing 7.5, notice how the call to `fopen()` is still prefaced with the `@` error suppression operator. If it fails, PHP will issue a warning that may or may not be reported or logged depending on the error reporting settings in `php.ini`. These settings are discussed at length in Chapter 25, but you need to know that this warning will still be issued regardless of whether you raise an exception.

Further Reading

Because exception handling is new to PHP, not much has been written on the subject. However, basic information about exception handling is plentiful. Sun has a good tutorial about what exceptions are and why you might want to use them (written from a Java perspective, of course) at http://java.sun.com/docs/books/tutorial/essential/exceptions/definition.html.

Next

The next part of the book deals with MySQL. We explain how to create and populate a MySQL database and then link what you've learned to PHP so that you can access your database from the Web.

II

Using MySQL

8

Designing Your Web Database

NOW THAT YOU ARE FAMILIAR WITH THE BASICS of PHP, you can begin looking at integrating a database into your scripts. As you might recall, Chapter 2, "Storing and Retrieving Data," described the advantages of using a relational database instead of a flat file. They include

- RDBMSs can provide faster access to data than flat files.
- RDBMSs can be easily queried to extract sets of data that fit certain criteria.
- RDBMSs have built-in mechanisms for dealing with concurrent access so that you, as a programmer, don't have to worry about it.
- RDBMSs provide random access to your data.
- RDBMSs have built-in privilege systems.

For some concrete examples, using a relational database allows you to quickly and easily answer queries about where your customers are from, which of your products is selling the best, or what types of customers spend the most. This information can help you improve the site to attract and keep more users but would be very difficult to distill from a flat file.

The database that you will use in this part of the book is MySQL. Before we get into MySQL specifics in the next chapter, we need to discuss

- Relational database concepts and terminology
- Web database design
- Web database architecture

You will learn the following in this part of the book:

- Chapter 9, "Creating Your Web Database," covers the basic configuration you will need to connect your MySQL database to the Web. You will learn how to create users, databases, tables, and indexes, and learn about MySQL's different storage engines.

- Chapter 10, "Working with Your MySQL Database," explains how to query the database and add, delete, and update records, all from the command line.
- Chapter 11, "Accessing Your MySQL Database from the Web with PHP," explains how to connect PHP and MySQL together so that you can use and administer your database from a web interface. You will learn two methods of doing this: using PHP's MySQL library and using the PEAR:DB database abstraction layer.
- Chapter 12, "Advanced MySQL Administration," covers MySQL administration in more detail, including details of the privilege system, security, and optimization.
- Chapter 13, "Advanced MySQL Programming," covers the storage engines in more detail, including coverage of transactions, full text search, and stored procedures.

Relational Database Concepts

Relational databases are, by far, the most commonly used type of database. They depend on a sound theoretical basis in relational algebra. You don't need to understand relational theory to use a relational database (which is a good thing), but you do need to understand some basic database concepts.

Tables

Relational databases are made up of relations, more commonly called *tables*. A table is exactly what it sounds like—a table of data. If you've used an electronic spreadsheet, you've already used a table.

Look at the sample table in Figure 8.1. It contains the names and addresses of the customers of a bookstore named Book-O-Rama.

CUSTOMERS

CustomerID	Name	Address	City
1	Julie Smith	25 Oak Street	Airport West
2	Alan Wong	1/47 Haines Avenue	Box Hill
3	Michelle Arthur	357 North Road	Yarraville

Figure 8.1   Book-O-Rama's customer details are stored in a table.

The table has a name (Customers); a number of columns, each corresponding to a different piece of data; and rows that correspond to individual customers.

Columns

Each column in the table has a unique name and contains different data. Additionally, each column has an associated data type. For instance, in the Customers table in Figure 8.1, you can see that CustomerID is an integer and the other three columns are strings. Columns are sometimes called *fields* or *attributes*.

Rows

Each row in the table represents a different customer. Because of the tabular format, each row has the same attributes. Rows are also called *records* or *tuples*.

Values

Each row consists of a set of individual values that correspond to columns. Each value must have the data type specified by its column.

Keys

You need to have a way of identifying each specific customer. Names usually aren't a very good way of doing this. If you have a common name, you probably understand why. Consider Julie Smith from the Customers table, for example. If you open your telephone directory, you may find too many listings of that name to count.

You could distinguish Julie in several ways. Chances are, she's the only Julie Smith living at her address. Talking about "Julie Smith, of 25 Oak Street, Airport West" is pretty cumbersome and sounds too much like legalese. It also requires using more than one column in the table.

What we have done in this example, and what you will likely do in your applications, is assign a unique CustomerID. This is the same principle that leads to your having a unique bank account number or club membership number. It makes storing your details in a database easier. An artificially assigned identification number can be guaranteed to be unique. Few pieces of real information, even if used in combination, have this property.

The identifying column in a table is called the *key* or the *primary key*. A key can also consist of multiple columns. If, for example, you choose to refer to Julie as "Julie Smith, of 25 Oak Street, Airport West," the key would consist of the Name, Address, and City columns and could not be guaranteed to be unique.

Databases usually consist of multiple tables and use a key as a reference from one table to another. Figure 8.2 shows a second table added to the database. This one stores orders placed by customers. Each row in the Orders table represents a single order, placed by a single customer. You know who the customer is because you store her CustomerID. You can look at the order with OrderID 2, for example, and see that the customer with CustomerID 1 placed it. If you then look at the Customers table, you can see that CustomerID 1 refers to Julie Smith.

CUSTOMERS

CustomerID	Name	Address	City
1	Julie Smith	25 Oak Street	Airport West
2	Alan Wong	1/47 Haines Avenue	Box Hill
3	Michelle Arthur	357 North Road	Yarraville

ORDERS

OrderID	CustomerID	Amount	Date
1	3	27.50	02-Apr-2000
2	1	12.99	15-Apr-2000
3	2	74.00	19-Apr-2000
4	3	6.99	01-May-2000

Figure 8.2   Each order in the Orders table refers to a customer from the Customers table.

The relational database term for this relationship is *foreign key*. CustomerID is the primary key in Customers, but when it appears in another table, such as Orders, it is referred to as a foreign key.

You might wonder why we chose to have two separate tables. Why not just store Julie's address in the Orders table? We explore this issue in more detail in the next section.

Schemas

The complete set of table designs for a database is called the database *schema*. It is akin to a blueprint for the database. A schema should show the tables along with their columns, and the primary key of each table and any foreign keys. A schema does not include any data, but you might want to show sample data with your schema to explain what it is for. The schema can be shown in informal diagrams as we have done, in *entity relationship diagrams* (which are not covered in this book), or in a text form, such as

Customers(CustomerID, Name, Address, City)

Orders(OrderID, CustomerID, Amount, Date)

Underlined terms in the schema are primary keys in the relation in which they are underlined. Italic terms are foreign keys in the relation in which they appear italic.

Relationships

Foreign keys represent a relationship between data in two tables. For example, the link from `Orders` to `Customers` represents a relationship between a row in the `Orders` table and a row in the `Customers` table.

Three basic kinds of relationships exist in a relational database. They are classified according to the number of elements on each side of the relationship. Relationships can be either one-to-one, one-to-many, or many-to-many.

A one-to-one relationship means that one of each thing is used in the relationship. For example, if you put addresses in a separate table from `Customers`, they would have a one-to-one relationship between them. You could have a foreign key from `Addresses` to `Customers` or the other way around (both are not required).

In a one-to-many relationship, one row in one table is linked to many rows in another table. In this example, one `Customer` might place many `Orders`. In these relationships, the table that contains the many rows has a foreign key to the table with the one row. Here, we put the `CustomerID` into the `Order` table to show the relationship.

In a many-to-many relationship, many rows in one table are linked to many rows in another table. For example, if you have two tables, `Books` and `Authors`, you might find that one book was written by two coauthors, each of whom had written other books, on their own or possibly with other authors. This type of relationship usually gets a table all to itself, so you might have `Books`, `Authors`, and `Books_Authors`. This third table would contain only the keys of the other tables as foreign keys in pairs, to show which authors are involved with which books.

How to Design Your Web Database

Knowing when you need a new table and what the key should be can be something of an art. You can read reams of information about entity relationship diagrams and database normalization, which are beyond the scope of this book. Most of the time, however, you can follow a few basic design principles. Let's consider them in the context of Book-O-Rama.

Think About the Real-World Objects You Are Modeling

When you create a database, you are usually modeling real-world items and relationships and storing information about those objects and relationships.

Generally, each class of real-world objects you model needs its own table. Think about it: You want to store the same information about all your customers. If a set of data has the same "shape," you can easily create a table corresponding to that data.

In the Book-O-Rama example, you want to store information about customers, the books that you sell, and details of the orders. The customers all have names and addresses. Each order has a date, a total amount, and a set of books that were ordered. Each book has an International Standard Book Number (ISBN), an author, a title, and a price.

This set of information suggests you need at least three tables in this database: Customers, Orders, and Books. This initial schema is shown in Figure 8.3.

CUSTOMERS

CustomerID	Name	Address	City
1	Julie Smith	25 Oak Street	Airport West
2	Alan Wong	1/47 Haines Avenue	Box Hill
3	Michelle Arthur	357 North Road	Yarraville

ORDERS

OrderID	CustomerID	Amount	Date
1	3	27.50	02-Apr-2000
2	1	12.99	15-Apr-2000
3	2	74.00	19-Apr-2000
4	3	6.99	01-May-2000

BOOKS

ISBN	Author	Title	Price
0-672-31697-8	Michael Morgan	Java 2 for Professional Developers	34.99
0-672-31745-1	Thomas Down	Installing GNU/Linux	24.99
0-672-31509-2	Pruitt, et al.	Teach Yourself GIMP in 24 Hours	24.99

Figure 8.3   The initial schema consists of Customers, Orders, and Books.

At present, you can't tell from the model which books were ordered in each order. We will deal with this situation shortly.

Avoid Storing Redundant Data

Earlier, we asked the question: "Why not just store Julie Smith's address in the Orders table?"

If Julie orders from Book-O-Rama on a number of occasions, which you hope she will, you will end up storing her data multiple times. You might end up with an Orders table that looks like the one shown in Figure 8.4.

OrderID	Amount	Date	CustomerID	Name	Address	City
12	199.50	25-Apr-2000	1	Julie Smith	25 Oak Street	Airport West
13	43.00	29-Apr-2000	1	Julie Smith	25 Oak Street	Airport West
14	15.99	30-Apr-2000	1	Julie Smith	25 Oak Street	Airport West
15	23.75	01-May-2000	1	Julie Smith	25 Oak Street	Airport West

Figure 8.4   A database design that stores redundant data takes up extra space and can cause anomalies in the data.

Such a design creates two basic problems:

- It's a waste of space. Why store Julie's details three times if you need to store them only once?

- It can lead to *update anomalies*—that is, situations in which you change the database and end up with inconsistent data. The integrity of the data is violated, and you no longer know which data is correct and which is incorrect. This scenario generally leads to losing information.

Three kinds of update anomalies need to be avoided: modification, insertion, and deletion anomalies.

If Julie moves to a new house while she has pending orders, you will need to update her address in three places instead of one, doing three times as much work. You might easily overlook this fact and change her address in only one place, leading to inconsistent data in the database (a very bad thing). These problems are called *modification anomalies* because they occur when you are trying to modify the database.

With this design, you need to insert Julie's details every time you take an order, so each time you must make sure that her details are consistent with the existing rows in the table. If you don't check, you might end up with two rows of conflicting information about Julie. For example, one row might indicate that Julie lives in Airport West, and another might indicate she lives in Airport. This scenario is called an *insertion anomaly* because it occurs when data is being inserted.

The third kind of anomaly is called a *deletion anomaly* because it occurs (surprise, surprise) when you are deleting rows from the database. For example, imagine that after an order has been shipped, you delete it from the database. After all Julie's current orders have been filled, they are all deleted from the Orders table. This means that you no longer have a record of Julie's address. You can't send her any special offers, and the next time she wants to order something from Book-O-Rama, you have to get her details all over again.

Generally, you should design your database so that none of these anomalies occur.

Use Atomic Column Values

Using atomic column values means that in each attribute in each row, you store only one thing. For example, you need to know what books make up each order. You could do this in several ways.

One solution would be to add a column to the Orders table listing all the books that have been ordered, as shown in Figure 8.5.

ORDERS

OrderID	CustomerID	Amount	Date	Books Ordered
1	3	27.50	02-Apr-2000	0-672-31697-8
2	1	12.99	15-Apr-2000	0-672-31745-1, 0-672-31509-2
3	2	74.00	19-Apr-2000	0-672-31697-8
4	3	6.99	01-May-2000	0-672-31745-1, 0-672-31509-2, 0-672-31697-8

Figure 8.5   With this design, the Books Ordered attribute in each row has multiple values.

This solution isn't a good idea for a few reasons. What you're really doing is nesting a whole table inside one column—a table that relates orders to books. When you set up your columns this way, it becomes more difficult to answer such questions as "How many copies of *Java 2 for Professional Developers* have been ordered?" The system can no longer just count the matching fields. Instead, it has to parse each attribute value to see whether it contains a match anywhere inside it.

Because you're really creating a table-inside-a-table, you should really just create that new table. This new table, called Order_Items, is shown in Figure 8.6.

ORDER_ITEMS

OrderID	ISBN	Quantity
1	0-672-31697-8	1
2	0-672-31745-1	2
2	0-672-31509-2	1
3	0-672-31697-8	1
4	0-672-31745-1	1
4	0-672-31509-2	2
4	0-672-31697-8	1

Figure 8.6   This design makes it easier to search for particular books that have been ordered.

This table provides a link between the Orders and Books tables. This type of table is common when a many-to-many relationship exists between two objects; in this case, one order might consist of many books, and each book can be ordered by many people.

Choose Sensible Keys

Make sure that the keys you choose are unique. In this case, we created a special key for customers (`CustomerID`) and for orders (`OrderID`) because these real-world objects might not naturally have an identifier that can be guaranteed to be unique. You don't need to create a unique identifier for books; this has already been done, in the form of an ISBN. For `Order_Item`, you can add an extra key if you want, but the combination of the two attributes `OrderID` and `ISBN` are unique as long as more than one copy of the same book in an order is treated as one row. For this reason, the table `Order_Items` has a `Quantity` column.

Think About the Questions You Want to Ask the Database

Continuing from the previous section, think about what questions you want the database to answer. (For example, what are Book-O-Rama's best-selling books?) Make sure that the database contains all the data required and that the appropriate links exist between tables to answer the questions you have.

Avoid Designs with Many Empty Attributes

If you wanted to add book reviews to the database, you could do so in at least two ways. These two approaches are shown in Figure 8.7.

BOOKS

ISBN	Author	Title	Price	Review
0-672-31697-8	Michael Morgan	Java 2 for Professional Developers	34.99	
0-672-31745-1	Thomas Down	Installing Debian GNU/Linux	24.99	
0-672-31509-2	Pruitt, et al.	Teach Yourself GIMP in 24 Hours	24.99	

BOOK_REVIEWS

ISBN	Review

Figure 8.7   To add reviews, you can either add a `Review` column to the Books table or add a table specifically for reviews.

The first way means adding a `Review` column to the `Books` table. This way, there is a field for the `Review` to be added for each book. If many books are in the database, and the reviewer doesn't plan to review them all, many rows won't have a value in this attribute. This is called *having a null value*.

Having many null values in your database is a bad idea. It wastes storage space and causes problems when working out totals and other functions on numerical columns. When a user sees a null in a table, he doesn't know whether it's because this attribute is irrelevant, whether the database contains a mistake, or whether the data just hasn't been entered yet.

You can generally avoid problems with many nulls by using an alternate design. In this case, you can use the second design proposed in Figure 8.7. Here, only books with a review are listed in the `Book_Reviews` table, along with their reviews.

Note that this design is based on the idea of having a single in-house reviewer; that is, a one-to-one relationship exists between `Books` and `Reviews`. If you want to include many reviews of the same book, this would be a one-to-many relationship, and you would need to go with the second design option. Also, with one review per book, you can use the ISBN as the primary key in the `Book_Reviews` table. If you have multiple reviews per book, you should introduce a unique identifier for each.

Summary of Table Types

You will usually find that your database design ends up consisting of two kinds of tables:

- Simple tables that describe a real-world object. They might also contain keys to other simple objects with which they have a one-to-one or one-to-many relationship. For example, one customer might have many orders, but an order is placed by a single customer. Thus, you put a reference to the customer in the order.

- Linking tables that describe a many-to-many relationship between two real objects such as the relationship between `Orders` and `Books`. These tables are often associated with some kind of real-world transaction.

Web Database Architecture

Now that we've discussed the internal architecture of the database, we can look at the external architecture of a web database system and discuss the methodology for developing a web database system.

Architecture

The basic operation of a web server is shown in Figure 8.8. This system consists of two objects: a web browser and a web server. A communication link is required between them. A web browser makes a request of the server. The server sends back a response. This architecture suits a server delivering static pages well. The architecture that delivers a database-backed website, however, is somewhat more complex.

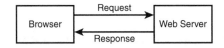

Figure 8.8   The client/server relationship between a web browser and web
server requires communication.

The web database applications you will build in this book follow a general web database
structure like the one shown in Figure 8.9. Most of this structure should already be
familiar to you.

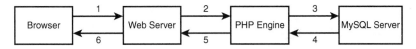

Figure 8.9   The basic web database architecture consists of the web browser,
web server, scripting engine, and database server.

A typical web database transaction consists of the following stages, which are numbered
in Figure 8.9. Let's examine the stages in the context of the Book-O-Rama example:

1. A user's web browser issues an HTTP request for a particular web page. For example, using an HTML form, she might have requested a search for all the books at
   Book-O-Rama written by Laura Thomson. The search results page is called
   `results.php`.

2. The web server receives the request for `results.php`, retrieves the file, and passes
   it to the PHP engine for processing.

3. The PHP engine begins parsing the script. Inside the script is a command to connect to the database and execute a query (perform the search for books). PHP
   opens a connection to the MySQL server and sends on the appropriate query.

4. The MySQL server receives the database query, processes it, and sends the results—
   a list of books—back to the PHP engine.

5. The PHP engine finishes running the script, which usually involves formatting the
   query results nicely in HTML. It then returns the resulting HTML to the web
   server.

6. The web server passes the HTML back to the browser, where the user can see the
   list of books she requested.

The process is basically the same regardless of which scripting engine or database server you use. Often the web server software, PHP engine, and database server all run on the same machine. However, it is also quite common for the database server to run on a different machine. You might do this for reasons of security, increased capacity, or load spreading. From a development perspective, this approach is much the same to work with, but it might offer some significant advantages in performance.

As your applications increase in size and complexity, you will begin to separate your PHP applications into tiers—typically, a database layer that interfaces to MySQL, a business logic layer that contains the core of the application, and a presentation layer that manages the HTML output. However, the basic architecture shown in Figure 8.9 still holds; you just add more structure to the PHP section.

Further Reading

In this chapter, we covered some guidelines for relational database design. If you want to delve into the theory behind relational databases, you can try reading books by some of the relational gurus such as C.J. Date. Be warned, however, that the material can be comparatively theoretical and might not be immediately relevant to a commercial web developer. The average web database tends not to be that complicated.

Next

In the next chapter, you start setting up your MySQL database. First, you learn how to set up a MySQL database for the web, how to query it, and then how to query it from PHP.

Creating Your Web Database

IN THIS CHAPTER, WE EXPLAIN HOW TO set up a MySQL database for use on a website.
Key topics covered in this chapter include

- Creating a database
- Setting up users and privileges
- Introducing the privilege system
- Creating database tables
- Creating indexes
- Choosing column types in MySQL

In this chapter, we follow through with the Book-O-Rama online bookstore application
discussed in the preceding chapter. As a reminder, here is the schema for the Book-O-
Rama application:

```
Customers(CustomerID, Name, Address, City)

Orders(OrderID, CustomerID, Amount, Date)

Books(ISBN, Author, Title, Price)

Order_Items(OrderID, ISBN, Quantity)

Book_Reviews(ISBN, Reviews)
```

Remember that each primary key is underlined and each foreign key is italic.
To use the material in this section, you must have access to MySQL. This usually
means that you

- Have completed the basic install of MySQL on your web server. This step includes
  - Installing the files
  - Setting up a user for MySQL to run as

- Setting up your path
- Running `mysql_install_db`, if required
- Setting the root password
- Deleting the anonymous user and test database
- Starting the MySQL server for the first time and setting it up to run automatically

If you've completed all these tasks, you can go right ahead and read this chapter. If you haven't, you can find instructions on how to do these things in Appendix A, "Installing PHP5 and MySQL5."

If you have problems at any point in this chapter, your MySQL system might not be set up correctly. If that is the case, refer to this list and Appendix A to make sure that your setup is correct.

- Have access to MySQL on a machine that you do not administer, such as a web hosting service, a machine at your workplace, and so on.

If this is the case, to work through the examples or to create your own database, you need to have your administrator set up a user and database for you to work with and tell you the username, password, and database name she has assigned to you.

You can either skip the sections of this chapter that explain how to set up users and databases or read them to better explain what you need to your system administrator. As a typical user, you cannot execute the commands to create users and databases.

The examples in this chapter were built and tested with the latest MySQL 5.0 version at the time of writing. Some earlier versions of MySQL have less functionality. You should install or upgrade to the most current stable release at the time of reading. You can download the current release from the MySQL site at
    http://mysql.com

In this book, we interact with MySQL using a command-line client called the MySQL monitor, which comes with every MySQL installation. However, you can use other clients. If you are using MySQL in a hosted web environment, for example, system administrators will often provide the phpMyAdmin browser-based interface for you to use. Different GUI clients obviously involve slightly different procedures from what we describe here, but you should be able to adapt these instructions fairly easily.

Using the MySQL Monitor

In the MySQL examples in this chapter and the next, each command ends with a semicolon (;). It tells MySQL to execute the command. If you leave off the semicolon, nothing will happen. This is a common problem for new users.

As a result of leaving off the semicolon, you can have new lines in the middle of a command. We used this scheme to make the examples easier to read. You can see where we have used this approach because MySQL provides a continuation symbol; it's an arrow that looks like this:

```
mysql> grant select
    ->
```

This symbol means MySQL expects more input. Until you type the semicolon, you get these characters each time you press Enter.

Another point to note is that SQL statements are not case sensitive, but database and table names can be (more on this topic later).

Logging In to MySQL

To log in to MySQL, go to a command-line interface on your machine and type the following:

```
mysql -h hostname -u username -p
```

The mysql command invokes the MySQL monitor, which is a command-line client that connects you to the MySQL server.

The -h switch specifies the host to which you want to connect—that is, the machine on which the MySQL server is running. If you're running this command on the same machine as the MySQL server, you can leave out this switch and the hostname parameter. If not, you should replace the hostname parameter with the name of the machine where the MySQL server is running.

The -u switch specifies the username you want to connect as. If you do not specify, the default will be the username you are logged in to the operating system as.

If you have installed MySQL on your own machine or server, you need to log in as root and create the database we'll use in this section. Assuming that you have a clean install, root is the only user you'll have to begin with. If you are using MySQL on a machine administered by somebody else, use the username that person gave you.

The -p switch tells the server you want to connect using a password. You can leave it out if a password has not been set for the user you are logging in as.

If you are logging in as root and have not set a password for root, we strongly recommend that you visit Appendix A right now. Without a root password, your system is insecure.

You don't need to include the password on this line. The MySQL server will ask you for it. In fact, it's better if you don't include it here. If you enter the password on the command line, it will appear as plain text on the screen and will be quite simple for other users to discover.

After you enter the previous command, you should get a response something like this:

```
Enter password:
```

(If this command doesn't work, verify that the MySQL server is running and the `mysql` command is somewhere in your path.)

You should then enter your password. If all goes well, you should see a response something like this:

```
Welcome to the MySQL monitor.  Commands end with ; or \g.
Your MySQL connection id is 1 to server version: 5.0.0-alpha-max-debug

Type 'help;' or '\h' for help. Type '\c' to clear the buffer.

mysql>
```

On your own machine, if you don't get a response similar to this, make sure that you have run `mysql_install_db` if required, you have set the `root` password, and you've typed it in correctly. If it isn't your machine, make sure that you typed in the password correctly.

You should now be at a MySQL command prompt, ready to create the database. If you are using your own machine, follow the guidelines in the next section. If you are using somebody else's machine, these steps should already have been done for you. You can jump ahead to the "Using the Right Database" section. You might want to read the intervening sections for general background, but you cannot run the commands specified there. (Or at least you shouldn't be able to!)

Creating Databases and Users

The MySQL database system can support many different databases. You will generally have one database per application. In the Book-o-Rama example, the database will be called `books`.

Creating the Database

Creating the database is the easiest part. At the MySQL command prompt, type

```
mysql> create database dbname;
```

You should substitute the name of the database you want to create for *dbname*. To begin creating the Book-O-Rama example, create a database called `books`.

That's it. You should see a response like this:

```
Query OK, 1 row affected (0.06 sec)
```

This means everything has worked. If you don't get this response, make sure that you typed the semicolon at the end of the line. A semicolon tells MySQL that you are finished, and it should actually execute the command.

Setting Up Users and Privileges

A MySQL system can have many users. The `root` user should generally be used for administration purposes only, for security reasons. For each user who needs to use the system, you need to set up an account and password. They do not need to be the same as usernames and passwords outside MySQL (for example, Unix or NT usernames and passwords). The same principle applies to `root`. Having different passwords for the system and for MySQL is a good idea, especially when it comes to the `root` password.

Setting up passwords for users isn't compulsory, but we strongly recommend that you set up passwords for all the users you create. For the purposes of setting up a web database, it's a good idea to set up at least one user per web application. You might ask, "Why would I want to do this?" The answer lies in privileges.

Introducing MySQL's Privilege System

One of the best features of MySQL is that it supports a sophisticated privilege system. A *privilege* is the right to perform a particular action on a particular object and is associated with a particular user. The concept is similar to file permissions. When you create a user within MySQL, you grant her a set of privileges to specify what she can and cannot do within the system.

Principle of Least Privilege

The principle of least privilege can be used to improve the security of any computer system. It's a basic but important principle that is often overlooked. The principle is as follows:

A user (or process) should have the lowest level of privilege required to perform his assigned task.

It applies in MySQL as it does elsewhere. For example, to run queries from the Web, a user does not need all the privileges to which `root` has access. You should therefore create another user who has only the necessary privileges to access the database you just created.

User Setup: The `GRANT` Command

The `GRANT` and `REVOKE` commands enable you to give rights to and take them away from MySQL users at these four levels of privilege:

- Global
- Database
- Table
- Column

We see shortly how each can be applied.

The GRANT command creates users and gives them privileges. The general form of the GRANT command is

```
GRANT privileges [columns]
ON item
TO user_name [IDENTIFIED BY 'password']
[REQUIRE ssl_options]
[WITH [GRANT OPTION | limit_options]  ]
```

The clauses in square brackets are optional. There are a number of placeholders in this syntax. The first, *privileges*, should be a comma-separated list of privileges. MySQL has a defined set of such privileges, which are described in the next section.

The *columns* placeholder is optional. You can use it to specify privileges on a column-by-column basis. You can use a single column name or a comma-separated list of column names.

The *item* placeholder is the database or table to which the new privileges apply. You can grant privileges on all the databases by specifying *.* as the *item*. This is called granting *global* privileges. You can also do this by specifying * alone if you are not using any particular database. More commonly, you can specify all tables in a database as *dbname.**, on a single table as *dbname.tablename*, or on specific columns by specifying *dbname.tablename* and some specific columns in the *columns* placeholder. These examples represent the three other levels of privilege available: *database*, *table*, and *column*, respectively. If you are using a specific database when you issue this command, *tablename* on its own will be interpreted as a table in the current database.

The *user_name* should be the name you want the user to log in as in MySQL. Remember that it does not have to be the same as a system login name. The *user_name* in MySQL can also contain a hostname. You can use this to differentiate between, say, laura (interpreted as laura@localhost) and laura@somewhere.com. This capability is quite useful because users from different domains often have the same name. It also increases security because you can specify where users can connect from, and even which tables or databases they can access from a particular location.

The *password* placeholder should be the password you want the user to log in with. The usual rules for selecting passwords apply. We discuss security more later, but a password should not be easily guessable. This means that a password should not be a dictionary word or the same as the username. Ideally, it should contain a mixture of upper- and lowercase and nonalphabetic characters.

The REQUIRE clause allows you to specify that the user must connect via Secure Sockets Layer (SSL) and specify other SSL options. For more information on SSL connections to MySQL, refer to the MySQL manual.

The WITH GRANT OPTION option, if specified, allows the specified user to grant her own privileges to others.

You can instead specify the WITH clause as

```
MAX_QUERIES_PER_HOUR n
```

or

```
MAX_UPDATES_PER_HOUR n
```

or

```
MAX_CONNECTIONS_PER_HOUR n
```

These clauses allow you to limit the number of queries, updates, or connections per hour a user may make. They can be useful for limiting individual user load on shared systems.

Privileges are stored in five system tables, in the database called `mysql`. These five tables are called `mysql.user`, `mysql.db`, `mysql.host`, `mysql.tables_priv`, and `mysql.columns_priv`. As an alternative to GRANT, you can alter these tables directly. We discuss exactly how these tables work and how you can alter them directly in Chapter 12, "Advanced MySQL Administration."

Types and Levels of Privileges

Three basic types of privileges exist in MySQL: privileges suitable for granting to regular users, privileges suitable for administrators, and a couple of special privileges. Any user can be granted any of these privileges, but it's usually sensible to restrict the administrator type privileges to administrators, according to the principle of least privilege.

You should grant privileges to users only for the databases and tables they need to use. You should not grant access to the `mysql` database to anyone except an administrator. This is the place where all the users, passwords, and so on are stored. (We look at this database in Chapter 12.)

Privileges for regular users directly relate to specific types of SQL commands and whether a user is allowed to run them. We discuss these SQL commands in detail in the next chapter. For now, let's look at a conceptual description of what they do. These privileges are shown in Table 9.1. The items under the Applies To column are the objects to which privileges of this type can be granted.

Table 9.1 **Privileges for Users**

Privilege	Applies To	Description
SELECT	tables, columns	Allows users to select rows (records) from tables.
INSERT	tables, columns	Allows users to insert new rows into tables.
UPDATE	tables, columns	Allows users to modify values in existing table rows.
DELETE	tables	Allows users to delete existing table rows.
INDEX	tables	Allows users to create and drop indexes on particular tables.
ALTER	tables	Allows users to alter the structure of existing tables by, for example, adding columns, renaming columns or tables, and changing data types of columns.

Table 9.1 **Continued**

Privilege	Applies To	Description
CREATE	databases, tables	Allows users to create new databases or tables. If a particular database or table is specified in GRANT, they can only create that database or table, which means they will have to drop it first.
DROP	databases, tables	Allows users to drop (delete) databases or tables.

Most of the privileges for regular users are relatively harmless in terms of system security. The ALTER privilege can be used to work around the privilege system by renaming tables, but it is widely needed by users. Security is always a trade-off between usability and safety. You should make your own decision when it comes to ALTER, but it is often granted to users.

In addition to the privileges listed in Table 9.1, the REFERENCES and EXECUTE privileges are currently unused, and a GRANT privilege is granted with WITH GRANT OPTION rather than in the *privileges* list.

Table 9.2 shows the privileges suitable for use by administrative users.

Table 9.2 **Privileges for Administrators**

Privilege	Description
CREATE TEMPORARY TABLES	Allows an administrator to use the keyword TEMPORARY in a CREATE TABLE statement.
FILE	Allows data to be read into tables from files and vice versa.
LOCK TABLES	Allows the explicit use of a LOCK TABLES statement.
PROCESS	Allows an administrator to view server processes belonging to all users.
RELOAD	Allows an administrator to reload grant tables and flush privileges, hosts, logs, and tables.
REPLICATION CLIENT	Allows use of SHOW STATUS on replication masters and slaves. Replication is explained in Chapter 12.
REPLICATION SLAVE	Allows replication slave servers to connect to the master server. Replication is explained in Chapter 12.
SHOW DATABASES	Allows a list of all databases to be seen with a SHOW DATABASES statement. Without this privilege, users see only databases on which they have other privileges.
SHUTDOWN	Allows an administrator to shut down the MySQL server.
SUPER	Allows an administrator to kill threads belonging to any user.

You are able to grant these privileges to nonadministrators, but you should use extreme caution if you are considering doing so.

The FILE privilege is a bit different. It is useful for users because loading data from files can save a lot of time re-entering data each time to get it into the database. However, file loading can be used to load any file that the MySQL server can see, including databases belonging to other users and, potentially, password files. Grant this privilege with caution or offer to load the data for the user.

Two special privileges also exist, and they are shown in Table 9.3.

Table 9.3   **Special Privileges**

Privilege	Description
ALL	Grants all the privileges listed in Tables 9.1 and 9.2. You can also write ALL PRIVILEGES instead of ALL.
USAGE	Grants no privileges. This privilege creates a user and allows her to log on, but it doesn't allow her to do anything. Usually, you will add more privileges later.

The REVOKE Command

The opposite of GRANT is REVOKE. You use it to take privileges away from a user. It is similar to GRANT in syntax:

```
REVOKE privileges [(columns)]
ON item
FROM user_name
```

If you have given the WITH GRANT OPTION clause, you can revoke this (along with all other privileges) by adding

```
REVOKE All PRIVILEGES, GRANT
FROM user_name
```

Examples Using GRANT and REVOKE

To set up an administrator, you can type

```
mysql> grant all
    -> on *
    -> to fred identified by 'mnb123'
    -> with grant option;
```

This command grants all privileges on all databases to a user called Fred with the password mnb123 and allows him to pass on those privileges.

Chances are you don't want this user in your system, so go ahead and revoke him:

```
mysql> revoke all privileges, grant
    -> from fred;
```

Now you can set up a regular user with no privileges:

```
mysql> grant usage
    -> on books.*
    -> to sally identified by 'magic123';
```

After talking to Sally, you know a bit more about what she wants to do, so you can give her the appropriate privileges:

```
mysql> grant select, insert, update, delete, index, alter, create, drop
    -> on books.*
    -> to sally;
```

Note that you don't need to specify Sally's password to give her privileges.

If you decide that Sally has been up to something in the database, you might decide to reduce her privileges:

```
mysql> revoke alter, create, drop
    -> on books.*
    -> from sally;
```

And later, when she doesn't need to use the database any more, you can revoke her privileges altogether:

```
mysql> revoke all
    -> on books.*
    -> from sally;
```

Setting Up a User for the Web

You need to set up a user for your PHP scripts to connect to MySQL. Again, you can apply the privilege of least principle: What should the scripts be able to do?

In most cases, they only need to run SELECT, INSERT, DELETE, and UPDATE queries. You can set up these privileges as follows:

```
mysql> grant select, insert, delete, update
    -> on books.*
    -> to bookorama identified by 'bookorama123';
```

Obviously, for security reasons, you should choose a better password than the one shown here.

If you use a web hosting service, you usually get access to the other user-type privileges on a database the service creates for you. It typically gives you the same *user_name* and *password* for command-line use (setting up tables and so on) and for web script connections (querying the database). Using the same username and password for both is marginally less secure. You can set up a user with this level of privilege as follows:

```
mysql> grant select, insert, update, delete, index, alter, create, drop
    -> on books.*
    -> to bookorama identified by 'bookorama123';
```

Go ahead and set up this second version of the user because you need to use it in the next section.

Logging Out as `root`

You can log out of the MySQL monitor by typing **quit**. You should log back in as your web user to test that everything is working correctly. If the GRANT statement that you ran was executed, but you are denied access when trying to log in, this usually means you have not deleted the anonymous users as part of the installation process. Log back in as `root` and consult Appendix A for instructions on how to delete the anonymous accounts. You should then be able to log in as the web user.

Using the Right Database

If you've reached this stage, you should be logged in to a user-level MySQL account ready to test the sample code, either because you've just set it up or because your web server administrator has set it up for you.

The first step you need to take when you log in is to specify which database you want to use. You can do this by typing

```
mysql> use dbname;
```

where *dbname* is the name of your database.

Alternatively, you can avoid the `use` command by specifying the database when you log in, as follows:

```
mysql -D dbname -h hostname -u username -p
```

In this example, you can use the `books` database:

```
mysql> use books;
```

When you type this command, MySQL should give you a response such as

```
Database changed
```

If you don't select a database before starting work, MySQL will give you an error message such as

```
ERROR 1046 (3D000): No Database Selected
```

Creating Database Tables

The next step in setting up the database is to actually create the tables. You can do this using the SQL command CREATE TABLE. The general form of a CREATE TABLE statement is

```
CREATE TABLE tablename(columns)
```

You should replace the *tablename* placeholder with the name of the table you want to create and the *columns* placeholder with a comma-separated list of the columns in your table. Each column will have a name followed by a data type.

Here's the Book-O-Rama schema again:

```
Customers(CustomerID, Name, Address, City)


Orders(OrderID, CustomerID, Amount, Date)


Books(ISBN, Author, Title, Price)


Order_Items(OrderID, ISBN, Quantity)


Book_Reviews(ISBN, Reviews)
```

Listing 9.1 shows the SQL to create these tables, assuming you have already created the database called books. You can find this SQL in the file chapter9/bookorama.sql on the CD-ROM accompanying this book.

You can run an existing SQL file, such as one loaded from the CD-ROM, through MySQL by typing

```
> mysql -h host -u bookorama -D books -p < bookorama.sql
```

(Remember to replace *host* with the name of your host.)

Using file redirection is handy for this task because it means that you can edit your SQL in the text editor of your choice before executing it.

Listing 9.1 bookorama.sql—SQL to Create the Tables for Book-O-Rama

```
create table customers
( customerid int unsigned not null auto_increment primary key,
  name char(50) not null,
  address char(100) not null,
  city char(30) not null
);

create table orders
( orderid int unsigned not null auto_increment primary key,
  customerid int unsigned not null,
  amount float(6,2),
  date date not null
);

create table books
(  isbn char(13) not null primary key,
   author char(50),
```

Listing 9.1   **Continued**

```
   title char(100),
   price float(4,2)
);

create table order_items
( orderid int unsigned not null,
  isbn char(13) not null,
  quantity tinyint unsigned,

  primary key (orderid, isbn)

);
create table book_reviews
(
  isbn char(13) not null primary key,
  review text
);
```

Each table is created by a separate CREATE TABLE statement. You can see that each table in the schema is created with the columns designed in the preceding chapter. Each column has a data type listed after its name, and some of the columns have other specifiers, too.

Understanding What the Other Keywords Mean

NOT NULL means that all the rows in the table must have a value in this attribute. If it isn't specified, the field can be blank (NULL).

AUTO_INCREMENT is a special MySQL feature you can use on integer columns. It means if you leave that field blank when inserting rows into the table, MySQL will automatically generate a unique identifier value. The value will be one greater than the maximum value in the column already. You can have only one of these in each table. Columns that specify AUTO_INCREMENT must be indexed.

PRIMARY KEY after a column name specifies that this column is the primary key for the table. Entries in this column have to be unique. MySQL automatically indexes this column. Where it is used with customerid in the customers table in Listing 9.1, it appears with AUTO_INCREMENT. The automatic index on the primary key takes care of the index required by AUTO_INCREMENT.

You can specify PRIMARY KEY after a column name only for single column primary keys. The PRIMARY KEY clause at the end of the order_items statement is an alternative form. We used it here because the primary key for this table consists of the two columns together. (This also creates an index based on the two columns together.)

UNSIGNED after an integer type means that it can have only a zero or positive value.

Understanding the Column Types

Let's consider the first table as an example:

```
create table customers
( customerid int unsigned not null auto_increment primary key,
  name char(50) not null,
  address char(100) not null,
  city char(30) not null
);
```

When creating any table, you need to make decisions about column types.

The `customers` table has four columns as specified in the schema. The first one, `customerid`, is the primary key, which is specified directly. We decided this will be an integer (data type `int`) and that these IDs should be `unsigned`. We've also taken advantage of the `auto_increment` facility so that MySQL can manage them for us; it's one less thing to worry about.

The other columns are all going to hold string type data. We chose the `char` type for them. This type specifies fixed-width fields. The width is specified in the brackets, so, for example, `name` can have up to 50 characters.

This data type will always allocate 50 characters of storage for the name, even if they're not all used. MySQL will pad the data with spaces to make it the right size. The alternative is `varchar`, which uses only the amount of storage required (plus one byte). There is a small trade-off: `varchar`s use less space on average, but `char`s are faster.

Note that all the columns are declared as NOT NULL. This is a minor optimization you can make wherever possible that also will make things run a bit faster. We address optimization in more detail in Chapter 12.

Some of the other CREATE statements have variations in syntax. Let's look at the `orders` table:

```
create table orders
( orderid int unsigned not null auto_increment primary key,
  customerid int unsigned not null,
  amount float(6,2) ,
  date date not null
);
```

The `amount` column is specified as a floating-point number of type `float`. With most floating-point data types, you can specify the display width and the number of decimal places. In this case, the order amount will be in dollars, so we allowed a reasonably large order total (width 6) and two decimal places for the cents.

The `date` column has the data type `date`.

This particular table specifies that all columns bar the amount as NOT NULL. Why? When an order is entered into the database, you need to create it in orders, add the items to `order_items`, and then work out the amount. You might not know the amount when the order is created, so you can allow for it to be NULL.

The `books` table has some similar characteristics:

```
create table books
(   isbn char(13) not null primary key,
    author char(50),
    title char(100),
    price float(4,2)
);
```

In this case, you don't need to generate the primary key because ISBNs are generated elsewhere. The other fields are left as NULL because a bookstore might know the ISBN of a book before it knows the `title`, `author`, or `price`.

The `order_items` table demonstrates how to create multicolumn primary keys:

```
create table order_items
( orderid int unsigned not null,
  isbn char(13) not null,
  quantity tinyint unsigned,

  primary key (orderid, isbn)
);
```

This table specifies the quantity of a particular book as a TINYINT UNSIGNED, which holds an integer between 0 and 255.

As mentioned previously, multicolumn primary keys need to be specified with a special primary key clause. This clause is used here.

Lastly, consider the `book_reviews` table:

```
create table book_reviews
(
  isbn char(13) not null primary key,
  review text
);
```

This table uses a new data type, `text`, which we have not yet discussed. It is used for longer text, such as an article. There are a few variants on this, which we discuss later in this chapter.

To understand creating tables in more detail, let's discuss column names and identifiers in general and then the data types we can choose for columns. First, though, let's look at the database we've created.

Looking at the Database with SHOW and DESCRIBE

Log in to the MySQL monitor and use the `books` database. You can view the tables in the database by typing

```
mysql> show tables;
```

MySQL then displays a list of all the tables in the database:

```
+-----------------+
| Tables in books |
+-----------------+
| book_reviews    |
| books           |
| customers       |
| order_items     |
| orders          |
+-----------------+
5 rows in set (0.06 sec)
```

You can also use show to see a list of databases by typing

```
mysql> show databases;
```

If you do not have the SHOW DATABASES privilege, you will see listed only the databases on which you have privileges.

You can see more information about a particular table, for example, books, using DESCRIBE:

```
mysql> describe books;
```

MySQL then displays the information you supplied when creating the database:

```
+--------+------------+------+-----+---------+-------+
| Field  | Type       | Null | Key | Default | Extra |
+--------+------------+------+-----+---------+-------+
| isbn   | char(13)   |      | PRI |         |       |
| author | char(50)   | YES  |     | NULL    |       |
| title  | char(100)  | YES  |     | NULL    |       |
| price  | float(4,2) | YES  |     | NULL    |       |
+--------+------------+------+-----+---------+-------+
4 rows in set (0.00 sec)
```

These commands are useful to remind yourself of a column type or to navigate a database that you didn't create.

Creating Indexes

We briefly mentioned indexes already, because designating primary keys creates indexes on those columns.

One common problem faced by new MySQL users is that they complain about poor performance from this database they have heard is lightning fast. This performance problem occurs because they have not created any indexes on their database. (It is possible to create tables with no primary keys or indexes.)

To begin with, the indexes that were created automatically for you will do. If you find that you are running many queries on a column that is not a key, you may want to add an index on that column to improve performance. You can do this with the CREATE INDEX statement. The general form of this statement is

```
CREATE [UNIQUE|FULLTEXT] INDEX index_name
ON table_name (index_column_name [(length)] [ASC|DESC], ...])
```

(FULLTEXT indexes are for indexing text fields; we discuss their use in Chapter 13, "Advanced MySQL Programming.")

The optional length field allows you to specify that only the first length characters of the field will be indexed. You can also specify that an index should be ascending (ASC) or descending (DESC); the default is ascending.

A Note on Table Types

You may be aware that MySQL offers more than one table type or storage engine, including some transaction-safe types. We discuss the table types in Chapter 13. At present, all the tables in the database use the default storage engine, MyISAM.

Understanding MySQL Identifiers

Five kinds of identifiers are used in MySQL: databases, tables, columns, and indexes, which you're already familiar with; and aliases, which we cover in the next chapter.

Databases in MySQL map to directories in the underlying file structure, and tables map to files. This mapping has a direct effect on the names you can give them. It also affects the case sensitivity of these names: If directory and filenames are case sensitive in your operating system, database and table names will be case sensitive (for example, in Unix); otherwise, they won't (for example, under Windows). Column names and alias names are not case sensitive, but you can't use versions of different cases in the same SQL statement.

As a side note, the location of the directory and files containing the data is wherever it was set in configuration. You can check the location on your system by using the mysqladmin facility as follows:

```
mysqladmin variables
```

Then look for the datadir variable.

A summary of possible identifiers is shown in Table 9.4. The only additional exception is that you cannot use ASCII(0), ASCII(255), or the quoting character in identifiers (and to be honest, we're not sure why you would want to).

Table 9.4 **MySQL Identifiers**

Type	Max Length	Case Sensitive?	Characters Allowed
Database	64	same as OS	Anything allowed in a directory name in your OS except the /, \, and . characters
Table	64	same as OS	Anything allowed in a filename in your OS except the / and . characters
Column	64	no	Anything
Index	64	no	Anything
Alias	255	no	Anything

These rules are extremely open.

Since MySQL 3.23.6, you can even have reserved words and special characters of all kinds in identifiers. The only limitation is that if you use anything unusual like this, you have to put it in backticks (located under the tilde key on the top left of most keyboards). For example,

```
create database `create database`;
```

The rules in versions of MySQL (prior to 3.23.6) are more restrictive and don't allow you to do this.

Of course, you should apply common sense to all this freedom. Just because you *can* call a database `create database` doesn't that mean that you *should*. The same principle applies here as in any other kind of programming: Use meaningful identifiers.

Choosing Column Data Types

The three basic column types in MySQL are numeric, date and time, and string. Within each of these categories are a large number of types. We summarize them here and go into more detail about the strengths and weaknesses of each in Chapter 12.

Each of the three types comes in various storage sizes. When you are choosing a column type, the principle is generally to choose the smallest type that your data will fit into.

For many data types, when you are creating a column of that type, you can specify the maximum display length. This is shown in the following tables of data types as M. If it's optional for that type, it is shown in square brackets. The maximum value you can specify for M is 255.

Optional values throughout these descriptions are shown in square brackets.

Numeric Types

The numeric types are either integers or floating-point numbers. For the floating-point numbers, you can specify the number of digits after the decimal place. This value is shown in this book as D. The maximum value you can specify for D is 30 or M-2 (that is, the maximum display length minus two—one character for a decimal point and one for the integral part of the number), whichever is lower.

For integer types, you can also specify whether you want them to be UNSIGNED, as shown in Listing 9.1.

For all numeric types, you can also specify the ZEROFILL attribute. When values from a ZEROFILL column are displayed, they are padded with leading zeros. If you specify a column as ZEROFILL, it will automatically also be UNSIGNED.

The integral types are shown in Table 9.5. Note that the ranges listed in this table show the signed range on one line and the unsigned range on the next.

Table 9.5 **Integral Data Types**

Type	Range	Storage (Bytes)	Description
TINYINT[(M)]	−127..128 or 0..255	1	Very small integers
BIT			Synonym for TINYINT
BOOL			Synonym for TINYINT
SMALLINT[(M)]	−32768..32767 or 0..65535	2	Small integers
MEDIUMINT[(M)]	−8388608.. 8388607 or 0..16777215	3	Medium-sized integers
INT[(M)]	$-2^{31}..2^{31}-1$ or $0..2^{32}-1$	4	Regular integers
INTEGER[(M)]			Synonym for INT
BIGINT[(M)]	$-2^{63}..2^{63}-1$ or $0..2^{64}-1$	8	Big integers

The floating-point types are shown in Table 9.6.

Table 9.6 **Floating-Point Data Types**

Type	Range	Storage (bytes)	Description
FLOAT(*precision*)	Depends on precision	Varies	Can be used to specify single or double precision floating-point numbers.

Table 9.6   **Continued**

Type	Range	Storage (bytes)	Description
FLOAT[(M,D)]	±1.175494351E–38 ±3.402823466E+38	4	Single precision floating-point number. These numbers are equivalent to FLOAT(4) but with a specified display width and number of decimal places.
DOUBLE[(M,D)]	±1. 7976931348623157E +308 ±2.2250738585072014E –308	8	Double precision floating-point number. These numbers are equivalent to FLOAT(8) but with a specified display width and number of decimal places.
DOUBLE PRECISION[(M,D)]	As above		Synonym for DOUBLE[(M, D)].
REAL[(M,D)]	As above		Synonym for DOUBLE[(M, D)].
DECIMAL[(M[,D])]	Varies	M+2	Floating-point number stored as char. The range depends on M, the display width.
NUMERIC[(M,D)]	As above		Synonym for DECIMAL.
DEC[(M,D)]	As above		Synonym for DECIMAL.
FIXED[(M,D)]	As above		Synonym for DECIMAL.

Date and Time Types

MySQL supports a number of date and time types; they are shown in Table 9.7. With all these types, you can input data in either a string or numerical format. It is worth noting that a TIMESTAMP column in a particular row will be set to the date and time of the most recent operation on that row if you don't set it manually. This feature is useful for transaction recording.

Table 9.7 **Date and Time Data Types**

Type	Range	Description
DATE	1000-01-01 9999-12-31	A date. Will be displayed as YYYY-MM-DD.
TIME	–838:59:59 838:59:59	A time. Will be displayed as HH:MM:SS. Note that the range is much wider than you will probably ever want to use.
DATETIME	1000-01-01 00:00:00 9999-12-31 23:59:59	A date and time. Will be displayed as YYYY-MM-DD HH:MM:SS.
TIMESTAMP[(*M*)]	1970-01-01 00:00:00	A timestamp, useful for transaction reporting. The display format depends on the value of *M* (see Table 9.8, which follows).
	Sometime in 2037 timestamps.	The top of the range depends on the limit on Unix.
YEAR[(*2*|*4*)]	70–69 (1970–2069) 1901–2155	A year. You can specify two- or four-digit format. Each has a different range, as shown.

Table 9.8 shows the possible different display types for TIMESTAMP.

Table 9.8 TIMESTAMP **Display Types**

Type Specified	Display
TIMESTAMP	YYYYMMDDHHMMSS
TIMESTAMP(14)	YYYYMMDDHHMMSS
TIMESTAMP(12)	YYMMDDHHMMSS
TIMESTAMP(10)	YYMMDDHHMM
TIMESTAMP(8)	YYYYMMDD
TIMESTAMP(6)	YYMMDD
TIMESTAMP(4)	YYMM
TIMESTAMP(2)	YY

String Types

String types fall into three groups. First, there are plain old strings—that is, short pieces of text. These are the CHAR (fixed-length character) and VARCHAR (variable-length character) types. You can specify the width of each. Columns of type CHAR are padded with spaces to the maximum width regardless of the size of the data, whereas VARCHAR columns vary in width with the data. (Note that MySQL strips the trailing spaces from CHARs when they are *retrieved* and from VARCHARs when they are *stored*.) There is a space versus speed trade-off with these two types, which we discuss in more detail in Chapter 12.

Second, there are TEXT and BLOB types. These types, which come in various sizes, are for longer text or binary data, respectively. BLOBs, or *binary large objects,* can hold anything you like—for example, image or sound data.

In practice, BLOB and TEXT columns are the same except that BLOB is case sensitive and TEXT is not. Because these column types can hold large amounts of data, they require some special considerations. We discuss this issue in Chapter 12.

The third group has two special types: SET and ENUM. The SET type specifies that values in this column must come from a particular set of specified values. Column values can contain more than one value from the set. You can have a maximum of 64 things in the specified set.

ENUM is an enumeration. It is very similar to SET, except that columns of this type can have only one of the specified values or NULL, and you can have a maximum of 65,535 things in the enumeration.

We summarized the string data types in Tables 9.9, 9.10, and 9.11. Table 9.9 shows the plain string types.

Table 9.9 **Regular String Types**

Type	Range	Description
[NATIONAL] CHAR(*M*) [BINARY | ASCII | UNICODE]	0 to 255 characters	Fixed-length string of length *M*, where *M* is between 0 and 255. The NATIONAL keyword specifies that the default character set should be used. This is the default in MySQL anyway, but is included because it is part of the ANSI SQL standard. The BINARY keyword specifies that the data should be treated as case sensitive. (The default is case sensitive.) The ASCII keyword specifies that the latin1 character set will be used for this column. The UNICODE keyword specifies that the ucs character set will be used.
CHAR		Synonym for CHAR(1).
[NATIONAL] VARCHAR(*M*) [BINARY]	1 to 255 characters	Same as above, except they are variable length.

Table 9.10 shows the TEXT and BLOB types. The maximum length of a TEXT field in characters is the maximum size in bytes of files that could be stored in that field.

Table 9.10   TEXT and BLOB Types

Type	Maximum Length (Characters)	Description
TINYBLOB	$2^8 - 1$ (that is, 255)	A tiny binary large object (BLOB) field
TINYTEXT	$2^8 - 1$ (that is, 255)	A tiny TEXT field
BLOB	$2^{16} - 1$ (that is, 65,535)	A normal-sized BLOB field
TEXT	$2^{16} - 1$ (that is, 65,535)	A normal-sized TEXT field
MEDIUMBLOB	$2^{24} - 1$ (that is, 16,777,215)	A medium-sized BLOB field
MEDIUMTEXT	$2^{24} - 1$ (that is, 16,777,215)	A medium-sized TEXT field
LONGBLOB	$2^{32} - 1$ (that is, 4,294,967,295)	A long BLOB field
LONGTEXT	$2^{32} - 1$ (that is, 4,294,967,295)	A long TEXT field

Table 9.11 shows the ENUM and SET types.

Table 9.11   ENUM and SET Types

Type	Maximum Values in Set	Description
ENUM('value1', 'value2',...)	65,535	Columns of this type can hold only *one* of the values listed or NULL.
SET('value1', 'value2',...)	64	Columns of this type can hold a set of the specified values or NULL.

Further Reading

For more information, you can read about setting up a database in the MySQL online manual at http://www.mysql.com/.

Next

Now that you know how to create users, databases, and tables, you can concentrate on interacting with the database. In the next chapter, we look at how to put data in the tables, how to update and delete it, and how to query the database.

10

Working with Your MySQL Database

IN THIS CHAPTER, WE DISCUSS STRUCTURED QUERY LANGUAGE (SQL) and its use in querying databases. You continue developing the Book-O-Rama database by learning how to insert, delete, and update data, and how to ask the database questions.

Key topics covered in this chapter include

- What is SQL?
- Inserting data into the database
- Retrieving data from the database
- Joining tables
- Using subqueries
- Updating records from the database
- Altering tables after creation
- Deleting records from the database
- Dropping tables

We begin by describing what SQL is and why it's a useful thing to understand.

If you haven't set up the Book-O-Rama database, you need to do that before you can run the SQL queries in this chapter. Instructions for doing this are in Chapter 9, "Creating Your Web Database."

What Is SQL?

SQL stands for *Structured Query Language*. It's the most standard language for accessing *relational database management systems (RDBMSs)*. SQL is used to store data to and retrieve it from a database. It is used in database systems such as MySQL, Oracle, PostgreSQL, Sybase, and Microsoft SQL Server, among others.

There's an ANSI standard for SQL, and database systems such as MySQL generally strive to implement this standard. There are some subtle differences between standard SQL and MySQL's SQL. Some of these differences are planned to become standard in future versions of MySQL, and some are deliberate differences. We point out the more important ones as we go. A complete list of the differences between MySQL's SQL and ANSI SQL in any given version can be found in the MySQL online manual. You can find this page at this URL and in many other locations:

    http://www.mysql.com/doc/en/Compatibility.html

You might have heard the terms *Data Definition Language (DDL)*, used for defining databases, and *Data Manipulation Language (DML)*, used for querying databases. SQL covers both of these bases. In Chapter 9, we looked at data definition (DDL) in SQL, so we've already been using it a little. You use DDL when you're initially setting up a database.

You will use the DML aspects of SQL far more frequently because these are the parts that you use to store and retrieve real data in a database.

Inserting Data into the Database

Before you can do a lot with a database, you need to store some data in it. The way you most commonly do this is to use the SQL INSERT statement.

Recall that RDBMSs contain tables, which in turn contain rows of data organized into columns. Each row in a table normally describes some real-world object or relationship, and the column values for that row store information about the real-world object. You can use the INSERT statement to put rows of data into the database.

The usual form of an INSERT statement is

```
INSERT [INTO] table [(column1, column2, column3,...)] VALUES
(value1, value2, value3,...);
```

For example, to insert a record into Book-O-Rama's customers table, you could type

```
insert into customers values
   (NULL, 'Julie Smith', '25 Oak Street', 'Airport West');
```

You can see that we've replaced *table* with the name of the actual table where we want to put the data and the *values* with specific values. The values in this example are all enclosed in quotation marks. Strings should always be enclosed in pairs of single or double quotation marks in MySQL. (We use both in this book.) Numbers and dates do not need quotes.

There are a few interesting things to note about the INSERT statement. The values specified here will be used to fill in the table columns in order. If you want to fill in only some of the columns, or if you want to specify them in a different order, you can list the specific columns in the columns part of the statement. For example,

```
insert into customers (name, city) values
('Melissa Jones', 'Nar Nar Goon North');
```

This approach is useful if you have only partial data about a particular record or if some fields in the record are optional. You can also achieve the same effect with the following syntax:

```
insert into customers
set name='Michael Archer',
    address='12 Adderley Avenue',
    city='Leeton';
```

Also notice that we specified a NULL value for the customerid column when adding Julie Smith and ignored that column when adding the other customers. You might recall that when you set up the database, you created customerid as the primary key for the customers table, so this might seem strange. However, you specified the field as AUTO_INCREMENT. This means that, if you insert a row with a NULL value or no value in this field, MySQL will generate the next number in the auto increment sequence and insert it for you automatically. This behavior is pretty useful.

You can also insert multiple rows into a table at once. Each row should be in its own set of parentheses, and each set of parentheses should be separated by a comma.

Only a few other variants are possible with INSERT. After the word INSERT, you can add LOW_PRIORITY or DELAYED. The LOW_PRIORITY keyword means the system may wait and insert later when data is not being read from the table. The DELAYED keyword means that your inserted data will be buffered. If the server is busy, you can continue running queries rather than having to wait for this INSERT operation to complete.

Immediately after this, you can optionally specify IGNORE. This means that if you try to insert any rows that would cause a duplicate unique key, they will be silently ignored. Another alternative is to specify ON DUPLICATE KEY UPDATE *expression* at the end of the INSERT statement. This can be used to change the duplicate value using a normal UPDATE statement (covered later in this chapter).

We've put together some simple sample data to populate the database. This is just a series of simple INSERT statements that use the multirow insertion approach. You can find the script that does this in the file \chapter10\book_insert.sql on the CD accompanying this book. It is also shown in Listing 10.1.

Listing 10.1 book_insert.sql—SQL to Populate the Tables for Book-O-Rama

```
use books;

insert into customers values
   (3, 'Julie Smith', '25 Oak Street', 'Airport West'),
   (4, 'Alan Wong', '1/47 Haines Avenue', 'Box Hill'),
   (5, 'Michelle Arthur', '357 North Road', 'Yarraville');

insert into orders values
   (NULL, 5, 69.98, '2000-04-02'),
   (NULL, 3, 49.99, '2000-04-15'),
```

Listing 10.1 **Continued**

```
  (NULL, 4, 74.98, '2000-04-19'),
  (NULL, 5, 24.99, '2000-05-01');

insert into books values
  ('0-672-31697-8', 'Michael Morgan',
   'Java 2 for Professional Developers', 34.99),
  ('0-672-31745-1', 'Thomas Down', 'Installing Debian GNU/Linux', 24.99),
  ('0-672-31509-2', 'Pruitt, et al.', 'Teach Yourself GIMP in 24 Hours', 24.99),
  ('0-672-31769-9', 'Thomas Schenk',
   'Caldera OpenLinux System Administration Unleashed', 49.99);

insert into order_items values
  (1, '0-672-31697-8', 2),
  (2, '0-672-31769-9', 1),
  (3, '0-672-31769-9', 1),
  (3, '0-672-31509-2', 1),
  (4, '0-672-31745-1', 3);

insert into book_reviews values
  ('0-672-31697-8', 'The Morgan book is clearly written and goes well beyond
                     most of the basic Java books out there.');
```

You can run this script from the command line by piping it through MySQL as follows:

```
> mysql -h host -u bookorama -p < book_insert.sql
```

Retrieving Data from the Database

The workhorse of SQL is the SELECT statement. It's used to retrieve data from a database by selecting rows that match specified criteria from a table. There are a lot of options and different ways to use the SELECT statement.

The basic form of a SELECT is

```
SELECT [options] items
[INTO file_details]
FROM tables
[ WHERE conditions ]
[ GROUP BY group_type ]
[ HAVING where_definition ]
[ ORDER BY order_type ]
[LIMIT limit_criteria ]
[PROCEDURE proc_name(arguments)]
[lock_options]
;
```

In the following sections, we describe each of the clauses of the statement. First, though, let's look at a query without any of the optional clauses, one that selects some items from a particular table. Typically, these items are columns from the table. (They can also be the results of any MySQL expressions. We discuss some of the more useful ones in a later section.) This query lists the contents of the name and city columns from the customers table:

```
select name, city
from customers;
```

This query has the following output, assuming that you've entered the sample data from Listing 10.1 and the other two sample INSERT statements from earlier in this chapter:

```
+-----------------+--------------------+
| name            | city               |
+-----------------+--------------------+
| Julie Smith     | Airport West       |
| Alan Wong       | Box Hill           |
| Michelle Arthur | Yarraville         |
| Melissa Jones   | Nar Nar Goon North |
| Michael Archer  | Leeton             |
+-----------------+--------------------+
```

As you can see, this table contains the items selected—name and city—from the table specified—customers. This data is shown for all the rows in the customers table.

You can specify as many columns as you like from a table by listing them after the SELECT keyword. You can also specify some other items. One useful item is the wildcard operator, *, which matches all the columns in the specified table or tables. For example, to retrieve all columns and all rows from the order_items table, you would use

```
select *
from order_items;
```

which gives the following output:

```
+---------+---------------+----------+
| orderid | isbn          | quantity |
+---------+---------------+----------+
|       1 | 0-672-31697-8 |        2 |
|       2 | 0-672-31769-9 |        1 |
|       3 | 0-672-31769-9 |        1 |
|       3 | 0-672-31509-2 |        1 |
|       4 | 0-672-31745-1 |        3 |
+---------+---------------+----------+
```

Retrieving Data with Specific Criteria

To access a subset of the rows in a table, you need to specify some selection criteria. You can do this with a WHERE clause. For example,

```
select *
from orders
where customerid = 5;
```

selects all the columns from the orders table, but only the rows with a customerid of 3. Here's the output:

```
+---------+------------+--------+------------+
| orderid | customerid | amount | date       |
+---------+------------+--------+------------+
|       1 |          5 |  69.98 | 2000-04-02 |
|       4 |          5 |  24.99 | 2000-05-01 |
+---------+------------+--------+------------+
```

The WHERE clause specifies the criteria used to select particular rows. In this case, we selected rows with a customerid of 5. The single equal sign is used to test equality; note that this is different from PHP, and you can easily become confused when you're using them together.

In addition to equality, MySQL supports a full set of operators and regular expressions. The ones you will most commonly use in WHERE clauses are listed in Table 10.1. Note that this list is not complete; if you need something not listed here, check the MySQL manual.

Table 10.1 **Useful Comparison Operators for WHERE Clauses**

Operator	Name (If Applicable)	Example	Description
=	Equality	customerid = 3	Tests whether two values are equal
>	Greater than	amount > 60.00	Tests whether one value is greater than another
<	Less than	amount < 60.00	Tests whether one value is less than another
>=	Greater than or equal	amount >= 60.00	Tests whether one value is greater than or equal to another
<=	Less than or equal	amount <= 60.00	Tests whether one value is less than or equal to another
!= or <>	Not equal	quantity != 0	Tests whether two values are not equal
IS NOT NULL	n/a	address is not null	Tests whether a field actually contains a value

Table 10.1   **Continued**

Operator	Name (If Applicable)	Example	Description
IS NULL	n/a	address is null	Tests whether a field does not contain a value
BETWEEN	n/a	amount between 0 and 60.00	Tests whether a value is greater than or equal to a minimum value and less than or equal to a maximum value
IN	n/a	city in ("Carlton", "Moe")	Tests whether a value is in a particular set
NOT IN	n/a	city not in ("Carlton", "Moe")	Tests whether a value is not in a set
LIKE	Pattern match	name like ("Fred %")	Checks whether a value matches a pattern using simple SQL pattern matching
NOT LIKE	Pattern match	name not like ("Fred %")	Checks whether a value doesn't match a pattern
REGEXP	Regular expression	name regexp	Checks whether a value matches a regular expression

The last three rows in the table refer to LIKE and REGEXP. They are both forms of pattern matching.

LIKE uses simple SQL pattern matching. Patterns can consist of regular text plus the % (percent) character to indicate a wildcard match to any number of characters and the _ (underscore) character to wildcard-match a single character.

The REGEXP keyword is used for regular expression matching. MySQL uses POSIX regular expressions. Instead of the keyword REGEXP, you can also use RLIKE, which is a synonym. POSIX regular expressions are also used in PHP. You can read more about them in Chapter 4, "String Manipulation and Regular Expressions."

You can test multiple criteria using the simple operators and the pattern matching syntax and combine them into more complex criteria with AND and OR. For example,

```
select *
from orders
where customerid = 3 or customerid = 4;
```

Retrieving Data from Multiple Tables

Often, to answer a question from the database, you need to use data from more than one table. For example, if you wanted to know which customers placed orders this month, you would need to look at the customers table and the orders table. If you also wanted to know what, specifically, they ordered, you would also need to look at the order_items table.

These items are in separate tables because they relate to separate real-world objects. This is one of the principles of good database design that we described in Chapter 8, "Designing Your Web Database."

To put this information together in SQL, you must perform an operation called a *join*. This simply means joining two or more tables together to follow the relationships between the data. For example, if you want to see the orders that customer Julie Smith has placed, you will need to look at the `customers` table to find Julie's customerid and then at the `orders` table for orders with that customerid.

Although joins are conceptually simple, they are one of the more subtle and complex parts of SQL. Several different types of joins are implemented in MySQL, and each is used for a different purpose.

Simple Two-Table Joins

Let's begin by looking at some SQL for the query about Julie Smith we just discussed:

```
select orders.orderid, orders.amount, orders.date
from customers, orders
where customers.name = 'Julie Smith'
and customers.customerid = orders.customerid;
```

The output of this query is

```
+---------+--------+------------+
| orderid | amount | date       |
+---------+--------+------------+
|       2 |  49.99 | 2000-04-15 |
+---------+--------+------------+
```

There are a few things to notice here. First, because information from two tables is needed to answer this query, you must list both tables.

By listing two tables, you also specify a type of join, possibly without knowing it. The comma between the names of the tables is equivalent to typing INNER JOIN or CROSS JOIN. This is a type of join sometimes also referred to as a *full join*, or the *Cartesian product* of the tables. It means, "Take the tables listed, and make one big table. The big table should have a row for each possible combination of rows from each of the tables listed, whether that makes sense or not." In other words, you get a table, which has every row from the `customers` table matched up with every row from the `orders` table, regardless of whether a particular customer placed a particular order.

That brute-force approach doesn't make a lot of sense in most cases. Often what you want is to see the rows that really do match—that is, the orders placed by a particular customer matched up with that customer.

You achieve this result by placing a *join condition* in the WHERE clause. This special type of conditional statement explains which attributes show the relationship between the two tables. In this case, the join condition is

```
customers.customerid = orders.customerid
```

which tells MySQL to put rows in the result table only if the customerid from the `customers` table matches the customerid from the `orders` table.

By adding this join condition to the query, you actually convert the join to a different type, called an *equi-join*.

Also notice the dot notation used to make it clear which table a particular column comes from; that is, `customers.customerid` refers to the `customerid` column from the `customers` table, and `orders.customerid` refers to the `customerid` column from the `orders` table.

This dot notation is required if the name of a column is ambiguous—that is, if it occurs in more than one table. As an extension, it can also be used to disambiguate column names from different databases. This example uses a `table.column` notation, but you can specify the database with a `database.table.column` notation, for example, to test a condition such as

```
books.orders.customerid = other_db.orders.customerid
```

You can, however, use the dot notation for all column references in a query. Using this notation can be a good idea, particularly when your queries begin to become complex. MySQL doesn't require it, but it does make your queries much more humanly readable and maintainable. Notice that we followed this convention in the rest of the previous query, for example, with the use of the condition

```
customers.name = 'Julie Smith'
```

The column `name` occurs only in the table `customers`, so we do not really need to specify what table it is from. MySQL will not be confused. For humans, though, the `name` on its own is vague, so it does make the meaning of the query clearer when you specify it as `customer.name`.

Joining More Than Two Tables

Joining more than two tables is no more difficult than a two-table join. As a general rule, you need to join tables in pairs with join conditions. Think of it as following the relationships between the data from table to table to table.

For example, if you want to know which customers have ordered books on Java (perhaps so you can send them information about a new Java book), you need to trace these relationships through quite a few tables.

You need to find customers who have placed at least one order that included an `order_item` that is a book about Java. To get from the `customers` table to the `orders` table, you can use the `customerid` as shown previously. To get from the `orders` table to the `order_items` table, you can use the `orderid`. To get from the `order_items` table to the specific book in the `Books` table, you can use the ISBN. After making all those links, you can test for books with *Java* in the title and return the names of customers who bought any of those books.

Let's look at a query that does all those things:

```
select customers.name
from customers, orders, order_items, books
where customers.customerid = orders.customerid
and orders.orderid = order_items.orderid
and order_items.isbn = books.isbn
and books.title like '%Java%';
```

This query returns the following output:

```
+------------------+
| name             |
+------------------+
| Michelle Arthur  |
+------------------+
```

Notice that this example traces the data through four different tables, and to do this with an equi-join, you need three different join conditions. It is generally true that you need one join condition for each pair of tables that you want to join, and therefore a total of join conditions one less than the total number of tables you want to join. This rule of thumb can be useful for debugging queries that don't quite work. Check off your join conditions and make sure you've followed the path all the way from what you know to what you want to know.

Finding Rows That Don't Match

The other main type of join that you will use in MySQL is the left join.

In the previous examples, notice that only the rows where a match was found between the tables were included. Sometimes you may specifically want the rows where there's no match—for example, customers who have never placed an order or books that have never been ordered.

One way to answer this type of question in MySQL is to use a left join. This type of join matches up rows on a specified join condition between two tables. If no matching row exists in the right table, a row will be added to the result that contains NULL values in the right columns.

Let's look at an example:

```
select customers.customerid, customers.name, orders.orderid
from customers left join orders
on customers.customerid = orders.customerid;
```

This SQL query uses a left join to join customers with orders. Notice that the left join uses a slightly different syntax for the join condition; in this case, the join condition goes in a special ON clause of the SQL statement.

The result of this query is

```
+------------+----------------+---------+
| customerid | name           | orderid |
+------------+----------------+---------+
|          1 | Melissa Jones  |    NULL |
|          2 | Michael Archer |    NULL |
|          3 | Julie Smith    |       2 |
|          4 | Alan Wong      |       3 |
|          5 | Michelle Arthur|       1 |
|          5 | Michelle Arthur|       4 |
+------------+----------------+---------+
```

This output shows that customers Melissa Jones and Michael Archer do not have matching `orderids` because the `orderids` for those customers are NULLs.

If you want to see only the customers who haven't ordered anything, you can check for those NULLs in the primary key field of the right table (in this case, `orderid`) because that should not be NULL in any real rows:

```
select customers.customerid, customers.name
from customers left join orders
using (customerid)
where orders.orderid is null;
```

The result is

```
+------------+----------------+
| customerid | name           |
+------------+----------------+
|          1 | Melissa Jones  |
|          2 | Michael Archer |
+------------+----------------+
```

Also notice that this example uses a different syntax for the join condition. Left joins support either the ON syntax used in the first example or the USING syntax in the second example. Notice that the USING syntax doesn't specify the table from which the join attribute comes; for this reason, the columns in the two tables must have the same name if you want to use USING.

You can also answer this type of question by using subqueries. We look at subqueries later in this chapter.

Using Other Names for Tables: Aliases

Being able to refer to tables by other names is often handy and occasionally essential. Other names for tables are called *aliases*. You can create them at the start of a query and then use them throughout. They are often handy as shorthand. Consider the huge query you saw earlier, rewritten with aliases:

```
select c.name
from customers as c, orders as o, order_items as oi, books as b
where c.customerid = o.customerid
and o.orderid = oi.orderid
and oi.isbn = b.isbn
and b.title like '%Java%';
```

As you declare the tables you are going to use, you add an AS clause to declare the alias for that table. You can also use aliases for columns; we return to this approach when we look at aggregate functions shortly.

You need to use table aliases when you want to join a table to itself. This task sounds more difficult and esoteric than it is. It is useful, if, for example, you want to find rows in the same table that have values in common. If you want to find customers who live in the same city—perhaps to set up a reading group—you can give the same table (customers) two different aliases:

```
select c1.name, c2.name, c1.city
from customers as c1, customers as c2
where c1.city = c2.city
and c1.name != c2.name;
```

What you are basically doing here is pretending that the table customers is two different tables, c1 and c2, and performing a join on the city column. Notice that you also need the second condition, c1.name != c2.name; this is to avoid each customer coming up as a match to herself.

Summary of Joins

The different types of joins we have described are summarized in Table 10.2. There are a few others, but these are the main ones you will use.

Table 10.2   **Join Types in MySQL**

Name	Description
Cartesian product	All combinations of all the rows in all the tables in the join. Used by specifying a comma between table names, and not specifying a WHERE clause.
Full join	Same as preceding.
Cross join	Same as above. Can also be used by specifying the CROSS JOIN keywords between the names of the tables being joined.
Inner join	Semantically equivalent to the comma. Can also be specified using the INNER JOIN keywords. Without a WHERE condition, equivalent to a full join. Usually, you specify a WHERE condition as well to make this a true inner join.
Equi-join	Uses a conditional expression with = to match rows from the different tables in the join. In SQL, this is a join with a WHERE clause.

Table 10.2   **Continued**

Name	Description
Left join	Tries to match rows across tables and fills in nonmatching rows with NULLs. Use in SQL with the LEFT JOIN keywords. Used for finding missing values. You can equivalently use RIGHT JOIN.

Retrieving Data in a Particular Order

If you want to display rows retrieved by a query in a particular order, you can use the ORDER BY clause of the SELECT statement. This feature is handy for presenting output in a good human-readable format.

The ORDER BY clause sorts the rows on one or more of the columns listed in the SELECT clause. For example,

```
select name, address
from customers
order by name;
```

This query returns customer names and addresses in alphabetical order by name, like this:

```
+-----------------+--------------------+
| name            | address            |
+-----------------+--------------------+
| Alan Wong       | 1/47 Haines Avenue |
| Julie Smith     | 25 Oak Street      |
| Melissa Jones   |                    |
| Michael Archer  | 12 Adderley Avenue |
| Michelle Arthur | 357 North Road     |
+-----------------+--------------------+
```

Notice that in this case, because the names are in *firstname, lastname* format, they are alphabetically sorted on the first name. If you wanted to sort on last names, you would need to have them as two different fields.

The default ordering is ascending (*a* to *z* or numerically upward). You can specify this if you like by using the ASC keyword:

```
select name, address
from customers
order by name asc;
```

You can also do it in the opposite order by using the DESC (descending) keyword:

```
select name, address
from customers
order by name desc;
```

In addition, you can sort on more than one column. You can also use column aliases or even their position numbers (for example, 3 is the third column in the table) instead of names.

Grouping and Aggregating Data

You may often want to know how many rows fall into a particular set or the average value of some column—say, the average dollar value per order. MySQL has a set of aggregate functions that are useful for answering this type of query.

These aggregate functions can be applied to a table as a whole or to groups of data within a table. The most commonly used ones are listed in Table 10.3.

Table 10.3 **Aggregate Functions in MySQL**

Name	Description
AVG(*column*)	Average of values in the specified column.
COUNT(*items*)	If you specify a column, this will give you the number of non-NULL values in that column. If you add the word DISTINCT in front of the column name, you will get a count of the distinct values in that column only. If you specify COUNT(*), you will get a row count regardless of NULL values.
MIN(*column*)	Minimum of values in the specified column.
MAX(*column*)	Maximum of values in the specified column.
STD(*column*)	Standard deviation of values in the specified column.
STDDEV(*column*)	Same as STD(*column*).
SUM(*column*)	Sum of values in the specified column.

Let's look at some examples, beginning with the one mentioned earlier. You can calculate the average total of an order like this:

```
select avg(amount)
from orders;
```

The output is something like this:

```
+-------------+
| avg(amount) |
+-------------+
|   54.985002 |
+-------------+
```

To get more detailed information, you can use the GROUP BY clause. It enables you to view the average order total by group—for example, by customer number. This information tells you which of your customers place the biggest orders:

```
select customerid, avg(amount)
from orders
group by customerid;
```

When you use a GROUP BY clause with an aggregate function, it actually changes the behavior of the function. Instead of giving an average of the order amounts across the table, this query gives the average order amount for each customer (or, more specifically, for each customerid):

```
+------------+-------------+
| customerid | avg(amount) |
+------------+-------------+
|          1 |   49.990002 |
|          2 |   74.980003 |
|          3 |   47.485002 |
+------------+-------------+
```

Here's one point to note when using grouping and aggregate functions: In ANSI SQL, if you use an aggregate function or GROUP BY clause, the only things that can appear in your SELECT clause are the aggregate function(s) and the columns named in the GROUP BY clause. Also, if you want to use a column in a GROUP BY clause, it must be listed in the SELECT clause.

MySQL actually gives you a bit more leeway here. It supports an *extended syntax*, which enables you to leave items out of the SELECT clause if you don't actually want them.

In addition to grouping and aggregating data, you can actually test the result of an aggregate by using a HAVING clause. It comes straight after the GROUP BY clause and is like a WHERE that applies only to groups and aggregates.

To extend the previous example, if you want to know which customers have an average order total of more than $50, you can use the following query:

```
select customerid, avg(amount)
from orders
group by customerid
having avg(amount) > 50;
```

Note that the HAVING clause applies to the groups. This query returns the following output:

```
+------------+-------------+
| customerid | avg(amount) |
+------------+-------------+
|          2 |   74.980003 |
+------------+-------------+
```

Choosing Which Rows to Return

One clause of the SELECT statement that can be particularly useful in Web applications is LIMIT. It is used to specify which rows from the output should be returned. This clause takes two parameters: the row number from which to start and the number of rows to return.

This query illustrates the use of LIMIT:

```
select name
from customers
limit 2, 3;
```

This query can be read as, "Select name from customers, and then return 3 rows, starting from row 2 in the output." Note that row numbers are zero indexed; that is, the first row in the output is row number zero.

This feature is very useful for Web applications, such as when the customer is browsing through products in a catalog, and you want to show 10 items on each page. Note, however, that LIMIT is not part of ANSI SQL. It is a MySQL extension, so using it makes your SQL incompatible with most other RDBMSs.

Using Subqueries

A subquery is a query that is nested inside another query. This feature is new in MySQL 4.1. While most subquery functionality can be obtained with careful use of joins and temporary tables, subqueries are often easier to read and write.

Basic Subqueries

The most common use of subqueries is to use the result of one query in a comparison in another query. For example, if you wanted to find the order in which the amount ordered was the largest of any of the orders, you could use the following query:

```
select customerid, amount
from orders
where amount = (select max(amount) from orders);
```

This query gives the following results:

```
+------------+--------+
| customerid | amount |
+------------+--------+
|          4 |  74.98 |
+------------+--------+
```

In this case, a single value is returned from the subquery (the maximum amount) and then used for comparison in the outer query. This is a good example of subquery use because this particular query cannot be elegantly reproduced using joins in ANSI SQL.

The same output, however, produced by this join query:

```
select customerid, amount
from orders
order by amount desc
limit 1;
```

Because it relies on LIMIT, this query is not compatible with most RDBMSs, but it executes more efficiently on MySQL than the subquery version.

One of the main reasons that MySQL did not get subqueries for so long was that there is very little that you cannot do without them. Technically, you can create a single, legal ANSI SQL query that has the same effect but relies on an inefficient, hack approach called the MAX-CONCAT trick.

You can use subquery values in this way with all the normal comparison operators. Some special subquery comparison operators are also available, detailed in the next section.

Subqueries and Operators

There are five special subquery operators. Four are used with regular subqueries, and one (EXISTS) is usually used only with correlated subqueries and is covered in the next section. The four regular subquery operators are shown in Table 10.4.

Table 10.4 **Subquery Operators**

Name	Sample Syntax	Description
ANY	SELECT c1 FROM t1 WHERE c1 > ANY (SELECT c1 FROM t2);	Returns true if the comparison is true for any of the rows in the subquery.
IN	SELECT c1 FROM t1 WHERE c1 IN (SELECT c1 from t2);	Equivalent to =ANY.
SOME	SELECT c1 FROM t1 WHERE c1 > SOME (SELECT c1 FROM t2);!	Alias for ANY; sometimes reads better to the human ear
ALL	SELECT c1 FROM t1 WHERE c1 > ALL (SELECT c1 from t2);	Returns true if the comparison is true for all of the rows in the subquery.

Each of these operators can appear only after a comparison operator, except for IN, which has its comparison operator (=) "rolled in," so to speak.

Correlated Subqueries

In correlated subqueries, things become a little more complicated. In correlated subqueries, you can use items from the outer query in the inner query. For example,

```
select isbn, title
 from books
 where not exists
  (select * from order_items where order_items.isbn=books.isbn);
```

This query illustrates both the use of correlated subqueries and the use of the last special
subquery operator, EXISTS. It retrieves any books that have never been ordered. (This is
the same information you found from doing a left join earlier.) Note that the inner
query includes the order_items table only in the FROM list but refers to books.isbn. In
other words, the inner query refers to data in the outer query. This is the definition of a
correlated subquery: You are looking for inner rows that match (or in this case don't
match) the outer rows.

The EXISTS operator returns true if there are any matching rows in the subquery.
Conversely, NOT EXISTS returns true if there are no matching rows in the subquery.

Row Subqueries

All the subqueries so far have returned a single value, although in many cases this value
is true or false (as with the preceding example using EXISTS). Row subqueries return
an entire row, which can then be compared to entire rows in the outer query. This
approach is generally used to look for rows in one table that also exist in another table.
There is not a good example of this in the books database, but a generalized example of
the syntax could be something like the following:

```
select c1, c2, c3
from t1
where (c1, c2, c3) in (select c1, c2, c3 from t2);
```

Using a Subquery as a Temporary Table

You can use a subquery in the FROM clause of an outer query. This approach effectively
allows you to query the output of the subquery, treating it as a temporary table.

In its simplest form, this is something like:

```
select * from
(select customerid, name from customers where city='Box Hill')
as box_hill_customers;
```

Note that we put the subquery in the FROM clause here. Immediately after the subquery's
closing parenthesis, you must give the results of the subquery an alias. You can then treat
it like any other table in the outer query.

Updating Records in the Database

In addition to retrieving data from the database, you often want to change it. For example, you might want to increase the prices of books in the database. You can do this using an UPDATE statement.

The usual form of an UPDATE statement is

```
UPDATE [LOW_PRIORITY] [IGNORE] tablename
SET column1=expression1,column2=expression2,...
[WHERE condition]
[ORDER BY order_criteria]
[LIMIT number]
```

The basic idea is to update the table called tablename, setting each of the columns named to the appropriate expression. You can limit an UPDATE to particular rows with a WHERE clause and limit the total number of rows to affect with a LIMIT clause. ORDER BY is usually used only in conjunction with a LIMIT clause; for example, if you are going to update only the first 10 rows, you want to put them in some kind of order first. LOW_PRIORITY and IGNORE, if specified, work the same way as they do in an INSERT statement.

Let's look at some examples. If you want to increase all the book prices by 10%, you can use an UPDATE statement without a WHERE clause:

```
update books
set price=price*1.1;
```

If, on the other hand, you want to change a single row—say, to update a customer's address—you can do it like this:

```
update customers
set address = '250 Olsens Road'
where customerid = 4;
```

Altering Tables After Creation

In addition to updating rows, you might want to alter the structure of the tables within your database. For this purpose, you can use the flexible ALTER TABLE statement. The basic form of this statement is

```
ALTER TABLE [IGNORE] tablename alteration [, alteration ...]
```

Note that in ANSI SQL you can make only one alteration per ALTER TABLE statement, but MySQL allows you to make as many as you like. Each of the alteration clauses can be used to change different aspects of the table.

If the IGNORE clause is specified and you are trying to make an alteration that causes duplicate primary keys, the first one will go into the altered table and the rest will be deleted. If it is not specified (the default), the alteration will fail and be rolled back.

The different types of alterations you can make with this statement are shown in Table 10.5.

Table 10.5 **Possible Changes with the** ALTER TABLE **Statement**

Syntax	Description
ADD [COLUMN] column_description [FIRST | AFTER column]	Adds a new column in the specified location (if not specified, then the column goes at the end). Note that column_descriptions need a name and a type, just as in a CREATE statement.
ADD [COLUMN] (column_description, column_description,...)	Adds one or more new columns at the end of the table.
ADD INDEX [index] (column,...)	Adds an index to the table on the specified column or columns.
ADD [CONSTRAINT [symbol]] PRIMARY KEY (column,...)	Makes the specified column or columns the primary key of the table. The CONSTRAINT notation is for tables using foreign keys. See Chapter 13"Advanced MySQL programming,"for more details.
ADD UNIQUE [CONSTRAINT [symbol]] [index] (column,...)	Adds a unique index to the table on the specified column or columns. The CONSTRAINT notation is for InnoDB tables using foreign keys. See Chapter 13 for more details.
ADD [CONSTRAINT [symbol]] FOREIGN KEY [index] (index_col,...) [reference_definition]	Adds a foreign key to an InnoDB table. See Chapter 13 for more details.
ALTER [COLUMN] column {SET DEFAULT value | DROP DEFAULT}	Adds or removes a default value for a particular column.
CHANGE [COLUMN] column new_column description	Changes the column called column so that it has the description listed. Note that this syntax can be used to change the name of a column because a column_description includes a name.
MODIFY [COLUMN] column_description	Similar to CHANGE. Can be used to change column types, not names.
DROP [COLUMN] column	Deletes the named column.
DROP PRIMARY KEY	Deletes the primary index (but not the column).
DROP INDEX index	Deletes the named index.
DROP FOREIGN KEY key	Deletes the foreign key (but not the column).

Table 10.5   **Possible Changes with the** ALTER TABLE **Statement**

Syntax	Description
DISABLE KEYS	Turns off index updating.
ENABLE KEYS	Turns on index updating.
RENAME [AS] new_table_name	Renames a table.
ORDER BY col_name	Re-creates the table with the rows in a particular order. (Note that after you begin changing the table, the rows will no longer be in order.)
CONVERT TO CHARACTER SET cs COLLATE c	Converts all text-based columns to the specified character set and collation.
[DEFAULT] CHARACTER SET cs COLLATE c	Sets the default character set and collation.
DISCARD TABLESPACE	Deletes the underlying tablespace file for an InnoDB table. (See Chapter 13 for more details on InnoDB.)
IMPORT TABLESPACE	Re-creates the underlying tablespace file for an InnoDB table. (See Chapter 13 for more details on InnoDB.)
table_options	Allows you to reset the table options. Uses the same syntax as CREATE TABLE.

Let's look at a few of the more common uses of ALTER TABLE.

You may frequently realize that you haven't made a particular column "big enough" for the data it has to hold. For example, previously in the customers table, you allowed names to be 50 characters long. After you start getting some data, you might notice that some of the names are too long and are being truncated. You can fix this problem by changing the data type of the column so that it is 70 characters long instead:

```
alter table customers
modify name char(70) not null;
```

Another common occurrence is the need to add a column. Imagine that a sales tax on books is introduced locally and that Book-O-Rama needs to add the amount of tax to the total order but keep track of it separately. You can add a tax column to the orders table as follows:

```
alter table orders
add tax float(6,2) after amount;
```

Getting rid of a column is another case that comes up frequently. You can delete the column you just added as follows:

```
alter table orders
drop tax;
```

Deleting Records from the Database

Deleting rows from the database is simple. You can do this using the DELETE statement, which generally looks like this:

```
DELETE [LOW_PRIORITY] [QUICK] [IGNORE] FROM table
[WHERE condition]
[ORDER BY order_cols]
[LIMIT number]
```

If you write

```
delete from table;
```

on its own, all the rows in a table will be deleted, so be careful! Usually, you want to delete specific rows, and you can specify the ones you want to delete with a WHERE clause. You might do this, if, for example, a particular book were no longer available or if a particular customer hadn't placed any orders for a long time and you wanted to do some housekeeping:

```
delete from customers
where customerid=5;
```

The LIMIT clause can be used to limit the maximum number of rows that are actually deleted. ORDER BY is usually used in conjunction with LIMIT.

LOW_PRIORITY and IGNORE work as they do elsewhere. QUICK may be faster on MyISAM tables.

Dropping Tables

At times, you may want to get rid of an entire table. You can do this with the DROP TABLE statement. This process is very simple, and it looks like this:

```
DROP TABLE table;
```

This query deletes all the rows in the table and the table itself, so be careful using it.

Dropping a Whole Database

You can go even further and eliminate an entire database with the DROP DATABASE statement, which looks like this:

```
DROP DATABASE database;
```

This query deletes all the rows, all the tables, all the indexes, and the database itself, so it goes without saying that you should be somewhat careful using this statement.

Further Reading

In this chapter, we provided an overview of the day-to-day SQL you will use when interacting with a MySQL database. In the next two chapters, we describe how to connect MySQL and PHP so that you can access your database from the Web. We also explore some advanced MySQL techniques.

If you want to know more about SQL, you can always fall back on the ANSI SQL standard for a little light reading. It's available from

http://www.ansi.org/

For more details on the MySQL extensions to ANSI SQL, you can look at the MySQL website:

http://www.mysql.com

Next

In Chapter 11, "Accessing Your MySQL Database from the Web with PHP," we cover how to make the Book-O-Rama database available over the Web.

11

Accessing Your MySQL Database from the Web with PHP

Previously, in our work with PHP, we used a flat file to store and retrieve data. When we looked at this file in Chapter 2, "Storing and Retrieving Data," we mentioned that relational database systems make a lot of these storage and retrieval tasks easier, safer, and more efficient in a web application. Now, having worked with MySQL to create a database, we can begin connecting this database to a web-based front end.

In this chapter, we explain how to access the Book-O-Rama database from the Web using PHP. You learn how to read from and write to the database and how to filter potentially troublesome input data.

Key topics covered in this chapter include

- How web database architectures work
- Querying a database from the Web using the basic steps
- Setting up a connection
- Getting information about available databases
- Choosing a database to use
- Querying the database
- Retrieving the query results
- Disconnecting from the database
- Putting new information in the database
- Using prepared statements
- Using other PHP–database interfaces
- Using a generic database interface: PEAR DB

How Web Database Architectures Work

In Chapter 8, "Designing Your Web Database," we outlined how web database architectures work. Just to remind you, here are the steps again:

1. A user's web browser issues an HTTP request for a particular web page. For example, the user might have requested a search for all the books written by Michael Morgan at Book-O-Rama, using an HTML form. The search results page is called `results.php`.

2. The web server receives the request for `results.php`, retrieves the file, and passes it to the PHP engine for processing.

3. The PHP engine begins parsing the script. Inside the script is a command to connect to the database and execute a query (perform the search for books). PHP opens a connection to the MySQL server and sends on the appropriate query.

4. The MySQL server receives the database query, processes it, and sends the results— a list of books—back to the PHP engine.

5. The PHP engine finishes running the script. This usually involves formatting the query results nicely in HTML. It then returns the resulting HTML to the web server.

6. The web server passes the HTML back to the browser, where the user can see the list of books she requested.

Now you have an existing MySQL database, so you can write the PHP code to perform the preceding steps. Begin with the search form. The code for this plain HTML form is shown in Listing 11.1.

Listing 11.1 `search.html`— **Book-O-Rama's Database Search Page**

```
<html>
<head>
  <title>Book-O-Rama Catalog Search</title>
</head>

<body>
  <h1>Book-O-Rama Catalog Search</h1>

  <form action="results.php" method="post">
    Choose Search Type:<br />
    <select name="searchtype">
      <option value="author">Author</option>
      <option value="title">Title</option>
      <option value="isbn">ISBN</option>
    </select>
    <br />
    Enter Search Term:<br />
```

Listing 11.1   **Continued**

```
  <input name="searchterm" type="text">
  <br />
  <input type="submit" value="Search">
</form>

</body>
</html>
```

This HTML form is reasonably straightforward. The output of this HTML is shown in Figure 11.1.

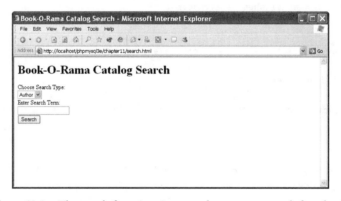

Figure 11.1   The search form is quite general, so you can search for a book on its title, author, or ISBN.

The script that will be called when the Search button is clicked is `results.php`. It is listed in full in Listing 11.2. Through the course of this chapter, we will discuss what this script does and how it works.

Listing 11.2   `results.php`—**This Script Retrieves Search Results from the MySQL Database and Formats Them for Display**

```
<html>
<head>
  <title>Book-O-Rama Search Results</title>
</head>
<body>
<h1>Book-O-Rama Search Results</h1>
<?php
  // create short variable names
  $searchtype=$_POST['searchtype'];
  $searchterm=$_POST['searchterm'];
```

Listing 11.2 **Continued**

```php
$searchterm= trim($searchterm);

if (!$searchtype || !$searchterm)
{
    echo 'You have not entered search details.  Please go back and try again.';
    exit;
}

if (!get_magic_quotes_gpc())
{
  $searchtype = addslashes($searchtype);
  $searchterm = addslashes($searchterm);
}

@ $db = new mysqli('localhost', 'bookorama', 'bookorama123', 'books');

if (mysqli_connect_errno())
{
    echo 'Error: Could not connect to database.  Please try again later.';
    exit;
}

$query = "select * from books where ".$searchtype." like '%".$searchterm."%'";
$result = $db->query($query);

$num_results = $result->num_rows;

echo '<p>Number of books found: '.$num_results.'</p>';

for ($i=0; $i <$num_results; $i++)
{
    $row = $result->fetch_assoc();
    echo '<p><strong>'.($i+1).'. Title: ';
    echo htmlspecialchars(stripslashes($row['title']));
    echo '</strong><br />Author: ';
    echo stripslashes($row['author']);
    echo '<br />ISBN: ';
    echo stripslashes($row['isbn']);
    echo '<br />Price: ';
    echo stripslashes($row['price']);
    echo '</p>';
}
```

Listing 11.2   **Continued**

```
$result->free();
$db->close();

?>
</body>
</html>
```

Note that this script allows you to enter the MySQL wildcard characters % and _
(underscore). This capability can actually be useful for the user. You can escape these
characters if it will cause a problem for your application.

Figure 11.2 illustrates the results of using this script to perform a search.

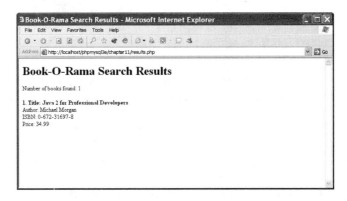

Figure 11.2   The results of searching the database for books about Java are
presented in a web page using the `results.php` script.

Querying a Database from the Web

In any script used to access a database from the Web, you follow some basic steps:

1. Check and filter data coming from the user.
2. Set up a connection to the appropriate database.
3. Query the database.
4. Retrieve the results.
5. Present the results back to the user.

These are the steps we followed in the script `results.php`, so now let's go through each
of them in turn.

Checking and Filtering Input Data

You begin the script by stripping any whitespace that the user might have inadvertently entered at the beginning or end of his search term. You do this by applying the function trim() to $searchterm:

```
$searchterm=trim($searchterm);
```

The next step is to verify that the user has entered a search term and search type. Note that you check whether he entered a search term after trimming whitespace from the ends of $searchterm. If you arrange these lines in the opposite order, you could encounter situations in which a user's search term is not empty and therefore does not create an error message; instead, it is all whitespace, so it is deleted by trim():

```
if (!$searchtype || !$searchterm)
{
    echo 'You have not entered search details.  Please go back and try again.';
    exit;
}
```

You check the $searchtype variable even though in this case it's coming from an HTML SELECT. You might ask why you should bother checking data that has to be filled in. It's important to remember that there might be more than one interface to your database. For example, Amazon has many affiliates who use its search interface. Also, it's sensible to screen data in case of any security problems that can arise because of users coming from different points of entry.

Also, when you plan to use any data input by a user, you need to filter it appropriately for any control characters. As you might remember, in Chapter 4, "String Manipulation and Regular Expressions," we described the functions addslashes(), stripslashes(), and get_magic_quotes_gpc(). You need to escape data when submitting any user input to a database such as MySQL.

In this case, you check the value of the get_magic_quotes_gpc() function. It tells you whether quoting is being done automatically. If it is not, you use addslashes() to escape the data:

```
if (!get_magic_quotes_gpc())
{
  $searchtype = addslashes($searchtype);
  $searchterm = addslashes($searchterm);
}
```

You also use stripslashes() on the data coming back from the database. If the magic quotes feature is turned on, the data will have slashes in it when it comes back from the database, so you need to take them out.

Here, you use the function `htmlspecialchars()` to encode characters that have special meanings in HTML. The current test data does not include any ampersands (&), less than (<), greater than (>), or double quotation mark (") symbols, but many fine book titles contain an ampersand. By using this function, you can eliminate future errors.

Setting Up a Connection

PHP5 has a new library for connecting to MySQL. This library is called mysqli (the *i* stands for improved). The mysqli library is suitable for use with MySQL version 4 and later. At version 4, a new connection protocol that is much faster was added to MySQL, and mysqli allows you to take advantage of it. The mysqli library allows you to use either an object-oriented or procedural syntax.

You use the following line in the script to connect to the MySQL server:

```
@ $db = new mysqli('localhost', 'bookorama', 'bookorama123', 'books');
```

This line instantiates the `mysqli` class and creates a connection to host `'localhost'` with username `'bookorama'`, and password `'bookorama123'`. The connection is set up to use the database called books.

Using this object-oriented approach, you can now invoke methods on this object to access the database. If you prefer a procedural approach, mysqli allows for this, too. To connect in a procedural fashion, you would use

```
@ $db = mysqli_connect('localhost', 'bookorama', 'bookorama123', 'books');
```

This function returns a resource rather than an object. This resource represents the connection to the database, and if you are using the procedural approach, you will need to pass this resource in to all the other mysqli functions. This is very similar to the way the file-handling functions, such as `fopen()`, work.

Most of the mysqli functions have an object-oriented interface and a procedural interface. Generally, the differences are that the procedural version function names start with `mysqli_` and require you to pass in the resource handle you obtained from `mysqli_connect()`. Database connections are an exception to this rule because they can be made by the mysqli object's constructor.

The result of your attempt at connection is worth checking because none of the rest of code will work without a valid database connection. You do this using the following code:

```
if (mysqli_connect_errno())
{
   echo 'Error: Could not connect to database.  Please try again later.';
   exit;
}
```

(This code is the same for the object-oriented and procedural versions.) The `mysqli_connect_errno()` function returns an error number on error, or zero on success.

Note that when you connect to the database, you begin the line of code with the error suppression operator, @. This way, you can handle any errors gracefully. (This could also be done with exceptions, which we have not used in this simple example.)

Bear in mind that there is a limit to the number of MySQL connections that can exist at the same time. The MySQL parameter `max_connections` determines what this limit is. The purpose of this parameter and the related Apache parameter `MaxClients` is to tell the server to reject new connection requests instead of allowing machine resources to be completely used up at busy times or when software has crashed.

You can alter both of these parameters from their default values by editing the configuration files. To set `MaxClients` in Apache, edit the `httpd.conf` file on your system. To set `max_connections` for MySQL, edit the file `my.conf`.

Choosing a Database to Use

Remember that when you are using MySQL from a command-line interface, you need to tell it which database you plan to use with a command such as

```
use books;
```

You also need to do this when connecting from the Web. The database to use is specified as a parameter to the `mysqli` constructor or the `mysqli_connect()` function. If you want to change the default database, you can do so with the `mysqli_select_db()` function. It can be accessed as either

```
$db->select_db(dbname)
```

or as

```
mysqli_select_db(db_resource, db_name)
```

Here, you can see the similarity between the functions that we described before: The procedural version begins with `mysqli_` and requires the extra database handle parameter.

Querying the Database

To actually perform the query, you can use the `mysqli_query()` function. Before doing this, however, it's a good idea to set up the query you want to run:

```
$query = "select * from books where $searchtype like '%$searchterm%'";
```

In this case, you search for the user-input value (`$searchterm`) in the field the user specified (`$searchtype`). Notice the use of `like` for matching rather than `equal`: it's usually a good idea to be more tolerant in a database search.

> **Tip**
>
> Remember that *the query you send to MySQL does not need a semicolon at the end of it*, unlike a query you type into the MySQL monitor.

You can now run the query:

```
$result = $db->query($query);
```

Or, if you wanted to use the procedural interface, you would use

```
$result = mysqli_query($db, $query);
```

You pass in the query you want to run and, in the procedural interface, the database link (again, in this case $db).

The object-oriented version returns a result object; the procedural version returns a result resource. (This is similar to the way the connection functions work.) Either way, you store the result in a variable ($result) for later use. This function returns `false` on failure.

Retrieving the Query Results

A large variety of functions is available to break the results out of the result object or identifier in different ways. The result object or identifier is the key to accessing the rows returned by the query.

In this example, you counted the number of rows returned and also used the `mysqli_fetch_assoc()` function.

When you use the object-oriented approach, the number of rows returned is stored in the `num_rows` member of the result object, and you can access it as follows:

```
$num_results = $result->num_rows;
```

When you use a procedural approach, the function `mysqli_num_rows()` gives you the number of rows returned by the query. You should pass it the result identifier, like this:

```
$num_results = mysqli_num_rows($result);
```

It's useful to know this—if you plan to process or display the results, as you now know how many there are and can loop through them:

```
for ($i=0; $i <$num_results; $i++)
{
  // process results
}
```

In each iteration of this loop, you call $result->fetch_assoc() (or mysqli_fetch_assoc()). The loop does not execute if no rows are returned. This is a function that takes each row from the resultset and returns the row as an array, with each key an attribute name and each value the corresponding value in the array:

```
$row = $result->fetch_assoc();
```

Or you can use a procedural approach:

```
$row = mysqli_fetch_assoc($result);
```

Given the array $row, you can go through each field and display it appropriately, as shown in this example:

```
echo '<br />ISBN: ';
echo stripslashes($row['isbn']);
```

As previously mentioned, you call `stripslashes()` to tidy up the value before displaying it.

Several variations can be used to get results from a result identifier. Instead of an array with named keys, you can retrieve the results in an enumerated array with `mysqli_fetch_row()`, as follows:

```
$row = $result->fetch_row($result);
```

or

```
$row = mysqli_fetch_row($result);
```

Here, the attribute values are listed in each of the array values `$row[0]`, `$row[1]`, and so on. (The `mysqli_fetch_array()` function allows you to fetch a row as either or both kinds of array.)

You could also fetch a row into an object with the `mysqli_fetch_object()` function:

```
$row = $result->fetch_object();
```

or

```
$row = mysqli_fetch_object($result);
```

You can then access each of the attributes via `$row->title`, `$row->author`, and so on.

Disconnecting from the Database

You can free up your resultset by calling either

```
$result->free();
```

or

```
mysqli_free_result($result);
```

You can then use

```
$db->close();
```

or

```
mysqli_close($db);
```

to close a database connection. Using this command isn't strictly necessary because the connection will be closed when a script finishes execution anyway.

Putting New Information in the Database

Inserting new items into the database is remarkably similar to getting items out of the database. You follow the same basic steps: make a connection, send a query, and check the results. In this case, the query you send is an INSERT rather than a SELECT.

Although this process is similar, looking at an example can sometimes be useful. In Figure 11.3, you can see a basic HTML form for putting new books into the database.

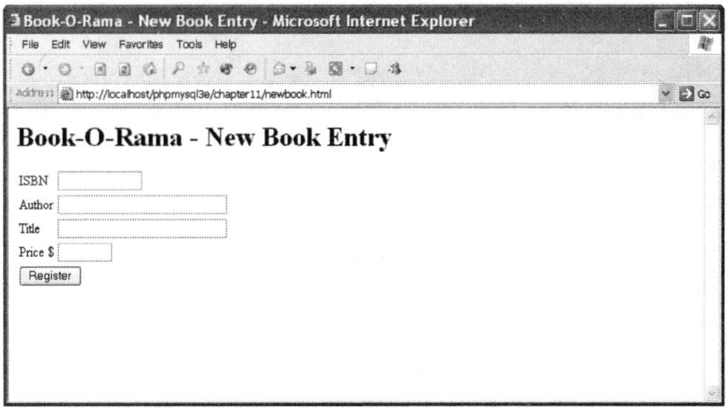

Figure 11.3   This interface for putting new books into the database could be used by Book-O-Rama's staff.

The HTML for this page is shown in Listing 11.3.

Listing 11.3   newbook.html— HTML for the Book Entry Page

```html
<html>
<head>
  <title>Book-O-Rama - New Book Entry</title>
</head>

<body>
  <h1>Book-O-Rama - New Book Entry</h1>

  <form action="insert_book.php" method="post">
    <table border="0">
      <tr>
        <td>ISBN</td>
         <td><input type="text" name="isbn" maxlength="13" size="13"></td>
      </tr>
      <tr>
        <td>Author</td>
        <td> <input type="text" name="author" maxlength="30" size="30"></td>
      </tr>
```

Listing 11.3 **Continued**

```
    <tr>
      <td>Title</td>
      <td> <input type="text" name="title" maxlength="60" size="30"></td>
    </tr>
    <tr>
      <td>Price $</td>
      <td><input type="text" name="price" maxlength="7" size="7"></td>
    </tr>
    <tr>
      <td colspan="2"><input type="submit" value="Register"></td>
    </tr>
  </table>
  </form>
</body>
</html>
```

The results of this form are passed along to `insert_book.php`, a script that takes the details, performs some minor validations, and attempts to write the data into the database. The code for this script is shown in Listing 11.4.

Listing 11.4 `insert_book.php`— **This Script Writes New Books into the Database**

```php
<html>
<head>
  <title>Book-O-Rama Book Entry Results</title>
</head>
<body>
<h1>Book-O-Rama Book Entry Results</h1>
<?php
  // create short variable names
  $isbn=$_POST['isbn'];
  $author=$_POST['author'];
  $title=$_POST['title'];
  $price=$_POST['price'];

  if (!$isbn || !$author || !$title || !$price)
  {
      echo 'You have not entered all the required details.<br />'
          .'Please go back and try again.';
      exit;
  }
  if (!get_magic_quotes_gpc())
  {
```

Listing 11.4   **Continued**

```php
   $isbn = addslashes($isbn);
   $author = addslashes($author);
   $title = addslashes($title);
   $price = doubleval($price);
 }

 @ $db = new mysqli('localhost', 'bookorama', 'bookorama123', 'books');

 if (mysqli_connect_errno())
 {
   echo 'Error: Could not connect to database.  Please try again later.';
   exit;
 }

 $query = "insert into books values
          ('".$isbn."', '".$author."', '".$title."', '".$price."')";
 $result = $db->query($query);
 if ($result)
     echo $db->affected_rows.' book inserted into database.';

 $db->close();
?>
</body>
</html>
```

The results of successfully inserting a book are shown in Figure 11.4.

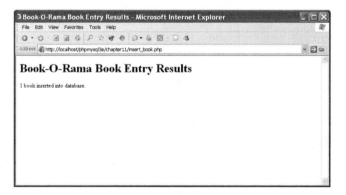

Figure 11.4   The script completes successfully and reports that the book has been added to the database.

If you look at the code for `insert_book.php`, you can see that much of it is similar to the script you wrote to retrieve data from the database. Here, you check that all the form fields were filled in, and you format them correctly for insertion into the database (if required) with `addslashes()`:

```
if (!get_magic_quotes_gpc())
{
  $isbn = addslashes($isbn);
  $author = addslashes($author);
  $title = addslashes($title);
  $price = doubleval($price);
}
```

Because the price is stored in the database as a float, you don't want to put slashes into it. You can achieve the same effect of filtering out any odd characters on this numerical field by calling `doubleval()`, which we discussed in Chapter 1, "PHP Crash Course." This also takes care of any currency symbols that the user might have typed in the form.

Again, you connect to the database by instantiating the `mysqli` object and setting up a query to send to the database. In this case, the query is an SQL `INSERT`:

```
$query = "insert into books values
          ('$isbn', '$author', '$title', '$price')";
$result = $db->query($query);
```

This query is executed on the database in the usual way by calling `$db->query()` (or `mysqli_query()` if you want to do things procedurally).

One significant difference between using `INSERT` and `SELECT` is in the use of `mysqli_affected_rows()`. This is a function in the procedural version or a class member variable in the object-oriented version:

```
echo $db->affected_rows.' book(s) inserted into database.';
```

In the previous script, you used `mysqli_num_rows()` to determine how many rows were returned by a `SELECT`. When you write queries that change the database such as `INSERT`s, `DELETE`s, and `UPDATE`s, you should use `mysqli_affected_rows()` instead.

We've now covered the basics of using MySQL databases from PHP.

Using Prepared Statements

The mysqli library supports the use of prepared statements. They are useful for speeding up execution when you are performing large numbers of the same query with different data. They also protect against SQL injection-style attacks.

The basic concept of a prepared statement is that you send a template of the query you want to execute to MySQL and then send the data separately. You can send multiple lots of the same data to the same prepared statement; this capability is particularly useful for bulk inserts.

You could use prepared statements in the `insert_book.php` script, as follows:

```
$query = "insert into books values(?, ?, ?, ?)";
$stmt = $db->prepare($query);
$stmt->bind_param("sssd", $isbn, $author, $title, $price);
$stmt->execute();
echo  $stmt->affected_rows.' book inserted into database.';
$stmt->close();
```

Let's consider this code line by line.

When you set up the query, instead of substituting in the variables as done previously, you put in question marks for each piece of data. You should not put any quotation marks or other delimiters around these question marks.

The second line is a call to `$db->prepare()`, which is called `mysqli_stmt_prepare()` in the procedural version. This line constructs a statement object or resource that you will then use to do the actual processing.

The statement object has a method called `bind_param()`. (In the procedural version, it is called `mysqli_stmt_bind_param()`.) The purpose of `bind_param()` is to tell PHP which variables should be substituted for the question marks. The first parameter is a format string, not unlike the format string used in `printf()`. The value you are passing here (`"sssd"`) means that the four parameters are a string, a string, a string, and a double, respectively. Other possible characters in the format string are `i` for integer and `b` for blob. After this parameter, you should list the same number of variables as you have question marks in your statement. They will be substituted in this order.

The call to `$stmt->execute()` (`mysqli_stmt_execute()` in the procedural version) actually runs the query. You can then access the number of affected rows and close the statement.

So how is this prepared statement useful? The clever thing is that you can change the values of the four bound variables and re-execute the statement without having to reprepare. This capability is useful for looping through bulk inserts.

As well as binding parameters, you can bind results. For SELECT type queries, you can use `$stmt->bind_result()` (or `mysqli_stmt_bind_result()`) to provide a list of variables that you would like the result columns to be filled in to. Each time you call `$stmt->fetch()` (or `mysqli_stmt_fetch()`), column values from the next row in the resultset are filled into these bound variables. For example, in the book search script you looked at earlier, you could use

```
$stmt->bind_result($isbn, $author, $title, $price);
```

to bind these four variables to the four columns that will be returned from the query. After calling

```
$stmt->execute();
```

you can call

```
$stmt->fetch();
```

in the loop. Each time this is called, it fetches the next result row into the four bound variables.

You can also use `mysqli_stmt_bind_param()` and `mysqli_stmt_bind_result()` in the same script.

Note that at the time of writing (PHP5RC2), prepared statements caused an Apache-crashing bug under Windows but worked fine on the Unix platforms.

Using Other PHP-Database Interfaces

PHP supports libraries for connecting to a large number of databases, including Oracle, Microsoft SQL Server, and PostgreSQL.

In general, the principles of connecting to and querying any of these databases are much the same. The individual function names vary, and different databases have slightly different functionality, but if you can connect to MySQL, you should be able to easily adapt your knowledge to any of the others.

If you want to use a database that doesn't have a specific library available in PHP, you can use the generic ODBC functions. ODBC, which stands for *Open Database Connectivity,* is a standard for connections to databases. It has the most limited functionality of any of the function sets, for fairly obvious reasons. If you have to be compatible with everything, you can't exploit the special features of anything.

In addition to the libraries that come with PHP, available database abstraction classes such as `PEAR::DB` allow you to use the same function names for each different type of database.

Using a Generic Database Interface: PEAR DB

Let's look at a brief example using the PEAR DB abstraction layer. This is one of the core components of PEAR and probably the most widely used of all the PEAR components. If you have PEAR installed, you should already have DB. If not, refer to the "PEAR Installation" section in Appendix A, "Installing PHP and MySQL."

For comparative purposes, let's look at how you could write the search results script differently using DB.

Listing 11.5 `results_generic.php`—**Retrieves Search Results from the MySQL Database and Formats Them for Display**

```
<html>
<head>
  <title>Book-O-Rama Search Results</title>
</head>
<body>
<h1>Book-O-Rama Search Results</h1>
<?php
  // create short variable names
```

Listing 11.5 **Continued**

```php
$searchtype=$_POST['searchtype'];
$searchterm=$_POST['searchterm'];

$searchterm= trim($searchterm);

if (!$searchtype || !$searchterm)
{
   echo 'You have not entered search details.  Please go back and try again.';
   exit;
}

if (!get_magic_quotes_gpc())
{
  $searchtype = addslashes($searchtype);
  $searchterm = addslashes($searchterm);
}

// set up for using PEAR DB
require_once('DB.php');
$user = 'bookorama';
$pass = 'bookorama123';
$host = 'localhost';
$db_name = 'books';

// set up universal connection string or DSN
$dsn = "mysqli://$user:$pass@$host/$db_name";

// connect to database
$db = &DB::connect($dsn) ;

// check if connection worked
if (DB::isError($db))
{
  echo $db->getMessage();
  exit;
}

// perform query
$query = "select * from books where ".$searchtype." like '%".$searchterm."%'";

$result = $db->query($query);
// check that result was ok
if (DB::isError($result))
{
  echo $db->getMessage();
```

Listing 11.5   **Continued**

```
    exit;
  }

  // get number of returned rows
  $num_results = $result->numRows();

  // display each returned row
  for ($i=0; $i <$num_results; $i++)
  {
     $row = $result->fetchRow(DB_FETCHMODE_ASSOC);
     echo '<p><strong>'.($i+1).'.'. Title: ';
     echo htmlspecialchars(stripslashes($row['title']));
     echo '</strong><br />Author: ';
     echo stripslashes($row['author']);
     echo '<br />ISBN: ';
     echo stripslashes($row['isbn']);
     echo '<br />Price: ';
     echo stripslashes($row['price']);
     echo '</p>';
  }

  // disconnect from database
  $db->disconnect();
?>
</body>
</html>
```

Let's examine what you do differently in this script.

To connect to the database, you use the line

```
$db = DB::connect($dsn);
```

This function accepts a universal connection string that contains all the parameters necessary to connect to the database. You can see this if you look at the format of the connection string:

```
$dsn = "mysqli://$user:$pass@$host/$db_name";
```

After this, you check to see whether the connection was unsuccessful using the isError() method and, if so, print the error message and exit:

```
if (DB::isError($db))
{
  echo $db->getMessage();
  exit;
}
```

Assuming everything has gone well, you then set up a query and execute it as follows:

```
$result = $db->query($query);
```

You can check the number of rows returned:

```
$num_results = $result->numRows();
```

You retrieve each row as follows:

```
$row = $result->fetchRow(DB_FETCHMODE_ASSOC);
```

The generic method `fetchRow()` can fetch a row in many different formats; the parameter `DB_FETCHMODE_ASSOC` tells it that you would like the row returned as an associative array.

After outputting the returned rows, you finish by closing the database connection:

```
$db->disconnect();
```

As you can see, this generic example is similar to the first script.

The advantages of using DB are that you need to remember only one set of database functions and that the code will require minimal changes if you decide to change the database software.

Because this is a MySQL book, we use the MySQL native libraries for extra speed and flexibility. You might want to use the DB package in your projects because sometimes the use of an abstraction layer can be extremely helpful.

Further Reading

For more information on connecting MySQL and PHP together, you can read the appropriate sections of the PHP and MySQL manuals.

For more information on ODBC, visit
http://www.webopedia.com/TERM/O/ODBC.html

Next

In the next chapter, we go into more detail about MySQL administration and discuss how to optimize databases.

## 12

Advanced MySQL Administration

IN THIS CHAPTER, WE COVER SOME MORE ADVANCED MySQL topics, including advanced privileges, security, and optimization.

Key topics covered in this chapter include

- Understanding the privilege system in detail
- Making your MySQL database secure
- Getting more information about databases
- Speeding things up with indexes
- Optimizing your database
- Backing up and recovering
- Implementing replication

Understanding the Privilege System in Detail

Chapter 9, "Creating Your Web Database," described the process of setting up users and granting them privileges. You saw how to do this with the GRANT command. If you're going to administer a MySQL database, understanding exactly what GRANT does and how it works can be useful.

When you issue a GRANT statement, it affects tables in the special database called mysql. Privilege information is stored in five tables in this database. Given this fact, when granting privileges on databases, you should be cautious about granting access to the mysql database.

One side note is that the GRANT command is available only from MySQL version 3.22.11 onward.

You can look at what's in the mysql database by logging in as an administrator and typing

```
use mysql;
```

If you do this, you can then view the tables in this database as usual by typing

show tables;

Your results look something like this:

```
+-----------------+
| Tables_in_mysql |
+-----------------+
| columns_priv    |
| db              |
| func            |
| help_category   |
| help_keyword    |
| help_relation   |
| help_topic      |
| host            |
| proc            |
| tables_priv     |
| user            |
+-----------------+
```

Each of these tables stores system information. Five of them—user, host, db, tables_priv, and columns_priv—store privilege information. They are sometimes called *grant tables*. These tables vary in their specific function but all serve the same general function, which is to determine what users are and are not allowed to do. Each of them contains two types of fields: scope fields, which identify the user, host, and part of a database that the privilege refers to; and privilege fields, which identify which actions can be performed by that user in that scope.

The user and host tables are used to decide whether a user can connect to the MySQL server at all and whether she has any administrator privileges. The db and host tables determine which databases the user can access. The tables_priv table determines which tables within a database a user can use, and the columns_priv table determines which columns within tables she has access to.

The user Table

The user table contains details of global user privileges. It determines whether a user is allowed to connect to the MySQL server at all and whether she has any global-level privileges—that is, privileges that apply to every database in the system.

You can see the structure of this table by issuing a describe user; statement. The schema for the user table is shown in Table 12.1.

Table 12.1   **Schema of the** user **Table in the** mysql **Database**

Field	Type
Host	varchar(60)
User	varchar(16)
Password	varchar(41)
Select_priv	enum('N','Y')
Insert_priv	enum('N','Y')
Update_priv	enum('N','Y')
Delete_priv	enum('N','Y')
Create_priv	enum('N','Y')
Drop_priv	enum('N','Y')
Reload_priv	enum('N','Y')
Shutdown_priv	enum('N','Y')
Process_priv	enum('N','Y')
File_priv	enum('N','Y')
Grant_priv	enum('N','Y')
References_priv	enum('N','Y')
Index_priv	enum('N','Y')
Alter_priv	enum('N','Y')
Show_db_priv	enum('N','Y')
Super_priv	enum('N','Y')
Create_tmp_table_priv	enum('N','Y')
Lock_tables_priv	enum('N','Y')
Execute_priv	enum('N','Y')
Repl_slave_priv	enum('N','Y')
Repl_client_priv	enum('N','Y')
ssl_type	enum('N','Y')
ssl_cipher	enum('N','Y')
x509_issuer	enum('N','Y')
x509_subject	enum('N','Y')
max_questions	enum('N','Y')
max_updates	enum('N','Y')
max_connections	enum('N','Y')

Each row in this table corresponds to a set of privileges for a User coming from a Host and logging in with the password Password. These are the *scope fields* for this table because they describe the scope of the other fields, called *privilege fields*.

The privileges listed in this table (and the others to follow) correspond to the privileges granted using GRANT in Chapter 9. For example, Select_priv corresponds to the privilege to run a SELECT command.

If a user has a particular privilege, the value in that column will be Y. Conversely, if a user has not been granted that privilege, the value will be N.

All the privileges listed in the user table are global; that is, they apply to *all the databases in the system* (including the mysql database). Administrators will therefore have some Ys in there, but the majority of users should have all Ns. Normal users should have rights to appropriate databases, not all tables.

The db and host Tables

Most of your average users' privileges are stored in the tables db and host.

The db table determines which users can access which databases from which hosts. The privileges listed in this table apply to whichever database is named in a particular row.

The host table supplements the user and db tables. If a user is to connect from multiple hosts, no host will be listed for that user in the user or db table. Instead, he will have a set of entries in the host table, one to specify the privileges for each user-host combination.

The schemas of these two tables are shown in Tables 12.2 and 12.3, respectively.

Table 12.2 Schema of the db Table in the mysql Database

Field	Type
Host	char(60)
Db	char(64)
User	char(16)
Select_priv	enum('N','Y')
Insert_priv	enum('N','Y')
Update_priv	enum('N','Y')
Delete_priv	enum('N','Y')
Create_priv	enum('N','Y')
Drop_priv	enum('N','Y')
Grant_priv	enum('N','Y')
References_priv	enum('N','Y')
Index_priv	enum('N','Y')
Alter_priv	enum('N','Y')
Create_tmp_tables_priv	enum('N','Y')
Lock_tables_priv	enum('N','Y')

Table 12.3   **Schema of the** host **Table in the** mysql **Database**

Field	Type
Host	char(60)
Db	char(64)
Select_priv	enum('N','Y')
Insert_priv	enum('N','Y')
Update_priv	enum('N','Y')
Delete_priv	enum('N','Y')
Create_priv	enum('N','Y')
Drop_priv	enum('N','Y')
Grant_priv	enum('N','Y')
References_priv	enum('N','Y')
Index_priv	enum('N','Y')
Alter_priv	enum ('N','Y')
Create_tmp_tables_priv	enum('N','Y')
Lock_tables_priv	enum('N','Y')

The tables_priv **and** columns_priv **Tables**

The tables_priv and columns_priv tables are used to store table-level privileges and column-level privileges, respectively. They work like the db table, except that they provide privileges for tables within a specific database and columns within a specific table, respectively.

These tables have a slightly different structure than the user, db, and host tables have. The schemas for the tables_priv table and columns_priv table are shown in Tables 12.4 and 12.5, respectively.

Table 12.4   **Schema of the** tables_priv **Table in the** mysql **Database**

Field	Type
Host	char(60)
Db	char(64)
User	char(16)
Table_name	char(60)
Grantor	char(77)
Timestamp	timestamp(14)
Table_priv	set('Select', 'Insert', 'Update', 'Delete', 'Create', 'Drop', 'Grant', 'References', 'Index', 'Alter')
Column_priv	set ('Select', 'Insert', 'Update', 'References')

Table 12.5   **Schema of the** `columns_priv` **Table in the** `mysql` **Database**

Field	Type
Host	char(60)
Db	char(64)
User	char(16)
Table_name	char(64)
Column_name	char(64)
Timestamp	timestamp(14)
Column_priv	set('Select', 'Insert', 'Update', 'References')

The `Grantor` column in the `tables_priv` table stores the name of the user who granted this privilege to this user. The `Timestamp` column in both of these tables stores the date and time when the privilege was granted.

Access Control: How MySQL Uses the Grant Tables

MySQL uses the grant tables to determine what a user is allowed to do in a two-stage process:

1. Connection verification. Here, MySQL checks whether you are allowed to connect at all, based on information from the `user` table, as shown previously. This authentication is based on username, hostname, and password. If a username is blank, it matches all users. Hostnames can be specified with a wildcard character (`%`). This character can be used as the entire field (that is, `%` matches all hosts) or as part of a hostname (for example, `%.tangledweb.com.au` matches all hosts ending in `.tangledweb.com.au`). If the password field is blank, no password is required. Your system is more secure if you avoid having blank users, wildcards in hosts, and users without passwords. If the hostname is blank, MySQL refers to the `host` table for a matching `user` and `host` entry.

2. Request verification. Each time you enter a request, after you have established a connection, MySQL checks whether you have the appropriate level of privileges to perform that request. The system begins by checking your global privileges (in the `user` table) and, if they are not sufficient, checks the `db` and `host` tables. If you still don't have sufficient privileges, MySQL will check the `tables_priv` table, and, if this is not enough, finally it will check the `columns_priv` table.

Updating Privileges: When Do Changes Take Effect?

The MySQL server automatically reads the grant tables when it is started and when you issue GRANT and REVOKE statements. However, now that you know where and how those privileges are stored, you can alter them manually. When you update them manually, the MySQL server *will not notice that they have changed.*

You need to point out to the server that a change has occurred, and you can do this in three ways. You can type

```
flush privileges;
```

at the MySQL prompt (you need to be logged in as an administrator to use this command). This is the most commonly used way of updating the privileges.

Alternatively, you can run either

```
mysqladmin flush-privileges
```

or

```
mysqladmin reload
```

from your operating system.

After this, global-level privileges will be checked the next time a user connects; database privileges will be checked when the next use statement is issued; and table- and column-level privileges will be checked on a user's next request.

Making Your MySQL Database Secure

Security is important, especially when you begin connecting your MySQL database to your website. The following sections explain the precautions you ought to take to protect your database.

MySQL from the Operating System's Point of View

Running the MySQL server (mysqld) as root is a bad idea if you are running a Unix-like operating system. Doing this gives a MySQL user with a full set of privileges the right to read and write files anywhere in the operating system. This is an important point, easily overlooked, which was famously used to hack Apache's website. (Fortunately, the crackers were "white hats" [good guys], and their only action was to tighten up security.)

Setting up a MySQL user specifically for the purpose of running mysqld is a good idea. In addition, you can then make the directories (where the physical data is stored) accessible only by the MySQL user. In many installations, the server is set up to run as userid mysql, in the mysql group.

You should also ideally set up your MySQL server behind your firewall. This way, you can stop connections from unauthorized machines. Check to see whether you can connect from outside to your server on port number 3306. This is the default port MySQL runs on and should be closed on your firewall.

Passwords

Make sure that all your users have passwords (especially root!) and that they are well chosen and regularly changed, as with operating system passwords. The basic rule to remember here is that passwords that are or contain words from a dictionary are a bad idea. Combinations of letters and numbers are best.

If you are going to store passwords in script files, make sure only the user whose password is stored can see that script.

PHP scripts that are used to connect to the database need access to the password for that user. This can be done reasonably securely by putting the login and password in a file called, for example, dbconnect.php, that you then include when required. This script can be carefully stored outside the web document tree and made accessible only to the appropriate user.

Remember that if you put these details in a file with .inc or some other extension in the web tree, you must be careful to check that your web server knows these files must be interpreted as PHP so that the details cannot be viewed in a web browser.

Don't store passwords in plain text in your database. MySQL passwords are not stored that way, but commonly in web applications, you additionally want to store website members' login names and passwords. You can encrypt passwords (one way) using MySQL's SHA1() function. Remember that if you insert a password in this format when you run SELECT (to log in a user), you will need to use the same function again to check the password a user has typed.

You will use this functionality when you implement the projects in Part V, "Building Practical PHP and MySQL Projects."

User Privileges

Knowledge is power. Make sure that you understand MySQL's privilege system and the consequences of granting particular privileges. Don't grant more privileges to any user than she needs. You should check them by looking at the grant tables.

In particular, don't grant the PROCESS, FILE, SHUTDOWN, and RELOAD privileges to any user other than an administrator unless absolutely necessary. The PROCESS privilege can be used to see what other users are doing and typing, including their passwords. The FILE privilege can be used to read and write files to and from the operating system (including, say, /etc/password on a Unix system).

The GRANT privilege should also be granted with caution because it allows users to share their privileges with others.

Make sure that when you set up users, you grant them access only from the hosts that they will be connecting from. If you have jane@localhost as a user, that's fine, but plain jane is pretty common and could log in from anywhere—and she might not be the jane you think she is. Avoid using wildcards in hostnames for similar reasons.

You can further increase security by using IPs rather than domain names in your host table. This way, you can avoid problems with errors or crackers at your DNS. You can enforce this by starting the MySQL daemon with the --skip-name-resolve option, which means that all host column values must be either IP addresses or localhost.

You should also prevent nonadministrative users from having access to the `mysqladmin` program on your web server. Because this program runs from the command line, access to it is an issue of operating system privilege.

Web Issues

Connecting your MySQL database to the Web raises some special security issues.

It's not a bad idea to start by setting up a special user just for the purpose of web connections. This way, you can give him the minimum privilege necessary and not grant, for example, `DROP`, `ALTER`, or `CREATE` privileges to that user. You might grant `SELECT` only on `catalog` tables and `INSERT` only on `order` tables. Again, this is an illustration of how to use the principle of least privilege.

> **Caution**
>
> In the preceding chapter, we described using PHP's `addslashes()` and `stripslashes()` functions to get rid of any problematic characters in strings. It's important to remember to do this and to do a general data cleanup before sending anything to MySQL. You might remember using the `doubleval()` function to check that the numeric data was really numeric. Forgetting this is a common error; people remember to use `addslashes()` but not to check numeric data.

You should always check all data coming in from a user. Even if your HTML form consists of select boxes and radio buttons, someone might alter the URL to try to crack your script. Checking the size of the incoming data is also worthwhile.

If users are typing in passwords or confidential data to be stored in your database, remember that it will be transmitted from the browser to the server in plain text unless you use Secure Sockets Layer (SSL). We discuss using SSL in more detail later in this book.

Getting More Information About Databases

So far, we've used `SHOW` and `DESCRIBE` to find out what tables are in the database and what columns are in them. In the following sections, we briefly look at other ways they can be used and at the use of the `EXPLAIN` statement to get more information about how a `SELECT` operation is performed.

Getting Information with SHOW

Previously, you used

```
show tables;
```

to get a list of tables in the database.

The statement

```
show databases;
```

displays a list of available databases. You can then use the SHOW TABLES statement to see a list of tables in one of those databases:

```
show tables from books;
```

When you use SHOW TABLES without specifying a database, it defaults to the one in use.

When you know what the tables are, you can get a list of the columns:

```
show columns from orders from books;
```

If you leave off the database name, the SHOW COLUMNS statement will default to the database currently in use. You can also use the *table.column* notation:

```
show columns from books.orders;
```

One other useful variation of the SHOW statement can be used to see what privileges a user has. For example, if you run

```
show grants for bookorama;
```

you get the following output:

```
+-----------------------------------------------------------------------+
| Grants for bookorama@%                                                |
+-----------------------------------------------------------------------+
| GRANT USAGE ON *.* TO 'bookorama'@'%'                                 |
| IDENTIFIED BY PASSWORD '*1ECE648641438A28E1910D0D7403C5EE9E8B0A85'    |
| GRANT SELECT, INSERT, UPDATE, DELETE, CREATE, DROP, INDEX, ALTER      |
| ON `books`.* TO 'bookorama'@'%'                                       |
+-----------------------------------------------------------------------+
```

The GRANT statements shown are not necessarily the ones that were executed to give privileges to a particular user, but rather summary equivalent statements that would produce the user's current level of privilege.

> **Note**
> The SHOW GRANTS statement was added in MySQL version 3.23.4. If you have an earlier version, this statement won't work.

Many other variations of the SHOW statement can be used as well. A summary of all the variations is shown in Table 12.6.

Table 12.6 **SHOW Statement Syntax**

Variation	Description
`SHOW DATABASES [LIKE database]`	Lists available databases, optionally with names like `database`.
`SHOW [OPEN] TABLES [FROM database] [LIKE table]`	Lists tables from the database currently in use, or from the database called `database` if specified, optionally with table names like `table`.
`SHOW COLUMNS FROM table [FROM database] [LIKE column]`	Lists all the columns in a particular table from the database currently in use, or from the database specified, optionally with column names like `column`. You might use `SHOW FIELDS` instead of `SHOW COLUMNS`.
`SHOW INDEX FROM table [FROM database]`	Shows details of all the indexes on a particular table from the database currently in use, or from the database called `database` if specified. You might use `SHOW KEYS` instead.
`SHOW STATUS [LIKE status_item]`	Gives information about a number of system items, such as the number of threads running. The `LIKE` clause is used to match against the names of these items, so, for example, `'Threads%'` matches the items `'Threads_cached'`, `'Threads_connected'`, and `'Threads_running'`.
`SHOW [GLOBAL|SESSION] VARIABLES [LIKE variable_name]`	Displays the names and values of the MySQL system variables, such as the version number. The `LIKE` clause can be used to match against them in a fashion similar to `SHOW STATUS`.
`SHOW [FULL] PROCESSLIST`	Displays all the running processes in the system—that is, the queries that are currently being executed. Most users will see their own threads, but if they have the `PROCESS` privilege, they can see everybody's processes—including passwords if they are in queries. The queries are truncated to 100 characters by default. Using the optional keyword `FULL` displays the full queries.
`SHOW TABLE STATUS [FROM database] [LIKE database]`	Displays information about each of the tables in the database currently being used, or the database called `database` if it is specified, optionally with a wildcard match. This information includes the table type and the time each table was last updated.
`SHOW GRANTS FOR user`	Shows the `GRANT` statements required to give the user specified in `user` his current level of privilege.
`SHOW PRIVILEGES`	Shows the different privileges that the server supports.
`SHOW CREATE DATABASE db`	Shows a `CREATE DATABASE` statement that would create the specified database.
`SHOW CREATE TABLE tablename`	Shows a `CREATE TABLE` statement that would create the specified table.
`SHOW [STORAGE] ENGINES`	Shows the storage engines that are available in this installation and which is the default. (We discuss storage engines further in Chapter 13, "Advanced MySQL Programming.")
`SHOW INNODB STATUS`	Shows data about the current state of the InnoDB storage engine.
`SHOW [BDB] LOGS`	Shows information about log files for the BDB storage engine.
`SHOW WARNINGS [LIMIT [offset,] row_count]`	Shows any errors, warnings, or notices generated by the last statement that was executed.
`SHOW ERRORS [LIMIT [offset,] row_count]`	Shows only the errors generated by the last statement that was executed.

Getting Information About Columns with DESCRIBE

As an alternative to the SHOW COLUMNS statement, you can use the DESCRIBE statement, which is similar to the DESCRIBE statement in Oracle (another RDBMS). The basic syntax for it is

```
DESCRIBE table [column];
```

This command gives information about all the columns in the table or a specific column if *column* is specified. You can use wildcards in the column name if you like.

Understanding How Queries Work with EXPLAIN

The EXPLAIN statement can be used in two ways. First, you can use

```
EXPLAIN table;
```

This command gives similar output to DESCRIBE *table* or SHOW COLUMNS FROM *table*.

The second and more interesting way you can use EXPLAIN allows you to see exactly how MySQL evaluates a SELECT query. To use it this way, just put the word EXPLAIN in front of a SELECT statement.

You can use the EXPLAIN statement when you are trying to get a complex query to work and clearly haven't got it quite right, or when a query is taking a lot longer to process than it should. If you are writing a complex query, you can check this in advance by running the EXPLAIN command before you actually run the query. With the output from this statement, you can rework your SQL to optimize it if necessary. It's also a handy learning tool.

For example, try running the following query on the Book-O-Rama database:

```
explain
select customers.name
from customers, orders, order_items, books
where customers.customerid = orders.customerid
and orders.orderid = order_items.orderid
and order_items.isbn = books.isbn
and books.title like '%Java%';
```

This query produces the following output. (Note that we are displaying this output vertically because the table rows are too wide to fit in this book. You can get this format by ending your query with \G instead of the semicolon.)

```
*************************** 1. row ***************************
          id: 1
 select_type: SIMPLE
       table: books
        type: ALL
```

```
    possible_keys: PRIMARY
              key: NULL
          key_len: NULL
              ref: NULL
             rows: 4
            Extra: Using where
*************************** 2. row ***************************
               id: 1
      select_type: SIMPLE
            table: order_items
             type: index
    possible_keys: PRIMARY
              key: PRIMARY
          key_len: 17
              ref: NULL
             rows: 4
            Extra: Using where; Using index
*************************** 3. row ***************************
               id: 1
      select_type: SIMPLE
            table: orders
             type: eq_ref
    possible_keys: PRIMARY
              key: PRIMARY
          key_len: 4
              ref: books.order_items.orderid
             rows: 1
            Extra:
*************************** 4. row ***************************
               id: 1
      select_type: SIMPLE
            table: customers
             type: eq_ref
    possible_keys: PRIMARY
              key: PRIMARY
          key_len: 4
              ref: books.orders.customerid
             rows: 1
            Extra:
```

This output might look confusing at first, but it can be very useful. Let's look at the columns in this table one by one.

The first column, id, gives the ID number of the SELECT statement within the query that this row refers to.

The column `select_type` explains the type of query being used. The set of values this column can have is shown in Table 12.7.

Table 12.7   **Possible Select Types as Shown in Output from** EXPLAIN

Type	Description
SIMPLE	Plain old SELECT, as in this example
PRIMARY	Outer (first) query where subqueries and unions are used
UNION	Second or later query in a union
DEPENDENT UNION	Second or later query in a union, dependent on the primary query
SUBQUERY	Inner subquery
DEPENDENT SUBQUERY	Inner subquery, dependent on the primary query (that is, a correlated subquery)
DERIVED	Subquery used in FROM clause

The column `table` just lists the tables used to answer the query. Each row in the result gives more information about how that particular table is used in this query. In this case, you can see that the tables used are `orders`, `order_items`, `customers`, and `books`. (You know this already by looking at the query.)

The `type` column explains how the table is being used in joins in the query. The set of values this column can have is shown in Table 12.8. These values are listed in order from fastest to slowest in terms of query execution. The table gives you an idea of how many rows need to be read from each table to execute a query.

Table 12.8   **Possible Join Types as Shown in Output from** EXPLAIN

Type	Description
const or system	The table is read from only once. This happens when the table has exactly one row. The type system is used when it is a system table, and the type const otherwise.
eq_ref	For every set of rows from the other tables in the join, you read one row from this table. This type is used when the join uses all the parts of the index on the table, and the index is UNIQUE or is the primary key.
ref	For every set of rows from the other tables in the join, you read a set of table rows that all match. This type is used when the join cannot choose a single row based on the join condition—that is, when only part of the key is used in the join, or if it is not UNIQUE or a primary key.
ref_or_null	This is like a ref query, but MySQL also looks for rows that are NULL. (This type is used mostly in subqueries.)

Table 12.8   **Possible Join Types as Shown in Output from** EXPLAIN

Type	Description
index_merge	A specific optimization, the Index Merge, has been used.
unique_subquery	This join type is used to replace ref for some IN subqueries where one unique row is returned.
index_subquery	This join type is similar to unique_subquery but is used for indexed nonunique subqueries.
range	For every set of rows from the other tables in the join, you read a set of table rows that fall into a particular range.
index	The entire index is scanned.
ALL	Every row in the table is scanned.

In the previous example, you can see that two of the tables are joined using eq_ref (orders and customers), one is joined using index (order_items), and the other one (books) is joined using ALL—that is, by looking at every single row in the table.

The rows column backs this up: It lists (roughly) the number of rows of each table that has to be scanned to perform the join. You can multiply these numbers together to get the total number of rows examined when a query is performed. You multiply these numbers because a join is like a product of rows in different tables. Check out Chapter 10, "Working with Your MySQL Database," for details. Remember that this is the number of rows examined, not the number of rows returned, and that it is only an estimate; MySQL can't know the exact number without performing the query.

Obviously, the smaller you can make this number, the better. At present, you have a negligible amount of data in the database, but when the database starts to increase in size, this query would increase in execution time. We return to this matter shortly.

The possible_keys column lists, as you might expect, the keys that MySQL might use to join the table. In this case, you can see that the possible keys are all PRIMARY keys.

The key column is either the key from the table MySQL actually used or NULL if no key was used. Notice that, although there is a possible PRIMARY key for the books table, it was not used in this query.

The key_len column indicates the length of the key used. You can use this number to tell whether only part of a key was used. The key length is relevant when you have keys that consist of more than one column. In this case, where the keys were used, the full key was used.

The ref column shows the columns used with the key to select rows from the table.

Finally, the Extra column tells you any other information about the way the join was performed. The possible values you might see in this column are shown in Table 12.9.

Table 12.9 **Possible Values for** `Extra` **Column as Shown in Output from** `EXPLAIN`

Value	Meaning
`Distinct`	After the first matching row is found, MySQL stops trying to find rows.
`Not exists`	The query has been optimized to use `LEFT JOIN`.
`Range checked for each record`	For each row in the set of rows from the other tables in the join, MySQL tries to find the best index to use, if any.
`Using filesort`	Two passes are required to sort the data. (This operation obviously takes twice as long.)
`Using index`	All information from the table comes from the index; that is, the rows are not actually looked up.
`Using temporary`	A temporary table needs to be created to execute this query.
`Using where`	A `WHERE` clause is being used to select rows.

You can fix problems you spot in the output from `EXPLAIN` in several ways. First, you can check column types and make sure they are the same. This applies particularly to column widths. Indexes can't be used to match columns if they have different widths. You can fix this problem by changing the types of columns to match or by building this in to your design from the start.

Second, you can tell the join optimizer to examine key distributions and therefore optimize joins more efficiently using the `myisamchk` utility or the `ANALYZE TABLE` statement, which are equivalent. You can invoke this utility by typing

```
myisamchk --analyze pathtomysqldatabase/table
```

You can check multiple tables by listing them all on the command line or by using

```
myisamchk --analyze pathtomysqldatabase/*.MYI
```

You can check all tables in all databases by running the following:

```
myisamchk --analyze pathtomysqldatadirectory/*/*.MYI
```

Alternatively, you can list the tables in an `ANALYZE TABLE` statement within the MySQL monitor:

```
analyze table customers, orders, order_items, books;
```

Third, you might want to consider adding a new index to the table. If this query is a) slow and b) common, you should seriously consider this fix. If it's a one-off query that you'll never use again, such as an obscure report requested once, this technique won't be worth the effort because it will slow down other things. We look at how to use this technique in the next section.

Speeding Up Queries with Indexes

If the `possible_keys` column from an EXPLAIN contains some NULL values, you might be able to improve the performance of your query by adding an index to the table in question. If the column you are using in your WHERE clause is suitable for indexing, you can create a new index for it using ALTER TABLE like this:

```
ALTER TABLE table ADD INDEX (column);
```

Optimizing Your Database

In addition to using the previous query optimization tips, you can do quite a few things to generally increase the performance of your MySQL database.

Design Optimization

Basically, you want everything in your database to be as small as possible. You can achieve this result, in part, with a decent design that minimizes redundancy. You can also achieve it by using the smallest possible data type for columns. You should also minimize NULLs wherever possible and make your primary key as short as possible.

Avoid variable length columns if at all possible (such as VARCHAR, TEXT, and BLOB). If your tables have fixed-length fields, they will be faster to use but might take up a little more space.

Permissions

In addition to using the suggestions mentioned in the previous section on EXPLAIN, you can improve the speed of queries by simplifying your permissions. Earlier, we discussed the way that queries are checked with the permission system before being executed. The simpler this process is, the faster your query will run.

Table Optimization

If a table has been in use for a period of time, data can become fragmented as updates and deletions are processed. This fragmentation increases the time taken to find things in this table. You can fix this problem by using the statement

```
OPTIMIZE TABLE tablename;
```

or by typing

```
myisamchk -r table
```

at the command prompt.

You can also use the `myisamchk` utility to sort a table index and the data according to that index, like this:

```
myisamchk --sort-index --sort-records=1 pathtomysqldatadirectory/*/*.MYI
```

Using Indexes

You should use indexes where required to speed up your queries. Keep them simple and don't create indexes that are not being used by your queries. You can check which indexes are being used by running EXPLAIN, as shown previously.

Using Default Values

Wherever possible, you should use default values for columns and insert data only if it differs from the default. This way, you reduce the time taken to execute the INSERT statement.

Other Tips

You can make many other minor tweaks to improve performance in particular situations and address particular needs. The MySQL website offers a good set of additional tips. You can find it at http://www.mysql.com.

Backing Up Your MySQL Database

In MySQL, there are several ways to do a backup. The first way is to lock the tables while you copy the physical files, using a LOCK TABLES command with the following syntax:

```
LOCK TABLES table lock_type [, table lock_type ...]
```

Each *table* should be the name of a table, and the *lock type* should be either READ or WRITE. For a backup, you only need a read lock. You need to execute a FLUSH TABLES; command to make sure any changes to your indexes have been written to disk before performing a backup.

Users and scripts can still run read-only queries while you make your backup. If you have a reasonable volume of queries that alter the database, such as customer orders, this solution is not practical.

The second, and superior, method is using the mysql_dump command. Usage is from the operating system command line, and is typically something such as

```
mysqldump --opt --all-databases > all.sql
```

This command dumps a set of all the SQL required to reconstruct the database to the file called all.sql.

You should then stop the mysqld process for a moment and restart it with the --log-bin[=*logfile*] option. The updates stored in the log file give you the changes made since your dump. (Obviously, you should back up the log files in any normal file backup.)

A third method is using the mysqlhotcopy script. You can invoke it with

```
mysqlhotcopy database /path/for/backup
```

You should then follow the process of starting and stopping the database as described earlier.

A final method of backup (and failover) is to maintain a replicated copy of the database. Replication is discussed later in this chapter.

Restoring Your MySQL Database

If you need to restore your MySQL database, there are, again, a couple of approaches. If the problem is a corrupted table, you can run `myisamchk` with the `-r` (repair) option.

If you used the first method from the preceding section for backup, you can copy the data files back into the same locations in a new MySQL installation.

If you used the second method for backup, there are a couple of steps. First, you need to run the queries in your dump file. This step reconstructs the database up to the point where you dumped that file. Second, you need to update the database to the point stored in the binary log. You can do this by running the command

```
mysqlbinlog hostname-bin.[0-9]* | mysql
```

More information about the process of MySQL backup and recovery can be found at the MySQL website at http://www.mysql.com.

Implementing Replication

Replication is a technology that allows you to have multiple database servers serving the same data. This way, you can load share and improve system reliability; if one server goes down, the others can still be queried. Once set up, it can also be used for making backups.

The basic idea is to have a master server and add to it a number of *slaves*. Each of the slaves mirrors the master. When you initially set up the slaves, you copy over a snapshot of all the data on the master at that time. After that, slaves request updates from the master. The master transmits details of the queries that have been executed from its binary log, and the slaves reapply them to the data.

The usual way of using this setup is to apply write queries to the master and read queries to the slaves. This is enforced by your application logic. More complex architectures are possible, such as having multiple masters, but we will only consider the setup for the typical example.

You need to realize that slaves usually do not have data that is as up to date as on the master. This occurs in any distributed database.

To begin setting up a master and slave architecture, you need to make sure binary logging is enabled on the master. Enabling binary logging is discussed in Appendix A, "Installing PHP and MySQL."

You need to edit your `my.ini` or `my.cnf` file on both the master and slave servers. On the master, you need the following settings:

```
[mysqld]
log-bin
server-id=1
```

The first setting turns on binary logging (so you should already have this one; if not, add it in now). The second setting gives your master server a unique ID. Each of the slaves also needs an ID, so you need to add a similar line to the `my.ini/my.cnf` files on each of the slaves. Make sure the numbers are unique! For example, your first slave could have `server-id=2`; the next, `server-id=3`; and so on.

Setting Up the Master

On the master, you need to create a user for slaves to connect as. There is a special privilege level for slaves called *replication slave*. Depending on how you plan to do the initial data transfer, you may need to temporarily grant some additional privileges.

In most cases, you will use a database snapshot to transfer the data, and in this case, only the special replication slave privilege is needed. If you decide to use the LOAD DATA FROM MASTER command to transfer data (you learn about it in the next section), this user will also need the RELOAD, SUPER, and SELECT privileges, but only for initial setup. As per the principle of least privilege, discussed in Chapter 9, you should revoke these other privileges after the system is up and running.

Create a user on the master. You can call it anything you like and give it any password you like, but you should make a note of the username and password you choose. In our example, we call this user `rep_slave`:

```
grant replication slave
on *.*
to 'rep_slave'@'%' identified by 'password';
```

Obviously, you should change the password to something else.

Performing the Initial Data Transfer

You can transfer the data from master to slave in several ways. The simplest is to set up the slaves (described in the next section) and then run a LOAD DATA FROM MASTER statement. The problem with this approach is that it will lock the tables on the master while the data is being transferred, and this can take some time, so we do not recommend it. (You can use this option only if you are using MyISAM tables.)

Generally, it is better to take a snapshot of the database at the current time. You can do this by using the procedures described for taking backups elsewhere in this chapter. You should first flush the tables with the following statement:

```
flush tables with read lock;
```

The reason for the read lock is that you need to record the place the server is up to in its binary log when the snapshot was taken. You can do this by executing this statement:

```
show master status;
```

You should see output similar to the following from this statement:

```
+----------------------+----------+--------------+------------------+
| File                 | Position | Binlog_Do_DB | Binlog_Ignore_DB |
+----------------------+----------+--------------+------------------+
| laura-ltc-bin.000001 |       95 |              |                  |
+----------------------+----------+--------------+------------------+
```

Note the File and Position; you will need this information to set up the slaves.

Now take your snapshot and unlock the tables with the following statement:

```
unlock tables;
```

If you are using InnoDB tables, the easiest way is to use the InnoDB Hot Backup tool, available from Innobase Oy at http://www.innodb.com. This is not Free Software, so there is a license cost involved. Alternatively, you can follow the procedure described here and, before unlocking the tables, shut down the MySQL server and copy the entire directory for the database you want to replicate before restarting the server and unlocking the tables.

Setting Up the Slave or Slaves

You have two optionsfor setting up the slave or slaves. If you have taken a snapshot of your database, begin by installing it on the slave server.

Next, run the following queries on your slave:

```
change master to
master-host='server',
master-user='user',
master-password='password',
master-log-file='logfile',
master-log-pos=logpos;
start slave;
```

You need to fill in the data shown in italics. The *server* is the name of the master server. The *user* and *password* come from the GRANT statement you ran on the master server. The *logfile* and *logpos* come from the output of the SHOW MASTER STATUS statement you ran on the master server.

You should now be up and running.

If you did not take a snapshot, you can load the data from the master after running the preceding query by executing the following statement:

```
load data from master;
```

Further Reading

In these chapters on MySQL, we have focused on the uses and parts of the system most relevant to web development and to linking MySQL with PHP. If you want to know more about MySQL administration, you can visit the MySQL website at http://www.mysql.com.

You might also want to consult the MySQL Press book *MySQL Administrator's Guide*, or Paul Dubois' book *MySQL, Third Edition*, available from Developer's Library.

Next

In the next chapter, "Advanced MySQL Programming," we look at some advanced features of MySQL that are useful when writing web applications, such as how to use the different storage engines, transactions, and stored procedures.

13

Advanced MySQL Programming

IN THIS CHAPTER, YOU LEARN ABOUT SOME more advanced MySQL topics, including table types, transactions, and stored procedures.

Key topics covered in this chapter include

- The LOAD DATA INFILE statement
- Storage engines
- Transactions
- Foreign keys
- Stored procedures

The LOAD DATA INFILE Statement

One useful feature of MySQL that we have not yet discussed is the LOAD DATA INFILE statement. You can use it to load table data in from a file. It executes very quickly. This flexible command has many options, but typical usage is something like the following:

```
LOAD DATA INFILE "newbooks.txt" INTO TABLE books;
```

This line reads row data from the file newbooks.txt into the table books. By default, data fields in the file must be separated by tabs and enclosed in single quotation marks, and each row must be separated by a newline (\n). Special characters must be escaped out with a slash (\). All these characteristics are configurable with the various options of the LOAD statement; see the MySQL manual for more details.

To use the LOAD DATA INFILE statement, a user must have the FILE privilege discussed in Chapter 9, "Creating Your Web Database."

Storage Engines

MySQL supports a number of different storage engines, sometimes also called *table types*. This means that you have a choice about the underlying implementation of the tables. Each table in your database can use a different storage engine, and you can easily convert between them.

You can choose a table type when you create a table by using

```
CREATE TABLE table TYPE=type ....
```

The possible table types are

- **MyISAM**—This type is the default and what we have used so far in the book. It is based on the traditional ISAM type, which stands for *Indexed Sequential Access Method*, a standard method for storing records and files. MyISAM adds a number of advantages over the ISAM type. Compared to the other storage engines, MyISAM has the most tools for checking and repairing tables. MyISAM tables can be compressed, and they support full text searching. They are not transaction safe and do not support foreign keys.

- **ISAM**—As described in the preceding bullet. The use of ISAM tables is deprecated.

- **MEMORY** (previously known as **HEAP**)—Tables of this type are stored in memory, and their indexes are hashed. This makes MEMORY tables extremely fast, but, in the event of a crash, your data will be lost. These characteristics make MEMORY tables ideal for storing temporary or derived data. You should specify MAX_ROWS in the CREATE TABLE statement; otherwise, these tables can hog all your memory. Also, they cannot have BLOB, TEXT, or AUTO INCREMENT columns.

- **MERGE**—These tables allow you to treat a collection of MyISAM tables as a single table for the purpose of querying. This way, you can work around maximum file size limitations on some operating systems.

- **BDB**—These tables are transaction safe; that is, they provide COMMIT and ROLLBACK capabilities. They are slower to use than the MyISAM tables, but they obviously give all the advantages of using transactions. These tables are based on the Berkeley DB.

- **InnoDB**—These tables are also transaction safe, and the same riders apply as for BDB. They also support foreign keys. InnoDB tables are faster and have more features than BDB tables, so if you need a transaction-safe storage engine, this is the one that we recommend.

In most web applications, you will generally use either MyISAM or InnoDB tables or a mix of the two.

You should use MyISAM when you are using a large number of SELECTs or INSERTs on a table (not both mixed together) because it is the fastest at doing this. For many web applications such as catalogs, MyISAM is the best choice. You should also use MyISAM if you need full text-searching capabilities. You should use InnoDB when transactions are important, such as for tables storing financial data or for situations in which INSERTs and SELECTs are being interleaved, such as online message boards or forums.

You can use MEMORY tables for temporary tables or to implement views, and MERGE tables if you need to deal with very large MyISAM tables.

You can change the type of a table after creation with an ALTER TABLE statement, as follows:

```
alter table orders type=innodb;
alter table order_items type=innodb;
```

We used MyISAM tables through most of this part of the book. We will now spend some time focusing on the use of transactions and ways they are implemented in InnoDB tables.

Transactions

Transactions are mechanisms for ensuring database consistency, especially in the event of error or server crash. In the following sections, you learn what transactions are and how to implement them with InnoDB.

Understanding Transaction Definitions

First, let's define the term *transaction*. A transaction is a query or set of queries guaranteed either to be completely executed on the database or not executed at all. The database is therefore left in a consistent state whether or not the transaction completed.

To see why this capability might be important, consider a banking database. Imagine the situation in which you want to transfer money from one account to another. This action involves removing the money from one account and placing it in another, which would involve at least two queries. It is vitally important that either these two queries are both executed or neither is executed. If you take the money out of one account and the power goes out before you put it into another account, what happens? Does the money just disappear?

You may have heard the expression *ACID compliance*. ACID is a way of describing four requirements that transactions should satisfy:

- **Atomicity**—A transaction should be atomic; that is, it should either be completely executed or not executed.
- **Consistency**—A transaction should leave the database in a consistent state.
- **Isolation**—Uncompleted transactions should not be visible to other users of the database; that is, until transactions are complete, they should remain isolated.
- **Durability**—Once written to the database, a transaction should be permanent or durable.

A transaction that has been permanently written to the database is said to be *committed*. A transaction that is not written to the database—so that the database is reset to the state it was in before the transaction began—is said to be *rolled back*.

Using Transactions with InnoDB

By default, MySQL runs in *autocommit mode*. This means that each statement you execute is immediately written to the database (committed). If you are using a transaction-safe table type, more than likely you don't want this behavior.

To turn autocommit off in the current session, type

```
set autocommit=0;
```

If autocommit is on, you need to begin a transaction with the statement

```
start transaction;
```

If it is off, you do not need this command because a transaction will be started automatically for you when you enter an SQL statement.

After you have finished entering the statements that make up a transaction, you can commit it to the database by simply typing

```
commit;
```

If you have changed your mind, you can revert to the previous state of the database by typing

```
rollback;
```

Until you have committed a transaction, it will not be visible to other users or in other sessions.

Let's look at an example. Execute the ALTER TABLE statements in the previous section of the chapter on your books database, as follows, if you have not already done so:

```
alter table orders type=innodb;
alter table order_items type=innodb;
```

These statements convert two of the tables to InnoDB tables. (You can convert them back later if you want by running the same statement but with type=MyISAM.)

Now open two connections to the books database. In one connection, add a new order record to the database:

```
insert into orders values
(5, 2, 69.98, '2004-06-18');
insert into order_items values
(5, '0-672-31697-8', 1);
```

Now check that you can see the new order:

```
select * from orders where orderid=5;
```

You should see the order displayed:

```
+---------+------------+--------+------------+
| orderid | customerid | amount | date       |
+---------+------------+--------+------------+
|       5 |          2 |  69.98 | 2004-06-18 |
+---------+------------+--------+------------+
```

Leaving this connection open, go to your other connection and run the same `select` query. You should not be able to see the order:

```
Empty set (0.00 sec)
```

(If you can see it, most likely you forgot to turn off autocommitting. Check this and that you converted the table in question to the InnoDB format.) The reason is that the transaction has not yet been committed. (This is a good illustration of transaction isolation in action.)

Now go back to the first connection and commit the transaction:

```
commit;
```

You should now be able to retrieve the row in your other connection.

Foreign Keys

InnoDB also supports foreign keys. You may recall that we discussed the concept of foreign keys in Chapter 8, "Designing Your Web Database." When you use MyISAM tables, you have no way to enforce foreign keys.

Consider, for example, inserting a row into the order_items table. You need to include a valid `orderid`. Using MyISAM, you need to ensure the validity of the `orderid` you insert somewhere in your application logic. Using foreign keys in InnoDB, you can let the database do the checking for you.

How do you set this up? To create the table initially using a foreign key, you could change the table DDL statement as follows:

```
create table order_items
( orderid int unsigned not null references orders(orderid),
  isbn char(13) not null,
  quantity tinyint unsigned,
  primary key (orderid, isbn)
) type=InnoDB;
```

We added the words `references orders(orderid)` after `orderid`. This means this column is a foreign key that must contain a value from the `orderid` column in the `orders` table.

Finally, we added the table type `type=InnoDB` at the end of the declaration. This is required for the foreign keys to work.

You can also make these changes to the existing table using ALTER TABLE statements, as follows:

```
alter table order_items type=InnoDB;
alter table order_items
add foreign key (orderid) references orders(orderid);
```

To see that this change has worked, you can try to insert a row with an orderid for which there is no matching row in the orders table:

```
insert into order_items values
(77, '0-672-31697-8', 7);
```

You should receive an error similar to

```
ERROR 1216 (23000): Cannot add or update a child row:
a foreign key constraint fails
```

Stored Procedures

MySQL5, currently in alpha at the time of writing, introduces *stored procedures*. This version should be the production version in 2005. In the following sections, we preview the stored procedures feature, which will be the major new feature in version 5.0.

A stored procedure is a programmatic function that is created and stored within MySQL. It can consist of SQL statements and a number of special control structures. It can be useful when you want to perform the same function from different applications or platforms, or as a way of encapsulating functionality. Stored procedures in a database can be seen as analogous to an object-oriented approach in programming. They allow you to control the way data is accessed.

Let's begin by looking at a simple example.

Basic Example

Listing 13.1 shows the declaration of a stored procedure.

Listing 13.1 `basic_stored_procedure.sql`— **Declaring a Stored Procedure**

```
# Basic stored procedure example
delimiter //

create procedure total_orders (out total float)
BEGIN
 select sum(amount) into total from orders;
END
//

delimiter ;
```

Let's go through this code line by line.

The first statement

```
delimiter //
```

changes the end-of-statement delimiter from the current value—typically a semicolon unless you have changed it previously—to a double forward slash. You do this so that you can use the semicolon delimiter within the stored procedure as you are entering the code for it without MySQL trying to execute the code as you go.

The next line

```
create procedure total_orders (out total float)
```

creates the actual procedure. The name of this procedure is `total_orders`. It has a single parameter called `total`, which is the value you are going to calculate. The word `OUT` indicates that this parameter is being passed out or returned.

Parameters can also be declared `IN`, meaning that a value is being passed into the procedure, or `INOUT`, meaning that a value is being passed in but can be changed by the procedure.

The word `float` indicates the type of the parameter. In this case, you return a total of all the orders in the `orders` table. The type of the `orders` column is `float`, so the type returned is also `float`. The acceptable data types map to the available column types.

If you want more than one parameter, you can provide a comma-separated list of parameters as you would in PHP.

The body of the procedure is enclosed within the `BEGIN` and `END` statements. They are analogous to the curly braces within PHP (`{}`)because they delimit a statement block.

In the body, you simply run a `SELECT` statement. The only difference from normal is that you include the clause `into total` to load the result of the query into the `total` parameter.

After you have declared the procedure, you return the delimiter back to being a semicolon with the line

```
delimiter ;
```

After the procedure has been declared, you can call it using the `call` keyword, as follows:

```
call total_orders(@t);
```

This statement calls the total orders and passes in a variable to store the result. To see the result, you need to then look at the variable:

```
select @t;
```

The result should be similar to

```
+-----------------+
| @t              |
+-----------------+
| 289.92001152039 |
+-----------------+
```

In a way similar to creating a procedure, you can create a function. A function accepts input parameters (only) and returns a single value. (At the time of writing, functions could not reference tables, but this limitation should change before version 5.0 becomes the production version.)

The basic syntax for this task is almost the same. A sample function is shown in Listing 13.2.

Listing 13.2 `basic_function.sql`— **Declaring a Stored Function**

```
# Basic syntax to create a function

delimiter //

create function add_tax (price float) returns float
return price*1.1;
//

delimiter ;
```

As you can see, this example uses the keyword `function` instead of `procedure`. There are a couple of other differences.

Parameters do not need to be specified as `IN` or `OUT` because they are all `IN`, or input parameters. After the parameter list, you can see the clause `returns float`. It specifies the type of the return value. Again, this value can be any of the valid MySQL types.

You return a value using the `return` statement, much as you would in PHP.

Notice that this example does not use the `BEGIN` and `END` statements. You could use them, but they are not required. Just as in PHP, if a statement block contains only one statement, you do not need to mark the beginning and end of it.

Calling a function is somewhat different from calling a procedure. You can call a stored function in the same way you would call a built-in function. For example,

```
select add_tax(100);
```

This statement should return the following output:

```
+-------------+
| add_tax(100) |
+-------------+
|         110 |
+-------------+
```

After you have defined procedures and functions, you can view the code used to define them by using, for example,

```
show create procedure total_orders;
```

or

```
show create function addtax;
```

You can delete them with

```
drop procedure total_orders;
```

or

```
drop function add_tax;
```

Stored procedures come with the ability to use control structures, variables, DECLARE handlers (like exceptions), and an important concept called *cursors*. We briefly look at each of these in the following sections.

Local Variables

You can declare local variables within a `begin...end` block by using a `declare` statement. For example, you could alter the `add_tax` function to use a local variable to store the tax rate, as shown in Listing 13.3.

Listing 13.3 `basic_function.sql`— **Declaring a Stored Function with Variables**

```
# Basic syntax to create a function

delimiter //

create function add_tax (price float) returns float
begin
  declare tax float default 0.10;
  return price*(1+tax);
end
//
delimiter ;
```

As you can see, you declare the variable using `declare`, followed by the name of the variable, followed by the type. The default clause is optional and specifies an initial value for the variable. You then use the variable as you would expect.

Cursors and Control Structures

Let's consider a more complex example. For this example, you'll write a stored procedure that works out which order was for the largest amount and returns the `orderid`. (Obviously, you could calculate this amount easily enough with a single query, but this simple example illustrates how to use cursors and control structures.) The code for this stored procedure is shown in Listing 13.4.

Listing 13.4 `control_structures_cursors.sql`— **Using Cursors and Loops to Process a Resultset**

```
# Procedure to find the orderid with the largest amount
# could be done with max, but just to illustrate stored procedure principles
```

Listing 13.4 **Continued**

```
delimiter //

create procedure largest_order(out largest_id int)
begin
  declare this_id int;
  declare this_amount float;
  declare l_amount float default 0.0;
  declare l_id int;

  declare done int default 0;
  declare continue handler for sqlstate '02000' set done = 1;
  declare c1 cursor for select orderid, amount from orders;

  open c1;
  repeat
    fetch c1 into this_id, this_amount;
    if not done then
      if this_amount > l_amount then
        set l_amount=this_amount;
        set l_id=this_id;
      end if;
    end if;
  until done end repeat;
  close c1;

  set largest_id=l_id;

end
//

delimiter ;
```

This code uses control structures (both conditional and looping), cursors, and declare handlers. Let's consider it line by line.

At the start of the procedure, you declare a number of local variables for use within the procedure. The variables this_id and this_amount store the values of orderid and amount in the current row. The variables l_amount and l_id are for storing the largest order amount and the corresponding ID. Because you will work out the largest amount by comparing each value to the current largest value, you initialize this variable to zero.

The next variable declared is done, initialized to zero (false). This variable is your loop flag. When you run out of rows to look at, you set this variable to 1 (true):

The line

```
declare continue handler for sqlstate '02000' set done = 1;
```

is called a *declare handler*. It is similar to an exception in stored procedures. At the time of writing, you could implement continue handlers and exit handlers. Continue handlers, like the one shown, take the action specified and then continue execution of the procedure. Exit handlers exit from the nearest `begin...end` block.

The next part of the declare handler specifies when the handler will be called. In this case, it will be called when `sqlstate '02000'` is reached. You may wonder what that means because it seems very cryptic! This means it will be called when no rows are found. You process a resultset row by row, and when you run out of rows to process, this handler will be called. You could also specify `FOR NOT FOUND` equivalently. Other options are `SQLWARNING` and `SQLEXCEPTION`.

The next thing is a *cursor*. A cursor is not dissimilar to an array; it retrieves a resultset for a query (such as returned by `mysqli_query()`) and allows you to process it a single line at a time (as you would with, for example, `mysqli_fetch_row()`). Consider this cursor:

```
declare c1 cursor for select orderid, amount from orders;
```

This cursor is called `c1`. This is just a definition of what it will hold. The query will not be executed yet.

The next line

```
open c1;
```

actually runs the query. To obtain each row of data, you must run a `fetch` statement. You do this in a `repeat` loop. In this case, the loop looks like this:

```
repeat
...
until done end repeat;
```

Note that the condition (until done) is not checked until the end. Stored procedures also support while loops, of the form

```
while condition do
...
end while;
```

There are also `loop` loops, of the form

```
loop
...
end loop
```

These loops have no built-in conditions but can be exited by means of a `leave;` statement.

Note that there are no `for` loops.

Continuing with the example, the next line of code fetches a row of data:

```
fetch c1 into this_id, this_amount;
```

This line retrieves a row from the cursor query. The two attributes retrieved by the query are stored in the two specified local variables.

You check whether a row was retrieved and then compare the current loop amount with the largest stored amount, by means of two IF statements:

```
if not done then
  if this_amount > l_amount then
    set l_amount=this_amount;
    set l_id=this_id;
  end if;
end if;
```

Note that variable values are set by means of the set statement.

In addition to if...then, stored procedures also support an if...then...else construct with the following form:

```
if condition then
    ...
    [elseif condition then]
    ...
    [else]
    ...
end if
```

There is also a case statement, which has the following form:

```
case value
    when value then statement
    [when value then statement ...]
    [else statement]
end case
```

Back to the example, after the loop has terminated, you have a little cleaning up to do:

```
close c1;
set largest_id=l_id;
```

The close statement closes the cursor.

Finally, you set the OUT parameter to the value you have calculated. You cannot use the parameter as a temporary variable, only to store the final value. (This usage is similar to some other programming languages, such as Ada.)

If you create this procedure as described here, you can call it as you did the other procedure:

```
call largest_order(@l);
select @l;
```

You should get output similar to the following:

```
+------+
| @1   |
+------+
| 3    |
+------+
```

You can check for yourself that the calculation is correct.

Further Reading

In this chapter, we took a cook's tour of the stored procedure functionality. You can find out more about stored procedures from the MySQL manual. Although not much is there at the time of writing, no doubt the documentation will become more fleshed out before this version of MySQL becomes the production version.

For more information on LOAD DATA INFILE, the different storage engines, and stored procedures, consult the MySQL manual.

If you want to find out more about transactions and database consistency, we recommend a good basic relational database text such as *An Introduction to Database Systems* by C. J. Date.

Next

We have now covered the fundamentals of PHP and MySQL. In Chapter 14, "Running an E-commerce Site," we look at the e-commerce and security aspects of setting up database-backed websites.

III

E-commerce and Security

14

Running an E-commerce Site

THIS CHAPTER INTRODUCES SOME OF THE ISSUES involved in specifying, designing, building, and maintaining an e-commerce site effectively. We examine the plan, possible risks, and some ways to make a website pay its own way.

Key topics you learn in this chapter include

- Deciding what you want to achieve with your e-commerce site
- Considering the types of commercial websites
- Understanding risks and threats
- Deciding on a strategy

Deciding What You Want to Achieve

Before spending too much time worrying about the implementation details of your website, you should have firm goals in mind and a reasonably detailed plan leading to those goals.

In this book, we make the assumption that you are building a commercial website. Presumably, then, making money is one of your goals.

There are many ways to take a commercial approach to the Internet. Perhaps you want to advertise your offline services or sell a real-world product online. Maybe you have a product that can be sold and provided online. Perhaps your site is not directly intended to generate revenue but instead supports offline activities or acts as a cheaper alternative to present activities.

Considering the Types of Commercial Websites

Commercial websites generally perform one or more of the following activities:

- Publish company information through online brochures
- Take orders for goods or services

- Provide services or digital goods
- Add value to goods or services
- Cut costs

Sections of many websites fit more than one of these categories. What follows is a description of each category and the usual way of making each generate revenue or other benefits for your organization.

The goal of this part of the book is to help you formulate your goals. Why do you want a website? How is each feature built in to your website going to contribute to your business?

Publishing Information Using Online Brochures

Nearly every commercial website in the early 1990s was simply an online brochure or sales tool. This type of site is still the most common form of commercial website. Either as an initial foray onto the Web or as a low-cost advertising exercise, this type of site makes sense for many businesses.

A *brochureware* site can be anything from a business card rendered as a web page to an extensive collection of marketing information. In any case, the purpose of the site, and its financial reason for existing, is to entice customers to make contact with your business. This type of site does not generate any income directly but can add to the revenue your business receives via traditional means.

Developing a site like this presents few technical challenges. The issues faced are similar to those in other marketing exercises. A few of the more common pitfalls with this type of site include

- Failing to provide important information
- Poor presentation
- Failing to answer feedback generated by the site
- Allowing the site to age
- Failing to track the success of the site

Failing to Provide Important Information

What are visitors likely to be seeking when they visit your site? Depending on how much they already know, they might want detailed product specifications, or they might just want very basic information such as contact details.

Many websites provide no useful information, or they miss crucial information. At the very least, your site needs to tell visitors what you do, what geographical areas your business services, and how to make contact.

Poor Presentation

"On the Internet, nobody knows you are a dog," or so goes the old saying.[1] In the same way that small businesses, or dogs, can look larger and more impressive when they are using the Internet, large businesses can look small, unprofessional, and unimpressive with a poor website.

Regardless of the size of your company, make sure that your website is of a high standard. Text should be written and proofread by somebody who has a very good grasp of the language being used. Graphics should be clean, clear, and fast to download. On a business site, you should carefully consider your use of graphics and color and make sure that they fit the image you want to present. Use animation carefully, if at all. Never play a sound without the user requesting it.

Although you cannot make your site look the same on all machines, operating systems, and browsers, you can make sure that it uses standard HTML so that the vast majority of users can view it without errors. Make sure that you test it with a wide variety of screen resolutions and the major browser/operating system combinations.

Failing to Answer Feedback Generated by the Website

Good customer service is just as vital in attracting and retaining customers on the Web as it is in the outside world. Large and small companies are guilty of putting an email address on a web page and then neglecting to check or answer that mail promptly.

People have different expectations of response times to email than to postal mail. If you do not check and respond to email daily, people will believe that their inquiry is not important to you.

Email addresses on web pages should usually be generic, addressed to job title or department rather than a specific person. What will happen to email sent to `fred.smith@example.com` when Fred leaves? Email addressed to `sales@example.com` is more likely to be passed to his successor. It could also be delivered to a group of people, which might help ensure that it is answered promptly.

You will probably receive a lot of spam sent to addresses that you put on web pages. Bear this fact in mind when deciding how to forward or handle emails sent to these addresses. You should consider using form-based feedback rather than directly giving out email addresses as this greatly reduces the incidence of spam.

Allowing the Site to Age

You need to be careful to keep your website fresh. Content needs to be changed periodically. Likewise, changes in the organization need to be reflected on the site. A "cobweb site" discourages repeat visits and leads people to suspect that much of the information might now be incorrect.

---

[1] Of course, an "old saying" about the Internet cannot really be very old. This is the caption from a cartoon by Peter Steiner originally published in the July 5, 1993, issue of *The New Yorker*.

One way to avoid a stale site is to update pages manually. Another is to use a scripting language such as PHP to create dynamic pages. If your scripts have access to up-to-date information, they can constantly generate up-to-date pages.

Failing to Track the Success of the Site

Creating a website is all well and good, but how do you justify the effort and expense? Particularly if the site is for a large company, you will be asked to demonstrate or quantify its value to the organization at some time.

For traditional marketing campaigns, large organizations spend tens of thousands of dollars on market research, both before launching a campaign and after the campaign to measure its effectiveness. Depending on the scale and budget of your web venture, these measures might be equally appropriate to aid in the design and measurement of your site.

Simpler or cheaper options include

- **Examining server logs**—Web servers store a lot of data about every request from your server. Much of this data is useless, and its sheer bulk makes it useless in its raw form. To distill your log files into a meaningful summary, you need a log file analyzer. Two of the better-known free programs are Analog, which is available from http://www.analog.cx/, and Webalizer, available from http://www.mrunix.net/webalizer/. Commercial programs such as Summary, available from http://summary.net, might be more comprehensive. A log file analyzer shows you how traffic to your site changes over time and what pages are being viewed.

- **Monitoring sales**—Your online brochure is supposed to generate sales. You should be able to estimate its effect on sales by comparing sales levels before and after the site launch. Your ability to monitor sales obviously becomes difficult if other kinds of marketing cause fluctuations in the same period.

- **Soliciting user feedback**—If you ask your users, they will tell you what they think of your site. By providing a feedback form, you can gather some useful opinions. To increase the quantity of feedback, you might like to offer a small inducement, such as entry into a prize drawing for all respondents.

- **Surveying representative users**—Holding focus groups can be an effective technique for evaluating your site or even a prototype of your intended site. To conduct a focus group, you simply need to gather some volunteers, encourage them to evaluate the site, and then interview them to gauge and record their opinions.

Focus groups can be expensive affairs, conducted by professional facilitators, who evaluate and screen potential participants to try to ensure that they accurately represent the spread of demographics and personalities in the wider community and then skillfully interview participants. Focus groups can also cost nothing, be run by an amateur, and be populated by a sample of people whose relevance to the target market is unknown.

Paying a specialist market research company is one way to get a well-run focus group and useful results, but it is not the only way. If you are running your own focus groups, choose a skillful moderator. The moderator should have excellent people skills and not have a bias or stake in the result of the research. Limit group sizes to 6 to 10 people. A recorder or secretary should assist the moderator to leave her free to facilitate discussion. The result that you get from your groups is only as relevant as the sample of people you use. If you evaluate your product only with friends and family of your staff, they are unlikely to represent the general community.

Taking Orders for Goods or Services

If your online advertising is compelling, the next logical step is to allow your customers to order while still online. Traditional salespeople know that it is important to get customers to make a decision now. The more time you give people to reconsider a purchasing decision, the more likely they are to shop around or change their mind. If customers want your product, it is in your best interest to make the purchase process as quick and easy as possible. Forcing people to step away from their computer and call a phone number or visit a store places obstacles in their way. If you have online advertising that has convinced viewers to buy, let them buy now, without leaving your website.

Taking orders on a website makes sense for many businesses. Every business wants orders. Allowing people to place orders online can either provide additional sales or reduce your salespeople's workload. Providing facilities for online orders obviously involves costs. Building a dynamic site, organizing payment facilities, and providing customer service all cost money.

Much of the appeal of online sales is that many of these costs stay the same regardless of whether you take 1,000 orders or 1,000,000 orders. To make the costs worthwhile though, you need to have products or services that will sell in reasonable numbers. Before you get too attached to the idea of online commerce, try to determine whether your products are suitable for an e-commerce site.

Products and services commonly bought using the Internet include books and magazines, computer software and equipment, music, clothing, travel, and tickets to entertainment events.

Just because your product is not in one of these categories, do not despair. These categories are already crowded with established brands. However, you would be wise to consider some of the factors that make these products big online sellers.

Ideally, an e-commerce product is nonperishable and easily shipped, expensive enough to make shipping costs seem reasonable, yet not so expensive that the purchaser feels compelled to physically examine the item before purchase.

The best e-commerce products are commodities. If a consumer buys an avocado, he will probably want to look at the particular avocado and perhaps feel it. All avocados are not the same. One copy of a book, CD, or computer program is usually identical to other copies of the same title. Purchasers do not need to see the particular item they will purchase.

In addition, e-commerce products should appeal to people who use the Internet. At the time of writing, this audience consists primarily of employed, younger adults, with above-average incomes, living in metropolitan areas. With time, though, the online population is beginning to look more like the whole population.

Some products are never going to be reflected in surveys of e-commerce purchases but are still a success. If you have a product that appeals only to a niche market, the Internet might be the ideal way to reach buyers. Even if only 10 people in your hometown collect 1980s action figures, a site selling them might work if 10 people in every other town collect them as well.

Some products are unlikely to succeed as e-commerce categories. Cheap, perishable items, such as groceries, seem a poor choice, although this has not deterred companies from trying, mostly unsuccessfully. Other categories suit brochureware sites very well but not online ordering. Big, expensive items fall into this category—items such as vehicles and real estate that require a lot of research before purchasing but that are too expensive to order without seeing and generally impractical to deliver.

Convincing prospective purchasers to complete an order presents a number of obstacles. They include

- Unanswered questions
- Trust
- Ease of use
- Compatibility

If users are frustrated by any of these obstacles, they are likely to leave without buying.

Unanswered Questions

If a prospective customer cannot find an immediate answer to one of her questions, she is likely to leave. This scenario has a number of implications. Make sure your site is well organized. Can a first-time visitor find what she wants easily? Also, make sure your site is comprehensive, without overloading visitors. On the Web, people are more likely to skim than to read carefully, so be concise. For most advertising media, there are practical limits on how much information you can provide. This is not true for a website. For a website, the two main limits are the cost of creating and updating information and limits imposed by how well you can organize, layer, and connect information so as not to overwhelm visitors.

Thinking of a website as an unpaid, never-sleeping, automatic salesperson is tempting, but customer service is still important. Encourage visitors to ask questions. Try to provide immediate or nearly immediate answers via phone, email, online chat, or some other convenient means.

Trust

If a visitor is not familiar with your brand name, why should he trust you? Anybody can put together a website. People do not need to trust you to read your brochureware site, but placing an order requires a certain amount of faith. How is a visitor to know whether you are a reputable organization or the aforementioned dog?

People are concerned about a number of issues when shopping online:

- **What are you going to do with their personal information?** Are you going to sell it to others, use it to send them huge amounts of advertising, or store it somewhere insecurely so that others can gain access to it? Telling people what you will and will not do with their data is important. Such information is called a *privacy policy* and should be easily accessible on your site.

- **Are you a reputable business?** If your business is registered with the relevant authority in a particular place; has a physical office, warehouse, and a phone number; and has been in business for a number of years, it is less likely to be a scam than a business that consists solely of a website and perhaps a post office box. Make sure that you display these details.

- **What happens if a purchaser is not satisfied with a purchase?** Under what circumstances will you give a refund? Who pays for shipping? Mail order retailers have traditionally had more liberal refund and return policies than traditional shops. Many offer an unconditional satisfaction guarantee. Consider the cost of returns against the increase in sales that a liberal return policy will create. Whatever your policy is, make sure that it is displayed on your site.

- **Should customers entrust their credit card information to you?** The single greatest trust issue for Internet shoppers is fear of transmitting their credit card details over the Internet. For this reason, you need to both handle credit cards securely and be seen as security conscious. At the very least, this means using Secure Sockets Layer (SSL) to transmit the details from the users' browser to your web server and ensuring that your web server is competently and securely administered. We discuss this topic in more detail later.

Ease of Use

Consumers vary greatly in their computer experience, language, general literacy, memory, and vision. Therefore, your site needs to be as easy as possible to use. Usability and user interface design principles fill many books on their own, but here are a few guidelines:

- **Keep your site as simple as possible.** The more options, advertisements, and distractions on each screen, the more likely a user is to get confused.

- **Keep text clear.** Use clear, uncomplicated fonts. Do not make text too small and bear in mind that it will be different sizes on different types of machines.

- **Make your ordering process as simple as possible.** Intuition and available evidence both support the idea that the more mouse clicks users have to make to place an order, the less likely they are to complete the process. Keep the number of steps to a minimum, but note that Amazon.com has a U.S. patent[2] on a process using only one click, which it calls 1-Click. This patent is strongly challenged by many website owners.

- **Try not to let users get lost.** Provide landmarks and navigational cues to tell users where they are. For example, if a user is within a subsection of the site, highlight the navigation for that subsection.

If you are using a shopping cart metaphor in which you provide a virtual container for customers to accumulate purchases prior to finalizing the sale, keep a link to the cart visible on the screen at all times.

Compatibility

Be sure to test your site in a number of browsers and operating systems. If the site does not work for a popular browser or operating system, you will look unprofessional and lose a section of your potential market.

If your site is already operating, your web server logs can tell you what browsers your visitors are using. As a rule of thumb, if you test your site in the last two versions of Microsoft Internet Explorer, a recent version of Internet Explorer and Safari on an Apple Mac, the current version of Mozilla on Linux, and a text-only browser such as Lynx, you will be visible to the vast majority of users. Remember to look at your site using a variety of screen resolutions. Some users have very large resolutions, but some use phones or PDAs. It is hard to make the same site look good on a screen that is 2,048 pixels wide and one that is 240 pixels wide.

Try to avoid features and facilities that are brand new, unless you are willing to write and maintain multiple versions of the site. Standards-compliant HTML or XHTML should work everywhere, but older features are more likely to be correctly supported on every browser and device.

Providing Services and Digital Goods

Many products or services can be sold over the Web and delivered to the customer via a courier. A smaller range can be delivered immediately online. If a service or good can be transmitted over a network, it can be ordered, paid for, and delivered instantly, without human interaction. The most obvious service provided this way is information.

---

[2]U.S. Patent and Trademark Office Patent Number 5,960,411. Method and system for placing a purchase order via a communications network.

Sometimes the information is entirely free or supported by advertising. Some information is provided via subscription or paid for on an individual basis.

Digital goods include e-books and music in electronic formats such as MP3. Stock library images also can be digitized and downloaded. Computer software does not always need to be on a CD, inside shrink-wrap. It can be downloaded directly. Services that can be sold this way include Internet access or web hosting and some professional services that can be replaced by an expert system.

If you are going to physically ship an item that was ordered from your website, you have both advantages and disadvantages over digital goods and services. Shipping a physical item costs money. Digital downloads are nearly free. This means that if you have something that can be duplicated and sold digitally, the cost to you is similar whether you sell 1 item or 1,000 items. Of course, there are limits; if you have a sufficient level of sales and traffic, you will need to invest in more hardware or bandwidth.

Digital products or services can be easy to sell as impulse purchases. If a person orders a physical item, delivery will take a day or more. In contrast, downloads are usually measured in seconds or minutes. As a result, immediacy can be a burden on merchants. If you are delivering a purchase digitally, you need to do it immediately. You cannot manually oversee the process or spread peaks of activity through the day. Immediate delivery systems are therefore more open to fraud and are more of a burden on computer resources.

Digital goods and services are ideal for e-commerce, but obviously only a limited range of goods and services can be delivered this way.

Adding Value to Goods or Services

Some successful areas of commercial websites do not actually sell any goods or services. Services such as courier companies' (UPS at www.ups.com or Fedex at www.fedex.com) tracking services are not generally designed to directly make a profit. They add value to the existing services offered by the organization. Providing a facility for customers to track their parcels or bank balances can give your company a competitive advantage if you do it early or can become an expected service in your industry.

Support forums also fall into this category. There are sound commercial reasons for giving customers a discussion area to share troubleshooting tips about your company's products. Customers might be able to solve their problems by looking at solutions given to others, international customers can get support without paying for long-distance phone calls, and customers might be able to answer one another's questions outside your office hours. Providing support in this way can increase your customers' satisfaction at a low cost.

Cutting Costs

One popular use of the Internet is to cut costs. Savings could result from distributing information online, facilitating communication, replacing services, or centralizing operations.

If you currently provide information to a large number of people, you could possibly do the same thing more economically via a website. Whether you are providing price lists, a catalog, documented procedures, specifications, or something else, making the same information available on the Web could be cheaper than printing and delivering paper copies. This is particularly true for information that changes regularly. The Internet can save you money by facilitating communication. Whether this means that tenders can be widely distributed and rapidly replied to, or whether it means that customers can communicate directly with a wholesaler or manufacturer, eliminating middlemen, the result is the same. Prices can come down, or profits can go up.

Replacing services that cost money to run with an electronic version can cut costs. A brave example was Egghead.com. The company chose to close its chain of computer stores and concentrate on its e-commerce activities. Although building a significant e-commerce site obviously costs money, a chain of 80 retail stores has much higher ongoing costs. Replacing an existing service also comes with risks. At the very least, you lose customers who do not use the Internet.

Egghead.com's new venture did not work out. The company closed its physical stores during the dot-com boom in 1998 and filed for Chapter 11 bankruptcy protection during the dot-com bust in 2001.

Centralization also can cut costs. If you have numerous physical sites, you need to pay numerous rents and overheads, staff at all of them, and the costs of maintaining inventory at each. An Internet business can be in one location but be accessible all over the world.

Understanding Risks and Threats

Every business faces risks, competitors, theft, fickle public preferences, and natural disasters, among other risks. The list is endless. However, many risks that e-commerce companies face are either less of a danger, or not relevant, to other ventures. These risks include

- Crackers
- Failure to attract sufficient business
- Computer hardware failure
- Power, communication, or network failures
- Reliance on shipping services
- Extensive competition
- Software errors
- Evolving governmental policies and taxes
- System-capacity limits

Crackers

The best-publicized threat to e-commerce comes from malicious computer users known as *crackers*. All businesses run the risk of becoming targets of criminals, but high-profile e-commerce businesses are bound to attract the attention of crackers with varying intentions and abilities.

Crackers might attack for the challenge, for notoriety, to sabotage your site, to steal money, or to gain free goods or services.

Securing your site involves a combination of

- Keeping backups of important information

- Having hiring policies that attract honest staff and keep them loyal because the most dangerous attacks can come from within

- Taking software-based precautions, such as choosing secure software and keeping it up to date

- Training staff to identify targets and weaknesses

- Auditing and logging to detect break-ins or attempted break-ins

Most successful attacks on computer systems take advantage of well-known weaknesses such as easily guessed passwords, common misconfigurations, and old versions of software. A few commonsense precautions can turn away nonexpert attacks and ensure that you have a backup if the worst happens.

Failure to Attract Sufficient Business

Although attacks by crackers are widely feared, most e-commerce failures relate to traditional economic factors. The effort of building and marketing a major e-commerce site costs a lot of money. Companies often are willing to lose money in the short term, however, based on assumptions that after the brand is established in the market place, customer numbers and revenue will increase.

The dot-com crash brought many companies crashing down as venture capital needed to support loss-making retailers dried up. The string of high-profile failures included European boo.com, which ran out of money and changed hands after burning $120 million in six months. The problem was not that Boo did not make sales; it was just that the company spent far, far more than it made.

Computer Hardware Failure

If your business relies on a website, obviously, the failure of a critical part of one of your computers will have an impact.

Busy or crucial websites justify having multiple redundant systems so that the failure of one does not affect the operation of the whole system. As with all threats, you need to determine whether the chance of losing your website for a day while waiting for parts or repairs justifies the expense of redundant equipment.

Multiple machines running Apache, PHP, and MySQL are reasonably easy to set up and, using MySQL's replication, easy to keep in sync, but they do significantly increase your hardware, network infrastructure, and hosting costs.

Power, Communication, Network, or Shipping Failures

If you rely on the Internet, you are relying on a complex mesh of service providers. If your connection to the rest of the world fails, you can do little other than wait for your supplier to reinstate service. The same goes for interruptions to power service and strikes or other stoppages by your delivery company.

Depending on your budget, you might choose to maintain multiple services from different providers. Doing so costs you more but means that, if one of your providers fails, you will still have another. Brief power failures can be overcome by investing in an uninterruptible power supply.

Extensive Competition

If you are opening a retail outlet on a street corner, you will probably be able to make a reasonably accurate survey of the competitive landscape. Your competitors will primarily be businesses that sell similar things in surrounding areas. New competitors will open occasionally. With e-commerce, the terrain is less certain.

Depending on shipping costs, your competitors could be anywhere in the world and subject to different currency fluctuations and labor costs. The Internet is fiercely competitive and evolving rapidly. If you are competing in a popular category, new competitors can appear every day.

You can do little to eliminate the risk of competition, but, by staying abreast of developments, you can try to ensure that your venture remains competitive.

Software Errors

When your business relies on software, you are vulnerable to errors in that software.

You can reduce the likelihood of critical errors by selecting software that is reliable, allowing sufficient time to test after changing parts of your system, having a formal testing process, and not allowing changes to be made on your live system without testing elsewhere first.

You can reduce the severity of outcomes by having up-to-date backups of all your data, keeping known working software configurations when making a change, and monitoring system operation to quickly detect problems.

Evolving Governmental Policies and Taxes

Depending on where you live, legislation relating to Internet-based businesses might be nonexistent, in the pipeline, or immature. This situation is unlikely to last. Some business models might be threatened, regulated, or eliminated by future legislation. Taxes might be added.

You cannot avoid these issues. The only way to deal with them is to keep up to date with what is happening and keep your site in line with the legislation. You might want to consider joining any appropriate lobby groups as issues arise.

System Capacity Limits

One issue to bear in mind when designing your system is growth. You certainly hope your system will get busier and busier. You should therefore design it in such a way that it can scale to cope with demand.

For limited growth, you can increase capacity by simply buying faster hardware, but there is a limit to how fast a computer you can buy. Is your software written so that after you reach this point, you can separate parts of it to share the load on multiple systems? Can your database handle multiple concurrent requests from different machines? Is your database connection code written so that you can later change it to write to a MySQL replication master and read from a variety of slaves?

Few systems cope with massive growth effortlessly, but if you design it with scalability in mind, you should be able to identify and eliminate bottlenecks as your customer base grows.

Deciding on a Strategy

Some people believe that the Internet changes too fast to allow effective planning. We would argue that this very changeability makes planning crucial. If you do not set goals and decide on a strategy, you will be left reacting to changes as they occur rather than being able to act in anticipation of change.

Now that you have examined some of the typical goals for a commercial website and some of the main threats, we hope you have some strategies for your own.

Your strategy will need to identify a business model. The model is usually something that has been shown to work elsewhere but is sometimes a new idea that you have faith in. Will you adapt your existing business model to the Web, mimic an existing competitor, or aggressively create a pioneering service?

Next

In the next chapter, we look specifically at security for e-commerce, providing an overview of security terms, threats, and techniques.

15

E-commerce Security Issues

THIS CHAPTER DISCUSSES THE ROLE OF SECURITY in e-commerce. We discuss who might be interested in your information and how they might try to obtain it, the principles involved in creating a policy to avoid these kinds of problems, and some of the technologies available for safeguarding the security of a website including encryption, authentication, and tracking.

Key topics covered in this chapter include

- The importance of your information
- Security threats
- Security policy creation
- Usability, performance, cost, and security
- Authentication principles
- Authentication on your site
- Encryption basics
- Private key encryption
- Public key encryption
- Digital signatures
- Digital certificates
- Secure web servers
- Auditing and logging
- Firewalls
- Data backups
- Physical security

How Important Is Your Information?

When considering security, you first need to evaluate the importance of what you are protecting. You need to consider its importance both to you and to potential crackers.

You might be tempted to believe that the highest possible level of security is required for all sites at all times, but protection comes at a cost. Before deciding how much effort or expense your security warrants, you need to decide how much your information is worth.

The value of the information stored on the computer of a hobby user, a business, a bank, and a military organization obviously varies. The lengths to which an attacker would be likely to go to obtain access to that information vary similarly. How attractive would the contents of your machines be to a malicious visitor?

Hobby users probably have limited time to learn about or work toward securing their systems. Given that information stored on their machines is likely to be of limited value to anyone other than the owners, attacks are likely to be infrequent and involve limited effort. However, all network computer users should take sensible precautions. Even the computer with the least interesting data still has significant appeal as an anonymous launching pad for attacks on other systems or as a vehicle for reproducing viruses and worms.

Military computers are obvious targets for both individuals and foreign governments. Because attacking governments might have extensive resources, it would be wise to invest in sufficient personnel and other resources to ensure that all practical precautions are taken in this domain.

If you are responsible for an e-commerce site, its attractiveness to crackers presumably falls somewhere between these two extremes, so the resources and efforts you devote should logically lie between the extremes, too.

Security Threats

What is at risk on your site? What threats are out there? We discussed some of the threats to an e-commerce business in Chapter 14, "Running an E-commerce Site." Many of them relate to security.

Depending on your website, security threats might include

- Exposure of confidential data
- Loss or destruction of data
- Modification of data
- Denial of Service
- Errors in software
- Repudiation

Let's run through each of these threats.

Exposure of Confidential Data

Data stored on your computers, or being transmitted to or from your computers, might be confidential. It might be information that only certain people are intended to see, such as wholesale price lists. It might be confidential information provided by a customer, such as his password, contact details, and credit card number.

We hope you are not storing information on your web server that you do not intend anyone to see. A web server is the wrong place for secret information. If you were storing your payroll records or your top secret plan for beating racing ferrets on a computer, you would be wise to use a computer other than your web server. The web server is inherently a publicly accessible machine and should contain only information that either needs to be provided to the public or has recently been collected from the public.

To reduce the risk of exposure, you need to limit the methods by which information can be accessed and limit the people who can access it. This process involves designing with security in mind, configuring your server and software properly, programming carefully, testing thoroughly, removing unnecessary services from the web server, and requiring authentication.

You need to design, configure, code, and test carefully to reduce the risk of a successful criminal attack and, equally important, to reduce the chance that an error will leave your information open to accidental exposure.

You also need to remove unnecessary services from your web server to decrease the number of potential weak points. Each service you are running might have vulnerabilities. Each one needs to be kept up to date to ensure that known vulnerabilities are not present. The services that you do not use might be more dangerous. If you never use the command rcp, for example, why have the service installed?[1] If you tell the installer that your machine is a network host, the major Linux distributions and Windows will install a large number of services that you do not need and should remove.

Authentication means asking people to prove their identity. When the system knows who is making a request, it can decide whether that person is allowed access. A number of possible methods of authentication can be employed, but only two forms are commonly used on public websites: passwords and digital signatures. We talk a little more about both later.

CD Universe offers a good example of the cost both in dollars and reputation of allowing confidential information to be exposed. In late 1999, a cracker calling himself Maxus reportedly contacted CD Universe, claiming to have 300,000 credit card numbers stolen from the company's site. He wanted a $100,000 (U.S.) ransom from the site to destroy the numbers. The company refused and found itself in embarrassing coverage on the front pages of major newspapers as Maxus doled out numbers for others to abuse.

Data is also at risk of exposure while it traverses a network. Although TCP/IP networks have many fine features that have made them the de facto standard for connecting

---

[1]Even if you do currently use rcp, you should probably remove it and use scp (secure copy) instead.

diverse networks together as the Internet, security is not one of them. TCP/IP works by chopping your data into packets and then forwarding those packets from machine to machine until they reach their destination. This means that your data is passing through numerous machines on the way, as illustrated in Figure 15.1. Any one of those machines could view your data as it passes by.

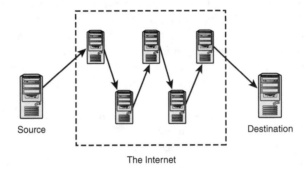

The Internet

Figure 15.1   Transmitting information via the Internet sends your information via a number of potentially untrustworthy hosts.

To see the path that data takes from you to a particular machine, you can use the command `traceroute` (on a Unix machine). This command gives you the addresses of the machines that your data passes through to reach that host. For a host in your own country, data is likely to pass through 10 different machines. For an international machine, it may pass through more than 20 intermediaries. If your organization has a large and complex network, your data might pass through 5 machines before it even leaves the building.

To protect confidential information, you can encrypt it before it is sent across a network and decrypt it at the other end. Web servers often use Secure Sockets Layer (SSL), developed by Netscape, to accomplish this as data travels between web servers and browsers. This is a fairly low-cost, low-effort way of securing transmissions, but because your server needs to encrypt and decrypt data rather than simply send and receive it, the number of visitors per second that a machine can serve drops dramatically.

Loss or Destruction of Data

Losing data can be more costly for you than having it revealed. If you have spent months building up your site, gathering user data and orders, how much would it cost you in time, reputation, and dollars to lose all that information? If you had no backups of any of your data, you would need to rewrite the website in a hurry and start from scratch. You would also have dissatisfied customers and fraudsters claiming that they ordered something that never arrived.

It is possible that crackers *will* break into your system and format your hard drive. It is fairly likely that a careless programmer or administrator *will* delete something by accident, but it is almost certain that you *will* occasionally lose a hard disk drive. Hard disk drives rotate thousands of times per minute, and, occasionally, they fail. Murphy's Law would tell you that the one that fails will be the most important one, long after you last made a backup.

You can take various measures to reduce the chance of data loss. Secure your servers against crackers. Keep the number of staff with access to your machine to a minimum. Hire only competent, careful people. Buy good quality drives. Use Redundant Array of Inexpensive Disks (RAID) so that multiple drives can act like one faster, more reliable drive.

Regardless of its cause, you have only one real protection against data loss: backups. Backing up data is not rocket science. On the contrary, it is tedious, dull, and—you hope—useless, but it is vital. Make sure that your data is regularly backed up and make sure that you have tested your backup procedure to be certain that you can recover. Make sure that your backups are stored away from your computers. Although the chances that your premises will burn down or suffer some other catastrophic fate are unlikely, storing a backup offsite is a fairly cheap insurance policy.

Modification of Data

Although the loss of data could be damaging, modification could be worse. What if somebody obtained access to your system and modified files? Although wholesale deletion will probably be noticed and can be remedied from your backup, how long will it take you to notice modification?

Modifications to files could include changes to data files or executable files. A cracker's motivation for altering a data file might be to graffiti your site or to obtain fraudulent benefits. Replacing executable files with sabotaged versions might give a cracker who has gained access once a secret backdoor for future visits or a mechanism to gain higher privileges on the system.

You can protect data from modification as it travels over the network by computing a signature. This approach does not stop somebody from modifying the data, but if the recipient checks that the signature still matches when the file arrives, she will know whether the file has been modified. If the data is being encrypted to protect it from unauthorized viewing, using the signature will also make it very difficult to modify en route without detection.

Protecting files stored on your server from modification requires that you use the file permission facilities your operating system provides and protect the system from unauthorized access. Using file permissions, users can be authorized to use the system but not be given free rein to modify system files and other users' files. The lack of a proper permissions system is one of the reasons that Windows 95, 98, and ME were never suitable as server operating systems.

Detecting modification can be difficult. If, at some point, you realize that your system's security has been breached, how will you know whether important files have been modified? Some files, such as the data files that store your databases, are intended to change over time. Many others are intended to stay the same from the time you install them, unless you deliberately upgrade them. Modification of both programs and data can be insidious, but although programs can be reinstalled if you suspect modification, you cannot know which version of your data was "clean."

File integrity assessment software, such as Tripwire, records information about important files in a known safe state, probably immediately after installation, and can be used at a later time to verify that files are unchanged. You can download commercial or conditional free versions from the following address:

http://www.tripwire.com

Denial of Service

One of the most difficult threats to guard against is Denial of Service. *Denial of Service (DoS)* occurs when somebody's actions make it difficult or impossible for users to access a service, or delay their access to a time-critical service.

Early in 2000, an infamous spate of *Distributed Denial of Service (DDoS)* attacks was made against high-profile websites. Targets included Yahoo!, eBay, Amazon, E-Trade, and Buy.com. These sites are accustomed to traffic levels that most of us can only dream of, but they are still vulnerable to being shut down for hours by a DoS attack. Although crackers generally have little to gain from shutting down a website, the proprietor might be losing money, time, and reputation.

Some sites have specific times when they expect to do most of their business. Online bookmaking sites experience huge demand just before major sporting events. One way that crackers attempted to profit from DDoS attacks in 2004 was by extorting money from online bookmakers with the threat of attacking during these peak demand times.

One of the reasons that these attacks are so difficult to guard against is that they can be carried out in a huge number of ways. Methods could include installing a program on a target machine that uses most of the system's processor time, reverse spamming, or using one of the automated tools. A *reverse spam* involves somebody sending out spam with the target listed as the sender. This way, the target will have thousands of angry replies to deal with.

Automated tools exist to launch distributed DoS attacks on a target. Without needing much knowledge, somebody can scan a large number of machines for known vulnerabilities, compromise a machine, and install the tool. Because the process is automated, an attacker can install the tool on a single host in less than five seconds. When enough machines have been co-opted, all are instructed to flood the target with network traffic.

Guarding against DoS attacks is difficult in general. With a little research, you can find the default ports used by the common DDoS tools and close them. Your router might provide mechanisms to limit the percentage of traffic that uses particular protocols such as ICMP. Detecting hosts on your network being used to attack others is easier than protecting your machines from attack. If every network administrator could be relied on to vigilantly monitor his own network, DDoS would not be such a problem.

Because there are so many possible methods of attack, the only really effective defense is to monitor normal traffic behavior and have a pool of experts available to take countermeasures when abnormal situations occur.

Errors in Software

Any software you have bought, obtained, or written may have serious errors in it. Given the short development times normally allowed to web projects, the likelihood is high that this software has some errors. Any business that is highly reliant on computerized processes is vulnerable to buggy software.

Errors in software can lead to all sorts of unpredictable behavior including service unavailability, security breaches, financial losses, and poor service to customers.

Common causes of errors that you can look for include poor specifications, faulty assumptions made by developers, and inadequate testing.

Poor Specifications

The more sparse or ambiguous your design documentation is, the more likely you are to end up with errors in the final product. Although it might seem superfluous to you to specify that when a customer's credit card is declined, the order should not be sent to the customer, at least one big-budget site had this bug. The less experience your developers have with the type of system they are working on, the more precise your specification needs to be.

Assumptions Made by Developers

A system's designers and programmers need to make many assumptions. Of course, you hope that they will document their assumptions and usually be right. Sometimes, though, people make poor assumptions. For example, they might assume that input data will be valid, will not include unusual characters, or will be less than a particular size. They might also make assumptions about timing, such as the likelihood of two conflicting actions occurring at the same time or that a complex processing task will always take more time than a simple task.

Assumptions like these can slip through because they are usually true. A cracker could take advantage of a buffer overrun because a programmer assumed a maximum length for input data, or a legitimate user could get confusing error messages and leave because your developers did not consider that a person's name might have an apostrophe in it. These sorts of errors can be found and fixed with a combination of good testing and detailed code review.

Historically, operating system or application-level weaknesses exploited by crackers have usually related either to buffer overflows or race conditions.

Poor Testing

Testing for all possible input conditions, on all possible types of hardware, running all possible operating systems with all possible user settings is rarely achievable. This situation is even more true than usual with web-based systems.

What is needed is a well-designed test plan that tests all the functions of your software on a representative sample of common machine types. A well-planned set of tests should aim to test every line of code in your project at least once. Ideally, this test suite should be automated so that it can be run on your selected test machines with little effort.

The greatest problem with testing is that it is unglamorous and repetitive. Although some people enjoy breaking things, few people enjoy breaking the same thing over and over again. It is important that people other than the original developers are involved in testing. One of the major goals of testing is to uncover faulty assumptions made by the developers. A person who can approach the project with fresh ideas is much more likely to have different assumptions. In addition, professionals are rarely keen to find flaws in their own work.

Repudiation

The final risk we will consider is repudiation. *Repudiation* occurs when a party involved in a transaction denies having taken part. E-commerce examples might include a person ordering goods off a website and then denying having authorized the charge on his credit card, or a person agreeing to something in email and then claiming that somebody else forged the email.

Ideally, financial transactions should provide the peace of mind of nonrepudiation to both parties. Neither party could deny their part in a transaction, or, more precisely, both parties could conclusively prove the actions of the other to a third party, such as a court. In practice, this rarely happens.

Authentication provides some surety about whom you are dealing with. If issued by a trusted organization, digital certificates of authentication can provide greater confidence.

Messages sent by each party also need to be tamperproof. There is not much value in being able to demonstrate that Corp Pty Ltd sent you a message if you cannot also demonstrate that what you received was exactly what the company sent. As mentioned previously, signing or encrypting messages makes them difficult to surreptitiously alter.

For transactions between parties with an ongoing relationship, digital certificates together with either encrypted or signed communications are an effective way of limiting repudiation. For one-off transactions, such as the initial contact between an e-commerce website and a stranger bearing a credit card, they are not so practical.

An e-commerce company should be willing to hand over proof of its identity and a few hundred dollars to a certifying authority such as VeriSign (http://www.verisign.com/) or Thawte (http://www.thawte.com/) to assure visitors of the company's bona fides. Would that same company be willing to turn away every customer who was not willing to do the same to prove her identity? For small transactions, merchants are generally willing to accept a certain level of fraud or repudiation risk rather than turn away business.

Usability, Performance, Cost, and Security

By its very nature, the Web is risky. It is designed to allow numerous anonymous users to request services from your machines. Most of those requests are perfectly legitimate requests for web pages, but connecting your machines to the Internet allows people to attempt other types of connections.

Although you might be tempted to assume that the highest possible level of security is appropriate, this is rarely the case. If you wanted to be really secure, you would keep all your computers turned off, disconnected from all networks, in a locked safe. To make your computers available and usable, some relaxation of security is required.

A trade-off needs to be made between security, usability, cost, and performance. Making a service more secure can reduce usability by, for instance, limiting what people can do or requiring them to identify themselves. Increasing security can also reduce the level of performance of your machines. Running software to make your system more secure—such as encryption, intrusion detection systems, virus scanners, and extensive logging—uses resources. Providing an encrypted session, such as an SSL connection to a website, takes more processing power than providing a normal one. These performance losses can be countered by spending more money on faster machines or hardware specifically designed for encryption.

You can view performance, usability, cost, and security as competing goals. You need to examine the trade-offs required and make sensible decisions to come up with a compromise. Depending on the value of your information, your budget, the number of visitors you expect to serve, and the obstacles you think legitimate users will be willing to put up with, you can come up with a compromise position.

Security Policy Creation

A security policy is a document that describes

- The general philosophy toward security in your organization
- The items to be protected—software, hardware, data
- The people responsible for protecting these items
- Standards for security and metrics, which measure how well those standards are being met

A good guideline for writing your security policy is that it's like writing a set of functional requirements for software. The policy shouldn't address specific implementations or solutions but instead should describe the goals and security requirements in your environment. It shouldn't need to be updated very often.

You should keep a separate document that sets out guidelines for how the requirements of the security policy are met in a particular environment. In this document, you can have different guidelines for different parts of your organization. This is more along the lines of a design document or a procedure manual that details what is actually done to ensure the level of security that you require.

Authentication Principles

Authentication attempts to prove that somebody is actually who she claims to be. You can provide authentication in many ways, but as with many security measures, the more secure methods are more troublesome to use.

Authentication techniques include passwords, digital signatures, biometric measures such as fingerprint scans, and measures involving hardware such as smart cards. Only two are in common use on the Web: passwords and digital signatures.

Biometric measures and most hardware solutions involve special input devices and would limit authorized users to specific machines with these features attached. Such measures might be acceptable, or even desirable, for access to an organization's internal systems, but they take away much of the advantage of making a system available over the Web.

Passwords are simple to implement, simple to use, and require no special input devices. They provide some level of authentication but might not be appropriate on their own for high-security systems.

A password is a simple concept. You and the system know your password. If a visitor claims to be you and knows your password, the system has reason to believe he is you. As long as nobody else knows or can guess the password, this system is secure. Passwords on their own have a number of potential weaknesses and do not provide strong authentication.

Many passwords are easily guessed. If left to choose their own passwords, around 50% of users will choose an easily guessed password. Common passwords that fit this description include dictionary words or the username for the account. At the expense of usability, you can force users to include numbers or punctuation in their passwords.

Educating users to choose better passwords can help, but even when educated, around 25% of users will still choose an easily guessed password. You could enforce password policies that stop users from choosing easily guessed combinations by checking new passwords against a dictionary, or requiring some numbers or punctuation symbols or a mixture of uppercase and lowercase letters. One danger is that strict password rules will lead to passwords that many legitimate users will not be able to remember, especially if different systems force them to follow different rules when creating passwords.

Hard-to-remember passwords increase the likelihood that users will do something unsecure such as write "username fred password rover" on a note taped to their monitors. Users need to be educated not to write down their passwords or to do other silly things such as give them over the phone to people who claim to be working on the system.

Passwords can also be captured electronically. By running a program to capture keystrokes at a terminal or using a packet sniffer to capture network traffic, crackers can—and do—capture usable pairs of login names and passwords. You can limit the opportunities to capture passwords by encrypting network traffic.

For all their potential flaws, passwords are a simple and relatively effective way of authenticating your users. They provide a level of secrecy that might not be appropriate for national security but is ideal for checking on the delivery status of a customer's order.

Authentication

Authentication mechanisms are built in to the most popular web browsers and web servers. A web server might require a username and password for people requesting files from particular directories on the server.

When challenged for a login name and password, your browser presents a dialog box similar to the one shown in Figure 15.2.

Figure 15.2   Web browsers prompt users for authentication when they attempt to visit a restricted directory on a web server.

Both the Apache web server and Microsoft's IIS enable you to very easily protect all or part of a site in this way. Using PHP or MySQL, you can achieve the same effect. Using MySQL is faster than the built-in authentication. Using PHP, you can provide more flexible authentication or present the request in a more attractive way.

We look at some authentication examples in Chapter 16, "Implementing Authentication with PHP and MySQL."

Encryption Basics

An *encryption algorithm* is a mathematical process to transform information into a seemingly random string of data.

The data that you start with is often called *plain text*, although it is not important to the process what the information represents—whether it is actually text or some other sort of data. Similarly, the encrypted information is called *ciphertext* but rarely looks anything like text. Figure 15.3 shows the encryption process as a simple flowchart. The plain text is fed to an encryption engine, which might have been a mechanical device, such as a World War II Engima machine, once upon a time but is now nearly always a computer program. The engine produces the ciphertext.

Figure 15.3   Encryption takes plain text and transforms it into seemingly random ciphertext.

To create the protected directory whose authentication prompt is shown in Figure 15.2, we used Apache's most basic type of authentication. (You see how to use it in the next chapter.) This encrypts passwords before storing them. We created a user with the password `password`; it was then encrypted and stored as `aWDuA3X3H.mc2`. You can see that the plain text and ciphertext bear no obvious resemblance to each other.

This particular encryption method is not reversible. Many passwords are stored using a one-way encryption algorithm. To see whether an attempt at entering a password is correct, you do not need to decrypt the stored password. You can instead encrypt the attempt and compare that to the stored version.

Many, but not all, encryption processes can be reversed. The reverse process is called *decryption*. Figure 15.4 shows a two-way encryption process.

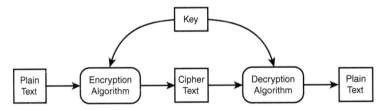

Figure 15.4   Encryption takes plain text and transforms it into seemingly random ciphertext. Decryption takes the ciphertext and transforms it back into plain text.

Cryptography is nearly 4,000 years old but came of age in World War II. Its growth since then has followed a similar pattern to the adoption of computer networks, initially being used only by military and finance corporations, being more widely used by companies starting in the 1970s, and becoming ubiquitous in the 1990s. In the past few years, encryption has gone from a concept that ordinary people saw only in World War II movies and spy thrillers to something that they read about in newspapers and use every time they purchase something with their web browsers.

Many different encryption algorithms are available. Some, like DES, use a secret or private key; some, like RSA, use a public key and a separate private key.

Private Key Encryption

Private key encryption, also called secret key encryption, relies on authorized people knowing or having access to a key. This key must be kept secret. If the key falls into the wrong hands, unauthorized people can also read your encrypted messages. As shown in Figure 15.4, both the sender (who encrypts the message) and the recipient (who decrypts the message) have the same key.

The most widely used secret key algorithm is the Data Encryption Standard (DES). This scheme was developed by IBM in the 1970s and adopted as the American standard for commercial and unclassified government communications. Computing speeds are orders of magnitudes faster now than in 1970, and DES has been obsolete since at least 1998.

Other well-known secret key systems include RC2, RC4, RC5, triple DES, and IDEA. Triple DES is fairly secure.[2] It uses the same algorithm as DES, applied three times with up to three different keys. A plain text message is encrypted with key one, decrypted with key two, and then encrypted with key three.

One obvious flaw of secret key encryption is that, to send somebody a secure message, you need a secure way to get the secret key to him. If you have a secure way to deliver a key, why not just deliver the message that way?

Fortunately, there was a breakthrough in 1976, when Diffie and Hellman published the first public key scheme.

Public Key Encryption

Public key encryption relies on two different keys: a public key and a private key. As shown in Figure 15.5, the public key is used to encrypt messages and the private key to decrypt them.

The advantage to this system is that the public key, as its name suggests, can be distributed publicly. Anybody to whom you give your public key can send you a secure message. As long as only you have your private key, then only you can decrypt the message.

The most common public key algorithm is RSA, developed by Rivest, Shamir, and Adelman at MIT and published in 1978. RSA was a proprietary system, but the patent expired in September 2000.

---

[2]Somewhat paradoxically, triple DES is twice as secure as DES. If you needed something three times as strong, you could write a program to implement a quintuple DES algorithm.

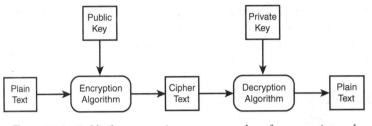

Figure 15.5   Public key encryption uses separate keys for encryption and decryption.

The capability to transmit a public key in the clear and not need to worry about it being seen by a third party is a huge advantage, but secret key systems are still in common use. Often, a hybrid system is used. A public key system is used to transmit the key for a secret key system that will be used for the remainder of a session's communication. This added complexity is tolerated because secret key systems are around 1,000 times faster than public key systems.

Digital Signatures

Digital signatures are related to public key cryptography but reverse the role of public and private keys. A sender can encrypt and digitally sign a message with her secret key. When the message is received, the recipient can decrypt it with the sender's public key. Because the sender is the only person with access to the secret key, the recipient can be fairly certain from whom the message came and that it has not been altered.

Digital signatures can be really useful. The recipient can be sure that the message has not been tampered with, and the signatures make it difficult for the sender to repudiate, or deny sending, the message.

It is important to note that although the message has been encrypted, it can be read by anybody who has the public key. Although the same techniques and keys are used, the purpose of encryption here is to prevent tampering and repudiation, not to prevent reading.

Because public key encryption is fairly slow for large messages, another type of algorithm, called a *hash function*, is usually used to improve efficiency. The hash function calculates a message digest or hash value for any message it is given. It is not important what value the algorithm produces. It is important that the output is deterministic—that is, that the output is the same each time a particular input is used, that the output is small, and that the algorithm is fast.

The most common hash functions are MD5 and SHA.

A hash function generates a message digest that matches a particular message. If you have a message and a message digest, you can verify that the message has not been tampered with, as long as you are sure that the digest has not been tampered with. To this end, the usual way of creating a digital signature is to create a message digest for the whole message using a fast hash function and then encrypt only the brief digest using a slow public key encryption algorithm. The signature can now be sent with the message via any normal unsecure method.

When a signed message is received, it can be checked. The signature is decrypted using the sender's public key. A hash value is then generated for the message using the same method that the sender used. If the decrypted hash value matches the hash value you generated, the message is from the sender and has not been altered.

Digital Certificates

Being able to verify that a message has not been altered and that a series of messages all come from a particular user or machine is good. For commercial interactions, being able to tie that user or server to a real legal entity such as a person or company would be even better.

A digital certificate combines a public key and an individual's or organization's details in a signed digital format. Given a certificate, you have the other party's public key, in case you want to send an encrypted message, and you have that party's details, which you know have not been altered.

The problem here is that the information is only as trustworthy as the person who signed it. Anybody can generate and sign a certificate claiming to be anybody he likes. For commercial transactions, it would be useful to have a trusted third party verify the identity of participants and the details recorded in their certificates.

These third parties are called *certifying authorities (CAs)*. They issue digital certificates to individuals and companies subject to identity checks. The two best known CAs are VeriSign (http://www.verisign.com/)and Thawte (http://www.thawte.com/), but you can use a number of other authorities. VeriSign and Thawte are both owned by the same company, and there is little practical difference between them. Some of the lesser-known authorities, such as Equifax Secure (www.equifaxsecure.com), are significantly cheaper.

The authorities sign a certificate to verify that they have seen proof of the person's or company's identity. It is worth noting that the certificate is not a reference or statement of creditworthiness. The certificate does not guarantee that you are dealing with some-body reputable. What it does mean is that if you are ripped off, you have a relatively good chance of having a real physical address and somebody to sue.

Certificates provide a network of trust. Assuming you choose to trust the CA, you can then choose to trust the people they choose to trust and then trust the people the certi-fied party chooses to trust.

The most common use for digital certificates is to provide an air of respectability to an e-commerce site. With a certificate issued by a well-known CA, web browsers can make SSL connections to your site without bringing up warning dialogs. Web servers that enable SSL connections are often called *secure web servers*.

Secure Web Servers

You can use the Apache web server, Microsoft IIS, or any number of other free or commercial web servers for secure communication with browsers via Secure Sockets Layer. Using Apache enables you to use a Unix-like operating system, which is almost certainly more reliable but harder to set up than IIS. You can also, of course, choose to use Apache on a Windows platform.

Using SSL on IIS simply involves installing IIS, generating a key pair, and installing your certificate. Using SSL on Apache requires installing three different packages: Apache, Mod_SSL, and OpenSSL.

You can have your cake and eat it too by purchasing Stronghold. Stronghold is a commercial product available from http://stronghold.redhat.com/ for around $1,000 (U.S.). Based on Apache, it comes as a self-installing binary preconfigured with SSL. This way, you get the reliability of Unix and an easy-to-install product with technical support from the vendor.

Installation instructions for the two most popular web servers, Apache and IIS, are in Appendix A, "Installing PHP5 and MySQL5." You can begin using SSL immediately by generating your own digital certificate, but visitors to your site will be warned by their web browsers that you have signed your own certificate. To use SSL effectively, you also need a certificate issued by a certifying authority.

The exact process to get this certificate varies between CAs, but in general, you need to prove to a CA that you are some sort of legally recognized business with a physical address and that the business in question owns the relevant domain name.

You also need to generate a certificate signing request (CSR). The process for this varies from server to server. You can find instructions on the CAs' websites. Stronghold and IIS provide a dialog box–driven process, whereas Apache requires you to type commands. However, the process is essentially the same for all servers. The result is an encrypted CSR. Your CSR should look something like this:

```
---BEGIN NEW CERTIFICATE REQUEST---
MIIBuwIBAAKBgQCLn1XX8faMHhtzStp9wY6BVTPuEU9bpMmhrb6vgaNZy4dTe6VS
84p7wGepq5CQjfOL4Hjda+g12xzto8uxBkCDO98Xg9q86CY45HZk+q6GyGOLZSOD
8cQHwh1oUP65s5Tz018OFBzpI3bHxfO6aYelWYziDiFKp1BrUdua+pK4SQIVAPLH
SV9FSz8Z7IHOg1Zr5H82oQOlAoGAWSPWyfVXPAF8h2GDb+cf97k44VkHZ+Rxpe8G
ghlfBn9L3ESWUZNOJMfDLlny7dStYU98VTVNekidYuaBsvyEkFrny7NCUmiuaSnX
4UjtFDkNhX9j5YbCRGLmsc865AT54KRu31O2/dKHLo6NgFPirijHy99HJ4LRY9Z9
HkXVzswCgYBwBFH2QfK88C6JKW3ah+6cHQ4Deoiltxi627WN5HcQLwkPGn+WtYSZ
jG5tw4tqqogmJ+IP2F/5G6FI2DQP7QDvKNeAU8jXcuijuWo27S2sbhQtXgZRTZvO
jGn89BC0mIHgHQMkI7vz35mx1Skk3VNq3ehwhGCvJlvoeiv2J8X2IQIVAOTRp7zp
En7QlXnXw1s7xXbbuKP0
---END NEW CERTIFICATE REQUEST---
```

Armed with a CSR, the appropriate fee, and documentation to prove that you exist, and having verified that the domain name you are using is in the same name as in the business documentation, you can sign up for a certificate with a CA.

When the CA issues your certificate, you need to store it on your system and tell your web server where to find it. The final certificate is a text file that looks a lot like the CSR shown here.

Auditing and Logging

Your operating system enables you to log all sorts of events. Events that you might be interested in from a security point of view include network errors, access to particular data files such as configuration files or the NT Registry, and calls to programs such as su (used to become another user, typically root, on a Unix system).

Log files can help you detect erroneous or malicious behavior as it occurs. They can also tell you how a problem or break-in occurred if you check them after noticing problems. The two main problems with log files are their size and veracity.

If you set the criteria for detecting and logging problems at their most paranoid levels, you will end up with massive logs that are very difficult to examine. To help with large log files, you really need to either use an existing tool or derive some audit scripts from your security policy to search the logs for "interesting" events. The auditing process could occur in real-time or could be done periodically.

In particular, log files are vulnerable to attack. If an intruder has root or administrator access to your system, she is free to alter log files to cover her tracks. Unix provides facilities to log events to a separate machine. This would mean that a cracker would need to compromise at least two machines to cover her tracks. Similar functionality is possible in Windows, but not as easy as in Unix.

Your system administrator might do regular audits, but you might like to have an external audit periodically to check the behavior of administrators.

Firewalls

Firewalls are designed to separate your network from the wider world. In the same way that firewalls in a building or a car stop fire from spreading into other compartments, network firewalls stop chaos from spreading into your network.

A firewall is designed to protect machines on your network from outside attack. It filters and denies traffic that does not meet its rules. It also restricts the activities of people and machines outside the firewall.

Sometimes, a firewall is also used to restrict the activities of those within it. A firewall can restrict the network protocols people can use, restrict the hosts they can connect to, or force them to use a proxy server to keep bandwidth costs down.

A firewall can either be a hardware device, such as a router with filtering rules, or a software program running on a machine. In any case, the firewall needs interfaces to two networks and a set of rules. It monitors all traffic attempting to pass from one network to the other. If the traffic meets the rules, it is routed across to the other network; otherwise, it is stopped or rejected.

Packets can be filtered by their type, source address, destination address, or port information. Some packets are merely discarded; other events can be set to trigger log entries or alarms.

Data Backups

You cannot underestimate the importance of backups in any disaster recovery plan. Hardware and buildings can be insured and replaced, or sites hosted elsewhere, but if your custom-developed web software is gone, no insurance company can replace it for you.

You need to back up all the components of your website—static pages, scripts, and databases—on a regular basis. Just how often you back up depends on how dynamic your site is. If it is all static, you can get away with backing it up when it has changed. However, the kinds of sites we talk about in this book are likely to change frequently, particularly if you are taking orders online.

Most sites of a reasonable size need to be hosted on a server with RAID, which can support mirroring. This covers situations in which you might have a hard disk failure. Consider, however, what might happen in situations in which something happens to the entire array, machine, or building.

You should run separate backups at a frequency corresponding to your update volume. These backups should be stored on separate media and preferably in a safe, separate location, in case of fire, theft, or natural disasters.

Many resources are available for backup and recovery. We concentrate on how you can back up a site built with PHP and a MySQL database.

Backing Up General Files

You can back up your HTML, PHP, images, and other nondatabase files fairly simply on most systems by using backup software.

The most widely used of the freely available utilities is AMANDA, the Advanced Maryland Automated Network Disk Archiver, developed by the University of Maryland. It ships with many Unix distributions and can also be used to back up Windows machines via SAMBA. You can read more about AMANDA at

http://www.amanda.org/

Backing Up and Restoring Your MySQL Database

Backing up a live database is more complicated than backing up general files. You need to avoid copying any table data while the database is in the middle of being changed.

Instructions on how to back up and restore a MySQL database can be found in Chapter 12, "Advanced MySQL Administration."

Physical Security

The security threats we have considered so far relate to intangibles such as software, but you should not neglect the physical security of your system. You need air conditioning and protection against fire, people (both the clumsy and the criminal), power failure, and network failure.

Your system should be locked up securely. Depending on the scale of your operation, your approach could be a room, a cage, or a cupboard. Personnel who do not need access to this machine room should not have it. Unauthorized people might deliberately or accidentally unplug cables or attempt to bypass security mechanisms using a bootable disk.

Water sprinklers can do as much damage to electronics as a fire. In the past, halon fire suppression systems were used to avoid this problem. The production of halon is now banned under the Montreal Protocol on Substances That Deplete the Ozone Layer, so new fire suppression systems must use other, less harmful, alternatives such as argon or carbon dioxide. You can read more about this issue at

http://www.epa.gov/Ozone/snap/fire/qa.html

Occasional brief power failures are a fact of life in most places. In locations with harsh weather and above-ground wires, long failures occur regularly. If the continuous operation of your systems is important to you, you should invest in an uninterruptible power supply (UPS). A UPS that can power a single machine for 10 minutes costs less than $300 (U.S.). Allowing for longer failures, or more equipment, can become expensive. Long power failures really require a generator to run air conditioning as well as computers.

Like power failures, network outages of minutes or hours are out of your control and bound to occur occasionally. If your network is vital, it makes sense to have connections to more than one Internet service provider. Having two connections costs more but should mean that, in case of failure, you have reduced capacity rather than becoming invisible.

These sorts of issues are some of the reasons you might like to consider co-locating your machines at a dedicated facility. Although one medium-sized business might not be able to justify a UPS that will run for more than a few minutes, multiple redundant network connections, and fire suppression systems, a quality facility housing the machines of a hundred similar businesses can.

Next

In Chapter 16, we look specifically at authentication—allowing users to prove their identity. We look at a few different methods, including using PHP and MySQL to authenticate site visitors.

16

Implementing Authentication with PHP and MySQL

IN THIS CHAPTER, WE DISCUSS HOW TO IMPLEMENT various PHP and MySQL techniques for authenticating users.

Key topics covered in this chapter include

- Identifying visitors
- Implementing access control
- Using basic authentication
- Using basic authentication in PHP
- Using Apache's `.htaccess` basic authentication
- Using basic authentication with IIS
- Using `mod_auth_mysql` authentication
- Creating your own custom authentication

Identifying Visitors

The Web is a fairly anonymous medium, but it is often useful to know who is visiting your site. Fortunately for visitors' privacy, you can find out very little about them without their assistance. With a little work, servers can find out quite a lot about the computers and networks that connect to them, however. A web browser usually identifies itself, telling the server what browser, browser version, and operating system a user is running. You can often determine what resolution and color depth visitors' screens are set to and how large their web browser windows are by using JavaScript.

Each computer connected to the Internet has a unique IP address. From a visitor's IP address, you might be able to deduce a little about her. You can find out who owns an IP and sometimes make a reasonable guess as to a visitor's geographic location. Some addresses are more useful than others. Generally, people with permanent Internet connections have a permanent address. Customers dialing into an ISP usually get only the temporary use of one of the ISP's addresses. The next time you see that address, it might be used by a different computer, and the next time you see that visitor, she will likely be using a different IP address. IP addresses are not as useful for identifying people as they might at first glance seem.

Fortunately for web users, none of the information that their browsers give out identifies them. If you want to know a visitor's name or other details, you will have to ask her.

Many websites provide compelling reasons to get users to provide their details. The *New York Times* newspaper (http://www.nytimes.com) provides its content free, but only to people willing to provide details such as name, sex, and total household income. Nerd news and discussion site Slashdot (http://www.slashdot.org) allows registered users to participate in discussions under a nickname and customize the interface they see. Most e-commerce sites record their customers' details when they make their first order. This means that a customer is not required to type her details every time.

Having asked for and received information from your visitor, you need a way to associate the information with the same user the next time she visits. If you are willing to make the assumption that only one person visits your site from a particular account on a particular machine and that each visitor uses only one machine, you could store a cookie on the user's machine to identify the user.

This arrangement is certainly not true for all users. Many people share a computer, and many people use more than one computer. At least some of the time, you need to ask a visitor who she is again. In addition to asking who a user is, you also need to ask her to provide some level of proof that she is who she claims to be.

As discussed in Chapter 15, "E-commerce Security Issues," asking a user to prove her identity is called *authentication*. The usual method of authentication used on websites is asking visitors to provide a unique login name and a password. Authentication is usually used to allow or disallow access to particular pages or resources, but can be optional, or used for other purposes such as personalization.

Implementing Access Control

Simple access control is not difficult to implement. The code shown in Listing 16.1 delivers one of three possible outputs. If the file is loaded without parameters, it will display an HTML form requesting a username and password. This type of form is shown in Figure 16.1.

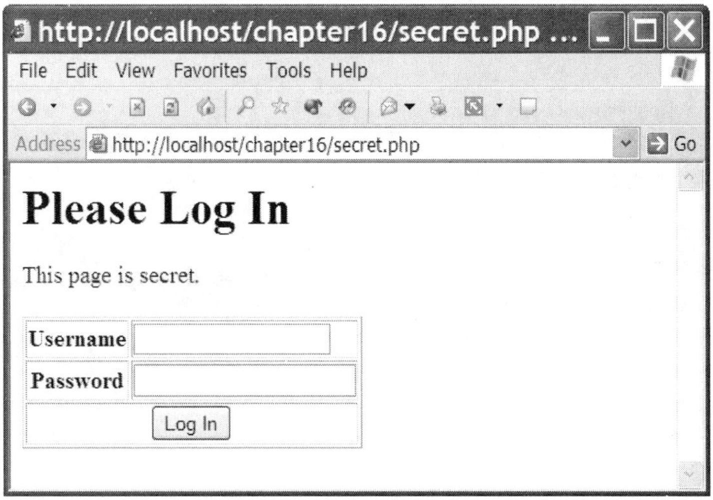

Figure 16.1 This HTML form requests that visitors enter a username and password for access.

If the parameters are present but not correct, it will display an error message. A sample error message is shown in Figure 16.2.

Figure 16.2 When users enter incorrect details, you need to give them an error message. On a real site, you might want to give a somewhat friendlier message.

If these parameters are present and correct, it will display the secret content. The sample test content is shown in Figure 16.3.

Figure 16.3   When provided with correct details, the script displays content.

The code to create the functionality shown in Figures 16.1, 16.2, and 16.3 is shown in Listing 16.1.

Listing 16.1   `secret.php`—**PHP and HTML to Provide a Simple Authentication Mechanism**

```php
<?php
  //create short names for variables
@ $name = $_POST['name'];
@ $password = $_POST['password'];

  if(empty($name)||empty($password))
  {
    //Visitor needs to enter a name and password
?>
    <h1>Please Log In</h1>
    This page is secret.
    <form method="post" action="secret.php">
    <table border="1">
    <tr>
      <th> Username </th>
      <td> <input type="text" name="name"> </td>
    </tr>
```

Listing 16.1   **Continued**

```
    <tr>
      <th> Password </th>
      <td> <input type="password" name="password"> </td>
    </tr>
    <tr>
      <td colspan="2" align="center">
        <input type="submit" value="Log In">
      </td>
    </tr>
    </table>
    </form>
<?php
  }
  else if($name=='user'&&$password=='pass')
  {
    // visitor's name and password combination are correct
    echo '<h1>Here it is!</h1>';
    echo 'I bet you are glad you can see this secret page.';
  }
  else
  {
    // visitor's name and password combination are not correct
    echo '<h1>Go Away!</h1>';
    echo 'You are not authorized to view this resource.';
  }
?>
```

The code from Listing 16.1 provides a simple authentication mechanism to allow authorized users to see a page, but it has some significant problems.

This script

- Has one username and password hard-coded into the script
- Stores the password as plain text
- Protects only one page
- Transmits the password as plain text

These issues can all be addressed with varying degrees of effort and success.

Storing Passwords

There are many better places to store usernames and passwords than inside the script. Inside the script, modifying the data is difficult. It is possible, but a bad idea, to write a script to modify itself. Doing so would mean having a script on your server that is executed on your server but that can be written or modified by others. Storing the data in another file on the server lets you more easily write a program to add and remove users and to alter passwords.

Inside a script or another data file, you are limited to the number of users you can have without seriously affecting the speed of the script. If you are considering storing and searching through a large number of items in a file, you should consider using a database instead, as previously discussed. As a rule of thumb, if you want to store and search through a list of more than 100 items, they should be in a database rather than a flat file.

Using a database to store usernames and passwords would not make the script much more complex but would allow you to authenticate many different users quickly. It would also allow you to easily write a script to add new users, delete users, and allow users to change their passwords.

A script to authenticate visitors to a page against a database is shown in Listing 16.2.

Listing 16.2 `secretdb.php`—**Using MySQL to Improve the Simple Authentication Mechanism**

```php
<?php
  $name = $_POST['name'];
  $password = $_POST['password'];

  if(!isset($_POST['name'])&&!isset($_POST['password']))
  {
    //Visitor needs to enter a name and password
?>
    <h1>Please Log In</h1>
    This page is secret.
    <form method="post" action="secretdb.php">
    <table border="1">
    <tr>
      <th> Username </th>
      <td> <input type="text" name="name"> </td>
    </tr>
    <tr>
      <th> Password </th>
      <td> <input type="password" name="password"> </td>
    </tr>
    <tr>
      <td colspan="2" align="center">
        <input type="submit" value="Log In">
      </td>
    </tr>
    </table>
    </form>
<?php
  }
  else
  {
```

Listing 16.2   **Continued**

```php
  // connect to mysql
  $mysql = mysqli_connect( 'localhost', 'webauth', 'webauth' );
  if(!$mysql)
  {
    echo 'Cannot connect to database.';
    exit;
  }
  // select the appropriate database
  $selected = mysqli_select_db( $mysql, 'auth' );
  if(!$selected)
  {
    echo 'Cannot select database.';
    exit;
  }

  // query the database to see if there is a record which matches
  $query = "select count(*) from authorized_users where
            name = '$name' and
            password = '$password'";

  $result = mysqli_query( $mysql, $query );
  if(!$result)
  {
    echo 'Cannot run query.';
    exit;
  }
  $row = mysqli_fetch_row( $result );
  $count = $row[0];

  if ( $count > 0 )
  {
    // visitor's name and password combination are correct
    echo '<h1>Here it is!</h1>';
    echo 'I bet you are glad you can see this secret page.';
  }
  else
  {
    // visitor's name and password combination are not correct
    echo '<h1>Go Away!</h1>';
    echo 'You are not authorized to view this resource.';
  }
}
?>
```

You can create the database used here by connecting to MySQL as the MySQL `root` user and running the contents of Listing 16.3.

Listing 16.3 `createauthdb.sql`— **These MySQL Queries Create the auth Database, the auth Table, and Two Sample Users**

```
create database auth;
use auth;
create table authorized_users ( name varchar(20),
                                password varchar(40),
                                        primary key    (name)
                       );
insert into authorized_users values ( 'username',
                                       'password' );

insert into authorized_users values ( 'testuser',
                                       sha1('password') );
grant select on auth.*
          to 'webauth'
          identified by 'webauth';
flush privileges;
```

Encrypting Passwords

Regardless of whether you store your data in a database or a file, storing the passwords as plain text is an unnecessary risk. A one-way hashing algorithm can provide better security with very little extra effort.

PHP provides a number of one-way hash functions. The oldest and least secure is the Unix Crypt algorithm, provided by the function `crypt()`. The Message Digest 5 (MD5) algorithm, implemented in the function `md5()`, is stronger and available in most versions of PHP. If you do not require compatibility with old PHP versions, use Secure Hash Algorithm 1 (SHA-1).

The PHP function `sha1()` provides a strong, one-way cryptographic hash function. The prototype for this function is

```
string sha1 ( string str [, bool raw_output])
```

Given the string `str`, the function will return a pseudo-random 40-character string. If you set `raw_output` to `true`, you will instead get a 20-character string of binary data. For example, given the string `"password"`, `sha1()` returns `"5baa61e4c9b93f3f0682250b6cf8331b7ee68fd8"`. This string cannot be decrypted and turned back into `"password"` even by its creator, so it might not seem very useful at first glance. The property that makes `sha1()` useful is that the output is deterministic. Given the same string, `sha1()` will return the same result every time it is run.

Rather than having PHP code like

```
if( $name == 'username' &&
    $password == 'password' )
{
```

```
   //OK passwords match
}
```

you can have code like

```
if( $name == 'username' &&
    sha1($password) == '5baa61e4c9b93f3f0682250b6cf8331b7ee68fd8' ) )
{
  //OK passwords match
}
```

You do not need to know what the password looked like before you used sha1() on it. You need to know only if the password typed in is the same as the one that was originally run through sha1().

As already mentioned, hard-coding acceptable usernames and passwords into a script is a bad idea. You should use a separate file or a database to store them.

If you are using a MySQL database to store your authentication data, you could either use the PHP function sha1() or the MySQL function SHA1(). MySQL provides an even wider range of hashing algorithms than PHP, but they are all intended for the same purpose.

To use SHA1(), you could rewrite the SQL query in Listing 16.2 as

```
select count(*) from authorized_users where
       name = '$username' and
       password = sha1('$password')
```

This query counts the number of rows in the table named authorized_users that have a name value equal to the contents of $name and a pass value equal to the output given by SHA1() applied to the contents of $password. Assuming that you force people to have unique usernames, the result of this query is either 0 or 1.

Keep in mind that the hash functions generally return data of a fixed size. In the case of SHA1, it is 40 characters when represented as a string. Make sure that your database column is this width.

Looking back at Listing 16.3, you can see that we created one user ('username') with an unencrypted password and another user with an encrypted one ('testuser') to illustrate the two possible approaches.

Protecting Multiple Pages

Making a script like the ones in Listings 16.1 and 16.2 protect more than one page is a little harder. Because HTTP is stateless, there is no automatic link or association between subsequent requests from the same person. This makes it harder to have data, such as authentication information that a user has entered, carry across from page to page.

The easiest way to protect multiple pages is to use the access control mechanisms provided by your web server. We look at these mechanisms shortly.

To create this functionality yourself, you could include parts of the script shown in Listing 16.1 in every page that you want to protect. Using `auto_prepend_file` and `auto_append_file`, you can automatically prepend and append the code required to every file in particular directories. The use of these directives was discussed in Chapter 5, "Reusing Code and Writing Functions."

If you use this approach, what happens when your visitors go to multiple pages within your site? Requiring them to re-enter their names and passwords for every page they want to view would not be acceptable.

You could append the details the users entered to every hyperlink on the page. Because they might have spaces or other characters that are not allowed in URLs, you should use the function `urlencode()` to safely encode these characters.

This approach still has a few problems, though. Because the data would be included in web pages sent to the users and the URLs they visit, the protected pages they visit will be visible to anybody who uses the same computer and steps back through cached pages or looks at the browser's history list. Because you are sending the password back and forth to the browser with every page requested or delivered, this sensitive information is being transmitted more often than necessary.

There are two good ways to tackle these problems: HTTP basic authentication and sessions. Basic authentication overcomes the caching problem, but the browser still sends the password to the server with every request. Session control overcomes both of these problems. We look at HTTP basic authentication now and examine session control in Chapter 22, "Using Session Control in PHP," and in more detail in Chapter 26, "Building User Authentication and Personalization."

Using Basic Authentication

Fortunately, authenticating users is a common task, so authentication facilities are built into HTTP. Scripts or web servers can request authentication from a web browser. The web browser is then responsible for displaying a dialog box or similar device to obtain required information from the user.

Although the web server requests new authentication details for every user request, the web browser does not need to request the user's details for every page. The browser generally stores these details for as long as the user has a browser window open and automatically resends them to the web server as required without user interaction.

This feature of HTTP is called *basic authentication*. You can trigger basic authentication using PHP or using mechanisms built into your web server. We look first at the PHP method, then the Apache method, and finally the IIS method.

Basic authentication transmits a user's name and password in plain text, so it is not very secure. HTTP 1.1 contains a more secure method known as *digest authentication*, which uses a hashing algorithm (usually MD5) to disguise the details of the transaction. Digest authentication is supported by many web servers and most current-version web browsers. Unfortunately, as with many recently implemented features, there are many older browsers still in use that do not support digest authentication and a version of the standard included in Microsoft IE and IIS that is not compatible with non-Microsoft products.

In addition to being poorly supported by installed web browsers, digest authentication is still not very secure. Both basic and digest authentication provide a low level of security. Neither gives the user any assurance that he is dealing with the machine he intended to access. Both might permit a cracker to replay the same request to the server. Because basic authentication transmits the user's password as plain text, it allows any cracker capable of capturing packets to impersonate the user for making any request.

Basic authentication provides a (low) level of security similar to that commonly used to connect to machines via Telnet or FTP, transmitting passwords in plaintext. Digest authentication is somewhat more secure, encrypting passwords before transmitting them.

When you combine basic authentication with SSL and digital certificates, all parts of a web transaction can be protected by strong security. If you want strong security, you should read Chapter 17, "Implementing Secure Transactions with PHP and MySQL." However, for many situations, a fast, but relatively insecure, method such as basic authentication is appropriate.

Basic authentication protects a named realm and requires users to provide a valid username and password. Realms are named so that more than one realm can be on the same server. Different files or directories on the same server can be part of different realms, each protected by a different set of names and passwords. Named realms also let you group multiple directories on the one host or virtual host as a realm and protect them all with one password.

Using Basic Authentication in PHP

PHP scripts are generally cross-platform, but using basic authentication relies on environment variables set by the server. For an HTTP authentication script to run on Apache using PHP as an Apache module or on IIS using PHP as an ISAPI module, it needs to detect the server type and behave slightly differently. The script in Listing 16.4 will run on both servers.

Listing 16.4 `http.php`—**PHP Can Trigger HTTP Basic Authentication**

```php
<?php

// if we are using IIS, we need to set $PHP_AUTH_USER and $PHP_AUTH_PW
if (substr($_SERVER['SERVER_SOFTWARE'], 0, 9) == 'Microsoft' &&
    !isset($_SERVER['PHP_AUTH_USER']) &&
    !isset($_SERVER['PHP_AUTH_PW']) &&
    substr($_SERVER['HTTP_AUTHORIZATION'], 0, 6) == 'Basic '
   )
{
  list($_SERVER['PHP_AUTH_USER'], $_SERVER['PHP_AUTH_PW']) =
    explode(':', base64_decode(substr($_SERVER['HTTP_AUTHORIZATION'], 6)));
}
```

Listing 16.4 **Continued**

```
// Replace this if statement with a database query or similar
if ($_SERVER['PHP_AUTH_USER'] != 'user' || $_SERVER['PHP_AUTH_PW'] != 'pass')
{
  // visitor has not yet given details, or their
  // name and password combination are not correct

  header('WWW-Authenticate: Basic realm="Realm-Name"');
  if (substr($_SERVER['SERVER_SOFTWARE'], 0, 9) == 'Microsoft')
    header('Status: 401 Unauthorized');
  else
    header('HTTP/1.0 401 Unauthorized');

  echo '<h1>Go Away!</h1>';
  echo 'You are not authorized to view this resource.';
}
else
{
  // visitor has provided correct details
  echo '<h1>Here it is!</h1>';
  echo '<p>I bet you are glad you can see this secret page.</p>';
}
?>
```

The code in Listing 16.4 acts similarly to the previous listings in this chapter. If the user has not yet provided authentication information, it will be requested. If she has provided incorrect information, she is given a rejection message. If she provides a matching name-password pair, she is presented with the contents of the page.

In this case, the user will see an interface somewhat different from the previous listings. This script does not provide an HTML form for login information. The user's browser presents her with a dialog box. Some people see this as an improvement; others would prefer to have complete control over the visual aspects of the interface. The login dialog box that Internet Explorer provides is shown in Figure 16.4.

Because the authentication is being assisted by features built into the browser, the browser chooses to exercise some discretion in how failed authorization attempts are handled. Internet Explorer lets the user try to authenticate three times before displaying the rejection page. Netscape Navigator lets the user try an unlimited number of times, popping up a dialog box to ask, "Authorization failed. Retry?" between attempts. Netscape displays the rejection page only if the user clicks Cancel.

As with the code given in Listings 16.1 and 16.2, you could include this code in pages you wanted to protect or automatically prepend it to every file in a directory.

Figure 16.4   The user's browser is responsible for the appearance of the dialog box when using HTTP authentication.

Using Basic Authentication with Apache's .htaccess **Files**

You can achieve similar results to the script in Listing 16.4 without writing a PHP script.

The Apache web server contains a number of different authentication modules that can be used to decide the validity of data entered by a user. The easiest to use is mod_auth, which compares name-password pairs to lines in a text file on the server.

To get the same output as the preceding script, you need to create two separate HTML files: one for the content and one for the rejection page. We skipped some HTML elements in the previous examples but really should include <html> and <body> tags when generating HTML.

Listing 16.5, named content.html, contains the content that authorized users see. Listing 16.6, called rejection.html, contains the rejection page. Having a page to show in case of errors is optional, but it is a nice, professional touch if you put something useful on it. Given that this page will be shown when a user attempts to enter a protected area but is rejected, useful content might include instructions on how to register for a password, or how to get a password reset and emailed if it has been forgotten.

Listing 16.5 `content.html`— **Sample Content**

```
<html><body>
<h1>Here it is!</h1>
<p>I bet you are glad you can see this secret page.</p>
</body></html>
```

Listing 16.6 `rejection.html`—**Sample 401 Error Page**

```
<html><body>
<h1>Go Away!</h1>
<p>You are not authorized to view this resource.</p>
</body></html>
```

There is nothing new in these files. The interesting file for this example is Listing 16.7. This file needs to be called `.htaccess` and will control accesses to files and any subdirectories in its directory.

Listing 16.7 `.htaccess`— **An** `.htaccess` **File Can Set Many Apache Configuration Settings, Including Activating Authentication**

```
ErrorDocument 401 /chapter16/rejection.html
AuthUserFile /home/book/.htpass
AuthGroupFile /dev/null
AuthName "Realm-Name"
AuthType Basic
require valid-user
```

Listing 16.7 is an `.htaccess` file to turn on basic authentication in a directory. Many settings can be made in an `.htaccess` file, but the six lines in this example all relate to authentication.

The first line

```
ErrorDocument 401 /chapter16/rejection.html
```

tells Apache what document to display for visitors who fail to authenticate (HTTP error number 401). You can use other `ErrorDocument` directives to provide your own pages for other HTTP errors such as 404. The syntax is

```
ErrorDocument error_number URL
```

For a page to handle error 401, it is important that the URL given is publicly available. It would not be very useful in providing a customized error page to tell people that their authorization failed if the page is locked in a directory in which they need to successfully authenticate to see.

The line

```
AuthUserFile /home/book/.htpass
```

tells Apache where to find the file that contains authorized users' passwords. This file is often named `.htpass`, but you can give it any name you prefer. It is not important what you call this file, but it is important where you store it. It should not be stored within the web tree—somewhere that people can download it via the web server. The sample `.htpass` file is shown in Listing 16.8.

As well as specifying individual users who are authorized, it is possible to specify that only authorized users who fall into specific groups may access resources. We chose not to, so the line

```
AuthGroupFile /dev/null
```

sets the `AuthGroupFile` to point to `/dev/null`, a special file on Unix systems that is guaranteed to be null.

Like the PHP example, to use HTTP authentication, you need to name the realm as follows:

```
AuthName "Realm-Name"
```

You can choose any realm name you prefer, but bear in mind that the name will be shown to your visitors. To make it obvious that the name in the example should be changed, we named ours `"Realm-Name"`.

Because a number of different authentication methods are supported, you need to specify which authentication method you are using. Here, you use `Basic` authentication, as specified by this directive:

```
AuthType Basic
```

You also need to specify who is allowed access. You could specify particular users, particular groups, or as we have done, simply allow any authenticated user access. The line

```
require valid-user
```

specifies that any valid user is to be allowed access.

Listing 16.8 `.htpass`— **The Password File Stores Usernames and Each User's Encrypted Password**

```
user1:0nRp9M80GS7zM
user2:nC13sOTOhp.ow
user3:yjQMCPWjXFTzU
user4:LOmlMEi/hAme2
```

Each line in the `.htpass` file contains a username, a colon, and that user's encrypted password.

The exact contents of your `.htpass` file will vary. To create it, you use a small program called `htpasswd` that comes in the Apache distribution.

The `htpasswd` program is used in one of the following ways:

```
htpasswd [-cmdps] passwordfile username
```

or

```
htpasswd -b[cmdps] passwordfile username password
```

The only switch that you need to use is `-c`. Using `-c` tells `htpasswd` to create the file. You must use this for the first user you add. Be careful not to use it for other users because, if the file exists, `htpasswd` will delete it and create a new one.

The optional `m`, `d`, `p`, or `s` switches can be used if you want to specify which encryption algorithm (including no encryption) you would like to use.

The `b` switch tells the program to expect the password as a parameter rather than prompt for it. This feature is useful if you want to call `htpasswd` noninteractively as part of a batch process, but you should not use it if you are calling `htpasswd` from the command line.

The following commands created the file shown in Listing 16.8:

```
htpasswd -bc /home/book/.htpass user1 pass1
htpasswd -b /home/book/.htpass user2 pass2
htpasswd -b /home/book/.htpass user4 pass3
htpasswd -b /home/book/.htpass user4 pass4
```

Note that `htpasswd` may not be in your path: If it is not, you may need to supply the full path to it. On many systems, you will find it in the `/usr/local/apache/bin` directory.

This sort of authentication is easy to set up, but there are a few problems with using an `.htaccess` file this way.

Users and passwords are stored in a text file. Each time a browser requests a file that is protected by the `.htaccess` file, the server must parse the `.htaccess` file and then parse the password file, attempting to match the username and password. Instead of using an `.htaccess` file, you could specify the same things in your `httpd.conf` file—the main configuration file for the web server. An `.htaccess` file is parsed every time a file is requested. The `httpd.conf` file is parsed only when the server is initially started. This approach is faster, but means that if you want to make changes, you need to stop and restart the server.

Regardless of where you store the server directives, the password file still needs to be searched for every request. This means that, like other techniques we have looked at that use a flat file, this would not be appropriate for hundreds or thousands of users.

Using Basic Authentication with IIS

Like Apache, IIS supports HTTP authentication. Apache uses the Unix approach and is controlled by editing text files, and as you might expect, selecting options in dialog boxes controls the IIS setup.

Using Windows XP, you change the configuration of Internet Information Server 5 (IIS5) using the Internet Information Services. You can find this utility by choosing Administrative Tools in the Control Panel.

The Internet Information Services application looks something like the window shown in Figure 16.5. The tree control on the left side shows that on the machine named W2, a number of services are running. The one of interest here is the default website. Within this website is a directory called `protected`. Inside this directory is a file called `content.html`.

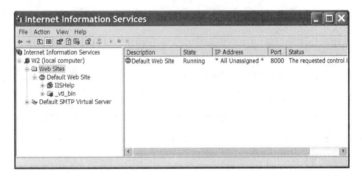

Figure 16.5   The Internet Information Services application allows you to configure Internet Information Server 5.

To add basic authentication to the `protected` directory, right-click on it and select Properties from the context menu. Using the Properties dialog, you can change many settings for this directory. The two tabs of interest here are Directory Security and Custom Errors. One of the options on the Directory Security tab is Anonymous Access and Authentication Control. Clicking this Edit button brings up the dialog box shown in Figure 16.6.

Within this dialog, you can disable anonymous access and turn on basic authentication. With the settings shown in Figure 16.6, only people who provide an appropriate name and password can view files in this directory.

To duplicate the behavior of the previous examples, you can also provide a page to tell users that their authentication details were not correct. Closing the Authentication Methods dialog box allows you to choose the Custom Errors tab.

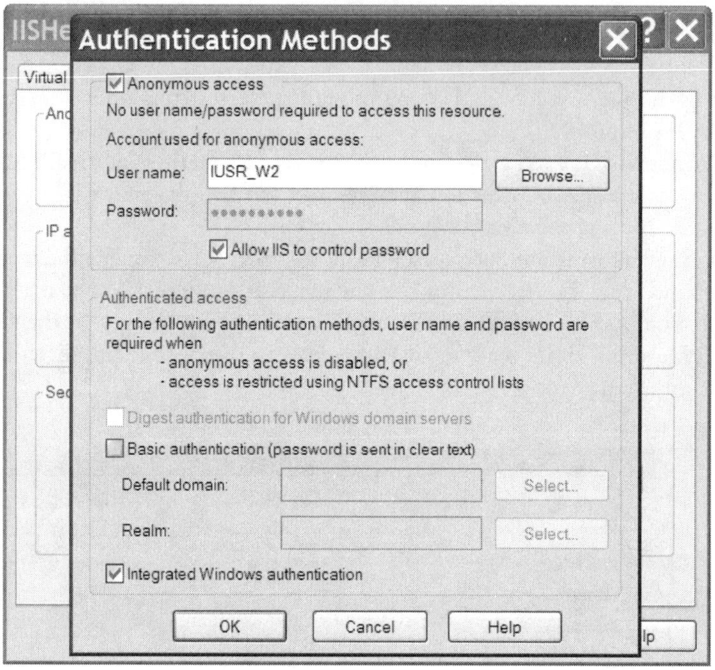

Figure 16.6 IIS5 allows anonymous access by default but allows you to turn
on authentication.

The Custom Errors tab, shown in Figure 16.7, associates errors with error messages.
Here, you store the same rejection file used earlier, `rejection.html`, shown in
Listing 16.6. IIS enables you to easily provide a more specific error message than Apache
does, providing the HTTP error code that occurred and a reason why it occurred. For
error 401, which represents failed authentication, IIS provides five different reasons. You
could provide different messages for each.

That is all you need to do to require authentication for this directory using IIS5. Like
a lot of Windows software, it is easier to set up than similar Unix software but harder to
copy from machine to machine or directory to directory. Accidentally setting it up in a
way that makes your machine insecure is also easy.

The major flaw with IIS's approach is that it authenticates web users by comparing
their login details to accounts on the machine. If you want to allow a user `"john"` to log
in with the password `"password"`, you need to create a user account on the machine, or
on a domain, with this name and password. You need to be very careful when you are
creating accounts for web authentication so that the users have only the account rights
they need to view web pages and do not have other rights such as Telnet access.

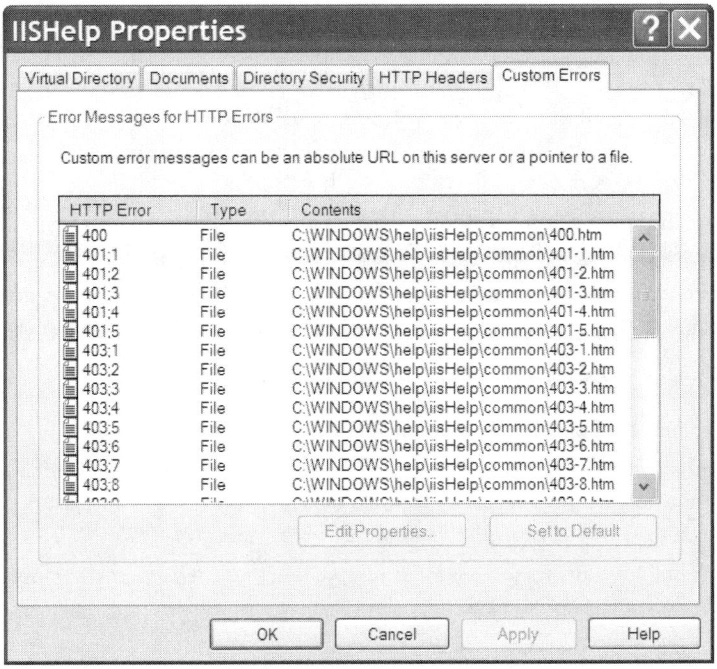

Figure 16.7 The Custom Errors tab lets you associate custom error pages
with error events.

Using `mod_auth_mysql` Authentication

As already mentioned, `mod_auth` is easy to set up with Apache and is effective. Because it
stores users in a text file, it is not really practical for busy sites with large numbers of
users.

Fortunately, you can have most of the ease of `mod_auth`, combined with the speed of
a database by using `mod_auth_mysql`. This module works in much the same way as
`mod_auth`, but because it uses a MySQL database instead of a text file, it can search large
user lists quickly.

To use it, you need to compile and install the module on your system or ask your system administrator to install it.

Installing `mod_auth_mysql`

To use `mod_auth_mysql`, you need to set up Apache and MySQL according to the
instructions in Appendix A, "Installing PHP and MySQL," but add a few extra steps. You

can find reasonable instructions in the files README and USAGE, which are in the distribution, but they refer to previous versions' behavior in some places. Here is a summary:

1. Obtain the distribution archive for the module. It is on the CD-ROM that came with this book, but you can always get the latest version from http://sourceforge.net/projects/mod-auth-mysql/.

2. Unzip and untar the source code.

3. Change to the mod_auth_mysql directory, run make, and then make install. You may need to change the install locations for MySQL in the make file (MakeFile).

4. Add this line to httpd.conf

   ```
   LoadModule mysql_auth_module libexec/mod_auth_mysql.so
   ```

   to dynamically load the module into Apache.

5. Create a database and table in MySQL to contain authentication information. It does not need to be a separate database or table; you can use an existing table such as the auth database from the example earlier in this chapter.

6. Add a line to your httpd.conf file to give mod_auth_mysql the parameters it needs to connect to MySQL. The directive will look like

   ```
   Auth_MySQL_Info hostname user password
   ```

Did It Work?

The easiest way to check whether your compilation worked is to see whether Apache will start. To start Apache, if you have SSL support, type

/usr/local/apache/bin/apachectl startssl

If you don't have SSL support, you can type
/usr/local/apache/bin/apachectl start

If it starts with the Auth_MySQL_Info directive in the httpd.conf file, mod_auth_mysql was successfully added.

Using mod_auth_mysql

After you have successfully installed the mod_auth_mysql module, using it is no harder than using mod_auth. Listing 16.9 shows a sample .htaccess file that will authenticate users with encrypted passwords stored in the database created earlier in this chapter.

Listing 16.9   .htaccess— **This** .htaccess **File Authenticates Users Against a MySQL Database**

```
ErrorDocument 401 /chapter16/rejection.html

AuthName "Realm Name"
AuthType Basic

Auth_MySQL_DB auth
Auth_MySQL_Encryption_Types MySQL
Auth_MySQL_Password_Table authorized_users
Auth_MySQL_Username_Field name
Auth_MySQL_Password_Field password

require valid-user
```

You can see that much of Listing 16.9 is the same as Listing 16.7. You still specify an error document to display in the case of error 401 (when authentication fails). You again specify basic authentication and give a realm name. As in Listing 16.7, you allow any valid, authenticated user access.

Because we are using mod_auth_mysql and did not want to use all the default settings, we used some directives to specify how this should work. Auth_MySQL_DB, Auth_MySQL_Password_Table, Auth_MySQL_Username_Field, and Auth_MySQL_Password_Field specify the name of the database, the table, the username field, and the password field, respectively.

We included the directive Auth_MySQL_Encryption_Types to specify that we want to use MySQL password encryption. Acceptable values are Plaintext, Crypt_DES, or MySQL. Crypt_DES is the default and uses standard Unix DES-encrypted passwords.

From the user perspective, this mod_auth_mysql example will work in exactly the same way as the mod_auth example. She will be presented with a dialog box by her web browser. If she successfully authenticates, she will be shown the content. If she fails, she will be given the error page.

For many websites, mod_auth_mysql is ideal. It is fast and relatively easy to implement, and it allows you to use any convenient mechanism to add database entries for new users. For more flexibility and the ability to apply fine-grained control to parts of pages, you might want to implement your own authentication using PHP and MySQL.

Creating Your Own Custom Authentication

In this chapter, you looked at creating your own authentication methods including some flaws and compromises and using built-in authentication methods, which are less flexible than writing your own code. Later in the book, after you learn about session control, you will be able to write your own custom authentication with fewer compromises than in this chapter.

In Chapter 22, we develop a simple user authentication system that avoids some of the problems we faced here by using sessions to track variables between pages.

In Chapter 26, we apply this approach to a real-world project and see how it can be used to implement a fine-grained authentication system.

Further Reading

The details of HTTP authentication are specified by RFC 2617, which is available at
http://www.rfc-editor.org/rfc/rfc2617.txt

The documentation for mod_auth, which controls basic authentication in Apache, can be found at
http://www.apache.org/docs/mod/mod_auth.html

The documentation for mod_auth_mysql is inside the download archive. It is a tiny download, so even if you just want to find out more about it, downloading the archive to look at the readme file is not silly.

Next

The next chapter explains how to safeguard data at all stages of processing from input, through transmission, and in storage. It includes the use of SSL, digital certificates, and encryption.

## 17

Implementing Secure Transactions with PHP and MySQL

I N THIS CHAPTER, WE EXPLAIN HOW TO DEAL with user data securely from input, through transmission, and in storage. This way, you can implement a transaction between your site and a user securely from end to end.

Key topics covered in this chapter include

- Providing secure transactions
- Using Secure Sockets Layer (SSL)
- Providing secure storage
- Determining whether to store credit card numbers
- Using encryption in PHP

Providing Secure Transactions

Providing secure transactions using the Internet is a matter of examining the flow of information in your system and ensuring that, at each point, your information is secure. In the context of network security, there are no absolutes. No system is ever going to be impenetrable. By *secure*, we mean that the level of effort required to compromise a system or transmission is high compared to the value of the information involved.

If you are to direct your security efforts effectively, you need to examine the flow of information through all parts of your system. The flow of user information in a typical application, written using PHP and MySQL, is shown in Figure 17.1.

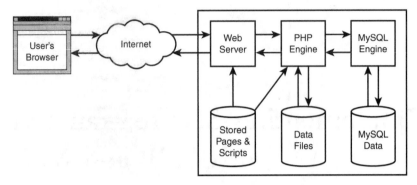

Figure 17.1   User information is stored or processed by these elements of a
typical web application environment.

The details of each transaction occurring in your system will vary, depending both on
your system design and on the user data and actions that triggered the transaction. You
can examine all of them in a similar way. Each transaction between a web application
and a user begins with the user's browser sending a request through the Internet to the
web server. If the page is a PHP script, the web server will delegate processing of the
page to the PHP engine.

The PHP script might read or write data to disk. It might also use the `include()` or
`require()` constructs to include other PHP or HTML files. It also sends SQL queries to
the MySQL daemon and receives responses. The MySQL engine is responsible for reading and writing its own data on disk.

This system has three main parts:

- The user's machine
- The Internet
- Your system

The following sections describe security considerations for each separately, but obviously
the user's machine and the Internet are largely out of your control.

The User's Machine

From your point of view, the user's machine is running a web browser. You have no control over other factors such as how securely the machine is set up. You need to bear in
mind that the machine might be very insecure or even a shared terminal at a library,
school, or café.

Many different browsers are available, each having slightly different capabilities. If you
consider only recent versions of the most popular two browsers, most of the differences
between them affect only how HTML will be rendered and displayed, but you also need
to consider security or functionality issues.

Note that some people disable features that they consider a security or privacy risk, such as Java, cookies, or JavaScript. If you use these features, you should either test that your application degrades gracefully for people without these features or consider providing a less feature-rich interface that allows these people to use your site.

Users outside the United States and Canada might have web browsers that support only 40-bit encryption. Although the U.S. Government changed the law in January 2000 to allow export of strong encryption (to nonembargoed countries) and 128-bit versions are now available to most users, some of them will not have upgraded. Unless you are making guarantees of security to users in the text of your site, this issue need not overly concern you as a web developer. SSL automatically negotiates for you to enable your server and the user's browser to communicate at the most secure level they both understand.

You cannot be sure that you are dealing with a web browser connecting to your site through your intended interface. Requests to your site might be coming from another site stealing images or content, or from a person using software such as cURL to bypass safety measures.

We look at the cURL library, which can be used to simulate connections from a browser, in Chapter 19, "Using Network and Protocol Functions." This tool is useful to you, as a developer, but can also be used maliciously.

Although you cannot change or control the way users' machines are set up, you do need to bear these issues in mind. The variability of user machines might be a factor in how much functionality you provide via server-side scripting (such as PHP) and how much you provide via client-side scripting (such as JavaScript).

Functionality provided by PHP can be compatible with every user's browser because the result is merely an HTML page. Using anything but very basic JavaScript involves taking into account the different capabilities of individual browser versions.

From a security perspective, you are better off using server-side scripting for such things as data validation because, that way, your source code is not visible to the user. If you validate data only in JavaScript, users can see the code and perhaps circumvent it.

Data that needs to be retained can be stored on your own machines, as files or database records, or on your users' machines as cookies. We look at using cookies for storing some limited data (a session key) in Chapter 22, "Using Session Control in PHP."

The majority of data you store should reside on the web server or in your database. There are a number of good reasons to store as little information as possible on a user's machine. If the information is outside your system, you have no control over how securely it is stored, you cannot be sure that the user will not delete it, and you cannot stop the user from modifying it in an attempt to confuse your system.

The Internet

As with the user's machine, you have very little control over the characteristics of the Internet, but this does not mean you can ignore these characteristics when designing your system.

The Internet has many fine features, but it is an inherently insecure network. When sending information from one point to another, you need to bear in mind that others could view or alter the information you are transmitting, as discussed in Chapter 15, "E-commerce Security Issues." With this point in mind, you can decide what action to take.

Your response might be to

- Transmit the information anyway, knowing that it might not be private and might not arrive unaltered.
- Digitally sign the information before transmitting it to protect it from tampering.
- Encrypt the information before transmitting it to keep it private and protect it from tampering.
- Decide that your information is too sensitive to risk any chance of interception and find another way to distribute your information.

The Internet is also a fairly anonymous medium. It is difficult to be certain whether the person you are dealing with is who he claims to be. Even if you can assure yourself about a user to your own satisfaction, proving this beyond a sufficient level of doubt in a forum such as a court might be difficult. This causes problems with repudiation, which we discussed in Chapter 15.

In summary, privacy and repudiation are important issues when conducting transactions over the Internet.

You can secure information flowing to and from your web server through the Internet in at least two different ways:

- Secure Sockets Layer (SSL)
- Secure Hypertext Transfer Protocol (S-HTTP)

Both these technologies offer private, tamper-resistant messages and authentication, but SSL is readily available and widely used, whereas S-HTTP has not really taken off. We look at SSL in detail later in this chapter.

Your System

The part of the universe that you do have control over is your system. Your system is represented by the components within the rectangular box shown previously in Figure 17.1. These components might be physically separated on a network or all exist on the one physical machine.

You are fairly safe in not worrying about the security of information while the various third-party products that you use to deliver your web content are handling it. The authors of those particular pieces of software have probably given them more thought than you have time to give them. As long as you are using an up-to-date version of a well-known product, you can find any well-known problems by judicious application of Google or your favorite web search engine. You should make it a priority to keep up to date with this information.

If installation and configuration are part of your role, you do need to worry about the way software is installed and configured. Many mistakes made in security are a result of not following the warnings in the documentation or involve general system administration issues that are topics for another book. We suggest you buy a good book on administering the operating system you intend to use or hire an expert system administrator.

One specific issue to consider when installing PHP is that installing PHP as a SAPI module for your web server is generally more secure, as well as much more efficient, than running it via the CGI interface.

The primary point you need to worry about as a web application developer is what your own scripts do or not do. What potentially sensitive data does your application transmit to the user over the Internet? What sensitive data do you ask users to transmit to you? If you are transmitting information that should be a private transaction between you and your users or that should be difficult for an intermediary to modify, you should consider using SSL.

We already discussed using SSL between the user's computer and the server. You should also think about the situation in which you are transmitting data from one component of your system to another over a network. A typical example arises when your MySQL database resides on a different machine from your web server. PHP connects to your MySQL server via TCP/IP, and this connection is unencrypted. If these machines are both on a private local area network, you need to ensure that the network is secure. If the machines are communicating via the Internet, your system will probably run slowly, and you need to treat this connection in the same way as other connections over the Internet.

It is important that when your users think they are dealing with you, they are, in fact, dealing with you. Registering for a digital certificate protects your visitors from spoofing (someone else impersonating your site), allows you to use SSL without users seeing a warning message, and provides an air of respectability to your online venture.

Do your scripts carefully check the data that users enter? Are you careful about storing information securely? We answer these questions in the next few sections of this chapter.

Using Secure Sockets Layer (SSL)

The Secure Sockets Layer protocol suite was originally designed by Netscape to facilitate secure communication between web servers and web browsers. It has since been adopted as the unofficial standard method for browsers and servers to exchange sensitive information.

Both SSL versions 2 and 3 are well supported. Most web servers either include SSL functionality or can accept it as an add-on module. Internet Explorer and Netscape Navigator have both supported SSL from version 3.

Networking protocols and the software that implements them are usually arranged as a stack of layers. Each layer can pass data to the layer above or below and request services of the layer above or below. Figure 17.2 shows such a protocol stack.

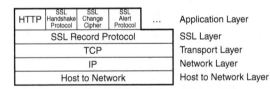

Figure 17.2   The protocol stack used by an application layer protocol such as
Hypertext Transfer Protocol.

When you use HTTP to transfer information, the HTTP protocol calls on the
Transmission Control Protocol (TCP), which in turn relies on the *Internet Protocol (IP)*. This
protocol in turn needs an appropriate protocol for the network hardware being used to
take packets of data and send them as an electrical signal to the destination.

HTTP is called an *application layer protocol*. There are many other application layer protocols such as FTP, SMTP, and Telnet (as shown in Figure 17.2), and others such as POP
and IMAP. TCP is one of two transport layer protocols used in TCP/IP networks. IP is
the protocol at the network layer. The host to network layer is responsible for connecting
the host (computer) to a network. The TCP/IP protocol stack does not specify the protocols used for this layer because you need different protocols for different types of networks.

When you send data, the data is sent down through the stack from an application to
the physical network media. When you receive data, it travels up from the physical network, through the stack, to the application.

Using SSL adds an additional transparent layer to this model. The SSL exists between
the transport layer and the application layer. This configuration is shown in Figure 17.3.
The SSL modifies the data from the HTTP application before giving it to the transport
layer to send it to its destination.

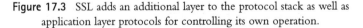

Figure 17.3   SSL adds an additional layer to the protocol stack as well as
application layer protocols for controlling its own operation.

SSL is capable of providing a secure transmission environment for protocols other than
HTTP. Other protocols can be used because SSL is essentially transparent. The SSL provides the same interface to protocols above it as the underlying transport layer. It then
transparently deals with handshaking, encryption, and decryption.

When a web browser connects to a secure web server via HTTP, the two need to follow a handshaking protocol to agree on what they will use for items such as authentication and encryption.

The handshake sequence involves the following steps:

1. The browser connects to an SSL-enabled server and asks the server to authenticate itself.

2. The server sends its digital certificate.

3. The server might optionally (and rarely) request that the browser authenticate itself.

4. The browser presents a list of the encryption algorithms and hash functions it supports. The server selects the strongest encryption that it also supports.

5. The browser and server generate session keys:

    a. The browser obtains the server's public key from its digital certificate and uses it to encrypt a randomly generated number.

    b. The server responds with more random data sent in plaintext (unless the browser has provided a digital certificate at the server's request, in which case the server will use the browser's public key).

    c. The encryption keys for the session are generated from this random data using hash functions.

Generating good quality random data, decrypting digital certificates, generating keys, and using public key cryptography take time, so this handshake procedure takes time. Fortunately, the results are cached, so if the same browser and server want to exchange multiple secure messages, the handshake process and the required processing time occur only once.

When data is sent over an SSL connection, the following steps occur:

1. It is broken into manageable packets.

2. Each packet is (optionally) compressed.

3. Each packet has a message authentication code (MAC) calculated using a hashing algorithm.

4. The MAC and compressed data are combined and encrypted.

5. The encrypted packets are combined with header information and sent to the network.

The entire process is shown in Figure 17.4.

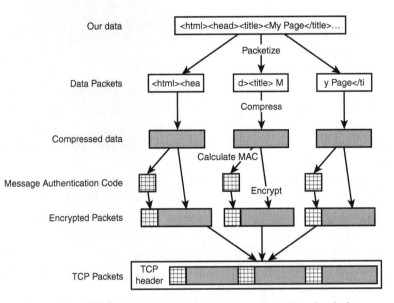

Figure 17.4 SSL breaks up, compresses, hashes, and encrypts data before sending it.

One thing you might notice from the diagram is that the TCP header is added after the data is encrypted. This means that routing information could still potentially be tampered with, and although snoopers cannot tell what information you are exchanging, they can see who is exchanging it.

The reason that SSL includes compression before encryption is that although most network traffic can be (and often is) compressed before being transmitted across a network, encrypted data does not compress well. Compression schemes rely on identifying repetition or patterns within data. Trying to apply a compression algorithm after data has been turned into an effectively random arrangement of bits via encryption is usually pointless. It would be unfortunate if SSL, which was designed to increase network security, had the side effect of dramatically increasing network traffic.

Although SSL is relatively complex, users and developers are shielded from most of what occurs because its external interfaces mimic existing protocols.

In the future, SSL 3.0 may be replaced by Transport Layer Security (TLS) 1.0, but at the time of writing, TLS is a draft standard and not supported by any servers or browsers. TLS is intended to be a truly open standard, rather than a standard defined by one organization but made available for others. It is based directly on SSL 3.0 but contains improvements intended to overcome weaknesses of SSL and offer further flexibility.

Screening User Input

One of the principles of building a safe web application is that you should never trust user input. Always screen user data before putting it in a file or database or passing it through a system execution command.

In several places throughout this book, we have described techniques you can use to screen user input. We've listed them briefly here as a reference:

- You should use the `addslashes()` function to filter user data before it is passed to a database. This function escapes out characters that might be troublesome to a database. You can use the `stripslashes()` function to return the data to its original form.

- You can switch on the `magic_quotes_gpc` and `magic_quotes_runtime` directives in your `php.ini` file. These directives automatically add and strip slashes for you. The `magic_quotes_gpc` applies this formatting to incoming `GET`, `POST`, and cookie variables, and the `magic_quote_runtime` applies it to data going to and from databases.

- You should use the `escapeshellcmd()` function when you are passing user data to a `system()` or `exec()` call or to backticks. This function escapes out any metacharacters that can be used to force your system to run arbitrary commands entered by a malicious user.

- You can use the `strip_tags()` function to strip out HTML and PHP tags from a string. This function prevents users from planting malicious scripts in user data that you might echo back to the browser.

- You can use the `htmlspecialchars()` function, which converts characters to their HTML entity equivalents. For example, < is converted to `&lt;`. This function converts any script tags to harmless characters.

Providing Secure Storage

The three different types of stored data (HTML or PHP files, script-related data, and MySQL data) are often stored in different areas of the same disk but are shown separately in Figure 17.1. Each type of storage requires different precautions and is examined separately.

The most dangerous type of data you store is executable content. On a website, this usually means scripts. You need to be very careful that your file permissions are set correctly within your web hierarchy. By this, we mean the directory tree starting from `htdocs` on an Apache server or `inetpub` on an IIS server. Others need to have permission to read your scripts to see their output, but they should not be able to write over or edit them.

The same proviso applies to directories within the web hierarchy. Only you should be able to write to these directories. Other users, including the user who the web server runs as, should not have permission to write or create new files in directories that can be loaded from the web server. If you allow others to write files here, they could write a malicious script and execute it by loading it through the web server.

If your scripts need permission to write to files, make a directory outside the web tree for this purpose. This is particularly true for file upload scripts. Scripts and the data that they write should not mix.

When writing sensitive data, you might be tempted to encrypt it first. This approach, however, usually provides little value. Let's put it this way: If you have a file called `creditcardnumbers.txt` on your web server and a cracker obtains access to your server and can read the file, what else can he read? To encrypt and decrypt data, you need a program to encrypt data, a program to decrypt data, and one or more key files. If the cracker can read your data, there is probably nothing stopping him from reading your key and other files.

Encrypting data could be valuable on a web server, but only if the software and key to decrypt the data were not stored on the web server, but were stored on another machine instead. One way of securely dealing with sensitive data would be to encrypt it on the server and then transmit it to another machine, perhaps via email.

Database data is similar to data files. If you set up MySQL correctly, only MySQL can write to its data files. This means that you need to worry only about accesses from users within MySQL. We already discussed MySQL's own permission system, which assigns particular rights to particular usernames at particular hosts.

One issue that needs special mention is that you will often need to write a MySQL password in a PHP script. Your PHP scripts are generally publicly loadable. This issue is not as much of a disaster as it might seem at first. Unless your web server configuration is broken, your PHP source is not visible from outside.

If your web server is configured to parse files with the extension .php using the PHP interpreter, outsiders will not be able to view the uninterpreted source. However, you should be careful when using other extensions. If you place .inc files in your web directories, anybody requesting them will receive the unparsed source. You either need to place include files outside the web tree, configure your server not to deliver files with this extension, or use .php as the extension on these files as well.

If you are sharing a web server with others, your MySQL password might be visible to other users on the same machine who can also run scripts via the same web server. Depending on how your system is set up, this situation might be unavoidable. You can avoid this problem by having a web server set up to run scripts as individual users or by having each user run her own instance of the web server. If you are not the administrator for your web server (as is likely the case if you are sharing a server), discussing this issue with your administrator and exploring security options might be worthwhile.

Determining Whether to Store Credit Card Numbers

Now that we've discussed secure storage for sensitive data, one type of sensitive data deserves special mention. Internet users are paranoid about their credit card numbers. If you are going to store them, you need to be very careful. You also need to ask yourself why you are storing them and whether it is really necessary.

What are you going to do with a card number? If you have a one-off transaction to process real-time card processing, you will be better off accepting the card number from your customer and sending it straight to your transaction processing gateway without storing it at all.

If you have periodic charges to make, such as the authority to charge a monthly fee to the same card for an ongoing subscription, this approach might not be an option. In this case, you should think about storing the numbers somewhere other than the web server.

If you are going to store large numbers of your customers' card details, make sure that you have a skilled and somewhat paranoid system administrator who has enough time to check up-to-date sources of security information for the operating system and other products you use.

Using Encryption in PHP

A simple, but useful, task you can use to demonstrate encryption is sending encrypted email. For many years, the de facto standard for encrypted email has been PGP, which stands for Pretty Good Privacy. Philip R. Zimmermann wrote PGP specifically to add privacy to email.

Freeware versions of PGP are available, but you should note that it is not Free Software. The freeware version can legally be used only for noncommercial use.

If you are a U.S. citizen residing in the United States or a Canadian citizen residing in Canada, you can obtain the freeware version from

http://web.mit.edu/network/pgp.html

If you want to use PGP for commercial use, you can get a commercial license from PGP Corporation. For details, see

http://www.pgp.com

To obtain the freeware version of PGP for use outside the United States and Canada, see the list of international download sites at the international PGP page:

http://www.pgpi.org

An open source alternative to PGP has more recently become available. Gnu Privacy Guard, known as GPG, is a *free* (as in beer) and *Free* (as in speech) replacement for PGP. It contains no patented algorithms and can be used commercially without restriction.

The two products perform the same task in fairly similar ways. If you intend to use the command-line tools, the differences might not matter, but each has different interfaces such as plug-ins for email programs that automatically decrypt email when it is received.

GPG is available from

http://www.gnupg.org

You can use the two products together, creating an encrypted message using GPG for somebody using PGP (as long as it is a recent version) to decrypt. Because we are interested in the creation of messages at the web server, we provide an example here using GPG. Using PGP instead does not require many changes.

As well as the usual requirements for examples in this book, you need to have GPG available for this code to work. GPG might already be installed on your system. If it is not, don't be concerned—the installation procedure is straightforward, but the setup can be a bit tricky.

Installing GPG

To add GPG to your Linux machine, you can download the appropriate archive file from www.gnupg.org. Depending on whether you choose the `.tar.gz` or `.tar.bz2` archive, you need to use `gunzip` or `tar` to extract the files from the archive.

To compile and install the program, use the same commands as for most Linux programs:

`configure` (or `./configure` depending on your system)

`make`

`make install`

If you are not the root user, you need to run the configure script with the `--prefix` option as follows:

`./configure --prefix=/path/to/your/directory`

You use this option because a nonroot user will not have access to the default directory for GPG.

If all goes well, GPG will be compiled and the executable copied to `/usr/local/bin/gpg` or the directory that you specified. You can change many options. See the GPG documentation for details.

For a Windows server, the process is even easier. Download the zip file, unzip it, and place `gpg.exe` somewhere in your PATH. (`C:\Windows\` or similar will be fine). Create a directory at `C:\gnupg`. Then open a command prompt and type **gpg**.

You also need to install GPG or PGP and generate a key pair on the system where you plan to check mail.

On the web server, you'll find very few differences between the command-line versions of GPG and PGP, so you might as well use GPG because it is free. On the machine where you read mail, you might prefer to buy a commercial version of PGP to have a nicer graphical user interface plug-in to your mail reader.

If you do not already have a key pair, generate one on your mail reading machine. Recall that a key pair consists of a public key, which other people (and your PHP script) use to encrypt mail before sending it to you, and a private key, which you use to either decrypt received messages or sign outgoing mail. It is important that you generate the key on your mail-reading machine rather than on your web server because your private key should not be stored on the web server.

If you are using the command-line version of GPG to generate your keys, enter the following command:

```
gpg --gen-key
```

You are prompted with a number of questions. Most of them have a default answer that you can accept. On separate lines, you are asked for your real name, your email address, and a comment, which will be used to name the key. (My key is named `'Luke Welling <luke@tangledweb.com.au>'`. I am sure that you can see the pattern. Had I provided a comment, too, it would be between the name and address.)

To export the public key from your new key pair, you can use the following command:

```
gpg --export > filename
```

This command gives you a binary file suitable for importing into the GPG or PGP key ring on another machine. If you want to email this key to people so that they can import it into their key rings, you can instead create an ASCII version like this:

```
gpg --export -a > filename
```

Having extracted the public key, you can upload the file to your account on the web server by using FTP.

The following commands assume that you are using Unix. The steps are the same for Windows, but directory names and system commands are different. First, log in to your account on the web server and change the permissions on the file so that other users will be able to read it. Type

```
chmod 644 filename
```

You need to create a key ring so that the user who your PHP scripts get executed as can use GPG. Which user this is depends on how your server is set up. It is often the user nobody but could be something else.

Change so that you are the web server user. You need to have root access to the server to do this. On many systems, the web server runs as nobody. The following examples assume this user. (You can change it to the appropriate user on your system.) If this is the case on your system, type

```
su root
su nobody
```

Create a directory where nobody can store his key ring and other GPG configuration information. It needs to be in nobody's home directory.

The home directory for each user is specified in `/etc/passwd`. On many Linux systems, `nobody`'s home directory defaults to `/`, which `nobody` does not have permission to write to. On many BSD systems, `nobody`'s home directory defaults to `/nonexistent`, which, because it doesn't exist, cannot be written to. On our system, `nobody` has been assigned the home directory `/tmp`. You need to make sure your web server user has a home directory that he can write to.

Type

```
cd ~
mkdir .gnupg
```

The user `nobody` needs a signing key of her own. To create this key, run this command again:

```
gpg --gen-key
```

Because your `nobody` user probably receives very little personal email, you can create a signing-only key for her. This key's only purpose is to allow you to trust the public key you extracted earlier.

To import the pubic key exported earlier, use the following command:

```
gpg --import filename
```

To tell GPG that you want to trust this key, you need to edit the key's properties using this command:

```
gpg --edit-key 'Luke Welling <luke@tangledweb.com.au>'
```

On this line, the text in single quotation marks is the name of the key. Obviously, the name of your key will not be `'Luke Welling <luke@tangledweb.com.au>'`, but a combination of the name, comment, and email address you provided when generating it.

Options within this program include `help`, which describes the available commands: `trust`, `sign`, and `save`.

Type **trust** and tell GPG that you trust your key fully. Type **sign** to sign this public key using `nobody`'s private key. Finally, type **save** to exit this program, keeping your changes.

Testing GPG

GPG should now be set up and ready to use. Creating a file containing some text and saving it as `test.txt` will allow you to test it.

Typing the following command (modified to use the name of your key)

```
gpg -a --recipient 'Luke Welling <luke@tangledweb.com.au>' --encrypt test.txt
```

should give you the warning

```
gpg: Warning: using insecure memory!
```

and create a file named `test.txt.asc`. If you open `test.txt.asc`, you should see an encrypted message like this:

```
-----BEGIN PGP MESSAGE-----
Version: GnuPG v1.0.3 (GNU/Linux)
Comment: For info see http://www.gnupg.org

hQEOA0DU7hVGgdtnEAQAhr4HgR7xpIBsK9CiELQw85+k1QdQ+p/FzqL8tICrQ+B3
0GJTEehPUDErwqUw/uQLTds0r1oPSrIAZ7c6GVkh0YEVBj2MskT81IIBvdo95OyH
K9PUCvg/rLxJ1kxe4Vp8QFET5E3FdII/ly8VP5gSTE7gAgm0SbFf3S91PqwMyTkD
/2oJEvL6e3cP384s0i81rBbDbOUAAhCjjXt2DX/uX9q6P18QW56UICUOn4DPaW1G
/gnNZCkcVDgLcKfBjbkB/TCWWhpA7o7kX4CIcIh7KlIMHY4RKdnCWQf271oE+8i9
cJRSCMsFIoI6MMNRCQHY6p9bfxL2uE39IRJrQbe6xoEe0nkB0uTYxiL0TG+FrNrE
tvBVMS0nsHu7HJey+oY4Z833pk5+MeVwYumJwlvHjdZxZmV6wz46GO2XGT17b28V
wSBnWOoBHSZsPvkQXHTOq65EixP8y+YJvBN3z4pzdH0Xa+NpqbH7q3+xXmd30hDR
+u7t6MxTLDbgC+NR
=gfQu
-----END PGP MESSAGE-----
```

You should be able to transfer this file to the system where you generated the key initially and run

```
gpg test.txt.asc
```

to retrieve your original text. The text will be written to a file with the same name as it had before—in this case, `test.txt`.

To have the text echoed to the screen, use the `-d` flag:

```
gpg -d test.txt.asc
```

To place the text in a file of your choice rather than the default name, you can use the `-o` flag as well and specify an output file like this:

```
gpg -do test.out test.txt.asc
```

Note that the output file is named first.

If you have GPG set up so that the user your PHP scripts run as can use it from the command line, you are most of the way there. If this setup is not working, see your system administrator or the GPG documentation.

Listings 17.1 and 17.2 enable people to send encrypted email by using PHP to call GPG.

Listing 17.1 `private_mail.php`— **The HTML Form to Send Encrypted Email**

```php
<html>
<body>
<h1>Send Me Private Mail</h1>

<?php
 // you might need to change this line, if you do not use
 // the default ports, 80 for normal traffic and 443 for SSL
 if($_SERVER['SERVER_PORT']!=443)
```

Listing 17.1 **Continued**

```
      echo '<p><font color = red>
              WARNING: you have not connected to this page using SSL.
              Your message could be read by others.</font></p>';
?>

<form method = post action = "send_private_mail.php"><br>
Your email address:<br>
<input type = text name = from size = 38><br>
Subject:<br>
<input type = text name = title size = 38><br>
Your message:<br>
<textarea name = body cols = 30 rows = 10>
</textarea><br>
<input type = submit value = "Send!">
</form>
</body>
</html>
```

Listing 17.2 `send_private_mail.php`— **The PHP Script to Call GPG and Send Encrypted Email**

```php
<?php
  //create short variable names
  $from = $_POST['from'];
  $title = $_POST['title'];
  $body = $_POST['body'];

  $to_email = 'luke@localhost';

  // Tell gpg where to find the key ring
  // On this system, user nobody's home directory is /tmp/
  putenv('GNUPGHOME=/tmp/.gnupg');

  //create a unique file name
  $infile = tempnam('', 'pgp');
  $outfile = $infile.'.asc';

  //write the user's text to the file
  $fp = fopen($infile, 'w');
  fwrite($fp, $body);
  fclose($fp);

  //set up our command
  $command = "/usr/local/bin/gpg -a \\
```

Listing 17.2   **Continued**

```
                  --recipient 'Luke Welling <luke@tangledweb.com.au>' \\
                  --encrypt -o $outfile $infile";

  // execute our gpg command
  system($command, $result);

  //delete the unencrypted temp file
  unlink($infile);

  if($result==0)
  {
    $fp = fopen($outfile, 'r');
    if(!$fp||filesize ($outfile)==0)
    {
      $result = -1;
    }
    else
    {
      //read the encrypted file
      $contents = fread ($fp, filesize ($outfile)) ;
      //delete the encrypted temp file
      unlink($outfile);

      mail($to_email, $title, $contents, "From: $from");
      echo '<h1>Message Sent</h1>
            <p>Your message was encrypted and sent.
            <p>Thank you.';
    }
  }

  if($result!=0)
  {
    echo '<h1>Error:</h1>
          <p>Your message could not be encrypted, so has not been sent.
          <p>Sorry.';
  }
?>
```

To make this code work for you, you need to change a few things. Email will be sent to the address in `$to_email`.

In Listing 17.2, you need to change the line

```
putenv('GNUPGHOME=/tmp/.gnupg');
```

to reflect the location of your GPG key ring. On our system, the web server runs as the user `nobody` and has the home directory `/tmp/`.

We used the function `tempnam()` to create a unique temporary filename. You can specify both the directory and a filename prefix. You are going to create and delete these files in around 1 second, so it's not very important what you call them as long as they are unique. We specified a prefix of `'pgp'` but let PHP use the system temporary directory.

The statement

```
$command = '/usr/local/bin/gpg -a '.
           '--recipient 'Luke Welling <luke@tangledweb.com.au>' '.
           '--encrypt -o $outfile $infile';
```

sets up the command and parameters that will be used to call GPG. You need to modify this statement to suit your situation. As when you used it on the command line, you need to tell GPG which key to use to encrypt the message.

The statement

```
system($command, $result);
```

executes the instructions stored in `$command` and stores the return value in `$result`. You could ignore the return value, but it lets you have an `if` statement and tells the user that something went wrong.

After you finish with the temporary files you use, you delete them using the `unlink()` function. This means that your user's unencrypted email is stored on the server for a short time. If the server fails during execution, it is even possible that the file could be left on the server.

While you are thinking about the security of your script, it is important to consider all flows of information within your system. GPG encrypts your email and allows your recipient to decrypt it, but how does the information originally come from the sender? If you are providing a web interface to send GPG-encrypted mail, the flow of information will look something like Figure 17.5.

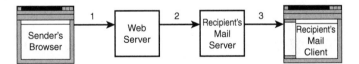

Figure 17.5   In the encrypted email application, the message is sent via the Internet three times.

In this figure, each arrow represents the message being sent from one machine to another. Each time the message is sent, it travels through the Internet and might pass through a number of intermediary networks and machines.

The script you are looking at here exists on the machine labeled *Web Server* in the diagram. At the web server, the message is encrypted using the recipient's public key. It is then sent via SMTP to the recipient's mail server. The recipient connects to his mail server, probably using POP or IMAP, and downloads the message using a mail reader. Here, he decrypts the message using his private key.

The data transfers in Figure 17.5 are labeled 1, 2, and 3. For stages 2 and 3, the information being transmitted is a GPG-encrypted message and is of little value to anybody who does not have the private key. For transfer 1, the message being transmitted is the text that the sender entered in the form.

If the information is important enough that you need to encrypt it for the second and third leg of its journey, sending it unencrypted for the first leg is a bit silly. Therefore, this script belongs on a server that uses SSL.

If you attempt connection to this script without SSL, it will provide a warning. You check this by checking the value of `$_SERVER['SERVER_PORT']`. SSL connections come in on port 443. Any other connection will cause an error.

Instead of providing an error message, you could deal with this situation in other ways. You could redirect the user to the same URL via an SSL connection. You could also choose to ignore it because it is not important if the form was delivered using a secure connection. What is usually important is that the details the user typed into the form are sent to you securely. You could simply have given a complete URL as the action of your form.

Currently, the open form tag looks like this:

```
<form method = post action = "send_private_mail.php">
```

You could alter it to send data via SSL even if the user connected without SSL, like this:

```
<form method = post action = "https://webserver/send_private_mail.php">
```

If you hard-code the complete URL like this, you can be assured that visitors' data will be sent using SSL, but you will need to modify the code every time you use it on another server or even in another directory.

Although in this case, and many others, it is not important that the empty form is sent to the user via SSL, sending it this way is usually a good idea. Seeing the little padlock symbol in the status bar of their browsers reassures people that their information will be sent securely. They should not need to look at your HTML source and see the action attribute of the form to know whether their data will be safe.

Further Reading

The specification for SSL version 3.0 is available from Netscape:

http://home.netscape.com/eng/ssl3/

If you would like to know more about how networks and networking protocols work, a classic introductory text is Andrew S. Tanenbaum's *Computer Networks*.

Next

We've wrapped up our discussion of e-commerce and security issues. In the next part of the book, we look at some more advanced PHP techniques, including interacting with other machines on the Internet, generating images on the fly, and using session control.

IV

Advanced PHP Techniques

## 18

Interacting with the File System and the Server

IN CHAPTER 2, "STORING AND RETRIEVING DATA," you saw how to read data from and write data to files on the web server. This chapter covers other PHP functions that enable you to interact with the file system on the web server.

Key topics covered in this chapter include

- Uploading files with PHP
- Using directory functions
- Interacting with files on the server
- Executing programs on the server
- Using server environment variables

To discuss the uses of these functions, we look at an example. Consider a situation in which you would like your client to be able to update some of a website's content—for instance, the current news about his company. (Or maybe you want a friendlier interface than FTP or SCP for yourself.) One approach is to let the client upload the content files as plain text. These files are then available on the site, through a template you have designed with PHP, as you did in Chapter 6, "Object-Oriented PHP."

Before we dive into the file system functions, let's briefly look at how file upload works.

Uploading Files

One useful piece of PHP functionality is support for HTTP upload. Instead of files coming from the server to the browser using HTTP, they go in the opposite direction— that is, from the browser to the server. Usually, you implement this configuration with an HTML form interface. The one used in this example is shown in Figure 18.1.

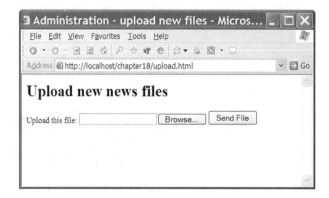

Figure 18.1 The HTML form used for this file upload has different fields and field types from those of a normal HTML form.

As you can see, the form has a box where the user can enter a filename or click the Browse button to browse files available to him locally. You might not have seen a file upload form before. We look at how to implement this form shortly.

After entering a filename, the user can click Send File, and the file will be uploaded to the server, where a PHP script is waiting for it.

HTML for File Upload

To implement file upload, you need to use some HTML syntax that exists specially for this purpose. The HTML for this form is shown in Listing 18.1.

Listing 18.1 upload.html—**HTML Form for File Upload**

```
<html>
<head>
  <title>Administration - upload new files</title>
</head>
<body>
<h1>Upload new news files</h1>
<form enctype="multipart/form-data" action="upload.php" method="post">
  <input type="hidden" name="MAX_FILE_SIZE" value="1000000">
  Upload this file: <input name="userfile" type="file">
  <input type="submit" value="Send File">
</form>
</body>
</html>
```

Note that this form uses POST. File uploads also work with the PUT method supported by Netscape Composer and Amaya although you would need to make significant changes to the code. They do not work with GET.

The extra features in this form are as follows:

- In the `<form>` tag, you must set the attribute `enctype="multipart/form-data"` to let the server know that a file is coming along with the regular form information.
- You must have a form field that sets the maximum size file that can be uploaded. This is a hidden field and is shown here as

```
<input type="hidden" name="MAX_FILE_SIZE" value=" 1000000">
```

  The name of this form field must be `MAX_FILE_SIZE`. The value is the maximum size (in bytes) of files you will allow people to upload. Here, we set this field to 1,000,000 bytes (roughly one megabyte). You may like to make it bigger or smaller for your application.

- You need an input of type `file`, shown here as

```
<input name="userfile" type="file">
```

You can choose whatever name you like for the file, but you should keep it in mind because you will use this name to access your file from the receiving PHP script.

A Note on Security

Before we go any further, it's worth noting that some versions of PHP have had security vulnerabilities in the file upload code. If you decide to use file upload on your production server, you should make sure you are using a recent version of PHP and keep your eyes open for patches.

This issue shouldn't deter you from using such a useful technology, but you should be careful about how you write your code and consider restricting access to file upload to, for example, site administrators and content managers.

Writing the PHP to Deal with the File

Writing the PHP to catch the file is reasonably straightforward but does depend on the PHP version and configuration settings. The function and variable names have changed over different versions and depend on whether you have `register_globals` turned on. The code here does not require `register_globals`, but it does require a PHP version of at least 4.1.

When the file is uploaded, it briefly goes into a temporary location on the web server. By default, this is the web server's main temporary directory. If you do not move, copy, or rename the file before your script finishes execution, it will be deleted when the script ends.

The data you need to handle in your PHP script is stored in the superglobal array `$_FILES`. If you have `register_globals` turned on, you can also access the information through direct variable names. However, this is probably the area in which it is most important to have `register_globals` turned off, or at least to act as though it is and use the superglobal array and ignore the globals.

The entries in $_FILES will be stored with the name of the <file> tag from your HTML form. Your form element is named userfile, so the array will have the following contents:

- The value stored in $_FILES['userfile']['tmp_name'] is the place where the file has been temporarily stored on the web server.
- The value stored in $_FILES['userfile']['name'] is the file's name on the user's system.
- The value stored in $_FILES['userfile']['size'] is the size of the file in bytes.
- The value stored in $_FILES['userfile']['type'] is the MIME type of the file—for example, text/plain or image/gif.
- The value stored in $_FILES['userfile']['error'] will give you any error codes associated with the file upload. This functionality was added at PHP 4.2.0.

Given that you know where the file is and what it's called, you can now copy it to somewhere useful. At the end of your script's execution, the temporary file will be deleted. Hence, you must move or rename the file if you want to keep it.

For the example, you will use the uploaded files as recent news articles, so you'll strip out any tags that might be in them and move them to a more useful directory. A script that performs this task is shown in Listing 18.2.

Listing 18.2 upload.php—**PHP to Catch the Files from the HTML Form**

```
<html>
<head>
  <title>Uploading...</title>
</head>
<body>
<h1>Uploading file...</h1>
<?php

  if ($_FILES['userfile']['error'] > 0)
  {
    echo 'Problem: ';
    switch ($_FILES['userfile']['error'])
    {
      case 1:  echo 'File exceeded upload_max_filesize';  break;
      case 2:  echo 'File exceeded max_file_size';  break;
      case 3:  echo 'File only partially uploaded';  break;
      case 4:  echo 'No file uploaded';  break;
    }
    exit;
  }
```

Listing 18.2 **Continued**

```php
  // Does the file have the right MIME type?
  if ($_FILES['userfile']['type'] != 'text/plain')
  {
    echo 'Problem: file is not plain text';
    exit;
  }

  // put the file where we'd like it
  $upfile = '/uploads/'.$_FILES['userfile']['name'] ;

  if (is_uploaded_file($_FILES['userfile']['tmp_name']))
  {
     if (!move_uploaded_file($_FILES['userfile']['tmp_name'], $upfile))
     {
        echo 'Problem: Could not move file to destination directory';
        exit;
     }
  }
  else
  {
    echo 'Problem: Possible file upload attack. Filename: ';
    echo $_FILES['userfile']['name'];
    exit;
  }

  echo 'File uploaded successfully<br><br>';

  // reformat the file contents
  $fp = fopen($upfile, 'r');
  $contents = fread ($fp, filesize ($upfile));
  fclose ($fp);

  $contents = strip_tags($contents);
  $fp = fopen($upfile, 'w');
  fwrite($fp, $contents);
  fclose($fp);

  // show what was uploaded
  echo 'Preview of uploaded file contents:<br><hr>';
  echo $contents;
  echo '<br><hr>';
?>
</body>
</html>
```

Interestingly enough, most of this script is error checking. File upload involves potential security risks, and you need to mitigate these risks where possible. You need to validate the uploaded file as carefully as possible to make sure it is safe to echo to your visitors.

Let's go through the main parts of the script. You begin by checking the error code returned in `$_FILES['userfile']['error']`. This error code was introduced at PHP 4.2.0. Since PHP 4.3, a constant is also associated with each of the codes. The possible constants and values are as follows:

- `UPLOAD_ERROR_OK`, value 0, means no error occurred.
- `UPLOAD_ERR_INI_SIZE`, value 1, means that the size of the uploaded file exceeds the maximum value specified in your `php.ini` file with the `upload_max_file-size` directive.
- `UPLOAD_ERR_FORM_SIZE`, value 2, means that the size of the uploaded file exceeds the maximum value specified in the HTML form in the `MAX_FILE_SIZE` element.
- `UPLOAD_ERR_PARTIAL`, value 3, means that the file was only partially uploaded.
- `UPLOAD_ERR_NO_FILE`, value 4, means that no file was uploaded.

If you want to use an older version of PHP, you can perform a manual version of some of these checks using sample code in the PHP manual or in older editions of this book.

You also check the MIME type. In this case, we want you to upload text files only, so test the MIME type by making sure that `$_FILES['userfile']['type']` contains `text/plain`. This is really only error checking. It is not security checking. The MIME type is inferred by the user's browser from the file extension and passed to your server. If there were some advantage to be obtained by passing a false one, it would not be hard for a malicious user to do so.

You then check that the file you are trying to open has actually been uploaded and is not a local file such as `/etc/passwd`. We come back to this topic in a moment.

If that all works out okay, you then copy the file into the include directory. We used `/uploads/` in this example; it's outside the web document tree and therefore a good place to put files that are to be included elsewhere.

You then open up the file, clean out any stray HTML or PHP tags that might be in the file using the `strip_tags()` function, and write the file back. Finally, you display the contents of the file so the user can see that her file uploaded successfully.

The results of one (successful) run of this script are shown in Figure 18.2.
In September 2000, an exploit was announced that could allow a cracker to fool PHP file upload scripts into processing a local file as if it had been uploaded. This exploit was documented on the BUGTRAQ mailing list. You can read the official security advisory at one of the many BUGTRAQ archives, such as http://lists.insecure.org/bugtraq/2000/Sep/0237.html.

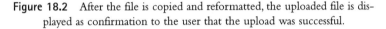

Figure 18.2   After the file is copied and reformatted, the uploaded file is displayed as confirmation to the user that the upload was successful.

To ensure that you are not vulnerable, this script uses the `is_uploaded_file()` and `move_uploaded_file()` functions to make sure that the file you are processing has actually been uploaded and is not a local file such as `/etc/passwd`. This function is available from PHP version 4.0.3 onward.

Unless you write your upload handling script carefully, a malicious visitor could provide his own temporary filename and convince your script to handle that file as though it were the uploaded file. Because many file upload scripts echo the uploaded data back to the user or store it somewhere that it can be loaded, this could lead to people being able to access any file that the web server can read. This could include sensitive files such as `/etc/passwd` and PHP source code including your database passwords.

Common Problems

Keep the following points in mind when performing file uploads:

- The previous example assumes that users have been authenticated elsewhere. You shouldn't allow just anybody to upload files to your site.

- If you are allowing untrusted or unauthenticated users to upload files, it's a good idea to be paranoid about the contents of the files. The last thing you want is a malicious script being uploaded and run. You should be careful, not just of the type and contents of the file as we are here, but of the filename itself. It's a good idea to rename uploaded files to something you know to be "safe."

- If you are using a Windows-based machine, be sure to use \\ or / instead of \ in file paths as per usual.

- Using the user-provided filename as we did in this script can cause a variety of problems. The most obvious one is that you run the risk of accidentally overwriting existing files if somebody uploads a file with a name that has already been used. A less obvious risk is that different operating systems and even different local language settings allow different sets of legal characters in filenames. A file being uploaded may have a filename that has illegal characters for your system.

- If you are having problems getting your file upload to work, check out your php.ini file. You need to have the upload_tmp_dir directive set to point to some directory that you have access to. You might also need to adjust the memory_limit directive if you want to upload large files; this determines the maximum file size in bytes that you can upload. Apache also has some configurable timeouts and transaction size limits that might need attention if you are having difficulties with large uploads.

Using Directory Functions

After the users have uploaded some files, it will be useful for them to be able to see what's been uploaded and manipulate the content files. PHP has a set of directory and file system functions that are useful for this purpose.

Reading from Directories

First, let's implement a script to allow directory browsing of the uploaded content. Browsing directories is actually straightforward in PHP. Listing 18.3 shows a simple script that can be used for this purpose.

Listing 18.3   browsedir.php—A Directory Listing of the Uploaded Files

```
<html>
<head>
  <title>Browse Directories</title>
</head>
<body>
<h1>Browsing</h1>
<?php
  $current_dir = '/uploads/';
  $dir = opendir($current_dir);

  echo "<p>Upload directory is $current_dir</p>";
  echo '<p>Directory Listing:</p><ul>';
  while ($file = readdir($dir))
  {
      echo "<li>$file</li>";
  }
```

Listing 18.3 **Continued**

```
  echo '</ul>';
  closedir($dir);
?>
</body>
</html>
```

This script makes use of the `opendir()`, `closedir()`, and `readdir()` functions.

The function `opendir()` opens a directory for reading. Its use is similar to the use of `fopen()` for reading from files. Instead of passing it a filename, you should pass it a directory name:

```
$dir = opendir($current_dir);
```

The function returns a directory handle, again in much the same way as `fopen()` returns a file handle.

When the directory is open, you can read a filename from it by calling `readdir($dir)`, as shown in the example. This function returns `false` when there are no more files to be read. (Note that it will also return `false` if it reads a file called `"0"`; you could, of course, test for this if it is likely to occur in your application.) Files aren't sorted in any particular order, so if you require a sorted list, you should read them into an array and sort that before displaying it.

When you are finished reading from a directory, you call `closedir($dir)` to finish. This is again similar to calling `fclose()` for a file.

Sample output of the directory browsing script is shown in Figure 18.3.

Figure 18.3   The directory listing shows all the files in the chosen directory, including the . (the current directory) and .. (one level up) directories. You can choose to filter them out.

If you are making directory browsing available via this mechanism, it is sensible to limit the directories that can be browsed so that a user cannot browse directory listings in areas not normally available to him.

An associated and sometimes useful function is `rewinddir($dir)`, which resets the reading of filenames to the beginning of the directory.

As an alternative to these functions, you can use the `dir` class provided by PHP. It has the properties `handle` and `path`, and the methods `read()`, `close()`, and `rewind()`, which perform identically to the nonclass alternatives.

Getting Information About the Current Directory

You can obtain some additional information given a path to a file.

The `dirname($path)` and `basename($path)` functions return the directory part of the path and filename part of the path, respectively. This information could be useful for the directory browser, particularly if you begin to build up a complex directory structure of content based on meaningful directory names and filenames.

You could also add to your directory listing an indication of how much space is left for uploads by using the `disk_free_space($path)` function. If you pass this function a path to a directory, it will return the number of bytes free on the disk (Windows) or the file system (Unix) on which the directory is located.

Creating and Deleting Directories

In addition to passively reading information about directories, you can use the PHP functions `mkdir()` and `rmdir()` to create and delete directories. You can create or delete directories only in paths that the user the script runs as has access to.

Using `mkdir()` is more complicated than you might think. It takes two parameters: the path to the desired directory (including the new directory name) and the permissions you would like that directory to have. Here's an example:

```
mkdir("/tmp/testing", 0777);
```

However, the permissions you list are not necessarily the permissions you are going to get. The inverse of the current umask will be combined with this value using AND to get the actual permissions. For example, if the umask is 022, you will get permissions of 0755.

You might like to reset the umask before creating a directory to counter this effect, by entering

```
$oldumask = umask(0);
mkdir("/tmp/testing", 0777);
umask($oldumask);
```

This code uses the `umask()` function, which can be used to check and change the current umask. It changes the current umask to whatever it is passed and returns the old umask, or, if called without parameters, it just returns the current umask.

Note that the umask() function has no effect on Windows systems.

The rmdir() function deletes a directory, as follows:

```
rmdir("/tmp/testing");
```

or

```
rmdir("c:\\tmp\\testing");
```

The directory you are trying to delete must be empty.

Interacting with the File System

In addition to viewing and getting information about directories, you can interact with and get information about files on the web server. You previously looked at writing to and reading from files. A large number of other file functions are available.

Getting File Information

You can alter the part of the directory browsing script that reads files as follows:

```
while ($file = readdir($dir)){
 echo '<a href="filedetails.php?file='.$file.'">'.$file.'</a><br>';
}
```

You can then create the script filedetails.php to provide further information about a file. The contents of this file are shown in Listing 18.4.

One warning about this script: Some of the functions used here are not supported under Windows, including posix_getpwuid(), fileowner(), and filegroup(), or are not supported reliably.

Listing 18.4 filedetails.php—**File Status Functions and Their Results**

```
<html>
<head>
  <title>File Details</title>
</head>
<body>
<?php
  $current_dir = '/uploads/';
  $file = basename($file);  // strip off directory information for security

  echo '<h1>Details of file: '.$file.'</h1>';
  $file = $current_dir.$file;

  echo '<h2>File data</h2>';
  echo 'File last accessed: '.date('j F Y H:i', fileatime($file)).'<br>';
  echo 'File last modified: '.date('j F Y H:i', filemtime($file)).'<br>';
```

Listing 18.4 **Continued**

```php
$user = posix_getpwuid(fileowner($file));
echo 'File owner: '.$user['name'].'<br>';

$group = posix_getgrgid(filegroup($file));
echo 'File group: '.$group['name'].'<br>';

echo 'File permissions: '.decoct(fileperms($file)).'<br>';

echo 'File type: '.filetype($file).'<br>';

echo 'File size: '.filesize($file).' bytes<br>';


echo '<h2>File tests</h2>';

echo 'is_dir: '.(is_dir($file)? 'true' : 'false').'<br>';
echo 'is_executable: '.(is_executable($file)? 'true' : 'false').'<br>';
echo 'is_file: '.(is_file($file)? 'true' : 'false').'<br>';
echo 'is_link: '.(is_link($file)? 'true' : 'false').'<br>';
echo 'is_readable: '.(is_readable($file)? 'true' : 'false').'<br>';
echo 'is_writable: '.(is_writable($file)? 'true' : 'false').'<br>';

?>
</body>
</html>
```

The results of one sample run of Listing 18.4 are shown in Figure 18.4.
Let's examine what each of the functions used in Listing 18.4 does. As mentioned previously, the `basename()` function gets the name of the file without the directory. (You can also use the `dirname()` function to get the directory name without the filename.)

The `fileatime()` and `filemtime()` functions return the timestamp of the time the file was last accessed and last modified, respectively. We reformatted the timestamp here using the `date()` function to make it more human readable. These functions return the same value on some operating systems (as in the example) depending on what information the system stores.

The `fileowner()` and `filegroup()` functions return the user ID (uid) and group ID (gid) of the file. These IDs can be converted to names using the functions `posix_getpwuid()` and `posix_getgrgid()`, respectively, which makes them a bit easier to read. These functions take the uid or gid as a parameter and return an associative array of information about the user or group, including the name of the user or group, as we have used in this script.

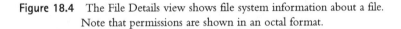

Figure 18.4   The File Details view shows file system information about a file.
Note that permissions are shown in an octal format.

The `fileperms()` function returns the permissions on the file. We reformatted them as an octal number using the `decoct()` function to put them into a format more familiar to Unix users.

The `filetype()` function returns some information about the type of file being examined. The possible results are `fifo`, `char`, `dir`, `block`, `link`, `file`, and `unknown`.

The `filesize()` function returns the size of the file in bytes.

The second set of functions—`is_dir()`, `is_executable()`, `is_file()`, `is_link()`, `is_readable()`, and `is_writable()`—all test the named attribute of a file and return `true` or `false`.

Alternatively, you could use the function `stat()` to gather a lot of the same information. When passed a file, this function returns an array containing similar data to these functions. The `lstat()` function is similar, but for use with symbolic links.

All the file status functions are quite expensive to run in terms of time. Their results are therefore cached. If you want to check some file information before and after a change, you need to call

```
clearstatcache();
```

to clear the previous results. If you want to use the previous script before and after changing some of the file data, you should begin by calling this function to make sure the data produced is up to date.

Changing File Properties

In addition to viewing file properties, you can alter them.

Each of the chgrp(`file, group`), chmod(`file, permissions`), and chown(`file, user`) functions behaves similarly to its Unix equivalent. None of these functions will work in Windows-based systems, although chown() will execute and always return true.

The chgrp() function changes the group of a file. It can be used to change the group only to groups of which the user is a member unless the user is root.

The chmod() function changes the permissions on a file. The permissions you pass to it are in the usual Unix chmod form. You should prefix them with a 0 (a zero) to show that they are in octal, as in this example:

```
chmod('somefile.txt', 0777);
```

The chown() function changes the owner of a file. It can be used only if the script is running as root, which should never happen, unless you are specifically running the script from the command line to perform an administrative task.

Creating, Deleting, and Moving Files

You can use the file system functions to create, move, and delete files.

First, and most simply, you can create a file, or change the time it was last modified, using the touch() function. This function works similarly to the Unix command touch. The function has the following prototype:

```
int touch (string file, [int time [, int atime]])
```

If the file already exists, its modification time will be changed either to the current time or the time given in the second parameter if it is specified. If you want to specify this time, you should give it in timestamp format. If the file doesn't exist, it will be created. The access time of the file will also change: by default to the current system time or alternatively to the timestamp you specify in the optional `atime` parameter.

You can delete files using the unlink() function. (Note that this function is not called delete—there is no delete.) You use it like this:

```
unlink($filename);
```

This is one of the functions that doesn't work with some older Windows versions. However, if it doesn't work on your setup, you can delete a file in Windows with

```
system("del filename.ext");
```

You can copy and move files with the copy() and rename() functions, as follows:

```
copy($source_path, $destination_path);
```

```
rename($oldfile, $newfile);
```

You might have noticed that we used copy() in Listing 18.2.

The `rename()` function does double duty as a function to move files from place to place because PHP doesn't have a move function. Whether you can move files from file system to file system and whether files are overwritten when `rename()` is used are operating system dependent, so check the effects on your server. Also, be careful about the path you use to the filename. If relative, this will be relative to the location of the script, not the original file.

Using Program Execution Functions

Let's move away from the file system functions now and look at the functions available for running commands on the server.

These functions are useful when you want to provide a web-based front end to an existing command-line–based system. For example, you previously used these commands to set up a front end for the mailing list manager `ezmlm`. You will use them again when you come to the case studies later in this book.

You can use four main techniques to execute a command on the web server. They are all relatively similar, but there are some minor differences:

1. `exec()`—The `exec()` function has the following prototype:

    ```
    string exec (string command [, array &result [, int &return_value]])
    ```

    You pass in the command that you would like executed, as in this example:

    ```
    exec("ls -la");
    ```

    The `exec()` function has no direct output. It returns the last line of the result of the command.

    If you pass in a variable as `result`, you will get back an array of strings representing each line of the output. If you pass in a variable as `return_value`, you will get the return code.

2. `passthru()`—The `passthru()` function has the following prototype:

    ```
    void passthru (string command [, int return_value])
    ```

    The `passthru()` function directly echoes its output through to the browser. (This functionality is useful if the output is binary—for example, some kind of image data.) It returns nothing.

    The parameters work the same way as `exec()`'s parameters do.

3. `system()`—The `system()` function has the following prototype:

    ```
    string system (string command [, int return_value])
    ```

    The function echoes the output of the command to the browser. It tries to flush the output after each line (assuming you are running PHP as a server module), which distinguishes it from `passthru()`. It returns the last line of the output (upon success) or `false` (upon failure).

    The parameters work the same way as in the other functions.

4. Backticks—We mentioned backticks briefly in Chapter 1, "PHP Crash Course." They are actually execution operators.

They have no direct output. The result of executing the command is returned as a string, which can then be echoed or whatever you like.

If you have more complicated needs, you can also use `popen()`, `proc_open()`, and `proc_close()`, which fork external processes and pipe data to and from them. The last two of these functions were added at PHP 4.3.

The script shown in Listing 18.5 illustrates how to use each of the four techniques in an equivalent fashion.

Listing 18.5   `progex.php`—**File Status Functions and Their Results**

```php
<?php

    chdir('/uploads/');

///// exec version
    echo '<pre>';

    // unix
    exec('ls -la', $result);
    // windows
    // exec('dir', $result);
    foreach ($result as $line)
      echo "$line\n";

    echo '</pre>';
    echo '<br><hr><br>';

///// passthru version
    echo '<pre>';

    // unix
    passthru('ls -la') ;
    // windows
    // passthru('dir');

    echo '</pre>';
    echo '<br><hr><br>';

///// system version

    echo '<pre>';
    // unix
    $result = system('ls -la');
```

Listing 18.5 **Continued**

```
   // windows
   // $result = system('dir');
   echo '</pre>';
   echo '<br><hr><br>';

/////backticks version

   echo '<pre>';
   // unix
   $result = `ls -al`;
   // windows0
   // $result = `dir`;
   echo $result;
   echo '</pre>';

? >
```

You could use one of these approaches as an alternative to the directory-browsing script you saw earlier. Note that one of the side effects of using external functions is amply demonstrated by this code: Your code is no longer portable. This script uses Unix commands, and the code will clearly not run on Windows.

If you plan to include user-submitted data as part of the command you're going to execute, you should always run it through the escapeshellcmd() function first. This way, you stop users from maliciously (or otherwise) executing commands on your system. You can call it like this:

```
system(escapeshellcmd($command));
```

You should also use the escapeshellarg() function to escape any arguments you plan to pass to your shell command.

Interacting with the Environment: getenv() and putenv()

Before we leave this discussion, let's look at how to use environment variables from within PHP. Two functions serve this purpose: getenv(), which enables you to retrieve environment variables, and putenv(), which enables you to set environment variables. Note that the environment we are talking about here is the environment in which PHP runs on the server.

You can get a list of all PHP's environment variables by running phpinfo(). Some are more useful than others; for example,

```
getenv("HTTP_REFERER");
```

returns the URL of the page from which the user came to the current page.

You can also set environment variables as required with `putenv()`, as in this example:

```
$home = "/home/nobody";
putenv (" HOME=$home ");
```

If you are a system administrator and would like to limit which environment variables programmers can set, you can use the `safe_mode_allowed_env_vars` directive in `php.ini`. When PHP runs in safe mode, users can set only environment variables whose prefixes are listed in this directive.

If you would like more information about what some of the environment variables represent, you can look at the CGI specification at http://hoohoo.ncsa.uiuc.edu/cgi/env.html.

Further Reading

Most of the file system functions in PHP map to underlying operating system functions of the same name. Try reading the `man` pages for more information if you're using Unix.

Next

In Chapter 19, "Using Network and Protocol Functions," you learn to use PHP's network and protocol functions to interact with systems other than your own web server. This again expands the horizons of what you can do with your scripts.

19

Using Network and Protocol Functions

IN THIS CHAPTER, WE LOOK AT THE NETWORK-ORIENTED functions in PHP that enable your scripts to interact with the rest of the Internet. A world of resources is available out there, and a wide variety of protocols is available for using them.

Key topics covered in this chapter include

- Examining available protocols
- Sending and reading email
- Using other websites via HTTP
- Using network lookup functions
- Using FTP

Examining Available Protocols

Protocols are the rules of communication for a given situation. For example, you know the protocol when meeting another person: You say hello, shake hands, communicate for a while, and then say goodbye. Different situations require different protocols. Also, people from other cultures may expect different protocols, which may make interaction difficult. Computer networking protocols are similar.

Like human protocols, different computer protocols are used for different situations and applications. You use the Hypertext Transfer Protocol (HTTP) to send and receive web pages. You probably also have used the File Transfer Protocol (FTP) for transferring files between machines on a network. Many others are available.

Protocols and other Internet standards are described in documents called *Requests For Comments (RFCs)*. These protocols are defined by the Internet Engineering Task Force (IETF). The RFCs are widely available on the Internet. The base source is the RFC Editor at http://www.rfc-editor.org/.

If you have problems when working with a given protocol, RFCs are the authoritative sources and are often useful for troubleshooting your code. They are, however, very detailed and often run to hundreds of pages.

Some examples of well-known RFCs are RFC2616, which describes the HTTP/1.1 protocol, and RFC822, which describes the format of Internet email messages.

In this chapter, we look at aspects of PHP that use some of these protocols. Specifically, we discuss sending mail with SMTP, reading mail with POP and IMAP, connecting to other web servers via HTTP, and transferring files with FTP.

Sending and Reading Email

The main way to send mail in PHP is to use the simple `mail()` function. We discussed the use of this function in Chapter 4, "String Manipulation and Regular Expressions," so we won't visit it again here. This function uses the Simple Mail Transfer Protocol (SMTP) to send mail.

You can use a variety of freely available classes to add to the functionality of `mail()`. In Chapter 30, "Building a Mailing List Manager," you use an add-on class to send HTML attachments with a piece of mail. SMTP is only for sending mail. The Internet Message Access Protocol (IMAP), described in RFC2060, and Post Office Protocol (POP), described in RFC1939 or STD0053, are used to read mail from a mail server. These protocols cannot send mail.

IMAP is used to read and manipulate mail messages stored on a server and is more sophisticated than POP, which is generally used simply to download mail messages to a client and delete them from the server.

PHP comes with an IMAP library. It can also be used to make POP and Network News Transfer Protocol (NNTP) as well as IMAP connections.

We look extensively at the use of the IMAP library in the project described in Chapter 29, "Building a Web-Based Email Service."

Using Other Websites

One of the great things you can do with the Web is use, modify, and embed existing services and information into your own pages. PHP makes this very easy. Let's look at an example to illustrate this use.

Imagine that the company you work for wants the company's stock quote displayed on its home page. This information is available on some stock exchange site somewhere, but how do you get at it?

Start by finding an original source URL for the information. When you know the URL, every time someone goes to your home page, you can open a connection to that URL, retrieve the page, and pull out the information you require.

As an example, we put together a script that retrieves and reformats a stock quote from the AMEX website. For the purpose of the example, we retrieved the current stock price of Amazon.com. (The information you want to include on your page might differ, but the principles are the same.)

This technique is known as *screen scraping* because you take information that is intended to be displayed on a screen and extract the parts that you need for presentation with a new interface. The script is shown in Listing 19.1.

Listing 19.1   `lookup.php`—**Script Retrieves a Stock Quote from the NASDAQ for the Stock with the Ticker Symbol Listed in** `$symbol`

```php
<html>
<head>
  <title>Stock Quote from NASDAQ</title>
</head>
<body>
<?php
  // choose stock to look at
  $symbol='AMZN';
  echo "<h1>Stock Quote for $symbol</h1>";

  $theurl="http://www.amex.com/equities/listCmp"
          ."/EqLCDetQuote.jsp?Product_Symbol=$symbol";

    if (!($contents = file_get_contents($theurl)))
  {
    echo 'Could not open URL';
    exit;
  }

  // find the part of the page we want and output it
  $pattern = '(\\$[0-9 ]+\\.[0-9]+)';

  if (eregi($pattern, $contents, $quote))
  {
    echo "<p>$symbol was last sold at: ";
    echo $quote[1];
    echo '</p>';
  }
  else
  {
    echo '<p>No quote available</p>';
  };
```

Listing 19.1 **Continued**

```
  // acknowledge source
  echo '<p>'
       .'This information retrieved from <br />'
       ."<a href=\"$theurl\">$theurl</a><br />"
       .'on '.(date('l jS F Y g:i a T')).'</p>';
?>
</body>
</html>
```

The output from one sample run of Listing 19.1 is shown in Figure 19.1.

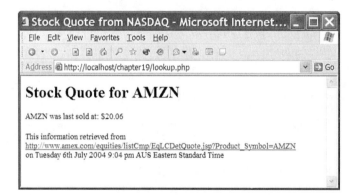

Figure 19.1 The `lookup.php` script uses a regular expression to pull out
the stock quote from information retrieved from the stock exchange.

The script itself is reasonably straightforward; in fact, it doesn't use any functions you
haven't seen before, just new applications of those functions.

You might recall that when we discussed reading from files in Chapter 2, "Storing
and Retrieving Data," we mentioned that you could use the file functions to read from
an URL. That's what we have done in this case. The call to `file_get_contents()`

```
$contents = file_get_contents($theurl)
```

returns the entire text of the web page at that URL stored in `$contents`.

The file functions can do a lot in PHP. The example here simply loads a web page via
HTTP, but you could interact with other servers via HTTPS, FTP, or other protocols in
exactly the same way. For some tasks, you might need to take a more specialized approach.
Some FTP functionality is available in the specific FTP functions, and not available via
`fopen()` and other file functions. There is an example using the FTP functions later in this
chapter. For some HTTP or HTTPS tasks, you may need to use the cURL library. With
cURL, you can log in to a website and mimic a user's progress through a few pages.

Having obtained the text of the page from `file_get_contents()`, you can then use a regular expression and the `eregi()` function to find the part of the page that you want:

```
$pattern = '(\\$[0-9 ]+\\.[0-9]+)';

if (eregi($pattern, $contents, $quote))
{
  echo "<p>$symbol was last sold at: ";
  echo $quote[1];
  echo '</p>';
}
```

That's it!

You can use this approach for a variety of purposes. Another good example is retrieving local weather information and embedding it in your page.

The best use of this approach is to combine information from different sources to add some value. You can see one good example of this approach in Philip Greenspun's infamous script that produces the Bill Gates Wealth Clock at http://philip.greenspun.com/WealthClock.

This page takes information from two sources. It obtains the current U.S. population from the U.S. Census Bureau's site. It also looks up the current value of a Microsoft share and combines these two pieces of information, adds a healthy dose of the author's opinion, and produces new information—an estimate of Bill Gates' current worth.

One side note: If you're using an outside information source such as this for a commercial purpose, it's a good idea to check with the source or take legal advice first. You might need to consider intellectual property issues in some cases.

If you're building a script like this, you might want to pass through some data. For example, if you're connecting to an outside URL, you might like to pass some parameters that would normally be typed in by the user. If you're doing this, it's a good idea to use the `urlencode()` function. This function takes a string and converts it to the proper format for an URL, for example, transforming spaces into plus signs. You can call it like this:

```
$encodedparameter = urlencode($parameter);
```

One problem with this overall approach is that the site you're getting the information from may change its data format, which will stop your script from working.

A better way of doing the same thing is to use Web Services. These services are like remote objects that you can connect to in order to retrieve data such as stock quotes. PHP's support for Web Services is growing. As well as technical advantages, using Web Services means that you are using an interface and a facility that the provider has implicitly or explicitly given you permission to access with a program.

Using Network Lookup Functions

PHP offers a set of "lookup" functions that can be used to check information about hostnames, IP addresses, and mail exchanges. For example, if you were setting up a directory site such as Yahoo! when new URLs were submitted, you might like to automatically check that the host of an URL and the contact information for that site are valid. This way, you can save some overhead further down the track when a reviewer comes to look at a site and finds that it doesn't exist or that the email address isn't valid.

Listing 19.2 shows the HTML for a submission form for a directory like this.

Listing 19.2 `directory_submit.html`—**HTML for the Submission Form**

```
<html>
<head>
  <title>Submit your site</title>
</head>
<body>
<h1>Submit site</h1>
<form method=post action="directory_submit.php">
URL: <input type=text name="url" size=30 value="http://"><br />
Email contact: <input type=text name="email" size=23><br />
<input type="submit" name="Submit site">
</form>
</body>
</html>
```

This is a simple form; the rendered version, with some sample data entered, is shown in Figure 19.2.

Figure 19.2   Directory submissions typically require your URL and some
contact details so directory administrators can notify you when
your site is added to the directory.

When the submit button is clicked, you want to check, first, that the URL is hosted on a real machine, and, second, that the host part of the email address is also on a real machine. We wrote a script to check these things, and the output is shown in Figure 19.3.

Figure 19.3 This version of the script displays the results of checking the hostnames for the URL and email address; a production version might not display these results, but it is interesting to see the information returned from the checks.

The script that performs these checks uses two functions from the PHP network functions suite: `gethostbyname()` and `dns_get_mx()`. The full script is shown in Listing 19.3.

Listing 19.3 `directory_submit.php`—**Script to Verify URL and Email Address**

```
<html>
<head>
  <title>Site submission results</title>
</head>
<body>
<h1>Site submission results</h1>
<?php

  // Extract form fields

  $url = $_REQUEST['url'];
  $email = $_REQUEST['email'];

  // Check the URL

  $url = parse_url($url);
  $host = $url['host'];
  if(!($ip = gethostbyname($host)) )
  {
```

Listing 19.3 **Continued**

```
    echo 'Host for URL does not have valid IP';
    exit;
  }

  echo "Host is at IP $ip <br>";

  // Check the email address

  $email = explode('@', $email);
  $emailhost = $email[1];

  // note that the dns_get_mx() function is *not implemented* in
  // Windows versions of PHP
  if (!dns_get_mx($emailhost, $mxhostsarr))
  {
    echo 'Email address is not at valid host';
    exit;
  }

  echo 'Email is delivered via: ';
  foreach ($mxhostsarr as $mx)
    echo "$mx ";

  // If reached here, all ok

  echo '<br>All submitted details are ok.<br>';
  echo 'Thank you for submitting your site.<br>'
       .'It will be visited by one of our staff members soon.'

  // In real case, add to db of waiting sites...
?>
</body>
</html>
```

Let's go through the interesting parts of this script.

First, you take the URL and apply the `parse_url()` function to it. This function returns an associative array of the different parts of an URL. The available pieces of information are the scheme, user, pass, host, port, path, query, and fragment. Typically, you don't need all these pieces, but here's an example of how they make up an URL.

Consider the following URL at http://nobody:secret@example.com:80/script.php?variable=value#anchor.

The values of each of the parts of the array are

- scheme: http
- user: nobody
- pass: secret
- host: example.com
- port: 80
- path: /script.php
- query: variable=value
- fragment: anchor

In the `directory_submit.php` script, you want only the host information, so you pull it out of the array as follows:

```
$url = parse_url($url);
$host = $url['host'];
```

After you've done this, you can get the IP address of that host, if it is in the domain name service (DNS). You can do this by using the `gethostbyname()` function, which returns the IP if there is one or `false` if not:

```
$ip = gethostbyname($host);
```

You can also go the other way by using the `gethostbyaddr()` function, which takes an IP as a parameter and returns the hostname. If you call these functions in succession, you might well end up with a different hostname from the one you began with. This can mean that a site is using a virtual hosting service where one physical machine and IP address host more than one domain name.

If the URL is valid, you then go on to check the email address. First, you split it into username and hostname with a call to `explode()`:

```
$email = explode('@', $email);
$emailhost = $email[1];
```

When you have the host part of the address, you can check to see whether there is a place for that mail to go by using the `dns_get_mx()` function:

```
dns_get_mx($emailhost, $mxhostsarr);
```

This function returns the set of Mail Exchange (MX) records for an address in the array you supply at `$mxhostarr`.

An MX record is stored at the DNS and is looked up like a hostname. The machine listed in the MX record isn't necessarily the machine where the email will eventually end up. Instead, it's a machine that knows where to route that email. (There can be more than one; hence, this function returns an array rather than a hostname string.) If you don't have an MX record in the DNS, there's nowhere for the mail to go.

Note that the `dns_get_mx()` function is not implemented in Windows versions of PHP. If you are using Windows, you should look into the PEAR::Net_DNS package, which will work for you.

If all these checks are okay, you can put this form data in a database for later review by a staff member.

In addition to the functions you just used, you can use the more generic function `checkdnsrr()`, which takes a hostname and returns `true` if any record of it appears in the DNS.

Using FTP

File Transfer Protocol, or FTP, is used to transfer files between hosts on a network. Using PHP, you can use `fopen()` and the various file functions with FTP as you can with HTTP connections, to connect to and transfer files to and from an FTP server. However, a set of FTP-specific functions also comes with the standard PHP install.

These functions are not built into the standard install by default. To use them under Unix, you need to run the PHP `configure` program with the `--enable-ftp` option and then rerun `make`. If you are using the standard Windows install, FTP functions are enabled automatically.

(For more details on configuring PHP, see Appendix A, "Installing PHP and MySQL.")

Using FTP to Back Up or Mirror a File

The FTP functions are useful for moving and copying files from and to other hosts. One common use you might make of this capability is to back up your website or mirror files at another location. Let's look at a simple example using the FTP functions to mirror a file. This script is shown in Listing 19.4.

Listing 19.4 `ftp_mirror.php`—**Script to Download New Versions of a File from an FTP Server**

```
<html>
<head>
  <title>Mirror update</title>
</head>
<body>
<h1>Mirror update</h1>
<?php
// set up variables - change these to suit application
$host = 'ftp.cs.rmit.edu.au';
$user = 'anonymous';
$password = 'me@example.com';
$remotefile = '/pub/tsg/teraterm/ttssh14.zip';
$localfile = '/tmp/writable/ttssh14.zip';
```

Listing 19.4 **Continued**

```php
// connect to host
$conn = ftp_connect($host);
if (!$conn)
{
  echo 'Error: Could not connect to ftp server<br />';
  exit;
}
echo "Connected to $host.<br />";

// log in to host
@ $result = ftp_login($conn, $user, $pass);
if (!$result)
{
  echo "Error: Could not log on as $user<br />";
  ftp_quit($conn);
  exit;
}
echo "Logged in as $user<br />";

// check file times to see if an update is required
echo 'Checking file time...<br />';
if (file_exists($localfile))
{
  $localtime = filemtime($localfile);
  echo 'Local file last updated ';
  echo date('G:i j-M-Y', $localtime);
  echo '<br />';
}
else
  $localtime=0;
$remotetime = ftp_mdtm($conn, $remotefile);
if (!($remotetime >= 0))
{
  // This doesn't mean the file's not there, server may not support mod time
  echo 'Can\'t access remote file time.<br />';
  $remotetime=$localtime+1;  // make sure of an update
}
else
{
  echo 'Remote file last updated ';
  echo date('G:i j-M-Y', $remotetime);
  echo '<br />';
}
```

Listing 19.4   **Continued**

```
if (!($remotetime > $localtime))
{
   echo 'Local copy is up to date.<br />';
   exit;
}

// download file
echo 'Getting file from server...<br />';
$fp = fopen ($localfile, 'w');
if (!$success = ftp_fget($conn, $fp, $remotefile, FTP_BINARY))
{
  echo 'Error: Could not download file';
  ftp_quit($conn);
  exit;
}
fclose($fp);
echo 'File downloaded successfully';

// close connection to host
ftp_quit($conn);

?>
</body>
</html>
```

The output from running this script on one occasion is shown in Figure 19.4.

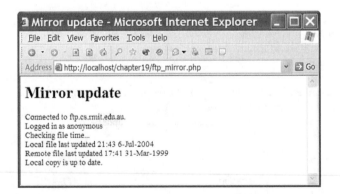

Figure 19.4   The FTP mirroring script checks whether the local version of a
file is up to date and downloads a new version if not.

The `ftp_mirror.php` script is quite generic. You can see that it begins by setting up some variables:

```
$host = 'ftp.cs.rmit.edu.au';
$user = 'anonymous';
$password = 'me@example.com';
$remotefile = '/pub/tsg/teraterm/ttssh14.zip';
$localfile = '/tmp/writable/ttssh14.zip';
```

The `$host` variable should contain the name of the FTP server you want to connect to, and the `$user` and `$password` correspond to the username and password you would like to log in with.

Many FTP sites support what is called *anonymous login*—that is, a freely available username that anybody can use to connect. No password is required, but it is a common courtesy to supply your email address as a password so that the system's administrators can see where their users are coming from. We followed this convention here.

The `$remotefile` variable contains the path to the file you would like to download. In this case, you are downloading and mirroring a local copy of Tera Term SSH, an SSH client for Windows. (SSH stands for secure shell. This is an encrypted form of Telnet.)

The `$localfile` variable contains the path to the location where you are going to store the downloaded file on your machine. In this case, you create a directory called `/tmp/writable` with permissions set up so that PHP can write a file there. Regardless of your operating system, you need to create this directory for the script to work. If your operating system has strong permissions, you will need to make sure that they allow your script to write. You should be able to change these variables to adapt this script for your purposes.

The basic steps you follow in this script are the same as if you wanted to manually transfer the file via FTP from a command-line interface:

1. Connect to the remote FTP server.

2. Log in (either as a user or anonymous).

3. Check whether the remote file has been updated.

4. If it has, download it.

5. Close the FTP connection.

Let's consider each of these steps in turn.

Connecting to the Remote FTP Server

The first step is equivalent to typing

```
ftp hostname
```

at a command prompt on either a Windows or Unix platform. You accomplish this step in PHP with the following code:

```
$conn = ftp_connect($host);
if (!$conn)
{
  echo 'Error: Could not connect to ftp server<br />';
  exit;
}
echo "Connected to $host.<br />";
```

The function call here is to `ftp_connect()`. This function takes a hostname as a parameter and returns either a handle to a connection or `false` if a connection could not be established. The function can also take the port number on the host to connect to as an optional second parameter. (We did not use this parameter here.) If you don't specify a port number, it will default to port 21, the default for FTP.

Logging In to the FTP Server

The next step is to log in as a particular user with a particular password. You can achieve this by using the `ftp_login()` function:

```
@ $result = ftp_login($conn, $user, $password);
if (!$result)
{
  echo "Error: Could not log on as $user<br />";
  ftp_quit($conn);
  exit;
}
echo "Logged in as $user<br />";
```

The function takes three parameters: an FTP connection (obtained from `ftp_connect()`), a username, and a password. It returns `true` if the user can be logged in and `false` if she can't. Notice that we put an `@` symbol at the start of the line to suppress errors. We did this because, if the user cannot be logged in, a PHP warning appears in the browser window. You can catch the error as we have done here by testing `$result` and supplying your own, more user-friendly error message.

Notice that if the login attempt fails, you actually close the FTP connection by using `ftp_quit()`. We discuss this function more later.

Checking File Update Times

Given that you are updating a local copy of a file, checking whether the file needs updating first is sensible because you don't want to have to redownload a file, particularly a large one, if it's up to date. This way, you can avoid unnecessary network traffic. Let's look at the code that checks file update times.

File times are the reason that you use the FTP functions rather than a much simpler call to a file function. The file functions can easily read and, in some cases, write files over network interfaces, but most of the status functions such as `filemtime()` do not work remotely. This will change in the future. The file system status functions are planned to support `ftp://` in PHP5.1. At that stage, you could reimplement this script using a simple `copy($remoteurl, $localurl)`.

To begin deciding whether you need to download a file, you check that you have a local copy of the file by using the `file_exists()` function. If you don't, obviously you need to download the file. If it does exist, you get the last modified time of the file by using the `filemtime()` function and store it in the `$localtime` variable. If it doesn't exist, you set the `$localtime` variable to 0 so that it will be "older" than any possible remote file modification time:

```
echo 'Checking file time...<br />';
if (file_exists($localfile))
{
  $localtime = filemtime($localfile);
  echo 'Local file last updated ';
  echo date('G:i j-M-Y', $localtime);
  echo '<br />';
}
else
  $localtime=0;
```

(You can read more about the `file_exists()` and `filemtime()` functions in Chapters 2, "Storing and Retrieving Data" and 18, "Interacting with the File System and the Server," respectively.)

After you have sorted out the local time, you need to get the modification time of the remote file. You can get this time by using the `ftp_mdtm()` function:

```
$remotetime = ftp_mdtm($conn, $remotefile);
```

This function takes two parameters—the FTP connection handle and the path to the remote file—and returns either the Unix timestamp of the time the file was last modified or −1 if there is an error of some kind. Not all FTP servers support this feature, so you might not get a useful result from the function. In this case, you can choose to artificially set the `$remotetime` variable to be "newer" than the `$localtime` variable by adding 1 to it. This way, you ensure that an attempt is made to download the file:

```
if (!($remotetime >= 0))
{
  // This doesn't mean the file's not there, server may not support mod time
  echo 'Can't access remote file time.<br>';
  $remotetime=$localtime+1;  // make sure of an update
}
```

```
else
{
  echo 'Remote file last updated ';
  echo date('G:i j-M-Y', $remotetime);
  echo '<br>';
}
```

When you have both times, you can compare them to see whether you need to download the file:

```
if (!($remotetime > $localtime))
{
  echo 'Local copy is up to date.<br>';
  exit;
}
```

Downloading the File

At this stage, you try to download the file from the server:

```
echo 'Getting file from server...<br>';
$fp = fopen ($localfile, 'w');
if (!$success = ftp_fget($conn, $fp, $remotefile, FTP_BINARY))
{
  echo 'Error: Could not download file';
  fclose($fp);
  ftp_quit($conn);
  exit;
}
fclose($fp);
echo 'File downloaded successfully';
```

You open a local file by using fopen(), as you learned previously. After you have done this, you call the function ftp_fget(), which attempts to download the file and store it in a local file. This function takes four parameters. The first three are straightforward: the FTP connection, the local file handle, and the path to the remote file. The fourth parameter is the FTP mode.

The two modes for an FTP transfer are ASCII and binary. The ASCII mode is used for transferring text files (that is, files that consist solely of ASCII characters), and the binary mode is used for transferring everything else. Binary mode transfers a file unmodified, whereas ASCII mode translates carriage returns and line feeds into the appropriate characters for your system (\n for Unix, \r\n for Windows, and \r for Macintosh).

PHP's FTP library comes with two predefined constants, FTP_ASCII and FTP_BINARY, that represent these two modes. You need to decide which mode fits your file type and pass the corresponding constant to ftp_fget() as the fourth parameter. In this case, you are transferring a ZIP file, so you use the FTP_BINARY mode.

The `ftp_fget()` function returns `true` if all goes well or `false` if an error is encountered. You store the result in `$success` and let the user know how it went.

After the download has been attempted, you close the local file by using the `fclose()` function.

As an alternative to `ftp_fget()`, you could use `ftp_get()`, which has the following prototype:

```
int ftp_get (int ftp_connection, string localfile_path,
       string remotefile_path, int mode)
```

This function works in much the same way as `ftp_fget()` but does not require the local file to be open. You pass it the system filename of the local file you would like to write to rather than a file handle.

Note that there is no equivalent to the FTP command `mget`, which can be used to download multiple files at a time. You must instead make multiple calls to `ftp_fget()` or `ftp_get()`.

Closing the Connection

After you have finished with the FTP connection, you should close it using the `ftp_quit()` function:

```
ftp_quit($conn);
```

You should pass this function the handle for the FTP connection.

Uploading Files

If you want to go the other way—that is, copy files from your server to a remote machine—you can use two functions that are basically the opposite of `ftp_fget()` and `ftp_get()`. These functions are called `ftp_fput()` and `ftp_put()`. They have the following prototypes:

```
int ftp_fput (int ftp_connection, string remotefile_path, int fp, int mode)

int ftp_put (int ftp_connection, string remotefile_path,
            string localfile_path, int mode)
```

The parameters are the same as for the `_get` equivalents.

Avoiding Timeouts

One problem you might face when transferring files via FTP is exceeding the maximum execution time. You know when this happens because PHP gives you an error message. This error is especially likely to occur if your server is running over a slow or congested network, or if you are downloading a large file, such as a movie clip.

The default value of the maximum execution time for all PHP scripts is defined in the `php.ini` file. By default, it's set to 30 seconds. This is designed to catch scripts that are running out of control. However, when you are transferring files via FTP, if your link to the rest of the world is slow or if the file is large, the file transfer could well take longer than this.

Fortunately, you can modify the maximum execution time for a particular script by using the `set_time_limit()` function. Calling this function resets the maximum number of seconds the script is allowed to run, starting from the time the function is called. For example, if you call

```
set_time_limit(90);
```

the script will be able to run for another 90 seconds from the time the function is called.

Using Other FTP Functions

A number of other FTP functions are useful in PHP. The function `ftp_size()` can tell you the size of a file on a remote server. It has the following prototype:

```
int ftp_size(int ftp_connection, string remotefile_path)
```

This function returns the size of the remote file in bytes or −1 if an error occurs. It is not supported by all FTP servers.

One handy use of `ftp_size()` is to work out the maximum execution time to set for a particular transfer. Given the file size and speed of your connection, you can take a guess as to how long the transfer ought to take and use the `set_time_limit()` function accordingly.

You can get and display a list of files in a directory on a remote FTP server by using the following code:

```
$listing = ftp_nlist($conn, dirname($remotefile));
foreach ($listing as $filename)
  echo "$filename <br>";
```

This code uses the `ftp_nlist()` function to get a list of names of files in a particular directory.

In terms of other FTP functions, almost anything that you can do from an FTP command line, you can do with the FTP functions. You can find the specific functions corresponding to each FTP command in the PHP online manual at http://php.net/manual/en/ref.ftp.php.

The exception is `mget` (multiple get), but you can use `ftp_nlist()` to get a list of files and then fetch them as required.

Further Reading

We covered a lot of ground in this chapter, and as you might expect, a lot of material is out there on these topics. For information on the individual protocols and how they work, you can consult the RFCs at http://www.rfc-editor.org/.

You might also find some of the protocol information at the World Wide Web Consortium interesting; go to http://www.w3.org/Protocols/.

You can also try consulting a book on TCP/IP such as *Computer Networks* by Andrew Tanenbaum.

Next

We ready to move on to Chapter 20, "Managing the Date and Time," and look at PHP's libraries of date and calendar functions. There, you see how to convert from user-entered formats to PHP formats to MySQL formats, and back again.

## 20

Managing the Date and Time

IN THIS CHAPTER, WE DISCUSS CHECKING AND FORMATTING the date and time and converting between date formats. These capabilities are especially important when you are converting between MySQL and PHP date formats, Unix and PHP date formats, and dates entered by the user in an HTML form.

Key topics covered in this chapter include

- Getting the date and time in PHP
- Converting between PHP and MySQL date formats
- Calculating dates
- Using the calendar functions

Getting the Date and Time from PHP

Way back in Chapter 1, "PHP Crash Course," we described using the `date()` function to get and format the date and time from PHP. Here, we discuss this function and some of PHP's other date and time functions in a little more detail.

Using the `date()` Function

As you might recall, the `date()` function takes two parameters, one of them optional. The first one is a format string, and the second, optional one is a Unix timestamp. If you don't specify a timestamp, `date()` will default to the current date and time. It returns a formatted string representing the appropriate date.

A typical call to the `date()` function could be

```
echo date('jS F Y');
```

This call produces a date in the format `29th October 2000`. The format codes accepted by `date()` are listed in Table 20.1.

Table 20.1 **Format Codes for PHP's** `date()` **Function**

Code	Description
a	Morning or afternoon, represented as two lowercase characters, either am or pm..
A	Morning or afternoon, represented as two uppercase characters, either AM or PM.
B	Swatch Internet time, a universal time scheme. More information is available at http://www.swatch.com/.
c	ISO 8601 date. A date is represented as YYYY-MM-DD. An uppercase T separates the date from the time. The time is represented as HH:MM:SS. Finally, the time zone is represented as an offset from Greenwich mean time (GMT)—for example, 2004-03-26T21:04:42+11:00. (This format code was added in PHP5.)
d	Day of the month as a two-digit number with a leading zero. The range is from 01 to 31.
D	Day of the week in three-character abbreviated text format. The range is from Mon to Sun.
F	Month of the year in full text format. The range is from January to December.
g	Hour of the day in 12-hour format without leading zeros. The range is from 1 to 12.
G	Hour of the day in 24-hour format without leading zeros. The range is from 0 to 23.
h	Hour of the day in 12-hour format with leading zeros. The range is from 01 to 12.
H	Hour of the day in 24-hour format with leading zeros. The range is from 00 to 23.
i	Minutes past the hour with leading zeros. The range is from 00 to 59.
I	Daylight savings time, represented as a Boolean value. This format code returns 1 if the date is in daylight savings and 0 if it is not.
j	Day of the month as a number without leading zeros. The range is from 1 to 31.
l	Day of the week in full-text format. The range is from Monday to Sunday.
L	Leap year, represented as a Boolean value. This format code returns 1 if the date is in a leap year and 0 if it is not.
m	Month of the year as a two-digit number with leading zeros. The range is from 01 to 12.
M	Month of the year in three-character abbreviated text format. The range is from Jan to Dec.
n	Month of the year as a number without leading zeros. The range is from 1 to 12.
O	Difference between the current time zone and GMT in hours—for example, +1600.
r	RFC822-formatted date and time—for example, Wed, 9 Oct 2002 18:45:30 +1600. (This code was added in PHP 4.0.4.)
s	Seconds past the minute with leading zeros. The range is from 00 to 59.
S	Ordinal suffix for dates in two-character format. It can be st, nd, rd, or th, depending on the number it follows.
t	Total number of days in the date's month. The range is from 28 to 31.
T	Time zone setting of the server in three-character format—for example, EST.
U	Total number of seconds from January 1, 1970, to this time; also known as a *Unix timestamp* for this date.

Table 20.1   **Continued**

Code	Description
w	Day of the week as a single digit. The range is from 0 (Sunday) to 6 (Saturday).
W	Week number in the year; ISO-8601 compliant. (This format code was added at PHP 4.1.0.)
y	Year in two-digit format—for example, 05.
Y	Year in four-digit format—for example, 2005.
z	Day of the year as a number. The range is 0 to 365.
Z	Offset for the current time zone in seconds. The range is -43200 to 43200.

Dealing with Unix Timestamps

The second parameter to the date() function is a Unix timestamp. In case you are wondering exactly what this means, most Unix systems store the current time and date as a 32-bit integer containing the number of seconds since midnight, January 1, 1970, GMT, also known as the *Unix Epoch*. This concept can seem a bit esoteric if you are not familiar with it, but it's a standard and integers are easy for computers to deal with.

Unix timestamps are a compact way of storing dates and times, but it is worth noting that they do not suffer from the year 2000 (Y2K) problem that affects some other compact or abbreviated date formats. They do have similar problems, though, because they can represent only a limited span of time using a 32-bit integer. If your software needs to deal with events before 1902 or after 2038, you will be in trouble.

On some systems including Windows, the range is more limited. A timestamp cannot be negative, so timestamps before 1970 cannot be used. To keep your code portable, you should bear this fact in mind.

You probably don't need to worry about your software still being used in 2038. Timestamps do not have a fixed size; they are tied to the size of a C long, which is at least 32 bits. If your software still happens to be in use in 2038, it is exceedingly likely that your compiler will be using a larger type.

Although this is a standard Unix convention, this format is still used by date() and a number of other PHP functions even if you are running PHP under Windows. The only difference is that, for Windows, the timestamp must be positive.

If you want to convert a date and time *to* a Unix timestamp, you can use the mktime() function. It has the following prototype:

```
int mktime ([int hour[, int minute[, int second[, int month[,
        int day[, int year [, int is_dst]]]]]]])
```

The parameters are fairly self-explanatory, with the exception of the last one, *is_dst*, which represents whether the date was in daylight savings time. You can set this parameter to 1 if it was, 0 if it wasn't, or -1 (the default value) if you don't know. This parameter is optional, so you will rarely use it anyway.

The main trap to avoid with this function is that the parameters are in a fairly unintuitive order. The ordering doesn't lend itself to leaving out the time. If you are not wor-
ried about the time, you can pass in 0s to the *hour*, *minute*, and *second* parameters. You
can, however, leave out values from the right side of the parameter list. If you don't provide parameters, they will be set to the current values. Hence, a call such as

```
$timestamp = mktime();
```

returns the Unix timestamp for the current date and time. You could also get this result
by calling

```
$timestamp = time();
```

The `time()` function does not take any parameters and always returns the Unix timestamp for the current date and time.

Another option is the `date()` function, as already discussed. The format string `"U"`
requests a timestamp. The following statement is equivalent to the two previous ones:

```
$timestamp = date("U");
```

You can pass in a two- or four-digit year to `mktime()`. Two-digit values from 0 to 69 are
interpreted as the years 2000 to 2069, and values from 70 to 99 are interpreted as 1970
to 1999.

Here are some other examples to illustrate the use of `mktime()`:

```
$time = mktime(12, 0, 0);
```

gives noon on today's date.

```
$time = mktime(0,0,0,1,1);
```

gives the 1st of January in the current year.

You can also use `mktime()` for simple date arithmetic. For example,

```
$time = mktime(12,0,0,$mon,$day+30,$year);
```

adds 30 days to the date specified in the components, even though (`$day+30`) will
usually be bigger than the number of days in that month.

To eliminate some problems with daylight savings time, use hour 12 rather than
hour 0. If you add (24 * 60 * 60) to midnight on a 25-hour day, you'll stay on the same
day. Add the same number to midday, and it'll give `11am` but will at least be the right day.

Using the `getdate()` Function

Another date-determining function you might find useful is `getdate()`. This function
has the following prototype:

```
array getdate ([int timestamp])
```

It takes an optional timestamp as a parameter and returns an array representing the parts of that date and time, as shown in Table 20.2.

Table 20.2   Array Key–Value Pairs from `getdate()` Function

Key	Value
seconds	Seconds, numeric
minutes	Minutes, numeric
hours	Hours, numeric
mday	Day of the month, numeric
wday	Day of the week, numeric
mon	Month, numeric
year	Year, numeric
yday	Day of the year, numeric
weekday	Day of the week, full-text format
month	Month, full-text format
0	Timestamp, numeric

After you have these parts in an array, you can easily process them into any required format. The 0 element in the array (the timestamp) might seem useless, but if you call `getdate()` without a parameter, it will give you the current timestamp.

Validating Dates

You can use the `checkdate()` function to check whether a date is valid. This capability is especially useful for checking user input dates. The `checkdate()` function has the following prototype:

```
int checkdate (int month, int day, int year)
```

It checks whether the `year` is a valid integer between 0 and 32,767, whether the `month` is an integer between 1 and 12, and whether the `day` given exists in that particular month. The function also takes leap years into consideration when working out whether a day is valid.

For example,

```
checkdate(9, 18, 1972)
```

returns `true`, whereas

```
checkdate(9, 31, 2000)
```

does not.

Converting Between PHP and MySQL Date Formats

Dates and times in MySQL are handled in ISO 8601 format. Times work relatively intuitively, but ISO 8601 requires you to enter dates with the year first. For example, you could enter August 29, 2005, either as 2005-08-29 or as 05-08-29. Dates retrieved from MySQL are also in this format by default.

Depending on your intended audience, you might not find this function very user friendly. To communicate between PHP and MySQL, then, you usually need to perform some date conversion. This operation can be performed at either end.

When putting dates into MySQL from PHP, you can easily put them into the correct format by using the date() function, as shown previously. One minor caution if you are creating them from your own code is that you should store the day and month with leading zeros to avoid confusing MySQL. You can use a two-digit year, but using a four-digit year is usually a good idea. If you want to convert dates or times in MySQL, two useful functions are DATE_FORMAT() and UNIX_TIMESTAMP().

The DATE_FORMAT() function works similarly to the PHP function but uses different formatting codes. The most common thing you want to do is format a date in normal American format (MM-DD-YYYY) rather than in the ISO format (YYYY-MM-DD) native to MySQL. You can do this by writing your query as follows:

```
SELECT DATE_FORMAT(date_column, '%m %d %Y')
FROM tablename;
```

The format code %m represents the month as a two-digit number; %d, the day as a two-digit number; and %Y, the year as a four-digit number. A summary of the more useful MySQL format codes for this purpose is shown in Table 20.3.

Table 20.3 **Format Codes for MySQL's** DATE_FORMAT() **Function**

Code	Description
%M	Month, full text
%W	Weekday name, full text
%D	Day of month, numeric, with text suffix (for example, 1st)
%Y	Year, numeric, four digits
%y	Year, numeric, two digits
%a	Weekday name, three characters
%d	Day of month, numeric, leading zeros
%e	Day of month, numeric, no leading zeros
%m	Month, numeric, leading zeros
%c	Month, numeric, no leading zeros

Table 20.3   **Continued**

Code	Description
%b	Month, text, three characters
%j	Day of year, numeric
%H	Hour, 24-hour clock, leading zeros
%k	Hour, 24-hour clock, no leading zeros
%h or %I	Hour, 12-hour clock, leading zeros
%l	Hour, 12-hour clock, no leading zeros
%i	Minutes, numeric, leading zeros
%r	Time, 12-hour (hh:mm:ss [AM|PM])
%T	Time, 24-hour (hh:mm:ss)
%S or %s	Seconds, numeric, leading zeros
%p	AM or PM
%w	Day of the week, numeric, from 0 (Sunday) to 6 (Saturday)

The UNIX_TIMESTAMP function works similarly but converts a column into a Unix timestamp. For example,

```
SELECT UNIX_TIMESTAMP(date_column)
FROM tablename;
```

returns the date formatted as a Unix timestamp. You can then do as you want with it in PHP.

You can easily perform date calculations and comparisons with the Unix timestamp. Bear in mind, however, that a timestamp can usually represent dates only between 1902 and 2038, whereas the MySQL date type has a much wider range.

As a rule of thumb, use a Unix timestamp for date calculations and the standard date format when you are just storing or showing dates.

Calculating Dates in PHP

A simple way to work out the length of time between two dates in PHP is to use the difference between Unix timestamps. We used this approach in the script shown in Listing 20.1.

Listing 20.1   `calc_age.php`—**Working Out a Person's Age Based on Birthdate**

```php
<?php
// set date for calculation
$day = 18;
$month = 9;
$year = 1972;
```

Listing 20.1 **Continued**

```
// remember you need bday as day month and year
$bdayunix = mktime (0, 0, 0, $month, $day, $year); // get ts for then
$nowunix = time(); // get unix ts for today
$ageunix = $nowunix - $bdayunix; // work out the difference
$age = floor($ageunix / (365 * 24 * 60 * 60)); // convert from seconds to years

echo "Age is $age";
?>
```

This script sets the date for calculating the age. In a real application, it is likely that this information might come from an HTML form. The script begins by calling mktime() to work out the timestamp for the birthday and for the current time:

```
$bdayunix = mktime (0, 0, 0, $month, $day, $year);
$nowunix = mktime(); // get unix ts for today
```

Now that these dates are in the same format, you can simply subtract them:

```
$ageunix = $nowunix - $bdayunix;
```

Now, the slightly tricky part: converting this time period back to a more human-friendly unit of measure. This is not a timestamp but instead the age of the person measured in seconds. You can convert it back to years by dividing by the number of seconds in a year. You then round it down by using the floor() function because a person is not said to be, for example, 20, until the end of his twentieth year:

```
$age = floor($ageunix / (365 * 24 * 60 * 60)); // convert from seconds to years
```

Note, however, that this approach is somewhat flawed because it is limited by the range of Unix timestamps (generally 32-bit integers). Birthdates are not an ideal application for timestamps. This example works on all platforms only for people born from 1970 onward. Windows cannot manage timestamps prior to 1970. Even then, this calculation is not always accurate because it does not allow for leap years and might fail if midnight on the person's birthday is the daylight savings switchover time in the local time zone.

Calculating Dates in MySQL

PHP does not have many date manipulation functions built in. Obviously, you can write your own, but ensuring that you correctly account for leap years and daylight savings time can be tricky. Another option is to download other people's functions. You can find many as user-contributed notes in the PHP manual, but only some of them are well thought out.

An option that may not seem immediately obvious is using MySQL. MySQL provides an extensive range of date manipulation functions that work for times outside the reliable range of Unix timestamps. You need to connect to a MySQL server to run a MySQL query, but you do not have to use data from the database.

The following query adds one day to the date February 28, 1700, and returns the resulting date:

```
select adddate('1700-02-28', interval 1 day)
```

The year 1700 is not a leap year, so the result is 1700-03-01.

You can find an extensive syntax for describing and modifying dates and times described in the MySQL manual; it is located at

http://www.mysql.com/doc/en/Date_and_time_functions.html

Unfortunately, there is not a simple way to get the number of years between two dates, so the birthday example is still a little flaky. You can get a person's age in days very easily, and Listing 20.2 converts that age to years imprecisely.

Listing 20.2 `mysql_calc_age.php`—**Using MySQL to Work Out a Person's Age Based on Birthdate**

```php
<?php
// set date for calculation
$day = 18;
$month = 9;
$year = 1972;

// format birthday as an ISO 8601 date
$bdayISO = date("c", mktime (0, 0, 0, $month, $day, $year));

// use mysql query to calculate an age in days
$db = mysqli_connect('localhost', 'user', 'pass');
$res = mysqli_query($db, "select datediff(now(), '$bdayISO')");
$age = mysqli_fetch_array($res);

// convert age in days to age in years (approximately)
echo "Age is ".floor($age[0]/365.25);
?>
```

After formatting the birthday as an ISO timestamp, you pass the following query to MySQL:

```
select datediff(now(), '1972-09-18T00:00:00+10:00')
```

The MySQL function `now()` always returns the current date and time. The MySQL function `datediff()` (added at version 4.1.1) subtracts one date from another and returns the difference in days.

It is worth noting that you are not selecting data from a table or even choosing a database to use for this script, but you do need to log in to the MySQL server with a valid username and password.

Because no specific built-in function is available for such calculations, an SQL query to calculate the exact number of years is fairly complex. Here, we took a shortcut and divided the age in days by 365.25 to give the age in years. This calculation can be one year out if run on somebody's birthday, depending on how many leap years there have been in that person's lifetime.

Using Microseconds

For some applications, measuring time in seconds is not precise enough to be useful. If you want to measure very short periods, such as the time taken to run some or all of a PHP script, you need to use the function `microtime()`.

If you are using PHP5, call `microtime()` with the parameter `get_as_float` set to `true`. This call returns a timestamp as a floating-point number ready for whatever use you have in mind. The timestamp is the same one returned by `mktime()`, `time()`, or `date()` but has a fractional component.

The statement

```
echo number_format(microtime(true), 10, '.', '');
```

produces something like 1080303003.1321949959.

On older versions, you cannot request the result as a float. It is provided as a string. A call to `microtime()` without a parameter returns a string of this form `"0.02149300 1080302326"`. The first number is the fractional part, and the second number is the number of whole seconds elapsed since January 1, 1970.

Dealing with numbers rather than strings is more useful, so if you don't mind your code requiring PHP 5.0 to run, it is easiest to call `microtime()` with the parameter `true`.

Using the Calendar Functions

PHP has a set of functions that enable you to convert between different calendar systems. The main calendars you will work with are the Gregorian, Julian, and Julian Day Count.

Most Western countries currently use the Gregorian calendar. The Gregorian date October 15, 1582, is equivalent to October 5, 1582, in the Julian calendar. Prior to that date, the Julian calendar was commonly used. Different countries converted to the Gregorian calendar at different times and some not until early in the twentieth century.

Although you may have heard of these two calendars, you might not have heard of the Julian Day Count (JD). It is similar in many ways to a Unix timestamp. It is a count of the number of days since a date around 4000 BC. In itself, it is not particularly useful, but it is useful for converting between formats. To convert from one format to another, you first convert to a Julian Day Count and then to the desired output calendar.

To use these functions under Unix, you first need to compile the calendar extension into PHP with `--enable-calendar`. These functions are built into the standard Windows install.

To give you a taste for these functions, consider the prototypes for the functions you would use to convert from the Gregorian calendar to the Julian calendar:

```
int gregoriantojd (int month, int day, int year)
string jdtojulian(int julianday)
```

To convert a date, you would need to call both of these functions:

```
$jd = gregoriantojd (9, 18, 1582);
echo jdtojulian($jd);
```

This call echoes the Julian date in a MM/DD/YYYY format.

Variations of these functions exist for converting between the Gregorian, Julian, French, and Jewish calendars and Unix timestamps.

Further Reading

If you would like to read more about date and time functions in PHP and MySQL, you can consult the relevant sections of the manuals at

http://php.net/manual/en/ref.datetime.php

http://www.mysql.com/doc/en/Date_and_time_functions.html

If you are converting between calendars, try the manual page for PHP's calendar functions:

http://php.net/manual/en/ref.calendar.php

Next

One of the unique and useful things you can do with PHP is create images on the fly. Chapter 21, "Generating Images," discusses how to use the image library functions to achieve some interesting and useful effects.

21

Generating Images

ONE OF THE USEFUL THINGS YOU CAN DO WITH PHP is create images on the fly. PHP has some built-in image information functions, and you can also use the GD2 library to create new images or manipulate existing ones. This chapter discusses how to use these image functions to achieve some interesting and useful effects.

Key topics covered in this chapter include

- Setting up image support in PHP
- Understanding image formats
- Creating images
- Using automatically generated images in other pages
- Using text and fonts to create images
- Drawing figures and graphing data

Specifically, we look at two examples: generating website buttons on the fly and drawing a bar chart using figures from a MySQL database.

We use the GD2 library here, but there is one other popular PHP image library. The ImageMagick library is not part of the standard PHP build but is easily installable from the PHP Extension Class Library (PECL). ImageMagick and GD2 have a lot of fairly similar features, but in some areas ImageMagick goes further. If you want to create GIFs (even animated GIFS), you should look at ImageMagick. If you want to work with true color images or render transparent effects, you should compare the offerings in both libraries.

See PECL for the PHP download of ImageMagick at http://pecl.php.net/package/imagick.

See the main ImageMagick site for demonstrations of its capabilities and detailed documentation at http://www.imagemagick.org.

Setting Up Image Support in PHP

Some of the image functions in PHP are always available, but most of them require the GD2 library. Detailed information about GD2 is available at http://www.boutell.com/gd/.

Since PHP 4.3, PHP comes with its own forked version of the GD2 library, supported by the PHP team. This version is easier to install with PHP and is usually more stable, so it's advisable to use this version. Under Windows, PNGs and JPEGs are automatically supported.

If you have Unix and want to work with PNGs, you need to install `libpng` from http://www.libpng.org/pub/png/ and `zlib` from http://www.gzip.org/zlib/.

You then need to configure PHP with the following options:

```
--with-png-dir=/path/to/libpng
--with-zlib-dir=/path/to/zlib
```

If you have Unix and want to work with JPEGs, you need to download `jpeg-6b` and recompile GD with JPEG support included. You can download it from ftp://ftp.uu.net/graphics/jpeg/.

You then need to reconfigure PHP with the following option and recompile it:

```
--with-jpeg-dir=/path/to/jpeg-6b
```

If you want to use TrueType fonts in your images, you also need the FreeType library. It also comes with PHP4. Alternatively, you can download it from http://www.freetype.org/.

If you want to use PostScript Type 1 fonts instead, you need to download `t1lib`, available from ftp://sunsite.unc.edu/pub/Linux/libs/graphics/.

You then need to run PHP's configure program with

```
--with-t1lib[=path/to/t1lib]
```

Finally, you will, of course, need to configure PHP using `--with-gd`.

Understanding Image Formats

The GD library supports JPEG, PNG, and WBMP formats. It no longer supports the GIF format. Let's briefly look at each of these formats.

JPEG

JPEG (pronounced "jay-peg") stands for *Joint Photographic Experts Group* and is really the name of a standards body, not a specific format. The file format we mean when we refer to JPEGs is officially called JFIF, which corresponds to one of the standards issued by JPEG.

In case you are not familiar with them, JPEGs are usually used to store photographic or other images with many colors or gradations of color. This format uses lossy compression; that is, to squeeze a photograph into a smaller file, some image quality is lost. Because JPEGs should contain what are essentially analog images, with gradations of color, the human eye can tolerate some loss of quality. This format is not suitable for line drawings, text, or solid blocks of color.

You can read more about JPEG/JFIF at the official JPEG site at http://www.jpeg.org/.

PNG

PNG (pronounced "ping") stands for *Portable Network Graphics*. This file format is the replacement for *GIF (Graphics Interchange Format)* for reasons we discuss shortly. The PNG website describes it as "a turbo-studly image format with lossless compression." Because it is lossless, this image format is suitable for images that contain text, straight lines, and blocks of color such as headings and website buttons—all the same purposes for which you previously might have used GIFs. A PNG-compressed version of the same image is generally similar in size to a GIF-compressed version. PNG also offers variable transparency, gamma correction, and two-dimensional interlacing. It does not, however, support animations; for this, you must use the extension format MNG, which is still in development.

Lossless compression schemes are good for illustrations but not generally a good way to store large photos because they tend to give large file sizes.

You can read more about PNG at the official PNG site at http://www.libpng.org/pub/png/.

WBMP

WBMP, which stands for *Wireless Bitmap*, is a file format designed specifically for wireless devices. It is not in wide use.

GIF

GIF stands for Graphics Interchange Format. It is a compressed lossless format widely used on the Web for storing images containing text, straight lines, and blocks of single color.

The question you are likely asking is, "Why doesn't GD support GIFs?" The answer is that it used to, up to version 1.3. For some older PHP versions, you could choose to download and install GD version 1.3. If you want this version, you can get it from http://www.linuxguruz.org/downloads/gd1.3.tar.gz.

Note, however, that the makers of GD discourage you from using this version and no longer support it, and it forces you to use an old version of PHP. Note also that this URL for the GIF version might not be available forever.

There is a good reason that GD no longer supports writing GIFs (although it does read GIFs). Standard GIFs use a form of compression known as *LZW (Lempel Ziv Welch)*, which was subject to a patent owned by UNISYS. After allowing the format to establish itself as a de facto standard for many years, UNISYS decided that providers of programs that read and write GIFs must pay licensing fees to UNISYS. For example, Adobe has paid a licensing fee for products such as Photoshop that are used to create GIFs. Code libraries appeared to be in the situation in which the writers of the code library must pay a fee, and, in addition, the users of the library must also pay a fee. Thus, if you used a GIF version of the GD library on your website, you might have owed UNISYS some fairly hefty licensing fees. The GIF reading functionality falls outside the license and is therefore still available.

This situation was unfortunate because GIFs were in use for many years before UNISYS chose to enforce licensing. Thus, the format became one of the standards for the Web. A lot of ill feeling exists about the patent in the web development community. You can read about this (and form your own opinion) at UNISYS's site at http://www.unisys.com/about_unisys/lzw/.

You can also read about it at Burn All Gifs, the opposition at http://burnallgifs.org/.

The U.S. version of the LZW patent expired on June 21, 2003, and the European and Asian ones at various times in 2004. We are not lawyers, and none of this should be interpreted as legal advice, but we think it is easier to use PNGs, regardless of the politics. Browser support for PNGs was variable a few years ago but is pretty good in all recent browsers. Advanced PNG feature support is still a bit patchy, but simple images should work everywhere.

It is expected (at this point in time) that GIF write support will be restored in PHP 5.0.1 and PHP 4.3.8 (which are each scheduled for release after the expiration date of the LZW patent).

Creating Images

The four basic steps to creating an image in PHP are as follows:

1. Creating a canvas image on which to work.
2. Drawing shapes or printing text on that canvas.
3. Outputting the final graphic.
4. Cleaning up resources.

Let's begin by looking at the simple image creation script shown in Listing 21.1.

Listing 21.1 `simplegraph.php`—**Outputs a Simple Line Graph with the Label** Sales

```php
<?php
// set up image
  $height = 200;
  $width = 200;
  $im = ImageCreateTrueColor($width, $height);
  $white = ImageColorAllocate ($im, 255, 255, 255);
  $blue = ImageColorAllocate ($im, 0, 0, 64);
```

Listing 21.1   **Continued**

```
// draw on image
  ImageFill($im, 0, 0, $blue);
  ImageLine($im, 0, 0, $width, $height, $white);
  ImageString($im, 4, 50, 150, 'Sales', $white);

// output image
  Header ('Content-type: image/png');
  ImagePng ($im);

// clean up
  ImageDestroy($im);
?>
```

The output from running this script is shown in Figure 21.1.

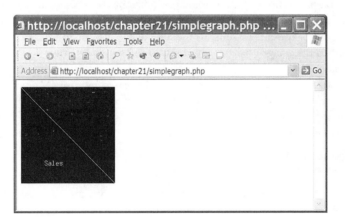

Figure 21.1   The script draws a blue background and then adds a line and a
text label for the image.

Now let's walk through the steps of creating this image one by one.

Creating a Canvas Image

To begin building or changing an image in PHP, you need to create an image identifier.
There are two basic ways to do this. One is to create a blank canvas, which you can do with
a call to the ImageCreateTrueColor() function, as done in this script with the following:

```
$im = ImageCreateTrueColor($width, $height);
```

You need to pass two parameters to `ImageCreateTrueColor()`. The first is the width of the new image, and the second is the height of the new image. The function will return an identifier for the new image. These identifiers work a lot like file handles.

An alternative way is to read in an existing image file that you can then filter, resize, or add to. You can do this with one of the functions `ImageCreateFromPNG()`, `ImageCreateFromJPEG()`, or `ImageCreateFromGIF()`, depending on the file format you are reading in. Each of these functions takes the filename as a parameter, as in this example:

```
$im = ImageCreateFromPNG('baseimage.png');
```

An example is shown later in this chapter using existing images to create buttons on the fly.

Drawing or Printing Text on the Image

Drawing or printing text on the image really involves two stages. First, you must select the colors in which you want to draw. As you probably already know, colors to be displayed on a computer monitor are made up of different amounts of red, green, and blue light. Image formats use a color palette that consists of a specified subset of all the possible combinations of the three colors. To use a color to draw in an image, you need to add this color to the image's palette. You must do this for every color you want to use, even black and white.

You can select colors for your image by calling the `ImageColorAllocate()` function. You need to pass your image identifier and the red, green, and blue (RGB) values of the color you want to draw into the function.

Listing 21.1 uses two colors: blue and white. You allocate them by calling

```
$white = ImageColorAllocate ($im, 255, 255, 255);
$blue = ImageColorAllocate ($im, 0, 0, 64);
```

The function returns a color identifier that you can use to access the color later.

Second, to actually draw into the image, you can use a number of different functions, depending on what you want to draw—lines, arcs, polygons, or text.

The drawing functions generally require the following as parameters:

- The image identifier
- The start and sometimes the end coordinates of what you want to draw
- The color you want to draw in
- For text, the font information

In this case, you use three of the drawing functions. Let's look at each one in turn.

First, you paint a blue background on which to draw using the `ImageFill()` function:

```
ImageFill($im, 0, 0, $blue);
```

This function takes the image identifier, the start coordinates of the area to paint (x and y), and the color to fill in as parameters.

> **Note**
> The coordinates of the image start from the top-left corner, which is x=0, y=0. The bottom-right corner of the image is x=$width, y=$height. This is normal for computer graphics, but the opposite of typical math graphing conventions, so beware!

Next, you draw a line from the top-left corner (0, 0) to the bottom-right corner ($width, $height) of the image:

```
ImageLine($im, 0, 0, $width, $height, $white);
```

This function takes the image identifier, the start point x and y for the line, the end point, and then the color as parameters.

Finally, you add a label to the graph:

```
ImageString($im, 4, 50, 150, 'Sales', $white);
```

The `ImageString()` function takes some slightly different parameters. The prototype for this function is

```
int imagestring (resource im, int font, int x, int y, string s, int col)
```

It takes as parameters the image identifier, the font, the x and y coordinates to start writing the text, the text to write, and the color.

The font is a number between 1 and 5. These numbers represent a set of built-in fonts. As an alternative to these fonts, you can use TrueType fonts or PostScript Type 1 fonts. Each of these font sets has a corresponding function set. We use the TrueType functions in the next example.

A good reason for using one of the alternative font function sets is that the text written by `ImageString()` and associated functions, such as `ImageChar()` (write a character to the image) is aliased. The TrueType and PostScript functions produce antialiased text.

If you're not sure what the difference is, look at Figure 21.2. Where curves or angled lines appear in the letters, the aliased text appears jagged. The curve or angle is achieved by using a "staircase" effect. In the antialiased image, when curves or angles appear in the text, pixels in colors between the background and the text color are used to smooth the text's appearance.

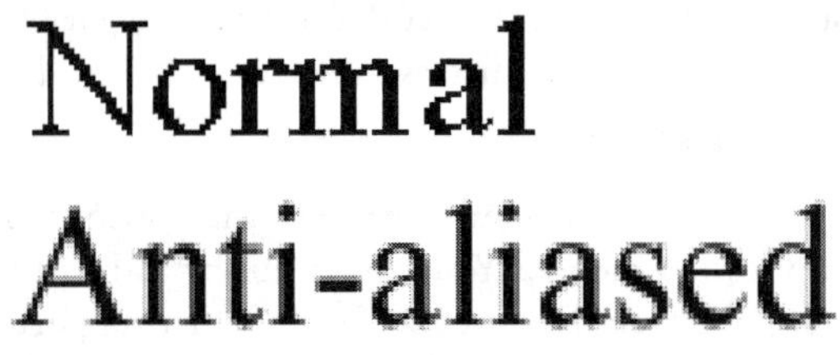

Figure 21.2   Normal text appears jagged, especially in a large font size.
Antialiasing smoothes the curves and corners of the letters.

Outputting the Final Graphic

You can output an image either directly to the browser or to a file.

In this example, you output the image to the browser. This is a two-stage process. First, you need to tell the web browser that you are outputting an image rather than text or HTML. You do this by using the Header() function to specify the MIME type of the image:

```
Header ('Content-type: image/png');
```

Normally, when you retrieve a file in your browser, the MIME type is the first thing the web server sends. For an HTML or PHP page (post execution), the first thing sent is

```
Content-type:  text/html
```

This tells the browser how to interpret the data that follows.

In this case, you want to tell the browser that you are sending an image instead of the usual HTML output. You can do this by using the Header() function, which we have not yet discussed.

This function sends raw HTTP header strings. Another typical application of this function is to do HTTP redirects. They tell the browser to load a different page instead of the one requested. They are typically used when a page has been moved. For example,

```
Header ('Location: http://www.domain.com/new_home_page.html ');
```

An important point to note when using the Header() function is that it cannot be executed if content has already been sent for the page. PHP will send an HTTP header automatically for you as soon as you output anything to the browser. Hence, if you have any echo statements, or even any whitespace before your opening PHP tag, the headers will be sent, and you will get a warning message from PHP when you try to call Header(). However, you can send multiple HTTP headers with multiple calls to the Header() function in the same script, although they must all appear before any output is sent to the browser.

After you have sent the header data, you output the image data with a call to

```
ImagePng ($im);
```

This call sends the output to the browser in PNG format. If you wanted it sent in a different format, you could call ImageJPEG()—if JPEG support is enabled. You would also need to send the corresponding header first, as shown here:

```
Header ('Content-type: image/jpeg');
```

The second option you can use, as an alternative to all the previous ones, is to write the image to a file instead of to the browser. You can do this by adding the optional second parameter to ImagePNG() (or a similar function for the other supported formats):

```
ImagePNG($im, $filename);
```

Remember that all the usual rules about writing to a file from PHP apply (for example, having permissions set up correctly).

Cleaning Up

When you're done with an image, you should return the resources you have been using to the server by destroying the image identifier. You can do this with a call to ImageDestroy():

```
ImageDestroy($im);
```

Using Automatically Generated Images in Other Pages

Because a header can be sent only once, and this is the only way to tell the browser that you are sending image data, it is slightly tricky to embed any images you create on the fly in a regular page. Three ways you can do it are as follows:

1. You can have an entire page consist of the image output, as we did in the previous example.

2. You can write the image out to a file, as previously mentioned, and then refer to it with a normal <IMG> tag.

3. You can put the image production script in an image tag.

We have covered methods 1 and 2 already. Let's briefly look at method 3 now. To use this method, you include the image inline in HTML by having an image tag along the lines of the following:

```
<img src="simplegraph.php" height="200" width="200" alt="Sales going down" />
```

Instead of putting in a PNG, JPEG, or GIF directly, put in the PHP script that generates the image in the SRC tag. It will be retrieved and the output added inline, as shown in Figure 21.3.

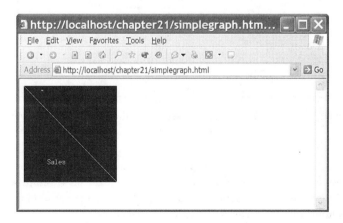

Figure 21.3   The dynamically produced inline image appears the same as a regular image to the end user.

Using Text and Fonts to Create Images

Let's look at a more complicated example. It is useful to be able to create buttons or other images for your website automatically. You can easily build simple buttons based on a rectangle of background color using the techniques we've already discussed. You can generate more complicated effects programmatically, too, but you can generally do it more easily in a paint program. This also makes it easier to get an artist to do the artwork and leave programmers programming.

In this example, you generate buttons using a blank button template. This allows you to have features such as beveled edges and so on, which are a good deal easier to generate using Photoshop, the GIMP, or some other graphics tool. With the image library in PHP, you can begin with a base image and draw on top of that.

You also use TrueType fonts in this example so that you can use antialiased text. The TrueType font functions have their own quirks, which we discuss.

The basic process is to take some text and generate a button with that text on it. The text will be centered both horizontally and vertically on the button, and will be rendered in the largest font size that will fit on the button.

We built a front end to the button generator for testing and experimenting. This interface is shown in Figure 21.4. (We did not include the HTML for this form here because it is very simple, but you can find it on the CD in `design_button.html`.)

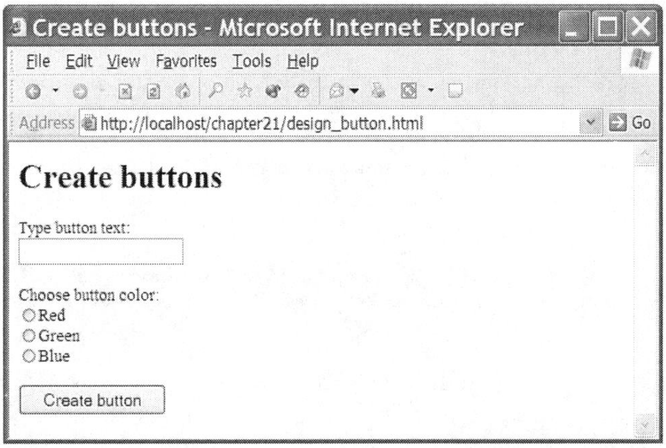

Figure 21.4   The front end lets a user choose the button color and type in the required text.

You could use this type of interface for a program to automatically generate websites. You could also call the script in an inline fashion, to generate all a website's buttons on the fly, but this would require caching to stop it becoming time consuming.

Typical output from the script is shown in Figure 21.5.

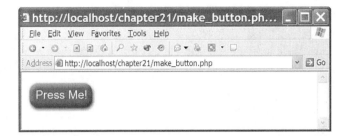

Figure 21.5 This button is generated by the make_button.php script.

The button is generated by the make_button.php script shown in Listing 21.2.

Listing 21.2 make_button.php—**Enables Calls from the Form in design_button.html or from Within an HTML Image Tag**

```php
<?php
// check we have the appropriate variable data
// variables are button-text and color

$button_text = $_REQUEST['button_text'];
$color = $_REQUEST['color'];

if ((empty($button_text) || empty($color)) || (!($color=='red'
    || $color=='blue' || $color=='green')))
{
  echo 'Could not create image - form not filled out correctly';
  exit;
}

// create an image of the right background and check size
$im = ImageCreateFromPNG ($color.'-button.png');
if (!$im)
{
  echo 'Could not create image';
  exit;
}

$width_image = ImageSX($im);
$height_image = ImageSY($im);

// Our images need an 18 pixel margin in from the edge of the image
$width_image_wo_margins = $width_image - (2 * 18);
$height_image_wo_margins = $height_image - (2 * 18);
```

Listing 21.2 **Continued**

```php
// Work out if the font size will fit and make it smaller until it does
// Start out with the biggest size that will reasonably fit on our buttons
$font_size = 33;

// you need to tell GD2 where your fonts reside
putenv('GDFONTPATH=C:\WINDOWS\Fonts');
$fontname = 'arial';

do
{
  $font_size--;

  // find out the size of the text at that font size
  $bbox=ImageTTFBBox ($font_size, 0, $fontname, $button_text);

  $right_text = $bbox[2];   // right co-ordinate
  $left_text = $bbox[0];    // left co-ordinate
  $width_text = $right_text - $left_text;  // how wide is it?
  $height_text = abs($bbox[7] - $bbox[1]);  // how tall is it?

}
while ( $font_size>8 &&
        ( $height_text>$height_image_wo_margins ||
          $width_text>$width_image_wo_margins )
      );

if ( $height_text>$height_image_wo_margins ||
     $width_text>$width_image_wo_margins )
{
  // no readable font size will fit on button
  echo 'Text given will not fit on button.<br />';
}
else
{
  // We have found a font size that will fit
  // Now work out where to put it

  $text_x = $width_image/2.0 - $width_text/2.0;
  $text_y = $height_image/2.0 - $height_text/2.0 ;

  if ($left_text < 0)
      $text_x += abs($left_text);    // add factor for left overhang
```

Listing 21.2 **Continued**

```
$above_line_text = abs($bbox[7]);   // how far above the baseline?
$text_y += $above_line_text;        // add baseline factor

$text_y -= 2;  // adjustment factor for shape of our template

$white = ImageColorAllocate ($im, 255, 255, 255);

ImageTTFText ($im, $font_size, 0, $text_x, $text_y, $white, $fontname,
              $button_text);

Header ('Content-type: image/png');
ImagePNG ($im);
}

ImageDestroy ($im);
?>
```

This is one of the longest scripts we've looked at so far. Let's step through it section by section. The script begins with some basic error checking and then sets up the canvas on which you're going to work.

Setting Up the Base Canvas

In Listing 21.2, instead of starting from scratch, you start with an existing image for the button. You provide a choice of three colors in the basic button: red (red-button.png), green (green-button.png), and blue (blue-button.png).

The user's chosen color is stored in the color variable from the form.

You begin by extracting the color from the superglobal $_REQUEST and setting up a new image identifier based on the appropriate button:

```
$color = $_REQUEST['color'];
...
$im = ImageCreateFromPNG ($color.'-button.png');
```

The function ImageCreateFromPNG() takes the filename of a PNG as a parameter and returns a new image identifier for an image containing a copy of that PNG. Note that this does not modify the base PNG in any way. You can use the ImageCreateFromJPEG() and ImageCreateFromGIF() functions in the same way if the appropriate support is installed.

Note

The call to ImageCreateFromPNG() creates the image in memory only. To save the image to a file or output it to the browser, you must call the ImagePNG() function. You'll come to that discussion shortly, but you have other work to do with the image first.

Fitting the Text onto the Button

Some text typed in by the user is stored in the $button_text variable. What you need to do is print that text on the button in the largest font size that will fit. You do this by iteration, or strictly speaking, by iterative trial and error.

You start by setting up some relevant variables. The first two are the height and width of the button image:

```
$width_image = ImageSX($im);
$height_image = ImageSY($im);
```

The second two represent a margin in from the edge of the button. The button images are beveled, so you need to leave room for that around the edges of the text. If you are using different images, this number will be different! In this case, the margin on each side is around 18 pixels:

```
$width_image_wo_margins = $width_image - (2 * 18);
$height_image_wo_margins = $height_image - (2 * 18);
```

You also need to set up the initial font size. You start with 32 (actually 33, but you decrement that in a minute) because this is about the biggest font that will fit on the button at all:

```
$font_size = 33;
```

With GD2, you need to tell it where your fonts live by setting the environment variable GDFONTPATH as follows:

```
putenv('GDFONTPATH=C:\WINDOWS\Fonts');
```

You also set up the name of the font you want to use. You're going to use this font with the TrueType functions, which will look for the font file in the preceding location and will append the filename with .ttf (TrueType Font):

```
$fontname = 'arial';
```

Note that depending on your operating system, you may have to add .ttf to the end of the font name.

If you don't have Arial (the font we used here) on your system, you can easily change it to another TrueType font.

Now you loop, decrementing the font size at each iteration, until the submitted text will fit on the button reasonably:

```
do
{
  $font_size--;
```

```
  // find out the size of the text at that font size
  $bbox=ImageTTFBBox ($font_size, 0, $fontname, $button_text);

  $right_text = $bbox[2];    // right co-ordinate
  $left_text = $bbox[0];     // left co-ordinate
  $width_text = $right_text - $left_text;  // how wide is it?
  $height_text = abs($bbox[7] - $bbox[1]);  // how tall is it?

}
while ( $font_size>8 &&
       ( $height_text>$height_image_wo_margins ||
         $width_text>$width_image_wo_margins )
     );
```

This code tests the size of the text by looking at what is called the *bounding box* of the text. You do this by using the `ImageGetTTFBBox()` function, which is one of the TrueType font functions. You will, after you have figured out the size, print on the button using a TrueType font (we used Arial, but you can use whatever you like) and the `ImageTTFText()` function.

The bounding box of a piece of text is the smallest box you could draw around the text. An example of a bounding box is shown in Figure 21.6.

(0,0) Our Company

Figure 21.6 Coordinates of the bounding box are given relative to the baseline. The origin of the coordinates is shown here as (0,0).

To get the dimensions of the box, you call

```
$bbox=ImageTTFBBox ($font_size, 0, $fontname, $button_text);
```

This call says, "For given font size `$font_size`, with text slanted on an angle of zero degrees, using the TrueType font Arial, tell me the dimensions of the text in `$button_text`."

Note that you actually need to pass the path to the file containing the font into the function. In this case, it's in the same directory as the script (the default), so we didn't specify a longer path.

The function returns an array containing the coordinates of the corners of the bounding box. The contents of the array are shown in Table 21.1.

Table 21.1 **Contents of the Bounding Box Array**

Array Index	Contents
0	x coordinate, lower-left corner
1	y coordinate, lower-left corner
2	x coordinate, lower-right corner
3	y coordinate, lower-right corner
4	x coordinate, upper-right corner
5	y coordinate, upper-right corner
6	x coordinate, upper-left corner
7	y coordinate, upper-left corner

To remember what the contents of the array are, just remember that the numbering starts at the bottom-left corner of the bounding box and works its way around counter-clockwise.

There is one tricky thing about the values returned from the ImageTTFBBox() function. They are coordinate values, specified from an origin. However, unlike coordinates for images, which are specified relative to the top-left corner, they are specified relative to a baseline.

Look at Figure 21.6 again. You will see that we have drawn a line along the bottom of most of the text. This is known as the *baseline*. Some letters hang below the baseline, such as *y* in this example. These parts of the letters are called *descenders*.

The left side of the baseline is specified as the origin of measurements—that is, x coordinate 0 and y coordinate 0. Coordinates above the baseline have a positive x coordinate, and coordinates below the baseline have a negative x coordinate.

In addition, text might actually have coordinate values that sit outside the bounding box. For example, the text might actually start at an x coordinate of −1.

What this all adds up to is the fact that care is required when you're performing calculations with these numbers.

You work out the width and height of the text as follows:

```
$right_text = $bbox[2];   // right co-ordinate
$left_text = $bbox[0];    // left co-ordinate
$width_text = $right_text - $left_text;  // how wide is it?
$height_text = abs($bbox[7] - $bbox[1]); // how tall is it?
```

After you have this information, you test the loop condition:

```
} while ( $font_size>8 &&
        ( $height_text>$height_image_wo_margins ||
          $width_text>$width_image_wo_margins )
      );
```

You test two sets of conditions here. The first is that the font is still readable; there's no point in making it much smaller than 8-point type because the button becomes too difficult to read. The second set of conditions tests whether the text will fit inside the drawing space you have available for it.

Next, you check to see whether the iterative calculations found an acceptable font size and report an error if not:

```
if ( $height_text>$height_image_wo_margins ||
     $width_text>$width_image_wo_margins )
{
  // no readable font size will fit on button
  echo 'Text given will not fit on button.<br />';
}
```

Positioning the Text

If all was okay, you next work out a base position for the start of the text. This is the midpoint of the available space.

```
$text_x = $width_image/2.0 - $width_text/2.0;
$text_y = $height_image/2.0 - $height_text/2.0 ;
```

Because of the complications with the baseline relative coordinate system, you need to add some correction factors:

```
  if ($left_text < 0)
      $text_x += abs($left_text);      // add factor for left overhang

  $above_line_text = abs($bbox[7]);    // how far above the baseline?
  $text_y += $above_line_text;         // add baseline factor

  $text_y -= 2;  // adjustment factor for shape of our template
```

These correction factors allow for the baseline and a little adjustment because the image is a bit "top heavy."

Writing the Text onto the Button

After that, it's all smooth sailing. You set up the text color, which will be white:

```
$white = ImageColorAllocate ($im, 255, 255, 255);
```

You can then use the ImageTTFText() function to actually draw the text onto the button:

```
ImageTTFText ($im, $font_size, 0, $text_x, $text_y, $white, $fontname,
              $button_text);
```

This function takes quite a lot of parameters. In order, they are the image identifier, the font size in points, the angle you want to draw the text at, the starting x and y coordinates of the text, the text color, the font file, and, finally, the actual text to go on the button.

> **Note**
>
> The font file needs to be available on the server and is not required on the client's machine because she will see it as an image.

Finishing Up

Finally, you can output the button to the browser:

```
Header ('Content-type: image/png');
ImagePNG ($im);
```

Then it's time to clean up resources and end the script:

```
ImageDestroy ($im);
```

That's it! If all went well, you should now have a button in the browser window that looks similar to the one you saw in Figure 21.5.

Drawing Figures and Graphing Data

In the preceding application, we looked at existing images and text. We haven't yet looked at an example with drawing, so let's do that now.

In this example, you run a poll on your website to test whom users will vote for in a fictitious election. You store the results of the poll in a MySQL database and draw a bar chart of the results using the image functions.

Graphing is the other thing these functions are primarily used for. You can chart any data you want—sales, web hits, or whatever takes your fancy.

For this example, we spent a few minutes setting up a MySQL database called `poll`. It contains one table called `poll_results`, which holds the candidates' names in the `candidate` column and the number of votes they received in the `num_votes` column. We also created a user for this database called `poll`, with password `poll`. This table is straightforward to set up, and you can create it by running the SQL script shown in Listing 21.3. You can do this piping the script through a root login using

```
mysql -u root -p < pollsetup.sql
```

Of course, you could also use the login of any user with the appropriate MySQL privileges.

Listing 21.3 `pollsetup.sql`—**Sets Up the Poll Database**

```
create database poll;
use poll;
create table poll_results (
  candidate varchar(30),
  num_votes int
);
insert into poll_results values
  ('John Smith', 0),
  ('Mary Jones', 0),
  ('Fred Bloggs', 0)
;
grant all privileges
on poll.*
to poll@localhost
identified by 'poll';
```

This database contains three candidates. You provide a voting interface via a page called
vote.html. The code for this page is shown in Listing21.4.

Listing 21.4 vote.html—**Allows Users to Cast Their Votes Here**

```
<html>
<head>
  <title>Polling</title>
<head>
<body>
<h1>Pop Poll</h1>
<p>Who will you vote for in the election?</p>
<form method="post" action="show_poll.php">
<input type="radio" name="vote" value="John Smith">John Smith<br />
<input type="radio" name="vote" value="Mary Jones">Mary Jones<br />
<input type="radio" name="vote" value="Fred Bloggs">Fred Bloggs<br /><br />
<input type="submit"  value="Show results">
</form>
</body>
</html>
```

The output from this page is shown in Figure 21.7.

The general idea is that, when users click the button, you will add their vote to the
database, get all the votes out of the database, and draw the bar chart of the current
results.

Typical output after some votes have been cast is shown in Figure 21.8.

Figure 21.7 Users can cast their votes here, and clicking the submit button will show them the current poll results.

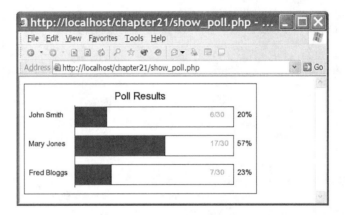

Figure 21.8 Vote results are created by drawing a series of lines, rectangles, and text items onto a canvas.

The script that generates this image is quite long. We split it into four parts, and we discuss each part separately. Most of the script is familiar; you have seen many MySQL examples similar to this one. You looked at how to paint a background canvas in a solid color and how to print text labels on it.

The new parts of this script relate to drawing lines and rectangles. We focus our attention on these sections. Part 1 (of this four-part script) is shown in Listing 21.5.1.

Listing 21.5.1 `show_poll.php`—**Part 1 Updates the Vote Database and Retrieves the New Results**

```php
<?php
/*********************************************
  Database query to get poll info
*********************************************/

// get vote from form
$vote=$_REQUEST['vote'];

// log in to database
if (!$db_conn = new mysqli('localhost', 'poll', 'poll', 'poll'))
{
  echo 'Could not connect to db<br />';
  exit;
}

if (!empty($vote))  // if they filled the form out, add their vote
{
  $vote = addslashes($vote);
  $query = "update poll_results
            set num_votes = num_votes + 1
            where candidate = '$vote'";
  if(!($result = @$db_conn->query($query)))
  {
    echo 'Could not connect to db<br />';
    exit;
  }
}

// get current results of poll, regardless of whether they voted
$query = 'select * from poll_results';
if(!($result = @$db_conn->query($query)))
{
  echo 'Could not connect to db<br />';
  exit;
}
$num_candidates = $result->num_rows;

// calculate total number of votes so far
$total_votes=0;
while ($row = $result->fetch_object())
{
    $total_votes +=  $row->num_votes;
}
$result->data_seek(0);  // reset result pointer
```

Part 1, shown in Listing 21.5.1, connects to the MySQL database, updates the votes according to the user's selection, and gets the stored votes. After you have that information, you can begin making calculations to draw the graph. Part 2 is shown in Listing 21.5.2.

Listing 21.5.2 show_poll.php—**Part 2 Sets Up All the Variables for Drawing**

```
/*********************************************
   Initial calculations for graph
*********************************************/
// set up constants
putenv('GDFONTPATH=C:\WINDOWS\Fonts');
$width=500;        // width of image in pixels - this will fit in 640x480
$left_margin = 50; // space to leave on left of graph
$right_margin= 50; // ditto right
$bar_height = 40;
$bar_spacing = $bar_height/2;
$font = 'arial';
$title_size= 16; // point
$main_size= 12; // point
$small_size= 12; // point
$text_indent = 10; // position for text labels from edge of image

// set up initial point to draw from
$x = $left_margin + 60;  // place to draw baseline of the graph
$y = 50;                 // ditto
$bar_unit = ($width-($x+$right_margin)) / 100;   // one "point" on the graph

// calculate height of graph - bars plus gaps plus some margin
$height = $num_candidates * ($bar_height + $bar_spacing) + 50;
```

Part 2 sets up some variables that you will use to actually draw the graph.

Working out the values for these sorts of variables can be tedious, but a bit of fore-thought about how you want the finished image to look will make the drawing process much easier. We arrived at the values used here by sketching the desired effect on a piece of paper and estimating the required proportions.

The $width variable is the total width of the canvas you will use. You also set up the left and right margins (with $left_margin and $right_margin, respectively); the "fat-ness" and spacing between the bars ($bar_height and $bar_spacing); and the font, font sizes, and label position ($font, $title_size, $main_size, $small_size, and $text_indent).

Given these base values, you can then make a few calculations. You want to draw a baseline that all the bars stretch out from. You can work out the position for this baseline by using the left margin plus an allowance for the text labels for the x coordinate and again an estimate from the sketch for the y coordinate. You could get the exact width of the longest name instead if flexibility is important.

You also work out two important values: first, the distance on the graph that represents one unit:

```
$bar_unit = ($width-($x+$right_margin)) / 100;    // one "point" on the graph
```

This is the maximum length of the bars—from the baseline to the right margin—divided by 100 because the graph is going to show percentage values.

The second value is the total height that you need for the canvas:

```
$height = $num_candidates * ($bar_height + $bar_spacing) + 50;
```

This value is basically the height per bar times the number of bars, plus an extra amount for the title. Part 3 is shown in Listing 21.5.3.

Listing 21.5.3 `show_poll.php` —**Part 3 Sets Up the Graph, Ready for the Data to Be Added**

```
/*******************************************
  Set up base image
*******************************************/
// create a blank canvas
$im = ImageCreateTrueColor($width,$height);

// Allocate colors
$white=ImageColorAllocate($im,255,255,255);
$blue=ImageColorAllocate($im,0,64,128);
$black=ImageColorAllocate($im,0,0,0);
$pink = ImageColorAllocate($im,255,78,243);

$text_color = $black;
$percent_color = $black;
$bg_color = $white;
$line_color = $black;
$bar_color = $blue;
$number_color = $pink;

// Create "canvas" to draw on
ImageFilledRectangle($im,0,0,$width,$height,$bg_color);

// Draw outline around canvas
ImageRectangle($im,0,0,$width-1,$height-1,$line_color);
```

Listing 21.5.3   **Continued**

```
// Add title
$title = 'Poll Results';
$title_dimensions = ImageTTFBBox($title_size, 0, $font, $title);
$title_length = $title_dimensions[2] - $title_dimensions[0];
$title_height = abs($title_dimensions[7] - $title_dimensions[1]);
$title_above_line = abs($title_dimensions[7]);
$title_x = ($width-$title_length)/2;  // center it in x
$title_y = ($y - $title_height)/2 + $title_above_line; // center in y gap
ImageTTFText($im, $title_size, 0, $title_x, $title_y,
            $text_color, $font, $title);

// Draw a base line from a little above first bar location
// to a little below last
ImageLine($im, $x, $y-5, $x, $height-15, $line_color) ;
```

In Part 3, you set up the basic image, allocate the colors, and then begin to draw the graph.

You fill in the background for the graph this time using

```
ImageFilledRectangle($im,0,0,$width,$height,$bg_color);
```

The `ImageFilledRectangle()` function, as you might imagine, draws a filled-in rectangle. The first parameter is, as usual, the image identifier. Then you must pass it the x and y coordinates of the start point and the end point of the rectangle. These points correspond to the upper-left corner and lower-right corner, respectively. In this case, you fill the entire canvas with the background color, which is the last parameter, and it's white.

You then call

```
ImageRectangle($im,0,0,$width-1,$height-1,$line_color);
```

to draw a black outline around the edge of the canvas. This function draws an outlined rectangle instead of a filled one. The parameters are the same. Notice that the rectangle is drawn to `$width-1` and `$height-1`—a canvas of width by height goes from (0, 0) to these values. If you drew it to `$width` and `$height`, the rectangle would be outside the canvas area.

You use the same logic and functions as in the preceding script to center and write the title on the graph.

Finally, you draw the baseline for the bars with

```
ImageLine($im, $x, $y-5, $x, $height-15, $line_color);
```

The `ImageLine()` function draws a line on the image you specify (`$im`) from one set of coordinates (`$x`, `$y-5`) to another (`$x`, `$height-15`), in the color specified by `$line_color`.

In this case, you draw the baseline from a little above where you want to draw the first bar, to a little above the bottom of the canvas.

You are now ready to fill in the data on the graph. Part 4 is shown in Listing 21.5.4.

Listing 21.5.4   `showpoll.php`—**Part 4 Draws the Actual Data onto the Graph and Finishes Up**

```
/*********************************************
  Draw data into graph
*********************************************/
// Get each line of db data and draw corresponding bars
while ($row = $result->fetch_object())
{
  if ($total_votes > 0)
    $percent = intval(($row->num_votes/$total_votes)*100);
  else
    $percent = 0;

  // display percent for this value
  $percent_dimensions = ImageTTFBBox($main_size, 0, $font, $percent.'%');
  $percent_length = $percent_dimensions[2] - $percent_dimensions[0];
  ImageTTFText($im, $main_size, 0, $width-$percent_length-$text_indent,
               $y+($bar_height/2), $percent_color, $font, $percent.'%');


  // length of bar for this value
  $bar_length = $x + ($percent * $bar_unit);

  // draw bar for this value
  ImageFilledRectangle($im, $x, $y-2, $bar_length, $y+$bar_height, $bar_color);

  // draw title for this value
  ImageTTFText($im, $main_size, 0, $text_indent, $y+($bar_height/2),
               $text_color, $font, "$row->candidate");

  // draw outline showing 100%
  ImageRectangle($im, $bar_length+1, $y-2,
                 ($x+(100*$bar_unit)), $y+$bar_height, $line_color);

  // display numbers
  ImageTTFText($im, $small_size, 0, $x+(100*$bar_unit)-50, $y+($bar_height/2),
               $number_color, $font, $row->num_votes.'/'.$total_votes);

  // move down to next bar
  $y=$y+($bar_height+$bar_spacing);
}
```

Listing 21.5.4 **Continued**

```
/******************************************
   Display image
******************************************/
Header('Content-type:  image/png');
ImagePNG($im);


/******************************************
   Clean up
******************************************/
ImageDestroy($im);
?>
```

Part 4 goes through the candidates from the database one by one, works out the percentage of votes, and draws the bars and labels for each candidate.

Again, you add labels using `ImageTTFText()` and draw the bars as filled rectangles
using `ImageFilledRectangle()`:

```
ImageFilledRectangle($im, $x, $y-2, $bar_length, $y+$bar_height, $bar_color);
```

You add outlines for the 100% mark using `ImageRectangle()`:

```
ImageRectangle($im, $bar_length+1, $y-2,
               ($x+(100*$bar_unit)), $y+$bar_height, $line_color);
```

After you have drawn all the bars, you again output the image using `ImagePNG()` and
clean up after yourself using `ImageDestroy()`.

This long-ish script can be easily adapted to suit your needs or to autogenerate polls
via an interface. One important feature that this script is missing is any sort of anticheat-
ing mechanism. Users would quickly discover that they can vote repeatedly and make
the result meaningless.

You can use a similar approach to draw line graphs, and even pie charts, if you are
good at mathematics.

Using Other Image Functions

In addition to the image functions used in this chapter, many others are available.
Drawing with a programming language takes a long time and some trial and error to get
right. Always begin by sketching what you want to draw, and then you can hit the manual for any extra functions you might need.

Further Reading

A lot of reading material is available online. If you're having trouble with the image functions, it sometimes helps to look at the source documentation for GD because the PHP functions are wrappers for this library. The GD documentation is available at http://www.boutell.com/gd/.

Remember, though, the PHP version of GD2 is a fork of the main library, so some details will vary.

You can also find some excellent tutorials on particular types of graph applications, particularly at Zend and Devshed at http://www.zend.com and http://devshed.com, respectively.

The bar chart application in this chapter was inspired by the dynamic bar graph script written by Steve Maranda, available from Devshed.

Next

In the next chapter, we tackle PHP's handy session control functionality.

22

Using Session Control in PHP

IN THIS CHAPTER, WE DISCUSS THE SESSION control functionality in PHP. Key topics covered in this chapter include

- What session control is
- Cookies
- Steps in setting up a session
- Session variables
- Sessions and authentication

What Session Control Is

You might have heard people say that "HTTP is a stateless protocol." This means that the protocol has no built-in way of maintaining state between two transactions. When a user requests one page, followed by another, HTTP does not provide a way for you to tell that both requests came from the same user.

The idea of session control is to be able to track a user during a single session on a website. If you can do this, you can easily support logging in a user and showing content according to her authorization level or personal preferences. You can track the user's behavior, and you can implement shopping carts.

Since version 4, PHP has included native session control functions. The approach to session control has changed slightly with the introduction of the superglobal variables; the $_SESSION superglobal is now available for use.

Understanding Basic Session Functionality

Sessions in PHP are driven by a unique session ID, a cryptographically random number. This session ID is generated by PHP and stored on the client side for the lifetime of a session. It can be either stored on a user's computer in a cookie or passed along through URLs.

The session ID acts as a key that allows you to register particular variables as so-called *session variables*. The contents of these variables are stored at the server. The session ID is the only information visible at the client side. If, at the time of a particular connection to your site, the session ID is visible either through a cookie or the URL, you can access the session variables stored on the server for that session. By default, the session variables are stored in flat files on the server. (You can change this to use a database if you are willing to write your own functions; you'll learn more on this topic in the section "Configuring Session Control.")

You have probably used websites that store a session ID in the URL. If your URL contains a string of random-looking data, it is likely to be some form of session control.

Cookies are a different solution to the problem of preserving state across a number of transactions while still having a clean-looking URL.

What Is a Cookie?

A *cookie* is a small piece of information that scripts can store on a client-side machine. You can set a cookie on a user's machine by sending an HTTP header containing data in the following format:

```
Set-Cookie: NAME=VALUE; [expires=DATE;] [path=PATH;]
 [domain=DOMAIN_NAME;] [secure]
```

This creates a cookie called NAME with the value VALUE. The other parameters are all optional. The expires field sets a date beyond which the cookie is no longer relevant. (Note that if no expiry date is set, the cookie is effectively permanent unless you or the user manually delete it.) Together, the path and domain can be used to specify the URL or URLs for which the cookie is relevant. The secure keyword means that the cookie will not be sent over a plain HTTP connection.

When a browser connects to an URL, it first searches the cookies stored locally. If any of them are relevant to the URL being connected to, they will be transmitted back to the server.

Setting Cookies from PHP

You can manually set cookies in PHP using the setcookie() function. It has the following prototype:

```
bool setcookie (string name [, string value [, int expire [, string path
[, string domain [, int secure]]]]])
```

The parameters correspond exactly to the ones in the Set-Cookie header mentioned previously.

If you set a cookie as

```
setcookie ('mycookie', 'value');
```

when the user visits the next page in your site (or reloads the current page), you will have access to the cookie via either `$_COOKIE['mycookie']` or `$HTTP_COOKIE_VARS["mycookie"]`. (Or, if you have `register_globals` turned on, you will have access directly as `$mycookie`.)

You can delete a cookie by calling `setcookie()` again with the same cookie name and an expiry time in the past. You can also set a cookie manually via the `header()` function and the cookie syntax given previously. One tip is that cookie headers must be sent *before any other headers*; otherwise, they will not work. (This is a cookie limitation rather than a PHP limitation.)

Using Cookies with Sessions

Cookies have some associated problems: Some browsers do not accept cookies, and some users might have disabled cookies in their browsers. This is one of the reasons PHP sessions use a dual cookie/URL method. (We discuss this method shortly.)

When you are using PHP sessions, you do not have to manually set cookies. The session functions take care of this task for you.

You can use the function `session_get_cookie_params()` to see the contents of the cookie set by session control. It returns an array containing the elements `lifetime`, `path`, `domain`, and `secure`.

You can also use

```
session_set_cookie_params($lifetime, $path, $domain [, $secure]);
```

to set the session cookie parameters.

If you want to read more about cookies, you can consult the cookie specification on Netscape's site:

http://wp.netscape.com/newsref/std/cookie_spec.html

(You can ignore the fact that this document calls itself a "preliminary specification"; it's been that way since 1995 and is as close to a standard as a document could be without actually being called a standard!)

Storing the Session ID

PHP uses cookies by default with sessions. If possible, a cookie will be set to store the session ID.

The other method it can use is adding the session ID to the URL. You can set this to happen automatically if you set the `session.use_trans_sid` directive in the `php.ini` file. It is off by default.

Alternatively, you can manually embed the session ID in links so that it is passed along. The session ID is stored in the constant SID. To pass it along manually, you add it to the end of a link similar to a GET parameter:

```
<A HREF="link.php?<?php echo strip_tags(SID); ?>">
```

(The `strip_tags()` function is used here to avoid cross-site scripting attacks.)

Compiling with `--enable-trans-sid` is generally easier, however.

Implementing Simple Sessions

The basic steps of using sessions are

- Starting a session
- Registering session variables
- Using session variables
- Deregistering variables and destroying the session

Note that these steps don't necessarily all happen in the same script, and some of them happen in multiple scripts. Let's examine each of these steps in turn.

Starting a Session

Before you can use session functionality, you need to actually begin a session. There are two ways you can do this.

The first, and simplest, is to begin a script with a call to the `session_start()` function:

```
session_start();
```

This function checks to see whether there is already a current session. If not, it will essentially create one, providing access to the superglobal `$_SESSION` array. If a session already exists, `session_start()` loads the registered session variables so that you can use them.

It's a good idea to call `session_start()` at the start of all your scripts that use sessions.

The second way you can begin a session is to set PHP to start one automatically when someone comes to your site. You can do this by using the `session.auto_start` option in your `php.ini` file; we look at this approach when we discuss configuration. This method has one big disadvantage: With `auto_start` enabled, you cannot use objects as session variables.

Registering Session Variables

The way you register session variables has recently changed in PHP. Session variables have been stored in the superglobal array `$_SESSION` since PHP 4.1, and also in the older `$HTTP_SESSION_VARS`. We recommend you use `$_SESSION`. To create a session variable, you simply set an element in this array, as follows:

```
$_SESSION['myvar'] = 5;
```

If you are using an older version of PHP, for a variable to be tracked from one script to another, you would have registered it with a call to `session_register()`. This use is now deprecated.

The session variable you have just created will be tracked until the session ends or until you manually unset it.

Using Session Variables

To bring session variables into scope so that they can be used, you must first start a session using `session_start()`. You can then access the variable via the `$_SESSION` superglobal array—for example, as `$_SESSION['myvar']`.

When you are using an object as a session variable, it is important that you include the class definition before calling `session_start()` to reload the session variables. This way, PHP knows how to reconstruct the session object.

If you have `register_globals` turned on, you can access session variables via their short form names—for example, `$myvar`—but this approach is not recommended. If you do have `register_globals` on, bear in mind that a session variable cannot be overridden by GET or POST data, which is a good security feature, but something to bear in mind when you're coding.

On the other hand, you need to be careful when checking whether session variables have been set (via, say, `isset()` or `empty()`). Remember that variables can be set by the user via GET or POST. You can check a variable to see whether it is a registered session variable by checking in `$_SESSION`.

You can check this directly using the following, for example:

```
if (isset($_SESSION['myvar'])) ...
```

Unsetting Variables and Destroying the Session

When you are finished with a session variable, you can unset it. You can do this directly by unsetting the appropriate element of the `$_SESSION` array, as in this example:

```
unset($_SESSION['myvar']);
```

Note that the use of `session_unregister()` and `session_unset()` is no longer required and is not recommended. These functions were used prior to the introduction of `$_SESSION`.

You should not try to unset the whole `$_SESSION` array because doing so will effectively disable sessions. To unset all the session variables at once, use

```
$_SESSION = array();
```

When you are finished with a session, you should first unset all the variables and then call

```
session_destroy();
```

to clean up the session ID.

Creating a Simple Session Example

Some of this discussion might seem abstract, so let's look at an example. Here, you'll implement a set of three pages.

On the first page, start a session and create the variable $_SESSION['sess_var']. The code to do this is shown in Listing 22.1.

Listing 22.1 `page1.php`—**Starting a Session and Creating a Session Variable**

```php
<?php
  session_start();

  $_SESSION['sess_var'] = "Hello world!";

  echo 'The content of $_SESSION[\'sess_var\'] is '
       .$_SESSION['sess_var'].'<br />';
?>
<a href="page2.php">Next page</a>
```

This script creates the variable and sets its value. The output of this script is shown in Figure 22.1.

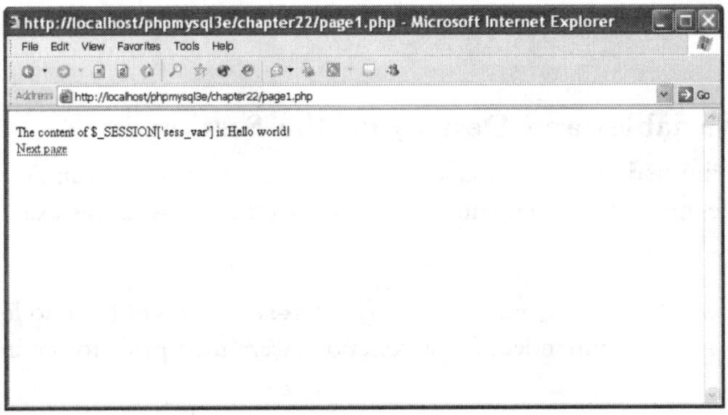

Figure 22.1   Initial value of the session variable shown by `page1.php`.

The *final* value of the variable on the page is the one that will be available on subsequent pages. At the end of the script, the session variable is *serialized*, or frozen, until it is reloaded via the next call to `session_start()`.

You can therefore begin the next script by calling `session_start()`. This script is shown in Listing 22.2.

Listing 22.2   page2.php—**Accessing a Session Variable and Unsetting It**

```php
<?php
  session_start();

  echo 'The content of $_SESSION[\'sess_var\'] is '
       .$_SESSION['sess_var'].'<br />';

  unset($_SESSION['sess_var']);
?>
<a href="page3.php">Next page</a>
```

After you call session_start(), the variable $_SESSION ['sess_var'] is available with its previously stored value, as you can see in Figure 22.2.

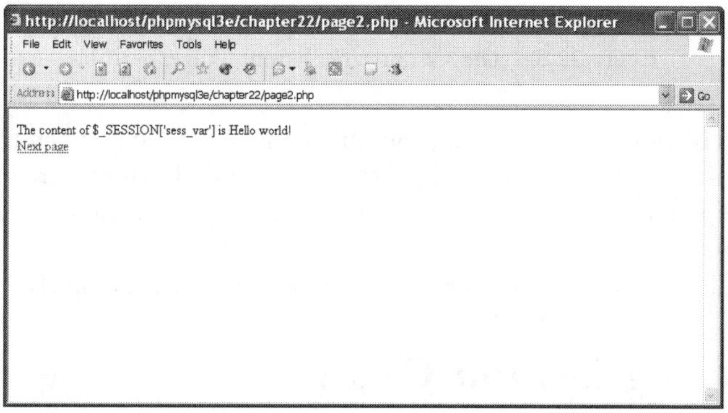

Figure 22.2   The value of the session variable is passed along via the session ID to page2.php.

After you have used the variable, you unset it. The session still exists, but the variable $_SESSIONx['sess_var'] no longer exists.

Finally, you pass along to page3.php, the final script in the example. The code for this script is shown in Listing 22.3.

Listing 22.3   page3.php—**Ending the Session**

```php
<?php

  session_start();

  echo 'The content of $_SESSION[\'sess_var\'] is '
       .$_SESSION['sess_var'].'<br />';

  session_destroy();
?>
```

As you can see in Figure 22.3, you no longer have access to the persistent value of $_SESSION['sess_var'].

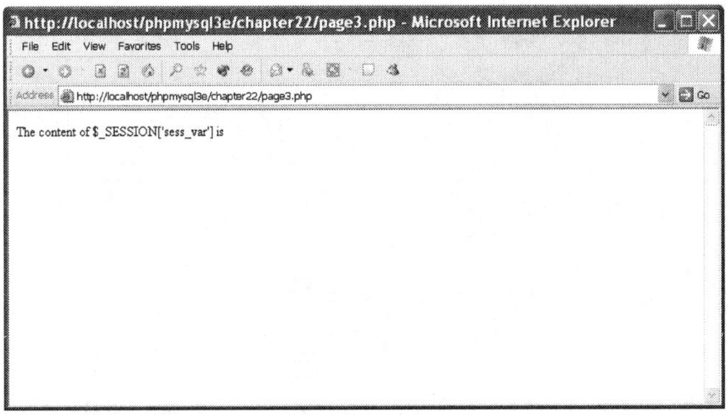

Figure 22.3   The session variable is no longer available.

With some PHP versions prior to 4.3, you might encounter a bug when trying to unset elements of $HTTP_SESSION_VARS or $_SESSION. If you find that you are unable to unset elements (that is, they stay set), you can revert to using session_unregister() to clear these variables.

You finish by calling session_destroy() to dispose of the session ID.

Configuring Session Control

There is a set of configuration options for sessions that you can set in your php.ini file. Some of the more useful options, and a description of each, are shown in Table 22.1.

Table 22.1   **Session Configuration Options**

Option Name	Default	Effect
session.auto_start	0 (disabled)	Automatically starts sessions.
session.cache_expire	180	Sets time-to-live for cached session pages, in minutes.
session.cookie_domain	none	Specifies the domain to set in the session cookie.
session.cookie_lifetime	0	Sets how long the session ID cookie will last on the user's machine. The default, 0, will last until the browser is closed.
session.cookie_path	/	Specifies the path to set in the session cookie.
session.name	PHPSESSID	Sets the name of the session that is used as the cookie name on a user's system.

Table 22.1   **Continued**

Option Name	Default	Effect
session.save_handler	files	Defines where session data is stored. You can set this option to point to a database, but you have to write your own functions.
session.save_path	/tmp	Sets the path where session data is stored. More generally, sets the argument passed to the save handled and defined by session.save_handler.
session.use_cookies	1 (enabled)	Configures sessions to use cookies on the client side.

Implementing Authentication with Session Control

Finally, we look at a more substantial example using session control.

Possibly the most common use of session control is to keep track of users after they have been authenticated via a login mechanism. In this example, you combine authentication from a MySQL database with use of sessions to provide this functionality. This functionality forms the basis of the project in Chapter 26, "Building User Authentication and Personalization," and will be reused in the other projects. You will reuse the authentication database you set up in Chapter 16, "Implementing Authentication with PHP and MySQL." You can check Listing 16.3 in that chapter for details of the database.

The example consists of three simple scripts. The first, authmain.php, provides a login form and authentication for members of the website. The second, members_only.php, displays information only to members who have logged in successfully. The third, logout.php, logs out a member.

To understand how this example works, look at Figure 22.4, which shows the initial page displayed by authmain.php.

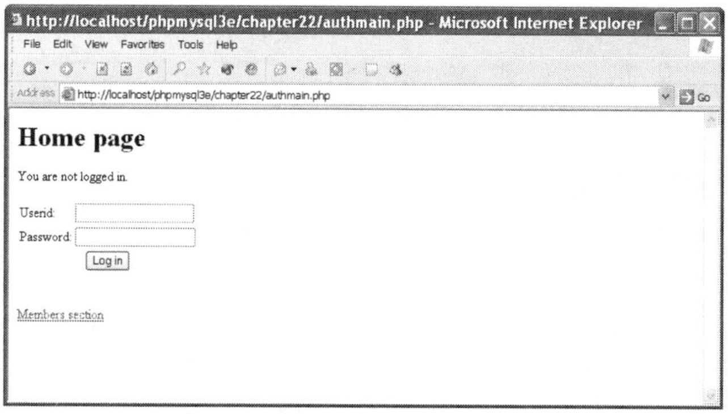

Figure 22.4   Because the user has not yet logged in, show her a login page.

This page gives the user a place to log in. If she attempts to access the Members section without logging in first, she will get the message shown in Figure 22.5.

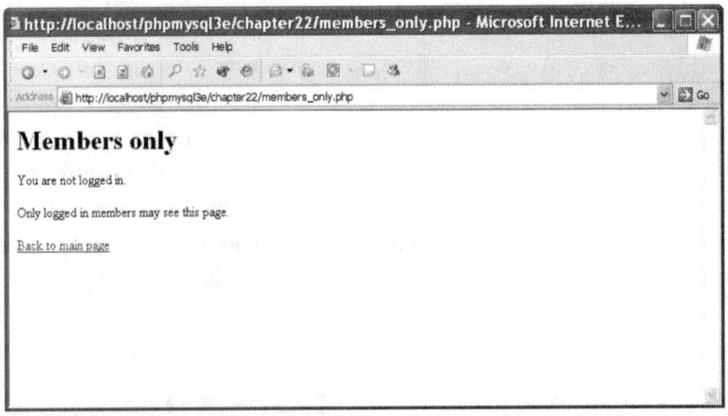

Figure 22.5   Users who haven't logged in can't see the site content; they will be shown this message instead.

If the user logs in first (with username: `testuser` and password: `password`, as set up in Chapter 16), however, and then attempts to see the Members page, she will get the output shown in Figure 22.6.

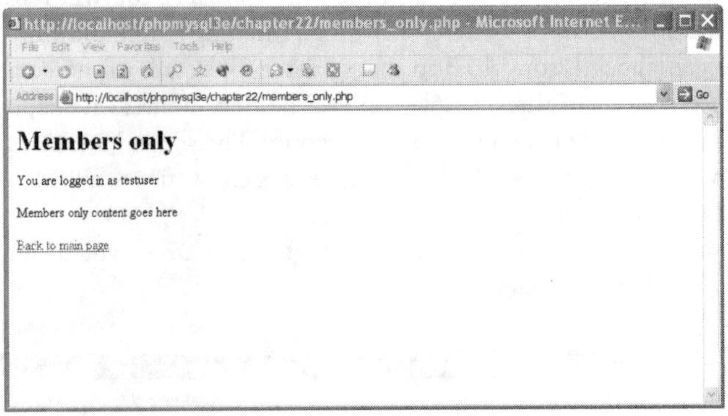

Figure 22.6   After the user has logged in, she can access the Members' areas.

First, let's look at the code for this application. Most of the code is in `authmain.php`, shown in Listing 22.4. Then we'll go through it bit by bit.

Listing 22.4 `authmain.php`—**The Main Part of the Authentication Application**

```php
<?php
session_start();

if (isset($_POST['userid']) && isset($_POST['password']))
{
  // if the user has just tried to log in
  $userid = $_POST['userid'];
  $password = $_POST['password'];

  $db_conn = new mysqli('localhost', 'webauth', 'webauth', 'auth');

  if (mysqli_connect_errno()) {
   echo 'Connection to database failed:'.mysqli_connect_error();
   exit();
  }

  $query = 'select * from authorized_users '
          ."where name='$userid' "
          ." and password=sha1('$password')";

  $result = $db_conn->query($query);
  if ($result->num_rows >0 )
  {
    // if they are in the database register the user id
    $_SESSION['valid_user'] = $userid;
  }
  $db_conn->close();
}
?>
<html>
<body>
<h1>Home page</h1>
<?
  if (isset($_SESSION['valid_user']))
  {
    echo 'You are logged in as: '.$_SESSION['valid_user'].' <br />';
    echo '<a href="logout.php">Log out</a><br />';
  }
  else
  {
    if (isset($userid))
    {
```

Listing 22.4 **Continued**

```
      // if they've tried and failed to log in
      echo 'Could not log you in.<br />';
    }
    else
    {
      // they have not tried to log in yet or have logged out
      echo 'You are not logged in.<br />';
    }

    // provide form to log in
    echo '<form method="post" action="authmain.php">';
    echo '<table>';
    echo '<tr><td>Userid:</td>';
    echo '<td><input type="text" name="userid"></td></tr>';
    echo '<tr><td>Password:</td>';
    echo '<td><input type="password" name="password"></td></tr>';
    echo '<tr><td colspan="2" align="center">';
    echo '<input type="submit" value="Log in"></td></tr>';
    echo '</table></form>';
  }
?>
<br />
<a href="members_only.php">Members section</a>
</body>
</html>
```

Some reasonably complicated logic is included in this script because it displays the login form, is also the action of the form, and contains HTML for a successful and failed login attempt.

The script's activities revolve around the valid_user session variable. The basic idea is that if someone logs in successfully, you will register a session variable called $_SESSION['valid_user'] that contains her userid.

The first thing you do in the script is call session_start(). This call loads in the session variable valid_user if it has been created.

In the first pass through the script, none of the if conditions apply, so the user falls through to the end of the script, where you tell her that she is not logged in and provide her with a form to do so:

```
echo '<form method="post" action="authmain.php">';
echo '<table>';
echo '<tr><td>Userid:</td>';
echo '<td><input type="text" name="userid"></td></tr>';
echo '<tr><td>Password:</td>';
echo '<td><input type="password" name="password"></td></tr>';
```

```
echo '<tr><td colspan="2" align="center">';
echo '<input type="submit" value="Log in"></td></tr>';
echo '</table></form>';
```

When the user clicks the submit button on the form, this script is reinvoked, and you start again from the top. This time, you will have a userid and password to authenticate, stored as $_POST['userid'] and $_POST['password']. If these variables are set, you go into the authentication block:

```
if (isset($_POST['userid']) && isset($_POST['password']))
{
  // if the user has just tried to log in
  $userid = $_POST['userid'];
  $password = $_POST['password'];

  $db_conn = new mysqli('localhost', 'webauth', 'webauth', 'auth');

  if (mysqli_connect_errno()) {
   echo 'Connection to database failed:'.mysqli_connect_error();
   exit();
  }

  $query = 'select * from authorized_users '
          ."where name='$userid' "
          ." and password=sha1('$password')";

  $result = $db_conn->query($query);
```

You connect to a MySQL database and check the userid and password. If they are a matching pair in the database, you create the variable $_SESSION['valid_user'], which contains the userid for this particular user, so you know who is logged in further down the track:

```
  if ($result->num_rows >0 )
  {
    // if they are in the database register the user id
    $_SESSION['valid_user'] = $userid;
  }
  $db_conn->close();
}
```

Because you now know who the user is, you don't need to show her the login form again. Instead, you can tell her you know who she is and give her the option to log out:

```
if (isset($_SESSION['valid_user']))
{
    echo 'You are logged in as: '.$_SESSION['valid_user'].' <br />';
    echo '<a href="logout.php">Log out</a><br />';
}
```

If you tried to log her in and failed for some reason, you'll have a userid but not a
`$_SESSION['valid_user']` variable, so you can give her an error message:

```
if (isset($userid))
{
  // if they've tried and failed to log in
  echo 'Could not log you in.<br />';
}
```

That's it for the main script. Now, let's look at the Members page. The code for this
script is shown in Listing 22.5.

Listing 22.5 `members_only.php`—**The Code for the Members' Section of the Website
Checks for Valid Users**

```
<?php
  session_start();

  echo '<h1>Members only</h1>';

  // check session variable

  if (isset($_SESSION['valid_user']))
  {
    echo '<p>You are logged in as '.$_SESSION['valid_user'].'</p>';
    echo '<p>Members only content goes here</p>';
  }
  else
  {
    echo '<p>You are not logged in.</p>';
    echo '<p>Only logged in members may see this page.</p>';
  }

  echo '<a href="authmain.php">Back to main page</a>';
?>
```

This code simply starts a session and checks whether the current session contains a registered user by checking whether the value of `$_SESSION['valid_user']` is set. If the
user is logged in, you show her the members' content; otherwise, you tell her that she is
not authorized.

Finally, the `logout.php` script signs a user out of the system. The code for this script
is shown in Listing 22.6.

Listing 22.6   `logout.php`— **This Script Deregisters the Session Variable and Destroys the Session**

```php
<?php
  session_start();

  // store to test if they *were* logged in
  $old_user = $_SESSION['valid_user'];
  unset($_SESSION['valid_user']);
  session_destroy();
?>
<html>
<body>
<h1>Log out</h1>
<?php
  if (!empty($old_user))
  {
    echo 'Logged out.<br />';
  }
  else
  {
    // if they weren't logged in but came to this page somehow
    echo 'You were not logged in, and so have not been logged out.<br />';
  }
?>
<a href="authmain.php">Back to main page</a>
</body>
</html>
```

This code is simple, but you need to do a little fancy footwork. You start a session, store the user's old username, unset the `valid_user` variable, and destroy the session. You then give the user a message that will be different if she was logged out or was not logged in to begin with.

This simple set of scripts forms the basis for a lot of the work we'll do in later chapters.

Further Reading

You can read more about cookies here:

http://home.netscape.com/newsref/std/cookie_spec.html

Next

We're almost finished with this part of the book. Before we move on to the projects, we briefly discuss some of the useful odds and ends of PHP that we haven't covered elsewhere.

## 23

Other Useful Features

Some useful PHP functions and features do not fit into any particular category. This chapter explains these features.

Key topics covered in this chapter include

- Using magic quotes
- Evaluating strings with `eval()`
- Terminating execution with `die` and `exit`
- Serializing variables and objects
- Getting information about the PHP environment
- Temporarily altering the runtime environment
- Loading PHP extensions
- Highlighting source code
- Using PHP on the command line

Using Magic Quotes

You have probably noticed that you need to be careful when using quotation marks (' and ") and back slashes (\) within strings. PHP gets confused by an attempted string statement like

```
echo "color = "#FFFFFF"";
```

and gives a parse error. To include quotation marks inside a string, use the quote type that is different from the quotes enclosing the string. For example, both

```
echo "color = '#FFFFFF'";
```

and

```
echo 'color = "#FFFFFF"';
```

are valid.

The same problem occurs with user input, as well as input and output to or from other programs.

Trying to run a `mysql` query like

```
insert into company values ('Bob's Auto Parts');
```

produces similar confusion in MySQL's parser.

We have already looked at the use of `addslashes()` and `stripslashes()` that escape out any single quotation mark, double quotation mark, backslash, and NULL characters.

PHP has a useful capability to automatically or magically add and strip slashes for you. With two settings in your `php.ini` file, you can turn on or off magic quoting for GET, POST, cookie data, and other sources.

The value of the `magic_quotes_gpc` directive controls whether magic quoting is used for GET, POST, and cookie operations.

With `magic_quotes_gpc` on, if somebody typed `"Bob's Auto Parts"` into a form on your site, your script would receive `"Bob\'s Auto Parts"` because the quote is escaped for you. This behavior can be very handy, but you need to know that it is happening so you can remember to remove the slashes before echoing the data back to your users. This is easy if your code runs on one server, but if you are writing code to distribute, you might want to make it work with or without magic quotes.

The function `get_magic_quotes_gpc()` returns either 1 or 0, telling you the current value of `magic_quotes_gpc`. This is most useful for testing if you need to use `stripslashes()` on data received from the user.

The value of `magic_quotes_runtime` controls whether magic quoting is used by functions that get data from databases and files. To get the value of `magic_quotes_runtime`, use the function `get_magic_quotes_runtime()`. This function returns either 1 or 0. Magic quoting can be turned on for a particular script using the function `set_magic_quotes_runtime()`.

By default, `magic_quotes_gpc` is on and `magic_quotes_runtime` is off.

Evaluating Strings: `eval()`

The function `eval()` evaluates a string as PHP code. For example,

```
eval ( "echo 'Hello World';" );
```

takes the contents of the string and executes it. This line produces the same output as

```
echo 'Hello World';
```

The function `eval()` can be useful in a variety of cases. You might want to store blocks of code in a database, retrieve them, and then evaluate them at a later point. You also might want to generate code in a loop and then use `eval()` to execute it.

The most common use for `eval()` is as part of a templating system. You can load a mixture of HTML, PHP, and plain text from a database. Your templating system can apply formatting to this content and then run it through `eval()` to execute any PHP code.

You can usefully use `eval()` to update or correct existing code. If you had a large collection of scripts that needed a predictable change, it would be possible (but inefficient) to write a script that loads an old script into a string, runs `regexp` to make changes, and then uses `eval()` to execute the modified script.

It is even conceivable that a very trusting person somewhere might want to allow PHP code to be entered in a browser and executed on her server.

Terminating Execution: `die` and `exit`

So far in this book, we have used the language construct `exit` to stop execution of a script. As you probably recall, it appears on a line by itself, like this:

```
exit;
```

It does not return anything. You can alternatively use its alias `die()`.

For a slightly more useful termination, you can pass a parameter to `exit()`. You can use this approach to output an error message or execute a function before terminating a script. This will be familiar to Perl programmers. For example,

```
exit('Script ending now');
```

More commonly, it is combined with OR with a statement that might fail, such as opening a file or connecting to a database:

```
mysql_query($query) or die('Could not execute query');
```

Instead of just printing an error message, you can run one last function before the script terminates:

```
function err_msg()
{
    return 'MySQL error was: '.mysql_error();
}

mysql_query($query) or die(err_msg());
```

This approach can be useful as a way of giving the user some reason why the script failed or as a way of closing HTML elements or clearing a half-completed page from the output buffer.

Alternatively, you could email yourself so that you know whether a major error has occurred, or you could add errors to a log file or throw an exception.

Serializing Variables and Objects

Serialization is the process of turning anything you can store in a PHP variable or object into a bytestream that can be stored in a database or passed along via a URL from page to page. Without this process, it is difficult to store or pass the entire contents of an array or object.

Serialization has decreased in usefulness since the introduction of session control. Serializing data is principally used for the types of things you would now use session control for. In fact, the session control functions serialize session variables to store them between HTTP requests.

However, you might still want to store a PHP array or object in a file or database. If you do, you need to know how to use these two functions: `serialize()` and `unserialize()`.

You can call the `serialize()` function as follows:

```
$serial_object = serialize($my_object);
```

If you want to know what the serialization actually does, look at what is returned from `serialize()`. This line turns the contents of an object or array into a string.

For example, you can look at the output of running `serialize()` on a simple employee object, defined and instantiated thus:

```
class employee
{
  var $name;
  var $employee_id;
}


$this_emp = new employee;
$this_emp->name = 'Fred';
$this_emp->employee_id = 5324;
```

If you serialize this and echo it to the browser, the output is

```
O:8:"employee":2:{s:4:"name";s:4:"Fred";s:11:"employee_id";i:5324;}
```

You can easily see the relationship between the original object data here and the serialized data.

Because the serialized data is just text, you can write it to a database or whatever you like. Be aware that you should use `addslashes()` on any data before writing it to a database, as per usual. You can see the need for this by noting the quotation marks in the previous serialized string.

To get the object back, call `unserialize()`:

```
$new_object = unserialize($serial_object);
```

Obviously, if you called `addslashes()` before putting the object into a database, you will need to call `stripslashes()` before unserializing the string.

Another point to note when serializing classes or using them as session variables: PHP needs to know the structure of a class before it can reinstantiate the class. Therefore, you need to include the class definition file before calling `session_start()` or `unserialize()`.

Getting Information About the PHP Environment

A number of functions can be used to find out information about how PHP is configured.

Finding Out What Extensions Are Loaded

You can easily see what function sets are available and what functions are available in each of those sets by using the get_loaded_extensions() and get_extension_funcs() functions.

The get_loaded_extensions() function returns an array of all the function sets currently available to PHP. Given the name of a particular function set or extension, get_extension_funcs() returns an array of the functions in that set.

The script in Listing 23.1 lists all the extension functions available to your PHP installation by using these two functions.

Listing 23.1 list_functions.php— **Lists All the Extensions Available to PHP and, with Each Extension, Provides a Bulleted List of Functions in That Extension**

```php
<?php
  echo 'Function sets supported in this install are:<br />';
  $extensions = get_loaded_extensions();
  foreach ($extensions as $each_ext)
  {
    echo "$each_ext <br />";
    echo '<ul>';
    $ext_funcs = get_extension_funcs($each_ext);
    foreach($ext_funcs as $func)
    {
      echo "<li> $func </li>";
    }
    echo '</ul>';
  }
?>
```

Note that the get_loaded_extensions() function doesn't take any parameters, and the get_extension_funcs() function takes the name of the extension as its only parameter.

This information can be helpful if you are trying to tell whether you have successfully installed an extension or if you are trying to write portable code that generates useful diagnostic messages when installing.

Identifying the Script Owner

You can find out the user who owns the script being run with a call to the
`get_current_user()` function, as follows:

```
echo get_current_user();
```

This information can sometimes be useful for solving permissions issues.

Finding Out When the Script Was Modified

Adding a last modification date to each page in a site is a fairly popular thing to do.

You can check the last modification date of a script with the `getlastmod()` (note the
lack of underscores in the function name) function, as follows:

```
echo date('g:i a, j M Y',getlastmod());
```

The function `getlastmod()` returns a Unix timestamp, which you can feed to `date()`,
as done here, to produce a human-readable date.

Loading Extensions Dynamically

You can actually load extension libraries at runtime, if they are not compiled in, by using
the `dl()` function. This function expects as a parameter the name of the file containing
the library. Under Unix, these are filenames ending in `.so`; under Windows, they end
in `.dll`.

An example of a call to `dl()` is

```
dl('php_gd2.dll');
```

This call dynamically loads the gd2 (image generation) extension (on a Windows
machine).

You shouldn't specify the directory where the file lives. Instead, you should configure
this in the `php.ini` file. A directive called `extension_dir` specifies the directory where
PHP will look for libraries to dynamically load.

If you find you are having trouble dynamically loading extensions, also check your
`php.ini` file for the `enable_dl` directive. If it's off, you won't be able to dynamically
load extensions. Particularly if the machine you work on is not your own, this directive
might be disabled for security reasons. You also cannot use `dl()` if PHP is running in
safe mode.

Temporarily Altering the Runtime Environment

You can view the directives set in the `php.ini` file or change them for the life of a single script. This capability can be particularly useful, for example, in conjunction with the
`max_execution_time` directive if you know your script will take some time to run.

You can access and change the directives using the twin functions `ini_get()` and
`ini_set()`. Listing 23.2 shows a simple script that uses these functions.

Listing 23.2   `iniset.php`— **Resets Variables from the** `php.ini` **File**

```php
<?php
  $old_max_execution_time = ini_set('max_execution_time', 120);
  echo "old timeout is $old_max_execution_time <br />";

  $max_execution_time = ini_get('max_execution_time');
  echo "new timeout is $max_execution_time <br />";
?>
```

The `ini_set()` function takes two parameters. The first is the name of the configuration directive from `php.ini` that you would like to change, and the second is the value you would like to change it to. It returns the previous value of the directive.

In this case, you reset the value from the default 30-second (or whatever is set in your `php.ini` file) maximum time for a script to run to 120 seconds.

The `ini_get()` function simply checks the value of a particular configuration directive. The directive name should be passed to it as a string. Here, it just checks that the value really did change.

Not all INI options can be set this way. Each option has a level at which it can be set. The possible levels are

- `PHP_INI_USER`—You can change these values in your scripts with `ini_set()`.

- `PHP_INI_PERDIR`—You can change these values in `php.ini` or in `.htaccess` or `httpd.conf` files if using Apache. The fact that you can change them in `.htaccess` files means that you can change these values on a per-directory basis—hence the name.

- `PHP_INI_SYSTEM`—You can change these values in the `php.ini` or `httpd.conf` files.

- `PHP_INI_ALL`—You can change these values in any of the preceding ways—that is, in a script, in an `.htaccess` file, or in your `httpd.conf` or `php.ini` files.

The full set of `ini` options and the levels at which they can be set is in the PHP manual at http://www.php.net/ini_set.

Highlighting Source Code

PHP comes with a built-in syntax highlighter, similar to many IDEs. In particular, it is useful for sharing code with others or presenting it for discussion on a web page.

The functions `show_source()` and `highlight_file()` are the same. (The `show_source()` function is actually an alias for `highlight_file()`.) Both of these functions accept a filename as the parameter. (This file should be a PHP file; otherwise, you won't get a very meaningful result.) Consider this example:

```php
show_source('list_functions.php');
```

The file is echoed to the browser with the text highlighted in various colors depending on whether it is a string, a comment, a keyword, or HTML. The output is printed on a background color. Content that doesn't fit into any of these categories is printed in a default color.

The `highlight_string()` function works similarly, but it takes a string as parameter and prints it to the browser in a syntax-highlighted format.

You can set the colors for syntax highlighting in your `php.ini` file. The section you want to change looks like this:

```
; Colors for Syntax Highlighting mode
highlight.string    =    #DD0000
highlight.comment   =    #FF9900
highlight.keyword   =    #007700
highlight.bg        =    #FFFFFF
highlight.default   =    #0000BB
highlight.html      =    #000000
```

The colors are in standard HTML RGB format.

Using PHP on the Command Line

You can usefully write or download many small programs and run them on the command line. If you are on a Unix system, these programs are usually written in a shell scripting language or Perl. If you are on a Windows system, they are usually written as a batch file.

You probably first came to PHP for a web project, but the same text processing facilities that make it a strong web language make it a strong command-line utility program.

There are three ways to execute a PHP script at the command line: from a file, through a pipe, or directly on the command line.

To execute a PHP script in a file, make sure that the PHP executable (`php` or `php.exe` depending on your operating system) is in your path and call it with the name of script as an argument. Here's an example:

```
php myscript.php
```

The file `myscript.php` is just a normal PHP file, so it contains any normal PHP syntax within PHP tags.

To pass code through a pipe, you can run any program that generates a valid PHP script as output and pipe that to the `php` executable. The following example uses the program `echo` to give a one-line program:

```
echo '<?php for($i=1; $i<10; $i++) echo $i; ?>' | php
```

Again, the PHP code here is enclosed in PHP tags (`<?php` and `?>`). Also note that this is the command-line program `echo`, not the PHP language construct.

A one-line program of this nature would be easier to pass directly from the command line, as in this example:

```
php -r 'for($i=1; $i<10; $i++) echo $i;'
```

The situation is slightly different here. The PHP code passed in this string is not enclosed in PHP tags. If you do enclose the string in PHP tags, you will get a syntax error.

The useful PHP programs that you can write for command-line use are unlimited. You can write installers for your PHP applications. You can knock together a quick script to reformat a text file before importing it to your database. You can even make a script do any repetitive tasks that you might need to do at the command line; a good candidate would be a script to copy all your PHP files, images, and MySQL table structures from your staging web server to your production one.

Next

Part V, "Building Practical PHP and MySQL Projects," covers a number of relatively complicated practical projects using PHP and MySQL. These projects provide useful examples for similar tasks you might have and demonstrate the use of PHP and MySQL on larger projects.

Chapter 24, "Using PHP and MySQL for Large Projects," addresses some of the issues you face when coding larger projects using PHP. They include software engineering principles such as design, documentation, and change management.

V

Building Practical PHP and MySQL Projects

24

Using PHP and MySQL for Large Projects

IN THE EARLIER PARTS OF THIS BOOK, WE DISCUSSED various components of and uses for PHP and MySQL. Although we tried to make all the examples interesting and relevant, they were reasonably simple, consisting of one or two scripts of up to 100 or so lines of code.

When you are building real-world web applications, writing code is rarely this simple. A few years ago, an "interactive" website had form mail and that was it. However, these days, websites have become web applications—that is, regular pieces of software delivered over the Web. This change in focus means a change in scale. Websites grow from a handful of scripts to thousands and thousands of lines of code. Projects of this size require planning and management just like any other software development.

Before we look at the projects in this part of the book, let's look at some of the techniques that can be used to manage sizable web projects. This is an emerging art, and getting it right is obviously difficult: You can see this by observation in the marketplace.

Key topics covered in this chapter include

- Applying software engineering to web development
- Planning and running a web application project
- Reusing code
- Writing maintainable code
- Implementing version control
- Choosing a development environment
- Documenting your project
- Prototyping
- Separating logic, content, and presentation: PHP, HTML, and CSS
- Optimizing code

Applying Software Engineering to Web Development

As you probably already know, software engineering is the application of a systematic, quantifiable approach to software development. That is, it is the application of engineering principles to software development.

Software engineering is also an approach that is noticeably lacking in many web projects for two main reasons. The first reason is that web development is often managed in the same way as the development of written reports. It is an exercise in document structure, graphic design, and production. This is a document-oriented paradigm. This approach is all well and good for static sites of small to medium size, but as the amount of dynamic content in websites is increased to the level in which the websites offer services rather than documents, this paradigm no longer fits. Many people do not think to use software engineering practices for a web project at all.

The second reason software engineering practices are not used is that web application development is different from normal application development in many ways. Developers deal with much shorter lead times, a constant pressure to have the site built *now*. Software engineering is all about performing tasks in an orderly, planned manner and spending time on planning. With web projects, often the perception is that you don't have the time to plan.

When you fail to plan web projects, you end up with the same problems you do when you fail to plan any software project: buggy applications, missed deadlines, and unreadable code.

The trick, then, is in finding the parts of software engineering that work in this new discipline of web application development and discarding the parts that don't.

Planning and Running a Web Application Project

There is no best methodology or project life cycle for web projects. There are, however, a number of things you should consider doing for your project. We list them here and discuss some of them in more detail in the following sections. These considerations are in a specific order, but you don't have to follow this order if it doesn't suit your project. The emphasis here is on being aware of the issues and choosing techniques that will work for you.

- Before you begin, think about what you are trying to build. Think about the goal. Think about who is going to use your web application—that is, your targeted audience. Many technically perfect web projects fail because nobody checked whether users were interested in such an application.

- Try to break down your application into components. What parts or process steps does your application have? How will each of those components work? How will they fit together? Drawing up scenarios, storyboards, or even use cases can be useful for figuring out this step.

- After you have a list of components, see which of them already exist. If a prewritten module has that functionality, look at using it. Don't forget to look inside and outside your organization for existing code. Particularly in the open source community, many preexisting code components are freely available for use. Decide what code you have to write from scratch and roughly how big that job is.

- Make decisions about process issues. This step is ignored too often in web projects. By process issues, we mean, for example, coding standards, directory structures, management of version control, development environment, documentation level and standards, and task allocations to team members.

- Build a prototype based on all the previous information. Show it to users. Iterate.

- Remember that, throughout this process, it is important and useful to separate content and logic in your application. We explain this idea in more detail shortly.

- Make any optimizations you think are necessary.

- As you go, test as thoroughly as you would with any software development project.

Reusing Code

Programmers often make the mistake of rewriting code that already exists. When you know what application components you need or—on a smaller scale—what functions you need, check what's available before beginning development.

One of the strengths of PHP as a language is its large built-in function library. Always check to see whether an existing function does what you are trying to do. Finding the one you want usually isn't too hard. A good way to do this is to browse the manual by function group.

Sometimes programmers rewrite functions accidentally because they haven't looked in the manual to see whether an existing function supplies the functionality they need. Always keep the manual bookmarked. Take note, however, that the online manual is updated quite frequently. The annotated manual is a fantastic resource because it contains comments, suggestions, and sample code from other users that often answer the same questions you might have after reading the basic manual page. It often contains bug reports and workarounds before they are fixed or documented in the documentation body.

You can reach the English language version at
http://www.php.net/manual/en/

Some programmers who come from a different language background might be tempted to write wrapper functions to essentially rename PHP's functions to match the language with which they are familiar. This practice is sometimes called *syntactic sugar*. It's a bad idea; it makes your code harder for others to read and maintain. If you're learning a new language, you should learn how to use it properly. In addition, adding a level of function call in this manner slows down your code. All things considered, you should avoid this approach.

If you find that the functionality you require is not in the main PHP library, you have two choices. If you need something relatively simple, you can choose to write your own function or object. However, if you're looking at building a fairly complex piece of functionality—such as a shopping cart, web email system, or web forums—you should not be surprised to find that somebody else has probably already built it. One of the strengths of working in the open source community is that code for application components such as these is often freely available. If you find a component similar to the one you want to build, even if it isn't exactly right, you can look at the source code as a starting point for modification or for building your own.

If you end up developing your own functions or components, you should seriously consider making them available to the PHP community after you have finished. This principle keeps the PHP developer community such a helpful, active, and knowledgeable group.

Writing Maintainable Code

The issue of maintainability is often overlooked in web applications, particularly because programmers often write them in a hurry. Getting started on the code and getting it finished quickly sometimes seem more important than planning it first. However, a little time invested up front can save you a lot of time further down the road when you're ready to build the next iteration of an application.

Coding Standards

Most large IT organizations have coding standards—guidelines to the house style for choosing file and variable names, guidelines for commenting code, guidelines for indenting code, and so on.

Because of the document paradigm often previously applied to web development, coding standards have sometimes been overlooked in this area. If you are coding on your own or in a small team, you can easily underestimate the importance of coding standards. Don't overlook such standards because your team and project might grow. Then you will end up not only with a mess on your hands, but also a bunch of programmers who can't make heads or tails of any of the existing code.

Defining Naming Conventions

The goals of defining a naming convention are

- To make the code easy to read. If you define variables and function names sensibly, you should be able to virtually read code as you would an English sentence, or at least pseudocode.
- To make identifier names easy to remember. If your identifiers are consistently formatted, remembering what you called a particular variable or function will be easier.

Variable names should describe the data they contain. If you are storing somebody's surname, call it $surname. You need to find a balance between length and readability. For example, storing the name in $n makes it easy to type, but the code is difficult to understand. Storing the name in $surname_of_the_current_user is more informative, but it's a lot to type (and therefore easier to make a typing error) and doesn't really add that much value.

You need to make a decision on capitalization. Variable names are case sensitive in PHP, as we've mentioned previously. You need to decide whether your variable names will be all lowercase, all uppercase, or a mix—for example, capitalizing the first letters of words. We tend to use all lowercase because this scheme is the easiest to remember for us.

Distinguishing between variables and constants with case is also a good idea. A common scheme is to use all lowercase for variables (for example, $result) and all uppercase for constants (for example, PI).

One bad practice some programmers use is to have two variables with the same name but different capitalization just because they can, such as $name and $Name. We hope it is obvious why this practice is a terrible idea.

It is also best to avoid amusing capitalization schemes such as $WaReZ because no one will be able to remember how it works.

You should also think about what scheme to use for multiword variable names. For example, we've seen all the following schemes:

```
$username
$user_name
$userName
```

It doesn't matter which you opt for, but you should try to be consistent about usage. You might also want to set a sensible maximum limit of two to three words in a variable name.

Function names have many of the same considerations, with a couple of extras. Function names should generally be verb oriented. Consider built-in PHP functions such as addslashes() or mysql_connect(), which describe what they are going to do to or with the parameters they are passed. This naming scheme greatly enhances code readability. Notice that these two functions have a different naming scheme for dealing with multiword function names. PHP's functions are inconsistent in this regard, partly as a result of having been written by a large group of people, but mostly because many function names have been adopted unchanged from various different languages and APIs.

Also remember that function names are not case sensitive in PHP. You should probably stick to a particular format anyway, just to avoid confusion.

You might want to consider using the module-naming scheme used in many PHP modules—that is, prefixing the name of functions with the module name. For example, all the improved MySQL functions begin with mysqli_, and all the IMAP functions begin with imap_. If, for example, you have a shopping cart module in your code, you could prefix the function in that module with cart_.

Note, however, that when PHP5 provides both a procedural and an object-oriented interface, the function names are different. Usually, the procedural ones use underlines (`my_function()`) and the object-oriented ones use what are called studlyCaps (`myFunction()`).

In the end, the conventions and standards you use when writing code don't really matter, as long as you apply some consistent guidelines.

Commenting Your Code

All programs should be commented to a sensible level. You might ask what level of commenting is sensible. Generally, you should consider adding a comment to each of the following items:

- **Files, whether complete scripts or include files**—Each file should have a comment stating what this file is, what it's for, who wrote it, and when it was updated.
- **Functions**—Function comments should specify what the function does, what input it expects, and what it returns.
- **Classes**—Comments should describe the purpose of the class. Class methods should have the same types and levels of comments as any other functions.
- **Chunks of code within a script or function**—We often find it useful to write a script by beginning with a set of pseudocode-style comments and then filling in the code for each section. So an initial script might resemble this:

```
<?
// validate input data
// send to database
// report results
?>
```

This commenting scheme is quite handy because after you've filled in all the sections with function calls or whatever, your code is already commented.

- **Complex code or hacks**—When performing some task takes you all day, or you have to do it in a weird way, write a comment explaining why you used that approach. This way, when you next look at the code, you won't be scratching your head and thinking, "What on earth was *that* supposed to do?"

Here's another general guideline to follow: Comment as you go. You might think you will come back and comment your code when you are finished with a project. We guarantee you this will not happen, unless you have far less punishing development timetables and more self-discipline than we do.

Indenting

As in any programming language, you should indent your code in a sensible and consistent fashion. Writing code is like laying out a resumé or business letter. Indenting makes your code easier to read and faster to understand.

In general, any program block that belongs inside a control structure should be indented from the surrounding code. The degree of indenting should be noticeable (that is, more than one space) but not excessive. We generally think the use of tabs should be avoided. Although easy to type, they consume a lot of screen space on many people's monitors. We use an indent level of two to three spaces for all projects.

The way you lay out your curly braces is also an issue. The two most common schemes follow:

Scheme 1:
```
if (condition) {
  // do something
}
```

Scheme 2:
```
if (condition)
{
  // do something else
}
```

Which one you use is up to you. The scheme you choose should, again, be used consistently throughout a project to avoid confusion.

Breaking Up Code

Giant monolithic code is awful. Some people create one huge script that does everything in one giant switch statement. It is far better to break up the code into functions and/or classes and put related items into include files. You can, for example, put all your database-related functions in a file called `dbfunctions.php`.

Reasons for breaking up your code into sensible chunks include the following:

- It makes your code easier to read and understand.

- It makes your code more reusable and minimizes redundancy. For example, with the previous `dbfunctions.php` file, you could reuse it in every script in which you need to connect to your database. If you need to change the way this works, you have to change it in only one place.

- It facilitates teamwork. If the code is broken into components, you can then assign responsibility for the components to team members. It also means that you can avoid the situation in which one programmer is waiting for another to finish working on `GiantScript.php` so that she can go ahead with her own work.

At the start of a project, you should spend some time thinking about how you are going to break up a project into planned components. This process requires drawing lines between areas of functionality, but you should not get bogged down in this because it might change after you start working on a project. You also need to decide which components need to be built first, which components depend on other components, and what your timeline will be for developing all of them.

Even if all team members will be working on all pieces of the code, it's generally a good idea to assign primary responsibility for each component to a specific person. Ultimately, this person would be responsible if something goes wrong with her component. Someone should also take on the job of build manager—that is, the person who makes sure that all the components are on track and working with the rest of the components. This person usually also manages version control; we discuss this task more later in the chapter. This person can be the project manager, or this task can be allocated as a separate responsibility.

Using a Standard Directory Structure

When starting a project, you need to think about how your component structure will be reflected in your website's directory structure. Just as it is a bad idea to have one giant script containing all functionality, it's also usually a bad idea to have one giant directory containing everything. Decide how you are going to split up your directory structure between components, logic, content, and shared code libraries. Document your structure and make sure that all the people working on the project have a copy so that they can find what they need.

Documenting and Sharing In-House Functions

As you develop function libraries, you need to make them available to other programmers on your team. Commonly, every programmer on a team writes his own set of database, date, or debugging functions. This scheme is a time waster. You should make functions and classes available to others.

Remember that even if code is stored in an area or directory commonly available to your team members, they won't know it's there unless you tell them. Develop a system for documenting in-house function libraries and make it available to programmers on your team.

Implementing Version Control

Version control is the art of concurrent change management as applied to software development. Version control systems generally act as a central *repository* or archive and supply a controlled interface for accessing and sharing your code (and possibly documentation).

Imagine a situation in which you try to improve some code but instead accidentally break it and can't roll it back to the way it was, no matter how hard you try. Or you or a client decides that an earlier version of the site was better. Or you need to go back to a previous version for legal reasons.

Imagine another situation in which two members of your programming team want to work on the same file. They both might open and edit the file at the same time, over-writing each other's changes. They both might have a copy that they work on locally and change in different ways. If you have thought about these things happening, one programmer might be sitting around doing nothing while she waits for another to finish editing a file.

You can solve all these problems with a version control system. Such systems can track changes to each file in the repository so that you can see not only the current state of a file, but also the way it looked at any given time in the past. This feature allows you to roll back broken code to a known working version. You can tag a particular set of file instances as a release version, meaning that you can continue development on the code but get access to a copy of the currently released version at any time.

Version control systems also assist multiple programmers in working on code together. Each programmer can get a copy of the code in the repository (called *checking it out*) and when he makes changes, these changes can be merged back into the repository (*checked in* or *committed*). Version control systems can therefore track who made each change to a system.

These systems usually have a facility for managing concurrent updates. This means that two programmers can actually modify the same file at the same time. For example, imagine that John and Mary have both checked out a copy of the most recent release of their project. John finishes his changes to a particular file and checks it in. Mary also changes that file and tries to check it in as well. If the changes they have made are not in the same part of the file, the version control system will merge the two versions of the file. If the changes conflict with each other, Mary will be notified and shown the two different versions. She can then adjust her version of the code to avoid the conflicts.

The version control system used by the majority of Unix and/or open source developers is the Concurrent Versions System (CVS). CVS, which is open source, comes bundled with virtually every version of Unix, and you can also get it for PCs running DOS or Windows and Macs. It supports a client/server model so that you can check code in or out from any machine with an Internet connection, assuming that the CVS server is visible on the Internet. It is used for the development of PHP, Apache, and Mozilla, among other high-profile projects, at least in part for this reason.

You can download CVS for your system from the CVS home page at
http://www.cvshome.org/

Although the base CVS system is a command-line tool, various add-ons give it a more attractive front end, including Java-based and Windows front ends. You can also access them from the CVS home page.

Bitkeeper is a rival version control product, used by a few high-profile open source projects including MySQL and the Linux kernel. It is available free to open source projects.

Commercial alternatives are also available. One of them is perforce, which runs on most common platforms and has PHP support. Although it is commercial, free licenses are offered for open source projects from the website at
http://www.perforce.com/

Choosing a Development Environment

This discussion of version control brings up the more general topic of development environments. All you really need are a text editor and browser for testing, but programmers are often more productive in an Integrated Development Environment (IDE).

You can find a number of emerging free projects to build a dedicated PHP IDE, including KPHPDevelop, for the KDE desktop environment under Linux, available from
   http://kphpdev.sourceforge.net/

Currently, though, the best PHP IDEs are all commercial. Zend Studio from zend.com, Komodo from activestate.com, and PHPEd from nusphere.com provide feature-rich IDEs. All have a trial download but require payment for ongoing use. Komodo offers a cheap noncommercial use license.

Documenting Your Projects

You can produce many different kinds of documentation for your programming projects, including, but not limited to, the following:

- Design documentation
- Technical documentation/developer's guide
- Data dictionary (including class documentation)
- User's guide (although most web applications have to be self-explanatory)

Our goal here is not to teach you how to write technical documentation but to suggest that you make your life easier by automating part of the process.

Some languages enable you to automatically generate some of these documents—particularly technical documentation and data dictionaries. For example, javadoc generates a tree of HTML files containing prototypes and descriptions of class members for Java programs.

Quite a few utilities of this type are available for PHP, including

- phpdoc, available from http://www.phpdoc.de/

  This system is used by PEAR for documenting code. Note that the term *phpDoc* is used to describe several projects of this type, of which this is one.

- PHPDocumentor, available from http://phpdocu.sourceforge.net

  PHPDocumentor gives similar output to javadoc and seems to work quite robustly. It also seems to have a more active developer team than the other two listed here.

- phpautodoc, available from http://sourceforge.net/projects/phpautodoc/

  Again, phpautodoc produces output similar to javadoc.

A good place to look for more applications of this type (and PHP components in general) is SourceForge:

http://sourceforge.net

SourceForge is primarily used by the Unix/Linux community, but many projects are available for other platforms.

Prototyping

Prototyping is a development life cycle commonly used for developing web applications. A prototype is a useful tool for working out customer requirements. Usually, it is a simplified, partially working version of an application that can be used in discussions with clients and as the basis of the final system. Often, multiple iterations over a prototype produce the final application. The advantage of this approach is that it lets you work closely with clients or end users to produce a system that they will be pleased with and have some ownership of.

To be able to "knock together" a prototype quickly, you need some particular skills and tools. A component-based approach works well in such situations. If you have access to a set of preexisting components, both in-house and publicly available, you will be able to do this much more quickly. Another useful tool for rapid development of prototypes is templates. We look at these tools in the next section.

You will encounter two main problems using a prototyping approach. You need to be aware of what these problems are so that you can avoid them and use this approach to its maximum potential.

The first problem is that programmers often find it difficult to throw away the code that they have written for one reason or another. Prototypes are often written quickly, and with the benefit of hindsight, you can see that you have not built a prototype in the optimal, or even in a near optimal, way. Clunky sections of code can be fixed, but if the overall structure is wrong, you are in trouble. The problem is that web applications are often built under enormous time pressure, and you might not have time to fix it. You are then stuck with a poorly designed system that is difficult to maintain.

You can avoid this problem by doing a little planning, as we discussed earlier in this chapter. Remember, too, that sometimes it is easier to scrap something and start again than to try to fix the problem. Although starting over might seem like something you don't have time for, it will often save you a lot of pain later.

The second problem with prototyping is that a system can end up being an eternal prototype. Every time you think you're finished, your client suggests some more improvements or additional functionality or updates to the site. This feature creep can stop you from ever signing off on a project.

To avoid this problem, draw up a project plan with a fixed number of iterations and a date after which no new functionality can be added without replanning, budgeting, and scheduling.

Separating Logic and Content

You are probably familiar with the idea of using HTML to describe a web document's structure and *cascading style sheets (CSS)* to describe its appearance. This idea of separating presentation from content can be extended to scripting. In general, sites will be easier to use and maintain in the long run if you can separate logic from content from presentation. This process boils down to separating your PHP and HTML.

For simple projects with a small number of lines of code or scripts, separating content and logic can be more trouble than it's worth. As your projects become bigger, it is essential to find a way to separate logic and content. If you don't do this, your code will become increasingly difficult to maintain. If you or the powers that be decide to apply a new design to your website and a lot of HTML is embedded in your code, changing the design will be a nightmare.

Three basic approaches to separating logic and content follow:

- Use include files to store different parts of the content. This approach is simplistic, but if your site is mostly static, it can work quite well. This type of approach was explained in the TLA Consulting example in Chapter 5, "Reusing Code and Writing Functions."

- Use a function or class API with a set of member functions to plug dynamic content into static page templates. We looked at this approach in Chapter 6, "Object-Oriented PHP."

- Use a template system. Such systems parse static templates and use regular expressions to replace placeholder tags with dynamic data. The main advantage of this approach is that if somebody else designs your templates, such as a graphics designer, she doesn't have to know anything about PHP code at all. You should be able to use supplied templates with minimum modification.

A number of template systems are available. Probably the most popular one is Smarty, available from

http://smarty.php.net/

Optimizing Code

If you come from a non-web programming background, optimization can seem really important. When PHP is used, most of a user's wait for a web application comes from connection and download times. Optimization of your code has little effect on these times.

Using Simple Optimizations

You can introduce a few simple optimizations that will make a difference in connection and download times. Many of these changes, described here, relate to applications that integrate a database such as MySQL with your PHP code:

- Reduce database connections. Connecting to a database is often the slowest part of any script.

- Speed up database queries. Reduce the number of queries that you make and make sure that they are optimized. With a complex (and therefore slow) query, there is usually more than one way to solve your problem. Run your queries from the database's command-line interface and experiment with different approaches to speed up things. In MySQL, you can use the EXPLAIN statement to see where a query might be going astray. (Use of this statement is discussed in Chapter 12, "Advanced MySQL Administration.") In general, the principle is to minimize joins and maximize use of indexes.

- Minimize generation of static content from PHP. If every piece of HTML you produce comes from echo or print(), page generation will take a good deal longer. (This is one of the arguments for shifting toward separate logic and content, as described previously.) This tip also applies to generating image buttons dynamically: You might want to use PHP to generate the buttons once and then reuse them as required. If you are generating purely static pages from functions or templates every time a page loads, consider running the functions or using the templates once and saving the result.

- Use string functions instead of regular expressions where possible. They are faster.

- Use single-quoted strings instead of double-quoted strings where possible. PHP evaluates double-quoted strings, looking for variables to replace. Single-quoted strings are not evaluated. On the other hand, if something is in single quotes, it's probably static content. Review what you are doing and see whether you can get rid of the string altogether by turning it into static HTML.

Using Zend Products

Zend Technologies owns the (open source) PHP scripting engine for use in PHP4 onward. In addition to the basic engine, you can also download the Zend Optimizer. This multi-pass optimizer can optimize your code for you and can increase the speed at which your scripts run from 40% to 100%. You need PHP 4.0.2 or higher to run the optimizer. Although closed source, it is free for download from Zend's site:

http://www.zend.com

This add-on works by optimizing the code produced by the runtime compilation of your script. Other Zend products include the Zend Studio, Zend Accelerator, Zend Encoder, and commercial support agreements.

Testing

Reviewing and testing code is another basic point of software engineering that is often overlooked in web development. It's easy enough to try running the system with two or three test cases and then say, "Yup, it works fine." This mistake is commonly made. Ensure that you have extensively tested and reviewed several scenarios before making the project production ready.

We suggest two approaches you can use to reduce the bug level of your code. (You can never eliminate bugs altogether, but you can certainly eliminate or minimize most of them.)

First, adopt a practice of code review. This is the process in which another programmer or team of programmers looks at your code and suggests improvements. This type of analysis often suggests

- Errors you have missed
- Test cases you have not considered
- Optimization
- Improvements in security
- Existing components you could use to improve a piece of code
- Additional functionality

Even if you work alone, finding a "code buddy" who is in the same situation and reviewing code for each other can be a good thing.

Second, we suggest you find testers for your web applications who represent the end users of the product. The primary difference between web applications and desktop applications is that anyone and everyone will use web applications. You shouldn't make assumptions that users will be familiar with computers. You can't supply them with a thick manual or quick reference card. You have to instead make web applications self-documenting and self-evident. You must think about the ways in which users will want to use your application. Usability is absolutely paramount.

Understanding the problems that naive end users will encounter can be really difficult if you are an experienced programmer or web surfer. One way to address this problem is to find testers who represent the typical user.

One way we have done this in the past is to release web applications on a beta-only basis. When you think you have the majority of the bugs out, publicize the application to a small group of test users and get a low volume of traffic through the site. Offer free services to the first 100 users in return for feedback about the site. We guarantee you that they will come up with some combination of data or usage you have not considered. If you are building a website for a client company, it can often supply a good set of naive users by getting staff at the company to work through the site. (This approach has the intrinsic benefit of increasing the client's sense of ownership in the site.)

Further Reading

There is a great deal of material to cover in this area; basically, we are talking about the science of software engineering, about which many, many books have been written.

A great book that explains the website-as-document versus website-as-application dichotomy is *Web Site Engineering: Beyond Web Page Design* by Thomas A. Powell. Any software engineering book you like will do as a backup.

For information on version control, visit the CVS website:

http://www.cvshome.org

You won't find many books on version control (this is surprising given how important it is!), but you can try either *Open Source Development with CVS* by Karl Franz Fogel or the *CVS Pocket Reference* by Gregor N. Purdy.

If you are looking for PHP components, IDEs, or documentation systems, try SourceForge:

http://sourceforge.net

Many of the topics we covered in this chapter are discussed in articles on Zend's site. You might consider going there for more information on the subject. You might also consider downloading the optimizer from the site when you are there:

http://www.zend.com

If you found this chapter interesting, you might want to look at Extreme Programming, which is a software development methodology aimed at domains where requirements change frequently, such as web development. You can access the website for Extreme Programming at

http://www.extremeprogramming.org

Next

In Chapter 25, "Debugging," we look at different types of programming errors, PHP error messages, and techniques for finding errors.

25

Debugging

THIS CHAPTER DEALS WITH DEBUGGING PHP scripts. If you have worked through some
of the examples in the book or used PHP before, you will probably already have developed some debugging skills and techniques of your own. As your projects get more
complex, debugging can become more difficult. Although your skills improve, the errors
are more likely to involve multiple files or interactions between code written by multiple
people.

Key topics covered in this chapter include

- Programming error types
    - Syntax errors
    - Runtime errors
    - Logic errors
- Error messages
- Error levels
- Triggering your own errors
- Handling errors gracefully

Programming Errors

Regardless of which language you are using, there are three general types of program
errors:

- Syntax errors
- Runtime errors
- Logic errors

We look briefly at each before discussing some tactics for detecting, handling, avoiding,
and solving errors.

Syntax Errors

Languages have a set of rules called the *syntax*, which statements must follow to be valid. This applies to both natural languages, such as English, and programming languages, such as PHP. If a statement does not follow the rules of a language, it is said to have a *syntax error*. Syntax errors are often also called *parser errors* when discussing interpreted languages, such as PHP, or *compiler errors* when discussing compiled languages, such as C or Java.

If you break the English language's syntax rules, there is a pretty good chance that people will still know what you intended to say. This usually is not the case with programming languages, however. If a script does not follow the rules of PHP's syntax—if it contains syntax errors—the PHP parser will not be able to process some or all of it. People are good at inferring information from partial or conflicting data. Computers are not.

Among many other rules, the syntax of PHP requires that statements end with semicolons, that strings are enclosed in quotation marks, and that parameters passed to functions be separated with commas and enclosed in parentheses. If you break these rules, your PHP script is unlikely to work and likely to generate an error message the first time you try to execute it.

One of PHP's great strengths is the useful error messages that it provides when things go wrong. A PHP error message usually tells you what went wrong, which file the error occurred in, and which line the error was found at.

An error message resembles the following:

```
Parse error: parse error, unexpected ''' in
/home/book/public_html/chapter25/error.php on line 2
```

This error was produced by the following script:

```php
<?php
    $date = date(m.d.y');
?>
```

You can see that we attempted to pass a string to the `date()` function but accidentally missed the opening quotation mark that would mark the beginning of the string.

Simple syntax errors such as this one are usually the easiest to find. You might make a similar but harder-to-find error by forgetting to terminate the string, as shown in this example:

```php
<?php
    $date = date('m.d.y);
?>
```

This script generates the following error message:

Parse error: parse error, unexpected $end in
/home/book/public_html/chapter25/error.php on line **4**

Obviously, because the script has only three lines, the error is not really on line four. Errors in which you open something but fail to close it often show up like this. You can run into this problem with single and double quotation marks and also with the various forms of brackets and parentheses.

The following script generates a similar syntax error:

```
<?php
  if (true)
  {
    echo 'error here';
?>
```

These errors can be hard to find if they result from a combination of multiple files. They can also be difficult to find if they occur in a large file. Seeing `parse error` on `line 1001` of a 1000-line file can be enough to spoil your day, but it should provide a subtle hint that you should try to write more modular code.

In general, though, syntax errors are the easiest type of error to find. If you make a syntax error and try to execute that block of code, PHP will give you a message telling you where to find your mistake.

Runtime Errors

Runtime errors can be harder to detect and fix. A script either contains a syntax error, or it does not. If the script contains a syntax error, the parser will detect it when that code is executed. Runtime errors are not caused solely by the contents of your script. They can rely on interactions between your scripts and other events or conditions.

The statement

```
require ('filename.php');
```

is a perfectly valid PHP statement. It contains no syntax errors.

This statement might, however, generate a runtime error. If you execute this statement and `filename.php` does not exist or the user who the script runs as is denied read permission, you will get an error resembling this one:

Fatal error: main() [function.require]: Failed opening required 'filename.php'
(include_path='.:/usr/local/lib/php') in
/home/book/public_html/chapter25/error.php on line **1**

Although nothing is wrong with the code here, because it relies on a file that might or might not exist at different times when the code is run, it can generate a runtime error.

The following three statements are all valid PHP. Unfortunately, in combination, they attempt to do the impossible—divide by zero:

```
$i = 10;
$j = 0;
$k = $i/$j;
```

This code snippet generates the following warning:

Warning: Division by zero in
/home/book/public_html/chapter25/div0.php on line **3**

This warning makes it very easy to correct. Few people would try to write code that attempted to divide by zero on purpose, but neglecting to check user input often results in this type of error.

The following code sometimes generates the same error but might be much harder to isolate and correct because it happens only some of the time:

```
$i = 10;
$k = $i/$_REQUEST['input'];
```

This is one of many different runtime errors that you might see while testing your code.
Common causes of runtime errors include the following:

- Calls to functions that do not exist
- Reading or writing files
- Interaction with MySQL or other databases
- Connections to network services
- Failure to check input data

We briefly discuss each of these causes in the following sections.

Calls to Functions That Do Not Exist

Accidentally calling functions that do not exist is easy. The built-in functions are often inconsistently named. Why does `strip_tags()` have an underscore, whereas `stripslashes()` does not?

It is also easy to call one of your own functions that does not exist in the current script but might exist elsewhere. If your code contains a call to a nonexistent function, such as

```
nonexistent_function();
```

or

```
mispeled_function();
```

you will see an error message similar to this:

Fatal error: Call to undefined function: nonexistent_function()
in **/home/book/public_html/chapter25/error.php** on line **1**

Similarly, if you call a function that exists but call it with an incorrect number of parameters, you will receive a warning.

The function `strstr()` requires two strings: a haystack to search and a needle to find. If instead you call it using

```
strstr();
```

you will get the following warning:

Warning: Wrong parameter count for strstr() in
/home/book/public_html/chapter25/error.php on line **1**

That same statement within the following script is equally wrong:

```php
<?php
  if($var == 4)
  {
    strstr();
  }
?>
```

Except in the possibly rare case in which the variable $var has the value 4, the call to strstr() will not occur, and no warning will be issued. The PHP interpreter does not waste time parsing sections of your code that are not needed for the current execution of the script. You need to be sure that you test carefully!

Calling functions incorrectly is easy to do, but because the resulting error messages identify the exact line and function call that are causing the problem, they are equally easy to fix. They are difficult to find only if your testing process is poor and does not test all conditionally executed code. When you test, one of the goals is to execute every line of code at least once. Another goal is to test all the boundary conditions and classes of input.

Reading or Writing Files

Although anything can go wrong at some point during your program's useful life, some problems are more likely than others. Because errors accessing files are likely enough to occur, you need to handle them gracefully. Hard drives fail or fill up, and human error results in directory permissions changing.

Functions such as fopen() that are likely to fail occasionally generally have a return value to signal that an error occurred. For fopen(), a return value of false indicates failure.

For functions that provide failure notification, you need to carefully check the return value of every call and act on failures.

Interaction with MySQL or Other Databases

Connecting to and using MySQL can generate many errors. The function mysqli_ connect() alone can generate at least the following errors:

- **Warning**: mysqli_connect() [function.mysqli-connect]: Can't connect to MySQL server on 'localhost' (10061)

- **Warning**: mysqli_connect() [function.mysqli-connect]: Unknown MySQL Server Host 'hostname' (11001)

- **Warning**: mysqli_connect() [function.mysqli-connect]: Access denied for user: 'username'@'localhost' (Using password: YES)

As you would probably expect, `mysqli_connect()` provides a return value of `false` when an error occurs. This means that you can easily trap and handle these types of common errors.

If you do not stop the regular execution of your script and handle these errors, your script will attempt to continue interacting with the database. Trying to run queries and get results without a valid MySQL connection results in your visitors seeing an unprofessional-looking screen full of error messages.

Many other commonly used MySQL-related PHP functions such as `mysqli_query()` also return `false` to indicate that an error occurred.

If an error occurs, you can access the text of the error message using the function `mysqli_error()`, or an error code using the function `mysqli_errno()`. If the last MySQL function did not generate an error, `mysqli_error()` returns an empty string and `mysqli_errno()` returns 0.

For example, assuming that you have connected to the server and selected a database for use, the code snippet

```
$result = mysqli_query($db, 'select * from does_not_exist' );
echo mysqli_errno($db);
echo '<br />';
echo mysqli_error($db);
```

might output

```
1146
Table 'dbname.does_not_exist' doesn't exist
```

Note that the output of these functions refers to the last MySQL function executed (other than `mysqli_error()` or `mysqli_errno()`). If you want to know the result of a command, make sure to check it before running others.

Like file interaction failures, database interaction failures will occur. Even after completing development and testing of a service, you will occasionally find that the MySQL daemon (`mysqld`) has crashed or run out of available connections. If your database runs on another physical machine, you are relying on another set of hardware and software components that could fail—another network connection, network card, routers, and so on between your Web server and the database machine.

You need to remember to check whether your database requests succeed before attempting to use the result. There is no point in attempting to run a query after failing to connect to the database and no point in trying to extract and process the results after running a query that failed.

It is important to note at this point that there is a difference between a query failing and a query that merely fails to return any data or affect any rows.

An SQL query that contains SQL syntax errors or refers to databases, tables, or columns that do not exist will fail. The query

```
select * from does_not_exist;
```

will fail because the table name does not exist, and it will generate an error number and message retrievable with `mysqli_errno()` and `mysqli_error()`.

A SQL query that is syntactically valid and refers only to databases, tables, and columns that exist generally does not fail. The query might, however, return no results if it is querying an empty table or searching for data that does not exist. Assuming that you have connected to a database successfully and have a table called `t1` and a column called `c1`, the query

```
select * from t1 where c1 = 'not in database';
```

will succeed but not return any results.

Before you use the result of the query, you need to check for both failure and no results.

Connections to Network Services

Although devices and other programs on your system will occasionally fail, they should fail rarely unless they are of poor quality. When using a network to connect to other machines and the software on those machines, you need to accept that some part of the system will fail often. To connect from one machine to another, you rely on numerous devices and services that are not under your control.

At the risk of our being repetitive, you really need to carefully check the return value of functions that attempt to interact with a network service.

A function call such as

```
$sp = fsockopen ( 'localhost', 5000 );
```

will provide a warning if it fails in its attempt to connect to port 5000 on the machine `localhost`, but it will display it in the default format and not give your script the option to handle it gracefully.

Rewriting the call as

```
$sp = @fsockopen ( 'localhost', 5000, &$errorno, &$errorstr );
if(!$sp)
  echo "ERROR: $errorno: $errorstr";
```

will suppress the built-in error message, check the return value to see whether an error occurred, and use your own code to handle the error message. As the code is written, it will display an error message that might help you solve the problem. In this case, it would produce the following output:

```
ERROR: 10035: A non-blocking socket operation could not be completed immediately.
```

Runtime errors are harder to eliminate than syntax errors because the parser cannot signal the error the first time the code is executed. Because runtime errors occur in response to a combination of events, they can be hard to detect and solve. The parser cannot automatically tell you that a particular line will generate an error. Your testing needs to provide one of the situations that create the error.

Handling runtime errors requires a certain amount of forethought—to check for different types of failure that might occur and then take appropriate action. Simulating each class of runtime error that might occur also takes careful testing.

We do not mean that you need to attempt to simulate every different error that might occur. MySQL, for example, can provide one of around 200 different error numbers and messages. You do need to simulate an error in each function call that is likely to result in an error and an error of each type that is handled by a different block of code.

Failure to Check Input Data

Often you make assumptions about the input data that will be entered by users. If this data does not fit your expectations, it might cause an error, either a runtime error or a logic error (detailed in the following section).

A classic example of a runtime error occurs when you are dealing with user input data and you forget to apply `addslashes()` to it. This means if you have a user with a name such as O'Grady that contains an apostrophe, you will get an error from the database function if you use the input in an insert statement inside single quotation marks.

We discuss errors because of assumptions about input data in more detail in the next section.

Logic Errors

Logic errors can be the hardest type of error to find and eliminate. This type of error occurs when perfectly valid code does exactly what it is instructed to do, but that was not what the writer intended.

Logic errors can be caused by a simple typing error, such as

```
for ( $i = 0; $i < 10; $i++ );
{
  echo 'doing something<br />';
}
```

This snippet of code is perfectly valid. It follows valid PHP syntax. It does not rely on any external services, so it is unlikely to fail at runtime. Unless you looked at it very carefully, it probably will not do what you think it will or what the programmer intended it to do.

At a glance, it looks as if it will iterate through the `for` loop 10 times, echoing `"doing something"` each time. The addition of an extraneous semicolon at the end of the first line means that the loop has no effect on the following lines. The `for` loop will iterate 10 times with no result, and then the `echo` statement will be executed once.

Because this snippet is a perfectly valid, but inefficient, way to write code to achieve this result, the parser will not complain. Computers are very good at some things, but they do not have any common sense or intelligence. A computer will do exactly as it is told. You need to make sure that what you tell it is exactly what you want.

Logic errors are not caused by any sort of failure of the code, but merely a failure of the programmer to write code that instructs the computer to do exactly what she wanted. As a result, errors cannot be detected automatically. You are not told that an error has occurred, and you are not given a line number where you can look for the problem. Logic errors are detected only by proper testing.

A logic error such as the previous trivial example is fairly easy to make, but also easy to correct because the first time your code runs, you will see output other than what you expected. Most logic errors are a little more insidious.

Troublesome logic errors usually result from developers' assumptions being wrong. Chapter 24, "Using PHP and MySQL for Large Projects," recommended using other developers to review code to suggest additional test cases and using people from the target audience rather than developers for testing. Assuming that people will enter only certain types of data is very easy to do and an error that is very easy to leave undetected if you do your own testing.

Let's say that you have an Order Quantity text box on a commerce site. Have you assumed that people will enter only positive numbers? If a visitor enters −10, will your software refund his credit card with 10 times the price of the item?

Suppose that you have a box to enter a dollar amount. Do you allow people to enter the amount with or without a dollar sign? Do you allow people to enter numbers with thousands separated by commas? Some of these things can be checked at the client side (using, for example, JavaScript) to take a little load off your server.

If you are passing information to another page, has it occurred to you that some characters might have special significance in a URL, such as spaces in the string you are passing?

An infinite number of logic errors is possible. There is no automated way to check for these errors. The only solution is, first, to try to eliminate assumptions that you have implicitly coded into the script and, second, test thoroughly with every type of valid and invalid input possible, ensuring that you get the anticipated result for all.

Variable Debugging Aid

As projects become more complex, having some utility code to help you identify the cause of errors can be useful. A piece of code that you might find useful is contained in Listing 25.1. This code echoes the contents of variables passed to your page.

Listing 25.1 `dump_variables.php`—**This Code Can Be Included in Pages to Dump the Contents of Variables for Debugging**

```php
<?php
  // these lines format the output as HTML comments
  // and call dump_array repeatedly

  echo "\n<!-- BEGIN VARIABLE DUMP -->\n\n";

  echo "<!-- BEGIN GET VARS -->\n";
```

Listing 25.1 **Continued**

```
  echo '<!-- '.dump_array($_GET)." -->\n";

  echo "<!-- BEGIN POST VARS -->\n";
  echo '<!-- '.dump_array($_POST)." -->\n";

  echo "<!-- BEGIN SESSION VARS -->\n";
  echo '<!-- '.dump_array($_SESSION)." -->\n";

  echo "<!-- BEGIN COOKIE VARS -->\n";
  echo '<!-- '.dump_array($_COOKIE)." -->\n";

  echo "\n<!-- END VARIABLE DUMP -->\n";

// dump_array() uses the builtin print_r
// and escapes out any HTML end comments

function dump_array($array)
{
  $output = print_r($array, true);
  $output = str_replace('-->', '-- >', $output);
  return $output;
}


?>
```

This code outputs four arrays of variables that a page receives. If a page was called with GET variables, POST variables, cookies, or it has session variables, they will be output.

Here, we put the output within an HTML comment so that it is viewable but does not interfere with the way the browser renders visible page elements. This is a good way to generate debugging information. Hiding the debug information in comments, as in Listing 25.1, allows you to leave in your debug code until the last minute. We used the dump_array() function as a wrapper to print_r(). The dump_array() function just escapes out any HTML end comment characters.

The exact output depends on the variables passed to the page, but when added to Listing 22.4, one of the authentication examples from Chapter 22, "Using Session Control in PHP," it adds the following lines to the HTML generated by the script:

```
<!-- BEGIN VARIABLE DUMP -->

<!-- BEGIN GET VARS -->
<!-- Array
(
)
 -->
```

```
<!-- BEGIN POST VARS -->
<!-- Array
(
    [userid] => testuser
    [password] => password
)
 -->
<!-- BEGIN SESSION VARS -->
<!-- Array
(
)
 -->
<!-- BEGIN COOKIE VARS -->
<!-- Array
(
    [PHPSESSID] => b2b5f56fad986dd73af33f470f3c1865
)
 -->


<!-- END VARIABLE DUMP -->
```

You can see that it displays the POST variables sent from the login form on the previous page: userid and password. It also shows the session variable used to keep the user's name in: valid_user. As discussed in Chapter 22, PHP uses a cookie to link session variables to particular users. The script echoes the pseudo-random number, PHPSESSID, which is stored in that cookie to identify a particular user.

Error Reporting Levels

PHP allows you to set how fussy it should be with errors. You can modify what types of events generate messages. By default, PHP reports all errors other than notices.

The error reporting level is assigned using a set of predefined constants, shown in Table 25.1.

Table 25.1 **Error Reporting Constants**

Value	Name	Meaning
1	E_ERROR	Report fatal errors at runtime
2	E_WARNING	Report nonfatal errors at runtime
4	E_PARSE	Report parse errors
8	E_NOTICE	Report notices, notifications that something you have done might be an error
16	E_CORE_ERROR	Report failures in the startup of the PHP engine
32	E_CORE_WARNING	Report nonfatal failures during the startup of the PHP engine

Table 25.1   **Continued**

Value	Name	Meaning
64	E_COMPILE_ERROR	Report errors in compilation
128	E_COMPILE_WARNING	Report nonfatal errors in compilation
256	E_USER_ERROR	Report user-triggered errors
512	E_USER_WARNING	Report user-triggered warnings
1024	E_USER_NOTICE	Report user-triggered notices
2047	E_ALL	Report all errors and warnings
2048	E_STRICT	Reports use of deprecated and unrecommended behavior; not included in E_ALL but very useful for code refactoring

Each constant represents a type of error that can be reported or ignored. If, for instance, you specify the error level as E_ERROR, only fatal errors will be reported. These constants can be combined using binary arithmetic, to produce different error levels.

The default error level—report all errors other than notices—is specified as follows:

```
E_ALL & ~E_NOTICE
```

This expression consists of two of the predefined constants combined using bitwise arithmetic operators. The ampersand (&) is the bitwise AND operator and the tilde (~) is the bitwise NOT operator. This expression can be read as E_ALL AND NOT E_NOTICE.

E_ALL itself is effectively a combination of all the other error types except for E_STRICT. It could be replaced by the other levels combined together using the bitwise OR operator (|):

```
E_ERROR | E_WARNING | E_PARSE | E_NOTICE | E_CORE_ERROR | E_CORE_WARNING |
E_COMPILE_ERROR |E_COMPILE_WARNING | E_USER_ERROR | E_USER_WARNING |
E_USER_NOTICE
```

Similarly, the default error reporting level could be specified by all error levels except E_NOTICE combined with OR:

```
E_ERROR | E_WARNING | E_PARSE | E_CORE_ERROR | E_CORE_WARNING | E_COMPILE_ERROR |
E_COMPILE_WARNING | E_USER_ERROR | E_USER_WARNING | E_USER_NOTICE
```

Altering the Error Reporting Settings

You can set the error reporting settings globally, in your php.ini file or on a per-script basis.

To alter the error reporting for all scripts, you can modify these four lines in the default php.ini file:

```
error_reporting =       E_ALL & ~E_NOTICE
display_errors  =       On
log_errors      =       Off
track_errors    =       Off
```

The default global settings are to

- Report all errors except notices
- Output error messages as HTML to standard output
- Not log error messages to disk
- Not track errors, storing the error in the variable `$php_errormsg`

The most likely change you will make is to turn the error reporting level up to `E_ALL | E_STRICT`. This change results in many notices being reported, for incidents that might indicate an error, or might just result from the programmer taking advantage of PHP's weakly typed nature and the fact that it automatically initializes variables to `0`.

While debugging, you might find it useful to set the `error_reporting` level higher. If you are providing useful error messages of your own, the production code would be more professional looking if you turn `display_errors` off and turn `log_errors` on, while leaving the `error_reporting` level high. You then can refer to detailed errors in the logs if problems are reported.

Turning `track_errors` on might help you to deal with errors in your own code, rather than letting PHP provide its default functionality. Although PHP provides useful error messages, its default behavior looks ugly when things go wrong.

By default, when a fatal error occurs, PHP outputs

```
<br>
<b>Error Type</b>: error message in <b>path/file.php</b>
on line <b>lineNumber</b><br>
```

and stops executing the script. For nonfatal errors, the same text is output, but execution is allowed to continue.

This HTML output makes the error stand out but looks poor. The style of the error message is unlikely to fit the rest of the site's look. It might also result in some users seeing no output at all if the page's content is being displayed within a table and their browser is fussy about valid HTML. HTML that opens but does not close table elements, such as

```
<table>
<tr><td>
<br>
<b>Error Type</b>:  error message in <b>path/file.php</b>
on line <b>lineNumber</b><br>
```

is rendered as a blank screen by some browsers.

You do not have to keep PHP's default error handling behavior or even use the same settings for all files. To change the error reporting level for the current script, you can call the function `error_reporting()`.

Passing an error report constant, or a combination of them, sets the level in the same way that the similar directive in php.ini does. The function returns the previous error reporting level. A common way to use the function is like this:

```
// turn off error reporting
$old_level = error_reporting(0);
// here, put code that will generate warnings
// turn error reporting back on
error_reporting($old_level);
```

This code snippet turns off error reporting, allowing you to execute some code that is likely to generate warnings that you do not want to see.

Turning off error reporting permanently is a bad idea because it makes finding your coding errors and fixing them more difficult.

Triggering Your Own Errors

The function trigger_error() can be used to trigger your own errors. Errors created in this way are handled in the same way as regular PHP errors.

The function requires an error message and can optionally be given an error type. The error type needs to be one of E_USER_ERROR, E_USER_WARNING, or E_USER_NOTICE. If you do not specify a type, the default is E_USER_NOTICE.

You use trigger_error() as follows:

```
trigger_error('This computer will self destruct in 15 seconds', E_USER_WARNING);
```

Handling Errors Gracefully

If you come from a C++ or Java background, you are probably comfortable using exceptions. Exceptions allow functions to signal that an error has occurred and leave dealing with the error to an exception handler. Exceptions were added to PHP only in version 5 but are an excellent way to handle errors in large projects. They were adequately covered in Chapter 7, "Exception Handling," so they will not be revisited here.

If you need your code to work on PHP4, you can simulate similar behavior with user-triggered errors and user-defined error handlers, but this behavior will become less important now that PHP supports exceptions. You have already seen how you can trigger your own errors. You can also provide your own error handlers to catch errors.

The function set_error_handler() lets you provide a function to be called when user-level errors, warnings, and notices occur. You call set_error_handler() with the name of the function you want to use as your error handler.

Your error handling function must take two parameters: an error type and an error message. Based on these two variables, your function can decide how to handle the error. The error type must be one of the defined error type constants. The error message is a descriptive string.

A call to `set_error_handler()` looks like this:

```
set_error_handler('my_error_handler');
```

Having told PHP to use a function called `my_error_handler()`, you must then provide a function with that name. This function must have the following prototype:

```
My_error_handler(int error_type, string error_msg
                 [, string errfile [, int errline [, array errcontext]]]))
```

What it actually does, however, is up to you.

The parameters passed to your handler function are

- The error type
- The error message
- The file the error occurred in
- The line the error occurred on
- The symbol table—that is, a set of all the variables and their values at the time the error occurred

Logical actions might include

- Displaying the error message provided
- Storing information in a log file
- Emailing the error to an address
- Terminating the script with a call to exit

Listing 25.2 contains a script that declares an error handler, sets the error handler using `set_error_handler()`, and then generates some errors.

Listing 25.2   `handle.php`—This Script Declares a Custom Error Handler and Generates Different Errors

```php
<?php
 // The error handler function
 function my_error_handler ($errno, $errstr, $errfile, $errline)
 {
   echo "<br /><table bgcolor='#cccccc'><tr><td>
        <p><strong>ERROR:</strong> $errstr</p>
        <p>Please try again, or contact us and tell us that
        the error occurred in line $errline of file '$errfile'</p>";
   if ($errno == E_USER_ERROR)
   {
     echo '<p>This error was fatal, program ending</p>';
     echo '</td></tr></table>';
     // close open resources, include page footer, etc
     exit;
```

Listing 25.2 **Continued**

```
  }
  echo '</td></tr></table>';
}
// Set the error handler
set_error_handler('my_error_handler');

//trigger different levels of error
trigger_error('Trigger function called', E_USER_NOTICE);
fopen('nofile', 'r');
trigger_error('This computer is beige', E_USER_WARNING);
include ('nofile');
trigger_error('This computer will self destruct in 15 seconds', E_USER_ERROR);
?>
```

The output from this script is shown in Figure 25.1.

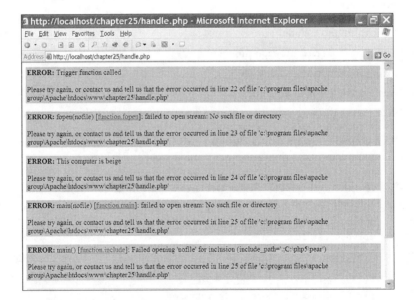

Figure 25.1 You can give friendlier error messages than PHP if you use your own error handler.

This custom error handler does not do any more than the default behavior. Because you write this code, you can make it do anything. You have a choice about what to tell your visitors when something goes wrong and how to present that information so that it fits the rest of the site. More importantly, you have the flexibility to decide what happens.

Should the script continue? Should a message be logged or displayed? Should tech support be alerted automatically?

It is important to note that your error handler will not have the responsibility for dealing with all error types. Some errors, such as parse errors and fatal runtime errors, still trigger the default behavior. If this behavior concerns you, make sure that you check parameters carefully before passing them to a function that can generate fatal errors and trigger your own `E_USER_ERROR` level error if your parameters are going to cause failure.

Here's a new feature in PHP5: If your error handler returns an explicit `false` value, PHP's built-in error handler will be invoked. This way, you can handle the `E_USER_*` errors yourself and let the built-in handler deal with the regular errors.

Next

In Chapter 26, "Building User Authentication and Personalization," you begin your first project. In this project, you look at how to recognize users who are coming back to your site and tailor your content appropriately.

## 26

Building User Authentication and Personalization

IN THIS PROJECT, YOU GET USERS TO REGISTER at your website. After they've done that, you can track what they're interested in and show them appropriate content. This behavior is called *user personalization*.

This particular project enables users to build a set of bookmarks on the Web and suggests other links they might find interesting based on their past behavior. More generally, user personalization can be used in almost any web-based application to show users the content they want in the format in which they want it.

In this project and the others to follow, you start by looking at a set of requirements similar to those you might get from a client. You develop those requirements into a set of solution components, build a design to connect those components together, and then implement each of the components.

In this project, you implement the following functionality:

- Logging in and authenticating users
- Managing passwords
- Recording user preferences
- Personalizing content
- Recommending content based on existing knowledge about a user

The Problem

For this project, your job is to build a prototype for an online bookmarking system, to be called PHPbookmark, similar (but more limited in functionality) to that available at Backflip at http://backflip.com.

This system should enable users to log in and store their personal bookmarks and to get recommendations for other sites that they might like to visit based on their personal preferences.

These solution requirements fall into three main categories:

- You need to be able to identify individual users. You should also have some way of authenticating them.

- You need to be able to store bookmarks for an individual user. Users should be able to add and delete bookmarks.

- You need to be able to recommend to users sites that might appeal to them, based on what you know about them already.

Solution Components

Now that you know the system requirements, you can begin designing the solution and its components. Let's look at possible solutions to each of the three main requirements listed in the preceding section.

User Identification and Personalization

Several alternatives can be used for user authentication, as you have seen elsewhere in this book. Because you want to tie users to some personalization information, you can store the users' logins and passwords in a MySQL database and authenticate against it.

If you are going to let users log in with usernames and passwords, you will need the following components:

- Users should be able to register their usernames and passwords. You need some restrictions on the length and format of each username and password. You should store passwords in an encrypted format for security reasons.

- Users should be able to log in with the details they supplied in the registration process.

- Users should be able to log out after they have finished using a site. This capability is not particularly important if people use the site from their home PC but is very important for security if they use the site from a shared PC.

- The site needs to be able to check whether a particular user is logged in and access data for a logged-in user.

- Users should be able to change their passwords as an aid to security.

- Users will occasionally forget their passwords. They should be able to reset their passwords without needing personal assistance from you. A common way of doing this is to send a user's password to him in an email address he has nominated at registration. This means you need to store his email address at registration. Because you store the passwords in an encrypted form and cannot decrypt the user's original password, you actually need to generate a new password, set it, and mail it to the user.

For purposes of this project, you will write functions for all these pieces of functionality. Most of them will be reusable, or reusable with minor modifications, in other projects.

Storing Bookmarks

To store a user's bookmarks, you need to set up some space in your MySQL database. You need the following functionality:

- Users should be able to retrieve and view their bookmarks.
- Users should be able to add new bookmarks. You should check that these are valid URLs.
- Users should be able to delete bookmarks.

Again, you can write functions for each of these pieces of functionality.

Recommending Bookmarks

You could take a number of different approaches to recommending bookmarks to a user. You could recommend the most popular overall or the most popular within a topic. For this project, you will implement a "like minds" suggestion system that looks for users who have a bookmark the same as your logged-in user and suggests their other bookmarks to your user. To avoid recommending any personal bookmarks, you will recommend only bookmarks stored by more than one other user.

You can again write a function to implement this functionality.

Solution Overview

After some doodling on napkins, we came up with a system flowchart you can use, as shown in Figure 26.1.

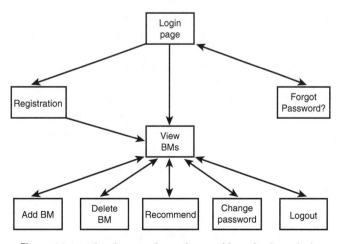

Figure 26.1   This diagram shows the possible paths through the PHPbookmark system.

You can build a module for each box on this diagram; some will need one script and others, two. You can also set up function libraries for

- User authentication
- Bookmark storage and retrieval
- Data validation
- Database connections
- Output to the browser. You can confine all the HTML production to this function library, ensuring that visual presentation is consistent throughout the site. (This is the function API approach to separating logic and content.)

You also need to build a back-end database for the system.

We describe the solution in some detail, but all the code for this application can be found on the CD-ROM in the `chapter26` directory. A summary of included files is shown in Table 26.1.

Table 26.1 **Files in the PHPbookmark Application**

Filename	Description
bookmarks.sql	SQL statements to create the PHPbookmark database
login.php	Front page with login form for the system
register_form.php	Form for users to register in the system
register_new.php	Script to process new registrations
forgot_form.php	Form for users to fill out if they've forgotten their passwords
forgot_passwd.php	Script to reset forgotten passwords
member.php	A user's main page, with a view of all his current bookmarks
add_bm_form.php	Form for adding new bookmarks
add_bms.php	Script to actually add new bookmarks to the database
delete_bms.php	Script to delete selected bookmarks from a user's list
recommend.php	Script to suggest recommendations to a user, based on users with similar interests
change_passwd_form.php	Form for members to fill out if they want to change their passwords
change_passwd.php	Script to change a user's password in the database
logout.php	Script to log a user out of the application
bookmark_fns.php	A collection of includes for the application
data_valid_fns.php	Functions to validate user-input data
db_fns.php	Functions to connect to the database
user_auth_fns.php	Functions for user authentication
url_fns.php	Functions for adding and deleting bookmarks and for making recommendations
output_fns.php	Functions that format output as HTML
bookmark.gif	Logo for PHPbookmark

You begin by implementing the MySQL database for this application because it is required for virtually all the other functionality to work.

Then you work through the code in the order it was written, starting from the front page, going through the user authentication, to bookmark storage and retrieval, and finally to recommendations. This order is fairly logical; it's just a question of working out the dependencies and building first the things that will be required for later modules.

> **Note**
>
> For the code in this project to work as written, you need to have switched on magic quotes. If you have not done this, you will need to use addslashes() on data being inserted to the MySQL database and stripslashes() on data retrieved from the database. We used this technique as a useful shortcut. You will also require a JavaScript-capable browser to view the application correctly.

Implementing the Database

The PHPbookmark database requires only a fairly simple schema. You need to store users and their email addresses and passwords. You also need to store the URL of a bookmark. One user can have many bookmarks, and many users can register the same bookmark. You therefore need two tables, user and bookmark, as shown in Figure 26.2.

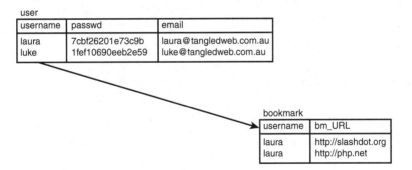

Figure 26.2 Database schema for the PHPbookmark system.

The user table stores each user's username (which is the primary key), password, and email address. The bookmark table stores username and bookmark (bm_URL) pairs. The username in this table refers to a username from the user table.

The SQL to create this database, and to create a user for connecting to the database from the Web, is shown in Listing 26.1. You should edit this file if you plan to use it on your system. Be sure to change the user's password to something more secure!

Listing 26.1 `bookmarks.sql`—**SQL File to Set Up the Bookmark Database**

```
create database bookmarks;
use bookmarks;

create table user  (
  username varchar(16) not null primary key,
  passwd char(40) not null,
  email varchar(100) not null
);

create table bookmark (
  username varchar(16) not null,
  bm_URL varchar(255) not null,
  index (username),
  index (bm_URL),
  primary key(username, bm_URL)
);

grant select, insert, update, delete
on bookmarks.*
to bm_user@localhost identified by 'password';
```

You can set up this database on your system by running this set of commands as the root MySQL user. You can do this with the following command on your system's command line:

```
mysql -u root -p < bookmarks.sql
```

You are then prompted to type in your password.

With the database set up, you're ready to go on and implement the basic site.

Implementing the Basic Site

The first page you'll build is called `login.php` because it provides users with the opportunity to log in to the system. The code for this first page is shown in Listing 26.2.

Listing 26.2 `login.php`—**Front Page of the PHPbookmark System**

```php
<?php
 require_once('bookmark_fns.php');
 do_html_header('');

 display_site_info();
 display_login_form();

 do_html_footer();
?>
```

This code looks very simple because it mostly calls functions from the function API that you will construct for this application. We look at the details of these functions shortly. Just looking at this file, you can see that it includes a file (containing the functions) and then calls some functions to render an HTML header, display some content, and render an HTML footer.

The output from this script is shown in Figure 26.3.

Figure 26.3   The front page of the PHPbookmark system is produced by the HTML rendering functions in `login.php`.

The functions for the system are all included in the file `bookmark_fns.php`, shown in Listing 26.3.

Listing 26.3   `bookmark_fns.php`—**Include File of Functions for the Bookmark Application**

```php
<?php
  // We can include this file in all our files
  // this way, every file will contain all our functions and exceptions
  require_once('data_valid_fns.php');
  require_once('db_fns.php');
  require_once('user_auth_fns.php');
  require_once('output_fns.php');
  require_once('url_fns.php');
?>
```

As you can see, this file is just a container for the five other include files you will use in this application. We structured the project like this because the functions fall into logical groups. Some of these groups might be useful for other projects, so we put each function group into a different file so you will know where to find it when you want it again. We constructed the bookmark_fns.php file because you will use most of the five function files in most of the scripts. Including this one file in each script is easier than having five require statements.

In this particular case, you use functions from the file output_fns.php. They are all straightforward functions that output fairly plain HTML. This file includes the four functions used in login.php—that is, do_html_header(), display_site_info(), display_login_form(), and do_html_footer(), among others.

Although we will not go through all these functions in detail, let's look at one as an example. The code for do_html_header() is shown in Listing 26.4.

Listing 26.4 do_html_header() **Function from** output_fns.php—**This Function Outputs the Standard Header That Will Appear on Each Page in the Application**

```
function do_html_header($title)
{
  // print an HTML header
?>
  <html>
  <head>
    <title><?php echo $title;?></title>
    <style>
      body { font-family: Arial, Helvetica, sans-serif; font-size: 13px }
      li, td { font-family: Arial, Helvetica, sans-serif; font-size: 13px }
      hr { color: #3333cc; width=300; text-align=left}
      a { color: #000000 }
    </style>
  </head>
  <body>
  <img src='bookmark.gif' alt='PHPbookmark logo' border=0
      align='left' valign='bottom' height = 55 width = 57 />
  <h1>  PHPbookmark</h1>
  <hr />
<?php
  if($title)
    do_html_heading($title);
}
```

As you can see, the only logic in the do_html_header() function is to add the appropriate title and heading to the page. The other functions used in login.php are similar. The function display_site_info() adds some general text about the site, display_login_form() displays the gray form shown in Figure 26.3, and do_html_footer() adds a standard HTML footer to the page.

The advantages to isolating or removing HTML from your main logic stream are discussed in Chapter 24, "Using PHP and MySQL for Large Projects." We use the function API approach here.

Looking at Figure 26.3, you can see that this page has three options: A user can register, log in if she has already registered, or reset her password if she has forgotten it. To implement these modules, we move on to the next section, user authentication.

Implementing User Authentication

There are four main elements to the user authentication module: registering users, logging in and logging out, changing passwords, and resetting passwords. In the following sections, we look at each of these elements in turn.

Registering

To register a user, you need to get his details via a form and enter him in the database.

When a user clicks on the Not a member? link on the login.php page, he is taken to a registration form produced by register_form.php. This script is shown in Listing 26.5.

Listing 26.5 register_form.php—**This Form Gives Users the Opportunity to Register with PHPbookmark**

```php
<?php
  require_once('bookmark_fns.php');
  do_html_header('User Registration');

  display_registration_form();

  do_html_footer();
?>
```

Again, you can see that this page is fairly simple and just calls functions from the output library in output_fns.php. The output of this script is shown in Figure 26.4.

The gray form on this page is output by the function display_registration_form(), contained in output_fns.php. When the user clicks on the Register button, he is taken to the script register_new.php, shown in Listing 26.6.

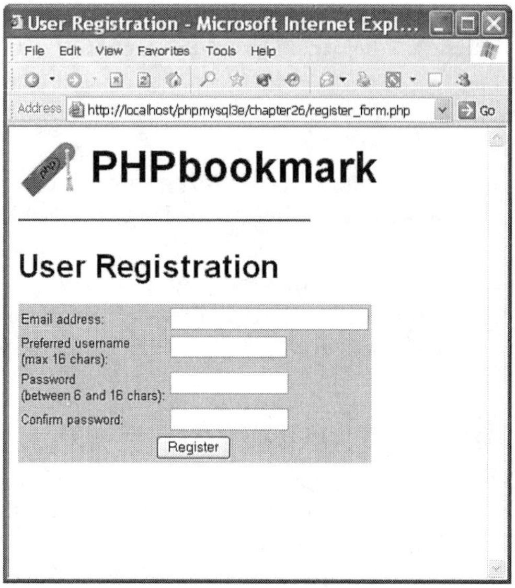

Figure 26.4 The registration form retrieves the details needed for the database. This form requires users to type their passwords twice, in case they make a mistake.

Listing 26.6 `register_new.php`— **This Script Validates the New User's Data and Puts It in the Database**

```php
<?php
  // include function files for this application
  require_once('bookmark_fns.php');

  //create short variable names
  $email=$_POST['email'];
  $username=$_POST['username'];
  $passwd=$_POST['passwd'];
  $passwd2=$_POST['passwd2'];
  // start session which may be needed later
  // start it now because it must go before headers
  session_start();
  try
  {
    // check forms filled in
    if (!filled_out($_POST))
    {
      throw new Exception('You have not filled the form out correctly '
                      .'- please go back and try again.');
    }
```

Listing 26.6   **Continued**

```
    // email address not valid
    if (!valid_email($email))
    {
      throw new Exception('That is not a valid email address.  Please go back '
                          .' and try again.');
    }

    // passwords not the same
    if ($passwd != $passwd2)
    {
      throw new Exception('The passwords you entered do not match
                          .' - please go back and try again.');
    }

    // check password length is ok
    if (strlen($passwd)<6)
    {
      throw new Exception('Your password must be at least 6 characters long.'
                          .'Please go back and try again.');
    }

    // check username length is ok
    if (strlen($username)>16)
    {
      throw new Exception('Your username must be less than 17 characters long.'
                          .'Please go back and try again.');
    }

    // attempt to register
    // this function can also throw an exception
    register($username, $email, $passwd);
    // register session variable
    $_SESSION['valid_user'] = $username;

    // provide link to members page
    do_html_header('Registration successful');
    echo 'Your registration was successful.  Go to the members page '
         .'to start setting up your bookmarks!';
    do_html_url('member.php', 'Go to members page');

  // end page
  do_html_footer();
}
catch (Exception $e)
{
```

Listing 26.6   **Continued**

```
      do_html_header('Problem:');
      echo $e->getMessage();
      do_html_footer();
      exit;
  }
?>
```

This is the first script with any complexity to it that we have looked at in this application. It begins by including the application's function files and starting a session. (When
the user is registered, you create his username as a session variable, as you did in
Chapter 22, "Using Session Control in PHP.")

The body of the script takes place in a try block because you check a number of
conditions. If any of them fail, execution will fall through to the catch block, which we
look at shortly.

Next, you validate the input data from the user. Here, you must test for the following
conditions:

- Check that the form is filled out. You test this with a call to the function
  filled_out(), as follows:

  ```
  if (!filled_out($_POST))
  ```

  We wrote this function ourselves. It is in the function library in the file
  data_valid_fns.php. We look at this function shortly.

- Check that the email address supplied is valid. You test this as follows:

  ```
  if (valid_email($email))
  ```

  Again, this is a function we wrote; it's in the data_valid_fns.php library.

- Check that the two passwords the user has suggested are the same, as follows:

  ```
  if ($passwd != $passwd2)
  ```

- Check that the username and password are the appropriate length, as follows:

  ```
  if (strlen($passwd)<6)
  ```

  and

  ```
  if (strlen($username)>16)
  ```

In the example, the password should be at least 6 characters long to make it harder
to guess, and the username should be fewer than 17 characters so that it will fit in
the database. Note that the maximum length of the password is not restricted in
this way because it is stored as an SHA1 hash, which will always be 40 characters
long no matter the length of the password.

The data validation functions used here, `filled_out()` and `valid_email()`, are shown in Listings 26.7 and 26.8, respectively.

Listing 26.7 `filled_out()` Function from `data_valid_fns.php`—This Function Checks That the Form Has Been Filled Out

```
function filled_out($form_vars)
{
  // test that each variable has a value
  foreach ($form_vars as $key => $value)
  {
    if (!isset($key) || ($value == ''))
      return false;
  }
  return true;
}
```

Listing 26.8 `valid_email()` Function from `data_valid_fns.php`—This Function Checks Whether an Email Address Is Valid

```
function valid_email($address)
{
  // check an email address is possibly valid
  if (ereg('^[a-zA-Z0-9 \._\-]+@([a-zA-Z0-9][a-zA-Z0-9\-]*\.)+
            [a-zA-Z]+$', $address))
    return true;
  else
    return false;
}
```

The function `filled_out()` expects to be passed an array of variables; in general, this is the `$_POST` or `$_GET` array. It checks whether the form fields are all filled out, and returns `true` if they are and `false` if they are not.

The `valid_email()` function uses a slightly more complex regular expression than the one developed in Chapter 4, "String Manipulation and Regular Expressions," for validating email addresses. It returns `true` if an address appears valid and `false` if it does not.

After you've validated the input data, you can actually try to register the user. If you look back at Listing 26.6, you can see that you do this as follows:

```
register($username, $email, $passwd);
// register session variable
$_SESSION['valid_user'] = $username;
```

```
      // provide link to members page
      do_html_header('Registration successful');
      echo 'Your registration was successful.  Go to the members page '
          .'to start setting up your bookmarks!';
      do_html_url('member.php', 'Go to members page');

      // end page
      do_html_footer();
```

As you can see, you call the `register()` function with the username, email address, and password that were entered. If this call succeeds, you register the username as a session variable and provide the user with a link to the main members page. (If it fails, this function will throw an exception that will be caught in the `catch` block.) The output is shown in Figure 26.5.

Figure 26.5   Registration was successful; the user can now go to the members page.

The `register()` function is in the included library called `user_auth_fns.php`. This function is shown in Listing 26.9.

Listing 26.9 register() **Function from** user_auth_fns.php—**This Function Attempts to Put the New User's Information in the Database**

```php
function register($username, $email, $password)
// register new person with db
// return true or error message
{
  // connect to db
  $conn = db_connect();

  // check if username is unique
  $result = $conn->query("select * from user where username='$username'");
  if (!$result)
    throw new Exception('Could not execute query');
  if ($result->num_rows>0)
    throw new Exception('That username is taken '
                        .'- go back and choose another one.') ;

  // if ok, put in db
  $result = $conn->query("insert into user values
                        ('$username', sha1('$password'), '$email')");
  if (!$result)
    throw new Exception('Could not register you in database '
                        .'- please try again later.');

  return true;
}
```

There is nothing particularly new in this function; it connects to the database you set up earlier. If the username selected is taken or the database cannot be updated, it will throw an exception. Otherwise, it will update the database and return true.

Note that you are performing the actual database connection with a function called db_connect(), which we wrote. This function simply provides a single location that contains the username and password to connect to the database. That way, if you change the database password, you need to change only one file in the application. The db_connect() function is shown in Listing 26.10.

Listing 26.10 db_connect() **Function from** db_fns.php—**This Function Connects to the MySQL Database**

```php
function db_connect()
{
  $result = new mysqli('localhost', 'bm_user', 'password', 'bookmarks');
  if (!$result)
    throw new Exception('Could not connect to database server');
  else
    return $result;
}
```

When users are registered, they can log in and out using the regular login and logout pages. You build them next.

Logging In

If users type their details into the form at login.php (see Figure 26.3) and submit it, they will be taken to the script called member.php. This script logs them in if they have come from this form. It also displays any relevant bookmarks to users who are logged in. It is the center of the rest of the application. This script is shown in Listing 26.11.

Listing 26.11 member.php—**This Script Is the Main Hub of the Application**

```php
<?php

// include function files for this application
require_once('bookmark_fns.php');
session_start();

//create short variable names
$username = $_POST['username'];
$passwd = $_POST['passwd'];

if ($username && $passwd)
// they have just tried logging in
{
  try
  {
    login($username, $passwd);
    // if they are in the database register the user id
    $_SESSION['valid_user'] = $username;
  }
  catch(Exception $e)
  {
    // unsuccessful login
    do_html_header('Problem:');
    echo 'You could not be logged in.
          You must be logged in to view this page.';
    do_html_url('login.php', 'Login');
    do_html_footer();
    exit;
  }
}

do_html_header('Home');
check_valid_user();
```

Listing 26.11 **Continued**

```
// get the bookmarks this user has saved
if ($url_array = get_user_urls($_SESSION['valid_user']))
  display_user_urls($url_array);

// give menu of options
display_user_menu();

do_html_footer();
?>
```

You might recognize the logic in the member.php script: It reuses some of the ideas from Chapter 22.

First, you check whether the user has come from the front page—that is, whether he has just filled in the login form—and try to log him in as follows:

```
if ($username && $passwd)
// they have just tried logging in
{
  try
  {
    login($username, $passwd);
    // if they are in the database register the user id
    $_SESSION['valid_user'] = $username;
  }
```

You try to log the user in by using a function called login(). It is defined in the user_auth_fns.php library, and we look at the code for it shortly.

If the user is logged in successfully, you register his session as you did before, storing the username in the session variable valid_user.

If all goes well, you then show the user the members page:

```
do_html_header('Home');
check_valid_user();
// get the bookmarks this user has saved
if ($url_array = get_user_urls($_SESSION['valid_user']))
  display_user_urls($url_array);

// give menu of options
display_user_menu();

do_html_footer();
```

This page is again formed using the output functions. Notice that the page uses several other new functions: check_valid_user() from user_auth_fns.php, get_user_urls() from url_fns.php, and display_user_urls() from output_fns.php. The check_valid_user() function checks that the current user has a registered session.

This is aimed at users who have *not* just logged in, but are mid-session. The `get_user_urls()` function gets a user's bookmarks from the database, and `display_user_urls()` outputs the bookmarks to the browser in a table. We look at `check_valid_user()` in a moment and at the other two in the section on bookmark storage and retrieval.

The `member.php` script ends the page by displaying a menu with the `display_user_menu()` function. Some sample output as displayed by `member.php` is shown in Figure 26.6.

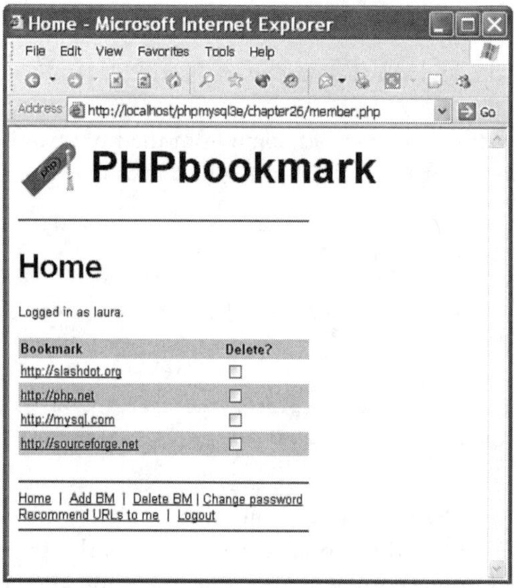

Figure 26.6 The `member.php` script checks that a user is logged in, retrieves and displays his bookmarks, and gives him a menu of options.

Let's look at the `login()` and `check_valid_user()` functions a little more closely now. The `login()` function is shown in Listing 26.12.

Listing 26.12 `login()` **Function from** `user_auth_fns.php`—**This Function Checks a User's Details Against the Database**

```
function login($username, $password)
// check username and password with db
// if yes, return true
// else throw exception
{
  // connect to db
  $conn = db_connect();
```

Listing 26.12   **Continued**

```
// check if username is unique
$result = $conn->query("select * from user
                        where username='$username'
                        and passwd = sha1('$password')");
if (!$result)
   throw new Exception('Could not log you in.');

if ($result->num_rows>0)
   return true;
else
   throw new Exception('Could not log you in.');
}
```

As you can see, the login() function connects to the database and checks that there is a user with the username and password combination supplied. It returns true if there is or throws an exception if there is not or if the user's credentials could not be checked.

The check_valid_user() function does not connect to the database again, but instead just checks that the user has a registered session—that is, that he has already logged in. This function is shown in Listing 26.13.

Listing 26.13   check_valid_user()**Function from** user_auth_fns.php—**This Function Checks That the User Has a Valid Session**

```
function check_valid_user()
// see if somebody is logged in and notify them if not
{
  if (isset($_SESSION['valid_user']))
  {
     echo 'Logged in as '.stripslashes($_SESSION['valid_user']).'.';
     echo '<br />';
  }
  else
  {
     // they are not logged in
     do_html_heading('Problem:');
     echo 'You are not logged in.<br />';
     do_html_url('login.php', 'Login');
     do_html_footer();
     exit;
  }
}
```

If the user is not logged in, the function will tell him he has to be logged in to see this page, and give him a link to the login page.

Logging Out

You might have noticed the link marked Logout on the menu in Figure 26.6. This is a link to the logout.php script; the code for this script is shown in Listing 26.14.

Listing 26.14   logout.php—**This Script Ends a User Session**

```php
<?php

// include function files for this application
require_once('bookmark_fns.php');
session_start();
$old_user = $_SESSION['valid_user'];
// store  to test if they *were* logged in
unset($_SESSION['valid_user']);
$result_dest = session_destroy();

// start output html
do_html_header('Logging Out');

if (!empty($old_user))
{
  if ($result_dest)
  {
    // if they were logged in and are now logged out
    echo 'Logged out.<br />';
    do_html_url('login.php', 'Login');
  }
  else
  {
   // they were logged in and could not be logged out
    echo 'Could not log you out.<br />';
  }
}
else
{
  // if they weren't logged in but came to this page somehow
  echo 'You were not logged in, and so have not been logged out.<br />';
  do_html_url('login.php', 'Login');
}

do_html_footer();

?>
```

Again, you might find that this code looks familiar. That's because it is based on the code you wrote in Chapter 22.

Changing Passwords

If a user follows the Change Password menu option, she will be presented with the form shown in Figure 26.7.

Figure 26.7   The change_passwd_form.php script supplies a form where users can change their passwords.

This form is generated by the script change_passwd_form.php. This simple script just uses the functions from the output library, so we did not include the source for it here.

When this form is submitted, it triggers the change_passwd.php script, which is shown in Listing 26.15.

Listing 26.15   change_passwd.php— **This Script Attempts to Change a User Password**

```php
<?php
  require_once('bookmark_fns.php');
  session_start();
  do_html_header('Changing password');

  // create short variable names
  $old_passwd = $_POST['old_passwd'];
  $new_passwd = $_POST['new_passwd'];
  $new_passwd2 = $_POST['new_passwd2'];
```

Listing 26.15   **Continued**

```
  try
  {
    check_valid_user();
    if (!filled_out($_POST))
      throw new Exception('You have not filled out the form completely.'
                          .' Please try again.');
    if ($new_passwd!=$new_passwd2)
      throw new Exception('Passwords entered were not the same.  Not changed.');
    if (strlen($new_passwd)<6)
      throw new Exception('New password must be at least 6 characters.'
                          .' Try again.');
    // attempt update
    change_password($_SESSION['valid_user'], $old_passwd, $new_passwd);
    echo 'Password changed.';
  }
  catch (Exception $e)
  {
    echo $e->getMessage();
  }
  display_user_menu();
  do_html_footer();
?>
```

This script checks that the user is logged in (using check_valid_user()), that she's filled out the password form (using filled_out()), and that the new passwords are the same and the right length. None of this is new. If all that goes well, the script will call the change_password() function as follows:

```
change_password($_SESSION['valid_user'], $old_passwd, $new_passwd);
echo 'Password changed.';
```

This function is from the user_auth_fns.php library, and the code for it is shown in Listing 26.16.

Listing 26.16   change_password() **Function from** user_auth_fns.php—**This Function Attempts to Update a User Password in the Database**

```
function change_password($username, $old_password, $new_password)
// change password for username/old_password to new_password
// return true or false
{
  // if the old password is right
  // change their password to new_password and return true
  // else throw an exception
  login($username, $old_password);
```

Listing 26.16   **Continued**

```
$conn = db_connect();
$result = $conn->query( "update user
                        set passwd = sha1('$new_password')
                        where username = '$username'");
if (!$result)
  throw new Exception('Password could not be changed.');
else
  return true;   // changed successfully
}
```

This function checks that the old password supplied was correct, using the login() function that you have already looked at. If it's correct, the function will connect to the database and update the password to the new value.

Resetting Forgotten Passwords

In addition to changing passwords, you need to deal with the common situation in which a user has forgotten her password. On the front page, login.php, you provide a link, marked Forgotten your password?, for users in this situation. This link takes users to the script called forgot_form.php, which uses the output functions to display a form, as shown in Figure 26.8.

Figure 26.8   The forgot_form.php script supplies a form in which users can ask to have their passwords reset and sent to them.

The `forgot_form.php` script is very simple—just using the output functions—so we did not include it here. When the form is submitted, it calls the `forgot_passwd.php` script, which is more interesting. This script is shown in Listing 26.17.

Listing 26.17 `forgot_passwd.php` —This Script Resets a User's Password to a Random Value and Emails Her the New One

```php
<?php
  require_once('bookmark_fns.php');
  do_html_header('Resetting password');

  // creating short variable name
  $username = $_POST['username'];

  try
  {
    $password = reset_password($username);
    notify_password($username, $password);
    echo 'Your new password has been emailed to you.<br />';
  }
  catch (Exception $e)
  {
    echo 'Your password could not be reset - please try again later.';
  }
  do_html_url('login.php', 'Login');
  do_html_footer();
?>
```

As you can see, this script uses two main functions to do its job: `reset_password()` and `notify_password()`. Let's look at each of these in turn.

The `reset_password()` function generates a random password for the user and puts it into the database. The code for this function is shown in Listing 26.18.

Listing 26.18 `reset_password()` Function from `user_auth_fns.php`—This Function Resets a User's Password to a Random Value and Emails Her the New One

```php
function reset_password($username)
// set password for username to a random value
// return the new password or false on failure
{
  // get a random dictionary word b/w 6 and 13 chars in length
  $new_password = get_random_word(6, 13);

  if($new_password==false)
    throw new Exception('Could not generate new password.');
  // add a number  between 0 and 999 to it
  // to make it a slightly better password
```

Listing 26.18   **Continued**

```
srand ((double) microtime() * 1000000);
$rand_number = rand(0, 999);
$new_password .= $rand_number;

// set user's password to this in database or return false
$conn = db_connect();
$result = $conn->query( "update user
                         set passwd = sha1('$new_password')
                         where username = '$username'");
if (!$result)
  throw new Exception('Could not change password.');  // not changed
else
  return $new_password;  // changed successfully
}
```

The reset_password() function generates its random password by getting a random word from a dictionary, using the get_random_word() function and suffixing it with a random number between 0 and 999. The get_random_word() function, shown in Listing 26.19, is also in the user_auth_fns.php library.

Listing 26.19   get_random_word() **Function from** user_auth_fns.php—**This Function Gets a Random Word from the Dictionary for Use in Generating Passwords**

```
function get_random_word($min_length, $max_length)
// grab a random word from dictionary between the two lengths
// and return it
{
  // generate a random word
  $word = '';
  // remember to change this path to suit your system
  $dictionary = '/usr/dict/words';  // the ispell dictionary
  $fp = @fopen($dictionary, 'r');
  if(!$fp)
    return false;
  $size = filesize($dictionary);

  // go to a random location in dictionary
  srand ((double) microtime() * 1000000);
  $rand_location = rand(0, $size);
  fseek($fp, $rand_location);

  // get the next whole word of the right length in the file
  while (strlen($word)< $min_length ||
         strlen($word)>$max_length || strstr($word, "'"))
  {
```

Listing 26.19 **Continued**

```
    if (feof($fp))
        fseek($fp, 0);          // if at end, go to start
    $word = fgets($fp, 80);  // skip first word as it could be partial
    $word = fgets($fp, 80);  // the potential password
  };
  $word=trim($word); // trim the trailing \n from fgets
  return $word;
}
```

To work, the get_random_word() function needs a dictionary. If you are using a Unix system, the built-in spell checker ispell comes with a dictionary of words, typically located at /usr/dict/words, as it is here, or at /usr/share/dict/words. If you don't find it in one of these places, on most systems you can find yours by typing

```
$ locate dict/words
```

If you are using some other system or do not want to install ispell, don't worry! You can download word lists as used by ispell from http://wordlist.sourceforge.net/.

This site also has dictionaries in many other languages, so if you would like a random, say, Norwegian or Esperanto word, you can download one of those dictionaries instead. These files are formatted with each word on a separate line, separated by newlines.

To get a random word from this file, you pick a random location between 0 and the filesize, and read from the file there. If you read from the random location to the next newline, you will most likely get only a partial word, so you skip the line you open the file to and take the next word as your word by calling fgets() twice.

The function has two clever bits. The first is that, if you reach the end of the file while looking for a word, you go back to the beginning:

```
if (feof($fp))
  fseek($fp, 0);          // if at end, go to start
```

The second is that you can seek for a word of a particular length: You check each word that you pull from the dictionary, and, if it is not between $min_length and $max_length, you keep searching. At the same time, you also dump words with apostrophes (single quotation marks) in them. You could escape them out when using the word, but just getting the next word is easier.

Back in reset_password(), after you have generated a new password, you update the database to reflect this and return the new password to the main script. This is then passed on to notify_password(), which emails it to the user. The notify_password() function is shown in Listing 26.20.

Listing 26.20 `notify_password()` **Function from** `user_auth_fns.php`**—This Function Emails a Reset Password to a User**

```
function notify_password($username, $password)
// notify the user that password has been changed
{
    $conn = db_connect();
    $result = $conn->query("select email from user
                            where username='$username'");
    if (!$result)
    {
      throw new Exception('Could not find email address.');
    }
    else if ($result->num_rows==0)
    {
      throw new Exception('Could not find '
                          .' email address.');    // username not in db
    }
    else
    {
      $row = $result->fetch_object();
      $email = $row->email;
      $from = "From: support@phpbookmark \r\n";
      $mesg = "Your PHPbookmark password has been changed to $password \r\n"
              ."Please change it next time you log in. \r\n";


      if (mail($email, 'PHPbookmark login information', $mesg, $from))
        return true;
      else
        throw new Exception('Could not send email.');
    }
}
```

In the `notify_password()` function, given a username and new password, you simply look up the email address for that user in the database and use PHP's `mail()` function to send it to her.

It would be more secure to give users a truly random password—made from any combination of upper and lowercase letters, numbers, and punctuation—rather than the random word and number. However, a password like `zigzag487` will be easier for users to read and type than a truly random one. It is often confusing for users to work out whether a character in a random string is 0 or O (zero or capital O), or 1 or l (one or a lowercase L)

On our system, the dictionary file contains about 45,000 words. If a cracker knew how we were creating passwords and knew a user's name, he would still have to try 22,500,000 passwords on average to guess one. This level of security seems adequate for this type of application even if our users disregard our emailed advice to change their password.

Implementing Bookmark Storage and Retrieval

Now let's move on and look at how users' bookmarks are stored, retrieved, and deleted.

Adding Bookmarks

Users can add bookmarks by clicking on the Add BM link in the user menu. This action takes them to the form shown in Figure 26.9.

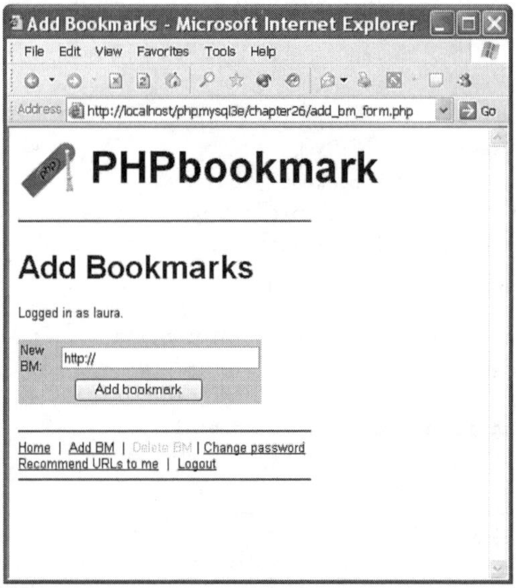

Figure 26.9   The add_bm_form.php script supplies a form where users can
add bookmarks to their bookmark pages.

Again, because the add_bm_form.php script is simple and uses just the output functions, we did not include it here. When the form is submitted, it calls the add_bms.php script, which is shown in Listing 26.21.

Listing 26.21 add_bms.php—This Script Adds New Bookmarks to a User's Personal Page

```php
<?php
 require_once('bookmark_fns.php');
 session_start();

  //create short variable name
  $new_url = $_POST['new_url'];

  do_html_header('Adding bookmarks');

  try
  {
    check_valid_user();
    if (!filled_out($_POST))
    {
      throw new Exception('Form not completely filled out.');
    }
    // check URL format
    if (strstr($new_url, 'http://')===false)
      $new_url = 'http://'.$new_url;

    // check URL is valid
    if (!(@fopen($new_url, 'r')))
      throw new Exception('Not a valid URL.');
    // try to add bm
    add_bm($new_url) ;
    echo 'Bookmark added.';

    // get the bookmarks this user has saved
    if ($url_array = get_user_urls($_SESSION['valid_user']))
      display_user_urls($url_array);
  }
  catch (Exception $e)
  {
    echo $e->getMessage();
  }
  display_user_menu();
  do_html_footer();
?>
```

Again, this script follows the pattern of validation, database entry, and output.

To validate, you first check whether the user has filled out the form using `filled_out()`. You then perform two URL checks. First, using `strstr()`, you see whether the URL begins with `http://`. If it doesn't, you add this to the start of the URL. After you've done this, you can actually check that the URL really exists. As you might recall from Chapter 19, "Using Network and Protocol Functions," you can use `fopen()` to open an URL that starts with `http://`. If you can open this file, you can assume the URL is valid and call the function `add_bm()` to add it to the database.

This function and the others relating to bookmarks are all in the function library `url_fns.php`. You can see the code for the `add_bm()` function in Listing 26.22.

Listing 26.22 `add_bm()` Function from `url_fns.php`—This Function Adds New Bookmarks to the Database

```
function add_bm($new_url)
{
  // Add new bookmark to the database

  echo "Attempting to add ".htmlspecialchars($new_url).'<br />';
  $valid_user = $_SESSION['valid_user'];

  $conn = db_connect();

  // insert the new bookmark
  if (!$conn->query( "insert into bookmark values
                          ('$valid_user', '$new_url')"))
    throw new Exception('Bookmark could not be inserted.');

  return true;
}
```

The `add_bm()` function is fairly simple. It checks that a user does not already have this bookmark listed in the database. (Although it is unlikely that users would enter a bookmark twice, it is possible and even likely that they might refresh the page.) If the bookmark is new, it is entered into the database.

Looking back at `add_bm.php`, you can see that the last thing it does is call `get_user_urls()` and `display_user_urls()`, the same as `member.php`. We look at these functions next.

Displaying Bookmarks

The `member.php` script and `add_bm()` function use the functions `get_user_urls()` and `display_user_urls()`. These functions get a user's bookmarks from the database and display them, respectively. The `get_user_urls()` function is in the `url_fns.php` library, and the `display_user_urls()` function is in the `output_fns.php` library.

The `get_user_urls()` function is shown in Listing 26.23.

Listing 26.23 `get_user_urls()` **Function from** `url_fns.php`—**This Function Retrieves a User's Bookmarks from the Database**

```
function get_user_urls($username)
{
  //extract from the database all the URLs this user has stored
  $conn = db_connect();
  $result = $conn->query( "select bm_URL
                          from bookmark
                          where username = '$username'");
  if (!$result)
    return false;

  //create an array of the URLs
  $url_array = array();
  for ($count = 0; $row = $result->fetch_row(); ++$count)
  {
    $url_array[$count] = $row[0];
  }
  return $url_array;
}
```

Let's briefly step through the `get_user_urls()` function. It takes a username as a parameter and retrieves the bookmarks for that user from the database. It returns an array of these URLs or `false` if the bookmarks could not be retrieved.

The array from `get_user_urls()` can be passed to `display_user_urls()`. This is again a simple HTML output function to print the user's URLs in a nice table format, so we didn't include it here. Refer to Figure 26.6 to see what the output looks like. The function actually puts the URLs into a form. Next to each URL is a check box that enables the user to mark bookmarks for deletion. We look at this capability next.

Deleting Bookmarks

When a user marks some bookmarks for deletion and clicks on the `Delete BM` link on the menu, the form containing the URLs is submitted. Each one of the check boxes is produced by the following code in the `display_user_urls()` function:

```
echo "<td><input type='checkbox' name='del_me[]'
          value='$url'></td>";
```

The name of each input is `del_me[]`. This means that, in the PHP script activated by this form, you have access to an array called `$del_me` that contains all the bookmarks to be deleted.

Clicking on the `Delete BM` option activates the `delete_bms.php` script, which is shown in Listing 26.24.

Listing 26.24   `delete_bms.php`— **This Script Deletes Bookmarks from the Database**

```php
<?php
  require_once('bookmark_fns.php');
  session_start();

  //create short variable names
  $del_me = $HTTP_POST_VARS['del_me'];
  $valid_user = $HTTP_SESSION_VARS['valid_user'];

  do_html_header('Deleting bookmarks');
  check_valid_user();
  if (!filled_out($HTTP_POST_VARS))
  {
    echo 'You have not chosen any bookmarks to delete.
        Please try again.';
    display_user_menu();
    do_html_footer();
    exit;
  }
  else
  {
    if (count($del_me) >0)
    {
      foreach($del_me as $url)
      {
        if (delete_bm($valid_user, $url))
          echo 'Deleted '.htmlspecialchars($url).'.<br />';
        else
          echo 'Could not delete '.htmlspecialchars($url).'.<br />';
      }
    }
    else
      echo 'No bookmarks selected for deletion';
  }
  // get the bookmarks this user has saved
  if ($url_array = get_user_urls($valid_user))
    display_user_urls($url_array);
```

Listing 26.24   **Continued**

```
  display_user_menu();
  do_html_footer();
?>
```

You begin this script by performing the usual validations. When you know that the user has selected some bookmarks for deletion, you delete them in the following loop:

```
foreach($del_me as $url)
{
  if (delete_bm($valid_user, $url))
    echo 'Deleted '.htmlspecialchars($url).'.<br />';
  else
    echo 'Could not delete '.htmlspecialchars($url).'.<br />';
}
```

As you can see, the `delete_bm()` function does the actual work of deleting the bookmark from the database. This function is shown in Listing 26.25.

Listing 26.25   `delete_bm()` **Function in** `url_fns.php`—**This Function Deletes a Single Bookmark from a User's List**

```
function delete_bm($user, $url)
{
  // delete one URL from the database
  $conn = db_connect();
  // delete the bookmark
  if (!$conn->query( "delete from bookmark
                      where username='$user' and bm_url='$url'"))
    throw new Exception('Bookmark could not be deleted');
  return true;
}
```

As you can see, `delete_bm()` is also a pretty simple function. It attempts to delete the bookmark for a particular user from the database. Note that you want to remove a particular username-bookmark pair in this case. Other users might still have this URL bookmarked.

Some sample output from running the deletion script on the system is shown in Figure 26.10.

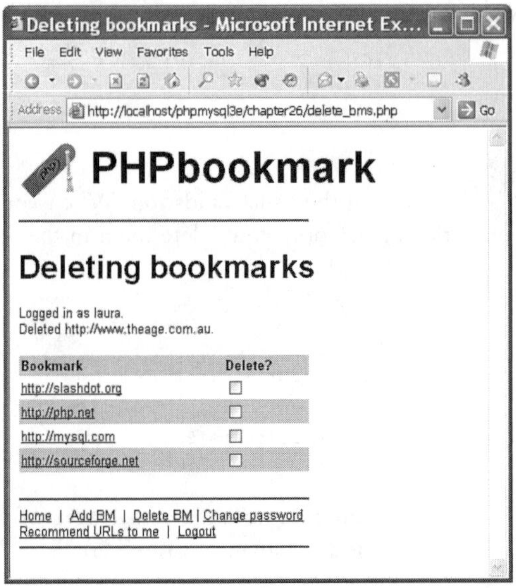

Figure 26.10   The deletion script notifies the user of deleted bookmarks and
then displays the remaining bookmarks.

As in the `add_bms.php` script, after the changes to the database have been made, you display the new bookmark list using `get_user_urls()` and `display_user_urls()`.

Implementing Recommendations

Finally, you're ready for the link recommender script, `recommend.php`. There are many different ways you could approach recommendations. You should perform what we call a "like minds" recommendation. That is, look for other users who have at least one bookmark the same as your given user. The other bookmarks of those other users might appeal to your given user as well.

The easiest way to implement this as an SQL query is to use subqueries. The first subquery looks like this:

```
select distinct(b2.username)
            from bookmark b1, bookmark b2
            where b1.username='$valid_user'
            and b1.username != b2.username
            and b1.bm_URL = b2.bm_URL
```

This query uses aliases to join the database table `bookmark` to itself—a strange but sometimes useful concept. Imagine that you actually have two bookmark tables, one called `b1` and one called `b2`. In `b1`, you look at the current user and his bookmarks. In the other table, you look at the bookmarks of all the other users. You are looking for other users (`b2.username`) who have an URL the same as the current user (`b1.bm_URL = b2.bm_URL`) and are not the current user (`b1.username != b2.username`).

This query gives you a list of like-minded people to your current user. Armed with this list, you can search for their other bookmarks with the outer query:

```
select bm_URL
from bookmark
where username in
                (select distinct(b2.username)
                 from bookmark b1, bookmark b2
                where b1.username='$valid_user'
                and b1.username != b2.username
                and b1.bm_URL = b2.bm_URL)
```

You add a second subquery to filter out the current user's bookmarks; if the user already has a bookmark, there's no point in recommending it to him. Finally, you add some filtering with the `$popularity` variable. You don't want to recommend any URLs that are too personal, so you suggest only URLs that a certain number of other users in the list of like-minded users have bookmarked. The final query looks like this:

```
select bm_URL
from bookmark
where username in
                (select distinct(b2.username)
                 from bookmark b1, bookmark b2
                where b1.username='$valid_user'
                and b1.username != b2.username
                and b1.bm_URL = b2.bm_URL)
and bm_URL not in
                (select bm_URL
                 from bookmark
                where username='$valid_user')
group by bm_url
having count(bm_url)>$popularity
```

If you were anticipating many users using your system, you could adjust `$popularity` upward to suggest only URLs that have been bookmarked by a large number of users. URLs bookmarked by many people might be higher quality and certainly have more general appeal than an average web page.

The full script for making recommendations is shown in Listings 26.26 and 26.27. The main script for making recommendations is called `recommend.php` (see Listing 26.26). It calls the recommender function `recommend_urls()` from `url_fns.php` (see Listing 26.27).

Listing 26.26 `recommend.php`— **This Script Suggests Some Bookmarks That a User Might Like**

```php
<?php
  require_once('bookmark_fns.php');
  session_start();
  do_html_header('Recommending URLs');
  try
  {
    check_valid_user();
    $urls = recommend_urls($_SESSION['valid_user']);
    display_recommended_urls($urls);
  }
  catch(Exception $e)
  {
    echo $e->getMessage();
  }
  display_user_menu();
  do_html_footer();
?>
```

Listing 26.27 `recommend_urls()` **Function from** `url_fns.php`—**This Function Works Out the Actual Recommendations**

```php
function recommend_urls($valid_user, $popularity = 1)
{
  // We will provide semi intelligent recommendations to people
  // If they have an URL in common with other users, they may like
  // other URLs that these people like
  $conn = db_connect();
```

Listing 26.27 **Continued**

```
// find other matching users
// with an url the same as you
// as a simple way of excluding people's private pages, and
// increasing the chance of recommending appealing URLs, we
// specify a minimum popularity level
// if $popularity = 1, then more than one person must have
// an URL before we will recommend it
$query = "select bm_URL
          from bookmark
          where username in
               (select distinct(b2.username)
                  from bookmark b1, bookmark b2
                where b1.username='$valid_user'
                and b1.username != b2.username
                and b1.bm_URL = b2.bm_URL)
          and bm_URL not in
                               (select bm_URL
                                from bookmark
                                where username='$valid_user')
          group by bm_url
          having count(bm_url)>$popularity";

if (!($result = $conn->query($query)))
   throw new Exception('Could not find any bookmarks to recommend.');
if ($result->num_rows==0)
   throw new Exception('Could not find any bookmarks to recommend.');

$urls = array();
// build an array of the relevant urls
for ($count=0; $row = $result->fetch_object(); $count++)
{
   $urls[$count] = $row->bm_URL;
}

return $urls;
}
```

Some sample output from recommend.php is shown in Figure 26.11.

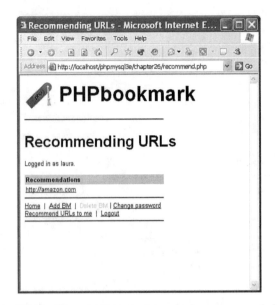

Figure 26.11   The `recommend.php` script has recommended that
this user might like amazon.com. At least two other users in the database who
both like amazon.com have this site bookmarked.

Wrapping Up and Considering Possible Extensions

In the preceding sections, we described the basic functionality of the PHPbookmark
application. There are many possible extensions. For example, you might consider adding

- A grouping of bookmarks by topic
- An "Add this to my bookmarks" link for recommendations
- Recommendations based on the most popular URLs in the database or on a particular topic
- An administrative interface to set up and administer users and topics
- Ways to make recommended bookmarks more intelligent or faster
- Additional error checking of user input

Experiment! It's the best way to learn.

Next

In the next project, you build a shopping cart that will enable users to browse your site,
adding purchases as they go, before finally checking out and making an electronic payment.

## 27

Building a Shopping Cart

IN THIS CHAPTER, YOU LEARN HOW TO BUILD a basic shopping cart. You add this on top of the Book-O-Rama database implemented in Part II, "Using MySQL." You also explore another option: setting up and using an existing open source PHP shopping cart.

In case you have not heard it before, the term *shopping cart* (sometimes also called a *shopping basket*) is used to describe a specific online shopping mechanism. As you browse an online catalog, you can add items to your shopping cart. After you've finished browsing, you check out of the online store—that is, purchase the items in your cart.

To implement the shopping cart for this project, you need to implement the following functionality:

- A database of the products you want to sell online
- An online catalog of products, listed by category
- A shopping cart to track the items a user wants to buy
- A checkout script that processes payment and shipping details
- An administration interface

The Problem

You probably remember the Book-O-Rama database developed in Part II. In this project, you get Book-O-Rama's online store up and going. The following are requirements for this system:

- You need to find a way of connecting the database to users' browsers. Users should be able to browse items by category.
- Users should also be able to select items from the catalog for later purchase. You need to be able to track which items they have selected.
- After users have finished shopping, you need to be able to total their order, take their delivery details, and process their payment.
- You should also build an administration interface to Book-O-Rama's site so that the administrator can add and edit books and categories on the site.

Solution Components

Let's look at the solutions to meeting each of the requirements listed in the preceding section.

Building an Online Catalog

You already have a database for the Book-O-Rama catalog. However, it probably needs some alterations and additions for this application. One of these is to add categories of books, as stated in the requirements.

You also need to add some information to the existing database about shipping addresses, payment details, and so on. You already know how to build an interface to a MySQL database using PHP, so this part of the solution should be pretty easy.

You should also use transactions while completing customers' orders. To do this, you need to convert your Book-O-Rama tables to use the InnoDB storage engine. This process is also reasonably straightforward.

Tracking Users' Purchases While They Shop

There are two basic ways you can track users' purchases while they shop. One is to put their selections into the database, and the other is to use a session variable.

Using a session variable to track selections from page to page is easier to write because it does not require you to constantly query the database for this information. By using this approach, you also avoid the situation in which you end up with a lot of junk data in the database from users who are just browsing and change their minds.

You need, therefore, to design a session variable or set of variables to store a user's selections. When a user finishes shopping and pays for her purchases, you will put this information in the database as a record of the transaction.

You can also use this data to give a summary of the current state of the cart in one corner of the page so that a user knows at any given time how much she is planning to spend.

Implementing a Payment System

In this project, you add the user's order and take the delivery details but do not actually process payments. Many, many payment systems are available, and the implementation for each one is different. For this project, you write a *dummy* function that can be replaced with an interface to your chosen system.

Payment systems are generally sold in more specific geographic areas than this book is. The way the different real-time processing interfaces work is generally similar. You need to organize a merchant account with a bank for the cards you want to accept. Your payment system provider will specify what parameters you need to pass to its system.

The payment system transmits your data to a bank and returns a success code or one of many different types of error codes. In exchange for passing on your data, the payment gateway charges you a setup or annual fee, as well as a fee based on the number or value of your transactions. Some providers even charge for declined transactions.

Your chosen payment system needs information from the customer (such as a credit card number), identifying information from you (to specify which merchant account is to be credited), and the total amount of the transaction.

You can work out the total of an order from a user's shopping cart session variable. You then record the final order details in the database and get rid of the session variable at that time.

Building an Administration Interface

In addition to the payment system and so on, you also need to build an administration interface that lets you add, delete, and edit books and categories from the database.

One common edit that you might make is to alter the price of an item (for example, for a special offer or sale). This means that when you store a customer's order, you should also store the price she paid for an item. It would make for an accounting nightmare if the only records you had were the items each customer ordered and the current price of each one. This also means that if the customer has to return or exchange the item, you will give her the right amount of credit.

You are not going to build a fulfillment and order tracking interface for this example. However, you can add one onto this base system to suit your needs.

Solution Overview

Let's put all the pieces together now. There are two basic views of the system: the user view and the administrator view. After considering the functionality required, we came up with two system flow designs you can use, one for each view. They are shown in Figures 27.1 and 27.2, respectively.

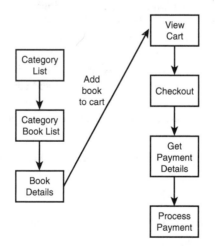

Figure 27.1   The user view of the Book-O-Rama system lets users browse books by category, view book details, add books to their cart, and purchase them.

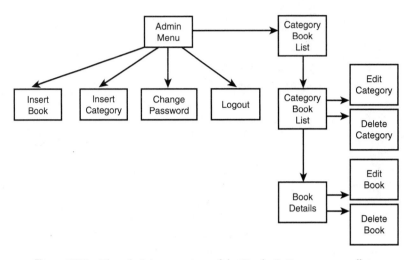

Figure 27.2   The administrator view of the Book-O-Rama system allows insertion, editing, and deletion of books and categories.

Figure 27.1 shows the main links between scripts in the user part of the site. A customer comes first to the main page, which lists all the categories of books in the site. From there, she can go to a particular category of books, and from there to an individual book's details.

You give the user a link to add a particular book to her cart. From the cart, she can check out of the online store.

Figure 27.2 shows the administration interface, which has more scripts but not much new code. These scripts let an administrator log in and insert books and categories.

The easiest way to implement editing and deletion of books and categories is to show the administrator a slightly different version of the user interface to the site. The administrator can still browse categories and books, but instead of having access to the shopping cart, he can go to a particular book or category and edit or delete that book or category. By making the same scripts suit both normal and administrator users, you can save yourself time and effort.

The three main code modules for this application are as follows:

- Catalog
- Shopping cart and order processing (We bundled them together because they are strongly related.)
- Administration

As in the project from Chapter 26, "Building User Authentication and Personalization," you also need to build and use a set of function libraries. For this project, you use a function API similar to the one in the previous project. Try to confine the parts of the code that output HTML to a single library to support the principle of separating logic and content and, more importantly, to make the code easier to read and maintain.

You also need to make some minor changes to the Book-O-Rama database for this project. We renamed the database `book_sc` (Shopping Cart) to distinguish the shopping cart database from the one built in Part II.

All the code for this project can be found on the CD-ROM. A summary of the files in the application is shown in Table 27.1.

Table 27.1   **Files in the Shopping Cart Application**

Name	Module	Description
index.php	Catalog	Main front page of site for users. Shows the users a list of categories in the system.
show_cat.php	Catalog	Page that shows the users all the books in a particular category.
show_book.php	Catalog	Page that shows the users details of a particular book.
show_cart.php	Shopping cart	Page that shows the users the contents of their shopping carts. Also used to add items to the cart.
checkout.php	Shopping cart	Page that presents the users with complete order details. Gets shipping details.
purchase.php	Shopping cart	Page that gets payment details from users.
process.php	Shopping cart	Script that processes payment details and adds the order to the database.
login.php	Administration	Script that allows the administrator to log in to make changes.
logout.php	Administration	Script that logs out the admin user.
admin.php	Administration	Main administration menu.
change_password_form.php	Administration	Form to let administrators change their log passwords.
change_password.php	Administration	Script that changes the administrator password.
insert_category_form.php	Administration	Form to let administrators add a new category to the database.
insert_category.php	Administration	Script that inserts a new category into the database.
insert_book_form.php	Administration	Form to let administrators add a new book to the system.
insert_book.php	Administration	Script that inserts a new book into the database.
edit_category_form.php	Administration	Form to let administrators edit a category.
edit_category.php	Administration	Script that updates a category in the database.

Table 27.1 **Continued**

Name	Module	Description
edit_book_form.php	Administration	Form to let administrators edit a book's details.
edit_book.php	Administration	Script that updates a book in the database.
delete_category.php	Administration	Script that deletes a category from the database.
delete_book.php	Administration	Script that deletes a book from the database.
book_sc_fns.php	Functions	Collection of include files for this application.
admin_fns.php	Functions	Collection of functions used by administrative scripts.
book_fns.php	Functions	Collection of functions for storing and retrieving book data.
order_fns.php	Functions	Collection of functions for storing and retrieving order data.
output_fns.php	Functions	Collection of functions for outputting HTML.
data_valid_fns.php	Functions	Collection of functions for validating input data.
db_fns.php	Functions	Collection of functions for connecting to the book_sc database.
user_auth_fns.php	Functions	Collection of functions for authenticating administrative users.
book_sc.sql	SQL	SQL to set up the book_sc database.
populate.sql	SQL	SQL to insert some sample data into the book_sc database.

Now, let's look at the implementation of each of the modules.

> **Note**
>
> This application contains a lot of code. Much of it implements functionality you have looked at already (particularly in Chapter 26), such as storing data to and retrieving it from the database, and authenticating the administrative user. We look briefly at this code but spend most of our time on the shopping cart functions.
>
> For the code in this project to work as written, you need to have magic_quotes_gpc switched on. If you have not done this, you will need to use addslashes() on data going to the MySQL database. We used this technique as a useful shortcut.
>
> You can enable magic quotes on a per-directory basis in an .htaccess file with the following directive:
>
> ```
> php_value magic_quotes_gpc on
> ```

Implementing the Database

As we mentioned earlier, we made some minor modifications to the Book-O-Rama database presented in Part II. The SQL to create the book_sc database is shown in Listing 27.1.

Listing 27.1   book_sc.sql—**SQL to Create the** book_sc **Database**

```
create database book_sc;

use book_sc;

create table customers
(
  customerid int unsigned not null auto_increment primary key,
  name char(60) not null,
  address char(80) not null,
  city char(30) not null,
  state char(20),
  zip char(10),
  country char(20) not null
) type=InnoDB;

create table orders
(
  orderid int unsigned not null auto_increment primary key,
  customerid int unsigned not null references customers(customerid),
  amount float(6,2),
  date date not null,
  order_status char(10),
  ship_name char(60) not null,
  ship_address char(80) not null,
  ship_city char(30) not null,
  ship_state char(20),
  ship_zip char(10),
  ship_country char(20) not null
) type=InnoDB;

create table books
(
   isbn char(13) not null primary key,
   author char(100),
   title char(100),
   catid int unsigned,
   price float(4,2) not null,
   description varchar(255)
) type=InnoDB;
```

Listing 27.1 **Continued**

```
create table categories
(
  catid int unsigned not null auto_increment primary key,
  catname char(60) not null
) type=InnoDB;

create table order_items
(
  orderid int unsigned not null references orders(orderid),
  isbn char(13) not null references books(isbn),
  item_price float(4,2) not null,
  quantity tinyint unsigned not null,
  primary key (orderid, isbn)
) type=InnoDB;

create table admin
 (
  username char(16) not null primary key,
  password char(40) not null
);

grant select, insert, update, delete
on book_sc.*
to book_sc@localhost identified by 'password';
```

Although nothing was wrong with the original Book-O-Rama interface, you must address a few other requirements now that you are going to make it available online.

The changes made to the original database are as follows:

- The addition of more address fields for customers. Having additional fields is more important now that you are building a more realistic application.

- The addition of a shipping address to an order. A customer's contact address might not be the same as the shipping address, particularly if she is using the site to buy a gift.

- The addition of a `categories` table and a `catid` to `books` table. Sorting books into categories makes the site easier to browse.

- The addition of `item_price` to the `order_items` table to recognize the fact that an item's price might change. You want to know how much the item cost when the customer ordered it.

- The addition of an `admin` table to store administrator login and password details.

- The removal of the reviews table. You could add reviews as an extension to this project. Instead, each book has a description field containing a brief blurb about the book.

- The change in storage engines to InnoDB. You do this so that you can use foreign keys and also so you can use transactions when entering customer order information.

To set up this database on your system, run the `book_sc.sql` script through MySQL as the root user, as follows:

```
mysql -u root -p < book_sc.sql
```

(You need to supply your root password.)

Beforehand, you should change the password for the `book_sc` user to something better than `'password'`. Note that if you change the password in `book_sc.sql`, you will also need to change it in `db_fns.php`. (You'll see where shortly.)

We also included a file of sample data called `populate.sql`. You can put the sample data into the database by running it through MySQL in this same way.

Implementing the Online Catalog

Three catalog scripts are used in this application: the main page, category page, and book details page.

The front page of the site is produced by the script called `index.php`. The output of this script is shown in Figure 27.3.

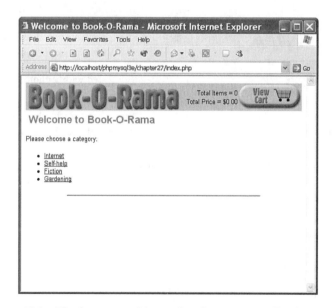

Figure 27.3 The front page of the site lists the categories of books available for purchase.

Notice that, in addition to the list of categories on the site, it has a link to the shopping cart in the top-right corner of the screen and some summary information about what's in the cart. These elements appear on every page while a user browses and shops.

If a user clicks one of the categories, she'll be taken to the category page, produced by the script show_cat.php. The category page for the Internet books section is shown in Figure 27.4.

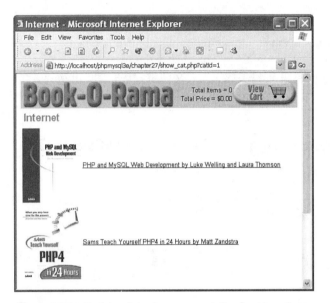

Figure 27.4   Each book in the category is listed with a photo.

All the books in the Internet category are listed as links. If a user clicks one of these links, she will be taken to the book details page. The book details page for one book is shown in Figure 27.5.

On this page, as well as the View Cart link, an Add to Cart link enables the user to select an item for purchase. We return to this feature when we look at how to build the shopping cart later.

Let's look at each of these three scripts.

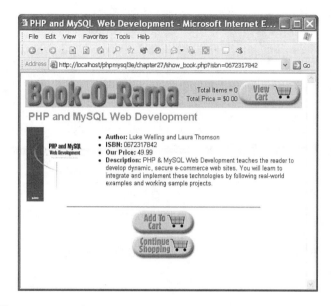

Figure 27.5   Each book has a details page that shows more information, including a long description.

Listing Categories

The first script used in this project, `index.php`, lists all the categories in the database. It is shown in Listing 27.2.

Listing 27.2   `index.php`—**Script to Produce the Front Page of the Site**

```php
<?php
  require ('book_sc_fns.php');
  // The shopping cart needs sessions, so start one
  session_start();
  do_html_header('Welcome to Book-O-Rama');

  echo '<p>Please choose a category:</p>';
```

Listing 27.2   **Continued**

```
  // get categories out of database
  $cat_array = get_categories();

  // display as links to cat pages
  display_categories($cat_array);

  // if logged in as admin, show add, delete, edit cat links
  if(isset($_SESSION['admin_user']))
  {
    display_button('admin.php', 'admin-menu', 'Admin Menu');
  }
  do_html_footer();
?>
```

This script begins by including `book_sc_fns.php`, the file that includes all the function libraries for this application.

After that, you must begin a session. This is required for the shopping cart functionality to work. Every page in the site will use the session.

The `index.php` script also contains some calls to HTML output functions such as `do_html_header()` and `do_html_footer()` (both contained in `output_fns.php`). It also contains some code that checks whether the user is logged in as an administrator and gives her some different navigation options if she is; we return to this feature in the section on the administration functions.

The most important part of this script is

```
// get categories out of database
$cat_array = get_categories();

// display as links to cat pages
display_categories($cat_array);
```

The functions `get_categories()` and `display_categories()` are in the function libraries `book_fns.php` and `output_fns.php`, respectively. The function `get_categories()` returns an array of the categories in the system, which you then pass to `display_categories()`. Let's look at the code for `get_categories()`, shown in Listing 27.3.

Listing 27.3   `get_categories()` **Function from** `book_fns.php`—**Function That Retrieves a Category List from the Database**

```
function get_categories()
{
    // query database for a list of categories
    $conn = db_connect();
```

Listing 27.3 **Continued**

```
  $query = 'select catid, catname
            from categories';
  $result = @$conn->query($query);
  if (!$result)
    return false;
  $num_cats = @$result->num_rows;
  if ($num_cats ==0)
      return false;
  $result = db_result_to_array($result);
  return $result;
}
```

As you can see, the get_categories() function connects to the database and retrieves a
list of all the category IDs and names. We wrote and used a function called
db_result_to_array(), located in db_fns.php. This function is shown in Listing 27.4.
It takes a MySQL result identifier and returns a numerically indexed array of rows,
where each row is an associative array.

Listing 27.4 db_result_to_array() **Function from** db_fns.php—**Function That
Converts a MySQL Result Identifier into an Array of Results**

```
function db_result_to_array($result)
{
  $res_array = array();

  for ($count=0; $row = $result->fetch_assoc(); $count++)
    $res_array[$count] = $row;

  return $res_array;
}
```

In this case, you return this array back all the way to index.php, where you pass it to the
display_categories() function from output_fns.php. This function displays each category as a link to the page containing the books in that category. The code for this function is shown in Listing 27.5.

Listing 27.5 display_categories() **Function from** output_fns.php—**Function
That Displays an Array of Categories as a List of Links to Those Categories**

```
function display_categories($cat_array)
{
  if (!is_array($cat_array))
  {
    echo 'No categories currently available<br />';
    return;
  }
```

Listing 27.5   **Continued**

```php
echo '<ul>';
foreach ($cat_array as $row)
{
  $url = 'show_cat.php?catid='.($row['catid']);
  $title = $row['catname'];
  echo '<li>';
  do_html_url($url, $title);
  echo '</li>';
}
echo '</ul>';
echo '<hr />';
}
```

The `display_categories()` function converts each category from the database into a link. Each link goes to the next script—`show_cat.php`—but each has a different parameter, the category ID or `catid`. (This unique number, generated by MySQL, is used to identify the category.)

This parameter to the next script determines which category you end up looking at.

Listing Books in a Category

The process for listing books in a category is similar. The script that does this, called `show_cat.php`, is shown in Listing 27.6.

Listing 27.6   `show_cat.php`—**Script That Shows the Books in a Particular Category**

```php
<?php
  require ('book_sc_fns.php');
  // The shopping cart needs sessions, so start one
  session_start();

  $catid = $_GET['catid'];
  $name = get_category_name($catid);

  do_html_header($name);

  // get the book info out from db
  $book_array = get_books($catid);

  display_books($book_array);


  // if logged in as admin, show add, delete book links
  if(isset($_SESSION['admin_user']))
  {
```

Listing 27.6 **Continued**

```
    display_button('index.php', 'continue', 'Continue Shopping');
    display_button('admin.php', 'admin-menu', 'Admin Menu');
    display_button("edit_category_form.php?catid=$catid",
      'edit-category', 'Edit Category');
  }
  else
    display_button('index.php', 'continue-shopping', 'Continue Shopping');

  do_html_footer();
?>
```

This script is similar in structure to the index page, except that you retrieve books instead of categories.

You start with `session_start()` as usual and then convert the category ID you have been passed into a category name by using the `get_category_name()` function as follows:

```
$name = get_category_name($catid);
```

This function, shown in Listing 27.7, looks up the category name in the database.

Listing 27.7 `get_category_name()` **Function from** `book_fns.php`—**Function That Converts a Category ID to a Category Name**

```
function get_category_name($catid)
{
  // query database for the name for a category id
  $catid = intval($catid);
  $conn = db_connect();
  $query = "select catname
            from categories
            where catid = $catid";
  $result = @$conn->query($query);
  if (!$result)
    return false;
  $num_cats = @$result->num_rows;
  if ($num_cats ==0)
    return false;
  $row = $result->fetch_object();
  return $row->catname;
}
```

After you have retrieved the category name, you can render an HTML header and proceed to retrieve and list the books from the database that fall into your chosen category, as follows:

```
$book_array = get_books($catid);
display_books($book_array);
```

The functions get_books() and display_books() are extremely similar to the get_categories() and display_categories() functions, so we do not go into them here. The only difference is that you retrieve information from the books table rather than the categories table.

The display_books() function provides a link to each book in the category via the show_book.php script. Again, each link is suffixed with a parameter. This time around, it's the ISBN for the book in question.

At the bottom of the show_cat.php script, there is some code to display additional functions if an administrator is logged in. We look at these functions in the section on administrative functions.

Showing Book Details

The show_book.php script takes an ISBN as a parameter and retrieves and displays the details of that book. The code for this script is shown in Listing 27.8.

Listing 27.8 show_book.php— **Script That Shows the Details of a Particular Book**

```php
<?php
  require ('book_sc_fns.php');
  // The shopping cart needs sessions, so start one
  session_start();

  $isbn = $_GET['isbn'];

  // get this book out of database
  $book = get_book_details($isbn);
  do_html_header($book['title']);
  display_book_details($book);

  // set url for "continue button"
  $target = 'index.php';
  if($book['catid'])
  {
    $target = 'show_cat.php?catid='.$book['catid'];
  }
  // if logged in as admin, show edit book links
  if( check_admin_user() )
  {
    display_button("edit_book_form.php?isbn=$isbn", 'edit-item', 'Edit Item');
    display_button('admin.php', 'admin-menu', 'Admin Menu');
    display_button($target, 'continue', 'Continue');
  }
  else
  {
```

Listing 27.8   **Continued**

```
    display_button("show_cart.php?new=$isbn", 'add-to-cart', 'Add '
                .$book['title'].' To My Shopping Cart');
    display_button($target, 'continue-shopping', 'Continue Shopping');
  }

  do_html_footer();
?>
```

Again with this script, you do similar things as in the previous two pages. You begin by starting the session and then use

```
$book = get_book_details($isbn);
```

to get the book information out of the database. Next, you use

```
display_book_details($book);
```

to output the data in HTML.

Note that `display_book_details()` looks for an image file for the book as `images/$isbn.jpg`. If this file does not exist, no image will be displayed.

The remainder of the `show_book.php` script sets up navigation. A normal user has the choices Continue Shopping, which takes her back to the category page, and Add to Cart, which adds the book to her shopping cart. If a user is logged in as an administrator, she will get some different options, which we look at in the section on administration.

We've completed the basics of the catalog system. Now let's look at the code for the shopping cart functionality.

Implementing the Shopping Cart

The shopping cart functionality all revolves around a session variable called `cart`. It is an associative array that has ISBNs as keys and quantities as values. For example, if you add a single copy of this book to your shopping cart, the array would contain

```
0672317842 => 1
```

That is, the array would contain one copy of the book with the ISBN 0672317842. When you add items to the cart, they are added to the array. When you view the cart, you use the `cart` array to look up the full details of the items in the database.

You also use two other session variables to control the display in the header that shows Total Items and Total Price. These variables are called `items` and `total_price`, respectively.

Using the `show_cart.php` Script

Let's examine how the shopping cart code is implemented by looking at the `show_cart.php` script. This script displays the page you will visit if you click on any View Cart or Add to Cart links. If you call `show_cart.php` without any parameters, you will get to see the contents of it. If you call it with an ISBN as a parameter, the item with that ISBN will be added to the cart.

To understand fully how this script operates, look first at Figure 27.6.

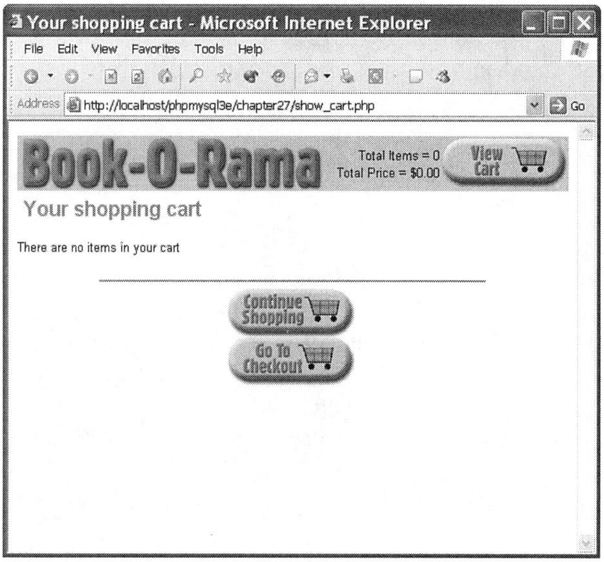

Figure 27.6 The `show_cart.php` script with no parameters just shows the contents of the cart.

In this case, we clicked the View Cart link when our cart was empty; that is, we had not yet selected any items to purchase.

Figure 27.7 shows the cart a bit further down the track after we selected two books to buy. In this case, we got to this page by clicking the Add to Cart link on the `show_book.php` page for this book, *PHP and MySQL Web Development*. If you look closely at the URL bar, you will see that we called the script with a parameter this time. The parameter is called `new` and has the value `0672317842`—that is, the ISBN for the book just added to the cart.

From this page, you can see that you have two other options. The Save Changes button can be used to change the quantity of items in the cart. To do this, the user can alter the quantities directly and click Save Changes. This is actually a submit button that takes the user back to the `show_cart.php` script again to update the cart.

Figure 27.7   The show_cart.php script with the new parameter adds a
new item to the cart.

In addition, the user can click the Go to Checkout button when she is ready to leave.
We come back to that shortly.

For now, let's look at the code for the show_cart.php script. This code is shown in
Listing 27.9.

Listing 27.9   show_cart.php— **Script That Controls the Shopping Cart**

```php
<?php
  require ('book_sc_fns.php');
  // The shopping cart needs sessions, so start one
  session_start();

  @ $new = $_GET['new'];

  if($new)
  {
    //new item selected
    if(!isset($_SESSION['cart']))
    {
      $_SESSION['cart'] = array();
      $_SESSION['items'] = 0;
      $_SESSION['total_price'] ='0.00';
    }
```

Listing 27.9 **Continued**

```php
    if(isset($_SESSION['cart'][$new]))
      $_SESSION['cart'][$new]++;
    else
      $_SESSION['cart'][$new] = 1;

    $_SESSION['total_price'] = calculate_price($_SESSION['cart']);
    $_SESSION['items'] = calculate_items($_SESSION['cart']);
  }

  if(isset($_POST['save']))
  {
    foreach ($_SESSION['cart'] as $isbn => $qty)
    {
      if($_POST[$isbn]=='0')
        unset($_SESSION['cart'][$isbn]);
      else
        $_SESSION['cart'][$isbn] = $_POST[$isbn];
    }
    $_SESSION['total_price'] = calculate_price($_SESSION['cart']);
    $_SESSION['items'] = calculate_items($_SESSION['cart']);
  }

  do_html_header('Your shopping cart') ;

  if($_SESSION['cart']&&array_count_values($_SESSION['cart']))
    display_cart($_SESSION['cart']);
  else
  {
    echo '<p>There are no items in your cart</p>';
    echo '<hr />';
  }
  $target = 'index.php';

  // if we have just added an item to the cart
  // continue shopping in that category
  if($new)
  {
    $details =  get_book_details($new);
    if($details['catid'])
      $target = 'show_cat.php?catid='.$details['catid'];
  }
```

Listing 27.9   **Continued**

```
display_button($target, 'continue-shopping', 'Continue Shopping');

// use this if SSL is set up
// $path = $_SERVER['PHP_SELF'];
// $server = $_SERVER['SERVER_NAME'];
// $path = str_replace('show_cart.php', '', $path);
// display_button('https://'.$server.$path.'checkout.php',
//                  'go-to-checkout', 'Go To Checkout');

// if no SSL use below code
display_button('checkout.php', 'go-to-checkout', 'Go To Checkout');


do_html_footer();
?>
```

This script has three main parts: displaying the cart, adding items to the cart, and saving changes to the cart. We cover these parts in the next three sections.

Viewing the Cart

No matter which page you come from, you display the contents of the cart. In the base case, when a user has just clicked View Cart, the only part of the code that will be executed follows:

```
if($_SESSION['cart']&&array_count_values($_SESSION['cart']))
    display_cart($_SESSION['cart']);
else
{
  echo '<p>There are no items in your cart</p>';
  echo '<hr />';
}
```

As you can see from this code, if you have a cart with some contents, you will call the display_cart() function. If the cart is empty, you'll give the user a message to that effect.

The display_cart() function just prints the contents of the cart as a readable HTML format, as you can see in Figures 27.6 and 27.7. The code for this function can be found in output_fns.php, which is included here as Listing 27.10. Although it is a display function, it is reasonably complex, so we chose to include it here.

Listing 27.10 `display_cart()` **Function from** `output_fns.php`—**Function That Formats and Prints the Contents of the Shopping Cart**

```
function display_cart($cart, $change = true, $images = 1)
{
  // display items in shopping cart
  // optionally allow changes (true or false)
  // optionally include images (1 - yes, 0 - no)

  echo '<table border = "0" width = "100%" cellspacing = "0">
       <form action = "show_cart.php" method = "post">
       <tr><th colspan = '. (1+$images) .' bgcolor="#cccccc">Item</th>
       <th bgcolor="#cccccc">Price</th><th bgcolor="#cccccc">Quantity</th>
       <th bgcolor="#cccccc">Total</th></tr>';

  //display each item as a table row
  foreach ($cart as $isbn => $qty)
  {
    $book = get_book_details($isbn);
    echo '<tr>';
    if($images ==true)
    {
      echo '<td align = left>';
      if (file_exists("images/$isbn.jpg"))
      {
        $size = GetImageSize('images/'.$isbn.'.jpg');
        if($size[0]>0 && $size[1]>0)
        {
          echo '<img src="images/'.$isbn.'.jpg" border="0" ';
          echo 'width = '. $size[0]/3 .' height = ' .$size[1]/3 . ' />';
        }
      }
      else
         echo ' ';
      echo '</td>';
    }
    echo '<td align = "left">';
    echo '<a href = "show_book.php?isbn='.$isbn.'">'
         .$book['title'].'</a> by '.$book['author'];
    echo '</td><td align = "center">$'.number_format($book['price'], 2);
    echo '</td><td align = "center">';
    // if we allow changes, quantities are in text boxes
    if ($change == true)
      echo "<input type = 'text' name = \"$isbn\" value = \"$qty\"
            size = \"3\" />";
    else
```

Listing 27.10   **Continued**

```
        echo $qty;
      echo '</td><td align = "center">$'.number_format($book['price']*$qty,2)
          ."</td></tr>\n";
    }
    // display total row
    echo "<tr>
            <th colspan = ". (2+$images) ." bgcolor=\"#cccccc\"> </td>
            <th align = \"center\" bgcolor=\"#cccccc\">
                ".$_SESSION['items']."
            </th>
            <th align = \"center\" bgcolor=\"#cccccc\">
                \$".number_format($_SESSION['total_price'], 2).
            '</th>
          </tr>';
    // display save change button
    if($change == true)
    {
      echo '<tr>
              <td colspan = '. (2+$images) .'> </td>
              <td align = "center">
                <input type = "hidden" name = "save" value = "true" />
                <input type = "image" src = "images/save-changes.gif"
                        border = "0" alt = "Save Changes" />
              </td>
              <td> </td>
            </tr>';
    }
    echo '</form></table>';
}
```

The basic flow of this function is as follows:

1. Loop through each item in the cart and pass the ISBN of each item to
   get_book_details() so that you can summarize the details of each book.

2. Provide an image for each book, if one exists. Use the HTML image height and
   width tags to resize the image a little smaller here. This means that the images will
   be a little distorted, but they are small enough that this isn't much of a problem. (If
   the distortion bothers you, you can always resize the images using the gd library
   discussed in Chapter 21, "Generating Images," or manually generate different-size
   images for each product.)

3. Make each cart entry a link to the appropriate book—that is, to show_book.php
   with the ISBN as a parameter.

4. If you are calling the function with the change parameter set to true (or not set— it defaults to true), show the boxes with the quantities in them as a form with the Save Changes button at the end. (When you reuse this function after checking out, you don't want the user to be able to change her order.)

Nothing is terribly complicated in this function, but it does quite a lot of work, so you might find reading it through carefully to be useful.

Adding Items to the Cart

If a user has come to the show_cart.php page by clicking an Add to Cart button, you have to do some work before you can show her the contents of her cart. Specifically, you need to add the appropriate item to the cart, as follows.

First, if the user has not put any items in her cart before, she will not have a cart, so you need to create one:

```
if(!isset($_SESSION['cart']))
{
  $_SESSION['cart'] = array();
  $_SESSION['items'] = 0;
  $_SESSION['total_price'] ='0.00';
}
```

To begin with, the cart is empty.

Second, after you know that a cart is set up, you can add the item to it:

```
if(isset($_SESSION['cart'][$new]))
  $_SESSION['cart'][$new]++;
else
  $_SESSION['cart'][$new] = 1;
```

Here, you check whether the item is already in the cart. If it is, you increment the quantity of that item in the cart by one. If not, you add the new item to the cart.

Third, you need to work out the total price and number of items in the cart. For this, you use the calculate_price() and calculate_items() functions, as follows:

```
$_SESSION['total_price'] = calculate_price($_SESSION['cart']);
$_SESSION['items'] = calculate_items($_SESSION['cart']);
```

These functions are located in the book_fns.php function library. The code for them is shown in Listings 27.11 and 27.12, respectively.

Listing 27.11 calculate_price() **Function from** book_fns.php— **Function That Calculates and Returns the Total Price of the Contents of the Shopping Cart**

```
function calculate_price($cart)
{
```

Listing 27.11   **Continued**

```
  // sum total price for all items in shopping cart
  $price = 0.0;
  if(is_array($cart))
  {
    $conn = db_connect();
    foreach($cart as $isbn => $qty)
    {
      $query = "select price from books where isbn='$isbn'";
      $result = $conn->query($query);
      if ($result)
      {
        $item = $result->fetch_object();
        $item_price = $item->price;
        $price +=$item_price*$qty;
      }
    }
  }
  return $price;
}
```

As you can see, the `calculate_price()` function works by looking up the price of each item in the cart in the database. This process is somewhat slow, so to avoid doing this more often than you need to, you store the price (and the total number of items, as well) as session variables and recalculate only when the cart changes.

Listing 27.12   `calculate_items()` **Function from** `book_fns.php`—**Function That Calculates and Returns the Total Number of Items in the Shopping Cart**

```
function calculate_items($cart)
{
  // sum total items in shopping cart
  $items = 0;
  if(is_array($cart))
  {
    $items=array_sum($cart);
  }
  return $items;
}
```

The `calculate_items()` function is simpler; it just goes through the cart and adds the quantities of each item to get the total number of items using the `array_sum()` function. If there's not yet an array (if the cart is empty), it just returns 0 (zero).

Saving the Updated Cart

If the user comes to the show_cart.php script by clicking the Save Changes button, the process is a little different. In this case, the user has arrived via a form submission. If you look closely at the code, you will see that the Save Changes button is the submit button for a form. This form contains the hidden variable save. If this variable is set, you know that you have come to this script from the Save Changes button. This means that the user has presumably edited the quantity values in the cart, and you need to update them.

If you look back at the text boxes in the Save Changes form part of the script, you will see that they are named after the ISBN of the item that they represent, as follows:

```
echo '<input type="text" name="$isbn" value="$qty" size="3">';
```

Now look at the part of the script that saves the changes:

```
if(isset($_POST['save']))
{
  foreach ($_SESSION['cart'] as $isbn => $qty)
  {
    if($_POST[$isbn]=='0')
      unset($_SESSION['cart'][$isbn]);
    else
      $_SESSION['cart'][$isbn] = $_POST[$isbn];
  }
  $_SESSION['total_price'] = calculate_price($_SESSION['cart']);
  $_SESSION['items'] = calculate_items($_SESSION['cart']);
}
```

Here, you work your way through the shopping cart, and for each isbn in the cart, you check the POST variable with that name. These variables are the form fields from the Save Changes form.

If any of the fields are set to zero, you remove that item from the shopping cart altogether, using unset(). Otherwise, you update the cart to match the form fields, as follows:

```
if($_POST[$isbn]=='0')
  unset($_SESSION['cart'][$isbn]);
else
  $_SESSION['cart'][$isbn] = $_POST[$isbn];
```

After these updates, you again use calculate_price() and calculate_items() to work out the new values of the total_price and items session variables.

Printing a Header Bar Summary

In the header bar of each page in the site, a summary of what's in the shopping cart is presented. This summary is obtained by printing out the values of the session variables total_price and items. This is done in the do_html_header() function.

These variables are registered when the user first visits the show_cart.php page. You also need some logic to deal with the cases in which a user has not yet visited that page. This logic is also included in the do_html_heaader() function:

```
if(!$_SESSION['items']) $_SESSION['items'] = '0';
if(!$_SESSION['total_price']) $_SESSION['total_price'] = '0.00';
```

Checking Out

When the user clicks the Go to Checkout button from the shopping cart, this action activates the checkout.php script. The checkout page and the pages behind it should be accessed via the Secure Sockets Layer (SSL), but the sample application does not force you to do this. (To read more about SSL, review Chapter 17, "Implementing Secure Transactions with PHP and MySQL.")

The checkout page is shown in Figure 27.8.

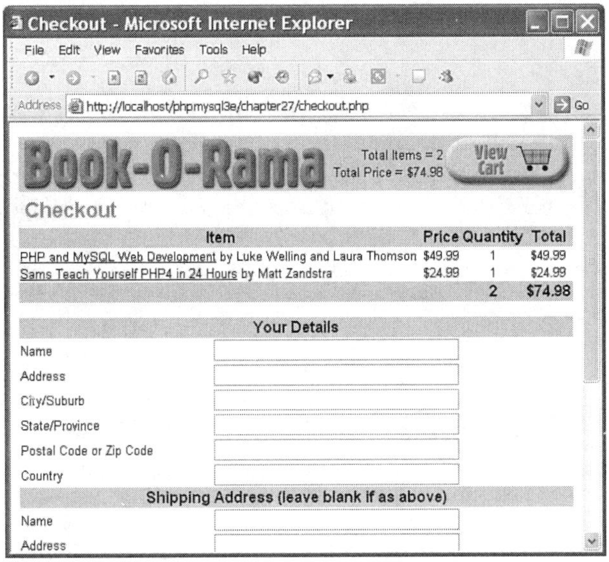

Figure 27.8   The checkout.php script gets the customer's details.

This script requires the customer to enter her address (and shipping address if it is different). It is quite a simple script, which you can see by looking at the code in Listing 27.13.

Listing 27.13   checkout.php— **Script That Gets the Customer Details**

```php
<?php
  //include our function set
  require ('book_sc_fns.php');
```

Listing 27.13 **Continued**

```
// The shopping cart needs sessions, so start one
session_start();

do_html_header('Checkout');

if($_SESSION['cart']&&count($_SESSION['cart']))
{
  display_cart($_SESSION['cart'], false, 0);
  display_checkout_form();
}
else
  echo '<p>There are no items in your cart</p>';

display_button('show_cart.php', 'continue-shopping', 'Continue Shopping');

do_html_footer();
?>
```

There are no great surprises in this script. If the cart is empty, the script will notify the customer; otherwise, it will display the form shown in Figure 27.8.

If a user continues by clicking the Purchase button at the bottom of the form, she will be taken to the purchase.php script. You can see the output of this script in Figure 27.9.

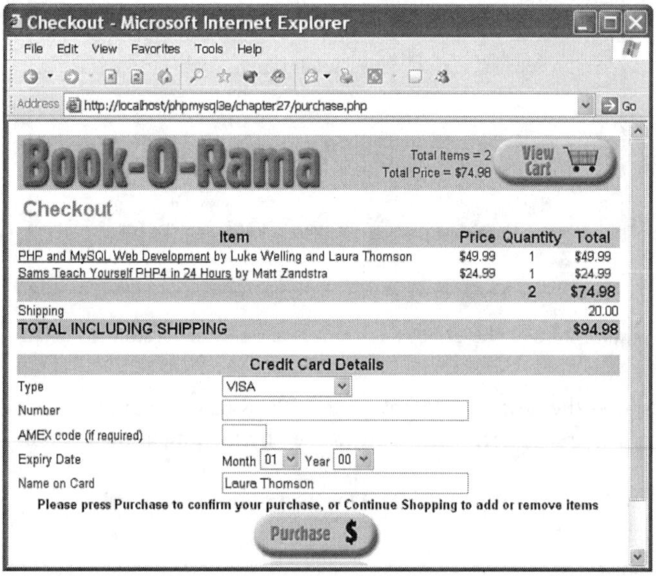

Figure 27.9   The purchase.php script calculates shipping and the final order total and gets the customer's payment details.

The code for the purchase.php script is slightly more complicated than the code for checkout.php. It is shown in Listing 27.14.

Listing 27.14   purchase.php—Script That Stores the Order Details in the Database and Gets the Payment Details

```php
<?php

  include ('book_sc_fns.php');
  // The shopping cart needs sessions, so start one
  session_start();

  do_html_header("Checkout");
  // create short variable names
  $name = $_POST['name'];
  $address = $_POST['address'];
  $city = $_POST['city'];
  $zip = $_POST['zip'];
  $country = $_POST['country'];

  // if filled out
  if($_SESSION['cart']&&$name&&$address&&$city&&$zip&&$country)
  {
    // able to insert into database
    if( insert_order($_POST)!=false )
    {
      //display cart, not allowing changes and without pictures
      display_cart($_SESSION['cart'], false, 0);

      display_shipping(calculate_shipping_cost());

      //get credit card details
      display_card_form($name);

      display_button('show_cart.php', 'continue-shopping', 'Continue Shopping');
    }
    else
    {
      echo 'Could not store data, please try again.';
      display_button('checkout.php', 'back', 'Back');
    }
  }
  else
  {
    echo 'You did not fill in all the fields, please try again.<hr />';
    display_button('checkout.php', 'back', 'Back');
  }
```

Listing 27.14 **Continued**

```
  do_html_footer();
?>
```

The logic here is straightforward: You check that the user filled out the form and inserted details into the database using a function called `insert_order()`. This simple function pops the customer details into the database. The code for it is shown in Listing 27.15.

Listing 27.15 `insert_order()` **Function from** `order_fns.php`**—Function That Inserts All the Details of the Customer's Order into the Database**

```
function insert_order($order_details)
{
  // extract order_details out as variables
  extract($order_details);

  // set shipping address same as address
  if(!$ship_name&&!$ship_address&&!$ship_city&&!$ship_state&&
    !$ship_zip&&!$ship_country)
  {
    $ship_name = $name;
    $ship_address = $address;
    $ship_city = $city;
    $ship_state = $state;
    $ship_zip = $zip;
    $ship_country = $country;
  }

  $conn = db_connect();

  // we want to insert the order as a transaction
  // start one by turning off autocommit
  $conn->autocommit(FALSE);

  // insert customer address
  $query = "select customerid from customers where
            name = '$name' and address = '$address'
            and city = '$city' and state = '$state'
            and zip = '$zip' and country = '$country'";
  $result = $conn->query($query);
  if($result->num_rows>0)
  {
    $customer = $result->fetch_object();
    $customerid = $customer->customerid;
  }
  else
```

Listing 27.15   **Continued**

```
{
  $query = "insert into customers values
          ('', '$name','$address','$city','$state','$zip','$country')";
  $result = $conn->query($query);
  if (!$result)
      return false;
}
$customerid = $conn->insert_id;

$date = date('Y-m-d');
$query = "insert into orders values
          ('', $customerid, ".$_SESSION['total_price']."., '$date',
           'PARTIAL', '$ship_name',
           '$ship_address','$ship_city','$ship_state','$ship_zip',
            '$ship_country')";

$result = $conn->query($query) ;
if (!$result)
  return false;

$query = "select orderid from orders where
              customerid = $customerid and
              amount > ".$_SESSION['total_price']."-.001 and
              amount < ".$_SESSION['total_price']."+.001 and
              date = '$date' and
              order_status = 'PARTIAL' and
              ship_name = '$ship_name' and
              ship_address = '$ship_address' and
              ship_city = '$ship_city' and
              ship_state = '$ship_state' and
              ship_zip = '$ship_zip' and
              ship_country = '$ship_country'";
$result = $conn->query($query);
if($result->num_rows>0)
{
  $order = $result->fetch_object();
  $orderid = $order->orderid;
}
else
  return false;

// insert each book
foreach($_SESSION['cart'] as $isbn => $quantity)
{
```

Listing 27.15   **Continued**

```
    $detail = get_book_details($isbn);
    $query = "delete from order_items where
             orderid = '$orderid' and isbn =  '$isbn'";
    $result = $conn->query($query);
    $query = "insert into order_items values
             ('$orderid', '$isbn', ".$detail['price'].", $quantity)";
    $result = $conn->query($query);
    if(!$result)
      return false;
  }


  // end transaction
  $conn->commit();
  $conn->autocommit(TRUE);


  return $orderid;
}
```

The insert_order() function is rather long because you need to insert the customer's details, order details, and details of each book she wants to buy.

You will note that the different parts of the insert are enclosed in a transaction, beginning with

```
$conn->autocommit(FALSE);
```

and ending with

```
$conn->commit();
$conn->autocommit(TRUE);
```

This is the only place in this application where you need to use a transaction. How do you avoid having to do it elsewhere? Look at the code in the db_connect() function:

```
function db_connect()
{
   $result = new mysqli('localhost', 'book_sc', 'password', 'book_sc');
   if (!$result)
      return false;
   $result->autocommit(TRUE);
   return $result;
}
```

Obviously, this is slightly different from the code used for this function in other chapters. After creating the connection to MySQL, you should turn on autocommit mode.

This ensures that each SQL statement is automatically committed, as we have previously discussed. When you actually want to use a multistatement transaction, you turn off auto-commit, perform a series of inserts, commit the data, and then re-enable autocommit mode.

You then work out the shipping costs to the customer's address and tell her how much it will be with the following line of code:

```
display_shipping(calculate_shipping_cost());
```

The code used here for `calculate_shipping_cost()` always returns $20. When you actually set up a shopping site, you must choose a delivery method, find out how much shipping costs for different destinations, and calculate those costs accordingly.

You then display a form for the user to fill in her credit card details by using the `display_card_form()` function from the `output_fns.php` library.

Implementing Payment

When the user clicks the Purchase button, you process her payment details using the `process.php` script. You can see the results of a successful payment in Figure 27.10.

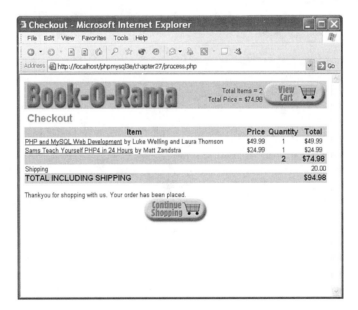

Figure 27.10   This transaction was successful, and the items will now be shipped.

The code for `process.php` can be found in Listing 27.16.

Listing 27.16   process.php— **Script That Processes the Customer's Payment and Tells Her the Result**

```php
<?php
  require ('book_sc_fns.php');
  // The shopping cart needs sessions, so start one
  session_start();

  do_html_header('Checkout');

  $card_type = $_POST['card_type'];
  $card_number = $_POST['card_number'];
  $card_month = $_POST['card_month'];
  $card_year = $_POST['card_year'];
  $card_name = $_POST['card_name'];

  if($_SESSION['cart']&&$card_type&&$card_number&&
     $card_month&&$card_year&&$card_name )
  {
    //display cart, not allowing changes and without pictures
    display_cart($_SESSION['cart'], false, 0);

    display_shipping(calculate_shipping_cost());

    if(process_card($_POST))
    {
      //empty shopping cart
      session_destroy();
      echo 'Thank you for shopping with us.  Your order has been placed.';
      display_button('index.php', 'continue-shopping', 'Continue Shopping');
    }
    else
    {
    echo 'Could not process your card. ';
    echo 'Please contact the card issuer or try again.';
      display_button('purchase.php', 'back', 'Back');
    }
  }
  else
  {
    echo 'You did not fill in all the fields, please try again.<hr />';
    display_button('purchase.php', 'back', 'Back');
  }
```

Listing 27.16 **Continued**

```
  do_html_footer();
?>
```

You process the user's card and, if all is successful, destroy her session.

The card processing function as it is written simply returns true. If you were actually implementing it, you would need to perform some validation (checking that the expiry date was valid and the card number well formed) and then process the actual payment.

When you set up a live site, you need to make a decision about what transaction clearing mechanism you want to use. You can

- Sign up with a transaction clearing provider. There are many, many alternatives here depending on the area you live in. Some of them offer real-time clearing, and others don't. Whether you need live clearing depends on the service you are offering. If you are providing a service online, you will most likely want it; if you are shipping goods, it's less crucial. Either way, these providers relieve you of the responsibility of storing credit card numbers.

- Send a credit card number to yourself via encrypted email, for example, by using Pretty Good Privacy (PGP) or Gnu Privacy Guard (GPG), as covered in Chapter 17. When you receive and decrypt the email, you can process these transactions manually.

- Store the credit card numbers in your database. We do not recommend this option unless you really, seriously know what you're doing with system security. Read Chapter 17 for more details about why this is a bad idea.

That's it for the shopping cart and payment modules.

Implementing an Administration Interface

The administration interface we implemented is very simple. We just built a Web interface to the database with some front-end authentication. This interface uses much of the same code as used in Chapter 26. We included it here for completeness, but with little discussion.

The administration interface requires a user to log in via the login.php file, which then takes him to the administration menu, admin.php. The login page is shown in Figure 27.11. (We omitted the login.php file here for brevity; it's almost exactly the same as the one in Chapter 26. If you want to look at it, it's on the CD-ROM.) The administration menu is shown in Figure 27.12.

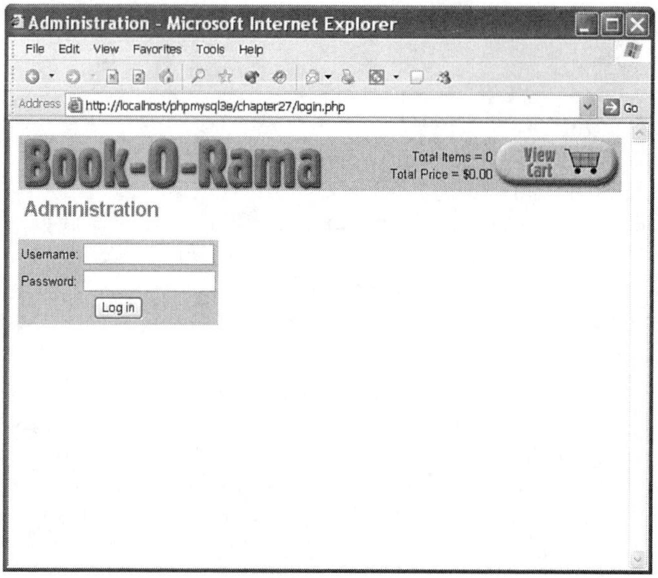

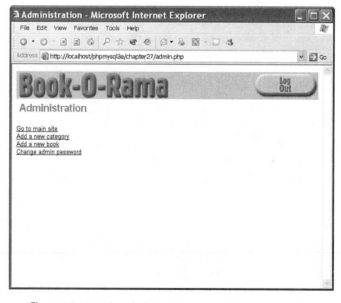

Figure 27.11   Users must pass through the login page to access the
administration functions.

Figure 27.12   The administration menu allows access to the
administration functions.

The code for the admin menu is shown in Listing 27.17.

Listing 27.17 admin.php—**Script That Authenticates the Administrator and Lets Him Access the Administration Functions**

```php
<?php

// include function files for this application
require_once('book_sc_fns.php');
session_start();


if ($_POST['username'] && $_POST['passwd'])
// they have just tried logging in
{
    $username = $_POST['username'];
    $passwd = $_POST['passwd'];

    if (login($username, $passwd))
    {
      // if they are in the database register the user id
      $_SESSION['admin_user'] = $username;
    }
    else
    {
      // unsuccessful login
      do_html_header('Problem:');
      echo 'You could not be logged in.
            You must be logged in to view this page.<br />';
      do_html_url('login.php', 'Login');
      do_html_footer();
      exit;
    }
}

do_html_header('Administration');
if (check_admin_user())
  display_admin_menu();
else
  echo 'You are not authorized to enter the administration area.';

do_html_footer();

?>
```

This code probably looks familiar; it is similar to a script from Chapter 26. After the administrator reaches this point, he can change his password or log out; this code is identical to the code in Chapter 26, so we did not include it here.

You identify the administration user after login by means of the `admin_user` session variable and the `check_admin_user()` function. This function and the others used by the administrative scripts can be found in the function library `admin_fns.php`.

If the administrator chooses to add a new category or book, he will go to either `insert_category_form.php` or `insert_book_form.php`, as appropriate. Each of these scripts presents the administrator with a form to fill in. Each is processed by a corresponding script (`insert_category.php` and `insert_book.php`), which verifies that the form is filled out and inserts the new data into the database. Here, we look at the book versions of the scripts only because they are similar to one another.

The output of `insert_book_form.php` is shown in Figure 27.13.

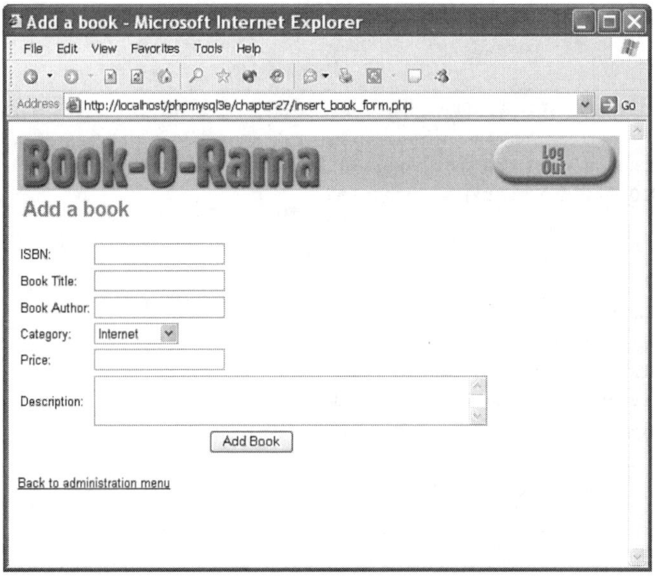

Figure 27.13   This form allows the administrator to enter new books into the online catalog.

Notice that the `Category` field for books is an HTML `SELECT` element. The options for this `SELECT` come from a call to the `get_categories()` function you looked at previously.

When the Add Book button is clicked, the `insert_book.php` script is activated. The code for this script is shown in Listing 27.18.

Listing 27.18   `insert_book.php`—**Script That Validates the New Book Data and Puts It into the Database**

```php
<?php

// include function files for this application
require_once('book_sc_fns.php');
session_start();

do_html_header('Adding a book');
if (check_admin_user())
{
  if (filled_out($_POST))
  {
    $isbn = $_POST['isbn'];
    $title = $_POST['title'];
    $author = $_POST['author'];
    $catid = $_POST['catid'];
    $price = $_POST['price'];
    $description = $_POST['description'];

    if(insert_book($isbn, $title, $author, $catid, $price, $description))
      echo "Book '".stripslashes($title)."' was added to the database.<br />";
    else
      echo "Book '".stripslashes($title).
          "' could not be added to the database.<br />";
  }
  else
    echo 'You have not filled out the form.  Please try again.';
  do_html_url('admin.php', 'Back to administration menu');
}
else
  echo 'You are not authorized to view this page.';

do_html_footer();

?>
```

You can see that this script calls the function `insert_book()`. This function and the others used by the administrative scripts can be found in the function library `admin_fns.php`.

In addition to adding new categories and books, the administrative user can edit and delete these items. We implemented this capability by reusing as much code as possible. When the administrator clicks the Go to Main site link in the administration menu, he goes to the category index at `index.php` and can navigate the site in the same way as a regular user, using the same scripts.

There is a difference in the administrative navigation, however: Administrators see different options based on the fact that they have the registered session variable admin_user. For example, if you look at the show_book.php page that you looked at previously in the chapter, you will see the different menu options shown in Figure 27.14.

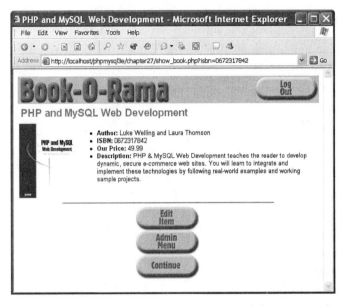

Figure 27.14   The show_book.php script produces different output for an administrative user.

The administrator has access to two new options on this page: Edit Item and Admin Menu. Notice that the shopping cart does not appear in the upper-right corner; instead, this page has a Log Out button.

The code for this page is all there, back in Listing 27.8, as follows:

```
if( check_admin_user() )
{
  display_button("edit_book_form.php?isbn=$isbn", 'edit-item', 'Edit Item');
  display_button('admin.php', 'admin-menu', 'Admin Menu');
  display_button($target, 'continue', 'Continue');
}
```

If you look back at the show_cat.php script, you will see that it also has these options built into it.

If the administrator clicks the Edit Item button, he will go to the edit_book_form.php script. The output of this script is shown in Figure 27.15.

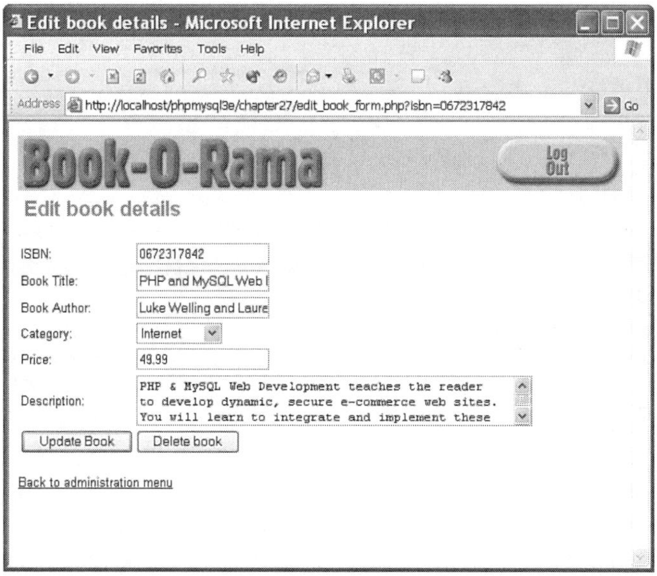

Figure 27.15   The edit_book_form.php script gives the administrator access to edit book details or delete a book.

This form is, in fact, the same one used to get the book's details in the first place. We built an option into that form to pass in and display existing book data. We did the same thing with the category form. To see what we mean, look at Listing 27.19.

Listing 27.19   display_book_form() Function from admin_fns.php—Form That Does Double Duty as an Insertion and Editing Form

```
function display_book_form($book = '')
// This displays the book form.
// It is very similar to the category form.
// This form can be used for inserting or editing books.
// To insert, don't pass any parameters.  This will set $edit
// to false, and the form will go to insert_book.php.
// To update, pass an array containing a book.  The
// form will be displayed with the old data and point to update_book.php.
// It will also add a "Delete book" button.
{

  // if passed an existing book, proceed in "edit mode"
  $edit = is_array($book);
```

Listing 27.19   **Continued**

```php
  // most of the form is in plain HTML with some
  // optional PHP bits throughout
?>
  <form method='post'
        action="<?php echo $edit?'edit_book.php':'insert_book.php';?>">
  <table border='0'>
  <tr>
    <td>ISBN:</td>
    <td><input type='text' name='isbn'
        value="<?php echo $edit?$book['isbn']:''; ?>" /></td>
  </tr>
  <tr>
    <td>Book Title:</td>
    <td><input type='text' name='title'
        value="<?php echo $edit?$book['title']:''; ?>" /></td>
  </tr>
  <tr>
    <td>Book Author:</td>
    <td><input type='text' name='author'
        value="<?php echo $edit?$book['author']:''; ?>" /></td>
  </tr>
  <tr>
      <td>Category:</td>
      <td><select name='catid'>
      <?php
          // list of possible categories comes from database
          $cat_array=get_categories();
          foreach ($cat_array as $thiscat)
          {
              echo '<option value="';
              echo $thiscat['catid'];
              echo '"';
              // if existing book, put in current catgory
              if ($edit && $thiscat['catid'] == $book['catid'])
                  echo ' selected';
              echo '>';
              echo $thiscat['catname'];
              echo "</option>\n";
          }
      ?>
      </select>
      </td>
  </tr>
  <tr>
   <td>Price:</td>
```

Listing 27.19 **Continued**

```php
    <td><input type='text' name='price'
            value="<?php echo $edit?$book['price']:''; ?>" /></td>
  </tr>
  <tr>
    <td>Description:</td>
    <td><textarea rows='3' cols='50'
        name='description'><?php
        echo $edit?$book['description']:''; ?></textarea></td>
  </tr>
  <tr>
    <td <?php if (!$edit) echo 'colspan=\'2\''; ?> align='center'>
      <?php
        if ($edit)
          // we need the old isbn to find book in database
          // if the isbn is being updated
          echo '<input type="hidden" name="oldisbn"
                value="'.$book['isbn'].'" />';
       ?>
      <input type='submit'
            value="<?php echo $edit?'Update':'Add'; ?> Book" />
      </form></td>
      <?php
        if ($edit)
        {
          echo '<td>';
          echo '<form method="post" action="delete_book.php">';
          echo '<input type="hidden" name="isbn"
                value="'.$book['isbn'].'" />';
          echo '<input type="submit"
                value="Delete book" />';
          echo '</form></td>';
        }
       ?>
      </td>
    </tr>
  </table>
  </form>
<?php
}
```

If you pass in an array containing the book data, the form will be rendered in edit mode and will fill in the fields with the existing data:

```php
<input type="text" name="price"
            value="<?php echo $edit?$book['price']:''; ?>" />
```

You even get a different submit button. In fact, for the edit form, you get two—one to update the book and one to delete it. These buttons call the scripts `edit_book.php` and `delete_book.php`, which update the database accordingly.

The category versions of these scripts work in much the same way, except for one thing. When an administrator tries to delete a category, it will not be deleted if any books are still in it. (This is checked with a database query.) This approach prevents any problems you might get with deletion anomalies. We discussed these anomalies in Chapter 8, "Designing Your Web Database." In this case, if a category that still had books in it was deleted, these books would become orphans. You wouldn't know what category they were in, and you would have no way of navigating to them!

That's the overview of the administration interface. For more details, refer to the code; it's all on the CD-ROM.

Extending the Project

If you followed along with this project, you have built a fairly simple shopping cart system. There are many additions and enhancements you could make:

- In a real online store, you would need to build some kind of order tracking and fulfillment system. At the moment, you have no way of seeing the orders that have been placed.

- Customers want to be able to check the progress of their orders without having to contact you. We feel that it is important that a customer does not have to log in to browse. However, providing existing customers a way to authenticate themselves enables them to see past orders and enables you to tie behaviors together into a profile.

- At present, the images for books have to be transferred via FTP to the image directory and given the correct name. You could add file upload to the book insertion page to make this process easier.

- You could add user login, personalization, and book recommendations; online reviews; affiliate programs; stock level checking; and so on. The possibilities are endless.

Using an Existing System

If you want to get a highly featured shopping cart up and running quickly, you might want to try using an existing shopping cart system. One well known open source cart implemented in PHP is FishCartSQL, available from

http://www.fishcart.org/

It has a lot of advanced features such as customer tracking, timed sales, multiple languages, credit card processing, and support for multiple online shops on one server. Of course, when you use an existing system, you always find there are things that it does not have that you want, and vice versa. The advantage of an open source product is that you can go in and change the things you don't like.

Next

In the next chapter, you learn how to build an online content management system suitable for managing digital assets. This system can be useful if you are running a content-based site.

## 28

Building a Content Management System

IN THIS CHAPTER, YOU LOOK AT A CONTENT management system (CMS) for storing, indexing, and searching text and multimedia content. Content management systems are extremely useful on websites where the site content is maintained by more than one author, where maintenance is performed by nontechnical staff, or where the content and graphic design are developed by different people or departments.

In this chapter, you build an application that helps authorized users to manage an organization's digital assets.

This chapter covers the following:

- Presenting web pages using a series of templates
- Building a search engine that indexes documents according to metadata

The Problem

Imagine that the busy web development team for SuperFastOnlineNews consists of excellent graphic designers and some award-winning writers. The site contains regularly updated news, sports, and weather pages. The main page shows the latest headline from each of the three category pages.

At SuperFastOnlineNews, the designers ensure that the website content looks great. This is what they do best. The writers, on the other hand, write excellent articles but can't draw well or build websites.

You need to allow all team members to concentrate on what they do best and bring their output together to provide the super-fast news service that the name implies.

Solution Requirements

For this project, you need to produce a system that

- Increases productivity by having the writers concentrate on writing and the designers on designing
- Allows the editor to review stories and decide which ones should be published
- Presents a consistent look and feel throughout the site using page templates
- Allows writers access only to their designated areas of the site
- Enables the look and feel to be easily changed for a section or throughout the site
- Prevents live content from being changed

Existing Systems

There are many existing CMSs—both free and commercial. Before writing your own, you would be well advised to evaluate some existing ones. The trade-off between using somebody else's and writing your own is similar to other projects.

Writing your own CMS gives you complete flexibility but requires a lot more work. You can decide exactly how the CMS output will integrate into the website and how dynamic content is handled.

Existing systems might give you very advanced features with very little work. They usually have very flexible output because that is one of the primary purposes of a CMS, but they often tie you to a particular workflow and may not handle dynamic content well.

Writing a simple CMS—with the types of features you will build in this chapter—does not take long, but the more features you require, the more difficult the task becomes and the more appealing adopting an existing system becomes.

Editing Content

First, you need to think about how you will get content into the system and how you will store and edit that content.

Getting Content into the System

You need to decide on the way that stories and design components will be submitted. There are many possibilities, but we describe three in the following sections.

FTP/SCP

The writers and designers could be given FTP or SCP access to areas on the web server, and they could then upload files from their local machine to the server. You would need to have a rigid naming standard for the uploaded files (to identify which pictures belonged to which stories) or a web-based system to deal with this separately from the FTP upload.

Unfortunately, giving detailed rights and permissions to different users via these methods would be difficult, so we do not use it in this example.

File Upload Method

As we discussed in Chapter 18, "Interacting with the File System and the Server," the HTTP protocol provides a method for files to be uploaded via the web browser. PHP is able to deal with these uploads very easily.

The file upload method also gives you the opportunity to handle the content in any way you like. You could store text in a database or in a file. The upload mechanism creates a temporary file. To store the data in a file, you copy it to a permanent location. To store it in a database, you read in the temporary file created by the upload mechanism and store its contents in the database. You will optionally use file upload for stories in this project but will need it for pictures.

Editing Online

You can let users create and edit documents without using FTP, SCP, or file upload. Instead, you can give the contributors a large text area input box on the screen in which their story content can be edited.

This method is simple but often effective. The web browser does not provide any text-editing facilities beyond the cut-and-paste functionality of the operating system. However, when you just need to make a small change—for instance, to correct a spelling mistake—you can quickly bring up the content and amend it. Unfortunately, because an HTML `textarea` cannot provide any advanced features such as real-time spell checking, you will more likely need to correct spelling mistakes.

Similar to file upload, the form data could either be written to a file or stored in a database.

Databases Versus File Storage

An important decision to make at an early stage is how the content will be stored after it has been uploaded into the system.

Because you will be storing metadata alongside the story text, you can put the text parts of the content into the database for this project. Although MySQL is capable of storing multimedia data, you are generally better off to store uploaded images on the file system, as we've done here. As discussed in Part II, "Using MySQL," using BLOB data in your MySQL database can reduce performance.

You can just store the image filename in the database. Using the file system, the `<IMG>` tag can reference the image file directly as usual.

Document Structure

The sample stories used in this project are short one- or two-paragraph news stories with a single optional image, designed for people in a hurry. They are structured documents in as much as they contain a headline and one or two paragraphs of text with an image.

The more structured a document is, the more easily it can be split up for storage in a database. The advantage of this technique is that all the documents can be presented in a consistent, structured manner. The corresponding disadvantage is that more structure leads to less flexibility.

Consider the news story example. You will store the headline in a field separate from the story text, and by its nature, the image is a separate component of the document.

With the headline as a separate item, you can define a standard typeface and style for it to be displayed in and can easily separate it from the rest of the story to form the main headlines page.

Another approach for large documents would be to have a one-to-many relationship with document components—that is, to store each paragraph, heading, or image as a separate row in the database, each linked to a master document ID. That kind of dynamic document structure would allow you much more flexibility in document structure and rendering.

Using Metadata

For this project, you already know that each story record comprises a headline, story text, and an image. However, there's no reason you can't store other data in the same record.

The system will automatically insert values for who created the story and when it was last modified. These values can be automatically displayed at the bottom of a story to sign and timestamp it without the author needing to worry about adding the information.

It might also be useful to add other data that is not displayed, known as *metadata*. A good example is storing keywords that would be used for the search engine index.

Rather than scan the entire text of every story, the search engine looks at the keyword metadata for each story and determines relevance solely from that. This way, the site administrator can have total control over which search words and phrases match which documents.

In the example, you will allow any number of keywords to be associated with a story and assign each keyword a weight value to indicate how relevant that keyword is on a scale from 1 to 10.

You can then develop a search engine algorithm that ranks matches according to this human-specified relevance for stories, rather than a complex algorithm that has to interpret English prose and make decisions based on its limited understanding and governed by fixed rules.

If your data is solely text stored in a database, MySQL's full text indexing and searching will be a better solution than rolling your own system, but the system developed here could be used for a simple search engine across multiple document types and multimedia files.

We aren't saying that you have to store metadata in the database. There's nothing to stop you from using the <META> tag in HTML or even using XML to build your documents. However, taking advantage of the database is worthwhile if you intend to search your metadata.

Formatting the Output

The news site example follows a simple but structured format when displaying a page. Each page contains several stories that are all formatted the same way. First, the headline is displayed in a large type, followed by the photograph underneath on the left, and then the story text on the right. The whole page is contained in a standard page template to preserve the site branding and consistency throughout.

Figure 28.1 shows the logical page structure you will be using.

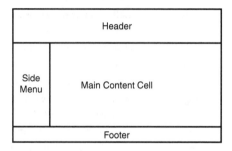

Figure 28.1   The logical page structure for the public pages of SFON follows common conventions and is easy to produce in HTML.

Implementing a simple templated structure such as this from a page design is not difficult. You simply split the page into three parts: a header, side menu, and footer that do not change and the content of the page that varies from page to page and day to day. Whenever you display a page for this site, you show the header and side menu first, the page content, and finally the footer.

The header and side menu are in one file (header.php), and the footer is in another (footer.php). The main content for each page is generated by an appropriate script.

Implementing the site with a header and footer template allows these template files to be easily changed if the site design is updated.

Solution Design/Overview

A summary of the files in this application is shown in Table 28.1.

Table 28.1 **Files in the Content Management Application**

Name	Type	Description
create_database.sql	SQL	SQL to set up the content database and some sample data
include_fns.php	Functions	Collection of include files for the admin section of this application
db_fns.php	Functions	Collection of functions for connecting to content database
select_fns.php	Functions	Collection of functions to aid creation of `<select>` drop-down lists from the database
user_auth_fns.php	Functions	Collection of functions for authenticating admin users
header.php	Template	Header shown at the top of every content page
footer.php	Template	Footer shown at the bottom of every content page
logo.gif	Image	Logo file displayed in `header.php`
index.php	Application	Summary that shows the most recent headline from each page of the site
admin/index.php	Application	Menu to the administrative functions for the site
page.php	Application	List of the headlines and story text for a particular page
resize_image.php	Application	Script that resizes an image on the fly for `index.php`
search_form.php	Application	Form to enter keywords for searching the site content
search.php	Application	Page that displays headlines of content matching keyword criteria
login.php	Application	Script that authenticates a user's password and logs her in to the system
logout.php	Application	Script that logs a user out of the system
writer.php	Application	List of stories that the logged-in user has written with an option to add, modify, or delete stories
story.php	Application	Story detail screen for editing or adding a new story
story_submit.php	Application	Script that adds a new story or commits changes from data entered in `story.php`
delete_story.php	Application	Script that processes a story delete request from `stories.php`
keywords.php	Application	List of keywords for a story with the option to add or delete keywords

Table 28.1   **Files in the Content Management Application**

Name	Type	Description
keyword_add.php	Application	Script that processes a keyword add request from keywords.php
keyword_delete.php	Application	Script that processes a keyword delete request from keywords.php
publish.php	Application	Editor's list of stories showing which ones are published with an option to toggle each one's status
publish_story.php	Application	Script that processes a publish request from publish.php
unpublish_story.php	Application	Script that processes an unpublish request from publish.php

Designing the Database

Listing 28.1 shows the SQL queries used to create the database for the content system. This listing is part of the file create_database.sql. The file on the CD-ROM also contains queries to populate the database with some sample users and stories.

Listing 28.1   **Excerpt from** create_database.sql—**SQL File to Set Up the Content Database**

```
drop database if exists content;

create database content;

use content;

drop table if exists writers;

create table writers (
  username   varchar(16) not null primary key,
  password   char(40) not null,
  full_name  text
);

drop table if exists stories;

create table stories (
  id         int not null primary key auto_increment,
  writer     varchar(16) not null,          # foreign key writers.username
  page       varchar(16) not null,          # foreign key pages.code
```

Listing 28.1 **Continued**

```
  headline    text,
  story_text  text,
  picture     text,
  created     int,
  modified    int,
  published   int
);

drop table if exists pages;

create table pages (
  code        varchar(16) primary key,
  description text
);

drop table if exists writer_permissions;

create table writer_permissions  (
  writer      varchar(16) not null,            # foreign key writers.username
  page        varchar(16) not null,            # foreign key pages.code
  primary key(writer, page)
);

drop table if exists keywords;

create table keywords (
  story       int not null,                    # foreign key stories.id
  keyword     varchar(32) not null,
  weight      int not null,
  primary key(story, keyword)
);

grant select, insert, update, delete
on content.*
to content@localhost identified by 'password';
```

You need to store a little information about each writer, including a login name and password, in the `writers` table. You store their full names for displaying after each article and for greeting them when they log in.

The `pages` table contains the page heading for each page on which stories can be displayed. The `writer_permissions` table implements a many-to-many relationship indicating for which pages a writer can submit stories.

The `stories` table contains separate fields for `headline`, `story_text`, and `picture`, as discussed previously. The `created`, `modified`, and `published` fields are integer fields and store the Unix timestamp values of the relevant times.

To create the database, run the following command:

```
mysql -u root < create_database.sql
```

Make sure that you do not already have a database called `content` that this will drop and replace.

Implementing the CMS

Now that you have a database, you can go about building the main part of the system.

Front End

Start by looking at `index.php`, shown in Listing 28.2, which will be the first page that a visitor to the site would see. You want to show her the headlines of the latest story from each page.

Listing 28.2 `index.php`—**Script That Shows the Most Recent Headline from Each Page**

```php
<?php
  include_once('db_fns.php');
  include_once('header.php');

  $handle = db_connect();

  $pages_sql = 'select * from pages order by code';
  $pages_result = $handle->query($pages_sql);

  echo '<table border="0" width="400">';

  while ($pages = $pages_result->fetch_assoc())
  {
    $story_sql = "select * from stories
                  where page = '{$pages['code']}'
                  and published is not null
                  order by published desc";

    $story_result = $handle->query($story_sql);

    if ($story_result->num_rows)
    {
```

Listing 28.2 **Continued**

```
    $story = $story_result->fetch_assoc();
    echo "<tr>
            <td>
              <h2>{$pages['description']}</h2>
              <p>{$story['headline']}</p>
              <p align='right' class='morelink'>
                <a href='page.php?page={$pages['code']}'>
                Read more {$pages['code']} ...
                </a>
              </p>
            </td>
            <td width='100'>";
    if ($story['picture'])
    {
      echo '<img src="resize_image.php?image=';
      echo urlencode($story['picture']);
      echo '&max_width=80&max_height=60"  />';
    }
    echo '</td></tr>';
  }
}
echo '</table>';

include_once('footer.php');
?>
```

The index.php script, as with all the public scripts, includes header.php at the start and
footer.php at the end. Any output generated by the script is therefore displayed within
the main content cell in the formatted page.

The hard work is done by two database queries. First,

```
select * from pages order by code
```

retrieves the list of pages in the database. Next inside the loop, the query

```
select * from stories
where page = '{$pages['code']}'
and published is not null
order by published desc
```

is executed to find the stories on that page in reverse order of the date published.
Because this string is in double quotation marks, {$pages['code']} will be replaced by
elements from the $page array.

Figure 28.2 shows the output from headline.php using the sample application data.

Figure 28.2 The `headline.php` script shows the headlines from each page within the site.

Next to each headline, a link is generated in the following form:

```
<p align='right' class='morelink'>
  <a href='page.php?page=news'>
  Read more news ...
  </a>
</p>
```

The link is generated within the previous loop so that the query string value of `page` and the page name are printed next to the relevant headline. Clicking this link takes the visitor to `page.php`—the full list of stories for the particular page. The source for `page.php` can be found in Listing 28.3.

Listing 28.3 `page.php`—**Script That Displays One Story or All Published Stories for a Page**

```php
<?php
  if (!isset($_REQUEST['page'])&&!isset($_REQUEST['story']))
  {
    header('Location: index.php');
    exit;
  }
```

Listing 28.3 **Continued**

```php
$page = $_REQUEST['page'];
$story = intval($_REQUEST['story']);

include_once('db_fns.php');
include_once('header.php');

$handle = db_connect();
if($story)
{
  $query = "select * from stories
          where id = '$story' and
                  published is not null";
}
else
{
  $query = "select * from stories
          where page = '$page' and
                  published is not null
          order by published desc";
}
$result = $handle->query($query);

while ($story = $result->fetch_assoc())
{
  // headline
  echo "<h2>{$story['headline']}</h2>";
  //picture
  if ($story['picture'])
  {
    echo '<div style="float:right; margin:0px 0px 6px 6px;">';
    echo '<img src="resize_image.php?image=';
    echo urlencode($story[picture]);
    echo '&max_width=200&max_height=120"  align = right/></div>';
  }
  // byline
  $w = get_writer_record($story['writer']);
  echo '<br /><p class="byline">';
  echo $w[full_name].', ';
  echo date('M d, H:i', $story['modified']);
  echo '</p>';
  // main text
  echo $story['story_text'];
}
include_once('footer.php');
?>
```

Note that `page.php` requires either a value for `page` or a value for `story`. In case `page.php` is ever called directly without the query string, the first condition

```
if (!isset($_REQUEST['page'])&&!isset($_REQUEST['story']))
{
  header('Location: index.php');
  exit;
}
```

will send the visitor back to the headline page so that the omission of `page` will not cause an error.

The first query is used if you are calling this page to display a single story:

```
select * from stories
where id = '$story' and
      published is not null
```

The second query is used to retrieve all stories for a particular page:

```
select * from stories
where page = '$page' and
      published is not null
order by published desc
```

The most recently published is retrieved first. Within each loop, the uploaded image and story text are printed to the screen, along with the writer's name and date of last change.

Figure 28.3 shows `page.php` in action, displaying all the news page items for the sample application.

Figure 28.3   The `page.php` script shows all published stories on the news page.

Image Manipulation

The writers who contribute stories will probably supply their own photographs to complement their stories. You want consistency, but what happens when one writer uploads a large, high-quality image and another writer uploads a small thumbnail?

Assuming that the pictures in question will primarily be photographs, you can insist on JPEG images only and take advantage of functions in PHP to manipulate the images. This topic was covered in detail in Chapter 21, "Generating Images."

We created a simple script called resize_image.php, shown in Listing 28.4, that you can use to resize an image on the fly so that it can be displayed with an <img> tag in a consistent size. Resizing images on the fly may not be appropriate for a busy site because it will be an expensive operation. Using it in this application allows you the flexibility to display the same image in different sizes on different pages—in this case, smaller images on the headline page and larger images on the specific pages. It also means that you can change the size of the images to suit a new layout if you change your template.

Listing 28.4 `resize_image.php`—**Script That Resizes a JPEG Image On the Fly**

```php
<?php

  $image = $_REQUEST['image'];
  $max_width = $_REQUEST['max_width'];
  $max_height = $_REQUEST['max_height'];

  if (!$max_width)
    $max_width = 80;
  if (!$max_height)
    $max_height = 60;

  $size = GetImageSize($image);
  $width = $size[0];
  $height = $size[1];

  $x_ratio = $max_width / $width;
  $y_ratio = $max_height / $height;

  if ( ($width <= $max_width) && ($height <= $max_height) ) {
    $tn_width = $width;
    $tn_height = $height;
  }
  else if (($x_ratio * $height) < $max_height) {
    $tn_height = ceil($x_ratio * $height);
    $tn_width = $max_width;
  }
  else {
    $tn_width = ceil($y_ratio * $width);
    $tn_height = $max_height;
  }
```

Listing 28.4   **Continued**

```
$src = ImageCreateFromJpeg($image);
$dst = ImageCreate($tn_width,$tn_height);
ImageCopyResized($dst, $src, 0, 0, 0, 0,
    $tn_width,$tn_height,$width,$height);
header('Content-type: image/jpeg');
ImageJpeg($dst, null, -1);
ImageDestroy($src);
ImageDestroy($dst);

?>
```

This script takes three parameters: the filename of the image to display, the maximum width, and the maximum height in pixels. This is not to say that if the maximum size specified is 200×200, the image will be scaled to 200×200. Rather, it will be scaled down in proportion so that the larger of the width or height is 200 pixels and the other dimension is 200 pixels or smaller. For instance, a 400×300 image would be reduced to 200×150. This way, the proportions of the image will be maintained.

Resizing on the server is a better option than just specifying height and width attributes to the <img> tag. The large, high-resolution image that a writer submitted might be several megabytes in size; but when scaled to a reasonable size, it could be less than 100KB. There is then no need to download the huge file and ask the browser to resize it, but you would need to cache the resized images for a moderately busy site.

The image manipulation functions are covered in detail in Chapter 21. Here, you use the ImageCopyResized() function to scale the image on the fly to the required size.

The key to the resize operation is the calculation of the new width and height parameters. You find the ratio between the actual and maximum dimensions. $max_width and $max_height can be passed in on the query string; otherwise, the default values specified at the top of the listing will be used:

```
$x_ratio = $max_width / $width;
$y_ratio = $max_height / $height;
```

If the image is already smaller than the specified maximum dimensions, the width and height are left unchanged. Otherwise, either the X or Y ratio is then used to scale both dimensions equally so that the reduced size image is not stretched or squashed, as follows:

```
if ( ($width <= $max_width) && ($height <= $max_height) ) {
  $tn_width = $width;
  $tn_height = $height;
}
else if (($x_ratio * $height) < $max_height) {
  $tn_height = ceil($x_ratio * $height);
  $tn_width = $max_width;
}
```

```
else {
  $tn_width = ceil($y_ratio * $width);
  $tn_height = $max_height;
}
```

After you have calculated the desired size, the image is resized and output to the browser. To function, this script is called from within `<img>` tags on a page, and it sends its output directly to the browser with an appropriate header directive.

A potential advantage of this approach that we did not make use of here is that the images do not need to be inside the web directory tree at all. This could have significant security advantages in this application in which you allow an administrative script to write to the image directories. Because the script passes the image out, only the script needs to be inside the web tree.

Back End

Let's look next at how stories can be added to the system. The admin menu (`/admin/index.php`) sends writers to `writer.php`. This script, after a writer is authenticated, displays a list of the stories the author has written. It displays the published date for live articles and offers the option to add a new story, edit or delete an existing one, and set the search keywords. An example is shown in Figure 28.4.

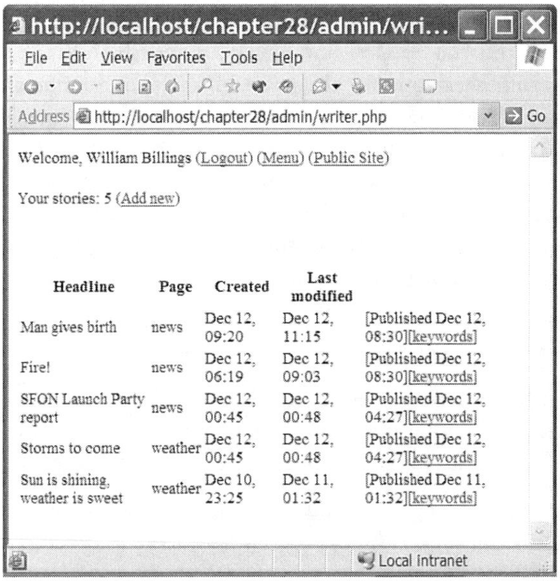

Figure 28.4   The `writer.php` script shows the story management page for writers.

These screens are not formatted inside the header and footer files, although they could be if desired. Because only the writers and editor will use these scripts, in the example we chose to format only as much as needed to create a usable system. The code for writer.php is shown in Listing 28.5.

Listing 28.5 writer.php— The Interface for Writers to Manage Their Stories

```php
<?php
  // writer.php Is the Interface for Writers to Manage Their Stories

  include_once('include_fns.php');

  if (!check_auth_user())
  {
    login_form();
  }
  else
  {
    $handle = db_connect();

    $writer = get_writer_record($_SESSION['auth_user']);

    echo '<p>Welcome, '.$writer['full_name'];
    echo ' (<a href="logout.php">Logout</a>)
          (<a href="index.php">Menu</a>)
          (<a href="../">Public Site</a>) </p>';
    echo '<p>';

    $query = 'select * from stories where writer = \''.
             $_SESSION['auth_user'].'\' order by created desc';
    $result = $handle->query($query);

    echo 'Your stories: ';
    echo $result->num_rows;
    echo ' (<a href="story.php">Add new</a>)';
    echo '</p><br /><br />';

    if ($result->num_rows)
    {
      echo '<table>';
      echo '<tr><th>Headline</th><th>Page</th>';
      echo '<th>Created</th><th>Last modified</th></tr>';
      while ($stories = $result->fetch_assoc())
      {
```

Listing 28.5 **Continued**

```php
      echo '<tr><td>';
      echo $stories['headline'];
      echo '</td><td>';
      echo $stories['page'];
      echo '</td><td>';
      echo date('M d, H:i', $stories['created']);
      echo '</td><td>';
      echo date('M d, H:i', $stories['modified']);
      echo '</td><td>';
      if ($stories['published'])
      {
        echo '[Published '.date('M d, H:i', $stories['published']).']';
      }
      else
      {
        echo '[<a href="story.php?story='.$stories['id'].'">edit</a>] ';
        echo '[<a href="delete_story.php?story='.$stories['id'].
            '">delete</a>] ';
      }
      echo '[<a href="keywords.php?story='.$stories['id'].'">keywords</a>]';
      echo '</td></tr>';
    }
    echo '</table>';
  }
}
?>
```

The first step is to check whether a user has been authenticated and, if not, to display only a login form.

The session variable `auth_user` will be set after a writer has logged in. The authentication here isn't particularly secure, and in reality you would take more care to ensure that the writers are properly authenticated. This topic is dealt with in detail in Chapter 16, "Implementing Authentication with PHP and MySQL."

The login form submits to `login.php`, which checks the username and password against database values. If the login is successful, the user is returned to the page she came from, using the `HTTP_REFERER` value. This means that the login script can be invoked from any calling page within the system.

Next, you welcome the writer by name and give her the opportunity to log out. This link will always appear at the top of `stories.php` so she can easily log out when she is done:

```
$writer = get_writer_record($_SESSION['auth_user']);

echo '<p>Welcome, '.$writer['full_name'];
echo ' (<a href="logout.php">Logout</a>)
       (<a href="index.php">Menu</a>)
       (<a href="../">Public Site</a>) </p>';
```

The function `get_writer_record()` is defined in `db_fns.php` and returns an array of all the fields in the `writer` table for the passed-in username. The script `logout.php` simply unsets the value of `auth_user`.

The following SQL in `writer.php` finds all a writer's stories, starting with the most recently added:

```
$query = 'select * from stories where writer = \''.
          $_SESSION['auth_user'].'\' order by created desc';
```

You store created, modified, and published timestamps against each story record. When a new story is added, both the created and modified timestamps are set to the system time. Each subsequent change updates only the modified field. You will not set the published timestamp until an editor publishes the story to make it part of the live site.

All this information is shown on the stories screen, first with

```
echo date('M d, H:i', $stories['created']);
```

and then

```
echo date('M d, H:i', $stories['modified']);
```

and finally

```
if ($stories['published'])
{
  echo '[Published '.date('M d, H:i', $stories['published']).']';
}
else
{
  echo '[<a href="story.php?story='.$stories['id'].'">edit</a>] ';
  echo '[<a href="delete_story.php?story='.$stories['id'].'">delete</a>] ';
}
echo '[<a href="keywords.php?story='.$stories['id'].'">keywords</a>]';
```

This code shows the published date if appropriate; otherwise, it shows links to edit or delete that story. Search keywords can be added to published and unpublished stories.

The script for entering a new story or editing an existing one is `story.php`. Figure 28.5 shows one of the stories being edited in the sample application database.

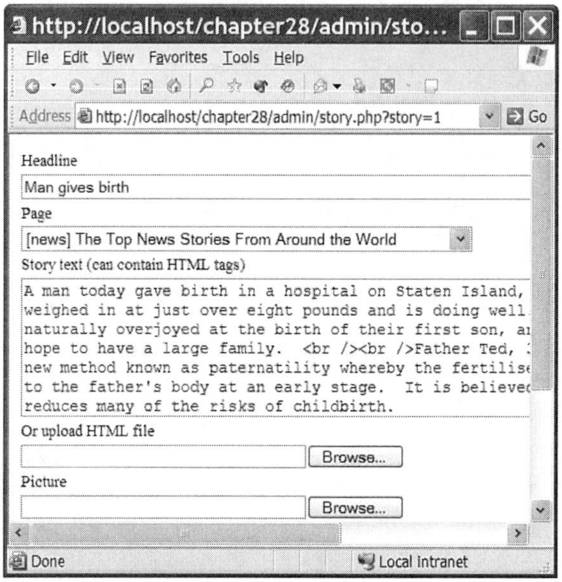

Figure 28.5   The story.php script enables you to edit a story.

The complete listing for story.php is shown in Listing 28.6.

Listing 28.6   story.php—**Script Used to Create or Edit a Story**

```php
<?php
  include ('include_fns.php');

  if (isset($_REQUEST['story']))
  {
    $story = get_story_record($_REQUEST['story']);
  }
?>

<form action="story_submit.php" method="post" enctype="multipart/form-data">
<input type="hidden" name="story" value="<?php echo $_REQUEST['story'];?>">
<input type="hidden" name="destination"
       value="<?php echo $_SERVER['HTTP_REFERER'];?>">
<table>

<tr>
  <td>Headline<td>
</tr>
```

Listing 28.6   **Continued**

```html
<tr>
  <td><input size="80" name="headline"
             value="<?php echo $story['headline'];?>"></td>
</tr>

<tr>
  <td>Page</td>
</tr>
<tr>
  <td>
<?php
  if(isset($_REQUEST['story']))
  {
    $query = "select p.code, p.description
              from pages p, writer_permissions wp, stories s
              where p.code = wp.page
                    and wp.writer = s.writer
                    and s.id =".$_REQUEST['story'];
  }
  else
  {
    $query = "select p.code, p.description
              from pages p, writer_permissions wp
              where p.code = wp.page
                    and wp.writer = '{$_SESSION['auth_user']}'";
  }
  echo query_select('page', $query, $story['page']);
?>
  </td>
</tr>

<tr>
  <td>Story text (can contain HTML tags)</td>
</tr>
<tr>
  <td><textarea cols="80" rows="7" name="story_text"
        wrap="virtual"><?php echo $story['story_text'];?></textarea>
  </td>
</tr>

<tr>
  <td>Or upload HTML file</td>
</tr>
```

Listing 28.6 **Continued**

```
<tr>
  <td><input type="file" name="html" size="40"></td>
</tr>

<tr>
  <td>Picture</td>
</tr>
<tr>
  <td><input type="file" name="picture" size="40"></td>
</tr>

<?php
  if ($story[picture])
  {
    $size   = getImageSize('../'.$story['picture']);
    $width  = $size[0];
    $height = $size[1];
?>
    <tr>
      <td>
        <img src="<?php echo '../'.$story['picture'];?>"
             width="<?php echo $width;?>" height="<?php echo $height;?>">
      </td>
    </tr>
<?php
  }
?>

<tr>
  <td align="center"><input type="submit" value="Submit"></td>
</tr>
</table>
</form>
```

The same script can be used whether adding or editing, and the action depends on whether story is set when the script is called:

```
if (isset($_REQUEST['story']))
{
  $story = get_story_record($_REQUEST['story']);
}
```

The function `get_story_record()` is defined in `db_fns.php` and returns an array of all the fields in the `stories` table for the specified story ID. If no story ID is passed in, `$story` will be `null` and `$story` will not contain the array elements:

```
<input size="80" name="headline"
    value="<?php echo $story['headline'];?>"></td>
```

If `story` is not set, the preceding code will produce no value from the PHP statement, so the headline input box will be blank. If `story` is set, it will contain the headline text for the story being edited.

The function `query_select()` is defined in `select_fns.php` and returns the HTML code to produce a `select` list from a given SQL query. The first parameter is the name attribute for the select. The SQL query in the second parameter selects two columns, where the first is the `value` part of each `option`, and the second appears after the `option` tag and is the text actually displayed in the list. The third parameter is optional. It adds a `selected` attribute to the option whose value matches the specified value. You use this function to generate a `select` that contains the pages this writer has permission to contribute to.

To store an edited article with the same ID as it had previously, you need to record this ID. You do it as a hidden variable:

```
<input type="hidden" name="story" value="<?php print $_REQUEST['story'];?>">
```

This line sets up a placeholder variable, setting the new value for `story` from the passed-in `story`. When the form is submitted, `story_submit.php` checks whether there is a value for `story` and generates an SQL `UPDATE` or `INSERT` statement accordingly.

The code for `story_submit.php` is shown in Listing 28.7.

Listing 28.7 `story_submit.php`—**Script Used to Insert or Update a Story in the Database**

```php
<?php
  // story_submit.php
  // add / modify story record

  include_once('include_fns.php');

  $handle = db_connect();

  $headline = $_REQUEST['headline'];
  $page = $_REQUEST['page'];
  $time = time();

  if ( (isset($_FILES['html']['name'])) &&
       (dirname($_FILES['html']['type']) == 'text') &&
       is_uploaded_file($_FILES['html']['tmp_name'])))
  {
```

Listing 28.7 **Continued**

```php
  $story_text = file_get_contents($_FILES['html']['tmp_name']);
}
else
{
  $story_text = $_REQUEST['story_text'];
}

$story_text = addslashes($story_text);

if (isset($_REQUEST['story']) && $_REQUEST['story']!='')
{   // It's an update
  $story = $_REQUEST['story'];

  $query = "update stories
           set headline = '$headline',
               story_text = '$story_text',
               page = '$page',
               modified = $time
           where id = $story";
}
else
{         // It's a new story
  $query = "insert into stories
               (headline, story_text, page, writer, created, modified)
           values
               ('$headline', '$story_text', '$page', '".
             $_SESSION['auth_user']."', $time, $time)";
}

$result = $handle->query($query);

if (!$result)
{
  echo "There was a database error when executing <pre>$query</pre>";
  echo mysqli_error();
  exit;
}

if ( (isset($_FILES['picture']['name']) &&
      is_uploaded_file($_FILES['picture']['tmp_name'])))
{
```

Listing 28.7 **Continued**

```php
  if (!isset($_REQUEST['story']) || $_REQUEST['story']=='')
  {
    $story = mysqli_insert_id($handle);
  }
  $type = basename($_FILES['picture']['type']);

  switch ($type) {
    case 'jpeg':
    case 'pjpeg':   $filename = "images/$story.jpg";
                    move_uploaded_file($_FILES['picture']['tmp_name'],
                                       '../'.$filename);
                    $query = "update stories
                                set picture = '$filename'
                                where id = $story";
                    $result = $handle->query($query);
                    break;
    default:        echo 'Invalid picture format: '.
                           $_FILES['picture']['type'];
  }
}

  header('Location: '.$_REQUEST['destination']);
?>
```

The delete story link calls delete_story.php, which executes a simple SQL delete statement and returns the writer to the calling page. The code for delete_story.php is shown in Listing 28.8.

Listing 28.8 delete_story.php— **Script Used to Delete a Story from the Database**

```php
<?php
  // delete_story.php

  include_once('include_fns.php');

  $handle = db_connect();

  $story = $_REQUEST['story'];
  if(check_permission($_SESSION['auth_user'], $story))
  {
    $query = "delete from stories where id = $story";
    $result = $handle->query($query);
  }
  header('Location: '.$_SERVER['HTTP_REFERER']);
?>
```

Note that the function `check_permission()` refers to the database to see that the logged-in user has permission to delete stories from this page. You use this function on many pages in the admin section. Even though unauthorized users will not be shown links to delete articles, it would not be very good if users could circumvent security by simply guessing an obvious URL.

Searches

Clicking the `keywords` link on the stories list brings up a new form for entering keywords against the story. There is no limit to the number of keywords that can be entered, and each keyword is given a weight value, with a higher value indicating that it is more relevant.

Figure 28.6 shows the screen used to set keywords against a particular story.

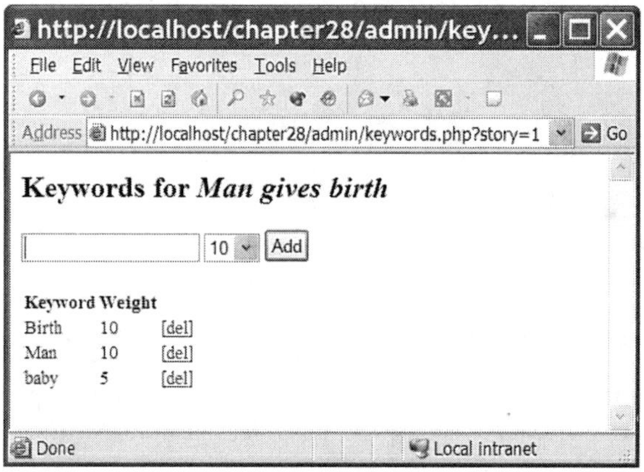

Figure 28.6   This screen enables you to set keywords for a story.

The script `keywords.php`, which is included on the CD-ROM, is fairly straightforward, so we don't describe it in any detail. This script triggers the `keyword_add.php` and `keyword_delete.php` scripts, which are also straightforward and are therefore not included here.

The script `keyword_add.php` uses the following query to add new keywords to the database:

```
insert into keywords (story, keyword, weight)
values ($story, '$keyword', $weight)
```

In a similar vein, `keyword_delete.php` uses the following query to remove a keyword:

```
delete from keywords where story = $story and keyword = '$keyword'
```

What is interesting is the way in which the weight values are used to calculate a percentage relevance figure when searching.

The search form in `search_form.php` contains a single field for keywords and submits to `search.php`, which queries the database of live stories to find matching content. The source for `search.php` is shown in Listing 28.9.

Listing 28.9   `search.php`—Script That Finds Matching Stories and Calculates a Percentage Match Score

```php
<?php
  include_once('db_fns.php');
  include_once('header.php');

  $handle = db_connect();

  if ($_REQUEST['keyword'])
  {
    $keywords = explode(' ', $_REQUEST['keyword']);
    $num_keywords = count($keywords);
    for ($i=0; $i<$num_keywords; $i++)
    {
      if ($i)
      {
        $keywords_string .= "or k.keyword = '".$keywords[$i]."' ";
      }
      else
      {
        $keywords_string .= "k.keyword = '".$keywords[$i]."' ";
      }
    }

    $query = "select s.id,
                     s.headline,
                     10 * sum(k.weight) / $num_keywords as score
              from stories s, keywords k
              where s.id = k.story
                    and ($keywords_string)
                    and published is not null
              group by s.id, s.headline
              order by score desc, s.id desc";


    $result = $handle->query($query);
  }
  echo '<h2>Search results</h2>';
```

Listing 28.9   **Continued**

```
  if ($result  && $result->num_rows)
  {
    echo '<table>';
    while ($matches = $result->fetch_assoc())
    {
      echo "<tr><td><a href='page.php?story={$matches['id']}'>
            {$matches['headline']}
            </td><td>";
      echo floor($matches['score']).'%';
      echo '</td></tr>';
    }
    echo '</table>';
  }
  else
  {
    echo 'No matching stories found';
  }
  include_once('footer.php');
?>
```

First, the keyword string passed into the search.php script is exploded into individual
search words. There is no facility for advanced search techniques in this example, such as
allowing the searcher to use AND or OR keywords or group words together into a phrase,
so all words in the string will be keywords.

```
if ($_REQUEST['keyword'])
{
  $keywords = split(' ', $_REQUEST['keyword']);
  $num_keywords = count($keywords);
  for ($i=0; $i<$num_keywords; $i++)
  {
    if ($i)
    {
      $keywords_string .= "or k.keyword = '".$keywords[$i]."' ";
    }
    else
    {
      $keywords_string .= "k.keyword = '".$keywords[$i]."' ";
    }
  }
}
```

This code uses the PHP function explode() to create an array containing each word in
the keyword string separated by a space character. If only one word is specified, it still
returns a single element array and the subsequent loop is executed once. Ultimately, the
condition stored in $keywords_string looks similar to

```
k.keyword = 'keyword1' or k.keyword = 'keyword2' or k.keyword = 'keyword3'
```

The search query built based on the previous code would be

```
select s.id,
       s.headline,
       10 * sum(k.weight) / $num_keywords as score
from stories s, keywords k
where s.id = k.story
and (k.keyword = 'keyword1'
  or k.keyword = 'keyword2'
  or k.keyword = 'keyword3')
group by s.id, s.headline
order by score desc, s.id desc
```

The calculation for the score is the sum of the weights from all matching keywords divided by the number of keywords searched for and then multiplied by 10. This weighting favors searches in which all the keywords entered match the keywords in the database.

Because the weights range from 1 to 10, the maximum value for the score is 100. A search for three keywords would be a 100% match with a story only if all three were found for that story and each had a weight of 10.

Editor Screen

The only part of the system we haven't covered is how a story actually is published after it has been written. The script publish.php, shown in Listing 28.10, makes a story live.

Listing 28.10 publish.php—**Script That Lists All Documents So the Editor Can Choose Which Ones Are Shown on the Live Site**

```php
<?php
  include_once('include_fns.php');

  if (!check_auth_user())
  {
    login_form();
  }
  else
  {
    $handle = db_connect();

    $writer = get_writer_record($_SESSION['auth_user']);

    echo '<p>Welcome, '.$writer['full_name'];
    echo ' (<a href="logout.php">Logout</a>) (<a href="index.php">Menu</a>)
          (<a href="../">Public Site</a>) </p>';
```

Listing 28.10   **Continued**

```php
$query = "select * from stories s, writer_permissions wp
          where wp.writer = '{$_SESSION['auth_user']}' and
                s.page = wp.page
          order by modified desc";
$result = $handle->query($query);

echo '<h1>Editor admin</h1>';

echo '<table>';
echo '<tr><th>Headline</th><th>Last modified</th></tr>';
while ($story = $result->fetch_assoc())
{
  echo '<tr><td>';
  echo $story['headline'];
  echo '</td><td>';
  echo date('M d, H:i', $story['modified']);
  echo '</td><td>';
  if ($story[published])
  {
    echo '[<a href="unpublish_story.php?story='.$story['id'].
        '">unpublish</a>] ';
  }
  else
  {
    echo '[<a href="publish_story.php?story='.$story['id'].'">publish</a>] ';
    echo '[<a href="delete_story.php?story='.$story['id'].'">delete</a>] ';
  }
  echo '[<a href="story.php?story='.$story['id'].'">edit</a>] ';

  echo '</td></tr>';
}
echo '</table>';
}
?>
```

This script should be made available only to the people who are authorized to publish stories to the live site. In the sample application, this is anybody who has permission to submit stories to a page. In a real system, it is quite likely to require a higher level of permission, or at least require somebody other than the original author to proofread and approve the material.

The publish.php script is similar to stories.php except that the editor is given a screen showing the stories for every writer, not just her own. The if statement ensures that appropriate options are presented for each story. Published stories can be unpublished, and unpublished stories can be published or deleted.

These three links submit to `unpublish_story.php`, `publish_story.php`, and `delete_story.php`, respectively.

The script `publish_story.php` uses the following SQL query:

```
update stories set published = $now
     where id = $story
```

This query marks a story as published and authorizes it for public viewing.

Similarly, `unpublish_story.php` uses the following query to mark a story as unpublished and stop it from being displayed to the public:

```
update stories set published = null
     where id = $story
```

The edit link appears regardless of whether a story is published, so the editor can always make changes. This is different to the writers' level of access, where they can modify a story only before it has been published.

Extending the Project

This project could be extended in several ways to make a more comprehensive content management system:

- You could allow groups of users to work on stories together (collaboration).
- You could implement a more flexible page layout so that editors can position text and images on the page.
- You could build an image library so that frequently used pictures are not duplicated and assign search keywords to images as well as story text.
- You could also add spell-checking functionality to the content editor. A check could be implemented using, for example, the Ispell or Aspell libraries.

Next

In the next project, you build a web-based interface that allows you to check and send email from the Web using IMAP.

29

Building a Web-Based
Email Service

MORE AND MORE OFTEN THESE DAYS, SITES WANT to offer web-based email to their users. This chapter explains how to implement a web interface to an existing mail server using the PHP IMAP library. You can use it to check your own existing mailbox through a web page or perhaps extend it to support many users for mass web-based email such as Hotmail.

In this project, you build an email client, Warm Mail, that will enable users to

- Connect to their accounts on POP3 or IMAP mail servers
- Read mail
- Send mail
- Reply to mail messages
- Forward mail messages
- Delete mail from their accounts

The Problem

For a user to be able to read his mail, you need to find a way to connect to his mail server. This generally isn't the same machine as the web server. You need a way to interact with the user's mailbox to see what messages have been received and to deal with each message individually.

Two main protocols are supported by mail servers for reading user mailboxes: Post Office Protocol version 3 (POP3) and Internet Message Access Protocol (IMAP). If possible, you should support both of them.

The main difference between these two is that POP3 is intended for, and usually used by, people who connect to a network for a short time to download and delete their mail from a server. IMAP is intended for online use, to interact with mail permanently kept on the remote server. IMAP has some more advanced features that we won't use here.

If you are interested in the differences between these protocols, you can consult the RFCs for them (RFC 1939 for POP version 3 and RFC 3501 for IMAP version 4 rev1). An excellent article comparing the two can be found at http://www.imap.org/papers/imap.vs.pop.brief.html.

Neither of these protocols is designed for sending mail; for that, you must use the Simple Mail Transfer Protocol (SMTP), which you used previously from PHP via the `mail()` function. This protocol is described in RFC 821.

Solution Components

PHP has excellent IMAP and POP3 support, but it is provided via the IMAP function library. To use the code presented in this chapter, you need to have installed the IMAP library. You can tell whether you already have it installed by looking at the output of the `phpinfo()` function.

If you are using Linux or Unix and do not have the IMAP library installed, you will need to download the required libraries. You can get the latest version via FTP from ftp://ftp.cac.washington.edu/imap/.

Under Unix, download the source and compile it for your operating system. Some users have reported difficulties with compiling newer versions of the IMAP library with PHP. If you experience difficulties, the solution seems to be to revert to using IMAP-2001, an older, stable version.

You should then create a directory for the IMAP files inside your system include directory, called, say `imap`. (Do *not* just copy the files across into the basic include directory because doing so may cause conflicts.) Inside your new directory, create two subdirectories called `imap/lib/` and `imap/include/`. Copy all the `*.h` files from your install to `imap/include/`. When you performed the compilation, a file called `c-client.a` was created. Rename it `libc-client.a` and copy it into your `imap/lib/` directory.

You then need to run PHP's configure script, adding the `--with-imap=`*dirname* directive (where *dirname* is the name of the directory you created) to any other parameters you use, and recompile PHP.

To use the IMAP extension with Windows, open your `php.ini` file and uncomment this line:

```
extension=php_imap.dll
```

Then restart the web server.

You can confirm that the IMAP extension is installed by running the `phpinfo()` function. A section for IMAP should be shown.

One interesting point to note is that, although they are called IMAP functions, they also work equally well with Post Office Protocol version 3 (POP3) and Network News Transfer Protocol (NNTP). For this example, you use them for IMAP and POP3, but you could easily extend the Warm Mail application to use NNTP and to be a news-reader as well as a mail client.

This library has several functions, but to implement the functionality in this application, you need to use only a few. We explain these functions as we use them, but you need to be aware that many more are available. See the documentation if your needs are different from ours or if you want to add extra features to the application.

You can build a fairly useful mail application with only a fraction of the built-in functions. This means that you need to plow through only a fraction of the documentation. The IMAP functions used in this chapter are

- imap_open()
- imap_close()
- imap_headers()
- imap_header()
- imap_fetchheader()
- imap_body()
- imap_delete()
- imap_expunge()

For a user to read his mail, you need to get his server and account details. Instead of getting these details from the user every time, you can set up a username and password database for the user so that you can store his details.

Often people have more than one email account (one for home and another for work, for example), and you should allow them to connect to any of their accounts. You should therefore allow them to have multiple sets of account information in the database.

You should enable users to read, reply to, forward, and delete existing emails, as well as send new ones. You can do all the reading parts using IMAP or POP3 and all the sending parts using SMTP with mail().

Now let's look at how to put all the pieces together.

Solution Overview

The general flow through this web-based system isn't much different from other email clients. Figure 29.1 shows a diagram illustrating the system flow and modules.

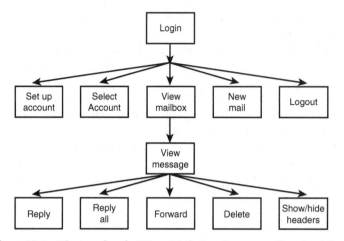

Figure 29.1   The interface for Warm Mail gives the user mailbox-level functionality and message-level functionality.

As you can see, you first require a user to log in and then give him a choice of options.
He can set up a new mail account or select one of his existing accounts for use. He also
can view his incoming mail—responding to, forwarding, or deleting it—and send new
mail.

You also give the user the option of viewing detailed headers for a particular message.
Viewing the complete headers can tell you a lot about a message. You can see which
machine the mail came from—a useful tool for tracking down spam. You can see which
machine forwarded it and at what time it reached each host—useful for assigning blame
for delayed messages. You might also be able to see which email client the sender used if
the application adds optional information to the headers.

This project uses a slightly different application architecture. Instead of having a set of
scripts, one for each module, this project has a slightly longer script, index.php, that
works like the event loop of a GUI-driven program. Each action taken on the site by
clicking a button brings you back to index.php, but with a different parameter.
Depending on the parameter, different functions are called to show the appropriate output to the user. The functions are in function libraries, as usual.

This architecture is suitable for small applications such as this. It suits applications that
are very event driven, where user actions trigger functionality. Using a single event handler is not suitable for larger architectures or projects being worked on by a team.

A summary of the files in the Warm Mail project is shown in Table 29.1.

Table 29.1 **Files in the Warm Mail Application**

Name	Type	Description
`index.php`	Application	The main script that runs the entire application
`include_fns.php`	Functions	Collection of include files for this application
`data_valid_fns.php`	Functions	Collection of functions for validating input data
`db_fns.php`	Functions	Collection of functions for connecting to the `mail` database
`mail_fns.php`	Functions	Collection of email-related functions for opening mailboxes, reading mail, and so on
`output_fns.php`	Functions	Collection of functions for outputting HTML
`user_auth_fns.php`	Functions	Collection of functions for authenticating users
`create_database.sql`	SQL	SQL to set up the `book_sc` database and set up a user

Let's look at the application now.

Setting Up the Database

The database for Warm Mail is fairly simple because it doesn't actually store any of the emails.

You need to store users of the system. For each user, you need to store the following fields:

- `username`—The user's preferred username for Warm Mail
- `password`—The user's preferred password for Warm Mail
- `address`—The user's preferred email address, which will appear in the From field of emails he sends from the system
- `displayname`—The "human-readable" name that the user would like displayed in emails from him to others

You also need to store each account that users would like to check with the system. For each account, you need to store the following information:

- `username`—The Warm Mail user who this account belongs to.
- `server`—The machine on which the account resides; for example, localhost or mail.tangledweb.com.au.
- `port`—The port to connect to when using this account. Usually, it is 110 for POP3 servers and 143 for IMAP servers.
- `type`—The protocol used to connect to this server, either `POP3` or `IMAP`.
- `remoteuser`—The username for connecting to the mail server.
- `remotepassword`—The password for connecting to the mail server.
- `accountid`—A unique key for identifying accounts.

You can set up the database for this application by running the SQL shown in Listing 29.1.

Listing 29.1 `create_database.sql`—**SQL to Create the Mail Database**

```
create database mail;

use mail;

create table users
(
  username char(16) not null primary key,
  password char(40) not null,
  address char(100) not null,
  displayname char(100) not null
);

create table accounts
(
  username char(16) not null,
  server char(100) not null,
  port int not null,
  type char(4) not null,
  remoteuser char(50) not null,
  remotepassword char(50) not null,
  accountid int unsigned not null auto_increment primary key
);

grant select, insert, update, delete
on mail.*
to mail@localhost identified by 'password';
```

Remember that you can execute this SQL by typing

```
mysql -u root -p < create_database.sql
```

You need to supply your root password. You also should change the password for the mail user in `create_database.sql` and in `db_fns.php` before running it.

On the CD-ROM, we provided an SQL file called `populate.sql`. In this application, we do not create a user registration or administration process. You can add one yourself if you want to use this software on a larger scale, but if you want it for personal use, you will just need to insert yourself into the database. The `populate.sql` script provides a template for doing this, so you can insert your details into it and run it to set yourself up as a user.

Examining the Script Architecture

As mentioned previously, the Warm Mail application uses one script to control everything. This script, called `index.php`, is shown in Listing 29.2. Although this script is quite
long, we go through it section by section.

Listing 29.2 `index.php`—**The Backbone of the Warm Mail System**

```php
<?php
// This file is the main body of the Warm Mail application.
// It works basically as a state machine and shows users the
// output for the action they have chosen.

//**************************************************************************
// Stage 1: pre-processing
// Do any required processing before page header is sent
// and decide what details to show on page headers
//**************************************************************************

  include ('include_fns.php');
  session_start();
  //create short variable names
  $username = $_POST['username'];
  $passwd = $_POST['passwd'];
  $action = $_REQUEST['action'];
  $account = $_REQUEST['account'];
  $messageid = $_GET['messageid'];

  $to =  $_POST['to'];
  $cc =  $_POST['cc'];
  $subject =  $_POST['subject'];
  $message =  $_POST['message'];

  $buttons = array();

  //append to this string if anything processed before header has output
  $status = '';

  // need to process log in or out requests before anything else
  if($username||$password)
  {
    if(login($username, $passwd))
    {
```

Listing 29.2 **Continued**

```
      $status .= '<p>Logged in successfully.</p><br /><br /><br /><br />
       <br /><br />';
      $_SESSION['auth_user'] = $username;
      if(number_of_accounts($_SESSION['auth_user'])==1)
      {
        $accounts = get_account_list($_SESSION['auth_user']);
        $_SESSION['selected_account'] = $accounts[0];
      }
    }
    else
     {
      $status .= '<p>Sorry, we could not log you in with that
                  username and password.</p><br /><br /><br /><br />
                  <br /><br />';
     }
  }
  if($action == 'log-out')
  {
    session_destroy();
    unset($action);
    $_SESSION=array();
  }

  //need to process choose, delete or store account before drawing header
  switch ( $action )
  {
    case 'delete-account' :
    {
      delete_account($_SESSION['auth_user'], $account);
      break;
    }
    case 'store-settings' :
    {
      store_account_settings($_SESSION['auth_user'], $_POST);
      break;
    }
    case 'select-account' :
    {
      // if have chosen a valid account, store it as a session variable
      if($account&&account_exists($_SESSION['auth_user'], $account))
      {
        $_SESSION['selected_account'] = $account;
      }
    }
  }
```

Listing 29.2   **Continued**

```php
  // set the buttons that will be on the tool bar
  $buttons[0] = 'view-mailbox';
  $buttons[1] = 'new-message';
  $buttons[2] = 'account-setup';
  //only offer a log out button if logged in
  if(check_auth_user())
  {
    $buttons[4] = 'log-out';
  }


//****************************************************************************
// Stage 2: headers
// Send the HTML headers and menu bar appropriate to current action
//****************************************************************************
  if($action)
  {
    // display header with application name and description of page or action
    do_html_header($_SESSION['auth_user'], "Warm Mail - ".
                   format_action($action),
                   $_SESSION['selected_account']);
  }
  else
  {
    // display header with just application name
    do_html_header($_SESSION['auth_user'], "Warm Mail",
     $_SESSION['selected_account'])   ;
  }

  display_toolbar($buttons);

//****************************************************************************
// Stage 3: body
// Depending on action, show appropriate main body content
//****************************************************************************
  //display any text generated by functions called before header
  echo $status;

  if(!check_auth_user())
  {
    echo '<p>You need to log in';
    if($action&&$action!='log-out')
      echo ' to go to '.format_action($action);
    echo '.</p><br /><br />';
    display_login_form($action);
  }
```

Listing 29.2 **Continued**

```
  else
  {
    switch ( $action )
    {
      // if we have chosen to setup a new account, or have just added or
      // deleted an account, show account setup page
      case 'store-settings' :
      case 'account-setup' :
      case 'delete-account' :
      {
        display_account_setup($_SESSION['auth_user']);
        break;
      }
      case 'send-message' :
      {
        if(send_message($to, $cc, $subject, $message))
          echo '<p>Message sent.</p><br /><br /><br /><br /><br />';
        else
          echo '<p>Could not send message.</p><br /><br /><br />
                <br /><br />';
        break;
      }
      case 'delete' :
      {
        delete_message($_SESSION['auth_user'],
                       $_SESSION['selected_account'], $messageid);
        //note deliberately no 'break' - we will continue to the next case
      }
      case 'select-account' :
      case 'view-mailbox' :
      {
        // if mailbox just chosen, or view mailbox chosen, show mailbox
        display_list($_SESSION['auth_user'],
          $_SESSION['selected_account']);
        break;
      }
      case 'show-headers' :
      case 'hide-headers' :
      case 'view-message' :
      {
```

Listing 29.2 **Continued**

```
    // if we have just picked a message from the list, or were looking at
    // a message and chose to hide or view headers, load a message
    $fullheaders = ($action=='show-headers');
    display_message($_SESSION['auth_user'],
                    $_SESSION['selected_account'],
                    $messageid, $fullheaders)  ;
  break;
}
case 'reply-all' :
{
  //set cc as old cc line
  if(!$imap)
    $imap = open_mailbox($_SESSION['auth_user'],
                         $_SESSION['selected_account']);
  if($imap)
  {
    $header = imap_header($imap, $messageid);
    if($header->reply_toaddress)
      $to = $header->reply_toaddress;
    else
      $to = $header->fromaddress;
    $cc = $header->ccaddress;
    $subject = 'Re: '.$header->subject;
    $body = add_quoting(imap_body($imap, $messageid));
    imap_close($imap);

    display_new_message_form($_SESSION['auth_user'],
    $to, $cc, $subject, $body);
  }
  break;
}
case 'reply' :
{
  //set to address as reply-to or from of the current message
  if(!$imap)
    $imap = open_mailbox($_SESSION['auth_user'],
                         $_SESSION['selected_account']);
  if($imap)
  {
```

Listing 29.2 **Continued**

```
           $header = imap_header($imap, $messageid);
           if($header->reply_toaddress)
             $to = $header->reply_toaddress;
           else
             $to = $header->fromaddress;
           $subject = 'Re: '.$header->subject;
           $body = add_quoting(stripslashes(imap_body($imap, $messageid)));
           imap_close($imap);

           display_new_message_form($_SESSION['auth_user'],
                                    $to, $cc, $subject, $body);
         }

         break;
       }
       case 'forward' :
       {
         //set message as quoted body of current message
         if(!$imap)
           $imap = open_mailbox($_SESSION['auth_user'],
                                $_SESSION['selected_account']);
         if($imap)
         {
           $header = imap_header($imap, $messageid)   ;
           $body = add_quoting(stripslashes(imap_body($imap, $messageid)));
           $subject = 'Fwd: '.$header->subject;
           imap_close($imap);

           display_new_message_form($_SESSION['auth_user'],
                                    $to, $cc, $subject, $body);
         }
         break;
       }
       case 'new-message' :
       {
         display_new_message_form($_SESSION['auth_user'],
                                  $to, $cc, $subject, $body);
         break;
       }
     }
   }
//****************************************************************************
// Stage 4: footer
//****************************************************************************
   do_html_footer();
?>
```

The `index.php` script uses an event handling approach. It contains the knowledge or logic about which function needs to be called for each event. The events in this case are triggered by the user clicking the various buttons in the site, each of which selects an action. Most buttons are produced by the `display_button()` function, but the `display_form_button()` function is used if it's a submit button. These functions are both in `output_fns.php`. They all jump to URLs of the form

```
index.php?action=log-out
```

The value of the `action` variable when `index.php` is called determines which event handler to activate.

The four main sections of the script are as follows:

1. You do some processing that must take place before you send the page header to the browser, such as starting the session, executing any preprocessing for the action the user has selected, and deciding what the headers will look like.

2. You process and send the appropriate headers and menu bar for the action the user has selected.

3. You choose which body of the script to execute, depending on the selected action. The different actions trigger different function calls.

4. You send the page footers.

If you look briefly through the code for the script, you will see that these four sections are marked with comments.

To understand this script fully, let's walk through actually using the site action by action.

Logging In and Out

When a user loads the page `index.php`, he will see the output shown in Figure 29.2.

Figure 29.2 The login screen for Warm Mail asks for a username and password.

Showing the login screen is the default behavior for the application. With no $action chosen yet, and no login details supplied, PHP will then execute the following parts of the code.

In the preprocessing stage, PHP first executes the following code:

```
include ('include_fns.php');
session_start();
```

These lines start the session that will be used to keep track of the $auth_user and $selected_account session variables, which we come to later.

As in the other applications, you create short variable names. You have done this in every form-related script since Chapter 1, "PHP Crash Course," so it barely needs mention except for the variable action. Depending on where in the application this variable comes from, it might be either a GET or POST variable. You therefore extract it from the $_REQUEST array. You have to do the same thing with the account variable because it is usually accessed via GET but is accessed via POST when deleting an account.

To save work when customizing the user interface, you use an array to control the buttons that appear on the toolbar. You declare an empty array as follows:

```
$buttons = array();
```

Then you set the buttons that you want on the page:

```
$buttons[0] = 'view-mailbox';
$buttons[1] = 'new-message';
$buttons[2] = 'account-setup';
```

If the user later logs in as an administrator, you will add more buttons to this array.

For the header stage, you print a plain vanilla header:

```
do_html_header($_SESSION['auth_user'], "Warm Mail",
    $_SESSION['selected_account']);
...
display_toolbar($buttons);
```

This code prints the title and header bar and then the toolbar of buttons you can see in Figure 29.2. These functions are located in the output_fns.php function library, but because you can easily see their effect in the figure, we don't go through them here.

Next comes the body of the code:

```
if(!check_auth_user())
{
  echo '<p>You need to log in</p>';
  if($action&&$action!='log-out')
    echo ' to go to '.format_action($action);
  echo '.<br /><br />';
  display_login_form($action);
}
```

The `check_auth_user()` function is from the `user_auth_fns.php` library. You used similar code in some of the previous projects; it checks whether the user is logged in. If he is not, which is the case here, you show him a login form, which you can see in Figure 29.2. You draw this form in the `display_login_form()` function from `output_fns.php`.

If the user fills in the form correctly and clicks the Log In button, he will see the output shown in Figure 29.3.

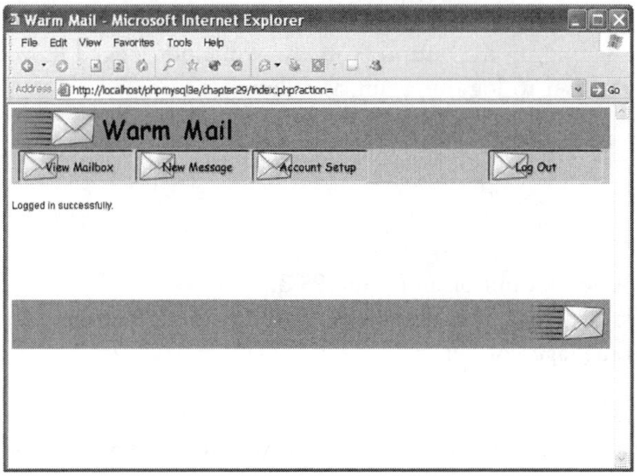

Figure 29.3   After successful login, the user can begin using the application.

On this execution of the script, you activate different sections of code. The login form has two fields: `$username` and `$password`. If they have been filled in, the following segment of preprocessing code will be activated:

```
if($username||$password)
{
  if(login($username, $passwd))
  {
    $status .= '<p>Logged in successfully.</p><br /><br /><br /><br />
    <br /><br />';
    $_SESSION['auth_user'] = $username;
    if(number_of_accounts($_SESSION['auth_user'])==1)
    {
      $accounts = get_account_list($_SESSION['auth_user']);
      $_SESSION['selected_account'] = $accounts[0];
    }
  }
  else
  {
```

```
$status .= '<p>Sorry, we could not log you in with that
          username and password.</p><br /><br /><br /><br />
          <br /><br />';
}
}
```

As you can see, the code calls the `login()` function, which is similar to the one used in Chapters 26, "Building User Authentication and Personalization," and 27, "Building a Shopping Cart." If all goes well, you register the username in the session variable `auth_user`.

In addition to setting up the buttons you saw while not logged in, you add another button to allow the user to log out again, as follows:

```
if(check_auth_user())
{
    $buttons[4] = 'log-out';
}
```

You can see this Log Out button in Figure 29.3.

In the header stage, you again display the header and the buttons. In the body, you display the status message you set up earlier:

```
echo $status;
```

After that, you just need to print the footer and wait to see what the user will do next.

Setting Up Accounts

When a user first starts using the Warm Mail system, he will need to set up some email accounts. If the user clicks on the Account Setup button, this will set the `action` variable to `account-setup` and recall the `index.php` script. The user will then see the output shown in Figure 29.4.

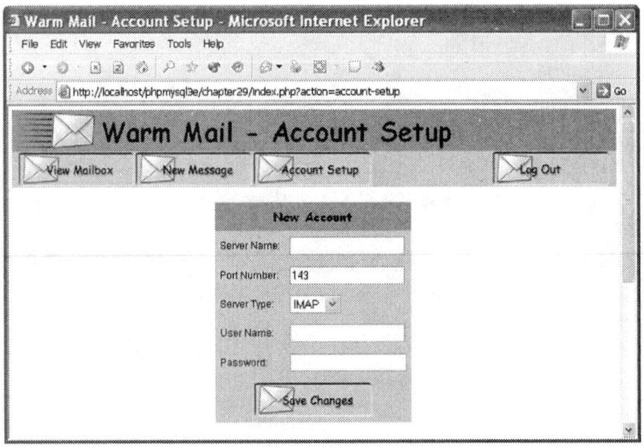

Figure 29.4   A user needs to set up his email account details before he can read his email.

Look back at the script in Listing 29.2. This time around because of the value of $action, you get different behavior. You get a slightly different header, as follows:

```
do_html_header($_SESSION['auth_user'], 'Warm Mail - '.
               format_action($action), $_SESSION['selected_account']);
```

More importantly, you get a different body, as follows:

```
case 'store-settings' :
case 'account-setup' :
case 'delete-account' :
{
  display_account_setup($_SESSION['auth_user']);
  break;
}
```

This is the typical pattern: Each command calls a function. In this case, you call the display_account_setup() function. The code for this function is shown in Listing 29.3.

Listing 29.3 display_account_setup() **Function from** output_fns.php—
Function to Get and Display Account Details

```
function display_account_setup($auth_user)
{
  //display empty 'new account' form

  display_account_form($auth_user);
  $list = get_accounts($auth_user);
  $accounts = sizeof($list);

  // display each stored account
  foreach($list as $key => $account)
  {
    // display form for each accounts details.
    // note that we are going to send the password for all accounts in the HTML
    // this is not really a very good idea
    display_account_form($auth_user, $account['accountid'],
                         $account['server'], $account['remoteuser'],
                         $account['remotepassword'], $account['type'],
                         $account['port']);
  }
}
```

When you call the display_account_setup() function, it displays a blank form to add a new account, followed by editable forms containing each of the user's current email accounts. The display_account_form() function displays the form shown in Figure 29.4. You use it in two different ways here: You use it with no parameters to display an empty form, and you use it with a full set of parameters to display an existing record.

This function is in the `output_fns.php` library; it simply outputs HTML, so we do not go through it here.

The function that retrieves any existing accounts is `get_accounts()`, from the `mail_fns.php` library. This function is shown in Listing 29.4.

Listing 29.4 `get_accounts()` **Function from** `mail_fns.php`—**Function to Retrieve All the Account Details for a Particular User**

```
function get_accounts($auth_user)
{
  $list = array();
  if($conn=db_connect())
  {
    $query = "select * from accounts where username = '$auth_user'";
    $result = $conn->query($query);
    if($result)
    {
      while($settings = $result->fetch_assoc())
        array_push($list, $settings);
    }
    else
      return false;
  }
  return $list;
}
```

As you can see, the `get_accounts()` function connects to the database, retrieves all the accounts for a particular user, and returns them as an array.

Creating a New Account

If a user fills out the account form and clicks the Save Changes button, the `store-settings` action will be activated. Let's look at the event handling code for this from `index.php`. In the preprocessing stage, you execute the following code:

```
case 'store-settings' :
{
  store_account_settings($_SESSION['auth_user'], $_POST);
  break;
}
```

The `store_account_settings()` function writes the new account details into the database. The code for this function is shown in Listing 29.5.

Listing 29.5 `store_account_settings()` **Function from** `mail_fns.php`—
Function to Save New Account Details for a User

```
function store_account_settings($auth_user, $settings)
{
  if(!filled_out($settings))
  {
    echo 'All fields must be filled in.  Try again.<br /><br />';
    return false;
  }
  else
  {
    if($settings['account']>0)
      $query = "update accounts  set server = '$settings[server]',
                  port = $settings[port], type = '$settings[type]',
                  remoteuser = '$settings[remoteuser]',
                  remotepassword = '$settings[remotepassword]'
                where accountid = $settings[account]
                  and username = '$auth_user'";
    else
      $query = "insert into accounts values ('$auth_user',
                  '$settings[server]', $settings[port],
                  '$settings[type]', '$settings[remoteuser]',
                  '$settings[remotepassword]', NULL)";
    if($conn=db_connect())
    {
      $result=$conn->query($query);
      if ($result)
        return true;
      else
        return false;
    }
    else
    {
      echo 'could not store changes.<br /><br /><br /><br /><br /><br />';
      return false;
    }
  }
}
```

As you can see, two choices within the `store_account_settings()` function correspond to inserting a new account or updating an existing account. The function executes
the appropriate query to save the account details.

After storing the account details, you go back to `index.php`, to the main body stage:

```
case 'store-settings' :
case 'account-setup' :
case 'delete-account' :
{
  display_account_setup($_SESSION['auth_user']);
  break;
}
```

As you can see, you then execute the `display_account_setup()` function as before to list the user's account details. The newly added account will now be included.

Modifying an Existing Account

The process for modifying an existing account is similar. The user can change the account details and click the Save Changes button. Again, this activity triggers the `store-settings` action, but this time it updates the account details instead of inserting them.

Deleting an Account

To delete an account, the user can click the Delete Account button shown under each account listing. Doing so activates the `delete-account` action.

In the preprocessing section of the `index.php` script, you execute the following code:

```
case 'delete-account' :
{
  delete_account($_SESSION['auth_user'], $account);
  break;
}
```

This code calls the `delete_account()` function. The code for this function is shown in Listing 29.6. Account deletion needs to be handled before the header because a choice of which account to use is located inside the header. The account list needs to be updated before it can be correctly drawn.

Listing 29.6 `delete_account()` **Function from** `mail_fns.php`**—Function to Delete a Single Account's Details**

```
function delete_account($auth_user, $accountid)
{
  //delete one of this user's accounts from the DB

  $query = "delete from accounts where accountid='$accountid' "
          ."and username = '$auth_user'";
  if($conn=db_connect())
  {
```

Listing 29.6   **Continued**

```
    $result = $conn->query($query);
  }
  return $result;
}
```

After execution returns to `index.php`, the body stage runs the following code:

```
case 'store-settings' :
case 'account-setup' :
case 'delete-account' :
{
  display_account_setup($_SESSION['auth_user']);
  break;
}
```

Notice that this is the same code you ran before; it just displays the list of the user's accounts.

Reading Mail

After the user has set up some accounts, you can move on to the main game: connecting to these accounts and reading mail.

Selecting an Account

You need to select one of the user's accounts to read mail from. The currently selected account is stored in the `$selected_account` session variable.

If the user has a single account registered in the system, it will be automatically selected when he logs in, as follows:

```
if(number_of_accounts($_SESSION['auth_user'])==1)
{
  $accounts = get_account_list($_SESSION['auth_user']);
  $_SESSION['selected_account'] = $accounts[0];
}
```

The `number_of_accounts()` function, from `mail_fns.php`, works out whether the user has more than one account; this function is shown in Listing 29.7. The `get_account_list()` function retrieves an array of the user's account IDs. In this case, there is exactly one, so you can access it as the array's `0` value.

Listing 29.7 `number_of_accounts()` **Function from** `mail_fns.php`—**Function to Work Out How Many Accounts a User Has Registered**

```
function number_of_accounts($auth_user)
{
  // get the number of accounts that belong to this user

  $query = "select count(*) from accounts where username = '$auth_user'";

  if($conn=db_connect())
  {
    $result = $conn->query($query);
      if($result)
      {
        $row = $result->fetch_array();
        return $row[0];
      }
  }
  return 0;
}
```

The `get_account_list()` function is similar to the `get_accounts()` function you looked at before except that it retrieves only the account names.

If a user has multiple accounts registered, he will need to select one to use. In this case, the headers contain a SELECT option that lists the available mailboxes. Choosing the appropriate one automatically displays the mailbox for that account. You can see this in Figure 29.5.

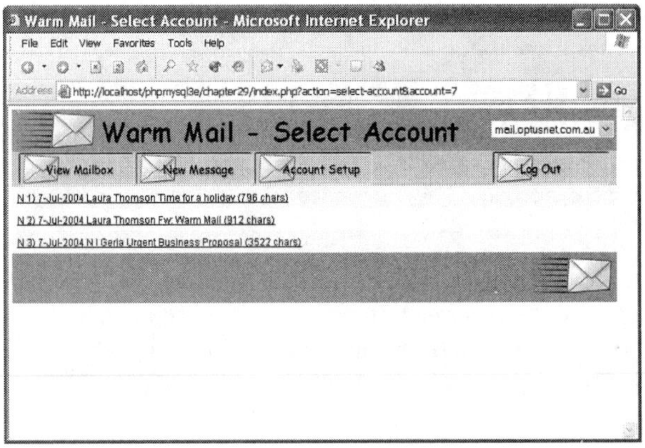

Figure 29.5 After the account is selected from the SELECT box, the mail from that account is downloaded and displayed.

This SELECT option is generated in the do_html_header() function from
output_fns.php, as shown in the following code fragment:

```
// include the account select box only if the user has more than one account
if(number_of_accounts($auth_user)>1)
{
  echo '<form target="index.php?action=open-mailbox" method="post">';
  echo '<td bgcolor="#ff6600" align="right" valign="middle">';
  display_account_select($auth_user, $selected_account);
  echo '</td>';
  echo '</form>';
}
```

We have generally avoided discussing the HTML used in the examples in this book, but
the HTML generated by the function display_account_select() bears a visit.

Depending on the accounts the current user has, display_account_select() generates HTML like this:

```
<select onchange="window.location=this.options[selectedIndex].value"
        name="account">
  <option value="0" selected>
    Choose Account</a>
  <option value="index.php?action=select-account&account=10">
    mail.domain.com
  </option>
  <option value="index.php?action=select-account&account=11">
    mail.server.com
  </option>
  <option value="index.php?action=select-account&account=9">
    localhost
  </option>
</select>
```

Most of this code is just an HTML select element, but it also includes a little
JavaScript. In the same way that PHP can generate HTML, it can also be used to generate client-side scripts.

Whenever a change event happens to this element, JavaScript sets window.location
to the value of the option. If your user selects the first option in the select,
window.location will be set to 'index.php?action=select-account&account=10'.
This results in this URL being loaded. Obviously, if the user has a browser that does not
support JavaScript or has JavaScript disabled, this code will have no effect.

The display_account_select() function, from output_fns.php, gets the available
account list and displays the SELECT. It also uses the get_account_list() function discussed previously.

Choosing one of the options in the SELECT activates the select_account event. If you look at the URL in Figure 29.5, you can see this event appended to the end of the URL, along with the account ID of the chosen account.

Appending these GET variables has two effects. First, in the preprocessing stage of index.php, the chosen account is stored in the session variable $selected_account, as follows:

```
case 'select-account' :
{
  // if have chosen a valid account, store it as a session variable
  if($account&&account_exists($_SESSION['auth_user'], $account))
  {
    $_SESSION['selected_account'] = $account;
  }
}
```

Second, when the body stage of the script is executed, the following code is executed:

```
case 'select-account' :
case 'view-mailbox' :
{
  // if mailbox just chosen, or view mailbox chosen, show mailbox
  display_list($_SESSION['auth_user'], $_SESSION['selected_account']);
  break;
}
```

As you can see, you take the same action here as if the user had chosen the View Mailbox option. We look at that action next.

Viewing Mailbox Contents

Mailbox contents can be viewed with the display_list() function. This function displays a list of all the messages in the mailbox. The code for this function is shown in Listing 29.8.

Listing 29.8 display_list() **Function from** output_fns.php—**Function to Display All Mailbox Messages**

```
function display_list($auth_user, $accountid)
{
  // show the list of messages in this mailbox

  global $table_width;

  if(!$accountid)
  {
```

Listing 29.8   **Continued**

```
    echo 'No mailbox selected<br /><br /><br /><br /><br />.';
  }
  else
  {

    $imap = open_mailbox($auth_user, $accountid);

    if($imap)
    {
      echo "<table width = $table_width cellspacing = 0
                 cellpadding = 6  border = 0>";

      $headers = imap_headers($imap);
      // we could reformat this data, or get other details using
      // imap_fetchheaders, but this is not a bad summary so we just echo each

      $messages = sizeof($headers);
      for($i = 0; $i<$messages; $i++)
      {
        echo '<tr><td bgcolor = "';
        if($i%2)
          echo '#ffffff';
        else
          echo '#ffffcc';
        echo '"><a href ="index.php?action=view-message&messageid='.($i+1).'">';
        echo $headers[$i];
        echo "</a></td></tr>\n";
      }
      echo '</table>';
    }
    else
    {
      $account = get_account_settings($auth_user, $accountid);
      echo 'could not open mail box '.$account['server'].
           '.<br /><br /><br /><br />';
    }
  }
}
```

In the `display_list()` function, you actually begin to use PHP's IMAP functions. The two key parts of this function are opening the mailbox and reading the message headers.

You open the mailbox for a user account with a call to the `open_mailbox()` function written in `mail_fns.php`. This function is shown in Listing 29.9.

Listing 29.9 open_mailbox() **Function from** mail_fns.php—**This Function Connects to a User Mailbox**

```
function open_mailbox($auth_user, $accountid)
{

  // select mailbox if there is only one
  if(number_of_accounts($auth_user)==1)
  {
    $accounts = get_account_list($auth_user);
    $_SESSION['selected_account'] = $accounts[0];
    $accountid = $accounts[0];
  }

  // connect to the POP3 or IMAP server the user has selected
  $settings = get_account_settings($auth_user, $accountid);
  if(!sizeof($settings)) return 0;
  $mailbox = '{'.$settings[server];
  if($settings[type]=='POP3')
    $mailbox .= '/pop3';

  $mailbox .= ':'.$settings[port].'}INBOX';

  // suppress warning, remember to check return value
@ $imap = imap_open($mailbox, $settings['remoteuser'],
                    $settings['remotepassword']);

  return  $imap;
}
```

You actually open the mailbox with the imap_open() function, which has the following prototype:

```
int imap_open (string mailbox, string username, string password [, int options])
```

The parameters you need to pass to it are as follows:

- *mailbox*—This string should contain the server name and mailbox name, and optionally a port number and protocol. The format of this string is

  {hostname/protocol:port}boxname

  If the protocol is not specified, it defaults to IMAP. In the code we wrote, you can see that we specify POP3 if the user has specified that protocol for a particular account.

For example, to read mail from the local machine using the default ports, you would use the following mailbox name for IMAP:

```
{localhost:143}INBOX
```

And you would use this one for POP3:

```
{localhost/pop3:110}INBOX
```

- *username*—The username for the account.
- *password*—The password for the account.

You can also pass it optional flags to specify options such as "open mailbox in read-only mode".

Note that we constructed the mailbox string piece by piece with the concatenation operator before passing it to imap_open(). You need to be careful how you construct this string because strings containing {$ can cause problems in PHP.

This function call returns an IMAP stream if the mailbox can be opened and false if it cannot.

When you are finished with an IMAP stream, you can close it by using imap_close(*imap_stream*). In this function, the IMAP stream is passed back to the main program. You then use the imap_headers() function to get the email headers for display:

```
$headers = imap_headers($imap);
```

This function returns header information for all mail messages in the mailbox you have connected to. The information is returned as an array, one line per message. This information has not been formatted. The function just outputs one line per message, so you can see from looking at Figure 29.5 what the output looks like.

You can get more information about email headers using the confusing, similarly named imap_header() function. In this case, though, the imap_headers() function gives you enough detail for the purposes of this project.

Reading a Mail Message

Each message in the previous display_list() function is set up to link to specific email messages. Each link is of the form

```
index.php?action=view-message&messageid=6
```

The messageid is the sequence number used in the headers retrieved earlier. Note that IMAP messages are numbered from 1, not 0.

If the user clicks one of these links, he will see output like that shown in Figure 29.6.

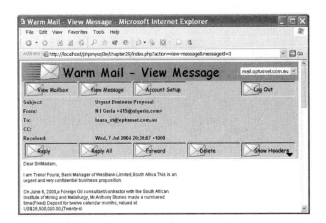

Figure 29.6   Using the view-message action shows a particular message; in this case, it's spam.

When you enter these parameters into the index.php script, you execute the following code:

```
case 'show-headers' :
case 'hide-headers' :
case 'view-message' :
{
  // if we have just picked a message from the list, or were looking at
  // a message and chose to hide or view headers, load a message
  $fullheaders = ($action=='show-headers');
  display_message($_SESSION['auth_user'],
                  $_SESSION['selected_account'],
                  $messageid, $fullheaders);
  break;
}
```

Here, you check the value of the $action being equal to 'show-headers'. In this case, it is false, and $fullheaders is set equal to false. We look at the 'show-headers' action in a moment.

The line

```
$fullheaders = ($action=='show-headers');
```

could have been more verbosely—but perhaps more clearly—written as

```
if($action=='show-headers')
  $fullheaders = true;
else
  $fullheaders = false;
```

Next, you call the display_message() function. Most of this function outputs plain HTML, so we do not go through it here. It calls the retrieve_message() function to get the appropriate message from the mailbox:

```
$message = retrieve_message($auth_user, $accountid, $messageid, $fullheaders);
```

The retrieve_message() function is in the mail_fns.php library. You can see the code for it in Listing 29.10.

Listing 29.10 retrieve_message() **Function from** mail_fns.php—**This Function Retrieves One Specific Message from a Mailbox**

```php
function retrieve_message($auth_user, $accountid, $messageid, $fullheaders)
{
  $message = array();

  if(!($auth_user && $messageid && $accountid))
    return false;

  $imap = open_mailbox($auth_user, $accountid);
  if(!$imap)
    return false;

  $header = imap_header($imap, $messageid);

  if(!$header)
    return false;

  $message['body'] = imap_body($imap, $messageid);
  if(!$message['body'])
    $message['body'] = "[This message has no body]\n\n\n\n\n\n";

  if($fullheaders)
    $message['fullheaders'] = imap_fetchheader($imap, $messageid);
  else
    $message['fullheaders'] = '';

  $message['subject'] = $header->subject;
  $message['fromaddress'] =  $header->fromaddress;
  $message['toaddress'] =   $header->toaddress;
  $message['ccaddress'] =   $header->ccaddress;
  $message['date'] =   $header->date;

  // note we can get more detailed information by using from and to
  // rather than fromaddress and toaddress, but these are easier

  imap_close($imap);
  return $message;
}
```

Again, you use `open_mailbox()` to open the user's mailbox. This time, however, you are after a specific message. Using this function library, you download the message headers and message body separately.

The three IMAP functions used here are `imap_header()`, `imap_fetchheader()`, and `imap_body()`. Note that the two header functions are distinct from `imap_headers()`, the one used previously. They are somewhat confusingly named. To summarize

- `imap_headers()`—Returns a summary of the headers for all the messages in a mailbox. It returns them as an array with one element per message.
- `imap_header()`—Returns the headers for one specific message in the form of an object.
- `imap_fetchheader()`—Returns the headers for one specific message in the form of a string.

In this case, you use `imap_header()` to fill out specific header fields and `imap_fetchheader()` to show the user the full headers if requested. (We come back to this topic later.)

You use `imap_header()` and `imap_body()` to build an array containing all the elements of a message that you are interested in. You call `imap_header()` as follows:

```
$header = imap_header($imap, $messageid);
```

You can then extract each of the fields you require from the object:

```
$message['subject'] = $header->subject;
```

You call `imap_body()` to add the message body to the array as follows:

```
$message['body'] = imap_body($imap, $messageid);
```

Finally, you close the mailbox with `imap_close()` and return the array you have built. The `display_message()` function can then display the message's fields in the form shown in Figure 29.6.

Viewing Message Headers

As you can see in Figure 29.6, the message contains a Show Headers button. It activates the `show-headers` option, which adds the full message headers to the message display. If the user clicks this button, he will see output similar to that shown in Figure 29.7.

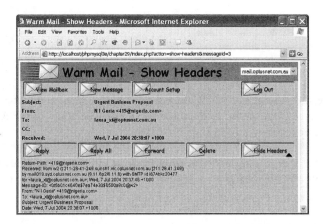

Figure 29.7   Using `show-headers` to see the full headers for this message
will help a user track down the source of the spam.

As you probably noticed, the event handling for `view-message` covers `show-headers`
(and its counterpart `hide-headers`), too. If this option is selected, you do the same
things as before. But in `retrieve_message()`, you also grab the full text of the headers,
as follows:

```
if($fullheaders)
    $message['fullheaders'] = imap_fetchheader($imap, $messageid);
```

You can then display these headers for the user.

Deleting Mail

If a user clicks the Delete button on a particular email, he will activate the `'delete'`
action. Doing so executes the following code from `index.php`:

```
case 'delete' :
{
    delete_message($_SESSION['auth_user'],
                   $_SESSION['selected_account'], $messageid);
    //note deliberately no 'break' - we will continue to the next case
}
case 'select-account' :
case 'view-mailbox' :
{
```

```
  // if mailbox just chosen, or view mailbox chosen, show mailbox
  display_list($_SESSION['auth_user'],
    $_SESSION['selected_account']);
  break;
}
```

As you can see, the message is deleted using the `delete_message()` function, and then the resulting mailbox is displayed as discussed previously. The code for the `delete_message()` function is shown in Listing 29.11.

Listing 29.11 `delete_message()` **Function from** `mail_fns.php`**—This Function Deletes One Specific Message from a Mailbox**

```
function delete_message($auth_user, $accountid, $message_id)
{
  // delete a single message from the server

  $imap = open_mailbox($auth_user, $accountid);
  if($imap)
  {
    imap_delete($imap, $message_id);
    imap_expunge($imap);
    imap_close($imap);
    return true;
  }
  return false;
}
```

As you can see, this function uses a number of the IMAP functions. The new ones are `imap_delete()` and `imap_expunge()`. Note that `imap_delete()` only marks messages for deletion. You can mark as many messages as you like. The call to `imap_expunge()` actually deletes the messages.

Sending Mail

Finally, we come to sending mail. You can do this in a few ways from this script: The user can send a new message, reply to, or forward mail. Let's see how these actions work.

Sending a New Message

The user can choose to send a new message by clicking the New Message button. Doing so activates the `'new-message'` action, which executes the following code in `index.php`:

```
case 'new-message' :
{
```

```
display_new_message_form($_SESSION['auth_user'],
                         $to, $cc, $subject, $body);
  break;
}
```

The new message form is just a form for sending mail. You can see what it looks like in Figure 29.8. This figure actually shows mail forwarding rather than new mail, but the form is the same. We look at forwarding and replies next.

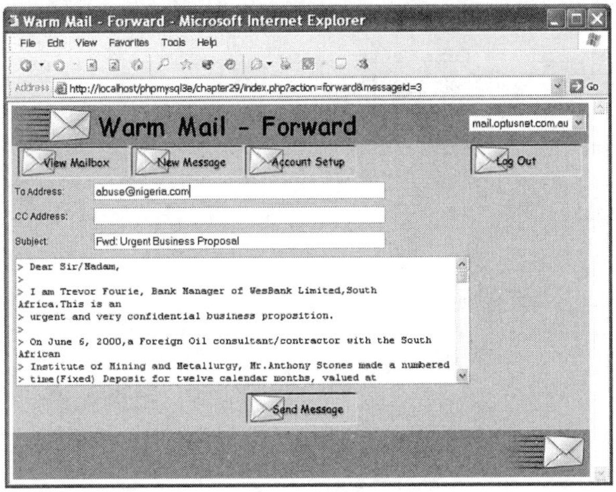

Figure 29.8   Using mail forwarding, you can report the spammer.

Clicking the Send Message button invokes the `'send-message'` action, which executes the following code:

```
case 'send-message' :
{
  if(send_message($to, $cc, $subject, $message))
    echo "<p>Message sent.</p><br /><br /><br /><br /><br /><br />";
  else
    echo "<p>Could not send message.</p><br /><br /><br /><br /><br /><br />";
  break;
}
```

This code calls the send_message() function, which actually sends the mail. This function is shown in Listing 29.12.

Listing 29.12   `send_message()` **Function from** `mail_fns.php`—**This Function Sends the Message That the User Has Typed In**

```
function send_message($to, $cc, $subject, $message)
{
  // send one email via PHP

  if (!$conn=db_connect())
  {
    return false;
  }
  $query = 'select address from users where '
          .'username=\''.$_SESSION['auth_user']."'";

  $result = $conn->query($query);
  if (!$result)
  {
    return false;
  }
  else if ($result->num_rows==0)
  {
    return false;
  }
  else
  {
    $row = $result->fetch_object();
    $other = 'From: '.$row->address;
    if (!empty($cc))
       $other.="\r\nCc: $cc";
    if (mail($to, $subject, $message, $other))
    {
      return true;
    }
    else
    {
      return false;
    }
  }
}
```

As you can see, this function uses `mail()` to send the email. First, however, it loads the user's email address out of the database to use in the From field of the email.

Replying To or Forwarding Mail

The Reply, Reply All, and Forward functions all send mail in the same way that New Message does. The difference in how they work is that they fill in parts of the new message form before showing it to the user. Look back at Figure 29.8. The message being forwarded has been indented with the > symbol, and the Subject line prefaced with To. Similarly, the Reply and Reply All options fill in the recipients, subject line, and indented message.

The code to reply to or forward mail is activated in the body section of index.php, as follows:

```
case 'reply-all' :
{
 //set cc as old cc line
   if(!$imap)
     $imap = open_mailbox($_SESSION['auth_user'],
                          $_SESSION['selected_account']);
   if($imap)
   {
     $header = imap_header($imap, $messageid);
     if($header->reply_toaddress)
       $to = $header->reply_toaddress;
     else
       $to = $header->fromaddress;
     $cc = $header->ccaddress;
     $subject = 'Re: '.$header->subject;
     $body = add_quoting(stripslashes(imap_body($imap, $messageid)));
     imap_close($imap);

     display_new_message_form($_SESSION['auth_user'],
     $to, $cc, $subject, $body);
   }
   break;
}
case 'reply' :
{
   //set to address as reply-to or from of the current message
   if(!$imap)
     $imap = open_mailbox($_SESSION['auth_user'],
                          $_SESSION['selected_account']);
   if($imap)
   {
```

```
    $header = imap_header($imap, $messageid);
    if($header->reply_toaddress)
      $to = $header->reply_toaddress;
    else
      $to = $header->fromaddress;
    $subject = 'Re: '.$header->subject;
    $body = add_quoting(stripslashes(imap_body($imap, $messageid)));
    imap_close($imap);

    display_new_message_form($_SESSION['auth_user'],
                             $to, $cc, $subject, $body) ;
  }

  break;
}
case 'forward' :
{
  //set message as quoted body of current message
  if(!$imap)
    $imap = open_mailbox($_SESSION['auth_user'],
                         $_SESSION['selected_account']);
  if($imap)
  {
    $header = imap_header($imap, $messageid);
    $body = add_quoting(stripslashes(imap_body($imap, $messageid)));
    $subject = 'Fwd: '.$header->subject;
    imap_close($imap);

    display_new_message_form($_SESSION['auth_user'],
                             $to, $cc, $subject, $body);
  }
  break;
}
```

You can see that each of these options sets up the appropriate headers, applies formatting as necessary, and calls the display_new_message_form() function to set up the form.

Now you've seen the full set of functionality for the web mail reader.

Extending the Project

There are many extensions or improvements you could make to this project. You can look to the mail reader you normally use for inspiration, but some useful additions are the following:

- Add the ability for users to register with this site. (You could reuse some of the code from Chapter 26, "Building User Authentication and Personalization," for this purpose.)

- Add the ability for users to have many addresses. Many users have more than one email address—perhaps a personal address and a work address. By moving their stored email address from the users table to the accounts table, you could allow them to use many addresses. You would need to change a limited amount of other code, too. The send mail form would need a drop-down box to select which address to use.

- Add the ability to send, receive, and view mail with attachments. If users are to be able to send attachments, you will need to build in file upload capabilities as discussed in Chapter 18, "Interacting with the File System and the Server." Sending mail with attachments is covered in Chapter 30, "Building a Mailing List Manager."

- Add address book capabilities.

- Add network newsreading capabilities. Reading from an NNTP server using the IMAP functions is almost identical to reading from a mailbox. You just need to specify a different port number and protocol in the `imap_open()` call. Instead of naming a mailbox such as INBOX, you name a newsgroup to read from instead. You could combine this with the thread-building capabilities from the project in Chapter 31, "Building Web Forums," to build a threaded web-based newsreader.

Next

In the next chapter, you build another email-related project. In this one, you build an application to support sending newsletters on multiple topics to people who subscribe through your site.

Building a Mailing List Manager

AFTER YOU'VE BUILT UP A BASE OF SUBSCRIBERS to your website, it's nice to be able to keep in touch with them by sending out a newsletter. In this chapter, you implement a front end for a mailing list manager (MLM). Some MLMs allow each subscriber to send messages to other subscribers. The program you create in this chapter is a newsletter system, in which only the list administrator can send messages. The system is named Pyramid-MLM.

This system is similar to others already in the marketplace. To get some idea of what we are aiming for, look at http://www.topica.com

Your application lets an administrator create multiple mailing lists and send newsletters to each of those lists separately. This application uses file upload to enable administrators to upload text and HTML versions of newsletters that they have created offline. This means administrators can use whatever software they prefer to create newsletters.

Users can subscribe to any of the lists at the site and select whether to receive newsletters in text or HTML.

We discuss the following topics:

- File upload with multiple files
- Mime-encoded email attachments
- HTML-formatted email
- Ways to manage user passwords without human interaction

The Problem

You want to build an online newsletter composition and sending system. This system should allow various newsletters to be created and sent to users, and allow users to subscribe to one or many of the newsletters.

Specifically, the requirements for this system are

- Administrators should be able to set up and modify mailing lists.
- Administrators should be able to send text and HTML newsletters to all the subscribers of a single mailing list.
- Users should be able to register to use the site, and enter and modify their details.
- Users should be able to subscribe to any of the lists on the site.
- Users should be able to unsubscribe from lists they are subscribed to.
- Users should be able to store their preference for either HTML-formatted or plain-text newsletters.
- For security reasons, users should not be able to send mail to the lists or to see each other's email addresses.
- Users and administrators should be able to view information about mailing lists.
- Users and administrators should be able to view past newsletters that have been sent to a list (the archive).

Solution Components

A number of components are needed to fulfill the requirements. The main ones are setting up a database of lists, subscribers, and archived newsletters; uploading newsletters that have been created offline; and sending mail with attachments.

Setting Up a Database of Lists and Subscribers

In this project, you track the usernames and passwords of all system users, as well as a list of the lists they have subscribed to. You also store each user's preference for receiving text or HTML email so that you can send a user the appropriate version of the newsletter.

An administrator is a specialized user with the ability to create new mailing lists and send newsletters to those lists.

A nice piece of functionality to have for a system like this is an archive of previous newsletters. Subscribers might not keep previous postings but might want to look up something. An archive can also act as a marketing tool for the newsletter because potential subscribers can see what the newsletters are like.

You will find nothing new or difficult in setting up this database in MySQL and an interface to it in PHP.

Using File Upload

You need an interface to allow the administrator to send newsletters, as mentioned previously. What we haven't discussed is how the administrator will create that newsletter.

You could provide him with a form `where` he could type or paste the newsletter content. However, it increases the user-friendliness of the system to let the administrator create a newsletter in his favorite editor and then upload the file to the web server. This also makes it easy for the administrator to add images to an HTML newsletter. For this, you can use the file upload capability discussed in Chapter 18, "Interacting with the File System and the Server."

You need to use a slightly more complicated form than you used in previous projects. For this project, you require the administrator to upload both text and HTML versions of the newsletter, along with any inline images that go into the HTML.

After the newsletter has been uploaded, you need to create an interface so that the administrator can preview the newsletter before sending it. This way, he can confirm that all the files were uploaded correctly.

Note that you also store all these files in an archive directory so that users can read back issues of newsletters. This directory needs to be writable by the user your web server runs as. The upload script will try to write the newsletters into `./archive/`, so you need to make sure you create that directory and set permissions on it appropriately.

Sending Mail with Attachments

For this project, you want to be able to send users either a plain-text newsletter or a "fancy" HTML version, according to their preference.

To send an HTML file with embedded images, you need to find a way to send attachments. PHP's simple `mail()` function doesn't easily support sending attachments. Instead, you can use the excellent `Mail_Mime` package from PEAR, originally created by Richard Heyes. It can deal with HTML attachments and can also be used to attach any images that are contained in the HTML file.

Installation instructions for this package are included under "Installing PEAR" in Appendix A, "Installing PHP and MySQL."

Solution Overview

For this project, you again use an event-driven approach to writing the code, as in Chapter 29, "Building a Web-Based Email Service."

To help you get started, we again began by drawing a set of system flow diagrams to show the paths users might take through the system. In this case, we drew three diagrams to represent the three different sets of interactions users can have with the system. Users have different allowable actions when they are not logged in, when they are logged in as regular users, and when they are logged in as administrators. These actions are shown in Figures 30.1, 30.2, and 30.3, respectively.

In Figure 30.1, you can see the actions that can be taken by a user who is not logged in. As you can see, he can log in (if he already has an account), create an account (if he doesn't already have one), or view the mailing lists available for signup (as a marketing tactic).

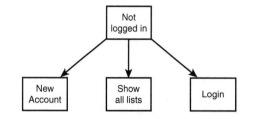

Figure 30.1   Users can choose only a limited number of actions when they are not logged in.

Figure 30.2 shows the actions a user can take after logging in. He can change his account setup (email address and preferences), change his password, and change which lists he is subscribed to.

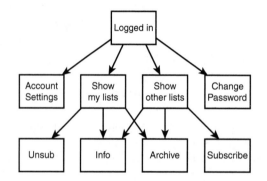

Figure 30.2   After logging in, users can change their preferences through a variety of options.

Figure 30.3 shows the actions available if an administrator has logged in. As you can see, an administrator has most of the functionality available to a user and some additional options. She can also create new mailing lists, create new messages for a mailing list by uploading files, and preview messages before sending them.

   Because this application uses an event-driven approach again, the backbone of the application is contained in one file, index.php, which calls on a set of function libraries. An overview of the files in this application is shown in Table 30.1.

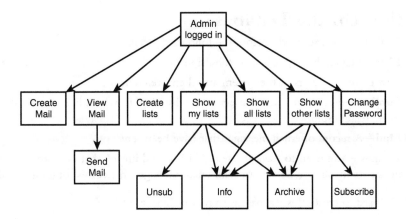

Figure 30.3 Administrators have additional actions available to them.

Table 30.1 **Files in the Mailing List Manager Application**

Filename	Type	Description
index.php	Application	The main script that runs the entire application
include_fns.php	Functions	Collection of include files for this application
data_valid_fns.php	Functions	Collection of functions for validating input data
db_fns.php	Functions	Collection of functions for connecting to the mlm database
mlm_fns.php	Functions	Collection of functions specific to this application
output_fns.php	Functions	Collection of functions for outputting HTML
upload.php	Component	Script that manages the file upload component of the administrator role; separated out to make security easier
user_auth_fns.php	Functions	Collection of functions for authenticating users
create_database.sql	SQL	SQL to set up the mlm database and set up a web user and an administrative user

Now let's work through the project implementation, beginning with the database in which you will store subscriber and list information.

Setting Up the Database

For this application, you need to store the following details:

- **Lists**—Mailing lists available for subscription
- **Subscribers**—Users of the system and their preferences
- **Sublists**—A record of which users have subscribed to which lists (a many-to-many relationship)
- **Mail**—A record of email messages that have been sent
- **Images**—You need to track the text, HTML, and images that go with each email because you want to be able to send email messages that consist of multiple files.

The SQL used to create this database is shown in Listing 30.1.

Listing 30.1 `create_database.sql`—**SQL to Create the** `mlm` **Database**

```
create database mlm;

use mlm;

create table lists
(
    listid int auto_increment not null primary key,
    listname char(20) not null,
    blurb varchar(255)
);

create table subscribers
(
  email char(100) not null primary key,
  realname char(100) not null,
  mimetype char(1) not null,
  password char(40) not null,
  admin tinyint not null
);

# stores a relationship between a subscriber and a list
create table sub_lists
(
  email char(100) not null,
  listid int not null
);

create table mail
(
```

Listing 30.1 **Continued**

```
  mailid int auto_increment not null primary key,
  email char(100) not null,
  subject char(100) not null,
  listid int not null,
  status char(10) not null,
  sent datetime,
  modified timestamp
);

#stores the images that go with a particular mail
create table images
(
  mailid int  not null,
  path char(100) not null,
  mimetype char(100) not null
);

grant select, insert, update, delete
on mlm.*
to mlm@localhost identified by 'password';

insert into subscribers values
('admin@localhost', 'Administrative User', 'H', sha1('admin'), 1);
```

Remember that you can execute this SQL by typing

```
mysql -u root -p < create_database.sql
```

You need to supply your root password. (You could, of course, execute this script via any MySQL user with the appropriate privileges; we just used root here for simplicity.) You should change the password for the mlm user and the administrator in your script before running it.

Some of the fields in this database require a little further explanation, so let's briefly run through them. The lists table contains a listid and listname. It also contains a blurb, which is a description of what the list is about.

The subscribers table contains email addresses (email) and names (realname) of the subscribers. It also stores their password and a flag (admin) to indicate whether a user is an administrator. You also store the type of mail they prefer to receive in mimetype. This can be either H for HTML or T for text.

The sublists table contains email addresses (email) from the subscribers table and listids from the lists table.

The `mail` table contains information about each email message that is sent through the system. It stores a unique ID (`mailid`), the address the mail is sent from (`email`), the subject line of the email (`subject`), and the `listid` of the list it has been sent to or will be sent to. The actual text or HTML of the message could be a large file, so you need to store the archive of the actual messages outside the database. You also track some general status information: whether the message has been sent (`status`), when it was sent (`sent`), and a timestamp to show when this record was last modified (`modified`).

Finally, you use the `images` table to track any images associated with HTML messages. Again, these images can be large, so you store them outside the database for efficiency. You need to keep track of the `mailid` they are associated with, the `path` to the location where the image is actually stored, and the MIME type of the image (`mimetype`)—for example, `image/gif`.

The SQL shown in Listing 30.1 also sets up a user for PHP to connect as and an administrative user for the system.

Defining the Script Architecture

As in the preceding project, this project uses an event-driven approach. The backbone of the application is in the file `index.php`. This script has the following four main segments:

1. Perform preprocessing. Do any processing that must be done before headers can be sent.

2. Set up and send headers. Create and send the start of the HTML page.

3. Perform an action. Respond to the event that has been passed in. As in the preceding example, the event is contained in the `$action` variable.

4. Send footers.

Almost all the application's processing is done in this file. The application also uses the function libraries listed in Table 30.1, as mentioned previously.

The full listing of the `index.php` script is shown in Listing 30.2.

Listing 30.2 `index.php`—**Main Application File for Pyramid-MLM**

```php
<?php

/**********************************************************************
* Section 1 : pre-processing
**********************************************************************/

  require_once ('include_fns.php');
  session_start();
```

Listing 30.2   **Continued**

```php
$action = $_GET['action'];
$buttons = array();

//append to this string if anything processed before header has output
$status = '';

// need to process log in or out requests before anything else
if($_POST['email']&&$_POST['password'])
{
  $login = login($_POST['email'], $_POST['password']);

  if($login == 'admin')
  {
    $status .= "<p><b>".get_real_name($_POST['email']).
               "</b> logged in"." successfully as <b>Administrator</b></p>
               <br /><br /><br /><br /><br />";
    $_SESSION['admin_user'] = $_POST['email'] ;
  }
  else if($login == 'normal')
  {
    $status .= "<p><b>".get_real_name($_POST['email'])."</b> logged in"
               ." successfully.</p><br /><br />";
    $_SESSION['normal_user'] = $_POST['email'];
  }
  else
  {
    $status .= "<p>Sorry, we could not log you in with that
               email address and password.</p><br />";
  }
}

if($action == 'log-out')
{
  unset($action);
  unset($_SESSION);
  session_destroy();
}

/**********************************************************************
* Section 2: set up and display headers
**********************************************************************/
```

Listing 30.2 **Continued**

```
// set the buttons that will be on the tool bar
if(check_normal_user())
{
  // if a normal user
  $buttons[0] = 'change-password';
  $buttons[1] = 'account-settings';
  $buttons[2] = 'show-my-lists';
  $buttons[3] = 'show-other-lists';
  $buttons[4] = 'log-out';
}
else if(check_admin_user())
{
  // if an administrator
  $buttons[0] = 'change-password';
  $buttons[1] = 'create-list';
  $buttons[2] = 'create-mail';
  $buttons[3] = 'view-mail';
  $buttons[4] = 'log-out';
  $buttons[5] = 'show-all-lists';
  $buttons[6] = 'show-my-lists';
  $buttons[7] = 'show-other-lists';
}
else
{
  // if not logged in at all
  $buttons[0] = 'new-account';
  $buttons[1] = 'show-all-lists';
  $buttons[4] = 'log-in';
}

if($action)
{
  // display header with application name and description of page or action
  do_html_header('Pyramid-MLM - '.format_action($action));
}
else
{
  // display header with just application name
  do_html_header('Pyramid-MLM');
}

display_toolbar($buttons);
```

Listing 30.2   **Continued**

```
  //display any text generated by functions called before header
  echo $status;

/**********************************************************************
 * Section 3: perform action
 **********************************************************************/

  // only these actions can be done if not logged in
  switch ( $action )
  {
    case 'new-account' :
    {
      // get rid of session variables
      session_destroy();
      display_account_form();
      break;
    }
    case 'store-account' :
    {
      if (store_account($_SESSION['normal_user'],
                $_SESSION['admin_user'], $_POST))
        $action = '';
      if(!check_logged_in())
        display_login_form($action);
      break;
    }
    case 'show-all-lists' :
    {
      display_items('All Lists', get_all_lists(), 'information',
                    'show-archive','');
      break;
    }
    case 'show-archive' :
    {
      display_items('Archive For '.get_list_name($_GET['id']),
                    get_archive($_GET['id']), 'view-html',
                    'view-text', '');
      break;
    }
    case 'information' :
    {
      display_information($_GET['id']);
      break;
    }
```

Listing 30.2 **Continued**

```
    default :
    {
      if(!check_logged_in())
        display_login_form($action);
      break;
    }
  }

  //all other actions require user to be logged in
  if(check_logged_in())
  {
    switch ( $action )
    {
      case 'account-settings' :
      {
        display_account_form(get_email(),
              get_real_name(get_email()), get_mimetype(get_email()));
        break;
      }
      case 'show-other-lists' :
      {
        display_items('Unsubscribed Lists',
                      get_unsubscribed_lists(get_email()), 'information',
                      'show-archive', 'subscribe');
        break;
      }
      case 'subscribe' :
      {
        subscribe(get_email(), $_GET['id']);
        display_items('Subscribed Lists', get_subscribed_lists(get_email()),
                      'information', 'show-archive', 'unsubscribe');
        break;
      }
      case 'unsubscribe' :
      {
        unsubscribe(get_email(), $_GET['id']);
        display_items('Subscribed Lists', get_subscribed_lists(get_email()),
                      'information', 'show-archive', 'unsubscribe');
        break;
      }
      case '':
      case 'show-my-lists' :
      {
```

Listing 30.2 **Continued**

```
        display_items('Subscribed Lists', get_subscribed_lists(get_email()),
                    'information', 'show-archive', 'unsubscribe');
        break;
    }
    case 'change-password' :
    {
      display_password_form();
      break;
    }
    case 'store-change-password' :
    {
      if(change_password(get_email(), $_POST['old_passwd'],
          $_POST['new_passwd'], $_POST['new_passwd2']))
      {
        echo '<p>OK: Password changed.</p>
              <br /><br /><br /><br /><br /><br />';
      }
      else
      {
        echo '<p>Sorry, your password could not be changed.</p>';
        display_password_form();
      }
      break;
    }
  }
}
// The following actions may only be performed by an admin user
if(check_admin_user())
{
  switch ( $action )
  {
    case 'create-mail' :
    {
      display_mail_form(get_email());
      break;
    }
    case 'create-list' :
    {
      display_list_form(get_email());
      break;
    }
    case 'store-list' :
    {
```

Listing 30.2 **Continued**

```
            if(store_list($_SESSION['admin_user'], $_POST))
            {
              echo '<p>New list added</p><br />';
              display_items('All Lists', get_all_lists(), 'information',
                            'show-archive','');
            }
            else
              echo '<p>List could not be stored, please try '
                    .'again.</p><br /><br /><br /><br /><br />';

            break;
          }
          case 'send' :
          {
            send($_GET['id'], $_SESSION['admin_user']);
            break;
          }
          case 'view-mail' :
          {
            display_items('Unsent Mail', get_unsent_mail(get_email()),
                          'preview-html', 'preview-text', 'send');
            break;
          }
        }
      }


  /*********************************************************************
   * Section 4: display footer
   *********************************************************************/

    do_html_footer();
  ?>
```

You can see the four segments of the code clearly marked in this listing. In the preprocessing stage, you set up the session and process any actions that need to be done before
headers can be sent. In this case, they include logging in and out.

In the header stage, you set up the menu buttons that the user will see and display the
appropriate headers using the do_html_header() function from output_fns.php. This
function just displays the header bar and menus, so we don't discuss it in detail here.

In the main section of the script, you respond to the action the user has chosen. These actions are divided into three subsets: actions that can be taken if not logged in, actions that can be taken by normal users, and actions that can be taken by administrative users. You check to see whether access to the latter two sets of actions is allowed by using the `check_logged_in()` and `check_admin_user()` functions. These functions are located in the `user_auth_fns.php` function library. The code for these functions and the `check_normal_user()` function are shown in Listing 30.3.

Listing 30.3   **Functions from** `user_auth_fns.php`**—These Functions Check Whether a User Is Logged In and at What Level**

```
function check_normal_user()
// see if somebody is logged in and notify them if not
{
  if (isset($_SESSION['normal_user']))
    return true;
  else
    return false;
}


function check_admin_user()
// see if somebody is logged in and notify them if not
{
  if (isset($_SESSION['admin_user']))
    return true;
  else
    return false;
}


function check_logged_in()
{
  return ( check_normal_user() || check_admin_user() );
}
```

As you can see, these functions use the session variables `normal_user` and `admin_user` to check whether a user has logged in. We explain how to set up these session variables shortly.

In the final section of the `index.php` script, you send an HTML footer using the `do_html_footer()` function from `output_fns.php`.

Let's look briefly at an overview of the possible actions in the system. These actions are shown in Table 30.2.

Table 30.2 **Possible Actions in the Mailing List Manager Application**

Action	Usable By	Description
log-in	Anyone	Gives a user a login form
log-out	Anyone	Ends a session
new-account	Anyone	Creates a new account for a user
store-account	Anyone	Stores account details
show-all-lists	Anyone	Shows a list of available mailing lists
show-archive	Anyone	Displays archived newsletters for a particular list
information	Anyone	Shows basic information about a particular list
account-settings	Logged-in users	Displays user account settings
show-other-lists	Logged-in users	Displays mailing lists to which the user is not subscribed
show-my-lists	Logged-in users	Displays mailing lists to which the user is subscribed
subscribe	Logged-in users	Subscribes a user to a particular list
unsubscribe	Logged-in users	Unsubscribes a user from a particular list
change-password	Logged-in users	Displays the change of password form
store-change-password	Logged-in users	Updates a user's password in the database
create-mail	Administrators	Displays a form to allow upload of newsletters
create-list	Administrators	Displays a form to allow new mailing lists to be created
store-list	Administrators	Stores mailing list details in the database
view-mail	Administrators	Displays newsletters that have been uploaded but not yet sent
send	Administrators	Sends newsletters to subscribers

One noticeable omission from Table 30.2 is an option along the lines of `store-mail`—that is, an action that actually uploads the newsletters entered via `create-mail` by administrators. This single piece of functionality is actually in a different file, `upload.php`. We put this functionality in a separate file because it makes keeping track of security issues a little easier on us, the programmers.

Next, we discuss the implementation of the actions in the three groups listed in Table 30.2—that is, actions for people who are not logged in, actions for logged-in users, and actions for administrators.

Implementing Login

When a brand-new user comes to your site, you would like him to do three things. First, you want the user to look at what you have to offer; second, to sign up with you; and third, to log in. We look at each of these tasks in turn.

Figure 30.4 shows the screen presented to users when they first come to the site.

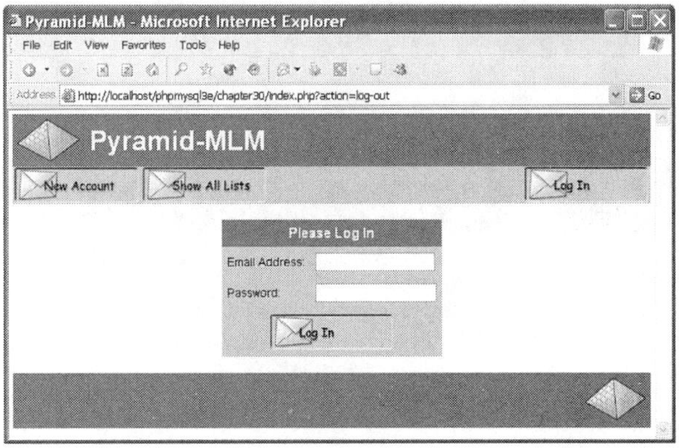

Figure 30.4   On arrival, users can create a new account, view available lists, or just log in.

We look at creating a new account and logging in now and then return to viewing list details in the "Implementing User Functions" and "Implementing Administrative Functions" sections.

Creating a New Account

If a user selects the New Account menu option, this selection activates the `new-account` action. This action, in turn, activates the following code in `index.php`:

```
case 'new-account' :
{
  // get rid of session variables
  session_destroy();
  display_account_form();
  break;
}
```

This code effectively logs out a user if she is currently logged in and displays the account details form, as shown in Figure 30.5.

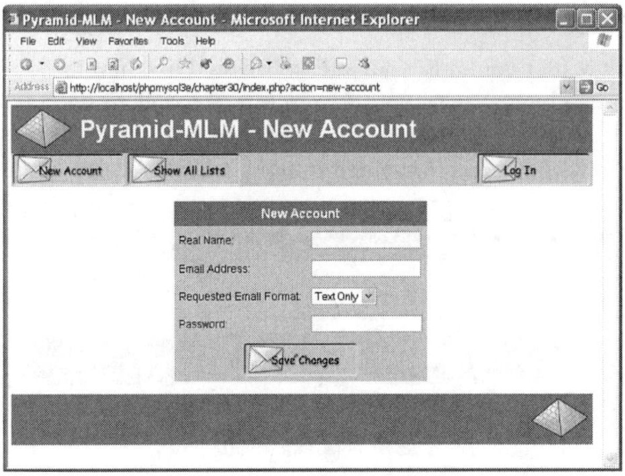

Figure 30.5   The new account creation form enables users to
enter their details.

This form is generated by the `display_account_form()` function from the
`output_fns.php` library. This function is used both here and in the `account-settings`
action to display a form to enable the user to set up an account. If the function is
invoked from the `account-settings` action, the form will be filled with the user's existing account data. Here, the form is blank, ready for new account details. Because this
function outputs only HTML, we do not go through the details here.

The submit button on this form invokes the `store-account` action. The code for this
action is as follows:

```
case 'store-account' :
{
  if (store_account($_SESSION['normal_user'],
          $_SESSION['admin_user'], $_POST))
    $action = '';
  if(!check_logged_in())
    display_login_form($action);
  break;
}
```

The `store_account()` function, shown in Listing 30.4, writes the account details to the
database.

Listing 30.4 `store_account()` **Function from** `mlm_fns.php`—**This Function Adds a New User to the Database or Stores Modified Details About an Existing User**

```
function store_account($normal_user, $admin_user, $details)
{
  if(!filled_out($details))
  {
    echo 'All fields must be filled in.  Try again.<br /><br />';
    return false;
  }
  else
  {
    if(subscriber_exists($details['email']))
    {
      //check logged in as the user they are trying to change
      if(get_email()==$details['email'])
      {
        $query = "update subscribers set realname = '{$details['realname']}',
                                        mimetype = '{$details['mimetype']}'
                  where email = '{$details['email']}'";
        if($conn=db_connect())
        {
          if ($conn->query($query))
            return true;
          else
            return false;
        }
        else
        {
          echo 'Could not store changes.<br /><br /><br /><br /><br /><br />';
          return false;
        }
      }
      else
      {
        echo '<p>Sorry, that email address is already registered here.</p>'.
             '<p>You will need to log in with that address to change '.
             ' its settings.</p>';
        return false;
      }
    }
    else // new account
    {
```

Listing 30.4   **Continued**

```
        $query = "insert into subscribers
                 values ('{$details['email']}',
                        '{$details['realname']}',
                        '{$details['mimetype']}',
                        sha1('{$details['new_password']}'),
                        0)";
    if($conn=db_connect())
    {
     if ($conn->query($query))
       return true;
     else
       return false;
    }
    else
    {
       echo 'Could not store new account.
            <br /><br /><br /><br /><br /><br />';
       return false;
    }
  }
 }
}
```

This function first checks that the user has filled in the required details. If this is okay, the function will then either create a new user or update the account details if the user already exists. A user can update only the account details of the user he is logged in as.

The logged-in user's identity is checked using the `get_email()` function, which retrieves the email address of the user who is currently logged in. We return to this function later because it uses session variables that are set up when the user logs in.

Logging In

If a user fills in the login form you saw in Figure 30.4 and clicks on the Log In button, she will enter the `index.php` script with the `email` and `password` variables set. This activates the login code, which is in the preprocessing stage of the script, as follows:

```
// need to process log in or out requests before anything else
if($_POST['email']&&$_POST['password'])
{
  $login = login($_POST['email'], $_POST['password']);

  if($login == 'admin')
  {
```

```
  $status .= "<p><b>".get_real_name($_POST['email']).
            "</b> logged in"." successfully as <b>Administrator</b></p>
            <br /><br /><br /><br /><br />";
  $_SESSION['admin_user'] = $_POST['email'];
}
else if($login == 'normal')
{
  $status .= "<p><b>".get_real_name($_POST['email'])."</b> logged in"
            ." successfully.</p><br /><br />";
  $_SESSION['normal_user'] = $_POST['email'];
}
else
{
  $status .= "<p>Sorry, we could not log you in with that
            email address and password.</p><br />";
}
}


if($action == 'log-out')
{
  unset($action);
  unset($_SESSION);
  session_destroy();
}
```

As you can see, you first try to log the user in by using the login() function from the
user_auth_fns.php library. This function is slightly different from the login functions
used elsewhere, so let's look at it more closely. The code for this function is shown in
Listing 30.5.

Listing 30.5   login() **Function from** user_auth_fns.php—**This Function Checks a**
User's Login Details

```
function login($email, $password)
// check username and password with db
// if yes, return login type
// else return false
{
  // connect to db
  $conn = db_connect();
  if (!$conn)
    return 0;

  $query = "select admin from subscribers
                    where email='$email'
                    and password = sha1('$password')";
```

Listing 30.5 **Continued**

```
$result = $conn->query($query);
if (!$result)
  return false;

if ($result->num_rows<1)
  return false;

$row = $result->fetch_array();

if($row[0] == 1)
  return 'admin';
else
  return 'normal';
}
```

In previous login functions, you returned `true` if the login was successful and `false` if it was not. In this case, you still return `false` if the login failed, but if it was successful, you return the user type, either `'admin'` or `'normal'`. You check the user type by retrieving the value stored in the `admin` column in the `subscribers` table, for a particular combination of email address and password. If no results are returned, you return `false`. If a user is an administrator, this value will be 1 (`true`), so you return `'admin'`. Otherwise, you return `'normal'`.

Returning to the main line of execution, you register a session variable to keep track of who the user is. She is either `admin_user` if she is an administrator or `normal_user` if she is a regular user. Whichever one of these variables you set will contain the email address of the user. To simplify checking for the email address of a user, you use the `get_email()` function mentioned earlier. This function is shown in Listing 30.6.

Listing 30.6 `get_email()` **function from** `user_auth_fns.php`— **This Function Returns the Email Address of the Logged-In User**

```
function get_email()
{
  if (isset($_SESSION['normal_user']))
    return $_SESSION['normal_user'];
  if (isset($_SESSION['admin_user']))
   return $_SESSION['admin_user'];

  return false;
}
```

Back in the main program, you report to the user whether she was logged in and at what level.

The output from one login attempt is shown in Figure 30.6.

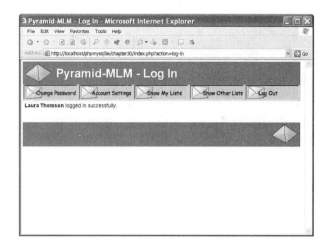

Figure 30.6   The system reports to the user that login was successful.

Now that you have logged in a user, you can proceed to the user functions.

Implementing User Functions

There are five things you want your users to be able to do after they have logged in:

- Look at the lists available for subscription
- Subscribe and unsubscribe from lists
- Change the way their accounts are set up
- Change their passwords
- Log out

You can see most of these options in Figure 30.6. Next, let's look at the implementation of each of these options.

Viewing Lists

In this project, you implement a number of options for viewing available lists and list details. In Figure 30.6, you can see two of these options: Show My Lists, which retrieves the lists this user is subscribed to, and Show Other Lists, which retrieves the lists the user is not subscribed to.

If you look back at Figure 30.4, you will see another option, Show All Lists, which retrieves all the available mailing lists on the system. For the system to be truly scalable, you should add paging functionality (to display, say, 10 results per page). We did not do this here for brevity.

These three menu options activate the `show-all-lists`, `show-other-lists`, and `show-my-lists` actions, respectively. As you have probably realized, all these actions work quite similarly. The code for these three actions is as follows:

```
case 'show-all-lists' :
{
  display_items('All Lists', get_all_lists(), 'information',
              'show-archive','');
  break;
}



case 'show-other-lists' :
{
  display_items('Unsubscribed Lists',
              get_unsubscribed_lists(get_email()), 'information',
              'show-archive', 'subscribe');
  break;
}



case '':
case 'show-my-lists' :
{
  display_items('Subscribed Lists', get_subscribed_lists(get_email()),
              'information', 'show-archive', 'unsubscribe');
  break;
}
```

As you can see, all these actions call the `display_items()` function from the `output_fns.php` library, but they each call it with different parameters. They all also use the `get_email()` function mentioned earlier to get the appropriate email address for this user.

To see what the `display_items()` function does, look at Figure 30.7, the Show Other Lists page.

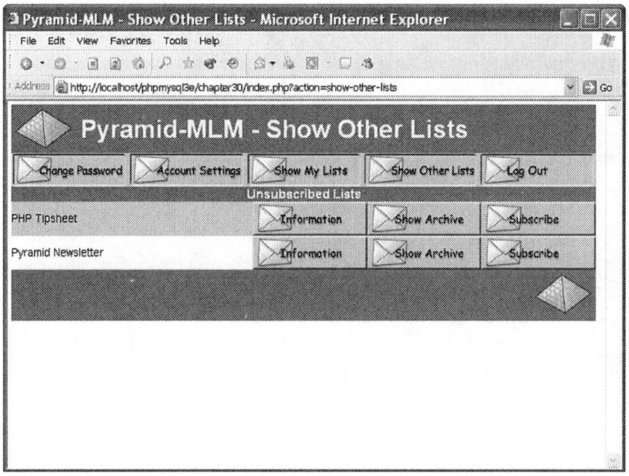

Figure 30.7   The `display_items()` function lays out a list of the lists that the user is not subscribed to.

Let's look at the code for the `display_items()` function, shown in Listing 30.7.

Listing 30.7   `display_items()`**Function from** `output_fns.php`**—This Function Displays a List of Items with Associated Actions**

```
function display_items($title, $list, $action1='', $action2='', $action3='')
{
  global $table_width;
  echo "<table width = '$table_width' cellspacing = '0' cellpadding = '0'
        border = '0'>";

  // count number of actions
  $actions = (($action1!='') + ($action2!='') + ($action3!=''));

  echo '<tr>
        <th colspan = \''. (1+$actions) ."' bgcolor='#5B69A6'> $title </th>
        </tr>";

  // count number of items
  $items = sizeof($list);
```

Listing 30.7 **Continued**

```
if($items == 0)
  echo '<tr>
      <td colspan = "'.(1+$actions).'" align = "center">
       No Items to Display</td>
      </tr>';
else
{
  // print each row
  for($i = 0; $items; $i++)
  {
    if($i%2) // background colors alternate
      $bgcolor = "'#ffffff'";
    else
      $bgcolor = "'#ccccff'";
    echo "<tr
        <td bgcolor = $bgcolor
         width = '". ($table_width - ($actions*149)) .'\'>';
    echo $list[$i][1];
    if($list[$i][2])
      echo ' - '.$list[$i][2];
    echo '</td>';

    // create buttons for up to three actions per line
    for($j = 1; $j<=3; $j++)
    {
      $var = 'action'.$j;
      if($$var)
      {
        echo "<td bgcolor = $bgcolor width = '149'>";
        // view/preview buttons are a special case as they link to a file
        if($$var == 'preview-html'||$$var == 'view-html'||
          $$var == 'preview-text'||$$var == 'view-text')
          display_preview_button($list[$i][3], $list[$i][0], $$var);
        else
          display_button( $$var, '&id=' . $list[$i][0] );
        echo '</td>';
      }
    }
    echo "</tr>\n";
  }
  echo '</table>';
}
}
```

This function outputs a table of items, with each item having up to three associated action buttons. The function expects the following five parameters, in order:

- `$title` is the title that appears at the top of the table. In the case shown in Figure 30.7, the title Unsubscribed Lists is passed in, as shown in the previously discussed code snippet for the action "Show Other Lists."

- `$list` is an array of items to display in each row of the table. In this case, it is an array of the lists the user is not currently subscribed to. You build this array (in this case) in the function `get_unsubscribed_lists()`, which we discuss shortly. This is a multidimensional array, with each row in the array containing up to four pieces of data about each row. In order, again:

  - `$list[n][0]` should contain the item ID, which is usually a row number. This gives the action buttons the ID of the row they are to operate on. In this case, you use IDs from the database; more on this later.

  - `$list[n][1]` should contain the item name. This is the text displayed for a particular item. For example, in the case shown in Figure 30.7, the item name in the first row of the table is PHP Tipsheet.

  - `$list[n][2]` and `$list[n][3]` are optional. You use them to convey that there is more information. They correspond to the more information text and the more information ID, respectively. We look at an example using these two parameters when we come to the View Mail action in the "Implementing Administrative Functions" section.

- The optional third, fourth, and fifth parameters to the function are used to pass in three actions that will be displayed on buttons corresponding to each item. In Figure 30.7, they are the three action buttons shown as Information, Show Archive, and Subscribe.

You get these three buttons for the Show All Lists page by passing in the action names `information`, `show-archive`, and `subscribe`. When you use the `display_button()` function, these actions are turned into buttons with those words on them and the appropriate action assigned to them.

Each of the Show actions calls the `display_items()` function in a different way, as you can see by looking back at their actions. In addition to having different titles and action buttons, each of the three uses a different function to build the array of items to display. Show All Lists uses the function `get_all_lists()`, Show Other Lists uses the function `get_unsubscribed_lists()`, and Show My Lists uses the function `get_subscribed_lists()`. All these functions work in a similar fashion and are all from the `mlm_fns.php` function library.

Let's look at `get_unsubscribed_lists()` because that's the example we've followed so far. The code for the `get_unsubscribed_lists()` function is shown in Listing 30.8.

Listing 30.8 `get_unsubscribed_lists()`**Function from** `mlm_fns.php`**—This Function Builds an Array of Mailing Lists That a User Is Not Subscribed To**

```
//get the lists that this user is *not* subscribed to
function get_unsubscribed_lists($email)
{
  $list = array();

  $query = "select lists.listid, listname, email
            from lists left
            join sub_lists
              on lists.listid = sub_lists.listid and
                 email='$email' where email is NULL order by listname";
  if($conn=db_connect())
  {
    $result = $conn->query($query);
    if(!$result)
    {
      echo '<p>Unable to get list from database.</p>';
      return false;
    }
    $num = $result->num_rows;
    for($i = 0; $i<$num; $i++)
    {
      $row = $result->fetch_array();
      array_push($list, array($row[0], $row[1]));
    }
  }
  return $list;
}
```

As you can see, this function requires an email address passed into it. This should be the email address of the subscriber that you are working with. The `get_subscribed_lists()` function also requires an email address as a parameter, but the `get_all_lists()` function does not for obvious reasons.

Given a subscriber's email address, you connect to the database and fetch all the lists the subscriber is not subscribed to. You use a LEFT JOIN to find unmatched items, and you loop through the result and build the array row by row using the `array_push()` built-in function.

Now that you know how this list is produced, let's look at the action buttons associated with these displays.

Viewing List Information

The Information button shown in Figure 30.7 triggers the `information` action, which is as follows:

```
case 'information' :
{
  display_information($_GET['id']);
  break;
}
```

To see what the `display_information()` function does, look at Figure 30.8.

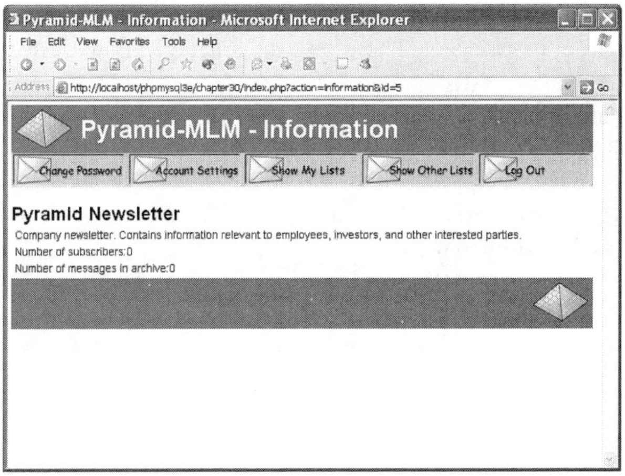

Figure 30.8   The `display_information()` function shows a blurb about a mailing list.

This function displays some general information about a particular mailing list and lists the number of subscribers and number of newsletters sent out to that list and available in the archive (more on that shortly). The code for this function is shown in Listing 30.9.

Listing 30.9   `display_information()` **Function from** `output_fns.php`—**This Function Displays List Information**

```
function display_information($listid)
{
  if(!$listid)
    return false;

  $info = load_list_info($listid);
```

Listing 30.9   **Continued**

```
  if($info)
  {
    echo '<h2>'.pretty($info['listname']).'</h2>';
    echo '<p>'.pretty($info['blurb']);
    echo '</p><p>Number of subscribers:' . $info['subscribers'];
    echo '</p><p>Number of messages in archive:' . $info['archive'].'</p>';
  }
}
```

The `display_information()` function uses two other functions to help it achieve its web task: `load_list_info()` and `pretty()`. The `load_list_info()` function actually retrieves the data from the database. The `pretty()` function simply formats the data from the database by stripping out slashes, turning newlines into HTML line breaks, and so on.

Let's look briefly at the `load_list_info()` function, which is in the `mlm_fns.php` function library. The code for it is shown in Listing 30.10.

Listing 30.10   `load_list_info()` **Function from** `mlm_fns.php`—**This Function Builds an Array of List Information**

```
function load_list_info($listid)
{
  if(!$listid)
    return false;

  if(!($conn=db_connect()))
    return false;

  $query = "select listname, blurb from lists where listid = $listid";
  $result = $conn->query($query);
  if(!$result)
  {
    echo 'Cannot retrieve this list';
    return false;
  }
  $info =  $result->fetch_assoc();

  $query = "select count(*) from sub_lists where listid = $listid";
  $result = $conn->query($query);
  if($result)
  {
    $row = $result->fetch_array();
    $info['subscribers'] = $row[0];
  }
```

Listing 30.10   **Continued**

```
$query = "select count(*) from mail where listid = $listid
         and status = 'SENT'";
$result = $conn->query($query);
if($result)
{
  $row = $result->fetch_array();
  $info['archive'] = $row[0];
}
return $info;
}
```

This function runs three database queries to collect the name and blurb for a list from the `lists` table, the number of subscribers from the `sub_lists` table, and the number of newsletters sent from the `mail` table.

Viewing List Archives

In addition to viewing the list blurb, users can look at all the mail that has been sent to a mailing list by clicking on the Show Archive button. This activates the `show-archive` action, which triggers the following code:

```
case 'show-archive' :
{
  display_items('Archive For '.get_list_name($_GET['id']),
                get_archive($_GET['id']), 'view-html',
                'view-text', '');
  break;
}
```

Again, this function uses the `display_items()` function to list the various items of mail that have been sent to the list. These items are retrieved using the `get_archive()` function from `mlm_fns.php`. This function is shown in Listing 30.11.

Listing 30.11   `get_archive()` **Function from** `mlm_fns.php`**—This Function Builds an Array of Archived Newsletters for a Given List**

```
function get_archive($listid)
{
  //returns an array of the archived mail for this list
  //array has rows like (mailid, subject)

  $list = array();
  $listname = get_list_name($listid);
```

Listing 30.11   **Continued**

```
$query = "select mailid, subject, listid
           from mail
           where listid = $listid and status = 'SENT' order by sent";

if($conn=db_connect())
{
  $result = $conn->query($query);
  if(!$result)
  {
    echo '<p>Unable to get list from database.</p>';
    return false;
  }
  $num = $result->num_rows;

  for($i = 0; $i<$num; $i++)
  {
    $row = $result->fetch_array();
    $arr_row = array($row[0], $row[1],
                $listname, $listid);
    array_push($list, $arr_row);
  }
}
return $list;
}
```

Again, this function gets the required information—in this case, the details of mail
that has been sent—from the database and builds an array suitable for passing to the
`display_items()` function.

Subscribing and Unsubscribing

On the list of mailing lists shown in Figure 30.7, each list has a button that enables users
to subscribe to it. Similarly, if users use the Show My Lists option to see the lists to
which they are already subscribed, they will see an Unsubscribe button next to each list.

These buttons activate the `subscribe` and `unsubscribe` actions, which trigger the
following two pieces of code, respectively:

```
case 'subscribe' :
{
  subscribe(get_email(), $_GET['id']);
  display_items('Subscribed Lists', get_subscribed_lists(get_email()),
                'information', 'show-archive', 'unsubscribe');
  break;
}
case 'unsubscribe' :
{
  unsubscribe(get_email(), $_GET['id']);
```

```
display_items('Subscribed Lists', get_subscribed_lists(get_email()),
             'information', 'show-archive', 'unsubscribe');
  break;
}
```

In each case, you call a function (`subscribe()` or `unsubscribe()`) and then redisplay a list of mailing lists the user is now subscribed to by using the `display_items()` function again.

The `subscribe()` and `unsubscribe()` functions are shown in Listing 30.12.

Listing 30.12 `subscribe()` **and** `unsubscribe()` **Functions from** `mlm_fns.php`—
These Functions Add and Remove Subscriptions for a User

```
function subscribe($email, $listid)
{
  if(!$email||!$listid||!list_exists($listid)||!subscriber_exists($email))
    return false;

  //if already subscribed exit
  if(subscribed($email, $listid))
    return false;

  if(!($conn=db_connect()))
    return false;

  $query = "insert into sub_lists values ('$email', $listid)";

  $result = $conn->query($query);
  return $result;
}

function unsubscribe($email, $listid)
{
  if(!$email||!$listid)
    return false;

  if(!($conn=db_connect()))
    return false;

  $query = "delete from sub_lists where email = '$email' and listid = $listid";

  $result = $conn->query($query);
  return $result;
}
```

The `subscribe()` function adds a row to the `sub_lists` table corresponding to the subscription; the `unsubscribe()` function deletes this row.

Changing Account Settings

The Account Settings button, when clicked, activates the `account-settings` action. The code for this action is as follows:

```
case 'account-settings' :
{
  display_account_form(get_email(),
        get_real_name(get_email()), get_mimetype(get_email()));
  break;
}
```

As you can see, you reuse the `display_account_form()` function used to create the account in the first place. However, this time you pass in the user's current details, which will be displayed in the form for easy editing. When the user clicks on the submit button in this form, the `store-account` action is activated as discussed previously.

Changing Passwords

Clicking on the Change Password button activates the `change-password` action, which triggers the following code:

```
case 'change-password' :
{
  display_password_form();
  break;
}
```

The `display_password_form()` function (from the `output_fns.php` library) simply displays a form for the user to change his password. This form is shown in Figure 30.9.

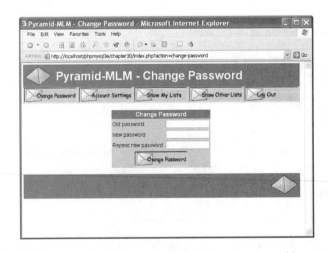

Figure 30.9   The `display_password_form()` function enables users to change their passwords.

When a user clicks on the Change Password button at the bottom of this form, the store-change-password action is activated. The code for this action is as follows:

```
case 'store-change-password' :
{
  if(change_password(get_email(), $_POST['old_passwd'],
    $_POST['new_passwd'], $_POST['new_passwd2']))
  {
    echo '<p>OK: Password changed.</p>
          <br /><br /><br /><br /><br /><br />';
  }
  else
  {
    echo '<p>Sorry, your password could not be changed.</p>';
    display_password_form();
  }
  break;
}
```

As you can see, this code tries to change the password using the change_password() function and reports success or failure to the user. The change_password() function, shown in Listing 30.13, can be found in the user_auth_fns.php function library.

Listing 30.13 change_password() **Function from** user_auth_fns.php—**This Function Validates and Updates a User's Password**

```
function change_password($email, $old_password, $new_password,
                         $new_password_conf)
// change password for email/old_password to new_password
// return true or false
{

  // if the old password is right
  // change their password to new_password and return true
  // else return false
  if (login($email, $old_password))
  {
    if($new_password==$new_password_conf)
    {
      if (!($conn = db_connect()))
        return false;
      $query = "update subscribers
                set password = sha1('$new_password')
                where email = '$email'";
      $result = $conn->query($query);
      return $result;
    }
```

Listing 30.13 **Continued**

```
    else
      echo '<p> Your passwords do not match. </p>';
  }
  else
    echo '<p> Your old password is incorrect. </p>';

  return false; // old password was wrong
}
```

This function is similar to other password setting and changing functions we have looked at. It compares the two new passwords entered by the user to make sure they are the same and, if they are, tries to update the user's password in the database.

Logging Out

When a user clicks on the Log Out button, the `log-out` action is triggered. The code executed by this action in the main script is actually in the preprocessing section of the script, as follows:

```
if($action == 'log-out')
{
  unset($action);
  unset($_SESSION);
  session_destroy();
}
```

This snippet of code disposes of the session variables and destroys the session. Notice that it also unsets the `action` variable; this means that you enter the main `case` statement without an action, triggering the following code:

```
default :
{
  if(!check_logged_in())
    display_login_form($action);
  break;
}
```

This code allows another user to log in or allows the user to log in as someone else.

Implementing Administrative Functions

If someone logs in as an administrator, she will get some additional menu options, which can be seen in Figure 30.10.

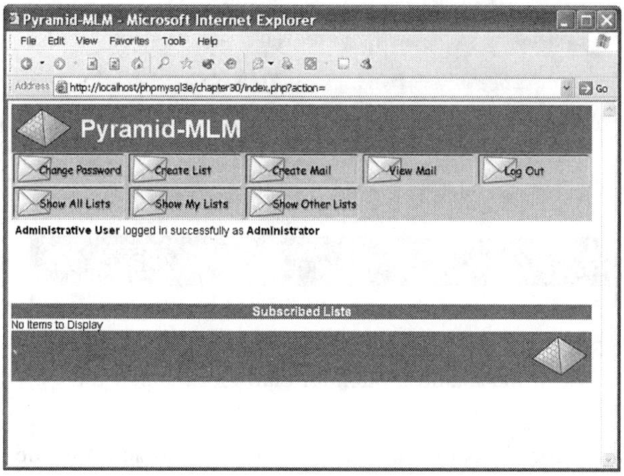

Figure 30.10   The administrator menu allows for mailing list creation and maintenance.

The extra options are Create List (create a new mailing list), Create Mail (create a new newsletter), and View Mail (view and send created newsletters that have not yet been sent). Now let's look at each of these options in turn.

Creating a New List

If the administrator chooses to set up a new list by clicking on the Create List button, she will activate the create-list action, which is associated with the following code:

```
case 'create-list' :
{
  display_list_form(get_email());
  break;
}
```

The display_list_form() function, found in the output_fns.php library, displays a form that enables the administrator to enter the details of a new list. It just outputs HTML, so we did not include it here. The output of this function is shown in Figure 30.11.

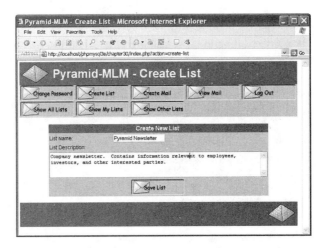

Figure 30.11   The Create List option requires the administrator to enter a
name and description (or blurb) for the new list.

When the administrator clicks on the Save List button, this activates the `store-list`
action, which triggers the following code in `index.php`:

```
case 'store-list' :
{
  if(store_list($_SESSION['admin_user'], $_POST))
  {
    echo '<p>New list added</p><br />';
    display_items('All Lists', get_all_lists(), 'information',
                  'show-archive','');
  }
  else
    echo '<p>List could not be stored, please try '
         .'again.</p><br /><br /><br /><br /><br />';

  break;
}
```

As you can see, the code tries to store the new list details and then displays the new list
of lists. The list details are stored with the `store_list()` function, which is shown in
Listing 30.14.

Listing 30.14 `store_list()`**Function from** `mlm_fns.php`—**This Function Inserts a New Mailing List into the Database**

```
function store_list($admin_user, $details)
{
  if(!filled_out($details))
  {
    echo 'All fields must be filled in.  Try again.<br /><br />';
    return false;
  }
  else
  {
    if(!check_admin_user($admin_user))
      return false;
      // how did this function get called by somebody not logged in as admin?

    if(!($conn=db_connect()))
    {
      return false;
    }

    $query = "select count(*)
              from lists
              where listname = '{$details['name']}'";
    $result = $conn->query($query);
    $row = $result->fetch_array();
    if($row[0] > 0)
    {
      echo 'Sorry, there is already a list with this name.';
      return false;
    }

    $query = "insert into lists values (NULL,
                                 '{$details['name']}',
                                 '{$details['blurb']}')";

    $result = $conn->query($query);
    return $result;
  }
}
```

This function performs a few validation checks before writing to the database: It checks that all the details were supplied, that the current user is an administrator, and that the list name is unique. If all goes well, the list is added to the `lists` table in the database.

Uploading a New Newsletter

Finally, we come to the main thrust of this application: uploading and sending newsletters to mailing lists.

When an administrator clicks on the Create Mail button, the `create-mail` action is activated, as follows:

```
case 'create-mail' :
{
  display_mail_form(get_email());
  break;
}
```

The administrator then sees the form shown in Figure 30.12.

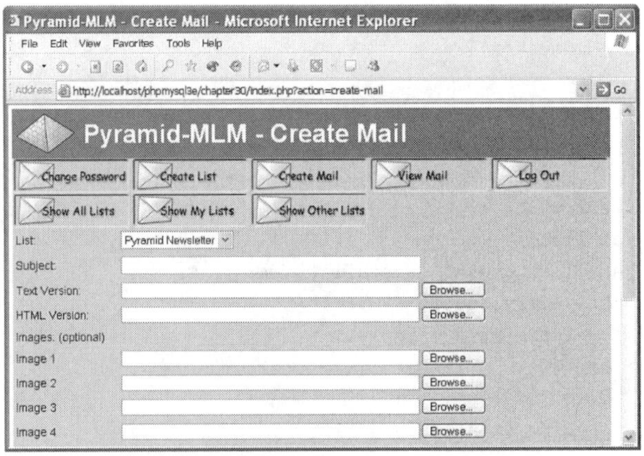

Figure 30.12   The Create Mail option gives the administrator an interface for
uploading newsletter files.

Remember that for this application you are assuming that the administrator has created a newsletter offline in both HTML and text formats and will upload both versions before sending. We chose to implement the application this way so that administrators can use their favorite software to create the newsletters. This makes the application more accessible.

This form has a number of fields for an administrator to fill out. At the top is a drop-down box of mailing lists to choose from. The administrator must also fill in a subject for the newsletter; this is the Subject line for the eventual email.

All the other form fields are file upload fields, which you can see from the Browse buttons next to them. To send a newsletter, an administrator must list both the text and HTML versions of this newsletter (although, obviously, you could change this to suit your needs). There are also a number of optional image fields where an administrator can upload any images that she has embedded in her HTML. Each of these files must be specified and uploaded separately.

The form you see is similar to a regular file upload form except that, in this case, you use it to upload multiple files. This use necessitates some minor differences in the form syntax and in the way you deal with the uploaded files at the other end.

The code for the `display_mail_form()` function is shown in Listing 30.15.

Listing 30.15 `display_mail_form()` **Function from** `output_fns.php`—**This Function Displays the File Upload Form**

```php
function display_mail_form($email, $listid=0)
{
  // display html form for uploading a new message
  global $table_width;
  $list = get_all_lists();
  $lists = sizeof($list);
?>
  <table cellpadding = '4' cellspacing = '0' border = '0'
        width = '<?php echo $table_width?>'>
  <form enctype='multipart/form-data' action='upload.php' method='post'>
  <tr>
    <td bgcolor = "#cccccc">
      List:
    </td>
    <td bgcolor = "#cccccc">
      <select name = "list">
      <?php
      for($i = 0; $i<$lists; $i++)
      {
        echo '<option value = '.$list[$i][0];
        if ($listid== $list[$i][0]) echo ' selected';
        echo '>'.$list[$i][1]."</option>\n";
      }
      ?>
      </select>
    </td>
  </tr>
  <tr>
    <td bgcolor = "#cccccc">
      Subject:
    </td>
    <td bgcolor = "#cccccc">
      <input type = "text" name = "subject" value = "<?php echo $subject?>"
        size = "60" ></td>
  </tr>
  <tr><td bgcolor = "#cccccc">
    Text Version:
  </td><td bgcolor = "#cccccc">
```

Listing 30.15   **Continued**

```
      <input type="file" name='userfile[0]' size = '60'>
    </td></tr>
    <tr><td bgcolor = "#cccccc">
      HTML Version:
    </td><td bgcolor = "#cccccc">
      <input type="file" name='userfile[1]' size = '60'>
    </td></tr>
    <tr><td bgcolor = '#cccccc' colspan ='2'>Images: (optional)
<?php
  $max_images = 10;
  for($i = 0; $i<10; $i++)
  {
    echo "<tr><td bgcolor = '#cccccc'>Image ". ($i+1) .' </td>';
    echo "<td bgcolor = '#cccccc'>";
    echo "<input type=\"file\" name='userfile[".($i+2)."]'
             size = '60'></td></tr>";
  }
?>
    <tr><td colspan = '2' bgcolor = '#cccccc' align = 'center'>
    <input type = "hidden" name = "max_images"  value = <?php echo $max_images?>>
    <input type = "hidden" name = "listid"  value = <?php echo $listid?>>
    <?php display_form_button('upload-files'); ?>
    </td>
    </form>
    </tr>
    </table>
<?php
}
```

Note that the files you want to upload will have their names entered in a series of inputs, each of type `file`, and with names that range from `userfile[0]` to `userfile[n]`. In essence, you treat these form fields in the same way that you would treat check boxes and name them using an array convention.

If you want to upload an arbitrary number of files through a PHP script and easily handle them as an array, you need to follow this convention.

In the script that processes this form, you actually end up with *three arrays*. Let's look at that script next.

Handling Multiple File Upload

You might remember that the file upload code is in a separate file. The complete listing of that file, `upload.php`, is shown in Listing 30.16.

Listing 30.16   upload.php—**This Script Uploads All the Files Needed for a Newsletter**

```php
<?php
  // this functionality is in a separate file to allow us to be
  // more paranoid with it

  // if anything goes wrong, we will exit

  $max_size = 50000;

  include ('include_fns.php');
  session_start();

  // only admin users can upload files
  if(!check_admin_user())
  {
    echo 'You do not seem to be authorized to use this page.';
    exit;
  }

  // set up the admin toolbar buttons
  $buttons = array();
  $buttons[0] = 'change-password';
  $buttons[1] = 'create-list';
  $buttons[2] = 'create-mail';
  $buttons[3] = 'view-mail';
  $buttons[4] = 'log-out';
  $buttons[5] = 'show-all-lists';
  $buttons[6] = 'show-my-lists';
  $buttons[7] = 'show-other-lists';

  do_html_header('Pyramid-MLM - Upload Files');

  display_toolbar($buttons);

  // check that the page is being called with the required data
  if(!$_FILES['userfile']['name'][0]
     ||!$_FILES['userfile']['name'][1]
     ||!$_POST['subject']||!$_POST['list'])
  {
      echo 'Problem: You did not fill out the form fully. The images are the
            only optional fields.  Each message needs a subject, text version
            and an HTML version.';
      do_html_footer();
      exit;
  }
```

Listing 30.16 **Continued**

```php
$list = $_POST['list'];
$subject = $_POST['subject'];

if(!($conn=db_connect()))
{
   echo '<p>Could not connect to db</p>';
   do_html_footer();
   exit;
}

// add mail details to the DB
$query = "insert into mail values (NULL,
                                   '{$_SESSION['admin_user']}',
                                   '$subject',
                                   '$list',
                                   'STORED', NULL, NULL)";
$result = $conn->query($query);
if(!$result)
{
  do_html_footer();
  exit;
}

//get the id MySQL assigned to this mail
$mailid = $conn->insert_id;

if(!$mailid)
{
  do_html_footer();
  exit;
}


// creating directory will fail if this is not the first message archived
// that's ok
@ mkdir('archive/'.$list, 0700);

// it is a problem if creating the specific directory for this mail fails
if(!mkdir('archive/'.$list."/$mailid", 0700))
{
  do_html_footer();
  exit;
}
```

Listing 30.16   **Continued**

```php
// iterate through the array of uploaded files
$i = 0;
while ($_FILES['userfile']['name'][$i]&&
       $_FILES['userfile']['tmp_name'][$i]!='none')
{
  echo '<p>Uploading '.$_FILES['userfile']['name'][$i].' - ';
  echo $_FILES['userfile']['size'][$i].' bytes.</p>';
  if ($_FILES['userfile']['size'][$i]==0)
  {
    echo 'Problem: '.$_FILES['userfile']['name'][$i].
         ' is zero length';
    $i++;
    continue;
  }

  if ($_FILES['userfile']['size'][$i]>$max_size)
  {
    echo 'Problem: '.$_FILES['userfile']['name'][$i].' is over '
         .$max_size.' bytes';
    $i++;
    continue;
  }

  // we would like to check that the uploaded image is an image
  // if getimagesize() can work out its size, it probably is.
  if($i>1&&!getimagesize($_FILES['userfile']['tmp_name'][$i]))
  {
    echo 'Problem: '.$_FILES['userfile']['name'][$i].
         ' is corrupt, or not a gif, jpeg or png';
    $i++;
    continue;
  }

  // file 0 (text message) and file 1 (html message) are special cases
  if($i==0)
    $destination = "archive/$list/$mailid/text.txt";
  else if($i == 1)
    $destination = "archive/$list/$mailid/index.html";
  else
  {
    $destination = "archive/$list/$mailid/"
```

Listing 30.16   **Continued**

```
                         .$_FILES['userfile']['name'][$i];
      $query = "insert into images
                 values ($mailid,
                         '".addslashes($_FILES['userfile']['name'][$i])."',
                         '".addslashes($_FILES['userfile']['type'][$i])."'
                         )";
      $result = $conn->query($query);
    }
    //if we are using PHP version >= 4.03

    if (!is_uploaded_file($_FILES['userfile']['tmp_name'][$i]))
    {
      // possible file upload attack detected
      echo 'Something funny happening with '
           .$_FILES['userfile']['name'].', not uploading.';
      do_html_footer();
      exit;
    }

    move_uploaded_file($_FILES['userfile']['tmp_name'][$i],
                       $destination);
/*
    // if version <= 4.02
    copy ($userfile[$i], $destination);

    unlink($userfile[$i]);
*/

    $i++;
  }

  display_preview_button($list, $mailid, 'preview-html');
  display_preview_button($list, $mailid, 'preview-text');
  display_button('send', "&id=$mailid");

  echo '<br /><br /><br /><br /><br />';
  do_html_footer();
?>
```

Let's walk through the steps in Listing 30.16. First, you start a session and check that the user is logged in as an administrator; you don't want to let anybody else upload files.

Strictly speaking, you should probably also check the list and mailid variables for unwanted characters, but we ignored this for the sake of brevity.

Next, you set up and send the headers for the page and validate that the form was filled in correctly. This step is important here because it's quite a complex form for the user to fill out.

Then you create an entry for this mail in the database and set up a directory in the archive for the mail to be stored in.

Next comes the main part of the script, which checks and moves each of the uploaded files. This is the part that is different when uploading multiple files. You now have four arrays to deal with; these arrays are called `$_FILES['userfile']['name']`, `$_FILES['userfile']['tmp_name']`, `$_FILES['userfile']['size']`, and `$_FILES['userfile']['type']`. They correspond to their similarly named equivalents in a single file upload, except that each of them is an array. The first file in the form is detailed in `$_FILES['userfile']['tmp_name'][0]`, `$_FILES['userfile']['name'][0]`, `$_FILES['userfile']['size'][0]`, and `$_FILES['userfile']['type'][0]`.

Given these three arrays, you perform the usual safety checks and move the files into the archive.

Finally, you give the administrator some buttons that she can use to preview the newsletter she has uploaded before she sends it and a button to send it. You can see the

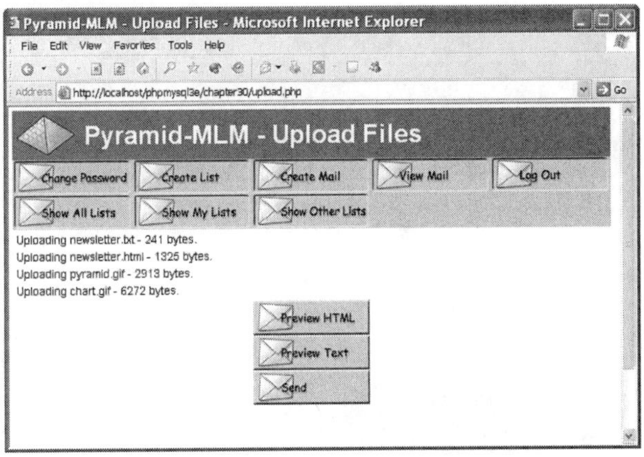

output from `upload.php` in Figure 30.13.

Figure 30.13 The upload script reports the files uploaded and their sizes.

Previewing the Newsletter

The administrator can preview a newsletter in two ways before sending it. She can access the preview functions from the upload screen if she wants to preview immediately after upload. The alternative is to click on the View Mail button, which will show her

all the unsent newsletters in the system, if she wants to preview and send mail later.
The View Mail button activates the `view-mail` action, which triggers the following
code:

```
case 'view-mail' :
{
  display_items('Unsent Mail', get_unsent_mail(get_email()),
                'preview-html', 'preview-text', 'send');
  break;
}
```

As you can see, this code again uses the `display_items()` function with buttons for the
`preview-html`, `preview-text`, and `send` actions.

Note that the Preview buttons do not actually trigger an action but instead link
directly to the newsletter in the archive. If you look back at Listings 30.7 and 30.16, you
will see that the `display_preview_button()` function creates these buttons instead of
the usual `display_button()` function.

The `display_button()` function creates an image link to a script with GET parameters where required; the `display_preview_button()` function gives a plain link into the
archive. This link pops up in a new window, achieved using the `target=new` attribute of
the HTML anchor tag. You can see the result of previewing the HTML version of a

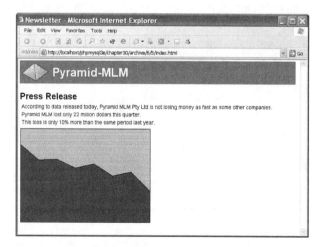

newsletter in Figure 30.14.

Figure 30.14 This preview of an HTML newsletter is shown complete with images.

Sending the Message

Clicking on the Send button for a newsletter activates the send action, which triggers the following code:

```
case 'send' :
{
  send($_GET['id'], $_SESSION['admin_user']);
  break;
}
```

This code calls the send() function, which you can find in the mlm_fns.php library. This long function, shown in Listing 30.17, is also the point at which you use the Mail_mime class.

Listing 30.17 send()**Function from** mlm_fns.php—**This Function Finally Sends Out a Newsletter**

```
function send($mailid, $admin_user)
{
  if(!check_admin_user($admin_user))
    return false;

  if(!($info = load_mail_info($mailid)))
  {
    echo "Cannot load list information for message $mailid";
    return false;
  }
  $subject = $info['subject'];
  $listid = $info['listid'];
  $status = $info['status'];
  $sent = $info['sent'];

  $from_name = 'Pyramid MLM';

  $from_address = 'return@address';
  $query = "select email from sub_lists where listid = $listid";

  $conn = db_connect();
  $result = $conn->query($query);
  if (!$result)
  {
    echo $query;
    return false;
```

Listing 30.17   **Continued**

```php
}
else if ($result->num_rows==0)
{
  echo "There is nobody subscribed to list number $listid";
  return false;
}

// include PEAR mail classes
require('Mail.php');
require('Mail/mime.php');

// instantiate MIME class and pass it the carriage return/line feed
// character used on this system
$message = new Mail_mime("\r\n");

// read in the text version of the newsletter
$textfilename = "archive/$listid/$mailid/text.txt";
$tfp = fopen($textfilename, "r");
$text = fread($tfp, filesize($textfilename));
fclose($tfp);

// read in the HTML version of the newsletter
$htmlfilename = "archive/$listid/$mailid/index.html";
$hfp = fopen($htmlfilename, "r");
$html = fread($hfp, filesize($htmlfilename));
fclose($hfp);

// add HTML and text to the mimemail object
$message->setTXTBody($text);
$message->setHTMLBody($html);

// get the list of images that relate to this message
$query = "select path, mimetype from images where mailid = $mailid";
$result = $conn->query($query);
if(!$result)
{
  echo '<p>Unable to get image list from database.</p>';
  return false;
}
$num = $result->num_rows;
for($i = 0; $i<$num; $i++)
{
  //load each image from disk
```

Listing 30.17   **Continued**

```php
    $row = $result->fetch_array();
    $imgfilename = "archive/$listid/$mailid/".$row[0];
    $imgtype = $row[1];
     // add each image to the object
    $message->addHTMLImage($imgfilename, $imgtype, $imgfilename, true);
}

// create message body
$body = $message->get();

// create message headers
$from = '"'.get_real_name($admin_user).'" <'.$admin_user.'>';
$hdrarray = array('From'    => $from,
                  'Subject' => $subject);

$hdrs = $message->headers($hdrarray);

// create the actual sending object
$sender =& Mail::factory('mail');

if($status == 'STORED')
{

  // send the HTML message to the administrator
  $sender->send($admin_user, $hdrs, $body);

  // send the plain text version of the message to administrator
  mail($admin_user, $subject, $text, 'From: "'.
      get_real_name($admin_user).
      '" <'.$admin_user."">");

  echo "Mail sent to $admin_user";

  // mark newsletter as tested
  $query = "update mail set status = 'TESTED' where mailid = $mailid";
  $result = $conn->query($query);

  echo '<p>Press send again to send mail to whole list.<center>';
  display_button('send', "&id=$mailid");
  echo '</center></p>';
}
else if($status == 'TESTED')
```

Listing 30.17   **Continued**

```
  {
    //send to whole list

    $query = "select subscribers.realname, sub_lists.email,
                     subscribers.mimetype
              from sub_lists, subscribers
              where listid = $listid and
                    sub_lists.email = subscribers.email";

    $result = $conn->query($query);
    if(!$result)
      echo '<p>Error getting subscriber list</p>';

    $count = 0;
    // for each subscriber
    while( $subscriber = $result->fetch_row())
    {
      if($subscriber[2]=='H')
      {
        //send HTML version to people who want it
        $sender->send($subscriber[1], $hdrs, $body);
      }
      else
      {
        //send text version to people who don't want HTML mail
        mail($subscriber[1], $subject, $text,
             'From: "'.get_real_name($admin_user).'" <'.$admin_user.">");
      }
      $count++;
    }

    $query = "update mail set status = 'SENT', sent = now()
              where mailid = $mailid";
    $result = $conn->query($query);
    echo "<p>A total of $count messages were sent.</p>";
  }
  else if($status == 'SENT')
  {
    echo '<p>This mail has already been sent.</p>';
  }
}
```

This function does several different things. It test-mails the newsletter to the administrator before sending it, and it keeps track of this test by tracking the status of a piece of mail in the database. When the upload script uploads a piece of mail, it sets the initial status of that mail to "STORED".

If the send() function finds that a mail has the status "STORED", it will update this status to "TESTED" and send it to the administrator. The status "TESTED" means the newsletter has been test-mailed to the administrator. If the status is "TESTED", it will be changed to "SENT" and sent to the whole list. This means each piece of mail must essentially be sent twice: once in test mode and once in real mode.

The function also sends two different kinds of email: the text version, which it sends using PHP's mail() function; and the HTML kind, which it sends using the Mail_mime class. We've used mail() many times in this book, so let's look at how to use the Mail_mime class. We do not cover this class comprehensively but instead explain how we used it in this fairly typical application.

You begin by including the class files and creating an instance of the Mail_mime class:

```
// include PEAR mail classes
include('Mail.php');
include('Mail/mime.php');

// instantiate MIME class and pass it the carriage return/line feed
// character used on this system
$message = new Mail_mime("\r\n");
```

Note that two class files are included here. You use the generic Mail class from PEAR later in this script to actually send the mail. This class comes with your PEAR installation.

The Mail_mime class is used to create the MIME format message that will be sent.

You next read in the text and HTML versions of the mail and add them to the Mail_mime class:

```
// read in the text version of the newsletter
$textfilename = "archive/$listid/$mailid/text.txt";
$tfp = fopen($textfilename, "r");
$text = fread($tfp, filesize($textfilename));
fclose($tfp);

// read in the HTML version of the newsletter
$htmlfilename = "archive/$listid/$mailid/index.html";
$hfp = fopen($htmlfilename, "r");
$html = fread($hfp, filesize($htmlfilename));
fclose($hfp);
```

```
// add HTML and text to the mimemail object
$message->setTXTBody($text);
$message->setHTMLBody($html);
```

You then load the image details from the database and loop through them, adding each image to the piece of mail you want to send:

```
$num = $result->num_rows;
for($i = 0; $i<$num; $i++)
{
  //load each image from disk
  $row = $result->fetch_array();
  $imgfilename = "archive/$listid/$mailid/".$row[0];
  $imgtype = $row[1];
   // add each image to the object
  $message->addHTMLImage($imgfilename, $imgtype, $imgfilename, true);
}
```

The parameters you pass to addHTMLImage() are the name of the image file (or you could also pass the image data), the MIME type of the image, the filename again, and true to signify that the first parameter is a filename rather than file data. (If you wanted to pass raw image data, you would pass the data, the MIME type, an empty parameter, and false.) These parameters are a little cumbersome.

At this stage, you need to create the message body before you can set up the message headers. You create the body as follows:

```
// create message body
$body = $message->get();
```

You can then create the message headers with a call to the Mail_mime class's headers() function:

```
// create message headers
$from = '"'.get_real_name($admin_user).'" <'.$admin_user.'>';
$hdrarray = array(
            'From'    => $from,
            'Subject' => $subject);
$hdrs = $message->headers($hdrarray);
```

Finally, having set up the message, you can send it. To do this, you need to instantiate the PEAR Mail class and pass to it the message you have created. You begin by instantiating the class, as follows:

```
// create the actual sending object
$sender =& Mail::factory('mail');
```

(The parameter `'mail'` here just tells the `Mail` class to use PHP's `mail()` function to send messages. You could also use `'sendmail'` or `'smtp'` as the value for this parameter for the obvious results.)

Next, you send the mail to each of your subscribers. You do this by retrieving and looping through each of the users subscribed to this list and using either the Mail `send()` or regular `mail()` depending on the user's MIME type preference:

```
if($subscriber[2]=='H')
{
  //send HTML version to people who want it
  $sender->send($subscriber[1], $hdrs, $body);
}
else
{
  //send text version to people who don't want HTML mail
  mail($subscriber[1], $subject, $text,
                'From: "'.get_real_name($admin_user).'" <'.$admin_user.">");
}
```

The first parameter of `$sender->send()` should be the user's email address; the second, the headers; and the third, the message body.

That's it! You have now completed building the mailing list application.

Extending the Project

As usual with these projects, there are many ways you could extend the functionality. You might like to

- Confirm membership with subscribers so that people can't be subscribed without their permission. You typically do this by sending email to their accounts and deleting those who do not reply. This approach also cleans out any incorrect email addresses from the database.

- Give the administrator powers to approve or reject users who want to subscribe to their lists.

- Add open list functionality that allows any member to send email to the list.

- Let only registered members see the archive for a particular mailing list.

- Allow users to search for lists that match specific criteria. For example, users might be interested in golf newsletters. When the number of newsletters grows past a particular size, a search would be useful to find specific ones.

- Make the program more efficient to handle a large mailing list. To do this, use a purpose-built mailing list manager such as exmlm that can queue and send messages in a multithreaded way. Calling `mail()` many times in PHP is not very efficient, making a PHP back end unsuitable for large subscriber lists. Of course, you could still build the front end in PHP but have ezmlm handle the grunt work.

Next

In the next chapter, you implement a web forum application that will enable users to have online discussions structured by topic and conversational threads.

31

Building Web Forums

O NE GOOD WAY TO GET USERS TO RETURN TO your site is to offer web forums. They can be used for purposes as varied as philosophical discussion groups and product technical support. In this chapter, you implement a web forum in PHP. An alternative is to use an existing package, such as Phorum, to set up your forums.

Web forums are sometimes also called *discussion boards* or *threaded discussion groups*. The idea of a forum is that people can post articles or questions to it, and others can read and reply to their questions. Each topic of discussion in a forum is called a *thread*.

For this project, you implement a web forum called blah-blah. Users will be able to

- Start new threads of discussion by posting articles
- Post articles in reply to existing articles
- View articles that have been posted
- View the threads of conversation in the forum
- View the relationship between articles—that is, see which articles are replies to other articles

The Problem

Setting up a forum is actually quite an interesting problem. You need some way of storing the articles in a database with author, title, date, and content information. At first glance, this database might not seem much different from the Book-O-Rama database.

The way most threaded discussion software works, however, is that, along with showing you the available articles, it shows you the relationship between articles. That is, you are able to see which articles are replies to other articles (and which article they're following up) and which articles are new topics of discussion.

You can see examples of discussion boards that implement this format in many places, including Slashdot:

http://slashdot.org

Deciding how to display these relationships requires some careful thought. For this system, users should be able to view an individual message, a thread of conversation with the relationships shown, or all the threads on the system.

Users must also be able to post new topics or replies. This is the easy part.

Solution Components

As we mentioned previously, the process of storing and retrieving the author and text of a message is easy. The most difficult part of this application is finding a database structure that will store the information you want and a way of navigating that structure efficiently.

The structure of articles in a discussion might look like the one shown in Figure 31.1.

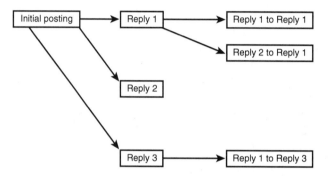

Figure **31.1**   An article in a threaded discussion might be the first article in a new topic, but more commonly it is a response to another article.

In this diagram, you can see that the initial posting starts off a topic, with three replies. Some of the replies have replies. These replies could also have replies, and so on.

Looking at the diagram gives you a clue as to how you can store and retrieve the article data and the links between articles. This diagram shows a *tree structure*. If you've done much programming, you'll know that this is one of the staple data structures used. In the diagram, there are *nodes*—or articles—and *links*—or relationships between articles—just as in any tree structure. (If you are not familiar with trees as a data structure, don't worry; we cover the basics as we go.)

The tricks to getting this all to work are

1. Finding a way to map this tree structure into storage—in this case, into a MySQL database

2. Finding a way to reconstruct the data as required

For this project, you begin by implementing a MySQL database that enables you to store articles between use. You then build simple interfaces to enable saving of articles.

When you load the list of articles for viewing, you will load the headers of each article into a `tree_node` PHP class. Each `tree_node` will contain an article's headers and a set of the replies to that article.

The replies will be stored in an array. Each reply will itself be a `tree_node` that can contain an array of replies to that article, which are themselves `tree_nodes`, and so on. This process continues until you reach the so-called *leaf nodes* of the tree, the nodes that do not have any replies. You then have a tree structure that looks like the one in Figure 31.1.

Some terminology: The message that you are replying to can be called the *parent* node of the current node. Any replies to the message can be called the *children* of the current node. If you imagine that this tree structure is like a family tree, this terminology will be easy to remember.

The first article in this tree structure—the one with no parent—is sometimes called the *root* node.

Note

Calling the first article the root can be unintuitive because you usually draw the root node at the top of diagrams, unlike the roots of real trees.

To build and display the tree structure for this project, you will write recursive functions. (We discussed recursion in Chapter 5, "Reusing Code and Writing Functions.")

We decided to use a class for this structure because it's the easiest way to build a complex, dynamically expanding data structure for this application. It also means you have quite simple, elegant code to do something quite complex.

Solution Overview

To really understand this project, it's probably a good idea to work through the code, which we do in a moment. This application has less bulk than some of the others, but the code is a bit more complex.

This application contains only three real pages. It has a main index page that shows all the articles in the forum as links to the articles. From here, you can add a new article, view a listed article, or change the way the articles are viewed by expanding and collapsing branches of the tree. (More on this shortly.) From the article view, you can post a reply to that article or view the existing replies to that article. The new article page enables you to enter a new post, either a reply to an existing message or a new, unrelated message.

The system flow diagram is shown in Figure 31.2.

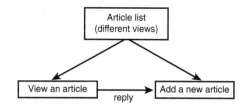

Figure 31.2   The blah–blah forum system has three main parts.

A summary of the files in this application is shown in Table 31.1.

Table 31.1   **Files in the Web Forum Application**

Name	Type	Description
index.php	Application	Main page the users see when they enter the site. Contains an expandable and collapsible list of all the articles on the site.
new_post.php	Application	Form used for posting new articles.
store_new_post.php	Application	StorPage where articles from the new_post.php form are stored.
view_post.php	Application	Page that displays an individual post and a list of the replies to that post.
treenode_class.php	Library	File that contains the treenode class, which you use to display the hierarchy of posts.
include_fns.php	Library	List of all the other function libraries for this application (the other Library-type files listed here).
data_valid_fns.php	Library	Collection of data validation functions.
db_fns.php	Library	Collection of database connectivity functions.
discussion_fns.php	Library	Collection of functions for dealing with storing and retrieving postings.
output_fns.php	Library	Collection of functions for outputting HTML.
create_database.sql	SQL	SQL to set up the database required for this application.

Now let's look at the implementation.

Designing the Database

There are a few attributes you need to store about each article posted to the forum: the name of the person who wrote it, called the *poster*; the title of the article; the time it was posted; and the article body. You therefore need a table of articles, and you need to create a unique ID for each article, called the postid.

Each article needs to have some information about where it belongs in the hierarchy. You could store information about an article's children with the article. However, each article can have many replies, so storing all this information can lead to some problems in database construction. Because each article can be a reply to only one other, it is easier to store a reference to the parent article—that is, the article that this article is replying to.

You therefore need to store the following data for each article:

- `postid`—A unique ID for each article
- `parent`—The `postid` of the parent article
- `poster`—The author of this article
- `title`—The title of this article
- `posted`—The date and time that the article was posted
- `message`—The body of the article

You will also add a couple of optimizations to this information.

When you are trying to determine whether an article has any replies, you have to run a query to see whether any other articles have this article as a parent. You need this information for every post that you list. The fewer queries you have to run, the faster the code will run. You can remove the need for these queries by adding a field to show whether there are any replies. You can call this field `children` and make it effectively Boolean: The value will be 1 if the node has children and 0 (zero) if it does not.

There is always a price to pay for optimizations. Here, you store redundant data. Because you are storing the data in two ways, you must be careful to make sure that the two representations agree with each other. When you add children, you must update the parent. If you allow the deletion of children, you need to update the parent node to make sure the database is consistent. In this project, you are not going to build a facility for deleting articles, so you avoid half of this problem. If you decide to extend this code, bear this issue in mind.

You will make one other optimization in this project: You will separate the message bodies from the other data and store them in a separate table. The reason for this is that this attribute will have the MySQL type `text`. Having this type in a table can slow down queries on that table. Because you will do many small queries to build the tree structure, using this type would slow it down quite a lot. With the message bodies in a separate table, you can just retrieve them when a user wants to look at a particular message.

MySQL can search fixed-size records faster than variable-sized records. If you need to use variable-sized data, you can help by creating indexes on the fields that will be used to search the database. For some projects, you would be best served by leaving the text field in the same record as everything else and specifying indexes on all the columns that you will search on. Indexes take time to generate, though, and the data in the forums is likely to be changing all the time, so you would need to regenerate your indexes frequently.

You will also add an `area` attribute in case you later decide to implement multiple forums with the one application. You won't implement this capability here, but this way it is reserved for future use.

Given all these considerations, the SQL to create the database for the forum database is shown in Listing 31.1.

Listing 31.1 `create_database.sql`—SQL to Create the Discussion Database

```
create database discussion;

use discussion;

create table header
(
  parent int not null,
  poster char(20) not null,
  title char(20) not null,
  children int default 0 not null,
  area int default 1 not null,
  posted datetime not null,
  postid int unsigned not null auto_increment primary key
);

create table body
(
  postid int unsigned not null primary key,
  message text
);



grant select, insert, update, delete
on discussion.*
to discussion@localhost identified by 'password';
```

You can create this database structure by running this script through MySQL as follows:

```
mysql -u root -p < create_database.sql
```

You need to supply your root password. You should probably also change the password we set up for the discussion user to something better.

To understand how this structure will hold articles and their relationship to each other, look at Figure 31.3.

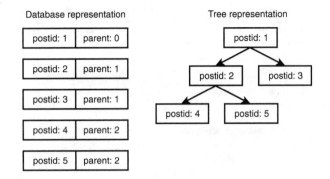

Figure 31.3   The database holds the tree structure in a flattened
relational form.

As you can see in the figure, the parent field for each article in the database holds the
`postid` of the article above it in the tree. The parent article is the article that is being
replied to.

You can also see that the root node, `postid 1`, has no parent. All new topics of discussion will be in this position. For articles of this type, you store their parent as a 0
(zero) in the database.

Viewing the Tree of Articles

Next, you need a way of getting information out of the database and representing it
back in the tree structure. You do this with the main page, `index.php`. For the purposes
of this explanation, we input some sample posts via the article posting scripts
`new_post.php` and `store_new_post.php`. We look at them in the next section.

We cover the article list first because it is the backbone of the site. After this, everything else will be easy.

Figure 31.4 shows the initial view of the articles in the site that a user would see.

This figure shows all the initiating articles. None of them are replies; each one is the
first article on a particular topic.

In this case, you have a number of options. The menu bar lets you add a new post and
expand or collapse your view of the articles.

To understand what these options mean, look at the posts. Some of them have plus
symbols next to them. This means that these articles have been replied to. To see the
replies to a particular article, you can click the plus symbol. The result of clicking one of
these symbols is shown in Figure 31.5.

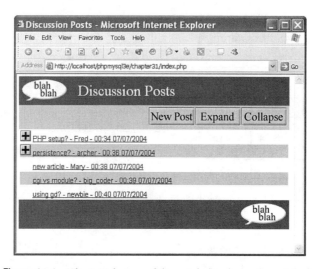

Figure 31.4   The initial view of the article list shows the articles in "collapsed" form.

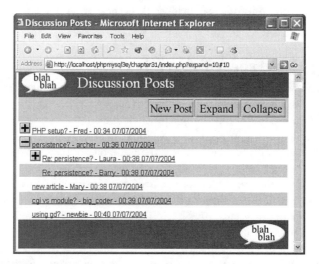

Figure 31.5   The thread of discussion about persistence has been expanded.

As you can see, clicking the plus symbol displays the replies to that first article. The plus symbol then turns into a minus symbol. If you click this symbol, all the articles in this thread will be collapsed, returning you to the initial view.

You might also notice that one of the replies in Figure 31.5 has a plus symbol next to it. This means that there are replies to this reply. The level of replies can continue to an arbitrary depth, and you can view each reply set by clicking on the appropriate plus symbol.

The two menu bar options Expand and Collapse expand all possible threads and collapse all possible threads, respectively. The result of clicking the Expand button is shown in Figure 31.6.

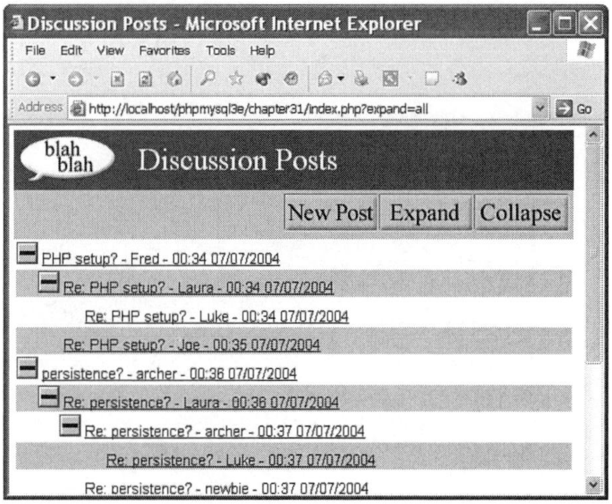

Figure 31.6   All the threads have now been expanded.

If you look closely at Figures 31.5 and 31.6, you can see that some parameters are passed back to `index.php` in the command line. In Figure 31.5, the URL looks as follows:

```
http://localhost/phpmysql3e/chapter31/index.php?expand=10#10
```

The script reads this line as "Expand the item with `postid` 10." The # is just an HTML anchor that scrolls the page down to the part that has just been expanded.

In Figure 31.6, the URL reads

```
http://localhost/phpmysql3e/chapter31/index.php?expand=all
```

Clicking the Expand button passes the parameter `expand` with the value `all`.

Expanding and Collapsing

To see how to create the article view, look at the `index.php` script, shown in Listing 31.2.

Listing 31.2 `index.php`—**Script to Create the Article View on the Main Page of the Application**

```php
<?php
  include ('include_fns.php');
  session_start();

  // check if we have created our session variable
  if(!isset($_SESSION['expanded']))
  {
    $_SESSION['expanded'] = array();
  }

  // check if an expand button was pressed
  // expand might equal 'all' or a postid or not be set
  if(isset($_GET['expand']))
  {
    if($_GET['expand'] == 'all')
      expand_all($_SESSION['expanded']);
    else
      $_SESSION['expanded'][$_GET['expand']] = true;
  }

  // check if a collapse button was pressed
  // collapse might equal all or a postid or not be set
  if(isset($_GET['collapse']))
  {
    if($_GET['collapse']=='all')
      $_SESSION['expanded'] = array();
    else
      unset($_SESSION['expanded'][$_GET['collapse']]);
  }

  do_html_header('Discussion Posts');

  display_index_toolbar();

  // display the tree view of conversations
  display_tree($_SESSION['expanded']);

  do_html_footer();
?>
```

This script uses the following three variables to do its job:

- The session variable `expanded`, which keeps track of which threads are expanded. This variable can be maintained from view to view, so you can have multiple threads expanded. The `expanded` variable is an associative array that contains the `postid` of articles that will have their replies expanded.
- The parameter `expand`, which tells the script which new threads to expand.
- The parameter `collapse`, which tells the script which threads to collapse.

When you click a plus or minus symbol or the Expand or Collapse button, this action recalls the `index.php` script with new parameters for `expand` or `collapse`. You use `expanded` from page to page to track which threads should be expanded in any given view.

The `index.php` script begins by starting a session and adding the `expanded` variable as a session variable if this has not already been done. After that, the script checks whether it has been passed an `expand` or `collapse` parameter and modifies the `expanded` array accordingly. Look at the code for the `expand` parameter:

```
if(isset($_GET['expand']))
{
  if($_GET['expand'] == 'all')
    expand_all($_SESSION['expanded']);
  else
    $_SESSION['expanded'][$_GET['expand']] = true;
}
```

If you click on the Expand button, the function `expand_all()` is called to add all the threads that have replies into the `expanded` array. (We look at this in a moment.)

If you try to expand a particular thread, you will be passed a `postid` via `expand`. You therefore add a new entry to the `expanded` array to reflect this.

The `expand_all()` function is shown in Listing 31.3.

Listing 31.3 `expand_all()` **Function from** `discussion_fns.php`—**Processes the** `$expanded` **Array to Expand All the Threads in the Forum**

```
function expand_all(&$expanded)
{
  // mark all threads with children as to be shown expanded
  $conn = db_connect();
  $query = 'select postid from header where children = 1';
  $result = $conn->query($query);
  $num = $result->num_rows;
  for($i = 0; $i<$num; $i++)
  {
    $this_row = $result->fetch_row();
    $expanded[$this_row[0]]=true;
  }
}
```

This function runs a database query to work out which of the threads in the forum have replies, as follows:

```
select postid from header where children = 1
```

Each of the articles returned is then added to the `expanded` array. You run this query to save time later. You could simply add all articles to the expanded list, but it would be wasteful to try processing replies that do not exist.

Collapsing the articles works in the opposite way, as follows:

```
if(isset($_GET['collapse']))
{
  if($_GET['collapse']=='all')
    $_SESSION['expanded'] = array();
  else
    unset($_SESSION['expanded'][$_GET['collapse']]);
}
```

You can remove items from the `expanded` array by unsetting them. You remove the thread that is to be collapsed or unset the entire array if the entire page is to be collapsed.

All this is preprocessing, so you know which articles should be displayed and which should not. The key part of the script is the call to `display_tree($_SESSION ['expanded'])`; which actually generates the tree of displayed articles.

Displaying the Articles

Let's look at the `display_tree()` function, shown in Listing 31.4.

Listing 31.4 `display_tree()` **Function from** `output_fns.php`—**Creates the Root Node of the Tree Structure**

```
function display_tree($expanded, $row = 0, $start = 0)
{
  // display the tree view of conversations

  global $table_width;
  echo "<table width = '$table_width'>";

  // see if we are displaying the whole list or a sublist
  if($start>0)
    $sublist = true;
  else
    $sublist = false;

  // construct tree structure to represent conversation summary
  $tree = new treenode($start, '', '', '', 1, true, -1, $expanded, $sublist);
```

Listing 31.4 **Continued**

```
  // tell tree to display itself
  $tree->display($row, $sublist);

  echo '</table>';
}
```

The main role of the display_tree() function is to create the root node of the tree structure. You use it to display the whole index and to create subtrees of replies on the view_post.php page. As you can see, it takes three parameters. The first, $expanded, is the list of article postids to display in an expanded fashion. The second, $row, is an indicator of the row number that will be used to work out the alternating colors of the rows in the list.

The third parameter, $start, tells the function where to start displaying articles. This is the postid of the root node for the tree to be created and displayed. If you are displaying the whole thing, as you are on the main page, this will be 0 (zero), meaning display all the articles with no parent. If this parameter is 0, you set $sublist to false and display the whole tree.

If the parameter is greater than 0, you use it as the root node of the tree to display, set $sublist to true, and build and display only part of the tree. (You use sublists in the view_post.php script.)

The most important task this function performs is instantiating an instance of the treenode class that represents the root of the tree. This is not actually an article, but it acts as the parent of all the first-level articles, which have no parent. After the tree has been constructed, you simply call its display function to actually display the list of articles.

Using the treenode Class

The code for the treenode class is shown in Listing 31.5. (You might find it useful at this stage to look over Chapter 6, "Object-Oriented PHP," to remind yourself how classes work.)

Listing 31.5 treenode **Class from** treenode_class.php— **The Backbone of the Application**

```
<?php
// functions for loading, contructing and
// displaying the tree are in this file

class treenode
{
```

Listing 31.5 **Continued**

```php
// each node in the tree has member variables containing
// all the data for a post except the body of the message
public $m_postid;
public $m_title;
public $m_poster;
public $m_posted;
public $m_children;
public $m_childlist;
public $m_depth;

public function __construct($postid, $title, $poster, $posted, $children,
                $expand, $depth, $expanded, $sublist)
{
  // the constructor sets up the member variables, but more
  // importantly recursively creates lower parts of the tree
  $this->m_postid = $postid;
  $this->m_title = $title;
  $this->m_poster = $poster;
  $this->m_posted = $posted;
  $this->m_children =$children;
  $this->m_childlist = array();
  $this->m_depth = $depth;

  // we only care what is below this node if it
  // has children and is marked to be expanded
  // sublists are always expanded
  if(($sublist||$expand) && $children)
  {
    $conn = db_connect();

    $query = "select * from header where parent = $postid order by posted";
    $result = $conn->query($query);

    for ($count=0; $row = @$result->fetch_assoc(); $count++)
    {
      if($sublist||$expanded[ $row['postid'] ] == true)
        $expand = true;
      else
        $expand = false;
      $this->m_childlist[$count]= new treenode($row['postid'],$row['title'],
                        $row['poster'],$row['posted'],
                        $row['children'], $expand,
                        $depth+1, $expanded, $sublist);
    }
  }
}
```

Listing 31.5 **Continued**

```php
function display($row, $sublist = false)
{
  // as this is an object, it is responsible for displaying itself

  // $row tells us what row of the display we are up to
  // so we know what color it should be

  // $sublist tells us whether we are on the main page
  // or the message page.  Message pages should have
  // $sublist = true.
  // On a sublist, all messages are expanded and there are
  // no "+" or "-" symbols.

  // if this is the empty root node skip displaying
  if($this->m_depth > -1)
  {
    //color alternate rows
    echo '<tr><td bgcolor = ';
    if ($row%2)
      echo "'#cccccc'>";
    else
      echo "'#ffffff'>";

    // indent replies to the depth of nesting
    for($i = 0; $i < $this->m_depth; $i++)
    {
      echo "<img src = 'images/spacer.gif' height = '22'
                      width = '22' alt = '' valign = 'bottom' />";
    }

    // display + or - or a spacer
    if ( !$sublist && $this->m_children && sizeof($this->m_childlist))
    // we're on the main page, have some children, and they're expanded
    {
      // we are expanded - offer button to collapse
      echo "<a href = 'index.php?collapse=".
                      $this->m_postid."#$this->m_postid'
          ><img src = 'images/minus.gif' valign = 'bottom'
          height = '22' width = '22' alt = 'Collapse Thread' border = '0'
          /></a>";
    }
```

Listing 31.5 **Continued**

```
    else if(!$sublist && $this->m_children)
    {
      // we are collapsed - offer button to expand
      echo "<a href = 'index.php?expand=".
          $this->m_postid."#$this->m_postid'><img src = 'images/plus.gif'
          height = '22' width = '22' alt = 'Expand Thread' border = '0'
          /></a>";
    }
    else
    {
      // we have no children, or are in a sublist, do not give button
      echo "<img src = 'images/spacer.gif' height = '22' width = '22'
              alt = '' valign = 'bottom' />";
    }


    echo " <a name = $this->m_postid ><a href =
          'view_post.php?postid=$this->m_postid'>$this->m_title -
          $this->m_poster - ".reformat_date($this->m_posted).'</a>';
    echo '</td></tr>';

    // increment row counter to alternate colors
    $row++;
  }
  // call display on each of this node's children
  // note a node will only have children in its list if expanded
  $num_children = sizeof($this->m_childlist);
  for($i = 0; $i < $num_children; $i++)
  {
    $row = $this->m_childlist[$i]->display($row, $sublist);
  }
  return $row;
  }


}

?>
```

This class contains the functionality that drives the tree view in this application.

One instance of the `treenode` class contains details about a single posting and links to all the reply postings of that class. This gives you the following member variables:

```
public $m_postid;
public $m_title;
public $m_poster;
public $m_posted;
public $m_children;
public $m_childlist;
public $m_depth;
```

Notice that the `treenode` does not contain the body of the article. There is no need to load the body until a user goes to the `view_post.php` script. You need to try to make this process relatively fast because you are doing a lot of data manipulation to display the tree list and need to recalculate when the page is refreshed or a button is pressed.

These variables follow a naming scheme commonly used in object-oriented applications—starting variables with `m_` to indicate that they are member variables of the class.

Most of these variables correspond directly to rows from the `header` table in the database. The exceptions are `$m_childlist` and `$m_depth`. You use the variable `$m_childlist` to hold the replies to this article. The variable `$m_depth` will hold the number of tree levels that you are down; this information will be used for creating the display.

The constructor function sets up the values of all the variables, as follows:

```
public function __construct($postid, $title, $poster, $posted, $children,
                  $expand, $depth, $expanded, $sublist)
{
  // the constructor sets up the member variables, but more
  // importantly recursively creates lower parts of the tree
  $this->m_postid = $postid;
  $this->m_title = $title;
  $this->m_poster = $poster;
  $this->m_posted = $posted;
  $this->m_children =$children;
  $this->m_childlist = array();
  $this->m_depth = $depth;
```

When you construct the root `treenode` from `display_tree()` from the main page, you actually create a *dummy* node with no article associated with it. You pass in some initial values as follows:

```
$tree = new treenode($start, '', '', '', 1, true, -1, $expanded, $sublist);
```

This line creates a root node with a `$postid` of 0 (zero). It can be used to find all the first-level postings because they have a parent of 0. You set the depth to -1 because this node isn't actually part of the display. All the first-level postings have a depth of 0 and are located at the far left of the screen. Subsequent depths step toward the right.

The most important thing that happens in this constructor is that the child nodes of this node are instantiated. You begin this process by checking whether you need to expand the child nodes. You perform this process only if a node has some children, and you have elected to display them:

```
if(($sublist||$expand) && $children)
{
  $conn = db_connect();
```

You then connect to the database and retrieve all the child posts, as follows:

```
$query = "select * from header where parent = $postid order by posted";
$result = $conn->query($query);
```

Next, you fill the array `$m_childlist` with instances of the `treenode` class, containing the replies to the post stored in this `treenode`, as follows:

```
for ($count=0; $row = @$result->fetch_assoc(); $count++)
{
  if($sublist||$expanded[ $row['postid'] ] == true)
    $expand = true;
  else
    $expand = false;
  $this->m_childlist[$count]= new treenode($row['postid'],$row['title'],
                            $row['poster'],$row['posted'],
                            $row['children'], $expand,
                            $depth+1, $expanded, $sublist);
}
```

This last line creates the new `treenode`s, following exactly the same process we just walked through, but for the next level down the tree. This is the recursive part: A parent tree node calls the `treenode` constructor, passes its own `postid` as parent, and adds one to its own depth before passing it.

Each `treenode`, in turn, is created and then creates its own children until you run out of replies or levels that you want to expand to.

After all that's done, you call the root `treenode`'s display function (back in `display_tree()`), as follows:

```
$tree->display($row, $sublist);
```

The `display()` function begins by checking whether this is the dummy root node:

```
if($this->m_depth > -1)
```

In this way, the dummy can be left out of the display. You don't want to completely skip the root node, though. You do not want it to appear, but it needs to notify its children that they need to display themselves.

The `display()` function then starts drawing the table containing the articles. It uses the modulus operator (`%`) to decide what color background this row should have (hence they alternate):

```
//color alternate rows
echo '<tr><td bgcolor = ';
if ($row%2)
  echo "'#cccccc'>";
else
  echo "'#ffffff'>";
```

It then uses the `$m_depth` member variable to work out how much to indent the current item. If you look back at the figures, you will see that the deeper the level a reply is on, the further it is indented. You code this as follows:

```
// indent replies to the depth of nesting
for($i = 0; $i < $this->m_depth; $i++)
{
    echo "<img src = 'images/spacer.gif' height = '22'
                    width = '22' alt = '' valign = 'bottom' />";
}
```

The next part of the function works out whether to supply a plus or minus button or nothing at all:

```
// display + or - or a spacer
if ( !$sublist && $this->m_children && sizeof($this->m_childlist))
// we're on the main page, have some children, and they're expanded
{
  // we are expanded - offer button to collapse
  echo "<a href = 'index.php?collapse=".
                  $this->m_postid."#$this->m_postid'
      ><img src = 'images/minus.gif' valign = 'bottom'
      height = '22' width = '22' alt = 'Collapse Thread' border = '0'
      /></a>";
}
else if(!$sublist && $this->m_children)
{
  // we are collapsed - offer button to expand
  echo "<a href = 'index.php?expand=".
      $this->m_postid."#$this->m_postid'><img src = 'images/plus.gif'
      height = '22' width = '22' alt = 'Expand Thread' border = '0'
      /></a>";
}
else
{
```

```
// we have no children, or are in a sublist, do not give button
echo "<img src = 'images/spacer.gif' height = '22' width = '22'
          alt = '' valign = 'bottom' />";
```

Next, you display the actual details of this node:

```
echo " <a name = $this->m_postid ><a href =
          'view_post.php?postid=$this->m_postid'>$this->m_title -
          $this->m_poster - ".reformat_date($this->m_posted).'</a>';
echo '</td></tr>';
```

You then change the color for the next row:

```
// increment row counter to alternate colors
$row++;
```

After that, you add some code that will be executed by all treenodes, including the root one, as follows:

```
// call display on each of this node's children
// note a node will only have children in its list if expanded
$num_children = sizeof($this->m_childlist);
for($i = 0; $i<$num_children; $i++)
{
  $row = $this->m_childlist[$i]->display($row, $sublist);
}
return $row;
```

Again, this is a recursive function call, which calls on each of this node's children to display themselves. You pass them the current row color and get them to pass it back when they are finished with it so that you can keep track of the alternating color.

That's it for this class. The code is fairly complex. You might like to experiment with running the application and then come back to look at it again when you are comfortable with what it does.

Viewing Individual Articles

The display_tree() call gives you links to a set of articles. If you click one of these articles, you will go to the view_post.php script, with a parameter of the postid of the article to be viewed. Sample output from this script is shown in Figure 31.7.

The view_post.php script, shown in Listing 31.6, shows the message body, as well as the replies to this message. The replies are again displayed as a tree but completely expanded this time, and without any plus or minus buttons. This is the effect of the $sublist switch coming into action.

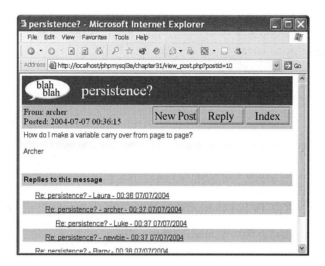

Figure 31.7   You can now see the message body for this posting.

Listing 31.6   `view_post.php`—**Displays a Single Message Body**

```php
<?php
  // include function libraries
  include ('include_fns.php');
  $postid = $_GET['postid'];
  // get post details
  $post = get_post($postid);

  do_html_header($post['title']);

  // display post
  display_post($post);

  // if post has any replies, show the tree view of them
  if($post['children'])
  {
    echo '<br /><br />';
    display_replies_line();
    display_tree($_SESSION['expanded'], 0, $postid);
  }

  do_html_footer();
?>
```

This script uses three main function calls to do its job: get_post(), display_post(), and display_tree(). The get_post() function, shown in Listing 31.7, pulls the function details out of the database.

Listing 31.7 get_post() Function from discussion_fns.php—Retrieves a Message from the Database

```
function get_post($postid)
{
  // extract one post from the database and return as an array

  if(!$postid) return false;

  $conn = db_connect();

  //get all header information from 'header'
  $query = "select * from header where postid = $postid";
  $result = $conn->query($query);
  if($result->num_rows!=1)
    return false;
  $post = $result->fetch_assoc();

  // get message from body and add it to the previous result
  $query = "select * from body where postid = $postid";
  $result2 = $conn->query($query);
  if($result2->num_rows>0)
  {
    $body = $result2->fetch_assoc();
    if($body)
    {
      $post['message'] = $body['message'];
    }
  }
  return $post;
}
```

This function, given a postid, performs the two queries required to retrieve the message header and body for that posting and puts them together into a single array, which it then returns.

The results of the get_post() function are then passed to the display_post() function from output_fns.php. This function just prints out the array with some HTML formatting, so we did not include it here.

Finally, the view_post.php script checks whether there are any replies to this article and calls display_tree() to show them in the sublist format—that is, fully expanded with no plusses or minuses.

Adding New Articles

After all that, we can now look at how a new post is added to the forum. A user can add a post in two ways: first, by clicking on the New Post button in the index page, and second, by clicking on the Reply button on the view_post.php page.

These actions both activate the same script, new_post.php, just with different parameters. Figure 31.8 shows the output from new_post.php after it is reached by clicking the Reply button.

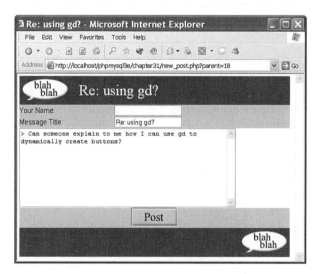

Figure 31.8   In replies, the text of the original message is automatically inserted and marked.

First, look at the URL shown in the figure:

```
http://localhost/phpmysql3e/chapter31/new_post.php?parent=18
```

The parameter passed in as parent will be the parent postid of the new posting. If you click New Post instead of Reply, you will get parent=0 in the URL.

Second, you can see that, in a reply, the text of the original message is inserted and marked with a > character, as is the case in most mail and news-reading programs.

Third, you can see that the title of this message defaults to the title of the original message prefixed with Re:.

Let's look at the code that produces this output; it is shown in Listing 31.8.

Listing 31.8 `new_post.php`—**Allows a User to Type a New Post or Reply to an Existing Post**

```php
<?php
  include ('include_fns.php');

  $title = $_POST['title'];
  $poster = $_POST['poster'];
  $message = $_POST['message'];

  if(isset($_GET['parent']))
     $parent = $_GET['parent'];
  else
    $parent = $_POST['parent'];


  if(!$area)
    $area = 1;

  if(!$error)
  {
    if(!$parent)
    {
      $parent = 0;
      if(!$title)
        $title = 'New Post';
    }
    else
    {
      // get post name
      $title = get_post_title($parent);

      // append Re:
      if(strstr($title, 'Re: ') == false )
        $title = 'Re: '.$title;

      //make sure title will still fit in db
      $title = substr($title, 0, 20);

      //prepend a quoting pattern to the post you are replying to
      $message = add_quoting(get_post_message($parent));
    }
  }
  do_html_header($title);

  display_new_post_form($parent, $area, $title, $message, $poster);
```

Listing 31.8   **Continued**

```
  if($error)
  {
    echo 'Your message was not stored.
          Make sure you have filled in all fields and try again.';
  }

  do_html_footer();
?>
```

After some initial setup, the new_post.php script checks whether the parent is 0 (zero) or otherwise. If it is 0, this topic is new, and little further work is needed.

If this message is a reply ($parent is the postid of an existing article), the script goes ahead and sets up the title and text of the original message, as follows:

```
// get post name
$title = get_post_title($parent);

// append Re:
if(strstr($title, 'Re: ') == false )
  $title = 'Re: '.$title;

//make sure title will still fit in db
$title = substr($title, 0, 20);

//prepend a quoting pattern to the post you are replying to
$message = add_quoting(get_post_message($parent));
```

The functions used here are get_post_title(), get_post_message(), and add_quoting(). These functions, all from the discussion_fns.php library, are shown in Listings 31.9, 31.10, and 31.11, respectively.

Listing 31.9   get_post_title() **Function from** discussion_fns.php—**Retrieves a Message's Title from the Database**

```
function get_post_title($postid)
{
  // extract one post's name from the database

  if(!$postid) return '';

  $conn = db_connect();
```

Listing 31.9 **Continued**

```
//get all header information from 'header'
$query = "select title from header where postid = $postid";
$result = $conn->query($query);
if($result->num_rows!=1)
  return '';
$this_row = $result->fetch_array();
return $this_row[0];


}
```

Listing 31.10 get_post_message() **Function from** discussion_fns.php—
Retrieves a Message's Body from the Database

```
function get_post_message($postid)
{
  // extract one post's message from the database

  if(!$postid) return '';

  $conn = db_connect();

  $query = "select message from body where postid = $postid";
  $result = $conn->query($query);
  if($result->num_rows>0)
  {
    $this_row = $result->fetch_array();
    return $this_row[0];
  }
}
```

These first two functions retrieve an article's header and body, respectively, from the database.

Listing 31.11 add_quoting() **Function from** discussion_fns.php—**Indents a Message Text with > Symbols**

```
function add_quoting($string, $pattern = '> ')
{
  // add a quoting pattern to mark text quoted in your reply
  return $pattern.str_replace("\n", "\n$pattern", $string);
}
```

The `add_quoting()` function reformats the string to begin each line of the original text with a symbol, which defaults to >.

After the user types in his reply and clicks the Post button, he is taken to the `store_new_post.php` script. Sample output from this script is shown in Figure 31.9.

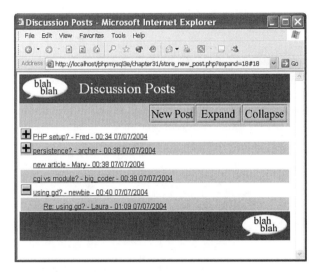

Figure 31.9   The new post is now visible in the tree.

The new post is shown in the figure, under `Re: using gd? - Laura - 01:09 07/07/2004`. Other than that, this page looks like the regular `index.php` page.

Let's look at the code for `store_new_post.php`, shown in Listing 31.12.

Listing 31.12   `store_new_post.php`—Puts the New Post in the Database

```php
<?php
  include ('include_fns.php');
  if($id = store_new_post($_POST))
  {
    include ('index.php');
  }
  else
  {
    $error = true;
    include ('new_post.php');
  }

?>
```

As you can see, this script is short. Its main task is to call the store_new_post() function, which is shown in Listing 31.13. This page has no visual content of its own. If storing succeeds, you see the index page. Otherwise, you go back to the new_post.php page
so that the user can try again.

Listing 31.13 store_new_post() **Function from** discussion_fns.php—**Validates
and Stores the New Post in the Database**

```
function store_new_post($post)
{
  // validate clean and store a new post

  $conn = db_connect();
  // check no fields are blank
  if(!filled_out($post))
  {
    return false;
  }
  $post = clean_all($post);

  //check parent exists
  if($post['parent']!=0)
  {
    $query = "select postid from header where postid = '".$post['parent']."'";
    $result = $conn->query($query);
    if($result->num_rows!=1)
    {
      return false;
    }
  }

  // check not a duplicate
  $query = "select header.postid from header, body where
            header.postid = body.postid and
            header.parent = ".$post['parent']." and
            header.poster = '".$post['poster']."' and
            header.title = '".$post['title']."' and
            header.area = ".$post['area']." and
            body.message = '".$post['message']."'";
  $result = $conn->query($query);
  if (!$result)
  {
    return false;
  }
  if($result->num_rows>0)
  {
```

Listing 31.13   **Continued**

```php
    $this_row = $result->fetch_array();
    return $this_row[0];
}
$query = "insert into header values
          ('".$post['parent']."',
           '".$post['poster']."',
           '".$post['title']."',
           0,
           '".$post['area']."',
           now(),
           NULL
          )";
$result = $conn->query($query);
if (!$result)
{
    return false;
}

// note that our parent now has a child
$query = 'update header set children = 1 where postid = '.$post['parent'];
$result = $conn->query($query);
if (!$result)
{
    return false;
}

// find our post id, note that there could be multiple headers
// that are the same except for id and probably posted time
$query = "select header.postid from header left join body
                on header.postid = body.postid
                where parent = '".$post['parent']."'
                and poster = '".$post['poster']."'
                and title = '".$post['title']."'
                and body.postid is NULL";
$result = $conn->query($query);
if (!$result)
{
    return false;
}
if($result->num_rows>0)
{
  $this_row = $result->fetch_array();
  $id = $this_row[0];
}
if($id)
```

Listing 31.13 **Continued**

```
{
    $query = "insert into body values ($id, '".$post['message']."')";
    $result = $conn->query($query);
    if (!$result)
    {
        return false;
    }

    return $id;
}

}
```

This function is long but not overly complex. It is only long because inserting a posting means inserting entries in the header and body tables and updating the parent article's row in the header table to show that it now has children.

That is the end of the code for the web forum application.

Adding Extensions

There are many extensions you could add to this project:

- You could add navigation to the view options so that from a post, you could navigate to the next message, the previous message, the next-in-thread message, or the previous-in-thread message.

- You could add an administration interface for setting up new forums and deleting old posts.

- You could add user authentication so that only registered users could post.

- You could add some kind of moderation or censorship mechanism.

Look at existing systems for ideas.

Using an Existing System

One noteworthy existing system is Phorum, an open source web forums project. It has different navigation and semantics from the one we created here, but its structure is relatively easily customized to fit into your own site. A notable feature of Phorum is that it can be configured by the actual user to display in either a threaded or flat view. You can find out more about it at

http://www.phorum.org

Next

In Chapter 32, "Generating Personalized Documents in Portable Document Format (PDF)," you use the PDF format to deliver documents that are attractive, print consistently, and are somewhat tamperproof. This capability is useful for a range of service-based applications, such as generating contracts online.

32

Generating Personalized Documents in Portable Document Format (PDF)

O N SERVICE-DRIVEN SITES, YOU SOMETIMES NEED TO deliver personalized documents, generated in response to input from your visitors. This input can be used to provide an automatically filled-in form or to generate personalized documents, such as legal documents, letters, or certificates.

The example in this chapter presents a user with an online skill assessment page and generates a certificate. We explain how to

- Use PHP string processing to integrate a template with a user's data to create a Rich Text Format (RTF) document
- Use a similar approach to generate a Portable Document Format (PDF) document
- Use PHP's PDFlib functions to generate a similar PDF document

The Problem

For this project, you give your visitors an exam consisting of a number of questions. If they answer enough of the questions correctly, you will generate a certificate for them to show that they have passed the exam.

So that a computer can mark the questions easily, they are multiple choice, consisting of a question and a number of potential answers. Only one of the potential answers for each question is correct.

If a user achieves a passing grade on the questions, he will be presented with a certificate.

Ideally, the file format for the certificate should

1. Be easy to design
2. Be able to contain a variety of different elements such as bitmap and vector images
3. Result in a high-quality printout
4. Require only a small file to be downloaded
5. Be generated almost instantly
6. Be at a low cost to produce
7. Work on many operating systems
8. Be difficult to fraudulently duplicate or modify
9. Not require any special software to view or print
10. Display and print consistently for all recipients

Like many decisions you need to make from time to time, you will probably need to compromise when choosing a delivery format to meet as many of these 10 attributes as possible.

Evaluating Document Formats

The most important decision you need to make is what format to deliver the certificate in. Options include paper, ASCII text, HTML, Microsoft Word or another word processor's format, Rich Text Format, PostScript, and Portable Document Format. Given the 10 attributes listed previously, you can consider and compare some of the options.

Paper

Delivering the certificate on paper has some obvious advantages. You retain complete control over the process. You can see exactly what each certificate output looks like before sending it to the recipient. Plus, you don't need to worry about software or bandwidth, and the certificate can be printed with anticounterfeiting measures.

Paper would meet all of your needs except for attributes 5 and 6: The certificate could not be created and delivered quickly. Postal delivery could take days or weeks depending on your and the recipient's location.

Each certificate would also cost a few cents to a few dollars in printing and postage costs and probably more in handling. Automatic electronic delivery would be cheaper.

ASCII

Delivering documents as ASCII or plain text comes with some advantages. Compatibility is no problem. Bandwidth required would be small, so cost would be very low. The simplicity of the result makes it easy to design and quick for a script to generate.

If you present your visitors with an ASCII file, however, you have very little control over the appearance of their certificates. You cannot control fonts or page breaks. You can only include text and have very little control over formatting. You have no control over a recipient's duplication or modification of the document. This is the method that makes it easiest for the recipient to fraudulently alter her certificate.

HTML

An obvious choice for delivering a document on the Web is HTML. Hypertext Markup Language is specifically designed for this purpose. As you are no doubt already aware, it includes formatting control, syntax to include objects such as images, and is compatible (with some variation) with a variety of operating systems and software. It is fairly simple, so it is both easy to design and quick for a script to generate and deliver.

Drawbacks to using HTML for this application include limited support for print-related formatting such as page breaks, little consistency in the output on different platforms and programs, and variable quality printing. In addition, although HTML can include any type of external element, the capability of the browser to display or use these elements cannot be guaranteed for unusual types.

Word Processor Formats

Particularly for intranet projects, providing documents as word processor documents makes some sense. However, for an Internet project, using a proprietary word processor format will exclude some visitors, but given its market dominance, Microsoft Word would make sense. Most users will either have access to Word or to a word processor that will try to read Word files such as OpenOffice Writer.

> Windows users without Word can download the freeware Word Viewer from
> http://www.microsoft.com/office/000/viewers.asp

Generating a document as a Microsoft Word document has some advantages. As long as you have a copy of Word, designing a document is easy. You have very good control over the printed appearance of your documents and a lot of flexibility with its contents. You can also make it relatively difficult for the recipient to modify by telling Word to ask for a password.

Unfortunately, Word files can be large, particularly if they contain images or other complex elements. There is also no easy way to generate them dynamically with PHP. The format is documented but is a binary format, and the format documentation comes with license conditions. It is possible to generate Word documents with a COM object, but it's definitely not simple.

Another new possibility you may now consider is OpenOffice Writer, which has the dual advantages of not being proprietary software and using an XML-based file format.

Word 2003 now also supports an XML file format natively. The Document Type Definition (DTD) for Word and other Office products can be downloaded from Microsoft.com. Look for "Office 2003 XML Reference Schemas." This would be a valid option, but not a simple one.

Rich Text Format

Rich Text Format (or RTF) gives you most of the power of Word, but the files are easier to generate. You still have flexibility over layout and formatting of the printed page. You can still include elements such as vector or bitmap images. Plus, you can still be fairly sure that the users will see a similar result to yours when they view or print the document.

RTF is Microsoft Word's text format. It is intended as an interchange format to transfer documents between different programs. In some ways, it is similar to HTML. It uses syntax and key words rather than binary data to convey formatting information. It is therefore relatively human readable.

The format is well documented. The specification is freely available and can be found here:

http://msdn.microsoft.com/library/default.asp?url=/library/en-us/dnrtfspec/html/ rtfspec.asp

The easiest way to generate an RTF document is to choose a Save As RTF option in your word processor. Because RTF files contain only text, it is possible to generate them directly, and existing ones can easily be modified.

Because the format is documented and freely available, RTF is readable by more software than Word's binary format. Be aware, though, that users opening a complex RTF file in older versions of Word or different word processors will often see somewhat different results. Each new version of Word introduces new keywords to RTF, so older implementations usually ignore controls they do not understand or have chosen not to implement.

From the original list, an RTF certificate would be easy to design using Word or another word processor; is able to contain a variety of different elements such as vector and bitmap images; gives a high-quality printout; can be generated easily and quickly; and can be delivered electronically at low cost.

This format works with a variety of applications and operating systems, although with somewhat variable results. On the downside, an RTF document can be easily and freely modified by anybody, which is a problem for a certificate and some other types of documents. The file size might be moderately large for complex documents.

RTF is a good option for many document delivery applications, so you can use it as one option here.

PostScript

PostScript, from Adobe, is a page description language. It is a powerful and complex programming language intended to represent documents in a device-independent way—that is, a description that will produce consistent results across different devices such as printers and screens. It is very well documented. At least three full-length books are available, as well as countless Web sites.

A PostScript document can contain very precise formatting, text, images, embedded fonts, and other elements. You can easily generate a PostScript document from an application by printing it to a PostScript printer driver. If you are interested, you can even learn to program in it directly.

PostScript documents are quite portable. They give consistent high-quality printouts from different devices and different operating systems.

There are a couple of significant downsides to using PostScript to distribute documents:

- The files can be huge.
- Many people will need to download additional software to use them.

Most Unix users can deal with PostScript files, but Windows users usually need to download a viewer such as GSview, which uses the Ghostscript PostScript interpreter. This software is available for a wide variety of platforms. Although it is available free, we do not really want to force people to download more software.

You can read more about Ghostscript at
http://www.ghostscript.com/

and download it from
http://www.cs.wisc.edu/~ghost/

For the current application, PostScript scores very well for consistent high-quality output but falls short on most of the other needs.

Portable Document Format

Fortunately, there is a format with most of the power of PostScript, but with significant advantages. The Portable Document Format (also from Adobe) was designed as a way to distribute documents that would behave consistently on different platforms and deliver predictable high-quality output onscreen or on paper.

Adobe describes PDF as "the open de facto standard for electronic document distribution worldwide. Adobe PDF is a universal file format that preserves all of the fonts, formatting, colors, and graphics of any source document, regardless of the application and platform used to create it. PDF files are compact and can be shared, viewed, navigated, and printed exactly as intended by anyone with a free Adobe Acrobat Reader."

PDF is an open format, and documentation is available from this site:
http://partners.adobe.com/asn/tech/pdf/specifications.jsp

It is also available from many other Web sites and an official book.

Judged against the desired attributes, PDF looks very good: PDF documents give consistent, high-quality output; are capable of containing elements such as bitmap and vector images; can use compression to create a small file; can be delivered electronically and cheaply; are usable on the major operating systems; and can include security controls.

Working against PDF is the fact that most of the software used to create PDF documents is commercial. A reader is required to view PDF files, but the Acrobat Reader is available free for Windows, Unix, and Macintosh from Adobe. Many visitors to your site will already be familiar with the .pdf extension and will most likely already have the reader installed.

PDF files are a good way to distribute attractive, printable documents, particularly ones that you do not want recipients to be able to easily modify.

Next, we look at two different ways to generate a PDF certificate.

Solution Components

To get the system working, you need to be able to examine users' knowledge and (assuming that they pass your test) generate a certificate reporting their performance. For this project, you experiment with generating this certificate in three different ways: two using PDF and one using RTF.

Let's look at the requirements of each of these components in some detail.

Question and Answer System

Providing a flexible system for online assessment that allows a variety of different question types, various media types for supporting information, useful feedback on wrong answers, and clever statistic gathering and reporting would be a complex task on its own.

In this chapter, we are mainly interested in the challenge of generating customized documents for delivery over the Web, so we explain how to build only a very simple quiz system. The quiz does not rely on any special software. It uses an HTML form to ask questions and a PHP script to process the answers. You have been doing this since Chapter 1, "PHP Crash Course."

Document Generation Software

No additional software is needed on the Web server to generate RTF or PDF documents from templates, but you need software to create the templates. To use the PHP PDF creation functions, you need to have compiled PDF support into PHP. (We discuss this topic shortly.)

Software to Create RTF Template

You can use the word processor of your choice to generate RTF files. We used Microsoft Word to create our certificate template, which is included on the CD-ROM in the Chapter 32 directory.

If you prefer another word processor, it would still be a good idea to test the output in Word because the majority of your visitors will be using this software.

Software to Create PDF Template

PDF documents are a little more difficult to generate. The easiest way is to purchase Adobe Acrobat. This software allows you to create high-quality PDFs from various applications. We used Acrobat to create the template file for this project.

To create the file, we used Microsoft Word to design a document. One of the tools in the Acrobat package is Adobe Distiller. Within Distiller, we needed to select a few non-default options. The file must be stored in ASCII format, and compression needs to be turned off. After these options are set, creating a PDF file is as easy as printing.

You can find out more about Acrobat here:

http://www.adobe.com/products/acrobat/

You can either buy it online or from a regular software retailer.

Another option to create PDFs is the conversion program `ps2pdf`, which, as the name suggests, converts PostScript files into PDF files. This option has the advantage of being free but does not always produce good output for documents with images or nonstandard fonts. The `ps2pdf` converter comes with the Ghostscript package mentioned previously.

Obviously, if you are going to create a PDF file this way, you will need to create a PostScript file first. Unix users typically use either the `a2ps` or `dvips` utilities for this purpose.

If you are working in a Windows environment, you can also create PostScript files without Adobe Distiller, albeit via a slightly more complicated process. You need to install a PostScript printer driver. For example, you can use the Apple LaserWriter IINT driver. If you don't have a PostScript driver installed, you can download one from Adobe at

http://www.adobe.com/support/downloads/product.jsp?product=44&platform=
Windows

To create your PostScript file, you need to select this printer and the Print to File option, typically found on the Print dialog box.

Most Windows applications then produce a file with a `.prn` extension. This should be a PostScript file. You should probably rename it to be a `.ps` file. You should then be able to view it using GSview or another PostScript viewer, or create a PDF file using the `ps2pdf` utility.

Be aware that different printer drivers produce PostScript output of varying quality. You might find that some of the PostScript files you produce give errors when run through the `ps2pdf` utility. We suggest using a different printer driver.

If you intend to create only a small number of PDF files, Adobe's online service might suit you. For $9.99 a month, you can upload files in a number of formats and download a PDF file. The service worked well for our certificate, but it does not let you select options that are important for this project. The PDF created will be stored as a binary file and compressed. This makes it very difficult to modify.

This service can be found at

https://createpdf.adobe.com/

A free trial option is available for this service if you want to test it.

You can also check out a free FTP-based interface to ps2pdf at the Net Distillery: http://www.babinszki.com/distiller/

A final option would be to encode the certificate in XML and use XML Style Sheet Transformations (XSLT) to convert it to PDF and any other desired formats. This method requires a good understanding of XSLT and is not covered here.

Software to Create PDF Programmatically

Support for creating PDF documents is available from within PHP. Several different function libraries are available, with similar intentions.

PHP's PDFlib functions use the PDFlib library, available from http://www.pdflib.com

The ClibPDF functions use the ClibPDF library, available from http://www.fastio.com/

Both of these libraries are similar. They provide an API of functions to generate a PDF document. We elected to use PDFlib for this project because it seems to be updated and maintained more regularly.

It is worth noting that neither library is Free Software. Both permit some noncommercial use without charge but require a license fee if you intend to provide a commercial service using them.

Some free libraries, such as FPDF, are starting to become available. FPDF is not yet as feature rich as the commercial libraries. Also, because FPDF is written in PHP (rather than in C as a PHP extension), it is a little slower than the other two. You can download FPDF from

http://www.fpdf.org/

In this chapter, we use PDFlib because it is probably the most commonly used extension.

You can see whether PDFlib is already installed on your system by checking the output of the function phpinfo(). Under the heading pdf, you can find out whether PDFlib support is enabled, as well as the version of PDFlib used.

If you intend to use TIFF or JPEG images in your PDF documents, you will also need to install the TIFF library, available from

http://www.libtiff.org/

and the JPEG library, available from
ftp://ftp.uu.net/graphics/jpeg/

On a Unix system, PDFlib now also contains prebuilt shared object libraries for PHP 4.3 and 5.0. They can be loaded from php.ini or with dl(), so there is no need to recompile to add this functionality.

On a Windows server, the PDFlib DLL is bundled in the PHP ZIP file, so you just need to uncomment the extension in your php.ini file.

Solution Overview

In this project, you produce a system with three possible outcomes. As you can see in Figure 32.1, you ask quiz questions, assess the answers, and then generate a certificate in one of three ways:

- You generate an RTF document from a blank template.
- You generate a PDF document from a blank template.
- You generate a PDF document programmatically via PDFlib.

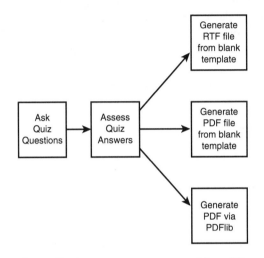

Figure 32.1   The certification system generates one of three different certificates.

A summary of the files in the certification project is shown in Table 32.1.

Table 32.1   **Files in the Certification Application**

Name	Type	Description
index.html	HTML page	HTML form that contains the quiz questions
score.php	Application	Script to assess users' answers
rtf.php	Application	Script to generate an RTF certificate from the template
pdf.php	Application	Script to generate a PDF certificate from the template
pdflib.php	Application	Script to generate a PDF certificate using PDFlib
signature.png	Image	Bitmap image of the signature to be included on the PDFlib certificate
PHPCertification.rtf	RTF	RTF certificate template
PHPCertification.pdf	PDF	PDF certificate template

Now let's look at the application.

Asking the Questions

The file `index.html` is straightforward. It needs to contain an HTML form asking the user for his name and the answers to a number of questions. In a real assessment application, you would most likely retrieve these questions from a database. Here, you focus on producing the certificate, so you just hard-code some questions into the HTML.

The `name` field is a text input. Each question has three radio buttons to allow the user to indicate his preferred answer. The form has an image button as a submit button.

The code for this page is shown in Listing 32.1.

Listing 32.1 `index.html`—**HTML Page Containing Quiz Questions**

```html
<html>
  <body>
    <h1><p align="center">
          <img src="rosette.gif" alt="">
          Certification
          <img src="rosette.gif" alt=""></p></h1>
    <p>You too can earn your highly respected PHP certification
       from the world famous Fictional Institute of PHP Certification.</p>
    <p>Simply answer the questions below:</p>

    <form action="score.php" method="post">

      <p>Your Name <input type="text" name="name" /></p>

      <p>What does the PHP statement echo do?</p>
      <ol>
        <li><input type="radio" name="q1" value="1" />
            Outputs strings.</li>
        <li><input type="radio" name="q1" value="2" />
            Adds two numbers together.</li>
        <li><input type="radio" name="q1" value="3" />
            Creates a magical elf to finish writing your code.</li>
      </ol>

      <p>What does the PHP function cos() do?</p>
      <ol>
        <li><input type="radio" name="q2" value="1" />
            Calculates a cosine in radians.</li>
        <li><input type="radio" name="q2" value="2" />
            Calculates a tangent in radians. </li>
        <li><input type="radio" name="q2" value="3" />
            It is not a PHP function. It is a lettuce. </li>
      </ol>
```

Listing 32.1   **Continued**

```
    <p>What does the PHP function mail() do?</p>
    <ol>
      <li><input type="radio" name="q3" value="1" />
          Sends a mail message.
      <li><input type="radio" name="q3" value="2" />
          Checks for new mail.
      <li><input type="radio" name="q3" value="3" />
          Toggles PHP between male and female mode.
    </ol>

    <p align="center"><input type="image" src="certify-me.gif" border="0"></p>

  </form>
 </body>
</html>
```

The result of loading index.html in a Web browser is shown in Figure 32.2.

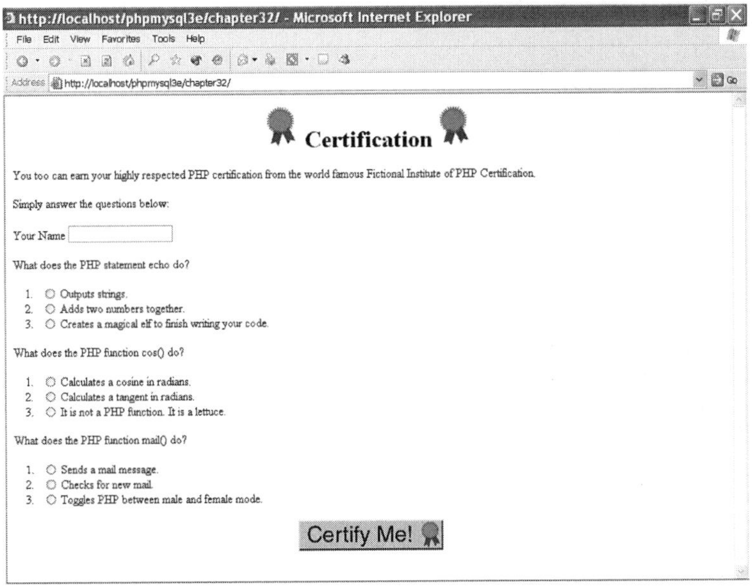

Figure 32.2   The index.html page asks the user to answer quiz questions.

Grading the Answers

When the user submits his answers to the questions in `index.html`, you need to grade him and calculate a score. This is done by the script called `score.php`, shown in Listing 32.2.

Listing 32.2 `score.php`—**Script to Mark Exams**

```php
<?php
  //create short variable names
  $q1 = $_POST['q1'];
  $q2 = $_POST['q2'];
  $q3 = $_POST['q3'];
  $name = $_POST['name'];

  // check that all the data was received
  if($q1==''||$q2==''||$q3==''||$name=='')
  {
    echo '<h1><p align = "center"><img src="rosette.gif" alt="">
                              Sorry:
                              <img src="rosette.gif" alt=""></p></h1>';
    echo '<p>You need to fill in your name and answer all questions</p>';
  }
  else
  {
    //add up the scores
    $score = 0;
    if($q1 == 1) // the correct answer for q1 is 1
      $score++;
    if($q2 == 1) // the correct answer for q2 is 1
      $score++;
    if($q3 == 1) // the correct answer for q3 is 1
      $score++;

    //convert score to a percentage
    $score = $score / 3 * 100;

    if($score < 50)
    {
      // this person failed
      echo '<h1 align="center"><img src="rosette.gif" alt="" />
                              Sorry:
                              <img src="rosette.gif" alt="" /></h1>';
      echo '<p>You need to score at least 50% to pass the exam</p>';
    }
    else
    {
```

Listing 32.2 **Continued**

```php
    // create a string containing the score to one decimal place
    $score = number_format($score, 1);

    echo '<h1 align="center"><img src="rosette.gif" alt="" />
                            Congratulations
                            <img src="rosette.gif" alt="" /></h1>';
    echo "<p>Well done $name, with a score of $score%,
            you have passed the exam.</p>";

    // provide links to scripts that generate the certificates
    echo '<p>Please click here to download your certificate as
            a Microsoft Word (RTF) file.</p>';
    echo '<form action="rtf.php" method="post">';
    echo '<center>
            <input type="image" src="certificate.gif" border="0">
            </center>';
    echo '<input type="hidden" name="score" value="'.$score.'">';
    echo '<input type="hidden" name="name" value="'.$name.'">';
    echo '</form>';

    echo '<p>Please click here to download your certificate as
            a Portable Document Format (PDF) file.</p>';
    echo '<form action="pdf.php" method="post">';
    echo '<center>
            <input type="image" src="certificate.gif" border="0">
            </center>';
    echo '<input type="hidden" name="score" value="'.$score.'">';
    echo '<input type="hidden" name="name" value="'.$name.'">';
    echo '</form>';

    echo '<p>Please click here to download your certificate as
            a Portable Document Format (PDF) file generated with PDFLib.</p>';
    echo '<form action="pdflib.php" method="post">';
    echo '<center>
            <input type="image" src="certificate.gif" border="0">
            </center>';
    echo '<input type="hidden" name="score" value="'.$score.'">';
    echo '<input type="hidden" name="name" value="'.$name.'">';
    echo '</form>';
    }
  }
?>
```

This script displays a message if the user did not answer all questions or scored less than the chosen pass mark.

If the user successfully answered the questions, he will be allowed to generate a certificate. The output of a successful visit is shown in Figure 32.3.

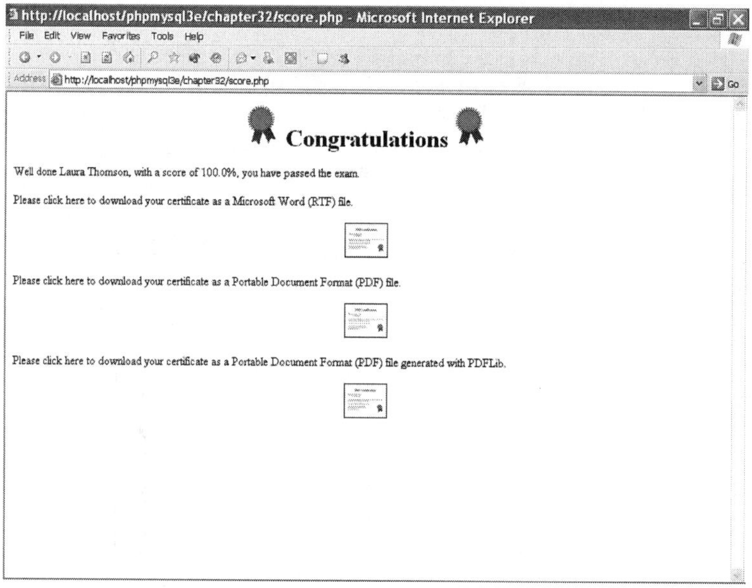

Figure 32.3   The `score.php` script presents successful visitors with the
option to generate a certificate in one of three ways.

From here, the user has three options: He can have an RTF certificate or one of two PDF certificates. Next, we look at the script responsible for each.

Generating an RTF Certificate

There is nothing to stop you from generating an RTF document by writing ASCII text to a file or a string variable, but doing so would mean learning yet another set of syntax.

Here is a simple RTF document:

```
{\rtf1
{\fonttbl {\f0 Arial;}{\f1 Times New Roman;}}
\f0\fs28 Heading\par
\f1\fs20 This is an rtf document.\par
}
```

This document sets up a font table with two fonts: Arial, to be referred to as f0, and Times New Roman, to be referred to as f1. It then writes Heading using f0 (Arial) in size 28 (14 point). The control \par indicates a paragraph break. It then writes This is an rtf document using f1 (Times New Roman) at size 20 (10 point).

You could generate a document like this manually, but no labor-saving functions are built into PHP to make the hard parts, such as incorporating graphics, easier. Fortunately, in many documents, the structure, style, and much of the text are static, and only small parts change from person to person. A more efficient way to generate a document is to use a template.

You can build a complex document, such as the one shown in Figure 32.4, easily using a word processor.

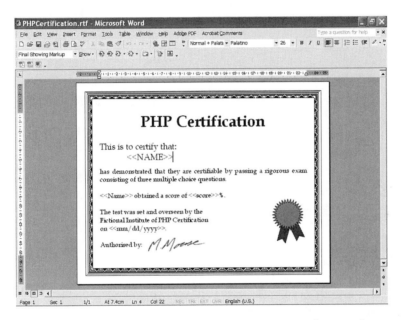

Figure 32.4 Using a word processor, you can create a complex, attractive
template easily.

The template includes placeholders such as <<NAME>> to mark the places where dynamic data will be inserted. It is not important what these placeholders look like. You use a meaningful description between two sets of angled braces. It is important that you choose placeholders that are highly unlikely to accidentally appear in the rest of the document. It will help you to lay out your template if the placeholders are roughly the same length as the data they will be replaced with.

The placeholders in this document are <<NAME>>, <<Name>>, <<score>>, and <<mm/dd/yyyy>>. Note that you use both NAME and Name because you will use a case-sensitive method to replace them.

Now that you have a template, you need a script to personalize it. This script, called rtf.php, is shown in Listing 32.3.

Listing 32.3 rtf.php—Script to Produce a Personalized RTF Certificate

```php
<?php
  //create short variable names
  $name = $_POST['name'];
  $score = $_POST['score'];
  // check we have the parameters we need
  if( !$name || !$score )
  {
    echo '<h1>Error:</h1><p>This page was called incorrectly</p>';
  }
  else
  {
    //generate the headers to help a browser choose the correct application
    header( 'Content-Type: application/msword' );
    header( 'Content-Disposition: inline, filename=cert.rtf');

    $date = date( 'F d, Y' );

    // open our template file
    $filename = 'PHPCertification.rtf';
    $output = file_get_contents($filename);

    // replace the place holders in the template with our data
    $output = str_replace( '<<NAME>>', strtoupper( $name ), $output );
    $output = str_replace( '<<Name>>', $name, $output );
    $output = str_replace( '<<score>>', $score, $output );
    $output = str_replace( '<<mm/dd/yyyy>>', $date, $output );

    // send the generated document to the browser
    echo $output;
  }
?>
```

This script performs some basic error checking to make sure that all the user details have been passed in and then moves to the business of creating the certificate.

The output of this script will be an RTF file rather than an HTML file, so you need to alert the user's browser to this fact. This is important so that the browser can attempt to open the file with the correct application or give a Save As... type dialog box if it doesn't recognize the .rtf extension.

You specify the MIME type of the file you are outputting by using PHP's `header()` function to send the appropriate HTTP header as follows:

```
header('Content-Type: application/msword');
header('Content-Disposition: inline, filename=cert.rtf');
```

The first header tells the browser that you are sending a Microsoft Word file (not strictly true, but the most likely helper application for opening the RTF file).

The second header tells the browser to automatically display the contents of the file and that its suggested filename is `cert.rtf`. This is the default filename the user will see if he tries to save the file from within his browser.

After the headers are sent, you open and read the template RTF file into the `$output` variable and use the `str_replace()` function to replace the placeholders with the actual data that you want to appear in the file. The line

```
$output = str_replace( '<<Name>>', $name, $output );
```

replaces any occurrences of the placeholder `<<Name>>` with the contents of the variable `$name`.

Having made your substitutions, it's just a matter of echoing the output to the browser. A sample result from the `rtf.php` script is shown in Figure 32.5.

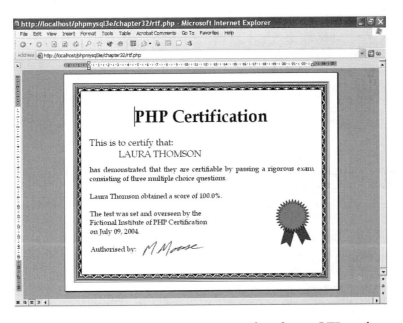

Figure 32.5 The `rtf.php` script generates a certificate from an RTF template.

This approach works very well. The calls to `str_replace()` run very quickly, even though the template and therefore the contents of $output are fairly long. The main problem from the point of view of this application is that the user will load the certificate in his word processor to print it. This is probably an invitation for people to modify the output. RTF does not allow you to make a read-only document.

Generating a PDF Certificate from a Template

The process of generating a PDF certificate from a template is similar. The main difference is that when you create the PDF file, some of the placeholders might be interspersed with formatting codes, depending on the version of Acrobat you are using. For example, if you look in the certificate template file you have created (using a text editor), you can see that the placeholders now look like this:

```
<<N)-13(AME)-10(>)-6(>
<<Na)-9(m)0(e)-18(>>
<)-11(<)1(sc)-17(or)-6(e)-6(>)-11(>
<)-11(<)1(m)-12(m)0(/d)-6(d)-19(/)1(yy)-13(yy)-13(>>
```

If you look through the file, you will see that, unlike RTF, this is not a format that humans can easily read through.

> **Note**
>
> The format of the PDF template file may vary depending on the version of Acrobat or other PDF generation tool you are using. The code supplied in this example may not work as written when you generate your own templates. Check your template and alter the code to suit. If you still have problems, use the PDFlib example given later in the chapter.

There are a few different ways you can deal with this situation. You could go through each of these placeholders and delete the formatting codes. Deleting them actually makes little difference to how the document looks in the end because the codes embedded in the previous template indicate how much space should be left between the letters of the placeholders that you are going to replace anyhow. However, if you take this approach, you must go through and hand-edit the PDF file and repeat this each time you change or update the file. Doing all this work is not a big deal when you're dealing with only four placeholders, but it becomes a nightmare when, for example, you have multiple documents with many placeholders, and you decide to change the letterhead on all the documents.

You can avoid this problem by using a different technique. You can use Adobe Acrobat to create a PDF form—similar to an HTML form with blank, named fields. You can then use a PHP script to create what is called an FDF (Forms Data Format) file, which is basically a set of data to be merged with a template. You can create FDFs using PHP's FDF function library: specifically, the `fdf_create()` function to create a file, the `fdf_set_value()` function to set the field values, and the `fdf_set_file()` function to set the associated template form file. You can then pass this file back to the browser with the appropriate MIME type—in this case, `vnd.fdf`—and the browser's Acrobat Reader plug-in should substitute the data into the form.

This way of doing things is neat, but it has two limitations. First, it assumes that you own a copy of Acrobat Professional (the full version, not the free reader, or even the Standard edition). Second, it is difficult to substitute in text that is inline rather than text that looks like a form field. This might or might not be a problem, depending on what you are trying to do. We largely use PDF generation for generating letters where many things must be substituted inline. FDFs do not work well for this purpose. If you are auto-filling, for example, a tax form online, this will not be a problem.

You can read more about the FDF format at Adobe's site:

http://partners.adobe.com/asn/developer/acrosdk/forms.html

You should also look at the FDF documentation in the PHP manual if you decide to use this approach:

http://www.php.net/manual/en/ref.fdf.php

We turn now to the PDF solution to the previous problem.

You can still find and replace the placeholders in the PDF file if you recognize that the additional format codes consist solely of hyphens, digits, and parentheses and can therefore be matched via a regular expression. We wrote a function, `pdf_replace()`, to automatically generate a matching regular expression for a placeholder and replace that placeholder with the appropriate text.

Note that with some versions of Acrobat, the placeholders are in plain text, and you can replace them with `str_replace()`, as you did before.

Other than this addition, the code for generating the certificate via a PDF template is similar to the RTF version. This script is shown in Listing 32.4.

Listing 32.4   `pdf.php`—**Script to Produce Personalized PDF Certificate via a Template**

```php
<?php
  set_time_limit( 180 ); // this script can be slow

  //create short variable names
  $name = $_POST['name'];
  $score = $_POST['score'];

  function pdf_replace( $pattern, $replacement, $string )
  {
    $len = strlen( $pattern ) ;
    $regex = '';
    for ( $i = 0; $i<$len; $i++ )
    {
      $regex .= $pattern[$i];
      if ($i<$len-1)
        $regex .= '(\)-?[0-9]+\()?';
    }
```

Listing 32.4 **Continued**

```php
    return ereg_replace ( $regex, $replacement, $string );
  }

  if(!$name||!$score)
  {
    echo '<h1>Error:</h1><p>This page was called incorrectly</p>';
  }
  else
  {
    //generate the headers to help a browser choose the correct application
    header( 'Content-Disposition:  filename=cert.pdf');
    header( 'Content-Type: application/pdf' );

    $date = date( 'F d, Y' );

    // open our template file
    $filename = 'PHPCertification.pdf';
    $output = file_get_contents($filename);

    // replace the place holders in the template with our data
    $output = pdf_replace( '<<NAME>>', strtoupper( $name ), $output );
    $output = pdf_replace( '<<Name>>', $name, $output );
    $output = pdf_replace( '<<score>>', $score, $output );
    $output = pdf_replace( '<<mm/dd/yyyy>>', $date, $output );

    // send the generated document to the browser

    echo $output;
  }
?>
```

This script produces a customized version of the PDF document. The document, shown in Figure 32.6, will print reliably on numerous systems, and is harder for the recipient to modify or edit. You can see that the PDF document in Figure 32.6 looks almost exactly like the RTF document in Figure 32.5.

One problem with this approach is that the code runs quite slowly because of the regular expression matching required. Regular expressions run much more slowly than `str_replace()` that you could use for the RTF version.

If you are going to match a large number of placeholders or try to generate many of these documents on the same server, you might want to look at other approaches. This issue would be less of a problem for a simpler template. Much of the bulk in this file is data representing the images.

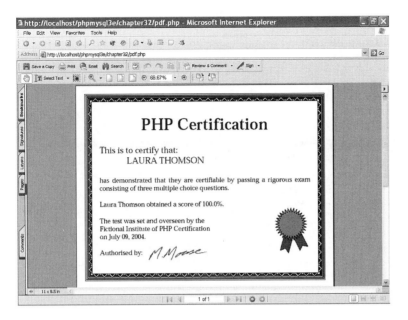

Figure 32.6   The pdf.php script generates a certificate from a
PDF template.

Generating a PDF Document Using PDFlib

PDFlib is intended for generating dynamic PDF documents via the Web. It is not strictly part of PHP, but rather a separate library, with a large number of functions intended to be called from a wide variety of programming languages. Language bindings are available for C, C++, Java, Perl, Python, Tcl, and ActiveX/COM.

Since PHP 4.0.5, PDFlib has been officially supported by PDFlib GmbH. This means that you can refer to either the PHP documentation at

http://www.php.net/en/manual/ref.pdf.php

or download the official documentation from pdflib.com.

A Hello World Script for PDFlib

After you have PHP and have installed it with PDFlib enabled, you can test it with a simple program such as the Hello World example in Listing 32.5.

Listing 32.5 `testpdf.php`—**Classic Hello World Example Using PDFlib via PHP**

```php
<?php

  // create a pdf document in memory
  $pdf = pdf_new();
  pdf_open_file($pdf, '');

  pdf_set_info($pdf, "Creator", "pdftest.php");
  pdf_set_info($pdf, "Author", "Luke Welling and Laura Thomson");
  pdf_set_info($pdf, "Title", "Hello World (PHP)");

  // US letter is 11" x 8.5" and there are 72 points per inch
  pdf_begin_page($pdf, 8.5*72, 11*72);

  // add a bookmark
  pdf_add_bookmark($pdf, 'Page 1', 0, 0);

  $font = pdf_findfont($pdf, 'Times-Roman', 'host', 0);
  pdf_setfont($pdf, $font, 24);
  pdf_set_text_pos($pdf, 50, 700);

  // write text
  pdf_show($pdf,'Hello,world!');
  pdf_continue_text($pdf,'(says PHP)');

  // end the document
  pdf_end_page($pdf);
  pdf_close($pdf);

  $data = pdf_get_buffer($pdf);

  // generate the headers to help a browser choose the correct application
  header('Content-Type: application/pdf') ;
  header('Content-Disposition: inline; filename=test.pdf');
  header('Content-Length: ' . strlen($data));

  // output PDF
  echo $data;

?>
```

The most likely error you will see if this script fails is the following:

```
Fatal error: Call to undefined function pdf_new()
in c:\program files\apache group\Apache\htdocs\phpmysql3e\chapter32\testpdf.php
on line 4
```

This message means that you do not have the PDFlib extension compiled or enabled into PHP.

The installation is fairly straightforward, but some details change depending on the exact versions of PHP and PDFlib that you are using. A good place to check for detailed suggestions is the user-contributed notes on the PDFlib page in the annotated PHP manual.

When you have this script up and running on your system, it is time to look at how it works. The lines

```
$pdf = pdf_new();
pdf_open_file($pdf, '');
```

initialize a PDF document in memory.

The function `pdf_set_info()` enables you to tag the document with a subject; title; creator; author; list of keywords; and one custom, user-defined field.

Here, you set a creator, author, and title. Note that all six info fields are optional:

```
pdf_set_info($pdf, 'Creator', 'pdftest.php');
pdf_set_info($pdf, 'Author', 'Luke Welling and Laura Thomson');
pdf_set_info($pdf, 'Title', 'Hello World (PHP)');
```

A PDF document consists of a number of pages. To start a new page, you need to call `pdf_begin_page()`. As well as the identifier returned by `pdf_open()`, `pdf_begin_page()` requires the dimensions of the page. Each page in a document can be a different size, but unless you have a good reason not to, you should use a common paper size.

PDFlib works in points, both for page size, and for locating coordinate locations on each page. For reference, A4 is approximately 595 by 842 points, and U.S. letter paper is 612 by 792 points. This means that the line

```
pdf_begin_page($pdf, 8.5*72, 11*72);
```

creates a page in the document, sized for U.S. letter paper.

A PDF document does not need to be just a printable document. Many PDF features can be included in the document, such as hyperlinks and bookmarks. The function `pdf_add_outline()` adds a bookmark to the document outline. The bookmarks in a document appear in a separate pane in Acrobat Reader, allowing you to skip straight to important sections.

The line

```
pdf_add_bookmark($pdf, 'Page 1', 0, 0);
```

adds a bookmark labeled Page 1, which refers to the current page.

Fonts available on systems vary from operating system to operating system and even from individual machine to machine. To guarantee consistent results, a set of core fonts works with every PDF reader. The 14 core fonts are

- Courier
- Courier-Bold
- Courier-Oblique
- Courier-BoldOblique
- Helvetica
- Helvetica-Bold
- Helvetica-Oblique
- Helvetica-BoldOblique
- Times-Roman
- Times-Bold
- Times-Italic
- Times-BoldItalic
- Symbol
- ZapfDingbats

Fonts outside this set can be embedded in documents, but this increases the file size and might not be acceptable under whatever license you own that particular font under. You can choose a font, its size, and character encoding as follows:

```
$font = pdf_findfont($pdf, 'Times-Roman', 'host', 0);
pdf_setfont($pdf, $font, 24);
```

Font sizes are specified in points. In this case, we chose host character encoding. The allowable values are winansi, builtin, macroman, ebcdic, or host. The meanings of the different values are as follows:

- winansi—Uses ISO 8859-1 plus special characters added by Microsoft, such as a Euro symbol.
- builtin—Uses the encoding built into the font. Normally used with non-Latin fonts and symbols.
- macroman—Uses Mac Roman encoding. The default Macintosh character set.
- ebcdic—Uses EBCDIC as used on IBM AS/400 systems.
- host—Automatically selects macroman on a Macintosh, ebcdic on an EBCDIC-based system, and winansi on all other systems.

If you do not need to include special characters, the choice of encoding is not important.

A PDF document is not like an HTML document or a word processor document. Text does not by default start at the top left and flow onto other lines as required. You need to choose where to place each line of text. As already mentioned, PDF uses points to specify locations. The origin (the x,y coordinate [0, 0]) is at the bottom-left corner of the page.

Given that the page is 612 by 792 points, the point (50, 700) is about two-thirds of an inch from the left of the page and about one-and-one-third inches from the top. To set the text position at this point, you use

```
pdf_set_text_pos($pdf, 50, 700);
```

Finally, having set up the page, you can write some text on it. To add text at the current position using the current font, you use `pdf_show()`.

The line

```
pdf_show($pdf,'Hello,world!');
```

adds the text `"Hello World!"` to the document.

To move to the next line and write more text, you use `pdf_continue_text()`. To add the string `"(says PHP)"`, you use

```
pdf_continue_text($pdf,'(says PHP)');
```

The exact location where this text will appear depends on the font and size selected.

If, rather than lines or phrases, you are using contiguous paragraphs, you might find the function `pdf_show_boxed()` more useful. It allows you to declare a text box and flow text into it.

After you have finished adding elements to a page, you need to call `pdf_end_page()` as follows:

```
pdf_end_page($pdf);
```

After you have finished the whole PDF document, you need to close it by using `pdf_close()`. When you are generating a file, you also need to close the file.

The line

```
pdf_close($pdf);
```

completes the generation of the Hello World document.

Now you can send the completed PDF to the browser:

```
$data = pdf_get_buffer($pdf);

// generate the headers to help a browser choose the correct application
header('Content-Type: application/pdf');
header('Content-Disposition: inline; filename=test.pdf');
header('Content-Length: ' . strlen($data));

// output PDF
echo $data;
```

You could also write this data to disk if you preferred. PDFlib allows you to do this by passing a filename as the second parameter to `pdf_open_file()`. At the time of writing, this feature was buggy under Windows (PHP 5.0.0). If you need to write the data to disk, you can do it manually.

This example was derived from the C language example in the PDFlib documentation and should provide a starting point.

Note that some PDFlib function parameters that are documented in the PHP manual as being optional are required in some versions of PDFlib. The document for the certificate is more complicated, including a border, a vector image, and a bitmap image. With the other two techniques, you can add these features using a word processor. With PDFlib, you must add them manually.

Generating a Certificate with PDFlib

To use PDFlib, we chose to make some compromises for this project. Although it is almost certainly possible to exactly duplicate the certificate used previously, a lot more effort would be required to generate and position each element manually rather than use a tool such as Microsoft Word to help lay out the document.

We want to use the same text as before, including the red rosette and the bitmap signature, but we are not going to try to duplicate the complex border. The complete code for this script is shown in Listing 32.6.

Listing 32.6 `pdflib.php`— **Generating a Certificate Using PDFlib**

```php
<?php

  // create short variable names
  $name = $_POST['name'];
  $score = $_POST['score'];

  if(!$name||!$score)
  {
    echo '<h1>Error:</h1><p>This page was called incorrectly</p>';
    exit;
  }
  else
  {
    $date = date( 'F d, Y' );

    // create a pdf document in memory
    $pdf = pdf_new();
    pdf_open_file($pdf, '');

    // set up name of font for later use
    $fontname = 'Times-Roman';
```

Listing 32.6   **Continued**

```php
// set up the page size in points and create page
// US letter is 11" x 8.5" and there are approximately 72 points per inch
$width = 11*72;
$height = 8.5*72;
pdf_begin_page($pdf, $width, $height);

// draw our borders
$inset = 20; // space between border and page edge
$border = 10; // width of main border line
$inner = 2; // gap within the border

//draw outer border
pdf_rect($pdf, $inset-$inner,
              $inset-$inner,
              $width-2*($inset-$inner),
              $height-2*($inset-$inner)) ;
pdf_stroke($pdf);

//draw main border $border points wide
pdf_setlinewidth($pdf, $border);
pdf_rect($pdf, $inset+$border/2,
              $inset+$border/2,
              $width-2*($inset+$border/2),
              $height-2*($inset+$border/2));
pdf_stroke($pdf);
pdf_setlinewidth($pdf, 1.0);

// draw inner border
pdf_rect($pdf, $inset+$border+$inner,
              $inset+$border+$inner,
              $width-2*($inset+$border+$inner),
              $height-2*($inset+$border+$inner));
pdf_stroke($pdf);

// add heading
$font = pdf_findfont($pdf, $fontname, 'host', 0);
if ($font)
  pdf_setfont($pdf, $font, 48);
$startx = ($width - pdf_stringwidth($pdf, 'PHP Certification',
          $font, 48))/2;
pdf_show_xy($pdf, 'PHP Certification', $startx, 490);
```

Listing 32.6 **Continued**

```
// add text
$font = pdf_findfont($pdf, $fontname, 'host', 0);
if ($font)
  pdf_setfont($pdf, $font, 26);
$startx = 70;
pdf_show_xy($pdf, 'This is to certify that:', $startx, 430);
pdf_show_xy($pdf, strtoupper($name), $startx+90, 391);

$font = pdf_findfont($pdf, $fontname, 'host', 0);
if ($font)
  pdf_setfont($pdf, $font, 20);

pdf_show_xy($pdf, 'has demonstrated that they are certifiable '.
                  'by passing a rigorous exam', $startx, 340);
pdf_show_xy($pdf, 'consisting of three multiple choice questions.',
                  $startx, 310) ;

pdf_show_xy($pdf, "$name obtained a score of $score".'%.', $startx, 260);

pdf_show_xy($pdf, 'The test was set and overseen by the ', $startx, 210);
pdf_show_xy($pdf, 'Fictional Institute of PHP Certification',
                  $startx, 180);
pdf_show_xy($pdf, "on $date.", $startx, 150);
pdf_show_xy($pdf, 'Authorized by:', $startx, 100);

// add bitmap signature image
// you may need to change the path to the signature file here
$path = 'C:/Program Files/Apache Group/Apache/htdocs/phpmysql3e/chapter32/';

// using gif version as PDFLib for Windows appears to have problems with GIFs
$signature = pdf_open_image_file($pdf, 'gif', $path.'signature.gif',
                                 'mask', 0);
pdf_place_image($pdf, $signature, 200, 75, 1);
pdf_close_image($pdf, $signature);

// set up colors for rosette
pdf_setcolor($pdf, 'fill', 'rgb', 0, 0, .4, 0);  // dark blue
pdf_setcolor($pdf, 'stroke', 'rgb', 0, 0, 0, 0); // black
```

Listing 32.6 **Continued**

```
// draw ribbon 1
pdf_moveto($pdf, 630, 150);
pdf_lineto($pdf, 610, 55);
pdf_lineto($pdf, 632, 69);
pdf_lineto($pdf, 646, 49);
pdf_lineto($pdf, 666, 150);
pdf_closepath($pdf);
pdf_fill($pdf);

// outline ribbon 1
pdf_moveto($pdf, 630, 150);
pdf_lineto($pdf, 610, 55);
pdf_lineto($pdf, 632, 69);
pdf_lineto($pdf, 646, 49);
pdf_lineto($pdf, 666, 150);
pdf_closepath($pdf);
pdf_stroke($pdf);

// draw ribbon 2
pdf_moveto($pdf, 660, 150);
pdf_lineto($pdf, 680, 49);
pdf_lineto($pdf, 695, 69);
pdf_lineto($pdf, 716, 55);
pdf_lineto($pdf, 696, 150);
pdf_closepath($pdf);
pdf_fill($pdf);

// outline ribbon 2
pdf_moveto($pdf, 660, 150);
pdf_lineto($pdf, 680, 49);
pdf_lineto($pdf, 695, 69);
pdf_lineto($pdf, 716, 55);
pdf_lineto($pdf, 696, 150) ;
pdf_closepath($pdf);
pdf_stroke($pdf);
pdf_setcolor($pdf, 'fill', 'rgb', .8, 0, 0, 0); // red

//draw rosette
draw_star(665, 175, 32, 57, 10, $pdf, true);
```

Listing 32.6 **Continued**

```
    //outline rosette
    draw_star(665, 175, 32, 57, 10, $pdf, false);

    // finish up the page and prepare to output
    pdf_end_page($pdf);
    pdf_close($pdf);
    $data = pdf_get_buffer($pdf);

    // generate the headers to help a browser choose the correct application
    header('Content-Type: application/pdf');
    header('Content-Disposition: inline; filename=certificate.pdf');
    header('Content-Length: ' . strlen($data));

    // output PDF
    echo $data;
}

function draw_star($centerx, $centery, $points, $radius,
                   $point_size, $pdf, $filled)
{
  $inner_radius = $radius-$point_size;

  for ($i = 0; $i<=$points*2; $i++ )
  {
    $angle= ($i*2*pi())/($points*2);

    if($i%2)
    {
      $x = $radius*cos($angle) + $centerx;
      $y = $radius*sin($angle) + $centery;
    }
    else
    {
      $x = $inner_radius*cos($angle) + $centerx;
      $y = $inner_radius*sin($angle) + $centery;
    }
    if($i==0)
      pdf_moveto($pdf, $x, $y) ;
    else if($i==$points*2)
      pdf_closepath($pdf);
    else
      pdf_lineto($pdf, $x, $y);
  }
```

Listing 32.6 **Continued**

```
   if($filled)
     pdf_fill_stroke($pdf);
   else
     pdf_stroke($pdf);
 }
?>
```

The certificate produced using this script is shown in Figure 32.7. As you can see, it is quite similar to the others, except that the border is simpler and the star looks a little different. The reason is that they are drawn into the document rather than taken from an existing clip art file.

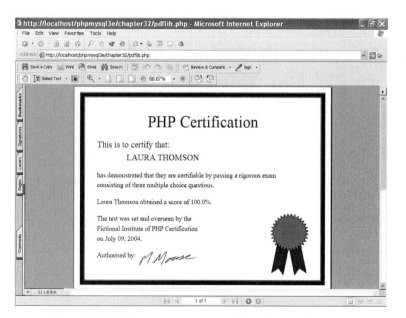

Figure 32.7   The pdflib.php script draws the certificate into a PDF document.

Now let's look at some of the parts of this script that are different from the previous examples.

Visitors need to get their own details on a certificate, so you create the document in memory rather than in a file. If you wrote it to a file, you would need to worry about mechanisms to create unique filenames, stop people from snooping into others' certificates, and determine a way to delete older certificate files to free hard drive space on the server.

To create a document in memory, you call pdf_new() without parameters followed by a call to pdf_open_file(), as follows:

```
$pdf = pdf_new();
pdf_open_file($pdf, '');
```

The simplified border consists of three stripes: a fat border and two thin borders, one inside the main border and one outside. You draw all of them as rectangles.

To position the borders in such a way that you can easily alter the page size or the appearance of the borders, you base all the border positions on the variables that you already have, $width and $height and a few new ones: $inset, $border, and $inner. You use $inset to specify how many points wide the border at the edge of the page is, $border to specify the thickness of the main border, and $inner to specify how wide the gap between the main border and the thin borders is.

If you have drawn with another graphics API, drawing with PDFlib will present few surprises. If you haven't read Chapter 21, "Generating Images," you might find it helpful to do so, because drawing images with the gd library is similar to drawing them with PDFlib.

The thin borders are easy. To create a rectangle, you use pdf_rect(), which requires as parameters the PDF document identifier, the x and y coordinates of the rectangle's lower-left corner, and the width and height of the rectangle. Because you want the layout to be flexible, you calculate these from the variables you have set:

```
pdf_rect($pdf, $inset-$inner,
                $inset-$inner,
                $width-2*($inset-$inner),
                $height-2*($inset-$inner));
```

The call to pdf_rect() sets up a path in the shape of a rectangle. To draw that shape, you need to call the pdf_stroke() function as follows:

```
pdf_stroke($pdf);
```

To draw the main border, you need to specify the line width. The default line width is 1 point. The following call to pdf_setlinewidth() sets it to $border (in this case, 10) points:

```
pdf_setlinewidth($pdf, $border);
```

With the width set, you again create a rectangle with pdf_rect() and call pdf_stroke() to draw it:

```
pdf_rect($pdf, $inset+$border/2,
                $inset+$border/2,
                $width-2*($inset+$border/2),
                $height-2*($inset+$border/2));
pdf_stroke($pdf);
```

After you have drawn the one wide line, you need to remember to set the line width back to 1 with this code:

```
pdf_setlinewidth($pdf, 1.0);
```

You use `pdf_show_xy()` to position each line of text on the certificate. For most lines of text, you use a configurable left margin (`$startx`) as the x coordinate and a value chosen by eye as the y coordinate. Because you want the heading centered on the page, you need to know its width so that you can position the left side of it. You can get the width by using `pdf_stringwidth()`. The call

```
pdf_stringwidth($pdf, 'PHP Certification', $font, 48);
```

returns the width of the string `'PHP Certification'` in the current font and font size.

As with the other versions of the certificate, you include a signature as a scanned bitmap. The three statements

```
$signature = pdf_open_image_file($pdf, 'gif', $path.'signature.gif',
                                 'mask', 0);
pdf_place_image($pdf, $signature, 200, 75, 1);
pdf_close_image($pdf, $signature);
```

open a GIF file containing the signature, add the image to the page at the specified location, and close the GIF file. Other file types can also be used. (We reverted to using GIF here because PNG support under Windows was buggy at the time of writing.) The only parameter that might not be self-explanatory is the fifth parameter to `pdf_place_image()`. This function is not limited to inserting the image at its original size. The fifth parameter is a scale factor. We chose to display the image at full size and used 1 as the scale factor, but you could use a larger number to enlarge the image or a fraction to shrink it.

The hardest item to add to the certificate using PDFlib is the rosette. You cannot automatically open and include a Windows meta file containing the rosette used previously, but you are free to draw any shapes you like.

To draw a filled shape such as one of the ribbons, you can write the following code. Here, you set the stroke or line color to be black and the fill or interior color to be navy blue:

```
pdf_setcolor($pdf, 'fill', 'rgb', 0, 0, .4, 0);  // dark blue
pdf_setcolor($pdf, 'stroke', 'rgb', 0, 0, 0, 0); // black
```

Here, you set up a five-sided polygon to be one of the ribbons and then fill it:

```
pdf_moveto($pdf, 630, 150);
pdf_lineto($pdf, 610, 55);
pdf_lineto($pdf, 632, 69);
pdf_lineto($pdf, 646, 49);
pdf_lineto($pdf, 666, 150);
pdf_closepath($pdf);
pdf_fill($pdf);
```

Because you want the polygon outlined as well, you need to set up the same path a second time but call `pdf_stroke()` instead of `pdf_fill()`.

Because the multipointed star is a complex repetitive shape, we wrote a function to calculate the locations in the path. Our function is called `draw_star()` and requires x and y coordinates for the center, the number of points required, the radius, the length of the points, a PDF document identifier, and a Boolean value to indicate whether the star shape should be filled in or just an outline.

The `draw_star()` function uses some basic trigonometry to calculate locations for a series of points to lay out a star. For each point you request your star to have, you find a point on the radius of the star and a point on a smaller circle `$point_size` within the outer circle and draw a line between them. One point worth noting is that PHP's trigonometric functions such as `cos()` and `sin()` work in radians rather than degrees.

Using a function and some mathematics, you can accurately generate a complex repetitive shape. Had you wanted a complicated pattern for the page border, you could have used a similar approach.

When all your page elements are generated, you need to end the page and the document.

Handling Problems with Headers

One minor issue to note in all these scripts is that you need to tell the browser what type of data you are going to send it. You do this by sending a content-type HTTP header, as in these examples:

```
header( 'Content-Type: application/msword' );
```

or

```
header( 'Content-Type: application/pdf' );
```

One point to be aware of is that browsers deal with these headers inconsistently. In particular, Internet Explorer often chooses to ignore the MIME type and attempt to automatically detect the type of file. (This particular problem seems to have improved in recent versions of Internet Explorer, so if you experience this issue, the easiest solution may be to upgrade your browser.)

Some of the headers seem to cause problems with session control headers. There are a few ways around this problem. We found that using GET parameters rather than POST or session variable parameters avoids the problem.

Another solution is not to use an inline PDF but to get the user to download it instead, as shown in the Hello World PDFlib example.

You can also avoid problems if you are willing to write two slightly different versions of your code, one for Netscape and one for Internet Explorer.

Extending the Project

Adding some more realistic assessment tasks to the examination obviously could extend this chapter's project, but we really intended it as an example of ways to deliver your own documents.

Customized documents that you might want to deliver online could include legal documents, partially filled-in order or application forms, or forms needed by government departments.

Further Reading

We suggest you visit Adobe's site if you want to know more about the PDF (and FDF) formats:

http://www.adobe.com

Next

In the next chapter, we examine PHP 5's new XML capabilities and use PHP to connect to Amazon's Web Services API using REST and SOAP.

33

Connecting to Web Services with XML and SOAP

IN THE PAST FEW YEARS, EXTENSIBLE MARKUP LANGUAGE (XML) has become an important means of communication. In this chapter, you use Amazon's Web Services interface to build a shopping cart on your website that uses Amazon as a back end. (This application is named Tahuayo, which is the name of an Amazonian tributary.) You use two different methods to do this: SOAP and REST. REST is also known as XML over HTTP. You use PHP's built-in SimpleXML library and the external NuSOAP library to implement these two methods.

In this chapter, we discuss the following topics:

- Understanding XML and SOAP basics
- Using XML to communicate with Amazon
- Parsing XML with PHP's SimpleXML library
- Caching responses
- Talking to Amazon with NuSOAP

The Problem

We have two goals with this project: The first is to help you gain an understanding of what XML and SOAP are and how to use them in PHP. The second is to put these technologies to use to communicate with the outside world. We chose the Amazon Web Services program as an interesting example that you might find useful for your own website.

Amazon has long offered an associate program that allows you to advertise Amazon's products on your website. Users can then follow a link to each product's page on Amazon's site. If someone clicks through from your site and then buys that product, you receive a small commission.

The Web Services program enables you to use Amazon more as an engine: You can search it and display the results via your own site, or fill a user's shopping cart directly with the contents of items he has selected while browsing your site. In other words, the customer uses your site until it is time to check out, which he then has to do via Amazon.

Communications between you and Amazon can take place in two possible ways. The first way is by using XML over HTTP, which is also known as Representational State Transfer (REST). If, for example, you want to perform a search using this method, you send a normal HTTP request for the information you require, and Amazon will respond with an XML document containing the information you requested. You can then parse this XML document and display the search results to the end user using an interface of your choice. The process of sending and receiving data via HTTP is very simple, but how easy it is to parse the resulting document depends on the complexity of the document.

The second way to communicate with Amazon is to use SOAP, which is one of the standard Web Services protocols. It used to stand for Simple Object Access Protocol, but it was decided that the protocol wasn't that simple and that the name was a bit misleading. The result is that the protocol is still called SOAP, but it is no longer an acronym.

In this project, you build a SOAP client that can send requests to and receive responses from the Amazon SOAP server. They contain the same information as the responses you get using the XML over HTTP method, but you will use a different approach to extract the data, namely the NuSOAP library.

Our final goal in this project is for you to build your own book-selling website that uses Amazon as a back end. You build two alternative versions: one using REST and one using SOAP.

Understanding XML

Let's spend a few moments examining XML and Web Services, in case you are not familiar with these concepts.

As mentioned previously, XML is the Extensible Markup Language. The specification is available from the W3C. Lots of information about XML can be found at the W3C's XML site at http://www.w3.org/XML/.

XML is derived from the Standard Generalized Markup Language, or SGML. If you already know Hypertext Markup Language, or HTML (and if you don't, you have started reading this book at the wrong end), you will have little difficulty with the concepts of XML.

XML is a tag-based text format for documents. As an example of an XML document, Listing 33.1 shows a response Amazon sends to an XML over HTTP request.

Listing 33.1 **XML Document Describing the First Edition of This Book**

```
<?xml version="1.0" encoding="UTF-8"?>
<ProductInfo xmlns:xsi="http://www.w3.org/2001/XMLSchema-instance"
xsi:noNamespaceSchemaLocation="http://xml.amazon.com/schemas2/ dev-heavy.xsd">
```

Listing 33.1 **Continued**

```
    <Details
url="http://www.amazon.com/exec/obidos/redirect?tag=tangledwebdesign%
26creative=XXXXXXXXXXXXXX%26camp=2025%26li
nk_code=xm2%26path=ASIN/0672317842">
        <Asin>0672317842</Asin>
        <ProductName>PHP and MySQL Web Development</ProductName>
        <Catalog>Book</Catalog>
        <Authors>
            <Author>Luke Welling</Author>
            <Author>Laura Thomson</Author>
        </Authors>
        <ReleaseDate>30 March, 2001</ReleaseDate>
        <Manufacturer>Sams</Manufacturer>
        <ImageUrlSmall>http://images.amazon.com/images/P/0672317842.01.
THUMBZZZ.jpg</ImageUrlSmall>
        <ImageUrlMedium>http://images.amazon.com/images/P/0672317842.01.
MZZZZZZZ.jpg</ImageUrlMedium>
        <ImageUrlLarge>http://images.amazon.com/images/P/0672317842.01.
LZZZZZZZ.jpg</ImageUrlLarge>
        <ListPrice>$49.99</ListPrice>
        <OurPrice>$34.99</OurPrice>
        <UsedPrice>$31.95</UsedPrice>
        <ThirdPartyNewPrice>$31.75</ThirdPartyNewPrice>
        <SalesRank>312</SalesRank>
        <Lists>
            <ListId>3KZW1EV9QMB5F</ListId>
            <ListId>22YCO1IGPIZJ3</ListId>
            <ListId>Y2I9B362QXVX</ListId>
        </Lists>
        <BrowseList>
          <BrowseNode>
             <BrowseName>PHP (Computer program language</BrowseName>
          </BrowseNode>
          <BrowseNode>
             <BrowseName>SQL (Computer program language</BrowseName>
          </BrowseNode>
          <BrowseNode>
             <BrowseName>Web sites</BrowseName>
          </BrowseNode>
          <BrowseNode>
             <BrowseName>Design</BrowseName>
          </BrowseNode>
          <BrowseNode>
             <BrowseName>SQL (Computer language)</BrowseName>
          </BrowseNode>
```

Listing 33.1   **Continued**

```
            <BrowseNode>
               <BrowseName>Sql (Programming Language)</BrowseName>
            </BrowseNode>
            <BrowseNode>
               <BrowseName>Computer Networks</BrowseName>
            </BrowseNode>
            <BrowseNode>
               <BrowseName>Computer Bks - Languages / Programming</BrowseName>
            </BrowseNode>
            <BrowseNode>
               <BrowseName>Computers</BrowseName>
            </BrowseNode>
            <BrowseNode>
               <BrowseName>Programming Languages - General</BrowseName>
            </BrowseNode>
            <BrowseNode>
               <BrowseName>Internet - Web Site Design</BrowseName>
            </BrowseNode>
            <BrowseNode>
               <BrowseName>Database Management - SQL Server</BrowseName>
            </BrowseNode>
            <BrowseNode>
               <BrowseName>Programming Languages - SQL</BrowseName>
            </BrowseNode>
         </BrowseList>
         <Media>Paperback</Media>
         <NumMedia>1</NumMedia>
         <Isbn>0672317842</Isbn>
         <Availability>Usually ships within 24 hours</Availability>
         <SimilarProducts>
            <Product>0735709211</Product>
            <Product>1861003730</Product>
            <Product>073570970X</Product>
            <Product>1861006918</Product>
            <Product>0596000413</Product>
         </SimilarProducts>
      </Details>
</ProductInfo>
```

The document begins with the following line:

```
<?xml version="1.0" encoding="UTF-8"?>
```

This standard declaration tells you the following document will be XML using UTF-8 character encoding.

Now look at the body of the document. The whole document consists of pairs of opening and closing tags, such as

```
<ProductName>PHP and MySQL Web Development</ProductName>
```

`ProductName` is an element, just as it would be in HTML. And, just as in HTML, you can nest elements:

```
<Authors>
  <Author>Luke Welling</Author>
  <Author>Laura Thomson</Author>
</Authors>
```

Also like HTML, elements can have attributes, as in this example:

```
<Details url="http://www.amazon.com/exec/obidos/redirect?tag=
➥tangledwebdesign%26creative=XXXXXXXXXXXXXX%26camp=2025%26link_code
➥=xm2%26path=ASIN/0672317842">
```

This `Details` element has a single attribute: `url`. Because the URL is very long, it has been broken over three lines here.

There are also some differences from HTML. The first is that each opening tag must have a closing tag. The exception to this rule is empty elements that open and close in a single tag because they do not enclose any text. If you are familiar with XHTML, you have seen the `<br />` tag used in place of `<br>` for this exact reason. In addition, all elements must be properly nested. You would probably get away with `<b><i>Text</b></i>` using an HTML parser, but to be valid XML or XHTML, the tags would need to be properly nested as `<b><i>Text</i></b>`.

The main difference you will notice between XML and HTML is that we seem to be making up our own tags as we go along! This is the flexibility of XML. You can structure your documents to match the data that you want to store. You can formalize the structure of XML documents by writing either a Document Type Definition (DTD) or an XML Schema. Both of these documents are used to describe the structure of a given XML document. If you like, you can think of the DTD or Schema as being like a class declaration and the XML document as being like an instance of that class. In this particular example, you do not use a DTD or Schema.

You can read Amazon's DTD for this document here:
http://xml.amazon.com/schemas2/dev-heavy.dtd

You can read the XML Schema for it here:
http://xml.amazon.com/schemas2/dev-heavy.xsd

You cannot open the DTD file in some browsers because they will try to parse the DTD as XML and get confused. You can, however, download it and read it in the editor of your choice. You should be able to open the XML Schema directly in your browser.

Notice that, other than the initial XML declaration, the entire body of the document is contained inside the `ProductInfo` element. This is called the *root element* of the document. Let's take a closer look:

```
<ProductInfo xmlns:xsi="http://www.w3.org/2001/XMLSchema-instance"
    xsi:noNamespaceSchemaLocation="http://xml.amazon.com/schemas2/
    dev-heavy.xsd">
```

This element has some slightly unusual attributes. They are *XML namespaces*. You do not need to understand namespaces for what you will do in this project, but they can be very useful. The basic idea is to qualify element and attribute names with a namespace so that common names do not clash when dealing with documents from different sources.

If you would like to know more about namespaces, you can read the document "Namespaces in XML Recommendation" at http://www.w3.org/TR/REC-xml-names/.

If you would like to know more about XML in general, a huge variety of resources is available. The W3C site is an excellent place to start, and there are also hundreds of excellent books and web tutorials. ZVON.org is one of the best web-based ones.

Understanding Web Services

Web Services are application interfaces made available via the World Wide Web. If you like to think in object-oriented terms, a Web Service can be seen as a class that exposes its public methods via the Web. Web Services are now becoming widespread, and some of the biggest names in the business are making some of their functionality available via Web Services.

For example, Google, Amazon, eBay, and PayPal all offer a range of Web Services. After you go through the process of setting up a client to the Amazon interface in this chapter, you should find it very straightforward to build a client interface to Google. You can find more information at http://www.google.com/apis/.

An ever-growing list of public Web Services is available at http://www.xmethods.net.

Several core protocols are involved in this remote function call methodology. Two of the most important ones are SOAP and WSDL.

SOAP

SOAP is a request-and-response–driven messaging protocol that allows clients to invoke Web Services and allows servers to respond. Each SOAP message, whether a request or response, is a simple XML document. A sample SOAP request you might send to Amazon is shown in Listing 33.2.

Listing 33.2 **SOAP Request for a Search Based on the ASIN**

```
<?xml version="1.0" encoding="UTF-8"?>
<SOAP-ENV:Envelope xmlns:SOAP-ENV="http://schemas.xmlsoap.org/soap/
➥envelope/"
                   xmlns:SOAP-ENC="http://schemas.xmlsoap.org/soap/
➥encoding/"
```

Listing 33.2 **Continued**

```
                    xmlns:xsi="http://www.w3.org/2001/XMLSchema-instance"
                    xmlns:xsd="http://www.w3.org/2001/XMLSchema"
 SOAP-ENV:encodingStyle="http://schemas.xmlsoap.org/soap/encoding/">
  <SOAP-ENV:Body>
    <namesp1:AsinSearchRequest xmlns:namesp1="urn:PI/DevCentral/
➥SoapService">
      <AsinSearchRequest xsi:type="m:AsinRequest">
        <asin >0060518057</asin>
        <tag >your-associate-id</tag>
        <type >heavy</type>
        <dev-tag >your-dev-tag</dev-tag>
      </AsinSearchRequest>
    </namesp1:AsinSearchRequest>
  </SOAP-ENV:Body>
</SOAP-ENV:Envelope>
```

The SOAP message begins with the declaration that this is an XML document. The root element of all SOAP messages is the SOAP envelope. Within it, you find the `Body` element that contains the actual request.

This request is an `AsinSearchRequest`, which asks the Amazon server to look up a particular item in its database based on the ASIN, which stands for Amazon.com Standard Item Number. This is a unique identifier given to every product in the Amazon.com database.

Think of `AsinSearchRequest` as a function call on a remote machine and the elements contained within this element as the parameters you are passing to that function. In this case, you pass an ASIN for the Dilbert book *Way of the Weasel*. You also need to pass in the tag, which is your Associate ID; the type of search to perform (`heavy` or `lite`); and the `dev-tag`, which is a developer token value Amazon will give you. The element type tells the service whether you want limited detail (`lite`) or all available information (`heavy`).

The response to this request is similar to the XML document you looked at in Listing 33.1, but it is enclosed in a SOAP envelope.

When dealing with SOAP, you usually generate SOAP requests and interpret responses programmatically using a SOAP library, regardless of the programming language you are using. This is a good thing because it saves on the effort of having to build the SOAP request and interpret the response manually.

WSDL

WSDL stands for *Web Services Description Language*. (It is often pronounced "wiz-dul.") This language is used to describe the interface to available services at a particular website. If you would like to see the WSDL document describing the Amazon Web Services used in this chapter, it is located at http://soap.amazon.com/schemas2/AmazonWebServices.wsdl.

As you will see if you follow this link, WSDL documents are significantly more complex than SOAP messages. You will always generate and interpret them programmatically, if given a choice.

If you would like to know more about WSDL, you can consult the W3C Draft at http://www.w3.org/TR/wsdl20/.

At the time of writing, WSDL is not yet a W3C Recommendation, so it is still subject to change. This has not stopped developers everywhere from using it enthusiastically. However, like all pieces of the Web Services puzzle, it is subject to change because the whole area is developing quickly.

Solution Components

There are a few parts you need to build your solution. As well as the most obvious parts—a shopping cart interface to show to customers and code to connect to Amazon via REST or SOAP—you need some ancillary parts. Having retrieved an XML document, your code needs to parse it to extract the information your cart will display. To meet Amazon's requirements and to improve performance, you need to consider caching. Finally, as the checkout activity needs to be done at Amazon, you need some functionality to hand over the contents of the user's cart to Amazon and pass the user over to that service.

Building a Shopping Cart

You obviously need to build a shopping cart as the front end for the system. You've done this before, in Chapter 27, "Building a Shopping Cart." Because shopping carts are not the main focus in this project, this chapter contains a simplified application. You just need to provide a basic cart so that you can track what the customer would like to buy and report it to Amazon upon checkout.

Using Amazon's Web Services Interfaces

To use the Amazon Web Services interface, you need to download the Amazon Web Services Developers' Kit. We got it from http://www.amazon.com/gp/aws/landing.html. This URL is subject to change, however.

You also need to sign up for a developer token. You can do this at the same site. This token is used to identify you to Amazon when your requests come in.

You might also like to sign up for an Amazon Associate ID. It enables you to collect commission if people buy any products via your interface.

When you download the developers' kit, read through it. It comes with documentation describing how the interface works and code samples in a variety of languages, including PHP.

Before you can download it, you need to agree to the license agreement. This is worth reading because it is not the usual yada-yada software license. Some of the license conditions that are important during implementation are the following:

- You must not make more than one request per second.

- You must cache data coming from Amazon.

- You may cache most data for 24 hours and some stable attributes for up to three months.

- If you cache prices and availability for more than an hour, you must display a disclaimer.

- You must link back to a page on Amazon.com and must not link text or graphics downloaded from Amazon to another commercial website.

With a hard-to-spell domain name, no promotion, and no obvious reason to use Tahuayo.com instead of going straight to Amazon.com, you do not need to take any further steps to keep requests below one per second.

In this project, you implement caching to meet the conditions at points 2 to 4. The application caches images for 24 hours and product data (which contains prices and availability) for 1 hour.

Your application also follows the fifth point. You want items on the main page to link to detailed pages on your site, but you link to Amazon when an order is complete.

Parsing XML

The first interface Amazon offers to its Web Services is via REST. This interface accepts a normal HTTP request and returns an XML document. To use this interface, you need to be able to parse the XML response Amazon sends back to you. You can do this by using PHP's SimpleXML library. This library requires at least PHP version 5.0.0 but is enabled by default.

Using SOAP with PHP

The other interface offering the same Web Services is SOAP. To access these services using SOAP, you need to use one of the various PHP SOAP libraries. There is a built-in SOAP library, but because it will not always be available, you can use the NuSOAP library. Because NuSOAP is written in PHP, it does not need compiling. It is just a single file to be called via `require_once()`.

NuSOAP is available from http://dietrich.ganx4.com/nusoap/. NuSOAP is available under the Lesser GPL; that is, you may use it in any application, including nonfree applications.

Caching

As we mentioned previously, one of the terms and conditions imposed upon developers by Amazon is that data downloaded from Amazon via Web Services must be cached. In this solution, you will need to find a way to store and reuse the data that you download until it has passed its use-by date.

Solution Overview

This project again uses an event-driven approach to run the code, as in Chapters 29, "Building a Web-Based Email Service," and 30, "Building a Mailing List Manager." We did not draw a system flow diagram for you in this example because there are only a few screens in the system, and the links between them are simple.

Users will begin at the main Tahuayo screen, shown in Figure 33.1.

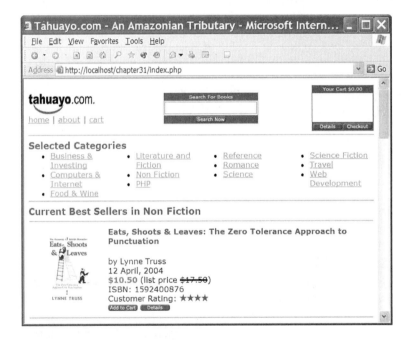

Figure 33.1   The first screen for Tahuayo shows all the main features of the site: category navigation, searching, and the shopping cart.

As you can see, the main features of the site are the Selected Categories display and the items in those categories. By default, you display the current best-sellers in the nonfiction category on the front page. If a user clicks on another category, she will see a similar display for that category.

A brief piece of terminology before we go further: Amazon refers to categories as *browse nodes*. You will see this expression used throughout our code and the official documentation.

The documentation provides a partial list of popular browse nodes. In addition, if you want a particular one, you can browse the normal Amazon.com site and read it from the URL, but there is no way to get a complete list. Frustratingly, some important categories, such as best-selling books, cannot be accessed as browse nodes.

More books and links to additional pages are available at the bottom of this page, but you can't see them in the screenshot. You will display 10 books on each page, along with links to up to 30 other pages. This 10-per page value is set by Amazon. The 30-page limit was our own arbitrary choice.

From here, users can click through to detailed information on individual books. This screen is shown in Figure 33.2.

Figure 33.2   The details page shows more information about a particular book, including similar products and reviews.

Although it does not all fit in a screenshot, the script shows most, but not all, of the information that Amazon sends with a heavy request on this page. We chose to ignore parts aimed at products other than books and the list of categories the book fits in.

If users click through the cover image, they will be able to see a larger version of the image.

You might have noticed the search box at the top of the screen in these figures. This feature runs a keyword search through the site and searches Amazon's catalog via its Web Services interface. An example of the output of a search is shown in Figure 33.3.

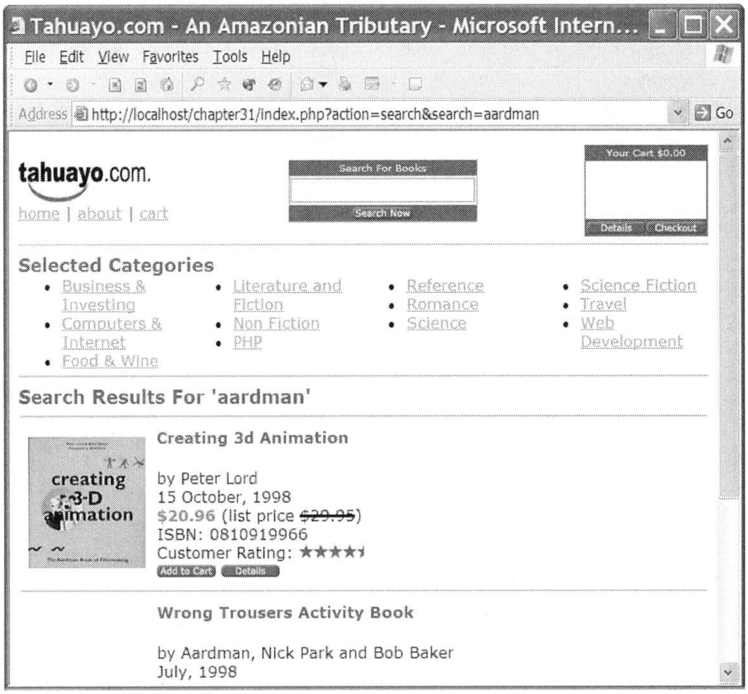

Figure 33.3 This screen shows the results of searching for aardman.

Although this project lists only a few categories, customers can get to any book by using the search facility and navigating to particular books.

Each individual book has an Add to Cart link with it. Clicking on this or the Details link in the cart summary takes the customer to a display of the cart contents. This page is shown in Figure 33.4.

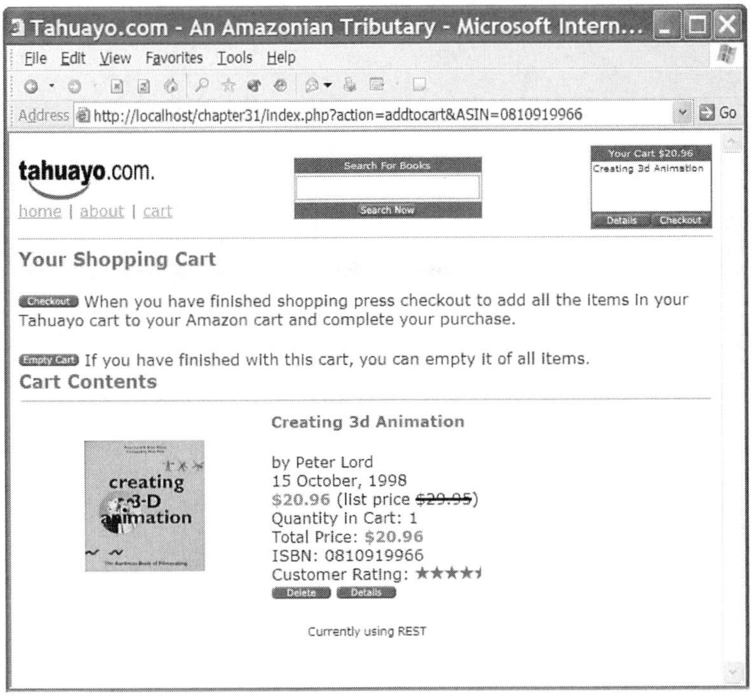

Figure 33.4 From the shopping cart page, the customer can delete items, clear the cart, or check out.

Finally, when a customer checks out by clicking on one of the Checkout links, you send the details of her shopping cart to Amazon and take her there. She will see a page similar to the one in Figure 33.5.

You should now understand what we mean by building your own front end and using Amazon as the back end.

Because this project also uses the event-driven approach, most of the core decision-making logic of the application is in one file, index.php. A summary of the files in the application is shown in Table 33.1.

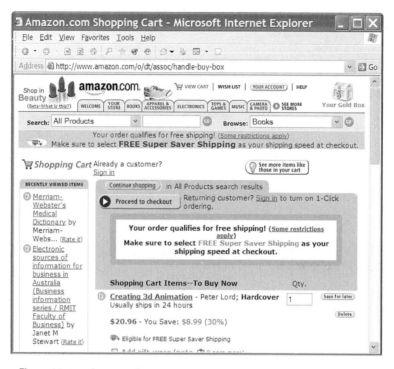

Figure 33.5 The items that were in the customer's Tahuayo cart are now in
her Amazon cart.

Table 33.1 **Files in the Tahuayo Application**

Filename	Type	Description
index.php	Application	Contains the main application file
about.php	Application	Shows the About page
constants.php	Include file	Sets up some global constants and variables
topbar.php	Include file	Generates the info bar across the top of each page and the CSS
bottom.php	Include file	Generates the footer at the bottom of each page
AmazonResultSet.php	Class file	Contains the PHP class that stores the result of each Amazon query
Product.php	Class file	Contains the PHP class that stores information on one particular book
bookdisplayfunctions.p	Functions	Contains functions that help display a book and lists of books

Table 33.1 **Continued**

Filename	Type	Description
cachefunctions.php	Functions	Contains functions to carry out the caching required by Amazon
cartfunctions.php	Functions	Contains shopping cart–related functions
categoryfunctions.php	Functions	Contains functions that help retrieve and display a category
utilityfunctions.php	Functions	Contains a few utility functions used throughout the application

You also need the nusoap.php file we mentioned previously because it is required in these files. NuSOAP is in the chapter33 directory on the CD-ROM at the back of the book, but if the author keeps maintaining it, you might like to replace it with a newer version from http://dietrich.ganx4.com/nusoap/index.php.

Let's begin this project by looking at the core application file index.php.

Core Application

The application file index.php is shown in Listing 33.3.

Listing 33.3 index.php—**The Core Application File**

```php
<?php
//we are only using one session variable 'cart' to store the cart contents
session_start();

require_once('constants.php');
require_once('Product.php');
require_once('AmazonResultSet.php');
require_once('utilityfunctions.php');
require_once('bookdisplayfunctions.php');
require_once('cartfunctions.php');
require_once('categoryfunctions.php');

// These are the variables we are expecting from outside.
// They will be validated and converted to globals
$external = array('action', 'ASIN', 'mode', 'browseNode', 'page', 'search');

// the variables may come via Get or Post
// convert all our expected external variables to short global names
foreach ($external as $e)
{
  if(@$_REQUEST[$e])
    $$e = $_REQUEST[$e];
  else
    $$e = '';
```

Listing 33.3 **Continued**

```
  $$e = trim($$e);
}

// default values for global variables
if($mode=='')
  $mode = 'books'; // No other modes have been tested
if($browseNode=='')
  $browseNode = 53; //53 is bestselling non-fiction books
if($page=='')
  $page = 1;  // First Page - there are 10 items per page

//validate/strip input
if(!eregi('^[A-Z0-9]+$', $ASIN)) // ASINS must be alpha-numeric
  $ASIN ='';
if(!eregi('^[a-z]+$', $mode)) // mode must be alphabetic
  $mode = 'books';
$page=intval($page); // pages and browseNodes must be integers
$browseNode = intval($browseNode);
// it may cause some confusion, but we are stripping characters out from
// $search it seems only fair to modify it now so it will be displayed
// in the heading
$search = safeString($search);

if(!isset($_SESSION['cart']))
{
  session_register('cart');
  $_SESSION['cart'] = array();
}

// tasks that need to be done before the top bar is shown
if($action == 'addtocart')
  addToCart($_SESSION['cart'], $ASIN, $mode) ;
if($action == 'deletefromcart')
  deleteFromCart($_SESSION['cart'], $ASIN) ;
if($action == 'emptycart')
  $_SESSION['cart'] = array();
// show top bar
require_once ('topbar.php');

// main event loop.  Reacts to user action on the calling page
switch ($action)
{
  case 'detail' :
    showCategories($mode);
    showDetail($ASIN, $mode);
  break;
```

Listing 33.3 **Continued**

```
case 'addtocart' :
case 'deletefromcart' :
case 'emptycart' :
case 'showcart' :
  echo '<hr /><h1>Your Shopping Cart</h1>';
  showCart($_SESSION['cart'], $mode);
break;

case 'image' :
  showCategories($mode);
  echo '<h1>Large Product Image</h1>';
  showImage($ASIN, $mode);
break;

case 'search' :
  showCategories($mode);
  echo "<h1>Search Results For '$search'</h1>";
  showSearch($search, $page, $mode);
break;

case 'browsenode':
default:
  showCategories($mode);
  $category = getCategoryName($browseNode);
  if(!$category||$category=='Best Selling Books')
  {
    echo '<h1>Current Best Sellers</h1>';
  }
  else
  {
    echo "<h1>Current Best Sellers in $category</h1>";
  }
  showBrowseNode($browseNode, $page, $mode) ;
break;
}
require ('bottom.php');
?>
```

Let's work our way through this file. You begin by creating a session. You store the customer's shopping cart as a session variable as you have done before.

You then include several files. Most of them are functions that we discuss later, but we need to address the first included file now. This file, constants.php, defines some important constants and variables that will be used throughout the application. The contents of constants.php can be found in Listing 33.4.

Listing 33.4   `constants.php`—**Declaring Key Global Constants and Variables**

```php
<?php
// this application can connect via REST (XML over HTTP) or SOAP
// define one version of METHOD to choose.
// define('METHOD', 'SOAP');
define('METHOD', 'REST');

// make sure to create a cache directory and make it writable
define('CACHE', 'cache'); // path to cached files
define('ASSOCIATEID', 'webservices-20'); //put your associate id here
define('DEVTAG', 'XXXXXXXXXXXXXX'); // put your developer tag here

//give an error if software is run with the dummy devtag
if(DEVTAG=='XXXXXXXXXXXXXX')
{
  die ('You need to sign up for an Amazon.com developer tag at<a href =
     "https://associates.amazon.com/exec/panama/associates/join/
➥developer/application.html/ref=sc_bb_1_0/002">Amazon</a>
       when you install this software.  You should probably sign up
       for an associate ID at the same time. Edit the file constants.php.');
}

// (partial) list of Amazon browseNodes.
$categoryList = array(5=>'Computers & Internet', 3510=>'Web Development',
                      295223=>'PHP', 17=>'Literature and Fiction',
                      3=>'Business & Investing', 53=>'Non Fiction',
                      23=>'Romance', 75=>'Science', 21=>'Reference',
                      6 =>'Food & Wine', 27=>'Travel',
                      16272=>'Science Fiction'
                      );
?>
```

This application has been developed to use either REST or SOAP. You can set which one it should use by changing the value of the METHOD constant.

The CACHE constant holds the path to the cache for the data you download from Amazon. Change this to the path you would like used on your system.

The ASSOCIATEID constant holds the value of your Associate ID. If you send this value to Amazon with transactions, you get a commission. Be sure to change it to your own Associate ID.

The DEVTAG constant holds the value of the developer token Amazon gives you when you sign up. You need to change this value to your own developer token; otherwise, the application will not work. You can sign up for a tag at

http://www.amazon.com/gp/aws/landing.html

Now let's look back at `index.php`. It contains some preliminaries and then the main event loop. You begin by extracting any incoming variables from the `$_REQUEST` super-global that came via `GET` or `POST`. You then set up some default values for some standard global variables that determine what will be displayed later, as follows:

```
// default values for global variables
if($mode=='')
  $mode = 'books'; // No other modes have been tested
if($browseNode=='')
  $browseNode = 53; //53 is bestselling non-fiction books
if($page=='')
  $page = 1;  // First Page - there are 10 items per page
```

You set the `mode` variable to `books`. Amazon supports many other modes (types of products), but for this application, you just need to worry about books. Modifying the code in this chapter to deal with other categories should not be too hard. The first step in this expansion would be to reset `$mode`. You would need to check the Amazon documentation to see what other attributes are returned for nonbook products and remove book-specific language from the user interface.

The `browseNode` variable specifies what category of books you would like displayed. This variable may be set if the user has clicked through one of the Selected Categories links. If it is not set—for example, when the user first enters the site—you will set it to 53. Amazon's browse nodes are simply integers that identify a category. The value 53 represents the category Non-Fiction Books, which seems as good a node as any other to display on the initial front page given that some of the best generic categories are not available as browse nodes.

The `page` variable tells Amazon which subset of the results you would like displayed within a given category. Page 1 contains results 1–10, page 2 has results 11–20, and so on. Amazon sets the number of items on a page, so you do not have control over this number. You could, of course, display two or more Amazon "pages" of data on one of your pages, but 10 is both a reasonable figure and the path of least resistance.

Next, you need to tidy up any input data you have received, whether through the search box or via `GET` or `POST` parameters:

```
//validate/strip input
if(!eregi('^[A-Z0-9]+$', $ASIN)) // ASINS must be alpha-numeric
  $ASIN ='';
if(!eregi('^[a-z]+$', $mode)) // mode must be alphabetic
  $mode = 'books';
$page=intval($page); // pages and browseNodes must be integers
$browseNode = intval($browseNode);
// it may cause some confusion, but we are stripping characters out from
// $search it seems only fair to modify it now so it will be displayed
// in the heading
$search = safeString($search) ;
```

This is nothing new. The safeString() function is in the utilityfunctions.php file. It simply removes any nonalphanumeric characters from the input string via a regular expression replacement. Because we have covered this topic before, we did not include it here in the text.

The main reason that you need to validate input in this application is that you use the customer's input to create filenames in the cache. You could run into serious problems if you allow customers to include .. or / in their input.

Next, you set up the customer's shopping cart, if she does not already have one:

```
if(!isset($_SESSION['cart']))
{
  session_register('cart');
  $_SESSION['cart'] = array();
}
```

You still have a few tasks to perform before you can display the information in the top information bar on the page (see Figure 33.1 for a reminder of what this looks like). A glimpse of the shopping cart is shown in the top bar of every page. It is therefore important that the cart variable is up to date before this information is displayed:

```
// tasks that need to be done before the top bar is shown
if($action == 'addtocart')
  addToCart($_SESSION['cart'], $ASIN, $mode);
if($action == 'deletefromcart')
  deleteFromCart($_SESSION['cart'], $ASIN) ;
if($action == 'emptycart')
  $_SESSION['cart'] = array();
```

Here, you add or delete items from the cart as necessary before displaying the cart. We come back to these functions when we discuss the shopping cart and checking out. If you want to look at them now, they are in the file cartfunctions.php. We are leaving them aside for a minute because you need to understand the interface to Amazon first.

Next, you include the file topbar.php. This file simply contains HTML and a style sheet and a single function call to the ShowSmallCart() function (from cartfunctions.php). It displays the small shopping cart summary in the top-right corner of the figures. We come back to this when we discuss the cart functions.

Finally, we come to the main event-handling loop. A summary of the possible actions is shown in Table 33.2.

Table 33.2 **Possible Actions in the Main Event Loop**

Action	Description
browsenode	Shows books in the specified category. This is the default action.
detail	Shows the details of one particular book.
image	Shows a large version of the book's cover.
search	Shows the results of a user search.

Table 33.2 **Continued**

Action	Description
addtocart	Adds an item to the user's shopping cart.
deletefromcart	Deletes an item from the shopping cart.
emptycart	Empties the shopping cart altogether.
showcart	Shows the contents of the cart.

As you can see, the first four actions in this table relate to retrieving and displaying information from Amazon. The second group of four deals with managing the shopping cart.

The actions that retrieve data from Amazon all work in a similar way. Let's consider retrieving data about books in a particular browsenode (category) as an example.

Showing Books in a Category

The code executed when the action is browsenode (view a category) is as follows:

```
showCategories($mode);
$category = getCategoryName($browseNode);
if(!$category||$category=='Best Selling Books')
{
  echo '<h1>Current Best Sellers</h1>';
}
else
{
  echo "<h1>Current Best Sellers in $category</h1>";
}
showBrowseNode($browseNode, $page, $mode);
```

The showCategories() function displays the list of selected categories you see near the top of most of the pages. The getCategoryName() function returns the name of the current category given its browsenode number. The showBrowseNode() function displays a page of books in that category.

Let's begin by considering the showCategories() function. The code for this function is shown in Listing 33.5.

Listing 33.5 showCategories() **Function from** categoryfunctions.php—**A List of Categories**

```
//display a starting list of popular categories
function showCategories($mode)
{
  global $categoryList;
  echo '<hr><h2>Selected Categories</h2>';

  if($mode == 'books')
  {
```

Listing 33.5 **Continued**

```php
  asort($categoryList);

  $categories = count($categoryList);
  $columns = 4;
  $rows = ceil($categories/$columns);

  echo '<table border = 0 cellpadding = 0 cellspacing=0 width = "100%"><tr>';

  reset($categoryList);

  for($col = 0; $col<$columns; $col++)
  {
    echo '<td width = "'.(100/$columns).'%" valign = top><ul>';
    for($row = 0; $row<$rows; $row++)
    {
      $category = each($categoryList);
      if($category)
      {
        $browseNode = $category['key'];
        $name = $category['value'];
        echo "<li><span class = 'category'><a href =
               'index.php?action=browsenode&browseNode=$browseNode'>$name</a>
               </span></li>";
      }
    }
    echo '</ul></td>';
  }
  echo '</tr></table><hr>';
  }
}
```

This function uses an array called `categoryList`, declared in the file `constants.php`, to map `browsenode` numbers to names. The desired `browsenodes` are simply hard-coded into this array. This function sorts the array and displays the various categories.

The `getCategoryName()` function called next in the main event loop looks up the name of the `browsenode` that you are currently looking at so you can display a heading on the screen such as Current Best Sellers in Business & Investing. It looks up this heading in the `categoryList` array mentioned previously.

The fun really starts when you get to the `showBrowseNode()` function, shown in Listing 33.6.

Listing 33.6   `showBrowseNode()` **Function from** `bookdisplayfunctions.php`—**A List of Categories**

```
// For a particular browsenode, display a page of products
function showBrowseNode($browseNode, $page, $mode)
{
  $ars = getARS('browse', array('browsenode'=>$browseNode,
                                'page' => $page,
                                'mode'=>$mode));
  showSummary($ars->products(), $page, $ars->totalResults(),
              $mode, $browseNode);
}
```

The `showBrowseNode()` function does exactly two things. First, it calls the `getARS()` function from `cachefunctions.php`. This function gets and returns an `AmazonResultSet` object (more on this in a moment). Then it calls the `showSummary()` function from `bookdisplayfunctions.php` to display the retrieved information.

The `getARS()` function is absolutely key to driving the whole application. If you work your way through the code for the other actions—viewing details, images, and searching—you will find that it all comes back to this.

Getting an `AmazonResultSet` Class

Let's look at that `getARS()` function in more detail. It is shown in Listing 33.7.

Listing 33.7   `getARS()` **Function from** `cachefunctions.php`—**A Resultset for a Query**

```
// Get an AmazonResultSet either from cache or a live query
// If a live query add it to the cache
function getARS($type, $parameters)
{
  $cache = cached($type, $parameters);
  if($cache)  // if found in cache
  {
    return $cache;
  }
  else
  {
    $ars = new AmazonResultSet;
    if($type == 'asin')
      $ars->ASINSearch(padASIN($parameters['asin']), $parameters['mode']);
    if($type == 'browse')
      $ars->browseNodeSearch($parameters['browsenode'], $parameters['page'],
                             $parameters['mode']);
```

Listing 33.7 **Continued**

```
   if($type == 'search')
     $ars->keywordSearch($parameters['search'], $parameters['page'],
                          $parameters['mode']);
    cache($type, $parameters, $ars);
  }
  return $ars;
}
```

This function is designed to drive the process of getting data from Amazon. It can do this in two ways: either from the cache or live from Amazon. Because Amazon requires developers to cache downloaded data, the function first looks for data in the cache. We discuss the cache shortly.

If you have not already performed this particular query, the data must be fetched live from Amazon. You do this by creating an instance of the AmazonResultSet class and calling the method on it that corresponds to the particular query you want to run. The type of query is determined by the $type parameter. In the category (or browse node) search example, you pass in browse as the value for this parameter (refer to Listing 33.6). If you want to perform a query about one particular book, you should pass in the value asin, and if you want to perform a keyword search, you should set the parameter to search.

Each of these parameters invokes a different method on the AmazonResultSet class. The individual item search calls the ASINSearch() method. The category search calls the browseNodeSearch() method. The keyword search calls the keywordSearch() method.

Let's take a closer look at the AmazonResultSet class. The full code for this class is shown in Listing 33.8.

Listing 33.8 AmazonResultSet.php—**A Class for Handling Amazon Connections**

```
<?php
// you can switch between REST and SOAP using this constant set in
// constants.php
if(METHOD=='SOAP')
{
  include_once('nusoap/nusoap.php');
}


// This class stores the result of queries
// Usually this is 1 or 10 instances of the Product class
class AmazonResultSet
{
  private $browseNode;
  private $page;
  private $mode;
  private $url;
  private $type;
```

Listing 33.8 **Continued**

```php
private $totalResults;
private $currentProduct = null;
private $products = array(); // array of Product objects

function products()
{
  return $this->products;
}

function totalResults()
{
  return $this->totalResults;
}

function getProduct($i)
{
  if(isset($this->products[$i]))
    return $this->products[$i] ;
  else
    return false;
}

// Perform a query to get a page full of products from a browse node
// Switch between XML/HTTP and SOAP in constants.php
// Returns an array of Products
function browseNodeSearch($browseNode, $page, $mode)
{
  if(METHOD=='SOAP')
  {
    $soapclient = new soapclient (
         'http://soap.amazon.com/schemas2/AmazonWebServices.wsdl',
         'wsdl');
    $soap_proxy = $soapclient->getProxy();
    $parameters['mode']=$mode;
    $parameters['page']=$page;
    $parameters['type']='heavy';
    $parameters['tag']=$this->assocID;
    $parameters['devtag']=$this->devTag;
    $parameters['sort']='+salesrank';
    $parameters['browse_node'] = $browseNode;
```

Listing 33.8 **Continued**

```
    // perform actual soap query
    $result = $soap_proxy->BrowseNodeSearchRequest($parameters);
    if(isSOAPError($result))
      return false;
    $this->totalResults = $result['TotalResults'];

    foreach($result['Details'] as $product)
    {
      $this->products[] = new Product($product);
    }
    unset($soapclient);
    unset($soap_proxy);
  }
  else
  {
    // form URL and call parseXML to download and parse it
    $this->type = 'browse';
    $this->browseNode = $browseNode;
    $this->page = $page;
    $this->mode = $mode;
    $this->url = 'http://xml.amazon.com/onca/xml2?t='.ASSOCIATEID
               .'&dev-t='.DEVTAG.'&BrowseNodeSearch='
               .$this->browseNode.'&mode='.$this->mode
               .'&type=heavy&page='.$this->page
               .'&sort=+salesrank&f=xml';
    $this->parseXML();
  }

  return $this->products;
}

// Given an ASIN, get the URL of the large image
// Returns a string
function getImageUrlLarge($ASIN, $mode)
{
  foreach($this->products as $product)
  {
    if( $product->ASIN()== $ASIN)
      return  $product->imageURLLarge();
  }
  // if not found
  $this->ASINSearch($ASIN, $mode);
    return $this->products(0)->imageURLLarge();
}
```

Listing 33.8 **Continued**

```php
// Perform a query to get a products with specified ASIN
// Switch between XML/HTTP and SOAP in constants.php
// Returns a Products object
function ASINSearch($ASIN, $mode = 'books')
{
  $this->type = 'ASIN';
  $this->ASIN=$ASIN;
  $this->mode = $mode;
  $ASIN = padASIN($ASIN);

  if(METHOD=='SOAP')
  {
    error_reporting(E_ALL & ~E_NOTICE);
    $soapclient = new soapclient (
          'http://soap.amazon.com/schemas2/AmazonWebServices.wsdl',
          'wsdl') ;
    $soap_proxy = $soapclient->getProxy();
    $parameters['asin']=$ASIN;
    $parameters['mode']=$mode;
    $parameters['type']="heavy";
    $parameters['tag']=$this->assocID;
    $parameters['devtag']=$this->devTag;

    // perform actual soap query

    $result = $soap_proxy->AsinSearchRequest($parameters);
    if(isSOAPError($result))
    {
      print_r($result);
      return false;
    }
    $this->products[0] = new Product($result['Details'][0]);
    $this->totalResults=1;
    unset($soapclient);
    unset($soap_proxy);
  }
  else
  {
    // form URL and call parseXML to download and parse it
    $this->url = 'http://xml.amazon.com/onca/xml2?t='.ASSOCIATEID
                  .'&dev-t='.DEVTAG.'&AsinSearch='
                  .$this->ASIN
                  .'&type=heavy&f=xml';
    $this->parseXML();
  }
  return $this->products[0];
}
```

Listing 33.8   **Continued**

```php
// Perform a query to get a page full of products with a keyword search
// Switch between XML/HTTP and SOAP in index.php
// Returns an array of Products
function keywordSearch($search, $page, $mode = 'books')
{
  if(METHOD=='SOAP')
  {
    error_reporting(E_ALL & ~E_NOTICE);
    $soapclient = new soapclient(
        'http://soap.amazon.com/schemas2/AmazonWebServices.wsdl','wsdl');
    $soap_proxy = $soapclient->getProxy();
    $parameters['mode']=$mode;
    $parameters['page']=$page;
    $parameters['type']="heavy";
    $parameters['tag']=$this->assocID;
    $parameters['devtag']=$this->devTag;
    $parameters['sort']='+salesrank';
    $parameters['keyword'] = $search;

    // perform actual soap request
    $result = $soap_proxy->KeywordSearchRequest($parameters);

    if(isSOAPError($result) )
      return false;

    foreach($result['Details'] as $product)
    {
      $this->products[] = new Product($product);
    }
    $this->totalResults = $result['TotalResults'] ;
    unset($soapclient);
    unset($soap_proxy);
  }
  else
  {
    $this->type = 'search';
    $this->search=$search;
    $this->page = $page;
    $search = urlencode($search);
    $this->mode = $mode;
```

Listing 33.8   **Continued**

```
      $this->url = 'http://xml.amazon.com/onca/xml2?t='.ASSOCIATEID
                  .'&dev-t='.DEVTAG.'&KeywordSearch='
                  .$search.'&mode='.$this->mode
                  .'&type=heavy&page='
                  .$this->page
                  .'&sort=+salesrank&f=xml';
      $this->parseXML();
    }
    return $this->products;
  }

  // Parse the XML into Product object(s)
  function parseXML()
  {
    // suppress errors because this will fail sometimes
    $xml = @simplexml_load_file($this->url);
    if(!$xml)
    {
      //try a second time in case just server busy
      $xml = @simplexml_load_file($this->url);
      if(!$xml)
      {
        return false;
      }

    }
    $this->totalResults = (integer)$xml->TotalResults;
    foreach($xml->Details as $productXML)
    {
      $this->products[] = new Product($productXML);
    }
  }
}
?>
```

This useful class does exactly the sort of thing classes are good for. It encapsulates the interface to Amazon in a nice black box. Within the class, the connection to Amazon can be made either via the REST method or the SOAP method. The method it uses is determined by the global METHOD constant you set in `constants.php`.

Let's begin by going back to the Category Search example. You use the `AmazonResultSet` class as follows:

```
$ars = new AmazonResultSet;
$ars->browseNodeSearch($parameters['browsenode'],
                       $parameters['page'],
                       $parameters['mode']);
```

This class has no constructor, so you go straight to that browseNodeSearch() method. Here, you pass it three parameters: the browsenode number you are interested in (corresponding to, say, Business & Investing or Computers & Internet); the page number, representing the records you would like retrieved; and the mode, representing the type of merchandise you are interested in. An excerpt of the code for this method is shown in Listing 33.9.

Listing 33.9 browseNodeSearch() **Method—Performing a Category Search**

```
function browseNodeSearch($browseNode, $page, $mode)
{
  if(METHOD=='SOAP')
  {
    $soapclient = new soapclient(
          'http://soap.amazon.com/schemas2/AmazonWebServices.wsdl',
          'wsdl');
    $soap_proxy = $soapclient->getProxy();
    $parameters['mode']=$mode;
    $parameters['page']=$page;
    $parameters['type']='heavy';
    $parameters['tag']=$this->assocID;
    $parameters['devtag']=$this->devTag;
    $parameters['sort']='+salesrank';
    $parameters['browse_node'] = $browseNode;

    // perform actual soap query
    $result = $soap_proxy->BrowseNodeSearchRequest($parameters);
    if(isSOAPError($result))
      return false;
    $this->totalResults = $result['TotalResults'];

    foreach($result['Details'] as $product)
    {
      $this->products[] = new Product($product);
    }
    unset($soapclient);
    unset($soap_proxy);
  }
  else
  {
    // form URL and call parseXML to download and parse it
    $this->type = 'browse';
    $this->browseNode = $browseNode;
    $this->page = $page;
    $this->mode = $mode;
```

Listing 33.9   **Continued**

```
    $this->url = 'http://xml.amazon.com/onca/xml2?t='.ASSOCIATEID
                .'&dev-t='.DEVTAG.'&BrowseNodeSearch='
                .$this->browseNode.'&mode='.$this->mode
                .'&type=heavy&page='.$this->page
                .'&sort=+salesrank&f=xml';
    $this->parseXML();
  }

  return $this->products;
}
```

Depending on the value of the METHOD constant, this method performs the query via REST or via SOAP. Next, we look at each of these methods separately.

Using REST/XML Over HTTP

To use REST/XML over HTTP, you begin by setting a few important class member variables:

- type—The type of search required. You are searching for books within a particular browsenode, so you set the value to browse.
- browse—The value of the particular browsenode you have been passed as a parameter.
- page—The page number that you have been passed as a parameter.
- mode—The type of item you are searching for (for example, books) that you have been passed as a parameter.
- url—The URL at Amazon that you need to connect to in order to perform this type of search.

The URLs that you make your HTTP connections to for different types of searches and the parameters they expect can be found in the Amazon.com Web Services API and Integration Guide in your developer's kit. Look closely at the GET parameters passed in here:

```
$this->_url = 'http://xml.amazon.com/onca/xml2?t='.ASSOCIATEID
                .'&dev-t='.DEVTAG.'&BrowseNodeSearch='
                .$this->_browseNode.'&mode='.$this->_mode
                .'&type=heavy&page='.$this->_page
                .'&sort=+salesrank&f=xml';
```

The parameters you need to pass to this URL are as follows:

- t—Your Associate ID.
- dev-t—Your developer token.
- BrowseNodeSearch—The browsenode number you want to search.
- mode—books, or another valid product type.
- type—Heavy or lite (note spelling!). Heavy gives more information.
- page—Group of 10 results.
- sort—The order you would like the results returned in. This parameter is optional. In this case, we set it to +salesrank because we wanted results in sales rank order.
- f—The format. This parameter should always contain the value 'xml'.

Valid sort types are as follows:

- Featured Items: +pmrank
- Bestselling: +salesrank
- Average Customer Review: +reviewrank
- Price (Low to High): +pricerank
- Price (High to Low): +inverse-pricerank
- Publication Date: +daterank
- Alphabetical (A-Z): +titlerank
- Alphabetical (Z-A): -titlerank

After you set all these parameters, you call

```
$this->parseXML();
```

to actually do the work. The parseXML() method is shown in Listing 33.10.

Listing 33.10 parseXML() **Method—Parsing the XML Returned from a Query**

```
// Parse the XML into Product object(s)
function parseXML()
{
  // suppress errors because this will fail sometimes
  $xml = @simplexml_load_file($this->url);
  if(!$xml)
  {
    //try a second time in case just server busy
    $xml = @simplexml_load_file($this->url);
    if(!$xml)
    {
      return false;
    }
}
```

Listing 33.10   **Continued**

```
  }
  $this->totalResults = (integer)$xml->TotalResults;
  foreach($xml->Details as $productXML)
  {
    $this->products[] = new Product($productXML);
  }
}
```

The function `simplexml_load_file()` does most of the work for you. It reads in the XML content from a file or, in this case, an URL. It provides an object-oriented interface to the data and the structure in the XML document. This is a useful interface to the data, but because you want one set of interface functions to work with data that has come in via REST or SOAP, you can build your own object-oriented interface to the same data in instances of the `Product` class. Note that you cast the attributes from the XML into PHP variable types in the REST version. You do not use the `cast` operator in PHP, but without it here, you would receive object representations of each piece of data that will not be very useful to you.

The `Product` class contains mostly accessor functions to access the data stored in its private members, so printing the entire file here is not worthwhile. The stucture of the class and constructor is worth visiting, though. Listing 33.11 contains part of the definition of `Product`.

Listing 33.11   **The Product Class Encapsulates the Information You Have About an Amazon Product**

```
class Product
{
  private $ASIN;
  private $productName;
  private $releaseDate;
  private $manufacturer;
  private $imageUrlMedium;
  private $imageUrlLarge;
  private $listPrice;
  private $ourPrice;
  private $salesRank;
  private $availability;
  private $avgCustomerRating;
  private $authors = array();
  private $reviews = array();
  private $similarProducts = array();
```

Listing 33.11 **Continued**

```php
function __construct($xml)
{
  if(METHOD=='SOAP')
  {
    $this->ASIN = $xml['Asin'];
    $this->productName = $xml['ProductName'];
    if($xml['Authors'])
    {
      foreach($xml['Authors'] as $author)
      {
        $this->authors[] = $author;
      }
    }
    $this->releaseDate = $xml['ReleaseDate'];
    $this->manufacturer = $xml['Manufacturer'];
    $this->imageUrlMedium = $xml['ImageUrlMedium'];
    $this->imageUrlLarge = $xml['ImageUrlLarge'];

    $this->listPrice = $xml['ListPrice'];
    $this->listPrice = str_replace('$', '', $this->listPrice);
    $this->listPrice = str_replace(',', '', $this->listPrice);
    $this->listPrice = floatval($this->listPrice);

    $this->ourPrice = $xml['OurPrice'];
    $this->ourPrice = str_replace('$', '', $this->ourPrice);
    $this->ourPrice = str_replace(',', '', $this->ourPrice);
    $this->ourPrice = floatval($this->ourPrice);

    $this->salesRank = $xml['SalesRank'];
    $this->availability = $xml['Availability'];
    $this->avgCustomerRating = $xml['Reviews']['AvgCustomerRating'];
    $reviewCount = 0;
    if($xml['Reviews']['CustomerReviews'])
    {
      foreach ($xml['Reviews']['CustomerReviews'] as $review)
      {
        $this->reviews[$reviewCount]['rating'] = $review['Rating'];
        $this->reviews[$reviewCount]['summary'] = $review['Summary'];
        $this->reviews[$reviewCount]['comment'] = $review['Comment'];
        $reviewCount++;
      }
    }
```

Listing 33.11   **Continued**

```php
    if($xml['SimilarProducts'])
    {
      foreach ($xml['SimilarProducts'] as $similar)
      {
        $this->similarProducts[] = $similar;
      }
    }
  }
  else // using REST
  {
    $this->ASIN = (string)$xml->Asin;
    $this->productName = (string)$xml->ProductName;
    if($xml->Authors->Author)
    {
      foreach($xml->Authors->Author as $author)
      {
        $this->authors[] = (string)$author;
      }
    }
    $this->releaseDate = (string)$xml->ReleaseDate;
    $this->manufacturer = (string)$xml->Manufacturer;
    $this->imageUrlMedium = (string)$xml->ImageUrlMedium;
    $this->imageUrlLarge = (string)$xml->ImageUrlLarge;

    $this->listPrice = (string)$xml->ListPrice;
    $this->listPrice = str_replace('$', '', $this->listPrice);
    $this->listPrice = str_replace(',', '', $this->listPrice);
    $this->listPrice = floatval($this->listPrice);

    $this->ourPrice = (string)$xml->OurPrice;
    $this->ourPrice = str_replace('$', '', $this->ourPrice);
    $this->ourPrice = str_replace(',', '', $this->ourPrice);
    $this->ourPrice = floatval($this->ourPrice);

    $this->salesRank = (string)$xml->SalesRank;
    $this->availability = (string)$xml->Availability;
    $this->avgCustomerRating = (float)$xml->Reviews->AvgCustomerRating;
    $reviewCount = 0;
    if($xml->Reviews->CustomerReview)
    {
      foreach ($xml->Reviews->CustomerReview as $review)
```

Listing 33.11   **Continued**

```
        {
          $this->reviews[$reviewCount]['rating'] = (float)$review->Rating;
          $this->reviews[$reviewCount]['summary'] = (string)$review->Summary;
          $this->reviews[$reviewCount]['comment'] = (string)$review->Comment;
          $reviewCount++;
        }
      }
      if($xml->SimilarProducts->Product)
      {
        foreach ($xml->SimilarProducts->Product as $similar)
        {
          $this->similarProducts[] = (string)$similar;
        }
      }
    }
  }
```

Again, this constructor takes two different forms of input data and creates one application interface. Note that while some of the handling code could be made more generic, some tricky attributes such as reviews have different names depending on the method.

Having gone through all this processing to retrieve the data, you now return control back to the getARS() function and hence back to showBrowseNode(). The next step is

```
showSummary($ars->products(), $page,
            $ars->totalResults(), $mode,
            $browseNode);
```

The showSummary() function simply displays the data in the AmazonResultSet, as you can see it all the way back in Figure 33.1. We therefore did not include the function here.

Using SOAP

Let's go back and look at the SOAP version of the browseNodeSearch() function. This section of the code is repeated here:

```
$soapclient = new soapclient(
      'http://soap.amazon.com/schemas2/AmazonWebServices.wsdl',
      'wsdl');
$soap_proxy = $soapclient->getProxy();
$parameters['mode']=$mode;
$parameters['page']=$page;
$parameters['type']='heavy';
$parameters['tag']=$this->assocID;
$parameters['devtag']=$this->devTag;
$parameters['sort']='+salesrank';
$parameters['browse_node'] = $browseNode;
```

```
// perform actual soap query
$result = $soap_proxy->BrowseNodeSearchRequest($parameters);
if(isSOAPError($result))
  return false;
$this->totalResults = $result['TotalResults'];

foreach($result['Details'] as $product)
{
  $this->products[] = new Product($product);
}
unset($soapclient);
unset($soap_proxy) ;
```

There are no extra functions to go through here; the SOAP client does everything for you.

You begin by creating an instance of the SOAP client:

```
$soapclient = new soapclient(
                  'http://soap.amazon.com/schemas2/AmazonWebServices.wsdl',
                  'wsdl');
```

Here, you provide the client with two parameters. The first is the WSDL description of the service, and the second parameter tells the SOAP client that this is a WSDL URL. Alternatively, you could just provide one parameter: the endpoint of the service, which is the direct URL of the SOAP Server.

We chose to do it this way for a good reason, which you can see right there in the next line of code:

```
$soap_proxy = $soapclient->getProxy();
```

This line creates a class according to the information in the WSDL document. This class, the SOAP proxy, will have methods that correspond to the methods of the Web Service. This makes life much easier. You can interact with the Web Service as though it were a local PHP class.

Next, you set up an array of the parameters you need to pass to the `browsenode` query:

```
$parameters['mode']=$mode;
$parameters['page']=$page;
$parameters['type']='heavy';
$parameters['tag']=$this->_assocID;
$parameters['devtag']=$this->_devTag;
$parameters['sort']='+salesrank';
$parameters['browse_node'] = $browseNode;
```

Using the `proxy` class, you can then just call the Web Service methods, passing in the array of parameters:

```
$result = $soap_proxy->BrowseNodeSearchRequest($parameters);
```

The data stored in $result is an array that you can directly store as a Product object in the products array in the AmazonResultSet class.

Caching the Data

Let's go back to the getARS() function and address caching. As you might recall, the function looks like this:

```
// Get an AmazonResultSet either from cache or a live query
// If a live query add it to the cache
function getARS($type, $parameters)
{
  $cache = cached($type, $parameters);
  if($cache)  // if found in cache
  {
    return  $cache;
  }
  else
  {
    $ars = new AmazonResultSet;
    if($type == 'asin')
      $ars->ASINSearch(padASIN($parameters['asin']), $parameters['mode']);
    if($type == 'browse')
      $ars->browseNodeSearch($parameters['browsenode'], $parameters['page'],
                             $parameters['mode']);
    if($type == 'search')
      $ars->keywordSearch($parameters['search'], $parameters['page'],
                          $parameters['mode']);
    cache($type, $parameters, $ars);
  }
  return $ars;
}
```

All the application's SOAP or XML caching is done via this function. You also use another function to cache images. You begin by calling the cached() function to see whether the required AmazonResultSet is already cached. If it is, you return that data instead of making a new request to Amazon:

```
$cache = cached($type, $parameters);
if($cache)  // if found in cache
{
  return  $cache;
}
```

If not, when you get the data back from Amazon, you add it to the cache:

```
cache($type, $parameters, $ars);
```

Let's look more closely at these two functions: cached() and cache(). These functions, shown in Listing 33.12, implement the caching Amazon requires as part of its terms and conditions.

Listing 33.12 cached() **and** cache() **Functions—Caching Functions from**
cachefunctions.php

```php
// check if Amazon data is in the cache
// if it is, return it
// if not, return false
function cached($type, $parameters)
{
  if($type == 'browse')
  {
    $filename =
➥CACHE.'/browse.'.$parameters['browsenode'].'.'.$parameters['page'].
              '.'.$parameters['mode'].'.dat';
  }
  if($type == 'search')
  {
    $filename = CACHE.'/search.'.$parameters['search'].'.'.$parameters['page'].
              '.'.$parameters['mode'].'.dat';
  }
  if($type == 'asin')
  {
    $filename = CACHE.'/asin.'.$parameters['asin'].'.'.$parameters['mode'].
              '.dat';
  }

  // is cached data missing or > 1 hour old?
  if(!file_exists($filename) ||
      ((mktime() - filemtime($filename)) > 60*60))
  {
    return false;
  }
  $data = file_get_contents($filename);
  return unserialize($data);
}

// add Amazon data to the cache
function cache($type, $parameters, $data)
{
  if($type == 'browse')
```

Listing 33.12   **Continued**

```
  {
    $filename = CACHE.'/browse.'.$parameters['browsenode'].
               '.'.$parameters['page'].'.'.$parameters['mode'].'.dat';
  }
  if($type == 'search')
  {
    $filename = CACHE.'/search.'.$parameters['search'].'.'.$parameters['page'].
               '.'.$parameters['mode'].'.dat';
  }
  if($type == 'asin')
  {
    $filename = CACHE.'/asin.'.$parameters['asin'].'.'.$parameters['mode'].
               '.dat';
  }
  $data = serialize($data);

  $fp = fopen($filename, 'wb');
  if(!$fp||(fwrite($fp, $data)==-1))
  {
    echo  ('<p>Error, could not store cache file');
  }
  fclose($fp);
}
```

Looking through this code, you can see that cache files are stored under a filename that consists of the type of query followed by the query parameters. The cache() function stores results by serializing them, and the cached() function deserializes them. The cached() function will also overwrite any data more than an hour old, as per the terms and conditions.

The function serialize() turns stored program data into a string that can be stored. In this case, you create a storable representation of an AmazonResultSet object. Calling unserialize() does the opposite, turning the stored version back into a data structure in memory. Note that unserializing an object like this means you need to have the class definition in the file so that the class is comprehendible and usable once reloaded.

In this application, retrieving a resultset from the cache takes a fraction of a second. Making a new live query takes up to 10 seconds.

Building the Shopping Cart

So, given all these amazing Amazon querying abilities, what can you do with them? The most obvious thing you can build is a shopping cart. Because we already covered this topic extensively in Chapter 27, we do not go into deep detail here.

The shopping cart functions are shown in Listing 33.13.

Listing 33.13 `cartfunctions.php`—**Implementing the Shopping Cart**

```php
<?php
require_once('AmazonResultSet.php');

// Using the function showSummary() in the file bookdisplay.php display
// the current contents of the shopping cart
function showCart($cart, $mode)
{
  // build an array to pass
  $products = array();
  foreach($cart as $ASIN=>$product)
  {
    $ars = getARS('asin', array('asin'=>$ASIN, 'mode'=>$mode));
    if($ars)
      $products[] = $ars->getProduct(0);
  }
  // build the form to link to an Amazon.com shopping cart
  echo '<form method="POST"
             action="http://www.amazon.com/o/dt/assoc/handle-buy-box">';
  foreach($cart as $ASIN=>$product)
  {
    $quantity = $cart[$ASIN]['quantity'];
    echo "<input type='hidden' name='asin.$ASIN' value='$quantity'>";
  }
  echo '<input type="hidden" name="tag-value" value="ASSOCIATEID">';
  echo '<input type="hidden" name="tag_value" value="ASSOCIATEID">';
  echo '<input type="image" src="images/checkout.gif"
                          name="submit.add-to-cart"
                          value="Buy From Amazon.com">';
  echo ' When you have finished shopping press checkout to add all the
         items in your Tahuayo cart to your Amazon cart and complete
         your purchase.<br />';
  echo '</form>';

  echo '<a href = "index.php?action=emptycart"><img
          src = "images/emptycart.gif" alt = "Empty Cart" border = 0></a>
        If you have finished with this cart, you can empty it of all items.
        <br />';
  echo '<h1>Cart Contents</h1>';
  showSummary($products, 1, count($products), $mode,  0, true);

}
```

Listing 33.13 **Continued**

```php
// show the small overview cart that is always on the screen
// only shows the last three items added
function showSmallCart()
{
  global $_SESSION;

  echo '<table border = 1 cellpadding = 1 cellspacing = 0>';
  echo '<tr><td class = cartheading>Your Cart $'.
       number_format(cartPrice(), 2).
       '</td></tr>';
  echo '<tr><td class = cart>'.cartContents().'</td></tr>';

  // form to link to an Amazon.com shopping cart
  echo '<form method="POST"
             action="http://www.amazon.com/o/dt/assoc/handle-buy-box">';
  echo '<tr><td class = cartheading><a href =
                          "index.php?action=showcart"><img
                          src="images/details.gif" border=0></a>';
  foreach($_SESSION['cart'] as $ASIN=>$product)
  {
    $quantity = $_SESSION['cart'][$ASIN]['quantity'];
    echo "<input type='hidden' name='asin.$ASIN' value='$quantity'>";
  }
  echo '<input type="hidden" name="tag-value" value="ASSOCIATEID">';
  echo '<input type="hidden" name="tag_value" value="ASSOCIATEID">';
  echo '<input type="image" src="images/checkout.gif"
             name="submit.add-to-cart" value="Buy From Amazon.com">';
  echo '</td></tr>';
  echo '</form>';

  echo '</table>';
}

// show last three items added to cart
function cartContents()
{
  global $_SESSION;

  $display = array_slice($_SESSION['cart'], -3, 3);
  // we want them in reverse chronological order
  $display = array_reverse($display, true);

  $result = '';
  $counter = 0;
```

Listing 33.13 **Continued**

```
  // abbreviate the names if they are long
  foreach($display as $product)
  {
    if(strlen($product['name'])<=40)
      $result .= $product['name'].'<br />';
    else
      $result .= substr($product['name'], 0, 37).'...<br />';
    $counter++;
  }

  // add blank lines if the cart is nearly empty to keep the
  // display the same
  for(;$counter<3; $counter++)
  {
    $result .= '<br />';
  }
  return $result;
}

// calculate total price of items in cart
function cartPrice()
{
  global $_SESSION;
  $total = 0.0;
  foreach($_SESSION['cart'] as $product)
  {
    $price = str_replace('$', '', $product['price']);
    $total += $price*$product['quantity'];
  }

  return $total;
}

// add a single item to cart
// there is currently no facility to add more than one at a time
function addToCart(&$cart, $ASIN, $mode)
{
  if(isset($cart[$ASIN] ))
  {
    $cart[$ASIN]['quantity'] +=1;
  }
  else
  {
```

Listing 33.13 **Continued**

```
    // check that the ASIN is valid and look up the price
    $ars = new AmazonResultSet;
    $product = $ars->ASINSearch($ASIN, $mode);

    if($product->valid())
      $cart[$ASIN] = array('price'=>$product->ourPrice(),
                    'name' => $product->productName(), 'quantity' => 1) ;
  }


}

// delete all of a particular item from cart
function deleteFromCart(&$cart, $ASIN)
{
  unset ($cart[$ASIN]);
}
?>
```

There are some differences about the way you do things with this cart. For example, look at the addToCart() function. When you try to add an item to the cart, you can check that it has a valid ASIN and look up the current (or at least, cached) price.

The really interesting issue here is this question: When customers check out, how do you get their data to Amazon?

Checking Out to Amazon

Look closely at the showCart() function in Listing 33.13. Here's the relevant part:

```
// build the form to link to an Amazon.com shopping cart
echo '<form method="POST"
     action="http://www.amazon.com/o/dt/assoc/handle-buy-box">';
foreach($cart as $ASIN=>$product)
{
  $quantity = $cart[$ASIN]['quantity'];
  echo "<input type='hidden' name='asin.$ASIN' value='$quantity'>";
}
echo '<input type="hidden" name="tag-value" value="ASSOCIATEID">';
echo '<input type="hidden" name="tag_value" value="ASSOCIATEID">';
echo '<input type="image" src="images/checkout.gif"
            name="submit.add-to-cart" value="Buy From Amazon.com">';
echo ' When you have finished shopping press checkout to add all the items
       in your Tahuayo cart to your Amazon cart and complete your purchase.
       <br />';
echo '</form>';
```

The checkout button is a form button that connects the cart to a customer's shopping cart on Amazon. You send ASINs, quantities, and your Associate ID through as POST variables. And hey, presto! You can see the result of clicking this button in Figure 33.5, earlier in this chapter.

One difficulty with this interface is that it is a one-way interaction. You can add items to the Amazon cart but cannot remove them. This means that people cannot browse back and forth between the sites easily without ending up with duplicate items in their carts.

Installing the Project Code

If you want to install the project code from this chapter, you will need to take a few steps beyond the norm. After you have the code in an appropriate location on your server, you need to do the following:

- Create a cache directory.
- Set the permissions on the cache directory so that the scripts will be able to write in it.
- Edit `constants.php` to provide the location of the cache.
- Sign up for an Amazon developer token.
- Edit `constants.php` to include your developer token and, optionally, your Associate ID.
- Make sure NuSOAP is installed. We included it inside the Tahuayo directory, but you could move it and change the code.
- Check that you have PHP5 compiled with simpleXML support.

Extending the Project

There are lots of fun things you could do to extend this project:

- You could expand the types of searches that are available via Tahuayo.
- You might like to experiment with Amazon's XSLT Web Service.
- You could check out the links to innovative sample applications in Amazon's Web Services How-To. Look at these applications for more ideas:

  http://associates.amazon.com/exec/panama/associates/ntg/browse/-/567634/

Shopping carts are the most obvious thing to build with this data, but they are not the only thing.

Further Reading

A million books and online resources are available on the topics of XML and Web Services. A great place to start is always at the W3C. You can look at the XML Working Group page at

http://www.w3.org/XML/Core/

and the Web Services Activity page at

http://www.w3.org/2002/ws/

just as a beginning.

VI

Appendixes

A

Installing PHP and MySQL

APACHE, PHP, AND MYSQL ARE AVAILABLE FOR MANY combinations of operating systems and web servers. In this appendix, we explain how to set up Apache, PHP, and MySQL on a few server platforms. We cover the most common options available for Unix and Windows XP.

Key topics covered in this appendix include

- Running PHP as a CGI interpreter or as a module
- Installing Apache, SSL, PHP, and MySQL under Unix
- Installing Apache, PHP, and MySQL under Windows
- Testing that it's working using `phpinfo()`
- Adding PHP to Microsoft Internet Information Server
- Installing PEAR
- Considering other configurations

Our goal in this appendix is to provide you with an installation guide for a web server that will enable you to host multiple websites. Some sites, like those in the examples, require Secure Sockets Layer (SSL) for e-commerce solutions. And most are driven via scripts to connect to a database (DB) server and extract and process data.

Many PHP users never need to install PHP on a machine, which is why this material is in an appendix rather than Chapter 1, "PHP Crash Course." The easiest way to get access to a reliable server with a fast connection to the Internet and PHP already installed is to simply sign up for an account at one of the thousands of hosting services or hosting service resellers around the globe.

Depending on why you are installing PHP on a machine, you might make different decisions. If you have a machine permanently connected to the network that you intend to use as a live server, performance will be important to you. If you are building a development server where you can build and test your code, having a similar configuration to the live server will be the most important consideration. If you intend to run ASP and PHP on the same machine, different limitations will apply.

Running PHP as a CGI Interpreter or Module

The PHP interpreter can be run as either a module or as a separate common gateway interface (CGI) binary. Generally, the module version is used for performance reasons. However, the CGI version is sometimes used for servers where a module version is not available or because it enables Apache users to run different PHP-enabled pages under different user IDs.

In this appendix, we primarily cover the module option as the method to run PHP.

Installing Apache, PHP, and MySQL Under Unix

Depending on your needs and your level of experience with Unix systems, you might choose to do a binary install or compile the programs directly from their source. Both approaches have their advantages.

A binary install will take an expert minutes and a beginner not much longer, but it will result in a system that is probably a version or two behind the current releases and one that is configured with somebody else's choices of options.

A source install will take some time to download, install, and configure, and such an approach is intimidating the first few times you do it. It does, however, give you complete control. You choose what to install, what versions to use, and what configuration directives to set.

Binary Installation

Most Linux distributions include a preconfigured Apache Web Server with PHP built in. The details of what is provided depend on your chosen distribution and version.

One disadvantage of binary installs is that you rarely get the latest version of a program. Depending on how important the last few bug fix releases are, getting an older version might not be a problem for you. The biggest issue is that you do not get to choose what options are compiled into your programs.

The most flexible and reliable path to take is to compile all the programs you need from their sources. This path will take a little more time than installing RPMs, so you might choose to use RPMs or other binary packages when available. Even if binary files are not available from official sources with the configuration you need, you might be able to find unofficial ones with a search engine.

Source Installation

Let's install Apache, PHP, and MySQL under a Unix environment. First, you need to decide which extra modules you will load under the trio. Because some of the examples covered in this book use a secure server for web transactions, you should install an SSL-enabled server.

For purposes of this book, the PHP configuration is more or less the default setup but also covers ways to enable the following two libraries under PHP:

- gd2
- PDFlib

These are just two of the many libraries available for PHP. We included them so that you can get an idea of what is required to enable extra libraries within PHP. Compiling most Unix programs follows a similar process.

You usually need to recompile PHP after installing a new library, so if you know what you need in advance, you can install all required libraries on your machine and then begin to compile the PHP module.

Here, we describe installation on an SuSE Linux server, but the description is generic enough to apply to other Unix servers.

Start by gathering the required files for the installation. You need these items:

- Apache (http://httpd.apache.org/)—The web server
- OpenSSL (http://www.openssl.org/)—Open source toolkit that implements the Secure Sockets Layer
- Mod_SSL (http://www.modssl.org/)—An Apache module interface to OpenSSL
- MySQL (http://www.mysql.com/)—The relational database
- PHP (http://www.php.net/)—The server-side scripting language
- http://www.pdflib.com/products/pdflib/download/index.html—Library for generating PDF documents on the fly
- ftp://ftp.uu.net/graphics/jpeg/—The JPEG library, needed for PDFlib and gd
- http://www.libpng.org/pub/png/libpng.html—The PNG library, needed for gd
- http://www.gzip.org/zlib/—The zlib library, needed for the PNG library, above
- http://www.libtiff.org/—The TIFF library, needed for PDFlib
- ftp://ftp.cac.washington.edu/imap/—The IMAP c client, needed for IMAP

If you want to use the `mail()` function, you will need to have an MTA (mail transfer agent) installed, although we do not go through this here.

We assume that you have root access to the server and the following tools installed on your system:

- `gzip` or `gunzip`
- `gcc` and GNU `make`

When you are ready to begin the installation process, you should start by downloading all `tar` file sources to a temporary directory. Make sure you put them somewhere with plenty of space. In our case, we chose `/usr/src` for the temporary directory. You should download them as root to avoid permissions problems.

Installing MySQL

In this section, we show you how to do a binary install of MySQL. This type of install automatically places files in various locations. We chose the following directories for the remainder of our trio:

- `/usr/local/apache`
- `/usr/local/ssl`

You can install the applications in different directories by changing the prefix option before installing.

Let's begin! Become root by using `su`:

```
$ su root
```

Then enter the user root's password. Next, change to the directory where you have stored the source files. For example, use

```
# cd /usr/src
```

MySQL recommends that you download a binary of MySQL instead of compiling from scratch. Which version to use depends on what you want to do. At the time of writing, the production version of MySQL was 4.0. You need 4.1 if you want to use subqueries and 5.0 if you want to use stored procedures. By the time you read this book, one of these versions may have become the production version. Although MySQL prerelease versions are generally very stable, you may choose not to use them on a production site. If you are learning and experimenting on your own machine, you may choose to use one of these versions.

You should download the following packages:

```
MySQL-server-VERSION.i386.rpm
MySQL-Max-VERSION.i386.rpm
MySQL-client-VERSION.i386.rpm
```

(The word *VERSION* is a placeholder for the version number. For whichever version you choose, make sure that you choose a matching set.) If you intend to run the MySQL client and server on this machine and to compile MySQL support into other programs such as PHP, you need all these packages.

Enter the following commands to install the MySQL servers and client:

```
rpm -i MySQL-server-VERSION.i386.rpm
rpm -i MySQL-Max-VERSION.i386.rpm
rpm -I MySQL-client-VERSION.i386.rpm
```

The MySQL server should now be up and running.

Now it's time to give the root user a password. Make sure you replace `new-password` in the following command with a password of your choice; otherwise, `new-password` will be your root password:

```
mysqladmin -u root password 'new-password'
```

When you install MySQL, it automatically creates two databases. One is the `mysql` table, which controls users, hosts, and DB permissions in the actual server. The other is a test DB. You can check your database via the command line like this:

```
# mysql -u root -p
Enter password:
mysql> show databases;
+--------------------+
| Database           |
+--------------------+
|  mysql             |
|  test              |
+--------------------+
2 rows in set (0.00 sec)
```

Type **quit** or **\q** to quit the MySQL client.

The default MySQL configuration allows any user access to the system without providing a username or password. This is obviously undesirable.

The final compulsory piece of MySQL housekeeping is deleting the anonymous accounts. Opening a command prompt and typing the following lines accomplish that task:

```
# mysql -u root -p
mysql> use mysql
mysql> delete from user where User='';
mysql> quit
```

You then need to type

```
mysqladmin -u root -p reload
```

for these changes to take effect.

You should also enable binary logging on your MySQL server because you will need it if you plan to use replication. To do this, first stop the server:

```
mysqladmin -u root -p shutdown
```

Create a file called `/etc/my.cnf` to be used as your MySQL options file. At the moment, you need only one option, but you can set several here. Consult the MySQL manual for a full list.

Open the file and type

```
[mysqld]
log-bin
```

Save the file and exit. Then restart the server by running `mysqld_safe`.

Installing PDFlib

If you do not want to use PDFlib to create PDF files, as discussed in Chapter 32, "Generating Personalized Documents in Portable Document Format (PDF)," you can skip this section.

Download PDFlib from http://www.pdflib.com/products/pdflib/download/index.html.

To extract the contents of the PDFlib archive, type

```
# gunzip -c PDFlib-6.0.0p1-Linux.tar.gz | tar xvf -
```

We do not use PDFlib directly, so we come back to it after PHP is running.

Installing PHP

You should still be acting as root; if not, use *su* to change back to root.

Before you can install PHP, you need to have Apache preconfigured so that it knows where everything is. (We come back to this topic later when setting up the Apache server.) Change back to the directory where you have the source code:

```
# cd /usr/src
# gunzip -c apache_1.3.31.tar.gz | tar xvf -
# cd apache_1.3.31
# ./configure --prefix=/usr/local/apache
```

Now you can start setting up PHP. Extract the source files and change to its directory:

```
# cd /usr/src
# gunzip -c php-5.0.0.tar.gz | tar xvf -
#  cd php-5.0.0
```

Again, many options are available with PHP's `configure` command. Use `./configure --help | less` to determine what you want to add. In this case, add support for MySQL, Apache, PDFlib, and gd.

Note that the following is all one command. You can put it all on one line or, as shown here, use the continuation character, the backslash (\). This character allows you to type one command across multiple lines to improve readability:

```
# ./configure --with-mysqli=mysql_config_path/mysql_config \
            --with-apache=../apache_1.3.31 \
            --with-jpeg-dir=/path/to/jpeglib \
            --with-tiff-dir=/path/to.tiffdir \
            --with-zlib-dir=/path/to/zlib \
            --with-imap=/path/to/imapcclient \
            --with-gd
```

Next, make and install the binaries:

```
# make
# make install
```

Copy an INI file to the `lib` directory:

```
# cp php.ini-dist /usr/local/lib/php.ini
```

or

```
# cp php.ini-recommended /usr/local/lib/php.ini
```

The two versions of `php.ini` in the suggested commands have different options set. The first, `php.ini-dist`, is intended for development machines. For instance, it has `display_errors` set to On. This makes development easier, but it is not really appropriate on a production machine. When we refer to a `php.ini` setting's default value in this book, we mean its setting in this version of `php.ini`. The second version, `php.ini-recommended`, is intended for production machines.

You can edit the `php.ini` file to set PHP options. There are any number of options that you might choose to set, but a few in particular are worth noting. You might need to set the value of `sendmail_path` if you want to send email from scripts.

Now it's time to set up OpenSSL. It is what you will use to create temporary certificates and CSR files. The `--prefix` option specifies the main installation directory:

```
# gunzip -c openssl-0.9.7d.tar.gz | tar xvf -
# cd openssl-0.9.7d
# ./config --prefix=/usr/local/ssl
```

Now make it, test it, and install it:

```
# make
# make test
# make install
```

Next, configure the mod_SSL module and specify it to be a loadable module with the Apache configuration:

```
# cd /usr/src/
# gunzip -c mod_ssl-2.8.18-1.3.31.tar.gz |tar xvf -
# cd mod_ssl-2.8.18-1.3.31
# ./configure --with-apache=../apache_1.3.31
```

Note that you can add more Apache modules to the Apache source tree. The optional `--enable-shared=ssl` option enables the building of mod_SSL as a dynamic shared object (DSO) `libssl.so`. Read the INSTALL and `htdocs/manual/dso.html` documents in the Apache source tree for more information about DSO support in Apache. It is strongly advised that ISPs and package maintainers use the DSO facility for maximum flexibility with mod_SSL. Notice, however, that Apache does not support DSO on all platforms.

```
# cd ../apache_1.3.31
#  SSL_BASE=../openssl-0.9.7d \
    ./configure \
    --enable-module=ssl \
    --activate-module=src/modules/php5/libphp5.a \
    --prefix=/usr/local/apache \
     --enable-shared=ssl
```

Finally, you can make Apache and the certificates and then install them:

```
# make
```

If you have done everything right, you will get a message similar to the following:

```
+--------------------------------------------------------------------+
| Before you install the package you now should prepare the SSL      |
| certificate system by running the 'make certificate' command.      |
| For different situations the following variants are provided:      |
|                                                                    |
| % make certificate TYPE=dummy     (dummy self-signed Snake Oil cert) |
| % make certificate TYPE=test      (test cert signed by Snake Oil CA) |
| % make certificate TYPE=custom    (custom cert signed by own CA)   |
| % make certificate TYPE=existing (existing cert)                   |
|        CRT=/path/to/your.crt [KEY=/path/to/your.key]               |
|                                                                    |
| Use TYPE=dummy    when you're a  vendor package maintainer,        |
| the TYPE=test     when you're an admin but want to do tests only,  |
| the TYPE=custom   when you're an admin willing to run a real server |
| and TYPE=existing when you're an admin who upgrades a server.      |
| (The default is TYPE=test)                                         |
|                                                                    |
| Additionally add ALGO=RSA (default) or ALGO=DSA to select          |
| the signature algorithm used for the generated certificate.        |
|                                                                    |
| Use 'make certificate VIEW=1' to display the generated data.       |
|                                                                    |
| Thanks for using Apache & mod_ssl.       Ralf S. Engelschall       |
|                                          rse@engelschall.com       |
|                                          www.engelschall.com       |
+--------------------------------------------------------------------+
```

Now you can create a custom certificate. This option prompts you for location, company, and a couple of other things. For contact information, it makes sense to use real data. For other questions during the process, the default answer is fine:

```
# make certificate TYPE=custom
```

Now install Apache:

```
# make install
```

If everything goes well, you should see a message similar to this:

```
+--------------------------------------------------------+
| You now have successfully built and installed the      |
| Apache 1.3 HTTP server. To verify that Apache actually |
| works correctly you now should first check the         |
| (initially created or preserved) configuration files   |
|                                                        |
|   /usr/local/apache/conf/httpd.conf                    |
|                                                        |
| and then you should be able to immediately fire up     |
| Apache the first time by running:                      |
|                                                        |
|   /usr/local/apache/bin/apachectl start                |
|                                                        |
| Or when you want to run it with SSL enabled use:       |
|                                                        |
|   /usr/local/apache/bin/apachectl startssl             |
|                                                        |
| Thanks for using Apache.       The Apache Group         |
|                                http://www.apache.org/   |
+--------------------------------------------------------+
```

Now it's time to see whether Apache and PHP are working. However, you need to edit the httpd.conf file to add the PHP type to the configuration.

httpd.conf **File: Snippets**

Look at the httpd.conf file. If you have followed the previous instructions, your httpd.conf file will be located in the /usr/local/apache/conf directory. The file has the addtype for PHP commented out. You should uncomment it at this time, so it looks like this:

```
AddType application/x-httpd-php .php
AddType application/x-httpd-php-source .phps
```

Now you are ready to start the Apache server to see whether it worked. First, start the server without the SSL support to see whether it comes up. Then check for PHP support and stop and start the server with the SSL support enabled to see whether everything is working.

Use configtest to check whether the configuration is set up properly:

```
# cd /usr/local/apache/bin
# ./apachectl configtest
Syntax OK
# ./apachectl start
   ./apachectl start: httpd started
```

If it worked correctly, you will see something similar to Figure A.1 when you connect to the server with a web browser.

Note

You can connect to the server by using a domain name or the actual IP address of the computer. Check both cases to ensure that everything is working properly.

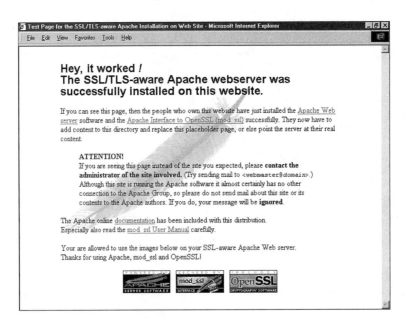

Figure A.1 The default test page provided by Apache.

Is PHP Support Working?

Now you can test for PHP support. Create a file named `test.php` with the following code in it. The file needs to be located in document root path, which should be set up, by default, to `/usr/local/apache/htdocs`. Note that this path depends on the directory prefix that you chose initially. However, you could change this in the `httpd.conf file`:

```
<?php phpinfo(); ?>
```

The output screen should look like Figure A.2.

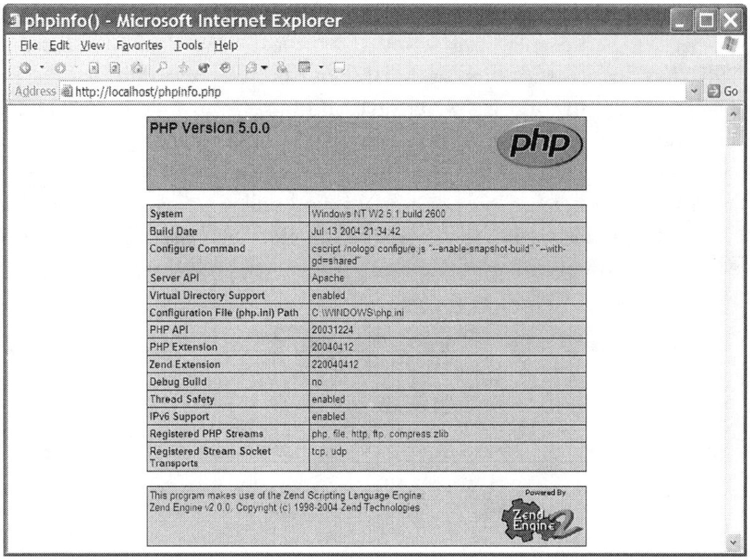

Figure A.2 The function `phpinfo()` provides useful configuration information.

Is SSL Working?

Now you are ready to test for SSL. First, stop the server and then restart with the SSL option enabled:

```
# /usr/local/apache/bin/apachectl stop
# /usr/local/apache/bin/apachectl startssl
```

Test to see whether it works by connecting to the server with a web browser and selecting the `https` protocol, like this:

```
https://yourserver.yourdomain.com
```

Try your server's IP address also, like this:

```
https://xxx.xxx.xxx.xxx
```

or

```
http://xxx.xxx.xxx.xxx:443
```

If it worked, the server will send the certificate to the browser to establish a secure connection. This makes the browser prompt you to accept the self-signed certificate. If it were a certificate from a certification authority your browser already trusts, the browser would not prompt you. In this case, we created and signed our own certificates. We didn't want to purchase one right away because we wanted to ensure that we could get everything working properly first.

If you are using Internet Explorer or Mozilla, you will see a padlock symbol in the status bar. This symbol tells you that a secure connection has been established. The icon used by Netscape is shown in Figure A.3.

Figure A.3 Web browsers display an icon to indicate the page you are viewing came via an SSL connection.

Final Steps

To use the PDFlib shared object and any other modules you installed in this way, you need to complete a few more steps.

First, copy the `libpdf_php` file (in `bind/php/php-50x` from wherever you extracted PDFLib) to the PHP `extensions` directory, which is probably

```
/usr/local/lib/php/extensions
```

Then add the following line to your `php.ini` file:

```
extension = libpdf_php.so
```

Installing Apache, PHP, and MySQL Under Windows

With Windows, the installation process is a little bit different because PHP is set up either as a CGI (`php.exe`) script or as an ISAPI module (`php5isapi.dll`). However, Apache and MySQL are installed in a similar fashion to the way they are installed under Unix. Make sure you have the latest operating system service patches applied to the machine before you begin the Windows installation.

You should start by downloading all the latest source files to a temporary directory with ample space. For our installation, we used `c:\temp\download` as the temporary directory.

If you have a slow network connection, you may prefer to use the versions from the CD, but they are likely to be a version or more out of date.

Installing MySQL Under Windows

The following instructions were written using Windows XP.

Begin by setting up MySQL. You can download the required ZIP file from http://www.mysql.com.

Unzip the MySQL ZIP file to the temporary directory and run the `Setup.exe` program. The installer is a standard InstallShield Wizard and should look like many other installers you have seen.

If you choose Typical Install, the wizard will not ask any questions other than where you would like MySQL installed. The directory where MySQL installs itself is, by default, `C:\mysql`. You can move it to a different directory if needed, after it's fully installed, but if you do, you will need to take some extra steps to keep everything working.

If you move MySQL and intend to run the MySQL executable, `mysqld`, you must tell it where everything is located by supplying command-line options. To display all options, use

```
C:\mysql\bin\mysqld --help
```

For example, if you moved the MySQL distribution to `D:\programs\mysql`, you must start `mysqld` with

```
D:\programs\mysql\bin\mysqld --basedir D:\programs\mysql
```

If you move the installation and are running it as a Windows service, you need to create an INI file called `my.ini` and place it in your main Windows directory. Your INI file will have content similar to the following:

```
[mysqld]
basedir=D:/programs/mysql/bin/
datadir= D:/programs/mysql/data/
```

In the NT/2000/XP setup, the name of the MySQL server is `mysqld-nt`, and it is normally installed as a service. A service is a program that runs constantly in the background to do work for other programs. Services usually run automatically when you start the machine, which saves you the effort of having to start them each time.

You can install the MySQL server as a service by going to the Windows command prompt and typing

```
cd c:\mysql\bin
mysqld-nt -install
```

The response you should get is

```
Service successfully installed.
```

Now you can start and stop the MySQL service from the command line using

```
NET START mysql
NET STOP mysql
```

Note that the executable's name is `mysqld-nt`, but the service's name is just `mysql`. If you run NET START `mysql`, you should see the following message:

```
The MySQL service was started successfully.
```

After the server has been installed, it can be stopped, started, or set to start automatically using the Services utility (found in Control Panel). To open Services, click Start and then select Control Panel. Double-click Administrative Tools and then double-click Services.

The Services utility is shown in Figure A.4. If you want to set any MySQL options, you must first stop the service and then specify them as *startup parameters* in the Services utility before restarting the MySQL service. The MySQL service can be stopped using the Services utility or using the commands NET STOP MySQL or `mysqladmin shutdown`.

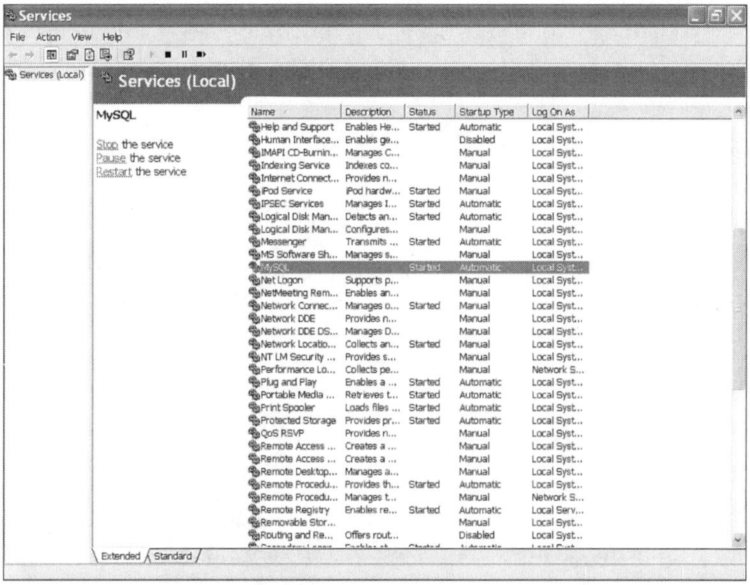

Figure A.4   The Services utility allows you to configure the services running on your machine.

To test whether MySQL is working, you can execute the following command:

```
C:\mysql\bin\mysqlshow
```

The default configuration is not really ideal, so you need to attend to a few loose ends:

- Setting your PATH
- Deleting the anonymous accounts
- Setting the root password

Setting Your PATH

MySQL comes with lots of command-line utilities. None of them are easy to get at unless the MySQL binary directory is in your PATH. The purpose of this environment variable is to tell Windows where to look for executable programs.

Many of the common commands you use at the Windows command prompt, such as dir and cd, are internal and built into cmd.exe. Others, such as format and ipconfig, have their own executables. Having to type **C:\WINNT\system32\format** would not be convenient if you wanted to format a disk. Having to type **C:\mysql\bin\mysql** to run the MySQL monitor also would not be convenient.

The directory where the executables for your basic Windows commands, such as format.exe, reside is automatically in your PATH, so you can simply type **format**. To have the same convenience with the MySQL command-line tools, you need to add it.

Click Start and choose Control Panel. Double-click System and go to the Advanced tab. If you click the Environment Variables button, you will be presented with a dialog box that allows you to view the environment variables for your system. Double-clicking PATH allows you to edit it.

Add a semicolon to the end of your current path to separate your new entry from the previous one; then add c:\mysql\bin. When you click OK, your addition will be stored in the machine's registry. The next time you restart your machine, you will be able to type **mysql** rather than **C:\mysql\bin\mysql**.

Deleting the Anonymous User

The default MySQL configuration allows any user access to the system without providing a username or password. This is obviously undesirable.

The first thing you should do is delete the anonymous user. By opening a command prompt and typing the following lines, you can accomplish that goal:

```
c:\mysql\bin\mysql -u root
use mysql
delete from user where User='';
quit
c:\mysql\bin\mysqladmin -u root reload
```

The anonymous user is now gone.

Setting the root Password

Even the superuser account, root, has no password yet. To set this user's password, type these lines:

```
c:\mysql\bin\mysqladmin -u root password your_password
c:\mysql\bin\mysqladmin -u root -h your_host_name password your_password
```

You should find that tasks that previously required no username or password will now fail without this information. Attempting to run

```
c:\mysql\bin\mysqladmin reload
```

or

```
c:\mysql\bin\mysqladmin shutdown
```

will now fail.

From now on, you will need to use the -u flag, provide a username, and add the -p flag to tell MySQL that you have a password, as in this example:

```
c:\mysql\bin\mysqladmin -u root -p reload
```

If you type this command, MySQL should now prompt you for the root password that you just set.

If you need more information, refer to the MySQL website at http://www.mysql.com.

You are now ready to install Apache under Windows. Let's begin!

Installing Apache Under Windows

Apache 1.3 and later versions are designed to run on Windows NT, 2000, and XP. The installer works only with the x86 family of processors, such as Intel's. Apache also runs on Windows 95 and 98. In all cases, TCP/IP networking must be installed. Make sure you use the Winsock 2 library if you decide to install it under either Windows 95 or 98.

Go to http://httpd.apache.org and download the Windows binary of the current version of Apache 1.3. (Apache 2.0 is threaded, and some PHP external libraries are not thread safe, so we recommend you use 1.3.)

We downloaded the apache_1.3.31-win32-x86-no_src.msi file. It contains the current version (within the 1.3 hierarchy) for Windows, without source code, packaged as an MSI file. MSI files are the package format used by the Windows installer.

Unless you have a really elusive bug or want to contribute to the development effort, it is unlikely that you will want to compile the source code yourself. This single file contains the Apache server ready to be installed.

Double-click the file you downloaded to start the process. The installation process should look familiar to you. As shown in Figure A.5, the installer looks similar to many other Windows installers.

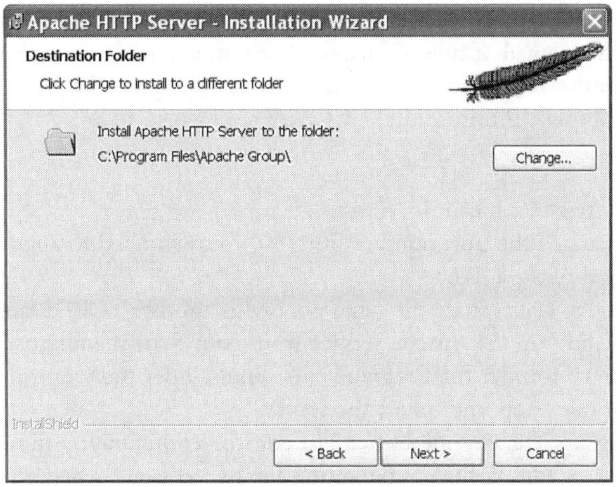

Figure A.5   The Apache installer is easy to use.

The install program prompts you for the following:

- The network name, server name, and administrator's email address. If you are building a server for real use, you should know the answers to these questions. If you are building a server for your own personal use, the answers are not particularly important.

- Whether you want Apache to run as a service. As with MySQL, setting it up this way is usually easier.

- The installation type. We recommend the Complete option, but you can choose Custom if you want to leave out some components such as the documentation.

- The directory in which to install Apache. (The default is `C:\Program Files\Apache Group\Apache`.)

After you choose all these options, the Apache server will be installed and started.

Apache listens to port 80 (unless you changed the Port, Listen, or BindAddress directives in the configuration files) after it starts. To connect to the server and access the default page, launch a browser and enter this URL:

`http://localhost/`

This should respond with a welcome page similar to the one shown in Figure A.1 and a link to the Apache manual. If nothing happens or you get an error, look in the `error.log` file in the `logs` directory. If your host isn't connected to the Internet, you might have to use this URL instead:

```
http://127.0.0.1/
```

This is the IP address that means localhost.

If you have changed the port number from 80, you will need to append `:port_number` on the end of the URL.

Note that Apache *cannot* share the same port with another TCP/IP application.

You can start and stop the Apache service from your Start menu: Apache adds itself as Apache HTTP Server under the Programs submenu. Under the Control Apache Server heading, you can start, stop, and restart the server.

After installing Apache, you might need to edit the configuration files in the `conf` directory. We look at editing the configuration file `httpd.conf` when we install PHP.

If you need to enable Apache with SSL in Windows, you should follow the excellent FAQ at http://tud.at/programm/apache-ssl-win32-howto.php3, but be aware that it is not for the fainthearted.

Installing PHP for Windows

To install PHP for Windows, begin by downloading the files for PHP5 from http://www.php.net.

Two files should be downloaded for a Windows installation. One is the ZIP file containing PHP (called something similar to `php-5.0.0-Win32.zip`) and one is a collection of libraries (`pecl-5.0.0-Win32.zip` or similar).

Begin by unzipping the ZIP file to the directory of your choice. The usual location is `c:\PHP`, and we use this location in the following explanation.

You can install the PECL libraries by unzipping the PECL file to your extensions directory. Using `C:\PHP` as your base directory, this will be `C:\PHP\ext\`.

Now follow these steps:

1. In the main directory, you will see a file called `php.exe` and one called `php5ts.dll`. You need these files to run PHP as a CGI. If you want to run it as a SAPI module instead, you can use the relevant DLL file for your web server. If you are using Apache, the file is called `php5apache.dll`, for example.

   The SAPI modules are faster and easier to secure; the CGI version allows you to run PHP from the command line. Again, the choice is up to you.

2. Copy all the DLLs to your Windows system directory, which is `C:\winnt\system32` on Windows NT or 2000 or `C:\windows\system32` on Windows XP.

3. Set up a `php.ini` configuration file. PHP comes with two prepared files: `php.ini-dist` and `php.ini-recommended`. We suggest you use `php.ini-dist` while you are learning PHP or on development servers and use `php.ini-recommended` on production servers. Make a copy of this file and rename it `php.ini`. Place your `php.ini` file in the `%SYSTEMROOT%` directory, which is usually `c:\winnt` or `c:\winnt40` on Windows NT or 2000 or `c:\windows` on Windows XP.

4. Edit your `php.ini` file. It contains many settings, most of which you can ignore for the time being. The settings you need to change now are as follows:

   - Change the `extension_dir` directive to point to the directory where your extension DLLs reside. In the normal install, this is `C:\PHP\ext`. Your `php.ini` will therefore contain

     `extension_dir = c:/php/ext`

   - Set the `doc_root` directive to point at the root directory from which your web server serves. This is likely to be

     `doc_root = "c:/Program Files/Apache Group/Apache/htdocs"`

     if you are using Apache or

     `doc_root = "c:/Inetpub/wwwroot"`

     if you are using IIS.

   - Choose some extensions to run. We suggest at this stage that you just get PHP working; you can add extensions as needed. To add an extension, look at the list under "Windows Extensions." You will see a lot of lines such as

     `;extension=php_pdf.dll`

     To turn on this extension, you can simply remove the semicolon at the start of the line (and do the opposite to turn it off). Note that if you want to add more extensions later, you should restart your web server after you have changed `php.ini` for the changes to take effect.

     In this book, you will use `php_pdf.dll`, `php_gd2.dll`, `php_imap.dll`, and `php_mysqli.dll`. You should uncomment these lines. You may find that `php_mysqli.dll` is missing. If so, add it as follows:

     `extension=php_mysqli.dll`

     Close and save your `php.ini` file.

5. If you are using NTFS, make sure the user that the web server runs as has permission to read your `php.ini` file.

Adding PHP to Your Apache Configuration

You may need to edit one of Apache's configuration files. Open the `httpd.conf` file in your favorite editor. This file is typically located in the `c:\Program Files\Apache Group\Apache\conf\` directory. Look for the following lines:

```
LoadModule php5_module c:/php/php5apache.dll
AddModule mod_php5.c
AddType application/x-httpd-php .php
Action application/x-httpd-php "/php/php.exe"
```

If you don't see these lines, add them to the file, save it, and restart your Apache server.

Adding PHP and MySQL to Microsoft IIS and PWS

This section covers how to add PHP and MySQL support to IIS with the ISAPI (`php5isapi.dll`) module. (You can also install it as a CGI, but we strongly recommend you use the ISAPI module because it is faster.) This section assumes that you have followed the steps in the preceding sections. The main difference is that the `doc_root` configuration directive is likely to be `c:/Inetpub/wwwroot`.

Next, you need to open Internet Information Services. If you have Windows 2000 or XP, you can find it in the Control Panel under Administrative Tools. If you don't see this option, you may need to install IIS from your original Windows CDs before continuing.

When IIS is open, you should see a tree view of services on the left side. Right-click the web server (usually called Default Web Server) and select Properties.

The resulting Properties dialog box contains quite a lot of information, but you need to change only a few things. Under Home Directory, click the Configuration button. Under Application Mappings, select Add to add PHP. You must then supply an executable. Supply the full path to the location of `php5isapi.dll` (probably `c:\php\php5isapi.dll`). In the Extension box, you should type **.php**. You also need to check the Script Engine box if it isn't already checked. Click OK.

If you want to be able to do HTTP Authentication (which we cover in this book), you should also look under ISAPI Filters. Select Add. You need to supply a filter name (in this case, type **PHP**) and an executable (here, supply the full path to the `php5isapi.dll` file as just shown). Click OK. Finally, close the Properties dialog box by clicking Apply.

You should now stop the web server (or check that it is stopped) and then restart it. You can do this from the Internet Information Services window by right-clicking on the web server and choosing Stop. You can restart in the same way by selecting Start.

Testing Your Work

The next step is to start your web server and test to ensure that you have PHP working. Create a `test.php` file and add the following line to it:

```
<? phpinfo(); ?>
```

Make sure the file is in the document root directory (typically `c:\Program File\Apache Group\Apache\htdocs` under Apache or `c:\Inetpub\wwwroot` under IIS); then pull it up on the browser, as follows:

`http://localhost/test.php`

or

`http://your-ip-number-here/test.php`

If you see a page similar to the one shown in Figure A.2, you know that PHP is working.

Installing PEAR

PHP5 comes with the PHP Extension and Application Repository (PEAR) package installer. If you are using Windows, go to the command line and type

`c:\php\go-pear`

The `go-pear` script asks you a few straightforward questions about where you would like the package installer and the standard PEAR classes installed and then downloads and installs them for you. (This first step is not required under Linux, but the rest of the installation is the same.)

At this stage, you should have an installed version of the PEAR package installer and the basic PEAR libraries. You can then simply install packages by typing

`pear install package`

where `package` is the name of the package you want to install.

To get a list of available packages, type

`pear list-all`

To see what you have installed currently, try

`pear list`

To install the MIME mail package used in Chapter 30, "Building a Mailing List Manager," type

`pear install Mail_Mime`

The DB package mentioned in Chapter 11, "Accessing Your MySQL Database from the Web with PHP," is installed automatically, but to make sure you have the newest version, you can type

`pear list-upgrades`

If a newer version is available, type

`pear upgrade DB`

If the preceding procedure does not work for you for whatever reason, we suggest you try downloading PEAR packages directly. To do this, go to http://pear.php.net/packages.php.

From here you can navigate through the various packages available. For example, in this book, we use Mail_Mime. Click through to the page for this package and click Download Latest to get a copy. You need to unzip the file you have downloaded and put it somewhere in your `include_path`.

You should have a `c:\php\pear` or similar directory. If you are downloading packages manually, we suggest you put the packages in the PEAR directory tree. PEAR has a standard structure, so we suggest you put things in the standard location; this is the place where the installer would put them. For example, the Mail_Mime package belongs in the Mail section, so in this example, we would place it in the `c:\php\pear\Mail` directory.

Setting Up Other Configurations

You can set up PHP and MySQL with other web servers such as Omni, HTTPD, and Netscape Enterprise Server. They are not covered in this appendix, but you can find information on how to set them up at the MySQL and PHP websites, http://www.mysql.com and http://www.php.net, respectively.

B

Web Resources

THIS APPENDIX LISTS SOME OF THE MANY resources available on the Web that you can use to find tutorials, articles, news, and sample PHP code. These resources are just some of the many out there. Obviously, there are far more than we could possibly list in one appendix, and many more are popping up daily as the usage of and familiarity with PHP and MySQL continue to increase among web developers.

Some of these resources are in different languages such as German or French or something other than your native language. We suggest using a translator like http://www.systransoft.com to browse the web resource in your native language.

PHP Resources

PHP.Net—http://www.php.net—The original site for PHP. Go to this site to download binary and source versions of PHP and the manual, to browse the mailing list archives, and to keep up to date with PHP news.

Zend.Com—http://www.zend.com—The source for the Zend engine that powers PHP. This portal site contains forums, articles, tutorials, and a database of sample classes and code that you can use.

PEAR—http://pear.php.net—The PHP Extension and Application Repository. This is the official PHP extension site.

PECL—http://pecl.php.net—The sister-site to PEAR. PEAR carries classes written in PHP; PECL (pronounced "pickle") carries extensions written in C. PECL classes are sometimes more difficult to install but perform a wider range of functionality and are almost always more powerful than their PHP-based counterparts.

PHPCommunity—http://www.phpcommunity.org/—A new community-based site.

php|architect—http://www.phparch.com—A PHP magazine. This website provides free articles, or you can subscribe to receive the magazine in either PDF or printed format.

PHP Magazine—http://www.phpmag.net/—Another PHP magazine, also available in electronic or printed format.

PHPWizard.net—http://www.phpwizard.net—The source of many cool PHP applications such as phpChat and phpIRC.

PHPMyAdmin.Net—http://www.phpmyadmin.net/—The home of the popular PHP-based web front end for MySQL.

PHPBuilder.com—http://www.phpbuilder.com—A portal for PHP tutorials. At this site, you can find tutorials on just about anything you can think of. The site also has a forum for people to post questions.

DevShed.com—http://www.devshed.com—Portal-type site that offers excellent tutorials on PHP, MySQL, Perl, and other development languages.

PX-PHP Code Exchange—http://px.sklar.com—A great place to start. Here, you can find many sample scripts and useful functions.

The PHP Resource—http://www.php-resource.de—A very nice source for tutorials, articles, and scripts. The only "problem" is that the site is in German. We recommend using a translator service site to view it. You can still read the sample code either way.

WeberDev.com—http://www.WeberDev.com—Formerly known as Berber's PHP sample page, this site grew and is now a place for tutorials and sample code. It targets PHP and MySQL users and covers security and general databases.

HotScripts.com—http://www.hotscripts.com—A great categorized selection of scripts. This site offers scripts in various languages such as PHP, ASP.NET, and Perl. It has an excellent collection of PHP scripts and is updated frequently. This site is a must-see if you are looking for scripts.

PHP Base Library—http://phplib.sourceforge.net—A site used by developers for large-scale PHP projects. It offers a library with numerous tools for an alternative session management approach, as well as templating and database abstraction.

PHP Center—http://www.php-center.de—Another German portal site used for tutorials, scripts, tips, tricks, advertising, and more.

PHP Homepage—http://www.php-homepage.de—Another German site about PHP with scripts, articles, news, and much more. It also has a quick reference section.

PHPIndex.com—http://www.phpindex.com—A nice French PHP portal with tons of PHP-related content. This site contains news, FAQs, articles, job listings, and much more.

WebMonkey.com—http://www.webmonkey.com—A portal with lots of web resources, real-world tutorials, sample code, and so on. The site covers design, programming, back end, multimedia stuff, and much more.

The PHP Club—http://www.phpclub.net—A site that offers many resources for PHP beginners. It has news, book reviews, sample code, forums, FAQs, and many tutorials for beginners.

PHP Classes Repository—http://phpclasses.org—A site that targets the distribution of freely available classes written in PHP. A must-see if you are developing code or your project will be composed of classes. It provides a nice search functionality, so you can find stuff easily.

The PHP Resource Index—http://php.resourceindex.com—Portal site for scripts, classes, and documentation. The cool thing about this site is that everything is nicely categorized, which can save you some time.

PHP Developer—http://www.phpdeveloper.org—Yet another PHP portal that provides PHP news, articles, and tutorials.

Evil Walrus—http://www.evilwalrus.com—A cool-looking portal for PHP scripts.

SourceForge—http://sourceforge.net—Extensive open source resources. SourceForge not only helps you find code that can be useful, but it also provides access to CVS, mailing lists, and machines for open source developers.

Codewalkers—http://codewalkers.com/—A site that contains articles, book reviews, tutorials, and the amazing PHP Contest through which you can win stuff with your new skills. The site offers a new code contest every two weeks.

PHP Developer's Network Unified Forums— http://forums.devnetwork.net/index.php—Discussion of all things PHP related.

PHP Kitchen—http://www.phpkitchen.com/—Articles, news, and PHP advocacy.

Postnuke—http://www.postnuke.com/—A frequently used PHP content-management system.

PHP Application Tools—http://www.php-tools.de/—A set of useful PHP classes.

MySQL and SQL Specific Resources

The MySQL site—http://www.mysql.com—The official MySQL website. It provides excellent documentation, support, and information. This site is a must-see if you are using MySQL, especially for the developer zone and mailing list archives.

The SQL Course—http://sqlcourse.com—A site that provides an introductory SQL tutorial with easy-to-understand instructions. It allows you to practice what you learn on an online SQL interpreter. An advanced version is provided at http://www.sqlcourse2.com.

SearchDatabase.com—http://searchdatabase.techtarget.com/—Nice portal with lots of useful information on DBs. It provides excellent tutorials, tips, white papers, FAQs, reviews, and so on. A must-see!

Apache Resources

Apache Software—http://www.apache.org—The place to start if you need to download the source or binaries for the Apache web server. The site provides online documentation.

Apache Week—http://www.apacheweek.com—Online weekly magazine that provides essential information for anyone running an Apache Server or anyone running Apache services.

Apache Today—http://www.apachetoday.com—A daily source of news and information about Apache. Users must subscribe to post questions.

Web Development

Philip and Alex's Guide to Web Publishing—http://philip.greenspun.com/panda/—A witty, irreverent guide to software engineering as it applies to the Web. One of the few books on the topic coauthored by a Samoyed.

Index

How can we make this index more useful? Email us at indexes@samspublishing.com

control, version (code)

    CVS (Concurrent Versions System), 515

    multiple programmers, 515

    repository, 514-515

control characters, 66

control structures

    alternate syntax, 54-55

    breaking out of, 54

    conditionals, 44-49

    declare, 55

    loops, 49-50

        break statement, 54

        do..while loops, 53-54

        for loops, 52-53

        foreach loops, 52-53

        while loops, 51-52

    stored procedures, 315-319

controlling visibility, 167-168

conversion specifications, 109-111

converting

    arrays to scalar variables, 103-104

    calendars, 449

    classes to strings, 188

cookies, 480-482

coordinates, bounding boxes, 465

copy() function, 414

correlated subqueries, 258

cos() function, 816

count() function, 102

COUNT(items) function, 254

counting array elements, 102

crackers, 333

CREATE privilege, 224

CREATE TABLE command (SQL), 227-229

CREATE TEMORARY TABLES privilege, 224

create_database.php files (Warm Mail application), 661

create_database.sql file, 631-633, 756

    content management systems, 630

    MLM application, 699

    Web forum application, 754

credit card numbers, storing, 389

criteria, retrieving specific data from databases, 246-247

cross join, 252

crypt() function, 364-365

cryptography, 348

CSR (Certificate Signing Request), 352-353

CSS (cascading style sheets), 518

curly braces ({}), regular expressions, 123

current() function, 100

cursors (stored procedures), 315-319

custom authentication, creating, 377

cutting costs (commercial websites), 331-332

CVS (Concurrent Versions System), 515, 521

D

data

    aggregating, 254-255

    encrypting, 388

    graphing, 468-476

    grouping, 254-255

    input, 530, 552-553

    inserting into databases, 242-244

    joins, 252-253

    loading, from files, 307

    metadata, content management systems, 628-629

    redundant data, avoiding (Web databases), 210-211

    retrieving

        from databases, 244-245

        from multiple tables, 247-248

        in a particular order, 253-254

        with specific criteria, 246-247

    rows, returning, 256

    sensitive data, 387-389

    tables

        aliases, 251-252

        joining, 249-250

        rows unmatched, 250-251

        two-table joins, 248-249

Data Definition Languages (DDL), 242

Data Encryption Standard (DES), 349

data hiding, OO (object-oriented) development, 158

Data Manipulation Languages (DML), 242

data transfer, database replication, 303-305

data types

    BLOB types (binary large objects), 238

    date and time data types, 236-237

    floating point data types (numeric column types), 235-236

Warm Mail application (email client), setting up, 661-662

Web forum application, 754-757

data_valid_fns.php files

MLM application, 699

PHPBookmark application, 544

Shopping Cart application, 584

Warm Mail application, 661

Web forum application, 754

date and time

calendars, converting, 449

converting between PHP and MySQL formats, 444-445

MySQL

date calculations, 446-448

DATE_FORMAT() function, 444-445

MySQL website, 449

UNIX_TIMESTAMP() function, 444-445

PHP

calendar functions, 448-449

checkdate() function, 443

date calculations, 445-446

date() function, 439-442

floor() function, 446

getdate() function, 442-443

microseconds, 448

mktime() function, 441-442

PHP website, 449

date and time column types, 236-237

date and time data types, 236-237

date() function, 19-20, 412

format codes, 439-441

Unix timestamps, 441-442

DATE_FORMAT() function, 444-445

db table, 286-289

db_connect() function, 555

db_fns.php files, 643

content management systems, 630

MLM application, 699

PHPBookmark application, 544

Shopping Cart application, 584

Warm Mail application, 661

Web forum application, 754

db_result_to_array() function, 591

DDL (Data Definition Languages), 242

DDoS (Distributed Denial of Service), 342

debugging variables, 531-533

declare control structure, 55

declare handlers, 317

declaring

functions, 142-143

stored functions, 314-315

stored procedures, 312-313

decoct() function, 413

decrement operators, 33-34

decryption, 348

default values, database optimization, 302

DELETE privilege, 223

DELETE statement, 262

delete_account() function, 676

delete_bm() function, 573

delete_bms.php files (PHPBookmark application), 544

delete_book.php files (Shopping Cart application), 584

delete_category.php files (Shopping Cart application), 584

delete_message() function, 688

delete_story.php files, 630, 649

deletion anomalies, avoiding (Web databases), 211

Denial of Service (DoS), 342-343

deregistering variables, 483

DES (Data Encryption Standard), 349

DESC keyword, 253

descenders (letters), 466

DESCRIBE command, 231-232

DESCRIBE statement, syntax, 296

describe user; statement, 286

designing

classes, 172-173

databases, content management systems, 631-633

Web databases

anomalies, avoiding, 211

atomic column values, 212

keys, creating, 213

null values, avoiding, 213

questions, formulating, 213

real-world objects, modeling, 209-210

redundant data, avoiding, 210-211

table types, 214

designs, database optimization, 301

design_button.html file, 460-463

How can we make this index more useful? Email us at indexes@samspublishing.com

P

How can we make this index more useful? Email us at indexes@samspublishing.com

How can we make this index more useful? Email us at indexes@sampublishing.com

How can we make this index more useful? Email us at indexes@samspublishing.com

What's on the CD?

The book's companion CD-ROM contains full versions of PHP, MySQL, Apache, several graphics libraries, files containing the code listings in the book, and the entire book in PDF format.

Windows

Appendix A, "Installing PHP and MySQL," describes setting up Apache, MySQL, and PHP on a Windows platform. We have included Windows versions of these products on the CD-ROM.

Apache 1.3.31 is located in the `Software\Apache\Windows\Binary` directory. Double-click on `apache_1.3.31-win32-x86-no_src.exe` to launch the Apache installer.

Both the current production version of MySQL (4.0—`mysql-4.0.20c-win.zip`) and the alpha version (5.0—`mysql-5.0.0a-alpha-win.zip`) are located in the `Software\MySQL\Windows\Binary` directory. Unzip and double-click on `SETUP.EXE` to start the MySQL installation program. Then follow the instructions in Appendix A to prepare your MySQL installation so that you can follow along with this book.

PHP5 is located in the `Software\PHP\Binary` directory. Follow the instructions in Appendix A to configure PHP for your particular system.

A collection of PECL modules for PHP5 is available for your use in the `Libraries` directory.

Linux/Unix

Many Linux distributions and some Unix workstations are already configured with Apache, MySQL, and PHP. They may not be the latest versions described in this book, however. Appendix A also describes setting up Apache, MySQL, and PHP on a Linux or Unix workstation if you need to install them. Source code for Apache, MySQL, and PHP and binary installers for MySQL on Linux are included on the CD-ROM.

The source code for Apache 1.3.31 is available in `Software/Apache/Unix/Source`. If you have GNU `tar` available, use `httpd-1.3.31.tar.gz`. Otherwise, use `httpd-1.3.31.tar.Z`.

Binary installers for MySQL Max4.0 and 5.0 for Linux are located in `Software\MySQL\Unix\Binary`. If your Linux system uses the RPM manager to install software, use `MySQL-Max-4.0.20-0.i386.rpm` or `MySQL-Max-5.0.0-0.i386.rpm` to install the server portion of MySQL and use `MySQL-client-4.0.20-0.i386.rpm` or `MySQL-client-5.0.0-0.i386.rpm` to install the client portion of MySQL. If your Linux system does not use the RPM manager to install software, use `mysql-max-4.0.20-pc-linux-i686.tar.gz` or `mysql-standard-5.0.0-alpha-pc-linux-i686.tar.gz` to install the client and server portions of MySQL.

The source code for MySQL 4.0.20 for Unix is located at `mysql-4.0.20.tar.gz`, and for 5.0, it is located at `mysql-5.0.0-alpha.tar.gz`. Solaris users should download GNU `tar` to extract these files because of a bug within the Solaris version of the `tar` program.

The source code for PHP 5.0 is included in `Software/PHP/Unix/Source/`.

A collection of PECL modules for PHP5 is available for your use in the Libraries directory.

License Agreement

By opening this package, you are agreeing to be bound by the following agreement:

You may not copy or redistribute the entire media as a whole. Copying and redistribution of individual software programs on the media is governed by terms set by individual copyright holders.

The installer and code from the author(s) are copyrighted by the publisher and author(s). Individual programs and other items on the media are copyrighted by their various authors or other copyright holders. Some of the programs included with this product may be governed by an Open Source license, which allows redistribution; see the license information for each product for more information.

Other programs are included on the media by special permission from their authors.

This software is provided as is without warranty of any kind, either expressed or implied, including but not limited to the implied warranties of merchantability and fitness for a particular purpose. Neither the publisher nor its dealers or distributors assume any liability for any alleged or actual damages arising from the use of this program. (Some states do not allow for the exclusion of implied warranties, so the exclusion may not apply to you.)